Contemporary British Politics

Visit the companion website for this
text at:
http://www.palgrave.com/politics/coxall/

Contemporary British Politics

4th edition

Bill Coxall
Lynton Robins
and
Robert Leach

First published 2003 by
PALGRAVE MACMILLAN
Houndmills, Basingstoke, Hampshire RG21 6XS and
175 Fifth Avenue, New York, N.Y. 10010
Companies and representatives throughout the world

PALGRAVE MACMILLAN is the global academic imprint of the
Palgrave Macmillan division of St. Martin's Press, LLC and of
Palgrave Macmillan Ltd. Macmillan® is a registered trademark in the
United States, United Kingdom and other countries. Palgrave is a
registered trademark in the European Union and other countries.

ISBN 1–4039–0507–X paperback

This book is printed on paper suitable for recycling and
made from fully managed and sustained forest sources.

A catalogue record for this book is available from the British Library.

Library of Congress Cataloging-in-Publication Data

Coxall, W. N.
    Contemporary British politics.– 4th ed. / Bill Coxall, Lynton Robins, and Robert Leach.
        p. cm
    Includes bibliographical references and index.
    ISBN 1-4039-0507-X (pbk.)
      1. Great Britain–Politics and government–1945- I. Robins, L. J. (Lynton J.) II. Leach,
    Robert, 1941- III. Title.

    JN231.C624 2003
    320.941–dc21

Editing and origination by Curran Publishing Services, Norwich

10 9   8   7   6   5   4   3   2   1
12 11 10 09 08 07 06 05 04 03

                                                                    2003042973

Printed and bound in Great Britain by
Ashford Colour Press Ltd, Gosport

This book is dedicated to the
memory of Bill Coxall

Contents

List of figures xii
List of tables xiii
List of boxes xv
Preface to the fourth edition xix
Acknowledgements xx
List of abbreviations xxi

PART I The Context of British Politics 1

1 Politics, Democracy and Power 3
What is politics? 3
Authority, power and influence 5
Democracy – power to the people? 5
Power in Britain 7
Perspectives on power 8
British politics? 11
Multi-level governance 12
Policies – who gets what, when, how? 13

2 Economy, Society and Politics 16
Political geography – nation, regions, town and country 16
Allegiance and identity 18
Ethnicity 19
Religion 21
Gender 23
Age 23
Inequalities in income and wealth 24
Occupation and social class 26
Changing class structure? 27
Economic inequality and political power 29
Economic and social divisions – the time dimension 30

3 The Historical Context: British Politics since 1945 32
The post-war years: the end of empire and the imperial legacy 33
The under-performing economy 36
Building a welfare state 37
The pendulum years: from crisis to doubt 39
Economic management: towards 'stagflation' 40
The Thatcher years 42

Thatcherite Britain in Europe 43
The welfare state and the free market 44
The impact of Thatcherism 45
Tony Blair and New Labour 45
Between Europe and the Atlantic 47
The new British state – changing political processes 48

4 Political Ideologies: The Battle of Ideas 50
Ideas and politics 50
The meaning and political significance of ideology 51
Ideological conflict and consensus 52
Classifying ideologies: left and right 52
Ideologies and political parties 52
Liberalism – core interests and values 53
Traditional Conservatism 56
Thatcherism and the New Right 59
Post-Thatcherism and modern Conservatism 60
British socialism or labourism 62
From old to New Labour 65
Nationalism 66
Racism 68
Feminism 69
Green thinking 71
Globalization and the 'end of ideology' 71

PART II Participating in Politics 73

5 Ways of Participating in Politics 75
Political participation 75
Who participates? 76
Why participate? 78
Do individuals need to vote? 79
Public opinion and participation 79
Political competence and participation 80
A changing political culture? 81
Political socialisation 83
Citizenship entitlements 85

6 Election Systems and Electoral Reform 88
Electoral statistics 88
Turnout and outcomes 89
Proportionality in general elections 90

Tactical voting 90
Electoral systems 91
Electoral reform in Britain 94
Referendums 96

7 Voting Behaviour 99
The decline of the two-party system 99
The primacy approach: the social basis of
   voting behaviour 101
Social class and voting behaviour 102
Gender and voting 103
Age and voting 104
Ethnicity and voting 105
The recency approach 105
The image of the party leader 107
Party images 108
Can issue preferences explain voting
   behaviour? 108
An econometric explanation of voting
   preference 109
The 2001 election: a campaign that changed
   nothing? 110
Measuring public opinion 113

8 Political Parties 115
Why parties? 115
Party systems 115
Types of party – cadre and mass parties 118
Ideological and pragmatic parties 118
Parties and interests 119
Party cohesion – factions and tendencies 120
The organisation of parties – power and
   decision making 121
The leadership 122
Parliamentary parties 126
Party conferences and the national
   organisation of the parties 128
The party membership and constituency
   parties 130
Power within the parties – the modern party
   and its membership 131
The finance of political parties 133
The future of the British party system 134

9 Pressure Groups 136
What are pressure groups? 136
Pressure groups and the political system:
   history and trends 138
New social movements 141

Pressure group targets 144
Pressure group influence 148
Pressure groups and democracy 151

10 The Mass Media and Politics 156
The mass media and society 156
The 'media as part of democracy' viewpoint 157
The 'media as a tool of the ruling class'
   viewpoint 159
Television politics 162
The 'tabloidisation' of the mass media 163
Tabloid television 164
Newspaper readership 165
The political impact of the mass media 166
More media, less politics? 169

PART III **British Government:
   Westminster and Whitehall** 171

11 The Evolving British Constitution 173
What is a constitution? 173
The classification of constitutions 174
The evolution of the British Constitution 175
The main characteristics of the British
   Constitution 177
Representative democracy 180
The rule of law 180
Ideological perceptions of the British
   Constitution 181
The movement for constitutional reform 183
Labour and the constitution: a government
   of radical reform? 184

12 Prime Minister and Cabinet 187
The prime minister 187
The role of the prime minister 189
The Prime Minister's Office 194
The Cabinet 195
The Cabinet Office 197
Prime ministerial government? 198
A 'Blair presidency'? 200
Constraints on prime ministerial
   government 200
Prime ministerial power: an irrelevant
   debate? 203
Criticism of the British core executive 203

**13 Ministers, Departments and the
   Civil Service** 206

The organisation of British central
  government 206
The internal organisation of central
  government departments – politicians
  and civil servants 208
The civil service – size and distribution 209
The British civil service – three major features 210
Recruitment of the higher civil service –
  issues of expertise and bias 210
From old public administration to new
  public management? 213
The Conservative reforms: a revolution in
  government? 213
The Blair government and the civil service 216
Standards in public life 217
Ministerial responsibility revisited 218
Where does power lie? Decision making
  within departments 222
The resurgence of the traditional model: do
  ministers decide after all? 224

**14 Parliament and the Legislative
  Process** **227**
The functions of the House of Commons 228
Representation 228
Legislation 233
Scrutiny and influence of the executive 238
Forum for national debate 240
Recruitment of a government 241
Executive dominance of Parliament 242
Reform of the House of Commons 243
The upper chamber 244
Powers and functions of the upper chamber 244
Composition of the upper chamber 246
Reform of the upper chamber 246
The Westminster Parliament and other
  parliaments 249

**15 The Law, Politics and the Judicial
  Process** **251**
The rule of law 251
Law in England, Scotland and Europe 253
The courts 253
The judiciary 254
The police and policing 256
Human rights and civil liberties 258
Administrative law: protecting civil liberties
  and redressing grievances 259
Judicial review 260

Administrative tribunals 261
Statutory inquiries 262
The ombudsman system 263
The European Convention on Human Rights
  and the Human Rights Act 264

**PART IV Multi-Level Governance:
  Government and Politics
  Above and Below Whitehall
  and Westminster** **267**

16 Britain and the European Union **269**
The European ideal, 1945–58 269
Britain and Europe, 1945–73 270
The development of the European ideal:
  integration and enlargement 271
Britain and Europe from 1973 to the
  present 273
The European Union: superstate or
  inter-governmental organisation? 276
The institutions and processes of the
  European Union 277
The impact of the European Union on the
  British state and government 281
The impact of EU membership on
  British politics: parties, pressure groups
  and voters 283
The impact of the European Union on UK
  policies 285
The future of the European Union and the
  relationship between the UK and the EU 286

17 Devolution: The Disunited Kingdom **288**
The British state 288
A confused national identity? 288
Northern Ireland and Irish nationalism 290
The troubles in Northern Ireland 291
The search for peace in Northern Ireland 294
Scottish nationalism and the pressure for
  devolution 297
The Scottish Parliament and government 298
Devolution in Wales 299
Asymmetrical devolution 302
The English question 303
English regional government 304
Devolution, federalism or separation? 305

18 Local Governance **308**
From local government to local governance 308

Representing communities and securing
accountability   311
The politics of local governance: local
interests and parties   313
Decision making within organisations: local
politicians, managers and professionals   314
Territory and community: the reorganisation
of structure   316
The delivery of services   320
Reforming the finance of local governance   322
Central–local and inter-authority relations
under 'multi-level governance'   325

**19 The New British State: Towards Multi-Level
   Governance**   327
Characterising the modern British state   327
The attack on government   329
Restructuring the state: quangos and
agencies   329
Privatisation, contracting out and
competition   332
New Labour and partnership with business
and the voluntary sector   333
Steering, not rowing: the enabling state   335
The regulatory state   335
Open government and the secret state   338
The disintegration of the British state or
towards multi-level governance?   341

PART V Policies and Issues   **343**

20 The Policy Process   **345**
Policy making and decision making   345
The political agenda   346
Decision making theory   347
The policy making process   349
Policy analysis   350
'Joined-up' policy making   351
Modernising policy making   352
Political leadership   352
Sources of policy advice   355
Policy and implementation   356

21 Managing the Economy   **358**
The tools of economic management   358
Management of the economy: the Thatcher
and Major years   361
Economic management under New Labour   363
A prudent or a gambling chancellor?   366

Britain's open economy   367

22 Delivering Public Services   **369**
The changing context of public service
delivery   369
Investment in the public services   371
Delivering healthcare   372
Delivering market-led education   374
Delivering law and order   375
Problems with performance   376

23 Tackling Poverty and Exclusion   **378**
Rich Britain, poor Britain   378
Explanations for poverty and inequality:
family breakdown   379
Explanations for poverty and inequality:
changes in the labour market – the
30/30/40 society   381
Fresh approaches: community and
stakeholding   381
New Labour's anti-poverty programme   383
Conservative rethinking   384
The pensions crisis and future poverty   385

24 The Politics of Diversity   **387**
Black and British   387
Countering racism and discrimination   389
Institutional racism   391
Multi-cultural Britain?   392
Including women: the impact of the women's
movement on policy   394
Achievements of the women's movement
and areas of controversy   397
The diversity of alternative lifestyles:
lesbian and gay rights   397

25 Politics and the Environment   **401**
The environmental debate   401
The 'tragedy of the commons'   402
Green ideology   402
The political agenda and the political
process   403
The Green Party   404
The greening of mainstream political
parties?   404
Britain and transnational pollution   406
The European Union and international
commitments   407
The GM debate   408

26 Foreign and Defence Policies 410
The differing nature of external policy 410
The making of British foreign and defence
  policies 411
The basis of Britain's foreign policy 412
The Commonwealth 412
The special relationship with the USA 413
Britain in Europe 414
The EU versus NATO in British foreign and
  defence policies 414
From new world order to the war on terror 416
Britain and Europe's evolving relationship
  with Russia 416
An ethical foreign policy for Britain? 416
The war on terror 419
British foreign and defence policies in the
  21st century 419

27 Who Governs? Power and the New British
  Politics 422
Who gets what, when, how? 422
Top-down and bottom-up approaches to
  politics 423
Participating in politics 423
The power of the centre 424
Government and governance 426
Multi-level governance 427
The segmentation of public policy – policy
  communities 428
Governance and democracy 429
Democracy, equality and power 430
The future of British politics 431

Bibliography 435
Index 445

List of figures

2.1 The population of the United Kingdom of Great Britain and Northern Ireland, 2000 — 16
2.2 Gross Domestic Product by head by nation and selected English regions, 1999 — 17
2.3 National identity in Scotland, 2000 — 18
2.4 Non-white ethnic minorities in Britain (total 4,045,000) in the year 2000 — 20
2.5 Unemployment levels by ethnic group — 21
2.6 Unemployment levels among 18–24 year olds by ethnic group — 21
2.7 Religious affiliation, Great Britain, 2000 — 22
2.8 Changing patterns of housing tenure in Britain — 29
3.1 Britain's changing political culture — 46
4.1 Left–right, conventional scale — 52
4.2 Tensions within Thatcherism and the New Right — 61
4.3 Influences on the ideology of the Labour Party — 64
5.1 A hierarchy of political participation — 77
6.1 Ballot paper for European Parliament East Midlands region — 95
7.1 Class percentages voting Labour and Conservative, 1945–58 — 100
7.2 A framework for analysis of voting behaviour — 101
7.3 Class voting in the 2001 general election (change since 1997 at head of each column) — 102
7.4 Party support by age in the 2001 general election — 104
7.5 Electoral churn — 106
7.6 The most important issues to the electorate, 2001 — 109
7.7 2001: a campaign with little impact? — 111
8.1 Spending by parties, 2001 general election — 134
9.1 Insider and outsider groups — 138
9.2 New social movements: typical composition — 142
9.3 Pressure group influence on Whitehall and Westminster: the main stages — 148

9.4 Pressure group power structure — 152
12.1 Prime Minister's Office, as reorganised following the 2001 election — 195
13.1 Structure of a typical department of state (civil servants italicised) — 208
13.2 Ministers in the Department for Education and Skills, 2002 — 209
13.3 Women employed in the civil service by grade, 2001 — 212
14.1 Principal stages in the legislative process for government bills — 235
14.2 Party affiliations of members of upper house, 2001 — 248
15.1 The system of courts in England and Wales — 254
18.1 The structure of elected local government in Britain — 318
18.2 The local authority map in England from 1998 — 319
18.3 The 32 unitary authorities in Scotland operational from April 1996 — 320
18.4 The 22 unitary authorities in Wales operational from April 1996 — 321
20.1 The policy making process — 350
20.2 The educational policy making process — 351
20.3 Shading opinion — 353
21.1 The 'stop–go' cycle of the political economy — 359
21.2 The British economy: key indicators, 1990–2002 (smoothed trends) — 364
21.3 The 2002 Budget: income, expenditure and borrowing plans — 367
24.1 The social class of ethnic minority and white males (percentage of each ethnic group in each class) — 391
24.2 Female representation in British parliaments and assemblies as a percentage of the total — 398
24.3 Women's employment and pay, 1952 and 2002 — 400
26.1 The British foreign policy making process — 411
26.2 Defence expenditure, 2000 — 415

List of tables

1.1 Models of the possible distribution of power 9
2.1 The distribution of marketable wealth (adults aged 20 or over), 1999 25
3.1 Post-war British prime ministers 32
4.1 The Whig-Liberal tradition in Britain 55
4.2 The evolution of conservatism in Britain 58
5.1 Recent levels of turnout 76
5.2 Membership of parties and pressure groups (based on figures for 2001 and 2002) 76
5.3 Falling electoral turnouts 78
5.4 Political 'generations' and the political culture, 1960s–1990s 85
6.1 The 1992, 1997 and 2001 general elections 89
6.2 Elections to the Scottish Parliament, 1999 96
6.3 Welsh Assembly Elections, 1999 96
7.1 When the voting decision was made in 1997 (per cent) 100
7.2 Sex and party choice in general elections, 1987–97 (per cent) 103
7.3 Black and Asian voting in the 2001 general election (per cent) 105
7.4 Voting intentions and perceived economic management competence, May–June 2001 (per cent) 110
7.5 The 2001 general election results for Great Britain 112
7.6 The 2001 general election: results for Northern Ireland (changes since 1997 shown in brackets) 112
7.7 The 2001 general election: results for Scotland (changes since 1997 shown in brackets) 113
8.1 'Crossing the Floor': recent changes of party by sitting MPs 121
8.2 Labour leadership election 1994 (first and only ballot) 125
8.3 How the parties choose their leaders 125
8.4 The new National Executive Committee of the Labour Party 130
9.1 Groups' ranking of influences on public policy 147
9.2 Pressure groups and democracy: for and against 154
10.1 Newspaper ownership and wider media interests 161
12.1 Cabinets compared 188
12.2 Prime ministerial power and constraints on prime ministerial power: a brief summary 204
14.1 Party composition of the House of Commons after the 1997 and 2001 general elections 230
14.2 Parliamentary stages of legislation 236
14.3 Main methods of Commons' scrutiny of the executive 239
14.4 Benefits and limitations of departmental select committees (DSCs) 240
15.1 Senior judges by gender, 1999 255
16.1 Europe: what's in a name? 271
16.2 Time chart: key dates in development of the EC/EU and in UK involvement 275
16.3 The location, composition and functions of key European Union institutions 279
16.4 MEPs elected to European Parliament by country (after 1995 enlargement) 280
16.5 Votes and seats for UK parties in European Parliament elections, 1979–99 280
16.6 Party representation in the European Parliament, 1999 283
16.7 Examples of Europe-wide interest groups 284
16.8 Turnout levels: elections for the European Parliament (excluding new member states in 1995) 285
17.1 Some of the political parties in Northern Ireland 293
17.2 The June 1998 elections to the Northern Ireland Assembly 295
17.3 Elections for the Scottish Parliament, May 1999 298
17.4 Welsh National Assembly: election results, May 1999 301

17.5 Devolution in Scotland and Wales compared 303

18.1 Who does what? English county councils and district councils (principal functions) 322

19.1 From old government to new governance: the shifting focus 328

19.2 Types and examples of quangos 331

19.3 Some of the principal privatisations 332

19.4 From the old Westminster model to the new British governance 341

19.5 The new multi-level governance, as applied to Britain 341

20.1 Differing approaches to policy making 352

22.1 Contrasting administrative cultures 369

22.2 Welfare services: the market and the state 370

24.1 Liberal and radical approaches to equal opportunities 390

27.1 The transport policy community in Britain: some key players 429

List of boxes

1.1 What is politics? 3
1.2 Politics, conflict and coercion 4
1.3 Power, authority and influence 5
1.4 Democracy – some definitions and observations 6
1.5 Conditions for representative democracy 7
2.1 Identity politics, an illustration 19
2.2 Some social or occupational class categories commonly used in Britain 27
2.3 Self-assigned class? 28
3.1 1956: twilight of empire 35
3.2 The welfare state: the main measures 38
3.3 Retreat from empire 39
3.4 The Falklands conflict: a metaphor for Thatcherism? 43
3.5 The nature of political consensus 47
3.6 Devolution 48
4.1 What are political ideologies? 51
4.2 Core liberal values 54
4.3 Clause Four of the Labour Party Constitution (1918–95) 63
4.4 From the New Clause Four (adopted 1995) 65
4.5 Comparative politics: 'separation nationalism' 67
4.6 Institutional racism: the Macpherson Inquiry's definition, 1999 68
4.7 Comparative politics: fascism and racism 69
5.1 The new politics of participation 82
5.2 Greenpeace: can direct action be justified in a liberal democracy? 83
5.3 The confused British citizen 86
6.1 Types of majoritarian system 92
6.2 Types of proportional representation system 93
6.3 The Jenkins Report 95
6.4 Comparative politics – elections in Germany – an AMS comparison 96
6.5 The merits and disadvantages of initiatives and referendums 97
8.1 Main functions of political parties 116
8.2 Comparative politics: party systems in other countries 117

8.3 The authority of Labour and Conservative leaders compared 123
8.4 How the Conservative Party elected its leader, 1965–98 124
8.5 Recommendations of the Neill Committee on party funding, 1998 134
9.1 The Countryside Alliance, September 2002 140
9.2 Comparative politics: left and right social movements in the UK and USA 142
9.3 The National Farmers Union (NFU) 152
9.4 The Royal Society for the Prevention of Cruelty to Animals (RSPCA) 153
10.1 Media values: anti-Semitism and pro-Israeli bias in reporting Middle Eastern affairs? 157
10.2 Do the British public's Euro-sceptic attitudes result from press hostility to the EU? 162
10.3 Comparative politics: the 'watchdog' role of the British and American press 163
10.4 The importance of timing in media political influence: the Zinoviev letter 167
10.5 Looking back to 1992 and 1997: did the *Sun* win it? 168
10.6 The lobby system 168
11.1 Comparative politics: federalism in the USA and other countries 176
11.2 The major sources of the British Constitution 177
11.3 Comparative politics: constitutional monarchies and republics 178
11.4 The main demands of Charter 88 183
11.5 Constitutional reform: the Labour–Liberal Democrat proposals, 1997 183
11.6 The Labour government's legislation on constitutional reform 184
11.7 The end of Parliamentary sovereignty and the unitary state? 185
12.1 The role of the prime minister: key aspects 189
12.2 Prime ministers and Parliament 193
12.3 The 'kitchen cabinet' 194
12.4 The role of the Cabinet 195

12.5 Some important Cabinet committees in Blair's government 197

12.6 The practical implications of collective Cabinet responsibility 199

12.7 President Blair? Two contrasting perspectives 200

12.8 Comparative politics: prime ministers and presidents 201

13.1 Departmental reorganisation under the Blair government 207

13.2 Features of the British civil service 210

13.3 Comparative politics – public bureaucracies in the USA and France, compared with Britain 211

13.4 Features of new public management 213

13.5 Example of an executive agency: the Driver and Vehicle Licensing Agency (set up 1990) 215

13.6 The impact of reform on key attributes of the traditional civil service 216

13.7 The Nolan Report, 1995: the seven principles of public life 217

13.8 Extracts from *Cabinet Practice: A Code of Conduct and Guidance on Procedure for Ministers* 218

13.9 The politics of individual and collective responsibility 220

13.10 The Scott Report (1996) – a case studyin the refusal to admit responsibility? 221

13.11 Constraints on the effective power of ministers 223

14.1 Unrepresentative MPs 229

14.2 Maintaining party cohesion and discipline in the House of Commons 231

14.3 MPs and the representation of interests – some areas of concern 232

14.4 Comparative politics: the UK Parliament and the US Congress 237

14.5 Limitations on Private Members' bills 238

14.6 Reasons for government control of the House of Commons 242

14.7 Old and interim reformed composition of the House of Lords, after House of Lords Act 1999 247

15.1 Types of law 252

15.2 Civil rights in the United Kingdom (and some limitations) 259

15.3 Grounds for judicial review 261

15.4 Rights under the European Convention on Human Rights and its Protocols (summarised) 265

16.1 Enlargement of the European Community/Union, 1952–2003 272

16.2 The principle of subsidiarity 277

16.3 Arguments for and against Britain joining the single European currency 286

17.1 The British state: core and periphery 290

17.2 The roots of conflict in Northern Ireland: different perspectives 292

17.3 The Northern Ireland Executive at the time of suspension (October 2002) 296

17.4 The Scottish Cabinet, June 2002 299

17.5 Comparative politics – the future of Scotland: the Quebec scenario or the Slovak scenario? 300

17.6 The Welsh Cabinet (June 2002) 301

17.7 The regional development agencies 304

18.1 Some of the appointed councils, authorities and trusts operating at local level, 2000 309

18.2 Some examples of 'joined-up' policy initiatives 311

18.3 The case for local democratic institutions 312

18.4 Comparative politics – running US cities – mayors and city managers 315

18.5 The community power debate 316

18.6 The government of London: the London Mayor and Greater London Authority 318

18.7 The poll tax – a policy disaster 324

19.1 Executive agencies and quangos 331

19.2 From Railtrack to Network Rail 334

19.3 Some important regulatory bodies 337

19.4 Britain's security services 338

20.1 Reshaping the political agenda: 'back to basics' 347

20.2 The Phillips Inquiry: lessons about policy making 353

20.3 Contrasting the Thatcher and Blair approaches 354

21.1 Prices and incomes policies in the 1960s and 1970s 359

21.2 The pro-business party loses the support of business 362

21.3 Labour and the euro 365

21.4 The radical Labour budget of 2002 367

22.1 Britain's largest PFI contracts (2002) 372
22.2 Nine key performance indicators for acute hospital trusts 373
22.3 Law and order 376
23.1 Political controversy over the meaning of poverty 380
23.2 New Labour's main anti-poverty measures 383
23.3 A profile of poverty in Britain 384
23.4 Identifying the poor 384
23.5 The pensions crisis: key factors 385
24.1 Blacks and Asians 388
24.2 Race riots in northern towns in Britain, 2001: the Ouseley Report 393
24.3 Islamophobia 395
24.4 The left, right and centre of good race relations 396
24.5 Women in Parliament 398
24.6 *The New Feminism* 399
25.1 Political concern about the environment: the five-stage cycle 404
25.2 A Green transport policy? 405
25.3 The Environment Agency 407
25.4 The Kyoto Agreement 408
26.1 Britain's 'special relationship' with the USA 413
26.2 The Western European Union 414
26.3 The views of Francis Fukuyama and Samuel Huntington 415
26.4 NATO membership status 417

26.5 The Ottawa Convention banning anti-personnel landmines 418
27.1 Parties and pressure groups: power, influence and democracy 425
27.2 People power or business power? 426

'In Focus' boxes

1.1 Representative democracy in action! 10
4.1 Margaret Thatcher 60
6.1 Replacing the Conservatives? 94
7.1 Leaders under fire 107
8.1 Competing for power 122
9.1 The country comes to town 141
10.1 The master of spin? 164
12.1 Where are they now? 188
12.2 The Cabinet, October 2002 190
12.3 The Cabinet in session 196
13.1 Whitehall 209
14.1 Mother of Parliaments? 227
15.1 Cherie Booth 256
16.1 Europe's new currency 273
17.1 Cooperation between devolved governments 306
18.1 The Mayor of London 317
19.1 David Shayler 339
21.1 Blair and Brown 363
22.1 Holding the purse strings 371
24.1 A war against terror or a war against Islam? 394
26.1 The special relationship survives? 420

Preface to the fourth edition

This edition of *Contemporary British Politics* has required more or less complete rewriting to take account of the dramatic changes in British politics since publication of the third edition just one year into New Labour's first term in office.

Most importantly the whole British system of government has been radically overhauled, largely as a consequence of New Labour's constitutional reform programme. Thus in this new edition we have had to not only incorporate extensive new material, but also rethink the analysis of British government in the light of developments which challenge long established constitutional principles and raise fundamental questions about the whole future of the British state.

The international context in which British politics takes place has been transformed by the events of 11 September 2001, the Afghanistan war and the crisis over Iraq. The introduction of the euro in most of the other EU member states and the agreement over enlargement have marked a step change in the development of the European Union, and posed new policy dilemmas for the British government. There have been significant changes in the process and content of British politics, with major developments in almost every field of policy.

The chapter structure of this edition has been modified to take account of the implications of devolution and the increasing significance of the EU, with analysis of the more familiar British government in Whitehall and Westminster in Part III complemented by an assessment of new patterns of multi-level governance in Part IV. The design and layout of the book has been reconsidered to make this edition as user-friendly as possible. Throughout we have tried to ensure that the illustrative material effectively complements the text. We have kept some of the tried and tested features, such as the definition boxes and other illustrative boxed material, although here have tried to make the boxes shorter and crisper. We have added 'comparative' boxes to illuminate our analysis of British politics by setting it in an international context. We have added more graphs and charts and tried to simplify the presentation of tables. However, to keep the overall length and cost of the book in reasonable proportions, and to avoid undue interference with the flow of the text, we decided to transfer some very useful features included in the old third edition to the new companion website.

New to this edition is a companion www site which can be found at <http://www.palgrave.com/politics/coxall> and performs a number of functions. One is obviously to provide regular updates on all the topics covered in the book as a result of on-going political events and developments, together with the latest scholarly analysis. We have also transferred to the website some of the features incorporated in previous editions, including additional teaching material, revision summaries, questions and assignments, which we have expanded and plan to continue to develop in future.

Bill Coxall, who wrote the first three editions of *Contemporary British Politics* with Lynton Robins, died in March 1999 shortly after publication of the third edition. This edition is dedicated to Bill, without whom it would not exist, and from whom it has inherited many of its most learned and fluent passages. He has been sadly missed in the preparation of this edition, for which the extensive new material has been written by Lynton Robins with Robert Leach, who has also taken over Bill Coxall's previous coordinating role.

Lynton Robins
Robert Leach

Acknowledgements

The authors and publishers are grateful to the following for permission to use copyright material: Steven Carroll for illustration in Table 3.1; PA photos for photographs in In Focus 1.1, 4.1, 6.1, 7.1, 9.1, 10.1, 12.3, 14.1, 15.1, 17.1, 18.1, 19.1, 21.1, 24.1, 26.1 ; COI for photograph in In Focus 12.1; Imagemakers London Ltd for photograph in In Focus 12.2; Steve Bell for cartoon in In Focus 22.1. Every effort has been made to trace all copyright holders of third party materials included in this work but if any have been inadvertently overlooked the publishers will be pleased to make the necessary arrangements at the first opportunity.

Robert Leach would like to thank his wife, Judith, for her understanding and forbearance throughout the preparation of this edition. Lynton Robins is grateful to his wife, Vivien, for her support. He would also like to thank his son Matthew, a Politics postgraduate, for his assistance in the library and for drafting possibilities for the final chapters.

List of abbreviations

ACEA	Association of European Automobile Companies	DHSS	Department of Health and Social Security
ACPO	Association of Chief Police Officers	DID	Department of International Development
AI	Amnesty International		
ALF	Animal Liberation Front	DMU	directly managed unit
AM	additional member system	DOE	Department of the Environment (now part of DEFRA)
APNI	Alliance Party of Northern Ireland		
ASH	Action on Smoking and Health	DSC	departmental select committee
AV	alternative vote	DTI	Department of Trade and Industry
AWM	Advantage West Midlands (development agency)	DUP	Democratic Unionist Party
		EAPC	Euro-Atlantic Partnership Council (replaced by NATO-RC)
BBC	British Broadcasting Corporation		
BEUC	European Bureau of Consumers' Associations	ECAS	European Citizen Action Service
		ECHR	European Court of Human Rights
BMA	British Medical Association	ECSC	European Coal and Steel Community
BMD	ballistic missile defence shield		
BNP	British National Party	EDM	Early Day Motion
BPPS	British Political Participation Survey	EEA	European Economic Area
BSA	British Social Attitudes	EEB	European Environmental Bureau
BSE	bovine spongiform encephalitis ('mad cow' disease)	EEC	European Economic Community
		EEDA	East of England Development Agency
BUF	British Union of Fascists		
CAP	Common Agricultural Policy	EFTA	European Free Trade Association
CBI	Confederation of British Industry	EGO	extra-governmental organisation
CCT	compulsory competitive tendering	EMDA	East Midlands Development Agency
CEFIC	European Chemistry Industry Council	EMS	European Monetary System
		EMU	economic and monetary union
CEMR	Council of European Municipalities and Regions	EP	European Parliament
		ERM	Exchange Rate Mechanism of the EMS
CLEAR	Campaign for Lead-Free Air		
CLP	Constituency Labour Party	ESC	Economic and Social Committee
CND	Campaign for Nuclear Disarmament	ETUC	European Trade Union Confederation
COPA	Committee of Professional Agricultural Organisations (EU)		
		EU	European Union
COREPER	Committee of Permanent Representatives (EU)	EUROBIT	European Association of Manufacturers of Business Machines and Information Technology
CPAG	Child Poverty Action Group		
CPGB	Communist Party of Great Britain	FCO	Foreign and Commonwealth Office
CPRE	Council for the Protection of Rural England	FPTP	first-past-the post
		FSA	Financial Services Authority
CRE	Commission for Racial Equality	GATT	General Agreement on Tariffs and Trade
DEFRA	Department of the Environment, Food and Rural Affairs		
		GCHQ	Government Communications Headquarters
DHA	District Health Authority		

GDP	Gross Domestic Product	Ofgem	Office of Gas and Electricity
GLA	Greater London Authority		Markets
GNP	Gross National Product	Ofsted	Office for Standards in Education
GOR	government offices for the regions	OFT	Office of Fair Trading
HAT	Housing Action Trust	Oftel	Office of Telecommunications
IMF	International Monetary Fund	Ofwat	Office of Water Services
IMRO	Investment Management Regulatory	OMOV	one man (person) one vote
	Organisation	ONE	One North East (development
INLA	Irish National Liberation Army		agency)
IPPR	Institute for Public Policy	OPEC	Organisation of Petroleum
	Research		Exporting Countries
IRA	Irish Republican Army	ORR	Office of the Rail Regulator
IRC	Industrial Reorganisation	PAC	Public Accounts Committee
	Corporation	PC	Plaid Cymru
ITA	Independent Television Authority	PESC	Public Expenditure Survey
LA	local authority		Committee
LSE	London School of Economics	PFI	private finance initiative
LMS	local management of schools	PfP	Partnership for Peace (for former
MAD	mutually assured destruction		Warsaw Pact members, now replaced
MAFF	Ministry of Agriculture, Fisheries		by EAPC)
	and Food (now subsumed into	PLP	Parliamentary Labour Party
	DEFRA)	PM	Prime Minister
MEP	member of the European	PMQT	Prime Minister's Question Time
	Parliament	PPP	public–private partnerships
MINIS	Management Information System for	PPS	Parliamentary Private Secretary
	Ministers	PR	proportional representation
MLR	Minimum Lending Rate	PSAs	public service agreements
MoD	Ministry of Defence	PSBR	Public Sector Borrowing
MP	Member of Parliament		Requirement
MSP	Member of the Scottish Parliament	PUP	Progressive Unionist Party
MWA	Member of the Welsh Assembly	QAA	Qualifications and Assessments
NATO	North Atlantic Treaty		Authority
	Organisation	QMV	qualified majority voting
NATO-RC	NATO-Russia Council	qualgo	quasi-autonomous local
NDO	non-departmental body		government organisation
NDPB	non-departmental public body	quango	quasi-autonomous non-governmental
NEB	National Enterprise Board		organisation
NEC	National Executive Committee	RDA	regional development agency
	(of the Labour Party)	RSPB	Royal Society for the Protection of
NEDC	National Economic Development		Birds
	Council (now defunct)	RSPCA	Royal Society for the Prevention of
NF	National Front		Cruelty to Animals
NFU	National Farmers' Union	SCS	Senior Civil Service
NHS	National Health Service	SDLP	Social Democratic and Labour Party
NIA	Northern Ireland Assembly	SDP	Social Democratic Party (now
NNDR	national non-domestic rates		subsumed into Liberal Democratic
NWDA	Northwest Development Agency		Party)
OECD	Organisation for Economic	SDR	strategic defence review
	Cooperation and Development	SEA	Single European Act

SEEDA	South East England Development Agency	UKIP	UK Independence Party
SF	Sinn Fein	UKUP	United Kingdom Unionist Party
SNP	Scottish National Party	UN	United Nations
SOLACE	Society of Local Authority Chief Executives	UNICE	Union of Industrial and Employers' Confederations of Europe
SSP	Scottish Socialist Party	USA	United States of America
STV	single transferable vote	UUP	Ulster Unionist Party
SWERDA	South West of England Regional Development Agency	UVF	Ulster Volunteer Force
		VAT	value added tax
SWP	Socialist Workers' Party	vCJD	variant Creutzfeld-Jacob disease (the human variant of 'mad cow' disease
TGWU	Transport and General Workers Union		
TUC	Trades Union Congress	WA	Welsh Assembly
UDA	Ulster Defence Association	WRP	Workers' Revolutionary Party
UDC	Urban Development Corporation	WTO	World Trade Organisation
UDP	Ulster Democratic Party	YF	Yorkshire Forward (development agency)
UK	United Kingdom		

Part I

THE CONTEXT OF BRITISH POLITICS

Politics is a controversial subject, which is what makes it fascinating. Those who like a good argument should enjoy the study of politics. Yet politics is also a social science, requiring a thorough detached analysis of political institutions, processes and behaviour. This book aims to provide scientific analysis without neglecting the controversy. Both elements of the study of politics are introduced in the first part of the book.

We begin in Chapter 1 with some big questions to which there are conflicting answers. What is politics? How is political power distributed, and who has power in Britain? What is democracy, and how far is British government and politics democratic? Should our central focus still be on the British state in these days of globalization and European integration on the one hand, and devolution and decentralisation on the other? Will the United Kingdom stay united? These questions, introduced at the start of the book, will be examined further in later chapters.

If political disagreement and conflict reflect divisions in the economy and society, it is important to examine their nature and extent. Chapter 2 therefore focuses on the social and economic context of British politics, and explores national, ethnic, religious, gender and class divisions within what is becoming a multi-cultural Britain. This chapter inevitably draws heavily on statistical analysis, but also points, more speculatively, to some of the implications for British politics and government.

Politics is dynamic rather than static. To understand the present and make plausible predictions of possible futures it is necessary to know something of the recent past. In Chapter 3 we identify some of the main themes and trends in British politics since 1945. This time dimension helps illuminate some of the key political issues of today: the management of the economy, the distribution of income and wealth, the delivery of public services, the relations of Britain with Europe and the wider world, and the relationship between the government in Whitehall and Westminster and the nations, regions and local communities that make up the United Kingdom. Many of the issues with which the Blair Labour government has been grappling since 1997 have been recurring themes in Britain's post-war history.

The fourth and final chapter of this opening part reflects the importance we attach to conflicting ideas, interests and values in the study of politics. While some assume that modern politics is all about presentation and 'spin' rather than substance, and that all politicians and parties are much the same, we maintain that widely different assumptions and interests continue to underlie contrasting perspectives on politics and to influence political attitudes and behaviour. We explore a range of ideological perspectives, including not only the 'mainstream' ideologies of liberalism, conservatism, socialism, which are loosely associated with political parties, but also nationalism, racism, feminism and green thinking, all of which underpin different ways of looking at politics. They help to explain not only party preferences and allegiances, but differing attitudes to political involvement, conflicting views on the scope and purpose of government, and widely varying positions on a wide range of policies.

Chapter 1

Politics, Democracy and Power

What is politics?	3
Authority, power and influence	5
Democracy – power to the people?	5
Power in Britain	7
Perspectives on power	8
British politics?	11
Multi-level governance	12
Policies – who gets what, when, how?	13

Politics is a subject that arouses conflicting emotions. Some are intensely interested in political issues and follow politics keenly. For others politics involves distant institutions, remote politicians and obscure complex issues with little direct relevance for immediate everyday life. Others again show a strong distaste towards political parties and politicians who are 'all the same' or 'on the make', and 'only interested in what they can get out of it'. Unsurprisingly such critics argue it would be much better if education, or health, or agriculture could be somehow 'taken out of politics'.

Yet politics is inescapable. Everyone is affected by it whether they like it or not. At the very least people have to pay taxes and obey laws, or suffer the penalties. They are obliged to register births, marriages and deaths, and fill in forms for countless other purposes. They can only drive their cars, exchange their houses or travel abroad if they fulfil the necessary requirements. In some states citizens are still liable to conscription into the armed forces. All this emphasises what may appear to be the downside of politics – the restraints on individual freedom, although of course these same restraints on others might help communities to enjoy peace, security, and the pursuit of their own lives without fear. More positively people receive various services provided or financed through the state in some form or other. Mostly these services are regarded as beneficial, although some may seem irksome or extravagant. Indeed, precisely what services should be provided by the state, the level of those services and how

they should be provided and paid for are political questions, which cannot be 'taken out of politics' because they have massive consequences for individuals and communities. Even the privatisation in Britain of some activities which were formerly state owned and run (such as rail transport) has not succeeded in depoliticising them.

What is politics?

Various answers have been given to the simple question 'What is politics?' Some of them are given in Box 1.1.

The first definition links politics and government in a common sense way. Clearly politics is about government, and this book analyses at some length the institutions of government. Yet this definition does seem to imply that politics is a rather remote activity, not for ordinary people. How far does politics include the governed as well as those doing the governing? And does it just imply the government of states? Some definitions of politics suggest that it is not only a universal human activity, as the ancient Greek philosopher Aristotle argued, but can take place at very different levels and in different spheres. Thus some talk of the politics of the golf club, or the

---

BOX 1.1

What is politics?

'The science and art of government.' (Shorter Oxford English Dictionary)

'Who gets what, when, how.' (H. Lasswell, American political scientist)

'The authoritative allocation of values.' (David Easton, another American political scientist)

'The art of the possible.' (R. A. Butler, British Conservative politician)

BOX 1.2

Politics, conflict and coercion

'Political power grows out of the barrel of a gun.' (Mao Zedong, Chinese Communist leader)

'War is nothing but a continuation of politics by other means.' (Von Clausewitz, Prussian military strategist)

'Every state is founded on force.' (Leon Trotsky, Russian Communist politician)

'The state is a human community that (successfully) claims the *monopoly of the legitimate use of physical force* within a given territory.' (Max Weber, German sociologist)

---

board room, or the university. However, the study of politics does in practice focus largely on government and public policy rather than what is sometimes called 'micro-politics'.

The two crisp American definitions suggest (in rather different language) that politics is about choosing between alternatives. Individuals, communities and governments cannot have everything they want, but must determine their priorities. Butler hints at the constraints involved in the political process. Compromise is often necessary because different sections of the community want different and often conflicting things. It is not possible to please everyone all the time. Decisions commonly produce winners and losers. Indeed some have seen disagreement and conflict as the essence of politics, and have emphasised the role of coercion and physical force. (See Box 1.2.)

All these quotations emphasise the coercive and violent side of politics, which is only too obvious in the modern world. Might matters more than right. Indeed, those who have physical force on their side may determine what is right. Justice appears to be merely 'what is in the interests of the stronger party' (as the sophist Thrasymachus declared in Plato's *Republic*, one of the earliest and most celebrated analyses of politics).

Yet such interpretations of politics do not tell the whole story. Power may be used for constructive as well destructive purposes. Politics may arise out of

disagreement and conflict, which may some times take a violent form, but it also involves the search for a peaceful resolution of conflict through compromise. Indeed a 'political solution' is commonly seen as an alternative to violence. Winston Churchill, famous largely as a great war leader, once observed, 'Jaw jaw is better than war war', while a noted French political scientist, Maurice Duverger (1972: 221), defined politics as 'a continual effort to eliminate physical violence'. Politics, he claimed, 'tends to replace fists, knives, clubs and rifles with other types of weapons', although he added sadly, 'it is not always successful in doing so'.

There are disagreements also over the scope of politics. Some liberals and conservatives would draw a clear distinction between the state and civil society, between a public or political sphere and a private sphere of life from which politics should be excluded – the family and other voluntary associations. Champions of the free market would seek to exclude the state and politics from much economic activity, and place firm limits on government intervention. By contrast, many socialists have sought to establish a political system in which the state controlled the economy. Fascism was associated with a totalitarian theory of the state, under which the state was all-embracing and excluded from no sphere of activity.

While some of these approaches to politics have become less fashionable, other contemporary political ideologies have involved a radical reinterpretation of the scope of politics. Thus feminists insist 'the personal is political'. They are not concerned just with formal legal equality in the public sphere, but with gender relations in the family, home and bedroom, because these are seen as central to the injustice and oppression suffered by women. Consequently, interpersonal relations,

---

Definitions
The state is a political and governmental unit – a compulsory association which is sovereign over a particular territory.
Civil society refers to the part of social life outside the control of the state, e.g. clubs, groups and associations, private business, the family.

sexual relations, and the division of labour within the home are not purely private matters but a legitimate sphere for political engagement. At another level Green ideas have politicised a whole range of issues which at one time were not seen as having much, if anything, to do with politics.

Authority, power and influence

Politics is clearly about power, but this key concept is difficult to define. Power suggests a capacity to achieve desired results, and compel obedience. It may be lawful or unlawful. An armed criminal may compel his victims to do things that they would not choose. He or she is clearly exercising power, although unlawfully. Others, such as a government minister, or a judge, may also wield effective power, but power that is generally recognised as rightful and legitimate. The term 'authority' is widely used to describe the rightful use of political power, or legitimate power. Power may compel obedience, while authority is widely accepted by those over whom it is exercised. We voluntarily obey those in authority because we accept the legitimacy of their power.

Why do we obey them? The German sociologist Max Weber distinguished between three main types or sources of authority: traditional, charismatic and legal-rational. Traditional authority rests on long-established custom – the authority of a tribal chief or hereditary monarch for example. Charismatic authority derives from the compelling personal qualities of an individual – the authority exercised by a Napoleon, Hitler or (more positively) Nelson Mandela. They are obeyed because of who they are, rather than because of what they are. Legal-rational authority is authority based on formal rules. Elected politicians and appointed government officials may be obeyed, not because of custom, nor because of their personal qualities, but because it is acknowledged that they legitimately hold their offices under accepted rules and procedures. It is the office or post rather than the person who occupies the post whose authority is obeyed. Weber considered that legal-rational authority is the characteristic form of authority in the modern world.

> **BOX 1.3**
> ## Power, authority and influence
>
> **Power** is the capacity to achieve desired goals.
> **Authority** is the rightful or legitimate use of power.
> **Influence** involves the ability to shape a decision or outcome through various forms of pressure.

Both modern bureaucracy and representative democracy involve legal-rational authority.

Power is sometimes also distinguished from influence. While 'power' implies a capacity to determine outcomes directly, 'influence' suggests the ability to shape outcomes indirectly, to exert pressure on those who are taking the decisions, persuading them to change their opinion and behaviour. The study of politics involves examining not just the formal institutions and offices directly involved in government, but also the influences on government and the policy process, the role for example of business organisations and trade unions, voluntary bodies and cause groups. Many political decisions taken by politicians or civil servants may have their origin and explanation in the successful influence of particular pressure groups or interests in society.

Democracy – power to the people?

Britain, along with most states in the modern western world, and many others elsewhere, claims to be a democracy. This near universal approval of democracy as a system of government is relatively recent. A form of democracy flourished in ancient Athens nearly 2,500 years ago, but from then until at least the late 18th century democracy scarcely existed anywhere, and was regarded as a remote and essentially impractical theoretical model. While direct rule by all the people themselves was just about possible in a small city state like ancient Athens, it was impractical for the extensive empires and large nation states that have flourished subsequently. Democracy became more feasible with the development of representative democracy rather than direct democracy.

Definitions
Direct democracy involves the direct and continuous participation of citizens in government.
Representative democracy involves indirect government by the people through representatives elected by the people.

Instead of the people themselves, the elected representatives of the people would rule.

Representative democracy has become so universally popular that even some of the most tyrannical and corrupt regimes lay claim to the title 'democratic' for form's sake. Even so, democracy has often been accorded only faint praise by some influential modern thinkers and politicians.

Whether modern representative democracy does ensure real government by the people, as Abraham Lincoln asserted, is far from clear. Indeed it does not even invariably result in a government chosen by the majority of the people (see Chapter 6). Yet at a minimum in mature democratic systems it does offer an element of real choice between rival parties and programmes, it does render opposition respectable rather than treasonable, and it does provide for the peaceful transfer of power between governments. These are very considerable benefits which should not be under-

rated, particularly when the alternatives are considered.

While the British like to think they invented modern representative democracy, the Americans and the French have a rather better claim. The American rebels against the British state and crown, through their successful Declaration of Independence of 1776, and the constitution they devised for the United States of America soon afterwards, effectively created the first modern democracy (despite the institution of slavery and the effective exclusion of black Americans from political rights long after the abolition of slavery). It was in France, following the revolution of 1789, that the ideas of popular sovereignty and liberty, equality and fraternity were substituted (initially only briefly) for the autocracy of the old French monarchy.

Britain only came to terms with democracy rather later. Although England boasts an ancient Parliament with over 700 years of near-continuous existence since it was established in 1265, even the lower house of that Parliament, the House of Commons, was not democratically elected until recently. Only a small proportion of adult males could participate in elections until a series of Reform Acts extended the vote to most men in the course of the 19th century. Even so, women could not vote until 1918, and they only obtained the vote on the same terms as men in 1928. Even today

---

BOX 1.4
Democracy – some definitions and observations

'Our constitution is called a democracy because power is in the hands not of a minority but of the whole people.' (Pericles of Athens, 431 B.C., as reported in Thucydides, *History of the Peloponnesian War* (Penguin edn,: 145)

'Government of the people, by the people, for the people.' (President Abraham Lincoln, Gettysburg address, 1863)

'Were there a people of gods, their government would be democratic. So perfect a government is not for men.' (Jean-Jacques Rousseau, *The Social Contract*, 1762)

'Democracy substitutes election by the incompetent many for appointment by the corrupt few.' (George Bernard Shaw, *Man and Superman*, 1903)

'Democracy is the worst form of government except all those other forms that have been tried from time to time.' (Winston Churchill, speech in House of Commons, 11 November 1947)

'So two cheers for democracy: one because it admits variety and two because it permits criticism. Two cheers are quite enough: there is no occasion to give three.' (E. M. Forster, *Two Cheers for Democracy*, 1951)

BOX 1.5

Conditions for representative democracy

- Full adult franchise – that is, all adults have the right to vote.
- A secret ballot – helps ensure voting without intimidation or bribery.
- Regular elections – governments and parliaments must not be able to postpone elections.
- Fair elections – each vote should count equally.
- An effective choice of candidates and parties for voters.
- A level playing field between rival parties and candidates contesting elections.
- A free and diverse media enabling a wide expression of views.

---

it is questionable how far Britain satisfies all the conditions to qualify as a full and fair system of representative democracy.

How far and fully Britain satisfies the conditions outlined in Box 1.5 will be discussed in more detail later in this book (particularly in Part II), although it would be generally conceded that British elections do involve a real choice and they are not patently rigged (as they are in some countries). Yet regardless of the extent of the right to vote and the mechanics of the electoral system, there are many who would question whether government 'of the people, by the people, for the people' is a reality in Britain. First, are the elected representatives of the people the real rulers of Britain? Second, and more importantly, how far do the right to vote, and other rights associated with the political system, give the people or the majority of the people real power?

Do elected politicians make the real decisions that affect the British people? Perhaps the real decision makers are not the politicians who tend to dominate the news but relatively faceless civil servants or advisers. Alternatively, more real power and influence may be exercised by individuals who are not part of the formal political process at all – businessmen (and they are usually still 'men'!), bankers, or owners of newspapers, television companies and other media, some of whom may not

even be British. Yet perhaps it is a mistake to think in terms of individual personalities, no matter how apparently influential and colourful. Real power may reside in organisations regardless of who currently appears to control them – corporate power. Again, many of these organisations transcend national boundaries.

However, if democracy is the rule of the many not the few, a more fundamental question is whether ordinary people have any real control or influence over these powerful individuals and organisations. Those who bother to use their vote may determine which of two or three rival teams of politicians occupy government posts for the next four or five years, but does this give voters significant influence over key government decisions and policies? What other opportunities do citizens have to participate in the political process? How far can 'ordinary people' hope to have a real voice in the many decisions that affect them? These questions will be addressed throughout this book, but particularly in chapters on elections and voting, parties and pressure groups, the media and public opinion, and the legislative process.

Power in Britain

While it may be possible to determine who has authority in a political system by examining the constitution, laws, written regulations and lists of office holders, it is much more difficult to assess power and influence. Newspapers and magazines sometimes attempt to compile lists of the most powerful people in Britain. These may generally be headed by the prime minister, as one might expect, but often include prominent businesspeople, media magnates and even sports personalities and pop idols, interspersed among some other elected politicians. Such lists are hardly scientific and may reflect little more than the highly subjective views of the journalists who compose them, but they do suggest that power is not just confined to those who hold some formal position in government, and that business tycoons such as Rupert Murdoch or Sir Richard Branson have more power than some Cabinet ministers.

One cynical conclusion might be that 'money talks': those with substantial wealth and income can use it to buy (sometimes literally) political influence. Yet there is no simple correlation between wealth and power. Newspapers also sometimes list the wealthiest people in Britain, but some of the names near the top of such lists, such as the Duke of Westminster or the Queen, do not figure prominently if at all in the lists of those with power. There are others, such as leading footballers and pop stars, who avoid any formal association with politics and lack significant economic power, but yet may have enormous influence as role models on behaviour, and perhaps contribute more to changing political attitudes on key issues than professional politicians. Yet again, it is possible that real power and influence is exercised by many who are not celebrities – 'faceless bureaucrats', or political advisers.

However, this whole approach may make too much of the power of particular individuals. Ministers and company chairs come and go, but the organisations they head generally last much longer. Perhaps we should be looking at the power of institutions. Perhaps the civil service, or the City of London, or multi-national corporations exercise far more effective power and influence in the British political process than any single personality. Alternatively, power may not lie with particular institutions but with more amorphous interests or elites, such as 'the ruling class' or 'the establishment', or 'big business' or 'the military-industrial complex' or 'global capitalism'. The implication behind such notions is that the individuals who hold formal positions of power, the official rulers, are driven by forces outside their control.

Definitions
Elite – an elite is a small dominant group. Elite theorists argue that power is inevitably exercised by the few (or by an elite or elites) even in nominally democratic organisations or states.
The establishment is a term sometimes used to describe the British elite, an unaccountable dominant social group largely educated at leading public schools and ancient universities.
The ruling class is a term used particularly by Marxists to describe those who own and control capital, and whose economic power gives them political power.

Definitions
Pluralism involves the belief that power is widely dispersed through society, rather than heavily concentrated in the hand of an elite or ruling class.
Neo-pluralism is a modified version of pluralism which still emphasises the dispersal of power while acknowledging the influence of key interests (e.g. business).
Democratic elitism is a modified form of elitism which still emphasises the importance of elites or leadership in politics, while acknowledging that competition between elites (e.g. through elections) encourages them to be responsive and accountable to the masses.

Alternatively we can seek to identify those who are effectively excluded from power. Thus it is often suggested that certain groups or interests might be marginalised in the political system – the unemployed, or ethnic minorities, or teenagers, or women, or those who live and work in the countryside. There may be sub-cultures, an underclass, or possibly a whole gender largely excluded from the political process.

All this implies that power may be rather or very unevenly distributed. Some, perhaps a small minority, appear to have a great deal of power, others relatively little influence, while others again may be virtually excluded from any effective participation in the decisions that affect their lives. Yet not everyone would agree that power is so narrowly concentrated; some would argue that ordinary people do have the capacity to influence and even determine key outcomes, in accordance with notions of democracy.

Perspectives on power

Who then rules Britain? It is a simple question, to which a variety of simple answers may be given: Britain has cabinet or prime ministerial government, Parliamentary sovereignty, an elected dictatorship, government by bureaucracy, business or corporate power, the dominance of an 'establishment' or 'ruling class'. All these answers, and others besides, have a certain plausibility and are worth giving serious consideration. Yet although it is certainly possible to provide a wealth of relevant information and analysis which should help towards an appreciation of who rules Britain, it should be acknowledged right away that it is impossible ultimately to give an authoritative and definitive answer to the question. Those answers that are given inevitably reflect different interpretations of the facts, and ultimately fundamentally different perspectives on politics, and different underlying ideological assumptions.

The term 'model' is often used in social science to describe a simplified version of reality. We try to make sense of a wide range of possibly relevant information by constructing simple hypotheses about the relationship between key variables, and see how far the real world fits the resulting models. Some simple models of the possible distribution of power in society are given in Table 1.1. The crucial question is how far power is dispersed or concentrated in the political system, but the different models also provide alternative explanations of the institutions and mechanisms involved.

They are not the only possible models, and indeed, different names or versions of these models may be encountered elsewhere. Moreover, not all the models are mutually exclusive. 'Pluralism', 'liberal capitalism' or 'liberal democracy' are the names often given to a composite version of the first three models listed in Table 1.1, suggesting a model where power is dispersed through a mixture of the ballot box, the free market and the influence of group interests on the policy process. Certainly these institutions and processes can be seen as playing a mutually reinforcing role. Yet they also reflect different and sometimes competing perspectives. Some old-fashioned liberals or those on the modern New Right place far more emphasis on the free market than the verdict of the ballot box, particularly if that results in interference with free market forces. Similarly, they may fear that group influences represent selfish sectional interests and illegitimate power which

Table 1.1 Models of the possible distribution of power

Name of model	Key players	Power	Evidence	Thinkers
Representative democracy model	individual voters through the ballot box	dispersed	formal political mechanisms, electoral system, written constitutions	Bentham, J.S. Mill
Market model	individual consumers and producers through the free market	dispersed	classical economic assumptions – evidence of working of market	Adam Smith, Hayek, Friedman
Pluralist model	interest groups	relatively dispersed	influence of groups in case studies of decision making	Bentley, Truman, Robert Dahl, neo-pluralists (e.g. Lindblom)
Elitist model	elites (e.g. social, business, military, bureaucratic, professional elites)	concentrated	reputation of key figures and relationships between them	Pareto, Mosca, Michels, Wright Mills
Marxist model	ruling class ('bourgeoisie' in a capitalist society)	highly concentrated	distribution of income and wealth – working of capitalist system	Marx, Lenin, Trotsky, Gramsci, Miliband, Poulantzas

Photograph: PA Photos.

IN FOCUS 1.1 Representative democracy in action!

Nigel Whiting enjoys a pint and a game of shove ha'penny with the landlady after voting in the 2001 general election at his local polling station, the Tichborne Arms, near Winchester. Making polling stations more accessible to voters is part of an initiative to boost turnout in elections (Representation of the People Act, 2000). Perhaps coincidentally, Winchester had the highest turnout in the UK. Mr Whiting, we assume, paid for his pint. There are no plans for a return to the widespread 19th-century custom of 'treating' voters to alcoholic beverages.

may distort the market. Similarly, while pluralists assume a role for elections and representative institutions, they tend to regard these as only providing a very limited, occasional and blunt instrument for popular political participation, and place much more emphasis on the continuous pressure of countless groups on the policy process.

How persuasive are these models? Which is the most convincing? The obvious answer is to look at the evidence, but the problem here is that each model begins from rather different assumptions, employs different methodologies and looks at different sorts of evidence. The representative government model largely assumes that political power lies where the constitutions, laws and other official documents say it does, so here it is important to examine the theory and practice of the key institutions. The market model derives its key assumptions from classical economics. It is countless individual producers and consumers operating through the market who determine the crucial questions of who gets what, when, how. The role of politics in this economic process is (and, they argue, should be) strictly limited, as government intervention can only distort the operation of the free market and lead to a less efficient allocation of resources. Evidence in support of these assumptions comes from analysis of market forces and government intervention in practice. Pluralists cite case studies in decision making to demonstrate the role of large numbers of different groups in the process. Elitists by contrast identify key individuals or groups who dominate decision

making in their communities. Marxists infer political power from economic power. They document the massive inequalities in income and wealth in modern capitalist society, and assume that it is those who control the means of production who will also control the political process.

At this point an intelligent reader coming to the study of politics for the first time might think, 'Hold on! Is this description or prescription? Science or ideology?' The answer is, inevitably, both. While writers on politics are conscientiously striving to provide an accurate picture of the way in which the political process actually operates, they are inevitably influenced by their own fundamental assumptions, and sometimes also by their ideals. Marx believed he was providing a dispassionate analysis of the underlying forces within capitalism, but it is difficult to divorce this analysis entirely from his condemnation of capitalism and hopes for a future socialist revolution. He wrote, 'Philosophers have only interpreted the world, the point however is to change it' (*Theses on Feuerbach*). There is a similar mixture of analysis and prescription among modern free marketeers. Like Marx, they too want to change the world, although in a quite different direction. Moreover, while much of the debate between pluralists and elitists apparently involves dispassionate social scientific research into the distribution of power, most of those involved are also defending or advancing theories of democracy, and implicitly or explicitly criticising or defending the processes they describe.

British politics?

This is a book that focuses primarily on British politics, although it is not wholly confined to Britain. Wherever relevant, comparisons with other countries will be made, particularly with the USA and with some of the leading European states. Many features of British politics are found elsewhere, although some are relatively rare or even unique. Both the similarities with and the differences from other states can be instructive. It is, for example, virtually impossible to discuss the system of voting in Britain, its advantages and disadvantages, and proposals for reform, without some reference to voting systems in other countries (see Chapter 6).

Nor does a focus on Britain preclude some discussion of politics both above and below the level of the British state. While many of the crucial decisions that affect British citizens are still resolved within Britain's central government around Whitehall and Westminster, other decisions are taken elsewhere, some above the level of the British state – for example, by the United Nations, the International Monetary Fund, the World Trade Organisation, the North Atlantic Treaty Organisation or the European Union – while some are taken by devolved government within the United Kingdom, by local councils, by appointed agencies, or particular institutions such as hospital trusts, schools and universities.

Needless to say, the level at which decisions should be taken is often an acutely controversial political question. Some would like to devolve or decentralise power as far down as possible to local councils or communities, to give people more say in those decisions that affect them. Others would stress the need for more cooperation between nations to resolve essentially global problems – peace and security, world poverty, population growth and resources, the future of the planet – that imply the need for decisions and compromises above state level. This raises some questions about the whole future of independent sovereign nation-states in an apparently increasingly interdependent globalized world. Perhaps formerly powerful and independent states like Britain are inevitably losing real power and influence in a new global or European politics.

The European Union raises some particularly important questions about levels of decision

> *Definitions*
> **An independent sovereign state** is a state that has a monopoly of supreme (or sovereign) power within its borders, not subject to interference in its internal affairs by any outside power.
> **Globalization** is a term that emphasises the increasing interdependence of people, organisations and states in the modern world, and the growing influence of global economic, cultural and political forces or trends. It implies limits to state sovereignty.

making and indeed the whole future of British politics. Britain's membership of what is now the EU has been acutely controversial since the British government first applied to join in 1961, and more particularly from 1973, when the Heath government signed the treaty of accession (Young, 1998). Some see the European Union as providing Britain with an opportunity to exert more political and economic influence, in cooperation with other member states, over decisions that affect all Britons. Others fear the absorption of Britain into a European superstate, which they see as a threat to British independence and identity. Whatever view is taken it is clear that the institutions and processes of the European Union are now an important element of the politics that affect us all. Indeed, the impact of Europe on British government and politics will be a running thread throughout this book (but see especially Chapter 16).

Yet the future of British politics is not just affected by the threat (real or exaggerated) of a European superstate. The very term 'Britain' and the notion of British politics are themselves increasingly contested (Davies, 2000: 853–86). The official title of the state (since 1922) is 'the United Kingdom of Great Britain and Northern Ireland'. It is often described more simply as 'the United Kingdom' or by the acronym 'UK'. 'Britain' or 'Great Britain' is simply the largest of those islands still often referred to as 'the British Isles', although the second largest of this group of islands, Ireland, is politically divided. Most of Ireland constitutes the Irish Republic, an independent sovereign state which is a member of the United

Nations and the European Union. Northern Ireland remains part of the United Kingdom, although its inhabitants are fiercely divided in their political allegiance. The majority insist they are 'British', rather more passionately than most people who live across the Irish Sea in 'Great Britain'. A large minority consider themselves Irish rather than British, and wish to belong to the Irish Republic rather than remain within the UK or British state. The political future of Northern Ireland remains acutely controversial.

Even without the long-running problem of Northern Ireland, the future of Britain and the British state is an open question. England is the largest of the constituent parts of Britain in territory and by far the largest in population. Many of those who live in England describe themselves almost interchangeably as 'English' or 'British', a confusion which can infuriate those who live in Scotland or Wales. Wales was absorbed by the English crown in the Middle Ages and was formally politically united with England in 1536. Scotland was an independent state until James VI of Scotland became also James I of England in 1603, although this union of the crowns did not involve full political union until 1707. The notion of a British state and the image of 'Britannia' effectively date from then. Some inhabitants of Scotland and Wales consider themselves to be both Scots or Welsh and British. Others consider themselves primarily or exclusively Scots or Welsh, and a significant minority would prefer to be part of an independent Scotland or Wales (see Chapters 2 and 17). Indeed, some have forecast the imminent 'break-up of Britain' (Nairn, 1981, 2000). This could happen. If the majority of those in Scotland and/or Wales clearly wished to be part of a separate state it would be impossible to maintain the union and 'Britain' would no longer exist as a meaningful political entity (although it would probably survive as a useful geographical term to describe the island). 'British politics' would be confined to the history books, to be replaced by the study of English (or Scottish or Welsh) politics (see Chapter 17).

Multi-level governance

However, the break-up of Britain has yet to take place and may never happen. For the present, and for the immediate future, the British state survives, although it has become more complicated. Scotland and Wales remain in a political union with England, although since 1999 Scotland has had its own Parliament and Executive, and Wales an Assembly and Executive. This involves what is described as a 'devolution' of power, rather than the total separation sought by nationalists or a fully federal system of government (as exists in the USA or Germany). Some people in England would like to see a similar devolution of power to English regions, leading to directly elected assemblies for the North East or South West, for example. This trend to devolve power away from central government to the regions is a feature of several other European states.

Whatever the future of devolved government, there has long been some form of local government in Britain, and there remains a complex system of elected local authorities in England, Wales and Scotland, that continue to employ large numbers of people, spend considerable amounts of public money, and preside over important public services, although it is widely alleged that local government has less discretion and effective control of services than it used to (Wilson and Game, 2002). Local councils are now increasingly expected to enable others to provide services that they previously provided themselves. Thus alongside elected local authorities there is a bewildering range of more specialist appointed public agencies, publicly funded partnerships and voluntary organisations. Yet this new and more complicated world of 'local governance' still has massive implications for the quality of people's lives (see Chapter 18, and also Leach and Percy-Smith, 2001).

Thus government and politics operate at a number of levels, both above and below the more familiar world of Whitehall and Westminster. These levels are far from self-contained, as is evident from any major policy area. For example, there is a significant local, regional, devolved national, UK and European input into British transport policy, as well as cross-cutting inputs from specialist government agencies, business interests, political parties, pressure groups and advisers. Here we are concerned with the whole political process that affects public policy and the delivery of public services in Britain. For most policies and services it is still the UK government that is particularly crucial in determining policy and allocating resources (see Part III). Thus it is inevitably still Whitehall and Westminster, rather than Brussels or Edinburgh or Cardiff or the local town hall, that remain the principal focuses of a book on British politics. Yet British politics involves them all and more besides.

Policies – who gets what, when, how?

Older books on politics concentrated on political institutions and processes, but often neglected the decisions, policies and services that are the product of the political process. This is like watching a game but ignoring the result. Who wins and who loses is crucial, in politics even more than in sport. So a study of politics must include not just the policy making process, but the outputs and outcomes of that process.

'It's the economy, stupid!' was the catchphrase of former US President Bill Clinton's Democrats, suggesting that politicians and governments are judged by how they run the economy. Of course it is possible that some of the most important economic developments are outside politicians' control, the consequence of national or global trends which may not be fully understood. Governments claim credit for the good times or pay the price for failure, when they may sometimes have little to do with either. Yet governments by their actions or inactions can help or hinder national prosperity. Political decisions are being taken regularly and routinely that may have critical implications for British industry, British jobs, prices and incomes and the standard of living. Governments can get things right, and sometimes they may get them badly wrong. Almost everyone may gain if the national economy prospers, and almost everyone may lose if there is a serious recession. However, within the country there will be relative winners and losers from national economic policy. This is most obvious at Budget time, when the media examine how various kinds of households (e.g. childless couples, one-parent families, pensioners) will be affected by changes in tax and spending. Over time some sections of the community may become progressively better off, while others become worse off. Inequality in the country as a whole may

grow or lessen. Economic policy clearly helps determine who gets what, where, how, and must be an important focus of any account of politics (see especially Chapter 21).

Health, education, transport, law and order: public services are now at the centre of political debate in Britain. Upon the quality of these services depends an important element of the quality of life of individuals and communities. Poor education in schools, colleges and universities ultimately affects everyone, not just the unfortunate recipients. People's lives can be blighted by crime. Thus it has long been recognised that such services cannot be left to the free market. Yet how far the state should intervene, the level of service, and the method of control, delivery and finance of services remain acutely controversial. Improvements may perhaps be possible by reforms in the delivery of services without additional resources, by eliminating waste, or introducing incentives, or making use of the private or voluntary sector. Yet ultimately it is a matter of how much governments (and ultimately citizens and taxpayers) are prepared to pay. Inevitably there is fierce competition arising from these demands on the public purse. More money for health may mean a lower priority for education or fighting crime. Behind the ministers, departments and agencies fighting for a higher share of public spending are all kinds of special interests: trade unions, professions, patients, consumers and clients, as well as the general mass of voters and taxpayers. Yet there may be important differences in the quality of services people obtain, depending on who they are or where they live. Some sections of the community may seem to get less than their fair share of vital services. A Briton's chance of finding a good school, or effective treatment for a medical condition, or any kind of NHS dentist, may depend on the 'postcode lottery'. Thus not just the management of the economy but specific policies on public services create winners and losers (see Chapter 22).

Can governments eradicate poverty? If the rich are getting richer, is that necessarily a bad thing? How far is it the role of government to promote equality and social justice? Such questions are at the centre of debate between socialists, liberals and conservatives, and the answers depend inevitably on ideological assumptions as well as economic analysis. Yet clearly the relative poverty of some can affect people generally: obviously and directly from the payment of taxes to fund social security benefits; less directly from the possible knock-on effects on national economic prosperity, health, education and crime. Child poverty, the problems of low income and one-parent families, run-down housing estates and deprived urban areas are problems that successive British governments have tried to tackle in different ways. The proposed remedies often reflect different perspectives on the nature of the problem (see Chapter 23).

Whole categories of people may be more systematically excluded from power and a share of general prosperity as a result of blatant or more subtle forms of discrimination, injustice and prejudice. British women were long excluded from the most basic civil and political rights, and from the opportunity to enter the main professions or compete on equal (or sometimes any) terms with men. Although women now enjoy formal political equality, they remain under-represented in Parliament and government, and despite equal pay and anti-discrimination legislation, women generally still earn less than men, and find it difficult to rise to the highest positions. They continue to shoulder a disproportionate share of domestic and child care duties. Some suffer physical violence, or constraints on their lives arising from the fear of violence. Feminists argue that women remain grossly unequal in a male-dominated society (see Chapter 24).

The rising number of black and Asian Britons often suffer more blatant forms of discrimination and prejudice. Most of the ethnic minorities have lower levels of pay and higher levels of unemployment than among the majority white community. Although they are far more liable to be stopped by the police, they are more likely to be victims of many forms of crime than whites. They remain grossly under-represented in politics, higher professional and managerial jobs. Ethnic divisions are often further complicated by religious differences. The attack on the World Trade Center in New York on 11 September 2001 exacerbated what has come to be called Islamophobia. As a consequence, some feel excluded from British society and have problems with their political identity. In some urban areas this has resulted in tension, a breakdown in community

relations, and sometimes violence. It remains a serious and potentially explosive political problem (see Chapter 24).

11 September 2001 provides a sharp reminder, if a reminder is needed, that politics transcends national boundaries. Any country may be profoundly affected by remote events and crises in far corners of the world. While Britain has not been involved in a major war since 1945, British troops have been engaged in active combat in Korea, the South Atlantic, the Persian Gulf, Kosovo and Afghanistan. British foreign policy has been guided by three main associations and interests; the 'special relationship' with the USA, the continuing (though declining) association with the Commonwealth, and the steadily increasing importance of the European Union. Balancing the cross-Atlantic ties with the USA and the cross-Channel ties with nearer neighbours in an expanding EU is likely to remain a dilemma for future British foreign policy. Yet a more fundamental problem for Britain and other advanced capitalist countries is the gross and intensifying differences in living standards across the world. It is global inequality rather than inequality within Britain that could now threaten a political explosion (see Chapter 26).

It is no longer only the threat of violent conflict between the 'haves' and the 'have-nots' that endangers the future of the planet. The relationship of humankind with its environment has only been widely recognised as a serious issue in relatively recent times, but for some this has become the supreme political problem facing this country and the world generally. Finite resources are being used up, and various forms of environmental pollution threaten irreversible changes to soil and climate. At best, future generations may suffer a heavy burden from our extravagance. At worst, 'spaceship earth' could be heading for catastrophe. There are some awkward ethical questions also. Much previous political debate has been about a fair division of resources between classes or categories of humans alive today – fair shares for the working class, women, or blacks. Yet the notion of inter-generational equity requires consideration of the needs of generations yet unborn. Moreover, many Greens would demand justice not just for humans yet unborn but for other species with whom humankind shares the planet, and indeed the earth itself. The politics of the environment has added a new dimension to ethical and political debate (see Chapter 25).

All this is politics. All these issues are on the agenda of British politics, whether the problems originate in Britain or elsewhere. They are all addressed further in the last part of this book. The issues are far from trivial. Indeed they may appear so frighteningly large and intractable that some may prefer to cut themselves off from politics and concentrate on their immediate lives and concerns. Yet ultimately we cannot exclude politics, unless we deny our common humanity, for we are political animals, as the philosopher Aristotle maintained. There is no subject more difficult, more important and ultimately more fascinating.

Further reading

There are few good accessible general introductions to the study of politics that can be recommended.

Crick (1993) is thought-provoking, if a little idiosyncratic. The French political scientist, Maurice Duverger's *The Study of Politics* (1972) is still worth reading.

Anthony Arblaster provides a readable short introduction to *Democracy* (1987). C. B. Macpherson's almost as brief *The Life and Times of Liberal Democracy* (1977) might also be consulted. Fuller and more ambitious is David Held's *Models of Democracy* (1987).

The rest of this book explores some of the themes discussed briefly in this chapter, and reading on each topic is recommended at the end of each chapter. However, anyone wishing to explore further some of the issues associated with the British state and the future of British politics might try looking at chapter 10, 'The post-imperial isles' of *The Isles: A History*, by Norman Davies (2000). This provides a thought-provoking non-Anglocentric perspective on the history and politics of the British Isles.

Chapter **2**

Economy, society and politics

Political geography – nation, regions,
    town and country   16
Allegiance and identity   18
Ethnicity   19
Religion   21
Gender   23
Age   23
Inequalities in income and wealth   24
Occupation and social class   26
Changing class structure?   27
Economic inequality and political
    power   29
Economic and social divisions – the time
    dimension   30

If politics arises out of disagreement and conflict, it is important to know something of the economic and social divisions in a country like the United Kingdom that can give rise to political differences. The population of the United Kingdom can be subdivided into numerous categories by statisticians and social scientists, and some of these divisions may have considerable political significance. Yet often it is not the (reasonably objective) categories into which people can be pigeon-holed that really matter in terms of political ideas and behaviour, but how people think about who they are – what is sometimes characterised as 'identity politics' (see Box 2.1). In this chapter we begin by looking at some of the relatively objective divisions within the United Kingdom, such as the distribution of the population by location, age and sex, but this inevitably merges into consideration of felt identities and distinctions, such as national and religious identities, ethnic differences, and gender relations. We conclude with an examination of inequalities in income and wealth, and the still highly contentious issue of social class and its implications for political attitudes and behaviour.

Political geography – nations, regions, town and country

England	49,997,000
Wales	22,946,000
Scotland	5,115,000
Northern Ireland	1,698,000
United Kingdom (total)	59,756,000

Source: taken from *Annual Abstract of Statistics*

Figure 2.1 The population of the United Kingdom of Great Britain and Northern Ireland, 2000

Although the United Kingdom is made up from four main component territories and national groups, most of its inhabitants (some 50 million out of close to 60 million) live in England. Thus the Union inevitably perhaps appears a rather lop-sided affair between the English and the much less numerous peoples inhabiting Scotland, Wales and Northern Ireland (see Figure 2.1). The preponderance of

'England' within 'Britain' and the 'United Kingdom' helps explain why these terms are often incorrectly used interchangeably. England is also much more densely populated than the other parts of the United Kingdom, particularly Scotland.

There are differences in culture and institutions arising out of past patterns of settlement and distinctive historical influences. Each country has its own religious traditions and divisions. Wales has its own language and a distinctive culture associated with that language. Scotland has its own legal and educational system. There are also important economic differences between the countries. Agriculture is rather more important to Scotland and Wales than England, although central Scotland, South Wales and Belfast were dependent on heavy industries which were adversely affected by Britain's industrial decline. However, although levels of income per head are substantially below the average for those for the UK as a whole in Wales and Northern Ireland, they are close to the average in Scotland (Figure 2.2).

There are also some significant differences in income and other economic indicators (such as unemployment) between English regions. England itself has been long divided into regions for purposes of statistical analysis and policy administration. However until recently the number and boundaries of those regions differed markedly, depending on which organisation or department was responsible for drawing them up. The regions in Figure 2.2 are those for Government Offices for the Regions, which are also the areas covered by regional development agencies (but do not match the old Treasury Standard Regions). They show some marked variations in regional prosperity, between a wealthy London and South East and the North East, which on 1999 figures is clearly the poorest English region, worse off than Scotland and Wales and only just on a level with Northern Ireland. The figures suggest that if anything regional inequalities are growing more pronounced. Regional disparities are a subject of some concern to economists and politicians in the UK and the European Union. While regional disparities impede European integration and have adverse consequences for national economic policy, they also have political implications, fuelling demands for more favourable treatment by the centre, assistance for inward investment, improvements to basic infrastructure, but also, sometimes, for more political autonomy.

These economic disparities in the performance of Britain's nations and regions have some implications for political allegiances – the talk of a North–South divide has become something of a cliché, but it is a cliché that has some basis in economic and political reality. Not only is the south richer than the north, but Labour's main political support (even after the 1997 and 2001 elections) still comes from the industrial north of England, central Scotland and south Wales, while Conservative strength lies in the south of England and particularly the South East. The industrial Midlands of England are politically contested. However, although the distinctive political allegiances of Wales, Northern Ireland and areas of Scotland can be explained partly in terms of economic inequality and relative deprivation, cultural factors and the politics of identity and allegiance have always been more significant in Northern Ireland and are increasingly significant in Scotland and Wales (see below).

It should be appreciated, however, that there remain more significant differences in economic activity and thus in income and wealth within than between nations and regions. Yorkshire and the

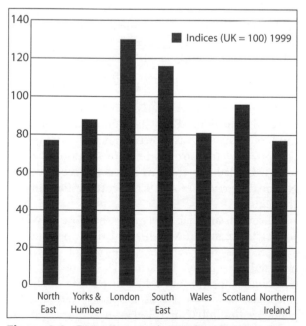

Figure 2.2 Gross Domestic Product per head by nation and selected English regions, 1999

Humber is for example one of the poorer of Britain's regions, but it contains Leeds which is relatively booming as a major financial, commercial and administrative centre, at least compared with Sheffield, Hull and neighbouring Bradford, now unhappily known for its deprivation, racial tension and riots rather than the wool on which its former wealth was based. Yet Bradford contains within its boundaries the small commuter town of Ilkley, over-whelmingly white, middle class and as comfortably prosperous as parts of the Surrey stockbroker belt, while Ilkley in turn is part of the Parliamentary constituency of Keighley, a formerly prosperous woollen town now shared between poor working class Asian and predominantly working class white communities which do not interrelate much. Similar comparisons between prosperity and deprivation, often close together, could be drawn all over Britain. There are differences between cities and towns and within them – including often marked differences between inner urban areas and outer suburbs and 'dormitory' towns. Some of the political implications of these economic differences can be charted in the party representation of Parliamentary constituencies and local government wards (see Waller and Criddle, 2002). However, where economic deprivation is particularly significant in a particular area there may be more serious political consequences in terms of alienation, anti-social and criminal behaviour, disturbances to public order, inter-community conflict and the rise of anti-system parties and movements, such as neo-fascist groups.

Allegiance and identity

Where people live is less significant for politics than how people think about where they live, and the nations or communities to which they think they belong. The national identity of the substantial majority of those who live in England is for the most part unproblematic, but there are divided loyalties among the non-English parts of the United Kingdom (see Curtis, in Hazell, 2000). This is particularly evident in Northern Ireland where the majority of Protestants (72 per cent in 1999) see themselves as British, and only 2 per cent see themselves as Irish, whereas among Catholics the figures are almost reversed: only 9 per cent think of themselves

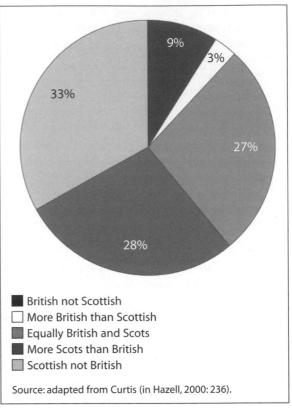

British not Scottish
More British than Scottish
Equally British and Scots
More Scots than British
Scottish not British

Source: adapted from Curtis (in Hazell, 2000: 236).

Figure 2.3 National identity in Scotland, 2000

as British while 68 per cent consider themselves Irish.

In Scotland opinion is rather less polarised, and many acknowledge a dual identity as Scots and British.

These felt identities clearly may be significant for political behaviour. Thus the figure for those who think of themselves as 'Scottish not British' (33 per cent) is not far from the level of support (29 per cent) recorded for the pro-independence Scottish National Party in the 1999 Scottish Parliament elections.

Indications are that rather more of those in Wales acknowledge a dual Welsh and British nationality – there was only a bare majority for a Welsh national assembly in the 1997 referendum (although support for it has increased somewhat since) and only 11 per cent supported Welsh independence in 2000 (Curtis in Hazell, 2000: 238). Of course, such felt identities and allegiances can shift over time, but they have some clear implications for the future of United Kingdom and British politics generally.

Regional consciousness remains relatively weak over most of England (with the partial exception of the North East and South West), which is one reason why there has, to date, been little popular demand for elected regional assemblies. There is rather more identification with the ancient counties (which go back a thousand years or more) in some parts of England at least, but county loyalties generally have more to do with sport than politics, and the counties (some would argue) make little sense as political and administrative units) as they hardly reflect the pattern of life and work in 21st-century Britain.

The cities may be rather more important in this respect, and city identities and loyalties may be stronger today. Rivalries between neighbouring cities are a feature of sub-national politics – between Glasgow and Edinburgh, Cardiff and Swansea, Manchester and Liverpool, Leeds and Sheffield. Yet there are important divisions within cities, between inner city areas and outer suburbs, for example, to the extent that some suburban dwellers who work in the city and depend on it for shopping and recreation still strenuously resist the notion that they are part of the city. Yet this may sometimes have more to do with financial self-interest and the fear of higher local government tax bills in city-dominated local authorities than any real sense of community identity. There are also continuing perceived differences between 'town' and 'country', even though only a tiny percentage of the UK working population is engaged in agriculture (around 2 per cent). However a rather larger number live in and/or identify with the country, which helps explain the apparent political strength and influence of bodies such as the Council for the Protection of Rural England and the Countryside Alliance.

Thus where people live sometimes gives rise to a sense of belonging to a particular community, and a sense of identity and allegiance. Yet some people will have no strong sense of allegiance to the place in which they just happen to live, and may have a greater sense of attachment to other kinds of community, bound together not by physical proximity, but by some other shared membership: for example of a particular ethnic group or faith community.

BOX 2.1
Identity politics, an illustration

Imagine, for example, a disabled woman of Pakistani descent who heads a one-parent family, is employed as a manual worker in Scotland, and has been brought up as a Muslim. All these aspects of her life may be fed into a range of statistical tables. Some may change over time, so she may appear in different categories when the next census is taken. Yet the bald facts do not tell us what she thinks about herself, and which of the various categories to which she belongs are important to her. Does she think of herself as British, Scottish, Asian or Pakistani, or a mixture of these identities? Is her Muslim religion the most important part of her self-identity or is it more incidental to her life? Is her gender, her family circumstances, her disability or her social class the most significant for her political attitudes and behaviour? How she thinks about herself will be influenced by all kinds of factors: family upbringing, education, work and social contacts, peer group pressure, the mass media. Her self-identity may change over time, depending on her experiences and contacts. She may decide, or be persuaded, to join a trade union, or a woman's group, or a support group for those who share her disability, and each of these may alter her outlook on life. Equally of course, how she is perceived and treated by others may affect her own sense of identity. If she suffers discrimination and prejudice as a 'Paki' or a Muslim, she may find it difficult to see herself as a Scot, or to experience a strong sense of solidarity with the working class or with her own sex.

Ethnicity

The definition of 'ethnicity' and how it is distinguished from terms such as 'nation', 'culture', 'community' and (most contentious of all) 'race' is, to say the least, problematic. The 'English' or 'British' are sometimes referred to as a 'mongrel' people, the product of waves of invasion and immigration from

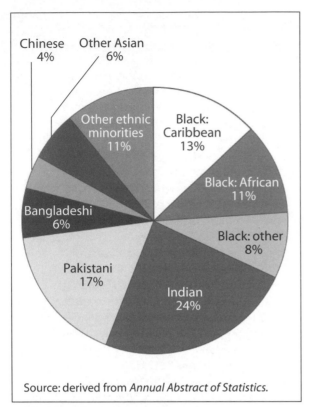

Source: derived from *Annual Abstract of Statistics.*

Figure 2.4 Non-white ethnic minorities in Britain (total 4,045,000) in the year 2000

different ethnic groups over the centuries – Celts, Angles, Saxons, Vikings, Norman French and so on. Some of these different ethnic origins can be evidenced in place names in different parts of the country, and in surviving surnames, yet they generally have no lasting political implications. When people talk of 'ethnic minorities' today, they are referring largely or exclusively to non-white ethnic groups, who are mainly the product of immigration over the last half century, because of persecution, or simply poverty and poor economic opportunities in their country of origin, coupled with labour shortages in particular regions and industries in the United Kingdom. Until very recently nearly all the immigration was from the territories of the former British Empire (now Commonwealth) and might be described as a legacy of empire. While in the early post Second World War period there was free entry to citizens of the British Commonwealth, from 1962 onwards there was a progressive tightening of immigration restrictions, on grounds that were effectively

racist, to reduce the growth of what was becoming a substantial non-white ethnic minority population. By the year 2000 this totalled just over 4 million, compared with nearly 55 million 'whites' out of total of 59 million.

Figure 2.4 involves some problematic issues of definition, and excludes 'white' groups who are sometimes categorised as ethnic minorities – Jews, Irish, Poles and so on – and who may suffer some of the discrimination and prejudice experienced by non-white minorities. Indeed, the reason 'ethnic minorities' are significant for politics is not that they are observably different (although many are, on the crude criteria of skin colour and dress) but the way they think and behave themselves, and, more critically, the way they are treated by other ethnic groups and particularly the 'white' majority.

Issues of identity and allegiance can be complicated for ethnic minorities. It is hardly surprising that many relatively recent immigrants and their immediate descendants should have some continuing positive sentiments towards their country of origin, particularly where they retain contacts with relatives there. The USA, which has long had a fairly successful programme of education to integrate immigrants into the American way of life and mould them into American citizens, still has thriving Irish-American, Spanish-American, Polish-American and Jewish-American communities. Similarly, there are thriving Polish, Italian and Ukrainian communities in some British cities. These hyphenated identities suggest that allegiances are not mutually exclusive – it is possible to be Irish and American. Similarly it is possible to be black or Asian and British, and such a dual allegiance is clearly felt by many. Yet a more exclusive allegiance may be felt as a consequence of rejection, prejudice and discrimination on the part of the majority, of which there is, unfortunately, considerable evidence. Thus ethnic minorities have generally been the first casualties of an economic downturn and unemployment. Today, unemployment levels remain significantly higher for most ethnic minorities (see Figure 2.5) with black and Asian school leavers in particular finding it much more difficult to secure jobs than their white counterparts (see Figure 2.6).

Other economic indicators tell a similar story. Blacks and Asians are less likely to be employed in occupations appropriate to their qualifications, and are more likely to be employed in part-time or casual labour, often involving working unsociable hours. They also encounter discrimination in the housing market, and are more likely to be victims of certain kinds of crime, and far more likely to be stopped by the police and questioned.

While parts of Britain, particularly some areas of London, have become multi-ethnic and genuinely multi-cultural, more commonly ethnic differences are reinforced by residential, social, and educational segregation. In some urban areas adversely affected by the decline of a staple industry and rising unemployment, economic deprivation has sharpened mutual suspicions and antagonisms between the white and ethnic minority population, and increased ethnic tensions. After 11 September 2001 prejudice and discrimination against some ethnic minorities were further complicated by Islamophobia. As a consequence it seems that ethnic divisions and tensions will have increasing rather than diminishing significance for British politics, certainly in terms of mainstream political activity – voting, representation, participation in pressure groups – but more seriously perhaps in terms of riots and violent disturbances.

Religion

Religion was once a major source of political division and conflict in Britain. Religious differences were a

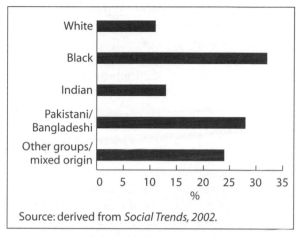

Source: derived from *Social Trends, 2002.*

Figure 2.6 Unemployment levels among 18–24 year olds by ethnic group

running thread in political history from the 16th century through to the 19th century. Yet apart from the persecution of the relatively small Jewish minority, religious divisions then were between variants of Christianity. Following the Protestant reformations in both England and Scotland in the 16th century, Roman Catholics became a feared, hated and persecuted minority in Britain, and an oppressed majority in Ireland. The further division between high Anglicanism and Puritanism or non-conformism in the 17th century was the major cause of the Civil War and a leading element among the subsequent political differences between the rival Tory and Whig parties. Later, while the Church of England was dubbed the 'Tory Party at prayer' it was the 'non-conformist conscience' that was the bedrock of British 19th-century Liberalism, and a key strand in the early Labour Party.

Yet if religion was once very important as a source of political inspiration and conflict, it was of fast-declining political significance for most of the 20th century. Today, Anglicans, nonconformists, Catholics and Jews can be found among the supporters of all modern mainstream political parties (in Britain, if not Ireland). Religion has ceased to be an indicator of political allegiance for most of England, with the partial exception of areas such as Liverpool, where the Protestant/Catholic divide remains important in sporting loyalties and has a significant if diminishing influence on party support. Such divisions are more important in Scotland, especially

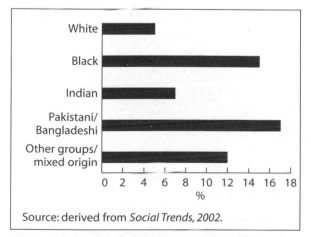

Source: derived from *Social Trends, 2002.*

Figure 2.5 Unemployment levels by ethnic group

Glasgow and parts of Edinburgh, where religious differences remain a key factor in explaining political allegiances, and also the rejection of separatist nationalism by working class Catholics. However the obvious exception to generalisations on the declining significance of religion for politics remains, of course, Northern Ireland, where religious affiliations continue to correlate closely with political loyalties – particularly for the fundamental Unionist/Nationalist divide (see above). A problem for Unionists is that the number of Catholics is steadily increasing as a proportion of the total population, to the extent that, on current trends, the Catholic minority could become a majority within 20 years or so. The political consequences hardly need spelling out.

Leaving Northern Ireland aside for the moment, there are some signs in the rest of Britain that religious differences may once more increase in political significance in the 21st century, not as formerly because of divisions within Christianity, but as a consequence of the enhanced importance of other religious faiths. Of these the Jewish faith continues to retain a high profile, and a strong Jewish identity is still felt by many of Jewish descent, even by those who retain little or no religious belief, partly as a consequence of the persecution Jews have suffered over the centuries. Muslim, Hindu and Sikh temples are also now features in British cities, providing additional physical evidence of the multifaith society that Britain has become. Of these faiths, Islam is the most visible and important, in terms of numbers of adherents, places of worship and political significance. Following 11 September 2001, Britain's Muslims have been subject to scrutiny, much of it hostile and ill-informed, stimulating the growth of what has been termed 'Islamophobia', and reinforcing racist prejudice among some of the white population. Inevitably, prejudice and discrimination has led some among the Muslim community to reconsider their own political allegiance and identity.

Until recently these new and renewed religious affiliations still had only marginal significance for politics. Yet recent political events have sharpened some religious antagonisms, while the demands of some religious groups for their own faith schools, following the precedent of 'church' schools and Catholic schools, may increase segregation and mutual suspicion between religions.

Figure 2.7 provides evidence for the increased variety of religious faith in Britain, without however really denting the assumption that Britain has become a predominantly secular society. Thus some two-fifths of the population belong to no religion, and many of those who still routinely claim to belong to the 'C of E' never attend church services. Religious observance is also declining among other Christian denominations. Although over half the population still claim to be Christian, far fewer are active members of religious congregations. Religion may be more important in the lives of those belonging to the small but growing non-Christian faith groups. However, all the non-Christian religions put together still only amount to less than 5 per cent of the population, and Muslims to just 2 per cent, underlining the absurdity of the fear of a British Islamic state promoted by British National Party propaganda.

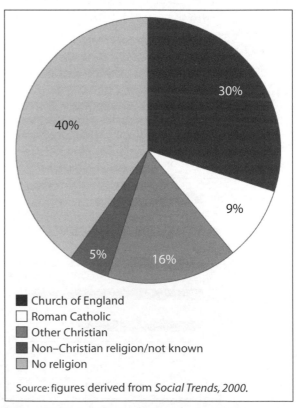

- ■ Church of England
- □ Roman Catholic
- ▨ Other Christian
- ■ Non–Christian religion/not known
- ▨ No religion

Source: figures derived from *Social Trends, 2000*.

Figure 2.7 Religious affiliation, Great Britain, 2000

Gender

The division between 'male' and 'female' is in many ways both the most obvious and the most persistent of social divisions. Although the position of women within British society and western society generally has been considerably transformed over the last two centuries, in ways which are too familiar to require repeating, and the equality of women is now formally recognised, females continue to suffer discrimination and inequality in many spheres, and gender is a social division of increasing importance for politics.

Women slightly outnumber men in the overall population, by 30,279,000 to 29,459,000. Men continue to outnumber women in the workforce, however, although the gap is fast closing, as women workers are up from 10 million in 1971 to 13.2 million in 2001, while the male labour force has remained relatively static at just over 16 million (figures from *Social Trends, 2002*). Despite this almost equal participation in paid work, women are still expected to undertake a disproportionate share of the burden of domestic work and child caring, and are far more likely to be involved in the care of elderly relatives (who themselves are more likely to be women, as they outnumber men by three to one among the population aged 85 and over). This dual burden of outside and domestic work may be one reason (besides prejudice) why relatively few women reach the highest and most well-paid managerial and professional posts. Women's average pay still lags well behind that of men, despite equal pay and equal opportunities legislation. As we shall see in more detail in subsequent chapters, men still substantially outnumber women in formal involvement in politics and government. One consequence of this continued male dominance of the political process, feminists would argue, is that policies are still skewed towards male interests and male economic dominance.

While gender divisions have not been expressed in terms of separate political parties, they have been expressed politically in a number of other ways. Thus women have worked in pressure groups, through and across existing parties and through the women's movement as a whole, to secure better representation in politics and government, and to secure specific reforms to improve the position of women. One problem for the women's movement is that many women feel that there is no longer a need for this kind of activity, or that other interests and causes are more pressing. The gender divide is cut across by numerous other divisions, including class, age, ethnicity and religion, and inevitably women find themselves on opposite sides on many political issues. (Feminism as an ideology is explored further in Chapter 4, and some policy issues are covered in Chapter 24.)

Age

Different age groups are an obvious social division. As a member of a particular arbitrarily-defined age group we may have some interests and attitudes in common. Yet as John Vincent (in Payne, 2000: 150) points out, age groups are an unusual social division, 'as we anticipate moving from one side of the division(s) to the other'. Thus most of us can expect to experience infancy, puberty, adulthood, parenthood, grandparenthood and retirement as we move between statistical age categories in the course of an average life-cycle. The old may remember how it feels to be young, while the young may anticipate how their needs, capacities and circumstances will change with age. Even so, the elderly can be the victims of negative stereotypes, and they may experience some of the same kinds of discrimination and prejudice felt by some other social categories. There are now increasing complaints over 'ageism' as well as over sexism and racism.

There have been significant changes in the age structure of the British population from the 19th century and even from the mid-20th century, with considerable implications for politics. Today, pensioners (10,789,000) comfortably outnumber children of compulsory school age (8,501,000). The implications of an ageing population are particularly obvious for pensions and health, and it is no accident that these two issues have shot up the political agenda in recent years. Adequate pensions and good health care are critical for the quality of life of the elderly, but have massive implications for public expenditure and taxation. Yet the elderly have potentially growing political weight. In the USA, for example, there is talk of 'grey power', involving the tacit assumption that the elderly have some interests in common that they seek to advance. In Britain 'grey power' is less evident, but already elderly voters not only outnumber young voters, and are more likely to use their vote (see Chapter 7), they also have the time and leisure to involve themselves in other political activities, in political parties and in a range of pressure groups (see Chapters 8 and 9).

Yet it should not assumed that the elderly, or for that matter any age group, have homogeneous interests. They will differ in family circumstances, mental and physical health, but most of all in income and wealth. Thus the elderly who are largely or wholly reliant on state benefits may experience real poverty, while those with good occupational pensions and the mortgage paid off may enjoy a very comfortable retirement, often including several holidays abroad annually, regular use of a car, frequent meals out and entertainment. They may indeed have a far better quality of life than when they were younger.

There are clear differences of attitude between age groups on a range of issues, some essentially economic, others based on formative influences when young (e.g. drugs, crime, sexual orientation, race relations). Some of the differences in attitudes witnessed among older people may simply be the consequence of the ageing process. Thus it is often assumed that, as they age, people become more set in their ways, less open to change, and conservative (with a small 'c', but perhaps with a large 'C' as well), and there is some evidence to support the assumption, although there are some conspicuous exceptions to the generalisation. It may also be the case that different generations, or age cohorts, may have different expectations because of the experiences they have gone through. Thus 'war babies' born in the Second World War may have markedly different expectations and attitudes from the 'sixties generation', or 'Thatcher's children' born into the 1980s. Prevailing values in society when people were young may condition their own attitudes for a lifetime. The convictions of anyone who is now over 65 and born and bred in Britain were formed at a time when the population was overwhelmingly white, when there was still a stigma attached to illegitimacy, when homosexuality and abortion were still crimes, and when most of today's 'recreational' drugs were largely unknown. This goes some way to explain the often considerable gap between the generations on issue of personal morality and freedom.

Inequalities in income and wealth

Some of the social divisions referred to above clearly have an economic dimension. Some nations or regions within the UK may have a lower standard of living than others. Above-average unemployment and lower than average wages are experienced by some ethnic minorities. Women are more likely to experience economic deprivation than men, while poverty is more prevalent among some age groups than others – particularly children and the elderly. Yet although poverty may be unevenly distributed between these different social categories, it is hardly gender or ethnicity or age or geographical location that largely explains poverty. The manifestation of poverty within some of these social divisions reflects a more fundamental division in economic circumstances.

A feature of almost all past and present societies has been gross inequality in income and wealth. The division between the rich and the poor has been seen as the crucial political divide, at least from the time of Plato and Aristotle onwards. Commonly, the rich have constituted a tiny minority, and poverty has been the common experience of the majority. Indeed, Plato and Aristotle assumed that democracy, the rule of the many, would be the rule of the poor, while the rule of the few, oligarchy, involved in practice the rule of the rich minority in their own interests. Until recently gross inequality, and poverty for the majority, were widely assumed to be unalterable aspects of human society. Economists such as Malthus argued that any improvement in the living standards of the poor would lead to an increase in population and a reduction in their circumstances to subsistence levels. While industrialisation raised the living standards of whole nations, including the poor, thus apparently disproving the gloomy assumptions of Malthus, and redistributed income and wealth between groups, it did not reduce inequality within society as a whole, and indeed may have increased it. However, it was no longer necessarily assumed that governments could or should do nothing about poverty and inequality. Indeed, it was widely reckoned that progressive taxation on the one hand and state welfare provision on the other were significantly reducing inequality and poverty in countries like Britain in the period after the Second World War.

This comfortable assumption of progress towards a more equal society was dented by revelations of the failures of the welfare state in certain areas: the rediscovery of child poverty, and the recognition of the economic deprivation suffered by some declining industrial urban areas from the 1960s onwards. It was more severely shaken by the economic problems of the 1970s, which not only involved the return of large-scale unemployment, but led to a more fundamental questioning of the role of the state. Some argued that it was the growth of government that was largely responsible for Britain's economic problems. Governments should not be in the business of redistribution. State welfare and high taxation sapped individual initiative and enterprise and created a dependency culture. Market forces, left alone, would create more wealth and prosperity for the nation as a whole, including the poorest. Attempts to reduce inequality were counter-productive. While this new orthodoxy was never fully acted upon, the growth of public spending was checked and the burden of taxation of the better off was substantially reduced. There is fairly clear evidence that some apparent progress towards a more equal society in Britain was checked in the last quarter of the 20th century, and partially reversed, for income inequality has grown.

As Table 2.1 demonstrates, Britain continues to be characterised by wide disparities in the distribution of wealth (which has changed little in recent years). The poorest half of the population own only 6 per cent of total marketable wealth. For much of the population the only significant wealth they own is bound up in their houses. If these are excluded from marketable wealth the figures are even more stark. In 1999 the top 1 per cent owned 34 per cent of marketable wealth excluding dwellings, and the top 50 per cent owned 97 per cent, leaving just 3 per cent of wealth to the other half of the population.

While it is difficult to make accurate comparisons with previous periods, it does appear that

Table 2.1 The distribution of marketable wealth (adults aged 20 or over), 1999

Category of population	Percentage of wealth owned
Most wealthy 1%	23%
Most wealthy 5%	43%
Most wealthy 10%	54%
Most wealthy 25%	74%
Most wealthy 50%	94%

Source: adapted from *Social Trends, 2002*, p. 102.

inequality in Britain is as marked as it ever was, and that democracy, involving the assumption of political equality, has not resulted in much greater economic and social equality. The sources of wealth may have changed considerably over the last 200 years, and there has been some significant social mobility, but the gulf between rich and poor remains. In so far as valid comparisons can be made with other countries, it does appear that inequality in Britain is more marked than in some other advanced industrial nations.

However, poverty in Britain today is clearly a relative concept. The poor in Britain suffer relative deprivation rather than absolute poverty. People feel deprived because they lack commodities or facilities that the bulk of the population take for granted. Where car ownership is almost universal, lack of access to a car does appear to have a severely adverse effect on the quality of life. Yet poor Britons clearly do not lack the basic necessities of life. In the mid-19th century it is reckoned that around a million people in Ireland died as a result of the potato famine, and the population was reduced by some 20 per cent as a result of starvation and emigration. This level of poverty is unthinkable in modern Britain or Ireland or any developed nation, although it is unfortunately common enough elsewhere. The problems of global inequality dwarf those within Britain, yet it is inequality in Britain that is more relevant for British politics and government. Thus it is important to examine in rather more detail the nature and extent of these social divisions by exploring the contentious concept of social class.

Occupation and social class

Sometimes it is suggested that Britain is already, or well on the way to becoming, a classless society. Others suggest not only that class differences are persistent, but that social inequality is increasing. Some foreign observers are struck by the extent to which Britain remains a class-conscious country. Class remains an important concept in social science in general and political science in particular. It is, for example, still regarded as an important factor in explaining voting behaviour and party allegiance (see Chapters 7 and 8). But if class is important, it is difficult to define. It is most commonly operationalised in terms of occupational categories, but different categories are used for different purposes, and these different categories hint at problems and ambiguities in fundamental concepts.

Class is a particularly important aspect of the Marxist perspective on power and state (discussed in Chapter 1). 'The history of all hitherto existing society is the history of class struggles' (*Communist Manifesto*, Marx and Engels, 1848). Marx, however, used the term 'class' in a distinctive way, linking it with the ownership of productive wealth rather than occupation. He assumed there was a fundamental conflict of interest in a capitalist society between the class that owned and controlled the means of production – the capitalists or bourgeoisie – and those who owned only their own labour, the proletariat. These were the two key classes that mattered in a modern capitalist society – others such as the old landed gentry, the petty bourgeoisie, and the peasants were becoming progressively less significant. Yet the actual ownership of the means of production may be less important in a modern capitalist society, where ownership may be divorced from effective control, and the key decisions are made by managers. Marx may also have underestimated the power of the professions and the growing state bureaucracy. These developments were more fully appreciated by Max Weber, writing rather later. While Weber acknowledged that the ownership of property was a key element in understanding social inequality, he also attached importance to differences in status between groups, particularly occupational groups.

Our modern understanding of class owes rather more to Weber than to Marx. In popular usage it is closely linked to hierarchies of social status. A simple three-class distinction – upper, middle and lower (or 'working') – is long established, although the 'upper class' is often relatively ignored. In so far as it is seriously treated, it is either linked with the old aristocracy and landed gentry, or used in a quasi-Marxist sense to mean those who are sufficiently wealthy not to have to depend on their own labour for a more than adequate income. The distinction between the middle and working class is most commonly associated with the division between 'white collar' (or non-manual) work and 'blue collar' (or manual) work.

The distinction between manual and non-manual work, although it is bound up closely with the popular understanding of class in Britain and also underpins some formal classifications for statistical purposes and much academic analysis, is not necessarily closely aligned with differences in income and wealth. Some 'white collar' jobs (e.g. junior clerical workers) are relatively poorly paid, while some manual workers (plumbers and builders in some parts of Britain) enjoy comparatively high wages. Moreover, it should be noted that the distinction between a manual working class and a non-manual middle class in no way corresponds to the Marxist distinction between the working class and the 'bourgeoisie' (although this term is often translated as 'middle class'). From a Marxist perspective both blue collar and white collar workers are 'working class'. The (essentially non-Marxist) British Labour Party similarly both referred to the familiar distinction between manual and non-manual work, and rejected its significance, in the phrase 'workers by hand or by brain' in the old Clause Four of its constitution. Academic commentators have often grouped junior white collar workers with the working class, along with various categories of manual workers, and this makes a great deal of sense in terms of income and economic inequality. Even so, the distinction in assumed social status between white collar and blue collar work has proved remarkably persistent, with implications for political behaviour. Thus many poorly paid white collar workers have declined to identify themselves with the 'interests of labour' which the Labour Party and its trade union allies claimed to champion.

BOX 2.2

Some social or occupational class categories commonly used in Britain

1. **Registrar General's classification formerly used in official surveys**

I   Professional
II Intermediate
III Skilled (subdivided into non-manual and manual)
IV Semi-skilled
V   Unskilled.

2. **System of classification used by Institute of Practitioners in Advertising (IPA) and commonly adopted by social scientists and political scientists, particularly in the analysis of voting and party allegiance**

A Higher managerial, administrative or professional
B Intermediate managerial, administrative or professional
C1 Supervisory or clerical, and junior white-collar workers
C2 Skilled manual workers
D Semi-skilled and unskilled manual workers
E State pensioners or widows (no other earnings), casual or lowest grade workers, long-term unemployed.

3. **New official classification to replace old Registrar General's classification for statistical purposes**

1. Higher managerial and professional occupations (e.g. company directors, barristers)
2. Lower managerial and professional occupations (e.g. nurses, police, journalists)
3. Intermediate occupations (e.g. clerks, secretaries)
4. Small employers and own account workers (e.g. publicans, farmers, decorators)
5. Lower supervisory, craft and related occupations (e.g. printers, plumbers, train drivers)
6. Semi-routine occupations (e.g. shop assistants, bus drivers, hairdressers)
7. Routine occupations (e.g. waiters, building labourers, refuse collectors)
8. Never worked and long-term unemployed.

Yet the terms 'working class' and 'middle class', particular the latter, cover too wide a range to be of much practical value unless broken down into further sub-categories. Thus the middle class is commonly taken to include business owners and directors, both salaried and self-employed professionals, clerical workers, shopkeepers and own-account workers (such as small builders). While some work in the private sector and some own their own businesses, many others work in the public sector. It should be clear that many of this diverse group scarcely share the same economic and political interests. While some of the 'middle class' have a strong interest in low taxation and reduced regulation of business enterprise, others have a vested interest in high public expenditure and thus high taxation, and some are professionally involved in the state intervention and regulation that other members of the middle class complain about. Similarly the manual working class is conventionally subdivided into skilled, semi-skilled and unskilled, and as with the middle class there is a cross-cutting distinction between those employed in the public and private sectors.

Yet it is increasingly questionable whether the old and familiar distinction between manual and non-manual work means much any more. Because of the decline of mining and heavy manufacturing industries, and the increased application of technology, much less work involves heavy physical labour. Many occupations require some manual and some non-manual labour. At the same time, some white collar and blue collar occupations have experienced an element of 'deskilling', while others require more complex skills and training than formerly.

Changing class structure?

There has been much academic debate on how Britain's class structure may be changing. Thus it is widely argued that class is not as important as it was. In particular the old manual working class is now relatively far smaller and more fragmented (class fragmentation). Others would claim that inequalities in income and wealth are as significant as ever and the basic class structure of Britain has not altered (class persistence). Others again would argue that old class divisions are being replaced by new ones (class realignment).

BOX 2.3
Self-assigned class?

The classifications above are for the most part objective – depending on occupational category. But individuals may think of themselves as working class or middle class, and this self-assigned class may not correspond with the categorisation of statisticians. Thus a manual worker who earns high wages, owns his own house and car, and adopts a middle class lifestyle, may think of himself as middle class. Similarly, a university lecturer (middle class by most objective qualifications) may have left wing political convictions and come from a manual working class family background, and proudly proclaim herself working class. Self-assigned class may be significant for political behaviour. For example, a manual worker who considers himself middle class may be more likely to vote Conservative, while it is probably safe to assume that the self-proclaimed working class lecturer will be on the left politically.

One of the reasons that there is so much disagreement about what is happening to the British class system relates back to differences in theoretical assumptions and classifications (discussed above). If the working class is identified with the old manual workers employed in mining and manufacturing, it is clear that numbers have declined, because these industrial sectors have declined, both relatively and absolutely, within the British economy. Moreover, many of the new jobs that have been created are in the services sector, and most of these jobs are commonly counted as middle class, because they appear to be 'white collar' and 'non-manual'. However, it is at best questionable whether, for example, work in call centres (one major growth area) should be regarded as 'middle class'. It is poorly paid, relatively unskilled work often undertaken on a short-term or casual basis. Yet if the decline of the working class is exaggerated, it is certainly true that there is a larger proportion of the population now employed in management and the professions. Moreover it is also true that the working class appears more fragmented – between employed and

unemployed, part-time and full-time, pubic sector and private sector, as well as along increasingly important gender and ethnic lines. These differences have clearly affected working class homogeneity and reduced traditional working class solidarity, with political repercussions.

Indeed, new social divisions may be becoming rather more important. It has been argued persuasively that there are now significant new divisions or 'cleavages' in British society, based not on differences within the production process but on differences in the consumption of goods and services. Thus it is claimed that there are significant differences in interest between those who are substantially reliant on public services – particularly public transport, and state-provided education, health and housing services – and those who are more reliant on their private cars, private health care and private schools, and privately owned houses. The former have a vested interest in public services and in higher public spending and taxation, while the latter have a vested interest in lower public spending and taxation. Indeed, the poorer public services are, the more their decision to opt out of them seems justified.

Housing tenure and the distribution of property

One of the most significant 'consumption cleavages' used to be housing tenure. A key division with social class and political implications was between 'home owners' (those who owned their house outright and those who were buying their house on a mortgage) and those who were renting a house from the local authority. While many from the 'working classes' lived in council houses, owner occupation was a badge of middle class respectability. The 'council estate' was among the most reliable source of Labour votes, while home owners were far more likely to vote Conservative. However, the sale of council houses and the transfer of substantial local authority housing to other landlords (largely voluntary housing associations), both encouraged by Conservative governments after 1979, has substantially altered the pattern of housing tenure.

Thus the number of council houses has been halved, a trend that has continued under Blair's Labour government, as some remaining council estates are in the process of being transferred to the

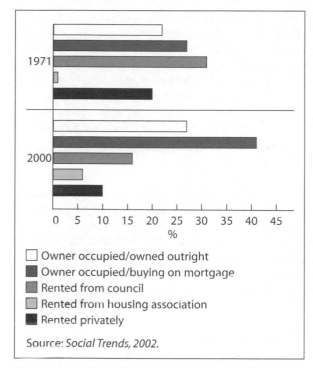

Owner occupied/owned outright
Owner occupied/buying on mortgage
Rented from council
Rented from housing association
Rented privately

Source: *Social Trends, 2002.*

Figure 2.8 Changing patterns of housing tenure in Britain

favoured 'third force' of housing associations. Owner occupation has become easily the majority form of housing tenure. It was widely anticipated that this would have politically damaging implications for the core vote of the Labour Party, and indeed there was evidence of increased Conservative voting initially among those who had bought their council homes. However, in the longer term it seems that these major changes in housing tenure have not led to commensurate changes in party allegiance (see Chapter 7).

Economic inequality and political power

The growth of home ownership is one aspect of what might be seen as a deliberate attempt to give more people a stake in property, not just in bricks and mortar but in stocks and shares. Indeed a growing proportion of the population has now acquired a large if indirect stake in the stock market through the investment of pension

and life insurance funds. Further encouragement was provided by the growth of the unit trust movement and government-sponsored investment schemes. However, the most high-profile stimulus to wider shareholding was provided through the heavily promoted privatisations and flotation of shares in former nationalised industries. The initial flotations were so successful that they were substantially over-subscribed. The cumulative effect was that share owners soon outnumbered the (declining) trade union members, which would not have been anticipated in the very different economic and political climate in the years immediately after the Second World War.

This suggests 'popular capitalism' has arrived. Yet the extent of the change can be exaggerated. While many more people seemed to have acquired a stake in property or capitalism, for most of them that stake has remained very small. As Table 2.1 on the distribution of wealth indicated, property ownership has not spread significantly, but remains heavily concentrated. Income inequality if anything has widened. Little significant progress has been made towards either the old Labour ideal of a more equal society or the Conservative 'property-owning democracy'.

The relationship between economic inequality and political power remains contentious. The norms of representative democracy – one person, one vote, one value – suggest political equality and the rule of the majority. To Marxists, the marked concentration of the distribution of income and wealth in the hands of the few reflects the effective concentration of political power in the hands of the ruling class. To neo-liberals, this inequality in income and wealth simply reflects market forces and the effects of the unequal distribution of talents and enterprise and initiative in society – thus the massive earnings of some company directors, and a few footballers and pop stars is simply the price placed on their scarcity. Both Marxists and neo-liberals assume the primacy of economics over politics. Social democrats, by contrast, implicitly assume that the political power of the majority can be mobilised to created a more equal society through the ballot box and representative government.

Economic and social divisions – the time dimension

It should already be clear that the importance attached to particular divisions in society not only varies from the perspective of different individuals and groups, but can change markedly over time. Take, for example, the following statement from a leading expert on British politics in the mid-20th century, Sir Ivor Jennings, in a book first published in 1941:

> Great Britain is a small island with a very homogeneous population. Few think of themselves as primarily English, Scots or Welsh. The sting has long been taken out of religious controversy. The country is so interdependent that there is little economic agitation on a regional basis, as there sometimes is in a large country like the United States. There are class divisions and (what is often the same thing) economic divisions, but they are not wide or deep, and they are tending to disappear through heavy taxation at the one end and high wage rates at the other. We are a closely knit economic unit, with a large measure of common interests and a long political tradition.
>
> (Jennings, 1966: 8–9)

Few would accept such an apparently complacent description of British politics today, although it may have reflected a mood of British national unity fairly accurately when first published in the Second World War.

Jennings was right then about religious controversy; for although it had been of critical importance for British politics until the early 20th century, its significance thereafter declined rapidly as religion played a diminishing role in people's lives in an increasingly secular society. Yet religious divisions are now beginning to appear rather more important once more (see section on religion, above). He was also right at the time about national and regional divisions – Scottish and Welsh nationalism, and the pressure for devolution, only began to take off from the late 1960s. Today, however, his observations on national identity would appear ludicrously wide of the mark (see Figure 2.3). Understandably, he made no observations about ethnic divisions, as what are now commonly described as 'ethnic minorities' are a product of post-war changes in the UK population. More contentiously, he ignored gender divisions, then more glaring than today (although war briefly provided nursery facilities and wider employment opportunities for women), yet this oversight on the part of Jennings reflected a then fairly common complacent view that 'votes for women' had secured their political equality. His assumptions over diminishing economic and class divisions now seem optimistic, although again they were widely shared at the time. Yet for a later generation of British political scientists, class divisions were all-important. Peter Pulzer wrote in 1967, 'class is the basis of British party politics; all else is embellishment and detail,' a bold generalisation which in turn appeared reasonably accurate when it was made, but now seems more questionable. (See section on changing class structure, above, and Chapter 7.)

The point is not to denigrate the work of Sir Ivor Jennings, an outstanding writer on politics of his time, but to emphasise how social divisions, and the importance attached to particular divisions, can change so markedly over a relatively short period. This book is concerned with contemporary British politics, and in this chapter therefore we have concentrated on the present, on providing a snapshot of British society and politics at a particular moment in time, near the start of the 21st century. It is important to emphasise, however, that politics is not static but dynamic. British politics has changed dramatically in the half century or so since the Second World War, reflecting in part the massive economic and social changes in Britain during that period, but also even more dramatic changes in the wider world. To understand fully British government and politics today it is necessary to know something of how the present was shaped by past developments, which may also provide some clues to the future. Thus in the next chapter we proceed to examine this time dimension.

Further reading

More extensive analysis of economic and social divisions in Britain can be found in standard textbooks on sociology, such as Bilton *et al.* (2002) and

Giddens (2001). Payne (2000) has edited a thoughtful collection of essays on *Social Divisions,* which examines in far more detail some of the theoretical and practical issues raised in this chapter.

Many of the implications of the social and economic divisions explored here for British politics as whole are addressed in later chapters of this book. The more specific implications of these divisions for Parliamentary constituencies and local government are explored in fascinating detail in Waller and Criddle (2002).

There is a wealth of official statistical information regularly published in the *Annual Abstract of Statistics, Social Trends, Regional Trends,* and so on. For even more up to date information see the website for the Office of National Statistics, <http://www.ons.gov.uk>.

Chapter **3**

The historical context: British politics since 1945

The post-war years: the end of empire and
  the imperial legacy   33
The under-performing economy   36
Building a welfare state   37
The pendulum years: from crisis to doubt   39
Economic management: towards
  'stagflation'   40
The Thatcher years   42
Thatcherite Britain in Europe   43
The welfare state and the free market   44
The impact of Thatcherism   45
Tony Blair and New Labour   45
Between Europe and the Atlantic   47
The new British state – changing political
  processes   48

This chapter rests squarely on the assumption that British politics today cannot be properly grasped without an understanding of the country's post-war history. British politics was transformed in the last half of the 20th century by an interplay of external and internal pressures. Britain's changing role in the world, resulting from loss of empire

and world power status, and its growing engagement with Europe, has involved a painful process of readjustment, which remains incomplete. The attempt of successive British governments to maintain a world role adversely affected the British economy, which was simultaneously stretched by a huge expansion in government spending at home from the 1939–45 war onwards. This involved the development of a new welfare state providing a system of social security 'from the cradle to the grave'.

These foreign and domestic policies, initially pursued by both Labour and Conservative governments, suggested there was a basic agreement or 'consensus' between the parties. This consensus came under strain in the 1970s and was eventually challenged by Margaret Thatcher and her Conservative administrations from 1979 onwards. Major divisions appeared over the role of the state and the delivery of public services, and over foreign and defence policies, including, increasingly, Britain's role in the European Union, particularly during the government of Thatcher's

Table 3.1 Post-war British prime ministers

1	Clement Attlee	1945–51
2	Sir Winston Churchill	1951–5
3	Sir Anthony Eden	1955–7
4	Harold Macmillan	1957–63
5	Sir Alec Douglas-Home	1963–4
6	Harold Wilson	1964–70, 1974–6
7	Edward Heath	1970–4
8	James Callaghan	1976–9
9	Margaret Thatcher	1979–90
10	John Major	1990–7
11	Tony Blair	1997–

> *Definition*
> Consensus means agreement. The term
> **consensus politics** implies a fundamental
> agreement between governments, parties
> (and, more questionably, the public) over
> values and policies. The post-war consensus in
> Britain was based on widespread acceptance
> of the social policies of Beveridge and the
> economic policies of Keynes (hence it is
> sometimes referred to as the
> 'Keynes–Beveridge' consensus) although the
> term has sometimes been used in a broader
> sense to cover agreement on constitutional
> issues, foreign and defence policies, and
> compromise in industrial relations. Some
> critics, however, have challenged the whole
> concept of consensus politics.

successor, John Major. The end of 18 years of Conservative rule, and the victory of Tony Blair's 'New Labour' in 1997, have involved both change and continuity. This heralded a still on-going constitutional revolution with massive implications for the future of the British state. Yet it did not involve the total repudiation of Thatcherism but rather a 'third way' of partnership between the public and private sectors, instead of the unrestricted free market associated with Thatcher, and the centralised state planning and public service delivery linked with 'old' Labour. Yet under Blair these important domestic policy issues seemed increasingly overshadowed by global politics – particularly after the events of 11 September 2001 and the 'war against terrorism'. These developments have dramatically revived the debate over Britain's role in the world, and its 'special relationship' with the United States on the one hand and its EU partners on the other.

The post-war years: the end of empire and the imperial legacy

Britain in 1945 saw itself and was perceived by others as a world power. Although far outmatched in population, industrial production and military capacity by the new superpowers, Britain was far in advance of the potentially second-rank countries

such as France, Italy, Germany or Japan. The distinctive features of Britain's international position in 1945 were:

- One of the three major victorious powers in the Second World War: Britain was one of the three major powers at the two conferences (Yalta and Potsdam) which, in the absence of a formal treaty, agreed the framework of the post-war world order. Moreover, in Churchill, the country had a towering leader who, by a combination of personal magnetism and bluff, seemed able to treat on equal terms with the American and Soviet leaders, Roosevelt and Truman, and Stalin.
- Possessor of a huge empire: at its peak in 1933, the British Empire covered nearly one-quarter of the world's land surface and contained almost one-quarter of its population. Although weakened by the growth of nationalist movements in Africa and Asia, the Empire remained of considerable economic and military significance.
- Having a 'special relationship' with the United States: strong historical, cultural and linguistic links between the two Anglo-Saxon powers underpinned their cooperation in both world wars. From 1942, Britain was a military ally of the United States in the war against Germany and Japan, but earlier the Lend-Lease Agreement (1941) provided a system of credits enabling Britain to obtain a continuous supply of American goods and materials in order to sustain its war effort.

Britain's post-war role in the world was powerfully shaped by Labour's Foreign Secretary, Ernest Bevin. A fervent patriot, Bevin based his policies on two principles – first, that a vigorous British foreign policy was vital to world peace; and second, that Britain was still a great power with important global interests to protect. To these ends, he presided over the development of a system of treaties for the global containment of communism (in alliance with the USA); the emergence of a complex imperial policy combining the development of the Empire, the creation of the Commonwealth, and a system of global bases and strong points; and powerful defence forces backed by a British atomic bomb. The Conservative government (1951–5) led by Winston Churchill with Anthony Eden as Foreign Secretary continued these policies.

The containment of communism

Bevin aimed at the close involvement of the United States in the defence of Western Europe against possible Soviet aggression. Hence he played a leading role in negotiating the formation of the North Atlantic Treaty Organisation (NATO) in 1949, which obliged the United States, Canada, Britain, France, the Netherlands, Belgium, Luxembourg and six other European countries to assist each other if attacked.

The Attlee government also allowed American strategic bombers (with atomic capability from 1949) to be stationed in Britain (1946), and when the Soviets blockaded Berlin (1948–9), participated with the USA in an airlift of supplies to keep the city open.

Defence and the British A-bomb

When the USA brought atomic collaboration with Britain to an end (1946), a Cabinet committee took the decision to develop a British A-bomb (successfully tested in 1952). The Churchill Cabinet later decided – in the wake of US and Soviet development of the more powerful H-bomb – that Britain should have this weapon too (1954).

Britain's extensive international security obligations and overseas commitments necessitated a large defence budget which rose to almost 8 per cent of GDP (Gross Domestic Product) in 1954, when Britain had a higher per capita burden of defence spending even than the United States.

European integration

Britain held back from taking part in talks about closer economic and political union with its continental neighbours. British governments were not involved in the establishment of the European Coal and Steel Community in 1951 (Treaty of Paris) which led on to the European Economic Community of 1957 (Treaty of Rome) between France, Germany, Italy and the Benelux countries. Several factors lay behind Britain's decision to hold aloof

from membership of the Common Market at its foundation:

- Britain's conception of itself as a great power with a world role;
- its unwillingness to compromise its national sovereignty and suspicion of the supranational, 'federalist' aspirations of the founders of the EEC;
- its belief that its most important international relationships were with the USA and the Commonwealth and that closer economic ties with continental Europe were not in its long-term interest.

Britain saw its empire as an important asset in the post-war period and sought to maximise its value in a number of ways:

- Strategic withdrawal from untenable positions: e.g. the granting of independence to India and Pakistan (1947) and Burma and Ceylon (1948).
- Fostering the emergence of the Commonwealth as a method enabling it to continue to exercise informal influence as formal empire receded. A Commonwealth Premiers' Conference was held in 1949.
- Providing financial assistance for colonial and Commonwealth development, e.g. by participating in the Colombo Plan (1951) to help India and its neighbours.
- Using force to defend its interests: e.g. the long war fought against communist terrorism in Malaysia, suppression of revolts in Kenya and Cyprus, and imprisonment of nationalist leaders such as Kwame Nkrumah (Gold Coast) and Dr Hastings Banda (Nyasaland).
- Preserving a worldwide system of naval and military bases, e.g. the Suez Canal Zone, Mombasa, Aden, Bahrein, Singapore and Hong Kong.

Although frequently stated, it is worth repeating that the British Empire was the largest empire the world has ever known. It is perhaps no wonder that the British people were slow to realise that the basis of their world power had declined. For in the post-war years warm sentiments were routinely expressed towards the Commonwealth (although some still referred to 'the Empire') by politicians from all parties as well as by the wider public. The British Dominions – the self-governing countries of white settlement, Canada, Australia, New Zealand and South Africa – remained loyal to Britain in both the First and Second World Wars. During the 1950s and 1960s many Conservatives took pride in their links with the 'old' Commonwealth and Labour was highly supportive of the 'new' Commonwealth, which offered emerging countries membership of a non-aligned alternative to the cold war power blocs. However, a reappraisal of Britain's world role was taking place as a reaction to both the implications of Britain's declining international competitiveness and political events abroad.

Decolonisation, which had slowed to a mere trickle in the 1950s, became a flood after 1960, with 17 colonial territories achieving their independence between 1960 and 1964. By 1979 the process was virtually complete, and little remained of the British Empire. Its dissolution was inevitable; only the factors underlying the timing of the process are in some dispute. Some historians attribute the post-1960 acceleration to the Suez affair (1956), when – in response to the nationalisation of the Suez Canal by the Egyptian leader, Gamal Abdel Nasser – Britain colluded with France and Israel to launch a joint military expedition against Egypt. However, the combination of a run on sterling, pressure from the USA, and international opinion forced Britain to withdraw before its object had been achieved, thereby dealing a shattering and long-lasting blow to the country's self-image as a great power.

Suez may well have been a less decisive influence on Prime Minister Macmillan's decision to speed up decolonisation in Africa after 1960 than President de Gaulle's decision to liquidate French colonial entanglements in north and west Africa after 1958, and the sudden decision of Belgium to withdraw from the Congo in mid-1960. Also, Britain was anxious to avoid further acute embarrassments such as the 1959 revelations of the Hola Camp 'massacres' in Kenya and of 'police state' conditions in Nyasaland (Holland, 1991: 298; Reynolds, 1991: 223).

However, Macmillan as prime minister, even in the aftermath of Suez, remained committed to a world role for Britain, as signalled by the search for a genuinely independent British nuclear deterrent, the attempt to broker peace between the super-

> **BOX 3.1**
> ## 1956: twilight of empire
>
> One of the more curious features of modern British history is that, while generally prepared to accept this transformation in respect of the Indian and Colonial Empires, successive British governments were to show extreme reluctance to abdicate control in the Middle East.... Thus the last dying convulsion of British imperialism was to be enacted in an area which, paradoxically, had never formed part of Britain's Empire. And the lesson of the decline in Britain's power to control events and dictate to governments which started in South Africa at the turn of the century [the Boer War] was to be completed in Egypt fifty years later.
>
> (Nutting, 1967: 7–8, 12)

powers at Summit meetings, and the adoption of a costly policing commitment 'East of Suez'.

In many ways, the 'writing was on the wall' regarding the need for Britain to relinquish its world role status for that of a less demanding regional status. The rise of nationalism throughout many British-governed countries and consequent demands for independence; increasing defence costs in the context of the cold war and their impact on the balance of payments; the spiralling costs of nuclear weapons and their delivery systems; the impact of Suez and the increasing role of the USA in maintaining global order, led to much rethinking regarding Britain's role in the world. Britain emerged from the Second World War, not as a superpower but as a world power. Some compared Britain as 'junior world policeman' cooperating with its senior partner, the USA, responsible for pursuing Western interests throughout its imperial sphere of influence, particularly in the Indian Ocean. Some within the British political elite began arguing that Britain's future role lay within Europe, not within the Commonwealth. For Britain no longer had the resources necessary to maintain a role east of Suez.

Europe, in the shape of the Common Market, was already an economic giant. Some argued that if it was to develop into something akin to the 'United States of Europe', it would become a political giant.

Furthermore Britain's world role could, indeed should, be played through influencing the politics of this new giant on the world stage.

The under-performing economy

Britain and its vast empire dominated the world economy during much of the 19th century. At this time the huge empire cost surprisingly little to maintain. For example, at the height of Britain's imperial history in the 1860s the costs of policing and defending the empire was no more than 2 per cent of GNP (Frankel, 1975: 289). A century later, the costs had risen to 9 per cent of GNP. Furthermore, whereas Britain's economy in the 1860s clearly benefited from having imperial markets, the benefits of Commonwealth trade in the post-war years were much less evident. Britain's dominance in world trade was challenged by the early years of the 20th century as other industrial nations increased their output and trade. From the end of the Second World War both Labour and Conservative governments became preoccupied with the pressing question of how to stop, and then reverse, Britain's relative economic decline. In other words, although Britain was progressively getting richer during the post-war years, her industrial rivals were getting richer quicker. The economies of Germany, France and then Italy gradually caught up with and then overtook Britain's economy.

Why was British capitalism under-performing compared with the economies of her European neighbours? Numerous hypotheses and explanations have been put forward to account for this failure. Some argued that British politicians, heavily influenced by memories of the 1930s, were too concerned with keeping unemployment at low levels. Keynesian economic policies were implemented in order to achieve high employment. It was argued that too much government intervention, designed to keep employment levels high, actually had the effect of reducing Britain's international competitiveness. Post-war governments intervened too much, it was argued, since capitalism generally worked best when left to itself. Some argued that cost of Britain's overseas commitments placed an unrealistic strain on the economy. Many historians argue that by the mid-1950s, Britain's overstretched global commitments and the huge burden of defence expenditure they necessitated were badly damaging the country's economy. British governments were well aware of the problem. In 1956 Harold Macmillan as Chancellor of the Exchequer observed that:

> for every rifle our comrades in Europe carried we were carrying two. If we were to follow the European example, we could save £700 million a year. If only half of these resources were shifted into exports the picture of our foreign balances would be transformed. If the other half were available for investment, there would be less critical comment about our low rate of investment compared to many other countries.
> (Chalmers, 1985: 65)

Others argued that vast resources devoted to paying for Britain's welfare state were the root cause of economic under-performance and relative decline. Resources, it was argued, that should have gone into reconstructing the economy at the end of the war went instead into fulfilling ambitious social policies.

The major theme of post-war economic policy in Britain was closer government involvement in running the economy than at any previous period. This greater state involvement had three main aspects:

- The creation of a mixed economy. This was done by a series of important nationalisation measures introduced by the Attlee government which, with the exceptions only of steel and road haulage, were retained by the Conservative governments of 1951–64. Major industries moving into public ownership included coal, the railways, iron and steel, gas, electricity and civil aviation.
- Government responsibility for economic management: Chancellors of the Exchequer – both Labour and Conservative – used a combination of fiscal techniques (i.e. manipulation of tax rates) and monetary methods (i.e. interest rate changes) to manage the economy in order to ensure full employment, stable prices, economic growth, protection of the value of sterling, and avoidance of balance of payments crises.
- 'Corporate bias': this is a phrase coined by the historian Keith Middlemas to describe the close relationship between government and the 'peak' organisations of industry and the trade unions, which was already embryonic in 1940, cemented

during the war, and continued after it. The advantage for both business and the unions was that they gained substantial influence over policy making, thereby increasing their capacity to serve the interests of their members.

The tasks facing British governments immediately after the war were: to achieve the smoothest possible transition from a wartime to a peacetime economy; to negotiate foreign loans on the best terms available in order to cover the huge balance-of-payments deficits predicted for 1946 and 1947 (themselves the result of Britain's massive loss of foreign assets and exports during the war); and to encourage the recovery of Britain's export trade. By the mid-1950s, under Labour Chancellors Hugh Dalton, Stafford Cripps and Hugh Gaitskell, and Conservative Chancellor R. A. Butler, these goals had been largely achieved. But they were not achieved without crises, the worst year being 1947, when Britain faced both a severe fuel crisis (coal having failed to regain its prewar levels of output) and even more damaging massive balance of payments and sterling convertibility crises.

However, assisted by the recovery in world trade, by a financial injection through the US Marshall Aid programme for European Recovery (1948) and by a large fall in the cost of imports (1953), Britain's current account balance of payments came back into surplus in 1948 and more decisively in 1952–4. Moreover, by the mid-1950s, the removal of the wartime regime of physical controls over the economy was virtually complete and Keynesian methods of economic management were effectively in place. The new fiscal and monetary methods of economic management had even acquired a name amongst journalists – 'Butskellism' (from the names of Labour and Conservative Chancellors, Gaitskell and Butler). Moreover, after a sharp increase in 1947 to over 1 million, unemployment fell to around 300,000 (1.5 per cent) for the next ten years.

Building a welfare state

Wartime changes prepared the way for the development of the post-war welfare state:

- The prominent role assumed by Labour – the party of radical change – in the wartime Coalition government: Labour held two posts in Churchill's War Cabinet and also key posts in home front ministries.

- A massive expansion in the role of government: The government took on large-scale powers over the production and distribution of resources and over the labour force – for example the allocation of raw materials to priority purposes, staff planning, price controls and rationing.

- The development of blueprints for vast new government responsibilities in the provision of welfare and the maintenance of full employment: The two main developments were the Beveridge Report (1942) and the White Paper on *Employment Policy* (1944). The Beveridge Report called for a new social security system based on compulsory social insurance and fixed subsistence-level benefits in return for flat-rate contributions. In the White Paper, the government accepted the maintenance of 'a high and stable level of employment' as one of the 'primary aims and responsibilities' of government after the war. The architects of these new policies were respectively W. H. Beveridge (1879–1963) and J. M. Keynes (1883–1946), both Liberals, both academics (Beveridge was a former Director of the London School of Economics (LSE) and Keynes a Cambridge don) and both temporary civil servants during the war. Beveridge assumed that in order to function properly his scheme would need to be accompanied by other sweeping changes: family allowances, a comprehensive national health service and full employment. Keynes allocated government a central role in maintaining consumer demand for goods and services at a level sufficient to achieve and preserve full employment.

- Government commitment to post-war social reconstruction: This was signalled by actual legislation, such as the 1944 Education Act and the introduction of family allowances (1945), and by the 1944 White Papers entitled *A National Health Service* (which envisaged a comprehensive health service with 'free' treatment financed by taxation) and *Social Insurance,* which accepted virtually the whole of the Beveridge Report and was quickly followed by the establishment of a new Ministry of National Insurance (1944).

- A leftward ideological shift in both elite opinion and public opinion: Post-war social reconstruction enjoyed widespread support from reformist intellectuals, civil servants, the political parties, leading figures in the churches, universities and media, and from public opinion, as indicated by the enthusiastic reception of the Beveridge Report, and the anti-Conservative trends in by-elections, the Mass Observation Survey, and opinion polls during the war.

The main welfare state measures introduced by the Labour governments (1945–51) – and by the wartime Coalition – and broadly continued by the Conservative governments in the 1950s are shown in Box 3.2.

BOX 3.2
The welfare state: the main measures

- **Family Allowances Act (1945):** 5 shillings (25p) per week to every family for the second and every subsequent child. Indicated state adoption of the principle of contributing financially to the upkeep of children regardless of parental means.
- **National Insurance (Industrial Injuries) Act (1946):** established four types of benefit – injury benefit (payable for six months); disablement benefit (payable after that according to the degree of disability); supplementary benefit (e.g. hardship allowances); and death benefits for dependants.
- **National Insurance Act (1946):** in return for flat-rate contributions, the state provided seven types of benefit – sickness; unemployment; retirement pension; maternity; widow's; guardian's allowance for orphans; and a death grant for funeral expenses. The new pension, 26 shillings (130p), represented an increase of 16 shillings (80p) on existing pensions and was more generous than Beveridge had recommended. This Act began the extensive state responsibility for citizen welfare often referred to at the time and later as 'cradle to grave' provision.
- **National Assistance Act (1948):** supplementary allowances payable on a means-tested basis to bring National Insurance benefits up to subsistence level or to provide for people not entitled to those benefits.
- **National Health Service Act (1946):** provided a comprehensive service available free to all at the point of receipt and financed mainly by taxation. The NHS was managed by three agencies: regional hospital boards appointed by the minister of health to run the former local authority and voluntary hospitals; local executive councils (half lay members, half professional) to administer the general practitioner and dental, ophthalmic and pharmaceutical services; and the local authorities whose health and welfare services included maternity and child care, vaccination and immunisation, domestic help, home nursing and home visiting.
- **Education Act (1944):** introduced a tripartite system of secondary education based on grammar, modern and technical schools, with selection by the 11+ examination; each type of school was intended to have 'parity of esteem'. Fee paying in secondary schools was abolished and the school leaving age was to be raised to 15 in 1945, and to 16 as soon as possible after that (in fact, these intentions were not achieved until 1947 (15) and 1973 (16)). The Act created the office of minister of education to whom it gave the duty of providing a national education service. It gave more state aid to the voluntary (i.e. church) schools but subjected them to stronger public control.
- **Employment policy:** government commitment to the maintenance after the war of 'a high and stable level of employment' (1944 White Paper) was seen by leading contemporaries such as Beveridge and Attlee to be as important as the measures described above in the attack on poverty and deprivation.

The pendulum years: from crisis to doubt

By the end of the 1960s policies that qualified Britain for a world power status had collapsed. The British attempt at real nuclear independence ended in the cancellation of the surface-to-surface missile 'Blue Streak' in 1960 and the negotiation of an agreement to purchase a new generation of nuclear weapons launched from Polaris submarines from the USA (Nassau Agreement, 1962). Denis Healey, as Defence Secretary, finally managed to wind down military commitments 'East of Suez' with the 1967 promise to withdraw British forces from Singapore and Malaysia in the mid-1970s.

The main themes of Britain's external relationships in the early post-war years were the collapse of the world role, the displacement of the Commonwealth by Europe, and the increasing reliance upon the USA. The major strand in Britain's domestic history was the continued reluctance to sacrifice its pursuit of national 'greatness' in order to dedicate itself to the goal of developing an efficient modern economy. However, by the 1960s, especially in light of Suez, many in Britain's political elite came around to accepting that Britain was no longer a world power. Dean Acheson quipped that Britain had 'lost its empire and not yet found a role'. Even as Acheson spoke these words, some felt that it was not necessarily true since a role existed for Britain as a middle-size European power.

If Britain's future role lay with Europe, that did not automatically imply, of course, that Britain should become a member of the European Economic Community. British politicians had distanced themselves from early experiments with European integration – such as the Schuman Plan – believing that Britain's interests were best served by international cooperation with European countries rather than by participating in supranationalist integration. As early as 1955 Britain proposed a 'grand design' to reorganise Western Europe. Britain wanted to create a wide free trade area which would embrace most of Western Europe, including the six countries of the EEC. This was opposed by EEC members on the grounds that free trade would destroy their 'common external tariff' and so threaten the process of integration. Once negotiations for a wider European Trade Area had collapsed, Britain organised an alternative

BOX 3.3
Retreat from empire

Rhodesia: a very British affair
The Foreign Office accepted the inevitability of white colonial governments in Africa being replaced by black self-government. Following the collapse of a multi-racial experiment in government, the Central Africa Federation, the British government was left with the problem of Southern Rhodesia, which had enjoyed near-independent rule under white control since 1923 and claimed dominion status. As a result of complex diplomacy, relatively liberal white governments in Rhodesia were replaced by increasingly right-wing administrations, culminating in an unilateral declaration of independence (UDI) and war against black insurgents. Britain ruled out military action against the rebel regime and organised international sanctions which the government knowingly broke at times. Rhodesia represented a special case of Pax Britannica in which peace had been brought to warring tribal groupings, but at the cost of unacceptable white supremacy. Few Rhodesians were surprised that once white controls had been removed, the black government of Robert Mugabe degenerated into genocide against the Matabele, state murders, lawlessness, corruption, economic chaos and famine.

(some would argue rival) trading bloc in 1959. The European Free Trade Association (EFTA) included Britain, Austria, Denmark, Norway, Portugal, Sweden and Switzerland. In contrast to the EEC, EFTA was a loosely knit, diverse organisation without any distinctive political goals.

In 1960 an interdepartmental assessment in Whitehall concluded that Britain's national interest would be served by full membership of the EEC. The following year Conservative Prime Minister Harold Macmillan announced that Britain intended to seek membership of the EEC. The Labour Opposition vacillated for a year, eventually supporting Britain's application only if five tough conditions could be met. In the event, the French vetoed Britain's application. Under the leadership of Harold Wilson, a Labour government first tried to 'bridge the gap' between EFTA and the EEC. When negotiations failed, the government decided on making a second application for EEC membership. Once again, however, the application failed as a result of another humiliating French veto. Wilson decided that Britain's application would not be withdrawn but 'lay on the table' until such time as it might be reactivated.

It was a Conservative government, under Edward Heath, that was responsible for pursuing the reactivated application which concluded successfully with Britain joining the EEC on 1 January 1973. From the opposition benches, Labour opposed the terms of membership negotiated by Heath. On returning to office, Labour purportedly renegotiated the terms of entry which were put to the electorate in referendum which supported continued membership by two to one.

Economic management: towards 'stagflation'

There was little change in the sectoral balance of the 'mixed economy' before 1970 but rather more after that date. Road haulage and steel were both denationalised in the 1950s by the Conservatives, but Labour returned steel to public ownership in 1967. After 1970 Labour nationalised aerospace and shipbuilding (1977) and formed the British National Oil Corporation in order to influence the exploitation of North Sea oil. The nationalisation of Rolls-Royce (1971) by the Conservatives and the acquisition of a majority shareholding in British Leyland (1975) by Labour were prompted by the desires of governments to ensure the survival of major ailing companies.

However, the consensus on economic management came under increasing strain during the 1970s, with new directions in economic policy being proposed by the Conservative New Right and the Labour left (alternative economic strategy). The challenge to the consensus emerged against a background of accelerating economic decline, with Britain slipping ever more rapidly down the international 'league table'.

In addition, hitherto favourable economic indicators took a sharp downward turn. The inflation rate,

> **Definition**
> **Stagflation** – a term coined in the 1970s to describe simultaneous inflation and economic stagnation, a combination previously considered almost impossible.

which had been running at 2–3 per cent in the 1950s and 4–5 per cent in the late 1960s, rose to over 9 per cent in the early 1970s and thence, after the quadrupling of OPEC (Organisation of Petroleum Exporting Countries) oil prices in 1973–4, to over 24 per cent in 1975. Unemployment, which had averaged an annual 335,000 in the 1950s and 447,000 in the 1960s, also increased sharply after 1970, rising to an annual average of 1.25 million (1974–9). Economic growth, which had averaged 2.8 per cent per annum between 1948 and 1973, plummeted to a mere 1.4 per cent between 1973 and 1979. A new term – 'stagflation' – was coined to describe this unprecedented situation of slow growth combined with both rising unemployment and accelerating inflation.

The years 1972–9 were the heyday of 'corporatist' economic management between government, employers and unions, with interventionist governments using incomes policies including wage freezes in order to contain inflationary pressures. This approach was symbolised by Labour's 'social contract' with the unions (1974–8), in which the unions agreed to voluntary restraint on wages in return for favourable government social and industrial policies. Whatever the final judgement of historians on incomes policies (whether statutory, 1972–4, or compulsory non-statutory, 1976–9), they had the undoubted disadvantage of politicising industrial relations. The Heath government's clash with the miners (1972–4) and the Callaghan government's battle with the public sector unions (1978–9) helped to bring about their downfall.

Rapidly rising inflation and unemployment, slowing economic growth, and high and increasing levels of public expenditure and taxation led the Labour government to move away to a certain extent from Keynesian methods and priorities of economic management in the late 1970s. First, Chancellor Denis Healey in his 1975 Budget refused to increase demand in the face of rising unemployment, thereby initiating a new emphasis

> *Definitions*
> **Corporatism** – in Britain is taken to mean a process of policy making involving government and the major economic interests, business and labour.
> **Tripartism** is another term with a similar usage to mean decision making by government, the Confederation of British Industry (CBI) (representing employers) and the Trades Union Congress (TUC) (representing workers), especially on incomes policy. Critics argued corporatism involved interference with the free market, the bypassing of parliament, and top-down decision making.

on control of inflation as the major goal of government policy, rather than the maintenance of a 'high and stable' level of employment. Dennis Kavanagh has called this policy shift 'a historic breach with one of the main planks of the post-war consensus' (Kavanagh, 1990: 127).

Second, during the sterling crisis of 1976, the government adopted formal targets for the growth of the money supply (notes and coins in circulation, plus sterling current accounts in the private sector and sterling deposit accounts held by British residents) as a way of reducing the rate of inflation. Finally, Labour also began the change from the Public Expenditure Survey Committee (PESC) method of controlling public spending to the use of cash limits. Under PESC, public spending plans were not adjusted when growth turned out to be lower or inflation higher than had been expected when the plans were drawn up. Under the cash limits methods, which began in 1976, each spending programme received a cash limit for the year and was expected to keep within its budget. However, although Labour initiated new priorities and methods in economic management, it was far from launching a new philosophy of government based on these new directions. That was the task the Thatcher government, coming to power in 1979, set itself to carry out.

Public spending: 'the party's over'

A generally bipartisan approach to the welfare state continued during the 1960s and early 1970s, with government social spending rising ever more rapidly as a proportion of GNP. But broad overall consensus was compatible with differing policy priorities and emphases, especially in education and housing. Thus in education Labour began a rapid movement towards comprehensive schools which was continued by the Conservatives after 1970, even though their preference for selectivity (and the preservation of the grammar schools) would have made them unlikely initiators of such a policy.

In housing, Labour stressed the need for increasing the stock of council houses whilst the Conservatives encouraged owner occupation. Both parties moved increasingly towards means-testing in their social security policies, but for Labour this was a regrettable departure from the principle of universality, whereas the Conservatives approved it as preserving work incentives and containing the growth of state welfare (Digby, 1989: 65, 69).

Severe economic difficulties experienced in the mid-1970s resulted in polarised opinion on the future of welfare. Labour attempted to tackle the problem of inflation in the economy by increasing welfare as a form of 'social wages', while curbing wage demands through establishing pay norms.

The welfare state was also under severe strain by the mid-1970s. In the 1950s, it had been expected that the rapid growth of the economy would enable welfare spending to rise without adding to the tax burden on households, but by the 1970s this expectation had been eroded. National income had failed to grow as rapidly as expected, but government welfare commitments had increased dramatically. The result was a steady rise in public expenditure which reached a post-war peak as a proportion of GDP of just under 46 per cent in 1975–6. The gap between public expenditure and revenue – which has to be filled by state borrowing (the Public Sector Borrowing Requirement) – increased dramatically even though the tax burden was at record levels. By 1975 even people officially classified as among the poorest in the community paid tax, and the average male wage earner with two children paid one-quarter of his income in direct taxes compared with 3.3 per cent in 1955. By the mid-1970s public expectations of the welfare state were running well ahead of public willingness and national capacity to finance it. On the political right, some voices were beginning to question assumptions about the desirability of having a welfare state.

The Thatcher years

The 1970s was a decade of crisis for the British economy. The shockwaves from the energy crisis which swept through the economy were intensified, rather than calmed, by the policies of successive governments. In both parties, the political centre was in retreat – in the Conservative Party because of the failure of Heathite statism between 1972 and 1974; in the Labour Party because of dissatisfaction with Labour's record on welfare and the economy, and the rise of radical single-issue groups representing feminists, blacks, gays, and CND (the Campaign for Nuclear Disarmament). Governments had lost political authority because of their apparent incapacity to reverse national decline. In particular, they were increasingly perceived by the public as at the mercy of over-mighty interest groups and as unable to deal with Britain's long-term problems of low productivity, backward industry and strife-torn management–union relations. Wilson's attempt at trade union reform had been blocked by his own party (1969), while Heath's industrial relations legislation had collapsed in a wave of industrial militancy (1971–2). The breakdown of government union reforms and wage restraint policies in the decade before 1979 engendered a sense of ungovernability, chaos and mounting public frustration. When first the Ford workers, then the lorry drivers, then the public sector unions in a series of well-publicised strikes, broke through the Callaghan government's 5 per cent pay norm in 1978–9, their actions seemed to symbolise the failure of consensus government.

The main objectives of Thatcherism between 1979 and 1990 were twofold: first, to restore British prestige and assert British interests more vigorously abroad, and second, to 'roll back the frontiers' of the state in economic and welfare (although not in law and order) policy. The full range of policies designed to implement the second of these goals was not present in its entirety in 1979, but emerged during the course of Thatcher's three administrations (privatisation, for example, mainly after 1983 and reform of the

welfare state after 1987). Policies on the economy, industrial relations and welfare represented a deliberate reversal of the post-war consensus, a change of political tack aimed at turning the country round and halting decline. They were continued under John Major (1990–7), who retained low inflation as the central target of macro-economic policy, implemented the more difficult privatisations and carried through the 'internal market' reforms in health and education.

Privatisation: the 1979 Conservative manifesto promised only modest denationalisation (of aerospace and shipbuilding), but privatisation emerged during the early 1980s as a central plank of the government's programme. Between 1979 and 1997 it carried out a massive transfer of assets from the public to the private sector, thereby virtually extinguishing the 'mixed economy' as it had existed since 1951. The goals were increased efficiency (the New Right believing as an article of faith that private enterprise was more efficient than public enterprise); the removal of a major burden from the taxpayer; and, more broadly, the creation of a free enterprise society in place of a 'socialist' society. By 1997 21 per cent of the adult population owned shares, compared with 7 per cent in 1979, and as a result of a large-scale sale of council houses, home ownership had risen from 52 per cent of households in 1979 to 67 per cent in 1997.

Both the nature and contents of Thatcherism became a much discussed topic among political scientists. Margaret Thatcher was projected as a 'conviction politician' determined to shape politics according to her own values. She had a reputation for 'handbagging' both political friends and enemies in order to gain their submission and acceptance of her preferred policies.

Thatcherism, however, was more than simply a 'warrior' style of leadership; it could also be defined as an ideology. Some argued that Thatcherism was a coherent set of ideas based on the thinking of the New Right. At times Thatcherite rhetoric did

---

Definition
Privatisation – the transfer of the ownership of assets from the public sector to the private sector.

reflect a mission to 'roll back the state and set the people free'. Her political instincts opposed the 'big government' of the welfare state and nationalised industries, both subsidised by presumed reluctant tax-payers. Government intervention – inspired by Keynes and Beveridge – had curtailed the freedom of the individual. It was argued that a larger market, and resulting smaller government financed by lower taxes, would best defend the freedom of the individual. In practical terms, this meant, (1), curtailing the public sector, which was seen as consuming wealth created by the private sector, and (2), stimulating the beleaguered private sector. Privatisation in its many forms, the introduction of competition into welfare services, lower income tax, as well as attempts to cut back on public spending, characterise the policies of Thatcherism

Others argued that Thatcherism was simply a set of 'Victorian values' which the Prime Minister proclaimed at one time or another. Influenced by her father when she was a young girl, Margaret Thatcher believed in self-reliance, the importance of the family, firm discipline, thrift, and in the nation and religion. These were seen as the values that had prevailed when Britain was at its imperial grandest. Unlike many of her generation, Thatcher rejected the permissive attitudes of the 1960s which appeared associated with national decline. (See Chapter 4 for a fuller discussion of Thatcherism.)

Thatcherite Britain in Europe

It was anticipated that Margaret Thatcher would be strongly committed to Britain's role in Europe. Her commitment was, however, to reduce Britain's contribution to the European Community budget. For a variety of reasons, including her combative style of conducting business, the European Community entered a period of decline – so-called 'Eurosclerosis'. A federalist-minded president of the European Commission, Jacques Delors, proposed accelerating the transition of the Community from a customs union to a single market. Twelve member states signed the Single European Act in 1986. Once it became argued in the corridors of Brussels that a single market required a single currency,

> ### BOX 3.4
> ## The Falklands conflict: a metaphor for Thatcherism?
>
> The Falkland Islands lie in the South Atlantic, some 400 miles off the coast of Argentina. Fewer than 2000 inhabitants, mostly of British stock, have lived on the islands for about 150 years. Argentina lay claim to the islands, known by it as the Islas Malvinas. When the Argentinian President General Galtieri invaded the Falkland Islands on 2 April 1982, the Thatcher government despatched a Task Force which successfully recaptured the islands at a cost of 255 British dead and 777 wounded. In addition, six British ships were sunk. A 'Fortress Falklands' policy was then put in place for the defence of the islands at a cost of £5 billion. Britain's victory in regaining the islands was imported into British politics as the 'Falklands factor' which transformed Margaret Thatcher's up until then failing political image. Many people concluded that although she took political risks, the spoils of victory justified those risks, and some were inclined to give her the benefit of the doubt over her economic policies also.

Thatcherites grew alarmed. As plans to rejuvenate the Community were discussed, so Margaret Thatcher's attitudes towards integration hardened. She attacked federal ambitions in a widely reported speech in Bruges, in which she criticised the workings of the Community across a broad front.

Against her judgement, her ministers persuaded her that sterling should enter the Exchange Rate Mechanism of the European Monetary System – a currency stabilisation scheme which was a forerunner of the creation of a single European currency. Her instincts, justified by the events of 'Black Wednesday', confirmed to Thatcherites the view that European integration was doomed to failure since 'you can't buck the market' and successfully integrate national currencies.

John Major led a deeply divided Conservative administration in which disagreements over the European Union reinforced other ideological splits within the party. While he proclaimed that he wanted Britain 'at the very heart of Europe', a significant number of his backbenchers were 'thinking the unthinkable': that Britain ought to leave the EU. They felt that the EU had developed beyond its original purpose of a trading organisation. As they saw it, the Maastricht Treaty of 1993 provided a blank cheque for a more federalist Europe, which extended the competence of the EU to new areas of policy as well as deepening the levels of cooperation and paving the way to full economic union.

European integration was not a development in tune with the Conservative mood, and subsequent divisions within government and party were among the principal reasons for the landslide Conservative defeat in the 1997 general election. Some speculated that the European issue had divided and weakened Conservatives in ways comparable to the Corn Laws in 1846 and tariff reform in 1903.

The welfare state and the free market

The Thatcher governments rejected full employment as the primary objective of economic policy in favour of the control of inflation. This meant the abandonment of Keynesian demand management in favour of monetarism (the control of the money supply) as the main mechanism of macroeconomic policy. By the mid-1980s, however, strict monetarism had been abandoned and the main counter-inflationary financial disciplines became first a stable exchange rate and then in 1990 entry to the European Exchange Rate Mechanism (ERM). Britain's ejection from the ERM in 1992, a devaluation of sterling from DM 2.95 to DM 2.65, led to the establishment of a new monetary framework involving publicly stated inflation targets and monthly meetings between the chancellor and the governor of the Bank of England to discuss monetary policy, the minutes of which were published six weeks later. By 1997, a low inflation economy seemed to have been achieved, with the inflation rate averaging 2.8 per cent between 1993 and 1997, still slightly higher than that of the UK's main trading partners (Kelly, in Dunleavy *et al.*, 1997: 284). However, over the 1979–96 period the annual rate of inflation averaged 6 per cent in Britain, considerably higher than in France, Germany, the United States and Japan (*Economist*, 1997).

Conservative governments in the 1980s would

> *Definition*
> **Monetarism** – strictly speaking, controlling inflation through controlling the money supply, although the term is sometimes used to describe free market economics and the whole economic approach of the Thatcher government.

have liked to cut back severely on state-provided welfare, but public support for the NHS, the social security system and free state education forced upon them a less directly anti-consensual approach. Nonetheless, the Thatcherite decade was a decisive one for social policy. Although the Thatcher administrations failed to reduce the share of GDP taken by welfare expenditure, they ended its century-long increase, and did so despite the need to spend substantially more on unemployment benefits. They had three main goals:

- the containment of costs and the search for greater efficiency and value for money in welfare provision;
- the targeting of benefits on the most needy;
- encouragement of an enhanced role for the private sector in housing, healthcare, education and pensions provision.

Before the late 1980s, housing represented the purest application of New Right principles, with significant but not revolutionary changes involving large-scale sales of council houses to sitting tenants, reductions in public sector house building, the scaling down of council rent subsidies and the encouragement of house purchase (with mortgage interest relief trebling down to 1987–8). But after 1988 fundamental changes in the health service, education, community care and housing were brought about by the introduction of 'quasi-markets' into these services. The Education Act (1988), Housing Act (1988) and National Health Service and Community Care Act (1990) constituted really important legislation which rivalled that of the years 1944–8 in significance and represented the biggest break with social policy tradition since 1945 (Glennerster, Power and Travers, 1991: 389–90). The changes were predominantly organisational and managerial, and sought greater cost-consciousness, efficiency and diversity in the delivery of services rather than any erosion of the principles of taxpayer financing or of free services at the point of use. The overall impact of the welfare reforms was to strengthen the role of central government, weaken the roles of local authorities and public sector professionals, and increase social inequality. They were continued by John Major, who added the 'Citizen's Charter' (1991), which sought to improve public sector services by establishing performance targets.

The Thatcherite mission to reduce public spending on welfare was not contained solely within an economic horizon. An increasing number on the political right came to see state welfare as imprisoning its beneficiaries into a 'culture of dependency'. The quest to reduce welfare was not, therefore, driven solely by economic imperatives, but was accompanied by a moral determination to return individualism to a nation of 'welfare junkies'.

The impact of Thatcherism

There were fluctuations apparent in the practice of Thatcherism. For example, the early monetarist targets, which were central to controlling the money supply in the fight against inflation, were abandoned. Yet inflation fell. Despite the initial Thatcherite determination to reduce public spending, actually policy was diluted into controlling the *growth* of public spending. Only by treating the proceeds of privatisation sales as 'negative' public spending was the rapid rate of growth in public spending obscured. Despite being the champion of the private sector, no economic miracle appeared to take place during Margaret Thatcher's period in Number Ten. Economic growth, at an average of 2 per cent a year, was barely above the preceding Labour governments' rate of 1.8 per cent a year. Although income tax was reduced significantly, increases in indirect taxes left average earners no better off. On the other hand, unemployment did reach record post-war levels. Some have argued that this is a harsh verdict on Thatcherite economics, and point to the languishing economies of European rivals, such as Germany, which did not experience a Thatcher-style revolution.

The 'enterprise culture' of Thatcherism influenced the economic behaviour of ordinary citizens in their everyday lives. Many purchased privatised shares or right-to-buy council houses, or both, so that share ownership and property ownership were widenened. However higher rates of unemployment, coupled with anti-trade-union legislation, transformed the labour market and increased insecurity for many workers. The free market values pursued through 18 years of Conservative government arguably also contributed to the weakening of old conservative values, such as tradition, stability and deference, and to an assault on institutions that Conservatives had in the past defended – the established professions, local government, the universities. While Margaret Thatcher believed that her Victorian values were also the values of capitalism, from an alternative perspective Victorian values can be seen as a backlash against the excesses of capitalism.

Tony Blair and New Labour

The transformation of Labour to New Labour began under the leadership of Neil Kinnock, continued under John Smith, and accelerated under Tony Blair. Internal reforms, constitutional amendments, policy reviews and a revised electoral strategy saw Labour pass through the final stages of being a 'mass bureaucratic party' to emerge as a 'electoral professional party' (Panebianco, 1988). Unlike the trade union-influenced, deal-making, socialist-flavoured old Labour, Tony Blair set out to forge New Labour as a democratic, market-oriented, efficiency-conscious, inclusive party of the radical centre.

New Labour's philosophy was summed up as a 'third way' between free market capitalism (associated with Margaret Thatcher) and centralised state socialism (associated with 'old' Labour). Unlike Thatcherism, the third way envisaged a large role for government; unlike social democracy, the third way stressed the responsibilities of individuals for their own welfare and the welfare of their families. The basic message of the third way was that New Labour would help individuals to help themselves.

Critics argued that the vague third way policy approach was no more than a post hoc rationalisation of policies, or possibly an electoral device to

Basis of the old consensus		Basis of the new consensus	
Old Labour Social democracy	**Old Conservative** One Nation Toryism	**New Labour** Third way	**Thatcherism** Neo-liberal New Right
Based on the big ideas of socialism and collectivism to advance the interests of the working class.	Based on a paternalistic philosophy, with the elite responsible for providing welfare for all.	Emerging philosophy based on 'cooperative self-help'. Reconstructed state with both more democracy and individual responsibility.	Populist pro-market philosophy based on individualism ('there is no such thing as society').
Concerned about protecting the interests of producers (workers and their trade unions) and the poor.	Protected the interests of the privileged and middle class, but also protection for the poor.	Concerned about the interests of consumers (especially middle Britain) and a new deal for citizens.	Concerned about helping the creators of wealth such as entrepreneurs. Much less concern for the poor.
Large welfare state as means of creating a more egalitarian society with more opportunity for all.	Pro-welfare state as a means of incorporating poor into society and providing mobility for the most able.	Pro-new style smaller welfare state (social investment state) based on a 'hand-up, not hand-out'.	Minimalist welfare state in order to attack the 'culture of dependency'. Privatise welfare services.
Pro-planning with public ownership as means of managing the mixed economy.	Pro-capitalist but accepts mixed economy. Excesses of the free market seen as 'unacceptable'.	Pro-free market but with strict regulation including a minimum wage.	Pro-market. Privatised much of the public sector with market forces shaping health and education
Nationalist, but with international rhetoric.	Nationalism.	Cosmopolitan nationalism.	Assertive nationalism.

Figure 3.1 Britain's changing political culture

beat the Conservatives in 1997. Others argued that third way policies had substance and were compelling many people into accepting low paid jobs, which perpetuated inequality in ways unacceptable to Labour supporters. This criticism may have been overly harsh, for where the New Right saw government as a source of problems for society, New Labour's third way recognised government in its traditional role of attempting to solve the problems of society. Where the New Right accepted the inevitability of poverty, third way policies are designed to eradicate poverty. If, in Labour's second term, the third way has given way to the 'third phase', then it may even comprise the transition of Labour into a modern 'tax and spend' party.

Tony Blair's determination to modernise the Labour Party was, once inside Number Ten, transferred to modernising the machinery of government. If third way policies were to be implemented, then a more efficient means of governing was necessary. A greater reliance on IT in delivering policy, greater recognition of female and ethnic minority talent in filling key posts, new government structures which bypassed old bureaucratic barriers, greater cooperation between the public, private and voluntary

> *Definition*
> **The third way** – a contentious term variously interpreted to mean:
>
> - a middle way between Thatcherism and 'old' Labour socialism (or between markets and hierarchy)
> - updated social democracy (or a third way between unrestricted free market capitalism and centralised state socialism)
> - partnerships or networks involving the public sector, private sector and voluntary (or 'third' sector).

BOX 3.5
The nature of political consensus

Political scientists have talked about a political consensus which existed during the early post-war years and another which was forged during the Thatcher years. This has been criticised by others for oversimplifying political reality and exaggerating the extent of policy overlap between the major parties. The term 'political consensus' is a rather vague political concept, and it may be this lack of precision that leads to disagreements over the degree of consensus that existed at any particular time.

Richard Heffernan has explored the nature of consensus politics and argued that a consensus is rather like a framework within which politicians work. This framework changes when challenges come in the shape of new events or fresh ideas, but the old consensus inevitably plays a large part in forming the new consensus. The framework of the consensus does not simply include certain policies, but is a constraint in so far as it also excludes specific policies. For the period under review in this chapter, he described the consensus framework as a 'compass, not necessarily a road map' for policy makers (Heffernan, 2002: 743).

Heffernan argued that there have been not one or two, but many consensus in Britain's post-war politics. This was because policies evolved, being both stable and changing at the same time. In reality, politics rarely swings from one extreme to the other when there is a change of government; while some policies might change, others continue. Furthermore, a political consensus contains a variety of ideas, which can result in differing interpretations. For example, although the ideas of John Maynard Keynes influenced the management of Britain's economy during many of the post-war years, Labour governments stressed Keynes' interests in equality, redistribution and planning, while Conservative governments emphasised his views on markets, freedom and opportunity. There were thus different interpretations of the consensus that journalists referred to as 'Butskellism'. It can also be argued that because New Labour has embraced neo-liberal ideas, this does not mean that Tony Blair is from the same political mould as Margaret Thatcher. Rather, both the governments of Blair and Thatcher have worked within a neo-liberal framework that has constrained as much as predetermined policy.

sectors, and above all, a stronger centre to drive through change, were seen as crucial elements of modern government. There has been some talk of a new 'Blairite' consensus.

Where Thatcherism was driven by free-market competition, New Labour relied on new patterns of collaboration. For example, the much used term 'joined-up' government was used to describe confronting policy problems which avoided the problems of 'departmentalitis'. New units of collaborative government, such as the Social Exclusion Unit, have been created outside the old departmental boundaries. The newly devolved legislatures – the Scottish Parliament and the Welsh Assembly – were expected to create new forms of collaborative government unknown at Westminster. Finally, collaborative government was reflected in the growth of public–private partnerships, in which the public and the private sectors enter long-term cooperative arrangements to supply hospitals, schools, prisons and other large civil engineering projects.

Between Europe and the Atlantic

New Labour has embraced the European Union to a greater extent than preceding Conservative administrations. Yet the same constraints that restricted the policy of the Major government still operate on Labour; specifically, finding the optimum balance between Europeanism and Atlanticism. Blair has shunned euro-federalism, calling for the EU to become 'a superpower, not a superstate'. At the same time, he has readily played Britain's

BOX 3.6

Devolution

Arguably the most radical measure taken by Tony Blair's first Labour government was to fulfil the promise to bring devolution to Scotland and Wales, and to Northern Ireland as part and parcel of the 'peace process'. Sixty per cent of the Scottish electorate turned out in a referendum in 1997, voting three to one in favour of setting up a parliament with limited powers of taxation. Fifty per cent of the Welsh electorate turned out, and with a wafer-thin majority voted for an assembly.

The arrangements for devolved government in Northern Ireland were different from those in Scotland and Wales because they take into account the special political circumstances found in the province. The Good Friday Agreement, basically the terms for a peaceful settlement in Northern Ireland, was put to the electorate in a referendum in which 81 per cent turned out, with four voters out of five endorsing its contents. At the same time a referendum was held in the Republic of Ireland in order to remove from the constitution claims to the North. Elections to the Northern Ireland Assembly resulted in nine parties winning representation.

The 'new politics' of devolution, especially in Scotland, has produced inter-party cooperation, resulting in distinctive policies for care of the elderly, student finance, and teacher remuneration. But there has also been some disenchantment with devolution, with claims that it has attracted only second-rate politicians. Those who once argued that devolution was the first step towards full independence accept that electoral disappointment with the former has weakened support for the latter.

An unexpected dimension of devolution has been the arousal of English nationalism. Inside Westminster it has been observed that Parliament has developed a sharper territorial dimension, with for example only MPs representing English constituencies sitting on certain select committees and rising to ministerial rank in associated ministries. (See Chapter 17 for a fuller account of devolution.)

traditional post-war role of 'junior partner' in enforcing Pax Americana.

The election of a Republican President, George W. Bush, supported by a like-minded Congress, has put the British prime minister in a delicate position, particularly in his relations with his European equals. The policies of 'America First' on the national missile defence system, the rejection of Kyoto, the restriction of steel imports to the USA and other trade issues have angered EU leaders. Differences have become more apparent over the conduct of the 'war against terrorism' and policy towards Iraq. Yet despite strained relations between the USA and the EU, Blair's ambition is for the UK to act as a bridge between the two, and avoid Britain ever being in a position of having to choose between Europe and America. However, there is a political dilemma in playing this role, for the US administration wants Britain to be at the heart of the EU, in a position to influence EU policy. Yet the more Britain becomes integrated into EU institutions, the more it will put strain on Britain's special relationship with the USA. Of course, this special relationship with the USA makes many EU governments suspicious of Britain's commitment to Europe.

The new British state – changing political processes

Complex processes have challenged long-held assumptions about the nation state. New post-war structures such as NATO and the EU have diluted monolithic national sovereignty, resulting from the interaction of thousands of national representatives 'engaged in multiple continuous negotiations, information exchange, coalition-building, informal trade-offs among like-minded officials and ministers in different governments' (Wallace, 1999). If these structures attacked sovereignty from above, devolution eroded it from below.

New technologies and other forces of globalization have reduced the significance of national borders. The advent of satellite television, the Internet, the ease of air travel, along with English becoming the dominant language of the world, draw people into sharing a global culture. Also some problems that are being faced, such as global warming and the threat of international terrorism, are too big for any single government to solve. Global problems tend to require global solutions, which further advance the globalizing process and further dilute national sovereignty.

The impact of these processes has contributed towards changes in the way Britain is governed. The nation-state of post-war Britain had a political system characterised by Parliamentary sovereignty; by local government being an agent of central government; by the same party system operating at local and national levels; and by a clear delineation between the public and the private sectors.

By the time New Labour was elected and Tony Blair entered Number Ten, much of the British state had become 'Europeanised'. New patterns of governance and partnerships involving the EU and frequent contacts with EU agencies reorientated political activity. Britain quickly signed up to the Social Chapter, a move unthinkable for Thatcherite Conservatives. A weaker nation-state structure with less clearly defined borders now practises multi-level governance. A system of complex networks characterises both policy making and service delivery. The once clear divide between the public and the private sectors is now blurred by transfers of assets and cooperation between the sectors in terms of partnerships and other forms of collaboration.

Discussion of Tony Blair developing a presidential style of leadership may in fact reflect a symptom of increasing weakness of the office of prime minister. Processes such as institutional fragmentation and privatisation have 'hollowed out' the state,

leaving the executive in a weaker position (Rhodes, 2000). In this sense, attempts to strengthen Number Ten and coordinate policy across departments may be interpreted as signs of a government trying to regain lost influence.

Further reading

On the post-war consensus, there is Kavanagh and Morris (1994), while Coxall and Robins (1998) includes a chapter on the post-war consensus alongside others on post-war politics and social, economic and foreign policy. A critical view of the consensus thesis is offered by Pimlott (1994). See Frankel (1975) for a thoughtful overview. On the emergence of a post-Thatcherite consensus, see Dunleavy *et al.* (2002), especially the introduction and the chapters on 'Britain, Europe and the world', 'Economic policy' and 'Social policy'. Information on both the Thatcher and Major governments is provided by Smith and Ludlam (1996) and Crewe (1996). See Panebianco (1988) for an account of modernising political parties. Wallace (1999) discusses recent developments in the nature of government. Rhodes (2000) discusses the research findings of the Whitehall Programme.

Morgan (1990) provides a valuable account of the post-war period, as in briefer compass does Dorey (1995). An excellent overview is provided by Morgan and Owen (2001).

Chapter 4

Political ideologies: the battle of ideas

Ideas and politics	**50**
The meaning and political significance of ideology	**51**
Ideological conflict and consensus	**52**
Classifying ideologies: left and right	**52**
Ideologies and political parties	**52**
Liberalism – core interests and values	**53**
Traditional Conservatism	**56**
Thatcherism and the New Right	**59**
Post-Thatcherism and modern Conservatism	**60**
British socialism or labourism	**62**
From old to New Labour	**65**
Nationalism	**66**
Racism	**68**
Feminism	**69**
Green thinking	**71**
Globalization and the 'end of ideology'	**71**

The study of politics from at least the time of Plato onwards has attached particular importance to political ideas. Ideas, it is suggested, can change the world. There is nothing so important as an idea whose time has come. In this chapter we explore political ideas, and the impact of particular political perspectives or ideologies on political behaviour. We examine the development of the British versions of the 'mainstream' ideologies, liberalism, conservatism and socialism, and their changing inter-relationship over time with the major political parties. We also look at other ideologies such as nationalism, racism, feminism and green thinking. We conclude with a discussion of the impact of globalization on political thinking, and the renewal of the 'end of ideology' debate.

Ideas and politics

Not everyone sees ideas as central to an understanding of politics. Marx stressed the importance of material circumstances and interests in influencing or determining values and ideas. Thus he argued that the ruling ideas in every age reflected the interests of the dominant class. Ideas may be considered as just rationalisations of class interest. Some feminists have similarly claimed that widely accepted 'mainstream' thinking is 'malestream' thinking, reflecting the power and interests of the dominant gender. Other ways of thinking might simply involve rationalisations of the self-interest of particular sections of humanity: white Europeans, for example. All this might suggest it is more important to understand how groups of people come to hold particular ideas, rather than analyse the logic, coherence and implications of the ideas themselves.

Much of the modern analysis of politics involves the study of political behaviour rather than ideas. The study of voting for example, suggests that most voting is habitual, and can be correlated with such factors as occupational class, age, gender, religion or ethnicity (Denver, 2002). Thus political parties appeal to particular interests. They seek to maximise their vote in the same way as firms seek to maximise profits, by appealing to as wide a section of the market as possible. In this context political convictions may appear a dangerous liability if they alienate important groups. Thus, it is argued, politicians and parties compete for the middle ground and abandon controversial ideas (Downs, 1957).

Some critics think modern politics is all 'spin' and no substance. Communication techniques are more important than the substance of the message. Successful promotion of a politician, party or policy is about mood music, tone, colour, packaging rather than ideas (Franklin, 1994; Kavanagh, 1995). Thus politicians are coached in dress, body language, interview techniques. In this context, an appearance of sincerity may be a useful asset, but passionately held convictions can seem embarrassing.

Others again have learned to distrust ideas. After the Second World War, following the defeat of fascism and the discrediting of Stalinist communism, all 'isms' seemed at best irrelevant, at worst dangerous. Thus the 'end of ideology' was proclaimed in the west. 'Pragmatism' was preferred to ideology. Pragmatists prefer to rely on instinct, habit, experience and common sense rather than elaborate political theories (Leach, 2002: 5–6, 17–18).

Yet what is regarded as 'common sense' reflects ideological assumptions. Instincts and habits do not come from thin air but are shaped by the social and political environment in which we are brought up. The economist John Maynard Keynes has observed:

> The ideas of economists and political philosophers, both when they are right and when they are wrong, are more powerful than is generally understood.... Practical men, who believe themselves to be quite exempt from any intellectual influences, are usually the slaves of some defunct economist.
>
> (Keynes, 1947, ch. 24)

It is a testament to the power of ideas that, long after Keynes himself died, his own ideas continued to shape the political attitudes of many who themselves had never read a word he had written, and many who had not even heard his name. Indeed, some of the major changes in direction in politics in Britain and elsewhere over the last century or two have involved an intellectual revolution – a significant transformation of ideas and assumptions. Thus the 'battle of ideas' remains crucial.

The meaning and political significance of ideology

The term 'ideology' has often been used – and is still sometimes employed – in a pejorative (or hostile, negative) sense, and equated with rigid adherence to political dogma. Most contemporary political scientists, however, prefer a neutral definition of the term. In this non-pejorative, comprehensive interpretation an ideology is any connected set of political beliefs (McLellan, 1995; Leach, 2002). On this definition, conservatism, liberalism, socialism, fascism, nationalism and feminism are all ideologies. What general characteristics do they have in common? What are the defining features of ideology? (See Box 4.1.)

The form taken by particular ideologies may vary somewhat from country to country. Thus British versions of ideologies may be distinctive. For example, socialism in Britain has generally been identified with the Parliamentary socialism of the Labour Party. By contrast in the former USSR it denoted the Marxist-Leninist version of socialism more usually described in Britain as communism or Bolshevism.

Ideologies may also change their function over time, the same ideology appearing as revolutionary in one age, but conservative in another. Thus liberalism was a revolutionary ideology in the late 18th and early 19th centuries when it was pitted against traditional absolute monarchies, but later in the 19th century became itself the dominant ideology, under attack from the new revolutionary ideology of socialism. Nationalism is another ideology that has involved both revolutionary or ultra-conservative implications in different times and places.

BOX 4.1
What are political ideologies?

Political ideologies are *action-oriented*. They shape political behaviour in particular directions, for example to bring about national independence or resurgence (nationalism) or sexual equality (feminism). In serving as guides to political action, ideologies provide pictures of contemporary society which show how it has come to be as it is, what it ought to be like (and what it ought not to be like) and how desirable changes can be brought about and undesirable changes avoided. In other words, ideologies normally contain three elements: *description and interpretation* of the past and present; *prescription of an ideal* to be attained in the future; and *recommendations of strategies and policies* on how to achieve their goals. Ideologies appeal to people as members of particular social groups – governing, business, ethnic, national, religious – as classes and as sexes. Typically, they combine conceptions of human nature, views on the process of history (including the roles of key social groupings such as class, race, gender and nation) and theories of the state.

Ideological conflict and consensus

Extensive and deep ideological conflict may be the exception rather than the rule. Often there appears to be a widespread agreement or consensus over prevailing values and assumptions in any society, a consensus only challenged by marginalised minorities. Thus it may appear for a time as if ideological conflict, or even ideology itself, is at an end, as Daniel Bell proclaimed in 1960, a point seemingly validated by the notion of a post-war consensus in the west in the 1950s. Similarly, Francis Fukuyama (1992) announced the 'end of history' following the collapse of Soviet Communism. The cold war was over, and western liberal capitalism had won.

Yet however securely established particular political creeds may appear, history suggests they will be ultimately susceptible to shock and challenge – and ultimately, displacement. Thus Soviet Communism successfully replaced Tsarism after the revolution in Russia, and Marxism-Leninism became so embedded in Russia and other Communist countries that it became difficult to imagine any circumstances in which it could be successfully challenged, yet ultimately these ideas too melted away with surprising swiftness. Rather less dramatic was the rise and subsequent eclipse of Keynesian assumptions in Britain and the west, displaced by the formerly unfashionable free market ideas of the New Right. Yet as this example indicates, ideologies can prove remarkably resilient. Ideas that were once apparently discredited or 'on the way out' have often subsequently made a comeback, although sometimes in modified form.

Classifying ideologies: left and right

The labels 'left' and 'right' are still widely used to classify ideologies and political parties, and to describe the position of individual thinkers and politicians. The terms derive from the seating positions in the National Assembly following the 1789 French Revolution, when the most revolutionary members sat on the left and the more conservative members on the right. Today on the conventional left–right political spectrum, communists are placed on the far left, socialists on the left, conservatives on the right and fascists on the far right. Liberals (including the British Liberal Democrats) might be located somewhere in the centre, although the term 'liberal' today covers a wide range.

Other ideologies are more difficult to place. Nationalism is today more commonly associated with the right, although in different times and places it has been linked with ideas and parties from across the spectrum, while many in Plaid Cymru (the Welsh nationalist party) and the Scottish National Party would place themselves on the left. Greens are generally linked with the left, although Greens themselves often claim to be off the scale – 'not left, not right but forward'. Indeed, if degrees of 'left' and 'right' can be marked on a scale, it is by no means clear what that scale is measuring. Attitudes to change? Attitudes to authority? Attitudes to capitalism and the free market? None of these seems to fit closely the way in which the terms 'left' and 'right' are actually used (see Leach, 2002: 11–13). Consequently, some argue the terms are confusing and should be abandoned (Brittan, 1968). Others have suggested a more complex two-dimensional system of classifying political ideas, with attitudes to authority on the vertical axis and attitudes to change on the horizontal axis (Eysenck, 1957; www.political compass.org). Whatever the merits of such more complex systems of classification of political attitudes, it is unlikely that they will ever displace the more familiar language of left and right.

Ideologies and political parties

Accounts of political ideologies may include creeds such as nationalism, fascism, feminism, anarchism or environmentalism, but they commonly focus on three 'mainstream' ideologies: liberalism, conservatism and socialism. In Britain these ideologies can be linked clearly with three significant political parties: the

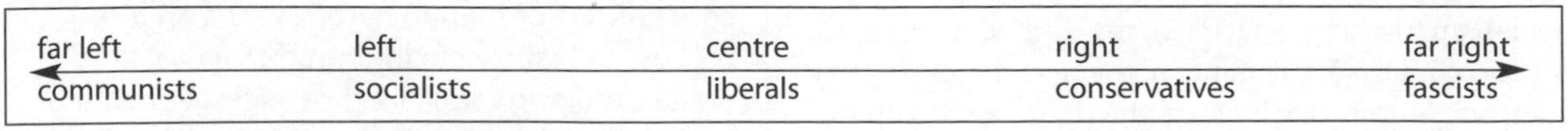

far left	left	centre	right	far right
communists	socialists	liberals	conservatives	fascists

Figure 4.1 Left–right, conventional scale

Liberal Democrats, the Conservatives and Labour. Yet the ideologies should not be confused altogether with the parties with which they are linked. The ideas associated with liberalism are much more important and much more influential than the values and policies adopted by the Liberal Party and its more recent Liberal Democrat successors. Indeed, liberalism is sometimes perceived as a 'hegemonic ideology', a system of ideas so influential that it has pervaded modern politics to such an extent that most modern ideologies, including the British interpretations of conservatism and socialism, may seem just 'variants of liberalism'. Yet the very breadth of liberalism suggests the extent of divisions within liberalism. Similarly, there are internal differences within conservatism, to the extent that Margaret Thatcher's brand of conservatism appears markedly different from some aspects of the conservatism that preceded it. As for socialism, its definition is hotly disputed, and many would deny that the British Labour Party is, or ever has been, a socialist party.

All this suggests that perhaps it would be preferable to examine political ideologies as theoretical models and avoid linking them with political parties that use their names and language. Yet this would not do either. The key point about political ideologies as opposed to traditional political theory is that they are 'action-oriented'. They do not involve pure abstract theory but have implications for political behaviour. As Marx said, 'Philosophers have only interpreted the world. The point however is to change it.' Political parties are one of the vehicles for translating ideas into practice. Thus parties that call themselves socialist seek to bring about, over time, their own version of a socialist society.

Moreover, political ideologies are not just articulated by a handful of great thinkers through recognised great books, but are expressed at a number of levels – by practising politicians who adapt the ideas of more original minds in speeches and slogans, by parties in election manifestos and programmes, and by the masses, if often in simplified and perhaps vulgarised form. Indeed, some ideologies, such as nationalism or fascism, are fairly thin in terms of sophisticated elaboration in key texts. While there are some important theoretical sources for British conservatism, much of it has to be inferred from the policy and practice of the British Conservative Party.

So it is neither possible nor desirable to separate the study of political ideologies from their often rather distinctive and sometimes highly contested expression by political parties. Yet it is a mistake to identify ideologies wholly with the parties with which they are often linked. Herbert Morrison, a leading Labour politician from the 1930s through to the 1950s, once declared that socialism is what the Labour government does. If that was so, there would be no point in studying socialism, only the performance of the Labour Party. Yet those who call themselves socialists within and outside the British Labour Party often disagree passionately over the nature and definition of socialism. Similarly, both Conservatives and Liberals sometimes agonise over the true meaning of conservatism and liberalism. All this argument would be totally pointless if it was not possible to envisage some ideal conception of conservatism, liberalism and socialism against which the programmes and policies and performance of parties can be measured.

Liberalism – core interests and values

With liberalism it is particularly important not to confuse the political ideology entirely with the expression of liberal ideas by the British Liberal Party and modern Liberal Democrats. Indeed, one of the problems for Liberals and Liberal Democrats is that liberal ideas have been so influential that they have permeated all mainstream British political parties. Thus it can be argued that liberalism has conquered while its former political vehicle, the Liberal Party, came close to extinction, before managing a partial recovery.

The term liberalism was not commonly used until the 19th century, although the foundations of liberal thought are much older, springing from the religious reformations of the 16th and 17th centuries, the 18th-century Enlightenment, the French Revolution, but most of all from the economic, social and political transformation brought about over time by industrialisation. Indeed the growth of liberalism is closely linked with the growth of capitalism, representative democracy, and the modern world. In that sense it is the hegemonic ideology of the modern age.

Liberalism can be linked closely with the class interests of the industrial bourgeoisie. In the early

19th century, following the arguments of classical economists such as Adam Smith and David Ricardo, liberals championed the free market and free trade, and opposed government intervention in the economy and the protection of agriculture. Their political programme involved an extension of the vote and Parliamentary representation to the new industrial centres, leading to a gradual transfer of power and influence from the old landowning aristocracy to the manufacturing classes. Yet to achieve and maintain themselves in power they had to appeal to a wider constituency, including the growing ranks of the professions and the skilled working class. This helps to explain some of the tensions within British liberalism as it evolved in the later 19th and early 20th century.

Ideologies evolve over time and can subdivide into different, and sometimes sharply conflicting, tendencies. While early, or classical, liberalism advocated limited constitutional government and free markets, over the course of the 19th-century British liberalism increasingly became identified with more intervention at both city and national level. New Liberals (e.g. T. H. Green, Leonard Hobhouse, John Hobson) argued that such intervention was not a restriction on freedom, but would enlarge the freedom of all individuals to make the most of their own potential. The Liberal government of 1906–14 introduced old age pensions, labour exchanges, and health and unemployment insurance, and laid some of the foundations for the welfare state, (later established on a more comprehensive basis by the 1945–51 Labour government).

The First World War and its aftermath led to splits among Liberals and the party's rapid decline. Many former Liberals moved to the Conservatives or Labour, and by the 1950s the party was reduced to just six MPs in the House of Commons. Yet New Liberal ideas permeated the other parties. Keynes and Beveridge, whose work and thought underpinned the post-Second World War political consensus, were both small and large 'l' liberals. The inspiration of the policies pursued by both Labour and Conservative governments owed more to New Liberalism than to traditional conservative or socialist thinking.

Ironically, when this ideological consensus was challenged in the 1970s, the challenge came from a revival of an older version of liberalism, the free market liberalism derived from Adam Smith and

---

BOX 4.2
Core liberal values

Individualism. Liberal analysis starts with individual men and women, rather than nations, races or classes. Individuals pursue their own self-interest. The interests or rights of individuals take priority over society, which is only the sum of individuals composing it any one time. Thus social behaviour is explained in terms of some fairly basic assumptions about individual human psychology. (Indeed some liberals even assumed that society and government had been deliberately created by individuals to further their own interests.)

Liberty or freedom. Individuals must be free to pursue their own self-interest. One practical application is the liberal demand for full freedom of thought and expression, and particularly religious toleration. Yet there have been some key differences between liberals over the interpretation and implementation of liberty. Early liberals emphasised freedom from tyranny and oppressive government (negative liberty), and followed Adam Smith and the classical economists in championing the free market. In the late 19th and early 20th centuries New Liberals sought the freedom to fulfil individual potential (positive liberty), which might require state welfare provision and state intervention to secure full employment.

Rationalism. Liberals also assume that humans are rational creatures and the best judge of their own self-interest. No one else, not rulers, priests or civil servants, can decide what is in individuals' interests better than they themselves. Liberals followed Jeremy Bentham in assuming that if everyone pursued his or her own rational self-interest this would lead to the greatest happiness of the greatest number.

Political and legal equality. Liberals have generally emphasised an equality of worth, advocating equality before the law and political equality (although some liberals were initially slow to accept votes for all men and women). In the economic sphere liberals have advocated equality of opportunity, but not equality of outcome. Indeed freedom in the economic sphere has commonly resulted in marked inequality.

Table 4.1 The Whig-Liberal tradition in Britain

Period		
17th century	**Puritanism and Parliamentarism**	
18th century	**The Whig tradition** 'Glorious Revolution' constitutional monarchy government by consent division of powers oligarchy	
Late 18th century Early 19th century	**Radicalism** revolution rationalism rights of man liberty, equality, fraternity **Classical liberalism** freedom of the individual free market economics utilitarianism and constitutional reform representative government	
Mid-19th century Later 19th century	**Gladstonian liberalism** free trade and balanced budgets national self-determination the 'nonconformist conscience' – temperance the municipal gospel and social reform democracy and Parliamentary reform	
Late 19th century Early 20th century	**New Liberalism** state intervention and social reform 'National efficiency' constitutional reform Liberal imperialism	
1920s–1970s	**Liberal Party decline** (but triumph of liberalism?) Post-war Keynes-Beveridge consensus 1960s progressive liberal consensus	
Late 20th century	**Liberal Party revival** 'New Liberal' tradition social reform constitutional reform and devolution civil liberties and human rights support for European integration Liberal Democrats	**Neo-liberal revival** Free market economics Thatcherism and New Right

Source: adapted from Leach, 2002: 26.

the classical economists. This neo-liberalism (not to be confused with New Liberalism!) was energetically promoted by Hayek and Friedman and taken up by Conservative politicians such as Keith Joseph and Margaret Thatcher. Thus the second half of the 20th century in Britain can be interpreted as much as a conflict between different versions of liberalism as a battle between conservatism and socialism.

Meanwhile the Liberal Party has achieved a modest revival of fortunes, initially on its own and then in alliance with a breakaway party from Labour, the Social Democratic Party, culminating ultimately in a merger to form the current Liberal Democrats. The Liberal Democrats retain a characteristic liberal interest in individual rights and civil liberties, support for New Liberal type welfare policies, a strong commitment to constitutional reform (particularly devolution and electoral reform) and an internationalist, humanitarian approach in foreign affairs. Yet much of this programme has been effectively taken over by the Labour Party, and it is difficult for the Liberal Democrats to find a distinctive ideological space to occupy to give them a clear identity in the struggle for electoral support in the early 21st century. The main questions that preoccupy the party now seem more tactical than ideological: coalition or competition with Labour.

Traditional Conservatism

Ideologies may evolve and change considerably over time. There are also significant internal tensions and contending schools of thought within all major ideologies. It is particularly important to bear these points in mind in making sense of modern conservatism. It may surprise those who are familiar with the free market ideas embraced by leading modern British Conservatives to learn that conservatism and the party that bears the name 'Conservative' were not always associated with these ideas. Yet in the 1950s and 1960s Conservative governments accepted the principles of Keynesian demand management, the welfare state, the mixed economy and even a form of economic planning (including incomes policy). Thatcher and her successors rejected much of this 'One Nation' Conservatism in pursuing neo-liberal or New Right free market ideas. While there are important elements of continuity between the ideas

of the modern party and older conservative thinking, Thatcher's leadership marks a watershed in the development of British conservatism. However, older interpretations of conservatism are not just of historical interest, but reflect continuing strands of thought within the party which could be important for its future. This section will concentrate on traditional conservatism, while the following section will focus on the New Right and contemporary conservatism.

Conservatism at its simplest suggests 'conserving', keeping things as they are. Whereas early liberalism favoured change and reform, old Toryism and 19th-century Conservatism were generally suspicious of, and resistant to, change. While liberalism was a product of the 18th-century Enlightenment, the American and French revolutions, and, most of all, industrial capitalism, Toryism and subsequently conservatism involved a reaction against all these. It was suspicious of the 'Age of Reason' and the threat this seemed to represent to traditional religious and secular authority. It was hostile to the language of freedom, equality and fraternity. It was fearful of many of the changes resulting from industrialization and the ideas associated with it. Many of these ideas were expressed by Edmund Burke, particularly in his critical essay *Reflections on the Revolution in France* (1790). Burke was a Whig politician increasing out of sympathy with thinking in his own party. He has come to be regarded as a key theorist of conservatism (although the term was not then used).

If liberalism was (initially at least) the ideology of the rising capitalist class, Toryism and conservatism reflected the interests of the declining but still powerful landed interest. Conservatives sought to maintain the current economic, social and political order against the pressures for change which could only result in a decline in their influence and power. Yet had conservatism remained wedded to a declining landed interest it would have fast faded as a political creed. Instead it held its own in conflict with liberalism in the 19th century and proceeded to dominate the 20th century in Britain. It achieved this remarkable success by flexible adaptation to new circumstances, although it can also be argued that some of its core principles have been fairly consistently maintained.

Thus although British conservatives have generally opposed radical change, they have often subsequently accepted change introduced by their political opponents rather than seeking to put the clock back, and indeed have sometimes initiated gradual reforms themselves. Flexibility, gradualism (a preference for gradual rather than radical reform) and pragmatism have been key aspects of British conservatism in action for most of the last two centuries.

To survive, Conservatives had to seek a wider base of support as the franchise was progressively extended to the middle classes, skilled workers and then the entire adult population. Increasingly, the Conservative Party came to be identified with the interests of property in general, rather than landed property, winning the support of many business people who would have once supported the liberals. Moreover, from the late 19th century the Conservatives under Benjamin Disraeli and subsequent leaders made a determined attempt to woo the working classes, particularly skilled workers, through social reform at home, combined with the pursuit of British national and imperial interests abroad. In the course of the 20th century they also sought to give the workers an increased stake in property, through encouraging home ownership and wider share ownership.

Much of this might be dismissed by their political opponents as a patent 'con trick', to persuade those with little or no property to support the cause and the party of substantial property, and to reject policies of extensive social reform and redistribution advocated by socialists. Conservatives themselves have generally argued that the various classes are bound together by ties of mutual dependence in an organic society, which is more than the sum of its individual parts. This organic theory of society and the state has often been contrasted with the individualism of liberalism. Disraeli had sought to transcend class differences and create 'one nation'. He argued that wealth carries with it obligations, including an obligation to assist those less fortunate. This 'paternalism' might entail a duty of voluntary charity, or an acceptance of state-sponsored social reform.

Such an approach marks off traditional conservatism from older forms of liberalism. While liberals thought individual human beings could be trusted to pursue their own self-interest to achieve social progress through free market forces, traditional conservatives did not generally share this optimistic

faith in human reason, goodness and progress, nor necessarily the benefits to be derived from increased human freedom in general and free market forces in particular. Conservatism has been described as a 'philosophy of imperfection'. Most conservatives do not believe in the perfectibility of humankind, but rather assume that there is an 'evil streak' (which Christians might describe as 'original sin') in human nature. This implies a need for authority – a strong state and strong government to maintain law and order and restrain violent and anti-social behaviour (Leach, 2002: 53–6).

Conservatives for most of the 19th and 20th centuries were far from being enthusiastic supporters of the free market and free trade. In the early 19th century Tories and Conservatives supported the Corn Laws and the protection of British agriculture. In the later 19th century many advocated what they called 'fair trade' as opposed to 'free trade', and in the early 20th century the party was converted by Joe Chamberlain to tariff reform and 'imperial preference', a policy which his son Neville Chamberlain sought to put into practice as Chancellor and later Prime Minister in the Conservative-dominated 'National Government' of the 1930s (Beer, 1982a, ch. 10).

In the post-Second World War era, modernisers in the Conservative Party adopted Disraeli's 'one nation' slogan to embrace social reform and state intervention. This 'one nation' conservatism became the new party orthodoxy. Thus Conservative governments between 1951 and 1964 appeared to have been fully converted to policies of Keynesian demand management, state welfare provision, the mixed economy, consensus and compromise in industrial relations and even, under Harold Macmillan, a form of state-led economic planning. For some modern conservatives this whole period is an aberration in the long history of the party, although for some others it remains the very essence of the authentic Tory and conservative tradition. Conservatism, according to one influential interpretation, involves an on-going tension between two rival libertarian and collectivist strands of thought, with each appearing to be dominant at different periods (Greenleaf, 1973, 1983). Indeed, such tensions and contradictions can be found in all mainstream ideologies. For others the contradictions are perhaps more apparent than real, and the core elements of

Table 4.2 The evolution of conservatism in Britain

Period	
Late 17th century 18th century	**Toryism** tradition monarchy Church of England landed interests
Late 18th century	**Edmund Burke** attack on values of French Revolution reassertion of tradition organic society gradual, pragmatic reform
Early 19th century	**Reactionary Toryism** fear of revolution repression protection of agriculture
1830s–1860s	**Peelite Conservatism** from Toryism to Conservatism acceptance of Parliamentary reform pragmatism gradualism
1860s–1870s	**Disraeli Conservatism** 'One Nation' paternalist social reform patriotism and imperialism Tory democracy
Mid-1880s–1930s	**Unionism** preservation of (Irish) Union imperial preference and protection social reform
1940s–1960s	**Post-Second World War 'One Nation' Conservatism** Keynesian demand management mixed economy and planning welfare state and social reform conciliation of unions corporatism end of Empire and into Europe
1970s–1980s	**Thatcherism** free market and competition privatisation and 'reining back the state' restoring authority of government defence of national sovereignty

Source: adapted from Leach, 2002: 50.

conservatism remain much as they have always been, although they have required some adaptation and reformulation over time.

Thatcherism and the New Right

The controversy over the nature of conservatism (outlined above) is at the heart of the continuing debate over Thatcherism and the New Right. Although ideologies are about ideas and interests rather than personalities, it is difficult to discuss conservatism after 1975 without extensive reference to the woman who gave her name to a political doctrine. Controversy surrounds Margaret Thatcher. For some, she and her allies hijacked the Conservative Party, and introduced alien individualist free market ideas at odds with the 'One Nation' tradition of social reform (Gilmour, 1978, 1992; Gilmour and Garnett, 1997). For others, Thatcherism involved the rediscovery of true conservatism. Yet both critics and true believers have perhaps exaggerated the break with the immediate past.

Margaret Thatcher is widely regarded as a conviction politician, who broke with the consensus politics of the post-war era, and rejected traditional conservative pragmatism for the ideology of the free market and competition. There is clearly some truth in this picture. Under Thatcher's leadership the neo-liberal ideas of Friedrich von Hayek and Milton Friedman became the new orthodoxy. Keynesian demand management was rejected and Adam Smith's 'invisible hand' of the free market restored to favour. Thatcher and some of her leading colleagues certainly embraced these ideas with some enthusiasm. Many of the policies pursued by her governments, such as the sale of council houses, the privatisation of the nationalised industries, the injection of competition into the public sector, and the attempts to 'rein back' the state and cut public spending and taxation, reflected free market ideas (Kavanagh, 1990).

Yet Thatcherism can be seen as the consequence rather than the cause of the breakdown of Keynesianism and the post-war consensus. Keynesian policies had been applied with some apparent success in the post-war decades, but by the 1970s they no longer seemed to work, and had been effectively abandoned by Callaghan's Labour government.

Similarly, concerns over the growth of government, the cost of the welfare state, trade union power and poor industrial relations were already widespread before Thatcher became leader of the Conservative Party. The party and its new leader adapted to altered circumstances as British Conservatives had managed so successfully in the past.

Moreover, while in office Thatcher was generally a more pragmatic and cautious Conservative than is sometimes imagined. Thus although she embraced the rhetoric of the free market with some fervour, she declared that the National Health Service is 'safe in our hands', rejected the privatisation of British Rail and the Post Office, and continued policies of state-financed urban regeneration (while slashing regional aid). Although there were some real cuts in public spending, and significant changes in the distribution of taxation, Conservative governments after 1979 were not particularly successful in reducing public spending and the overall burden of taxation. The state was restructured rather than 'reined back'. It was only more towards the end of her premiership that she dogmatically and disastrously pursued policies such as the poll tax (incautiously described as 'the flagship of Thatcherism') which ultimately helped to bring her down.

Indeed, the ideology of Thatcherism (or the New Right as interpreted in Britain) is best seen not as a pure free market doctrine but as a blend of these ideas with some traditional conservative elements, a mix of neo-liberalism and neo-conservatism, 'the free economy and the strong state' (Gamble, 1994). Thus 'reining back the state' in the economic sphere did not entail weakening government. On the contrary, Thatcherism involved a reaffirmation of the traditional Tory commitment to strong government, leadership, defence, law and order and the authority of the state. Thatcher and her successors continued to exploit the sentiments of nationalism and patriotism which had appealed so well in the past to the British electorate, most obviously in relation to the Falklands, the Gulf War and Europe. Both Margaret Thatcher and John Major strongly opposed devolution, emphasising the traditional Tory insistence on the Union of the United Kingdom. Both also employed the rhetoric of traditional family values which always played well with the Conservative Party.

For a period Thatcherism played well with the electorate also. Thatcherism was populist rather than

Photograph: PA Photos.

IN FOCUS 4.1 Margaret Thatcher

Margaret Thatcher, Prime Minister 1979–90, and the inspiration for 'Thatcherism'. Although not a particularly original thinker herself, she enthusiastically embraced the free market ideas of others and sought to apply them in government, and dominated the British political scene in the last quarter of the 20th century.

paternalist, appealing to the straight-talking 'common sense' of the readers of the tabloid press. Ideologies are held at various levels. While the elaborate sophisticated version of Thatcherism reflected the economic theories of Smith, Hayek and Friedman, the popular version was more about vivid imagery and slogans – 'the Iron Lady', 'Stand on your own two feet', 'the nanny state', 'Get on your bike'. Some of this rhetoric appealed to sections of the working class as well as the Conservative Party rank and file, although the popularity of Thatcherism can be exaggerated. Indeed, Parliamentary landslides depended more on the weaknesses and divisions in the opposition than on positive support for Thatcherism.

Moreover, this blend of neo-conservative and neo-liberal ideas inevitably involved some tensions and contradictions. One example, which caused a rare defeat for the Thatcher government, was over the symbolic issue of Sunday opening of shops, which involved an extension of competition and choice, and thus pleased neo-liberal advocates of the free market, but at the same time upset those traditional conservatives who wanted 'to keep Sunday special'. A much more important and damaging illustration of the problems of reconciling free market and traditional conservative ideas was over Britain's relations with the European Union. Thatcher had supported joining the European Community and she was an enthusiastic advocate of the 'single market', which seemed to fulfil her own free market values. Indeed, membership of the EC had been sold to the Conservative Party and the British people as a 'common market' entailing economic benefits for Britain. However, closer European integration threatened another core Conservative value, national and Parliamentary sovereignty. Conservative schizophrenia over Europe was intensified by the Maastricht Treaty and the drive towards European monetary union.

Altogether, Thatcherism was less original and distinctive and Thatcher herself rather more compatible with the mainstream Tory and Conservative tradition than is sometimes imagined. Even so, in one respect at least Thatcher was atypical of mainstream conservatism. Her instincts were radical rather than gradualist. She was a warrior rather than a healer. She was impatient with dissent to the extent of quarrelling not only with her ideological opponents within her party but with many of her earlier allies, including Nigel Lawson and Geoffrey Howe. Ultimately she was brought down by a coalition of the enemies she had made in the Cabinet and on the back benches, yet the bitterness caused by the circumstances of her departure has left a legacy of internal division in a party whose unity was once declared its secret weapon.

Post-Thatcherism and modern Conservatism

The strength of conservatism in the past has been its flexible pragmatism, its ability to adapt to new circumstances. While it might fairly be claimed that Thatcher successfully reinterpreted conservatism for a new age, she has made it more difficult for her successors to perform a similar feat. Her

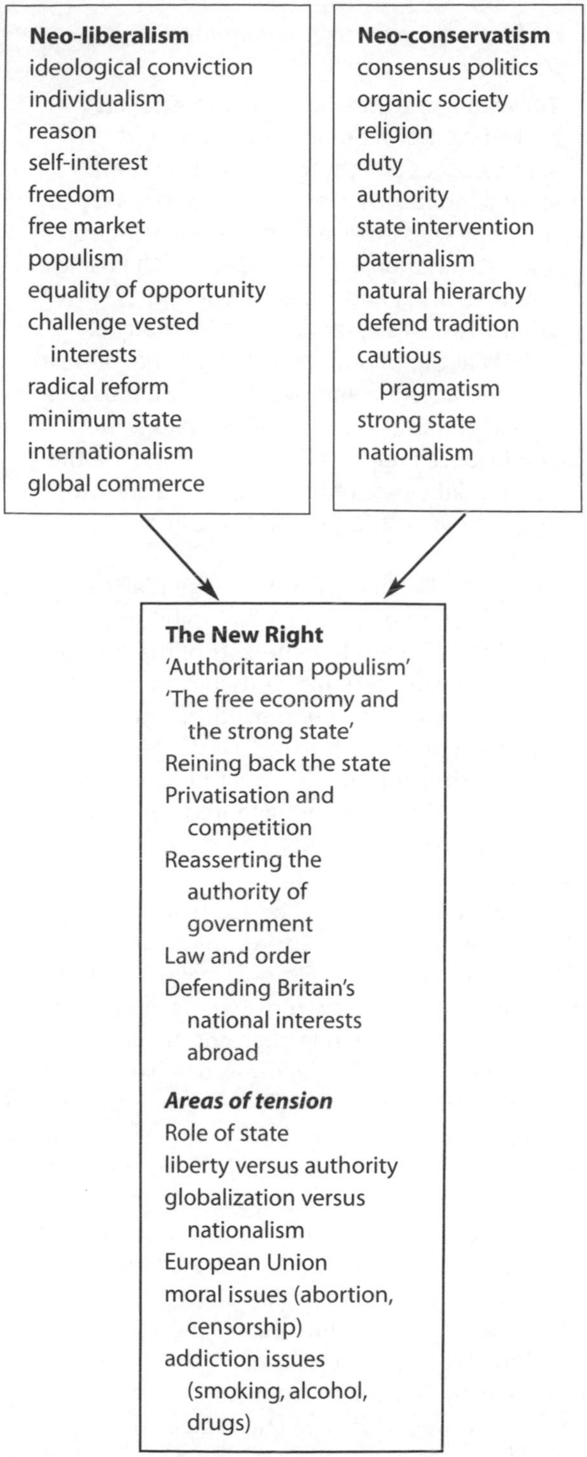

Neo-liberalism
ideological conviction
individualism
reason
self-interest
freedom
free market
populism
equality of opportunity
challenge vested
    interests
radical reform
minimum state
internationalism
global commerce

Neo-conservatism
consensus politics
organic society
religion
duty
authority
state intervention
paternalism
natural hierarchy
defend tradition
cautious
    pragmatism
strong state
nationalism

The New Right
'Authoritarian populism'
'The free economy and
    the strong state'
Reining back the state
Privatisation and
    competition
Reasserting the
    authority of
    government
Law and order
Defending Britain's
    national interests
    abroad

Areas of tension
Role of state
liberty versus authority
globalization versus
    nationalism
European Union
moral issues (abortion,
    censorship)
addiction issues
    (smoking, alcohol,
    drugs)

Figure 4.2 Tensions within Thatcherism and the New Right

Source: adapted from Leach, 2002: 199.

own influence helped tip the scales against candidates for the party leadership who might have changed direction – Heseltine, Clarke and Portillo – and in favour of those more likely to protect her legacy – Major, Hague and Duncan Smith.

While John Major's more consensual style of conservatism, provoked some early discussion of a distinctive 'Majorism', his premiership did not mark a significant break from Thatcherism, although Thatcher herself became sufficiently disappointed with her chosen successor to effectively disown him. Yet apart from scrapping the poll tax, Major continued and extended his predecessor's policies, privatising the railways, developing the internal market in the health service and competition in schools, pursuing managerial centralisation through executive agencies in the civil service, and resisting devolution. Of his own initiatives the Citizen's Charter was widely if not entirely fairly dismissed as an essentially cosmetic exercise, 'back to basics' was misinterpreted, and local government reorganisation disastrously backfired, but none of these could be interpreted as a departure from the Thatcher legacy. He received most criticism over Europe from Thatcherite loyalists who conveniently forget that it was Thatcher who had signed the Single European Act and accepted UK entry into the Exchange Rate Mechanism. If he appeared weak it was because his Parliamentary position after the 1992 election was weak, leaving him at the mercy of a handful of Euro-sceptic rebels (Seldon and Kavanagh, 1994).

William Hague, the unexpected victor from the leadership contest after John Major resigned following the 1997 landslide defeat, sought to make his party more internally democratic and initially tried to promote a more caring, inclusive conservatism. The two aims proved mutually incompatible. He had to satisfy two very different audiences, a socially diverse electorate and a dwindling ageing Conservative Party membership whose views on most issues were diametrically opposed to those of the disillusioned ex-voters and new voters the party had to woo. Obliged to disown any apparent retreat from Thatcherism, Hague tried to unite his party on the single issue of 'saving the pound', which was also an issue on which party members and most voters were apparently united. Yet this only served to highlight the divisions among leading Conservatives, and distract attention from other potentially more electorally profitable issues. Thus despite, or perhaps because of, the continued enthusiastic endorsement of Thatcher, Hague failed to reinvent conservatism.

Iain Duncan Smith, Hague's even more unexpected successor, won (like Major and Hague before him) because of who he was not rather than who he was. Although his Thatcherite credentials are even stronger than those of his predecessors, he has found it easier to distance himself from Thatcher, if only because Conservative activists have finally realised that the party has to change if it is to have any hope of recovery. Thus despite his past record as a Euro-sceptic rebel, Duncan Smith has played down opposition to the euro, and made positive noises about public services, ethnic minorities and alternative lifestyles, but otherwise the Conservative shadow cabinet has largely confined itself to attacking government policy without making too many specific commitments.

It is too early to tell whether Duncan Smith or anyone else will be able to revive Conservative fortunes, and whether this will entail another successful reinvention of conservative ideology. Margaret Thatcher successfully changed the terms of political debate to the extent that the Labour Party were eventually obliged to accept and adopt much of her free market ideology. One problem for the Conservatives now is that Blair and Brown have similarly shifted the argument back towards improved public services, with an apparent public acceptance of the need for higher taxation to fund them. Thus Conservatives either have to embrace Labour's agenda, simply promising better delivery, or come up with radical alternatives (such as a different method of funding health).

British socialism or labourism

While conservatism involved a defence of traditional social arrangements, and liberalism a justification and support for industrialisation and moderate social and political reform in the interests of capital, socialism developed as a radical or revolutionary ideology involving a fundamental challenge to both traditional interests and industrial capitalism. As the first country to industrialise, at some initial cost to the living conditions of the labouring poor in both town

---

> **Definitions: mainstream ideologies and industrialisation**
>
> **Toryism** and **traditional conservativism** harked back to a pre-industrial, ordered society. Tories sought to protect traditional landed interests and agriculture, were wary of the upheavals involved with industrialisation and urbanisation, and suspicious of the rising manufacturing and mercantile interests.
>
> **Liberalism** was essentially the ideology of industrial capitalism, and reflected the interests of manufacturing and commerce. Liberals were critical of traditional institutions and values, and favoured reforms that would increase the political influence of growing towns and cities, and remove restrictions on trade and enterprise.
>
> **Socialism**, like liberalism, was essentially a product of modern industrial capitalism, but socialists reflected the interests of the growing industrial workforce rather than capital, and sought to overthrow or transform capitalism. While not normally hostile to industrialisation as such, they sought a radical redistribution of income and wealth, and favoured a planned rather than a free market economy.

and country, it might be expected that Britain would be a fertile environment for revolutionary ideas. Yet the British working class largely rejected the periodic revolutionary movements which swept through much of the European continent.

Robert Owen (1771–1858) secured some popular support for his early version of socialism, derived initially from his own experiences of running a model factory, but subsequently from his involvement in early British trade unionism in the 1830s and the cooperative movement from the 1840s. Thus his socialism depended on grass roots working class self-help rather than the total overthrow of the existing economic and political system demanded by revolutionary socialists. Owen was criticised by Marx as a 'utopian socialist' with no realistic strategy for the achievement of socialism. Yet Marx's own socialism found less support in Britain (the country where he spent the bulk of his working life) than in Germany, France, Italy or even (but ultimately especially) Russia. British workers gave more support to the political reforms demanded by Chartists from the 1830s through to the 1850s, and then the practical improvements in wages and conditions pursued by moderate trade unionism in the latter half of the 19th century.

The mainstream British version of socialism, the socialism of the Labour Party, developed relatively late and was distinctly unusual. Indeed, some question whether it should be called socialism at all, and prefer to use the term 'labourism' to describe Labour's ideology. The Labour Party was effectively formed in 1900 as the Labour Representation Committee from an alliance between some trade unions seeking Parliamentary representation to protect trade union rights and interests and three small socialist societies, of which one, the Social Democratic Federation, which was Marxist inspired, left within a year. The other two involved the tiny Fabian Society, committed to gradual, evolutionary, Parliamentary state-sponsored socialism, and the Independent Labour Party, which preached a quasi-religious ethical socialism based on the universal brotherhood of man rather than the revolution arising from inevitable class conflict taught by Marxists. In practice, Labour's reformist ideas were not so dissimilar from those of radical Liberals, some of whom were to switch subsequently to the new party.

Trade union ideas and interests dominated the early history of the Labour Party, which had 'emerged from the bowels of the trade union movement' in Ernest Bevin's graphic description. The Parliamentary Labour Party had been established to serve the wider interests of the labour movement rather than other way around. Yet the bulk of trade unionists seemed more concerned with improvements in wages and conditions through 'free collective bargaining' within the existing capitalist economic system than with the overthrow of capitalism. Beyond that, the largely moderate trade union leadership was content to leave Parliamentary tactics and policy to the Parliamentary Labour Party and its leaders.

While socialists of sorts were part of the broad labour coalition from the start, the Labour Party only became formally committed to a socialist programme in 1918 with the adoption of Clause Four, and the celebrated commitment to the 'common ownership of means of production' ('distribution

---

BOX 4.3

Clause Four of the Labour Party Constitution (1918–95)

To secure for the workers by hand or by brain the full fruits of their industry and the most equitable distribution thereof that may be possible, upon the basis of the common ownership of the means of production, distribution, and exchange, and the best obtainable system of popular administration and control of each industry and service.

---

and exchange' were added subsequently), although the detailed plans for implementing this ambitious goal were never formulated. Instead the Labour Party in practice remained committed to gradual Parliamentary reform rather than a fundamental transformation of the economic, social and political order, as was demonstrated by the cautious record of the two minority Labour governments of 1924 and 1929–31, as well as the whole labour movement's peaceful and constitutional record in the General Strike of 1926. Socialism for the Labour Party was a distant aspiration, dependent on the achievement of a Parliamentary majority, to be followed by step by step gradual reform. Other variants of socialism, including Marxism, syndicalism, guild socialism, cooperation, and local socialism, were marginalised. Critics suggested the Labour Party was always more committed to parliamentarism than to socialism (Miliband, 1972), and that its moderate trade unionist and reformist programme was better described as 'labourism' rather than 'socialism' (Saville, 1988).

The Labour Party achieved its first Parliamentary majority in 1945, and the record of the Attlee government has come to define the Labour interpretation of socialism: both what it was, and what it was not. Common ownership of the 'commanding heights of the economy' (largely fuel and transport) involved an extensive and controversial extension of the role of the state, although not the wholesale nationalisation envisaged by some socialists. Some of the industries taken into state ownership were already largely municipalised (electricity, gas) and/or perceived to be declining (gas, rail, iron and steel). Left-wing critics complained that the method of

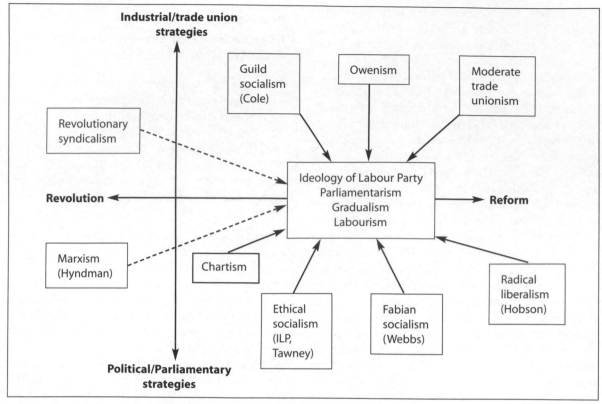

Figure 4.3 Influences on the ideology of the Labour Party

Source: adapted from Leach, 2002: 84.

nationalisation (through public corporations) involved state capitalism rather than workers' control. Labour's economic policy followed the principles of Keynesian demand management rather than the detailed socialist planning of a command economy. Thus Labour operated a mixed but essentially still capitalist economy, albeit with more government regulation. It pursued town planning, established New Towns and tried to influence the location of industry. The government's most important achievement was the establishment of the welfare state. It not only largely implemented the welfare proposals of the 1942 Beveridge Report, but also established the National Health Service, and expanded municipal housing.

The second half of the 20th century saw a long battle between the Labour left and right for the soul of the party. The split effectively began with the resignation of Bevan, Wilson and Freeman from the Attlee government in protest against the Labour Chancellor Gaitskell's imposition of charges

for teeth and spectacles on the health service. Bevan became the unofficial leader of the left, which championed socialism and more nationalisation at home, and opposition to German rearmament and nuclear weapons in foreign and defence policy. Revisionists or social democrats on the right were convinced that the party had to modernise, and abandon further nationalisation, which was considered electorally unpopular. Crosland's (1956) seminal book *The Future of Socialism* argued that ownership of industry was irrelevant. Instead, socialists should pursue greater equality through progressive taxation and welfare benefits. Gaitskell, who defeated Bevan for the leadership of the party in 1955, sought to scrap Clause Four, and even considered changing the party's name. He fought to reverse a party conference decision in favour of unilateral nuclear disarmament.

The conflict if anything became more bitter following the death of Bevan in 1960 and Gaitskell in 1963, after which Harold Wilson, the candidate of the left, became leader, while Roy Jenkins eventually emerged as the standard bearer of the Gaitskellites. The problems faced in government by the Wilson and Callaghan administrations further polarised opinion with the party. The left-wing socialists favoured more nationalisation, unilateral nuclear disarmament and internal party democracy, and mostly opposed membership of the European Community. The right supported NATO, nuclear weapons, and EC membership while opposing further nationalisation. After the election of the old Bevanite, Michael Foot, as leader in 1980, some of the 'moderates' left Labour to form the Social Democratic Party (Crewe and King, 1995), while others such as Healey and Hattersley stayed to fight from within. Healey narrowly defeated Tony Benn (by now the standard bearer of the left) for the deputy leadership in 1981, but the party went on to its most disastrous defeat in 1983 on a left-wing manifesto which included commitments to further nationalisation, nuclear disarmament and leaving the European Community.

From old to New Labour

Under the leadership of Neil Kinnock, John Smith and finally Tony Blair the Labour Party gradually restored its electoral fortunes. Kinnock faced down the hard left Militant Tendency which had infiltrated the party, instituted a policy review which led to the abandonment of the pledges that some considered had lost the party support, and modernised the image and presentation of the party (including the introduction of the red rose logo). Smith introduced 'one person one vote' and Blair daringly persuaded the party to change Clause Four, which Gaitskell had earlier sought and failed to scrap. Blair's modernisation programme involved an (unofficial) rebranding of the party as New Labour.

Much ink has already been spent on the transition from old to New Labour. The party's programme has clearly changed considerably from the election defeat in 1983. Some would see the change in terms of a shift from socialism to social democracy. Indeed, New Labour has embraced many of the policies of the old SDP. Others argue that Blair has abandoned not only socialism but social democracy as well, and is effectively Thatcher's heir. Certainly Blair had

> **BOX 4.4**
> ## From the New Clause Four (adopted 1995)
>
> The Labour Party is a democratic socialist party. It believes that by the strength of our common endeavour we achieve more than we achieve alone, so as to create for each of us the means to realise our true potential and for all of us a community in which power, wealth and opportunity are in the hands of the many not the few, where the rights we enjoy reflect the duties we owe, and where we live together, freely, in a spirit of solidarity, tolerance and respect.

accepted the free market, has not reversed the Conservative privatisation programme and has made controversial use of public–private partnerships and the Private Finance Initiative to fund public sector investment. Yet at the same time the Blair government has pursued a whole raft of policies that the Conservatives opposed, including devolution as part of a radical programme of constitutional reform, a national minimum wage, ratification of the Social Chapter of the Maastricht Treaty, the New Deal of welfare into work, the incorporation of the European Convention of Human Rights into English law, and most recently a massive injection of funds into the NHS funded largely by increases in National Insurance contributions.

The rejection of 'old Labour' involves the rejection not just of old left-wing socialism but of 'labourism', the moderate trade unionist and working class values and interests which permeated the old Labour Party. In this sense, the most symbolic change was not the redrafting of Clause Four, which had never really reflected the aims of Labour in practice, but the dropping of the old Labour Party logo with its manual workers' tools for the red rose. While the party had never preached class conflict, it had been identified mainly with the interests of (largely male-dominated and white) manual workers and trade unionists, although increasingly led by middle class graduates and professionals. The problem for Labour was that the working class had become both a smaller proportion of the population and more fragmented on gender and ethnic lines, as well as between skilled and unskilled, public and private sector workers (see Chapter 2). It was no longer possible for Labour to win elections by appealing to the old manual working class of Britain's industrial heartlands. Blair's repositioning of this party to win the votes of middle England was thus an electoral necessity.

It is perhaps easier to explain how and why Labour has changed than to indicate what the party now stands for. Blair himself has used 'buzz words' which have been part of Labour's vocabulary since its beginnings – 'society', 'community' 'solidarity', 'cooperation', 'partnership', 'fairness'. He has argued that Labour's values are unchanged, but they need reinterpretation in the modern world. A number of fashionable concepts and strands of thought have been attached to the New Labour project (see definitions).

New Labour has borrowed extensively not only from the socialist and social democratic tradition but from other ideologies. Thus there is much in common between New Labour and the New Liberal ideas of a century ago. Blair talked of the need to rebuild the 'progressive alliance' between Labour and the Liberals. Although the project for coalition with the Liberal Democrats failed to materialise at Westminster, it did take shape in Edinburgh and, eventually, Cardiff. Blair has also drawn on the ideas of 'one nation' Conservatism, and on the pragmatism that was once a hallmark of conservatives. 'What matters is what works.' Thus he has sometimes been castigated for not having a clear political philosophy. To critics, New Labour involves a retreat from ideology.

Nationalism

Nationalism is the doctrine that the world is divided into national communities which should form states (Gellner, 1983; Breuilly, 1993). It emerged from the political upheavals linked with the French Revolution, and it began as a revolutionary ideology with particularly damaging implications for multi-national states ruled by traditional dynasties (such as the Hapsburg Austrian empire or Tsarist Russia). The radical notion of popular sovereignty was linked with the idea of national sovereignty. Supreme power should not rest with an absolute monarch but with the people, or the nation. Nationalism was initially closely

> *Definitions: New Labour ideas*
>
> **Communitarianism:** a school of philosophy critical of liberal individualism, and stressing the importance of community interests and values. Communitarian ideas were developed by a number of thinkers but popularised by Amitae Etzioni (1995).
>
> **Stakeholding:** a concept made fashionable by the political economist Will Hutton (1995) and taken up for a time by Blair (1996: 291–321). It goes beyond the concept of shareholding to suggest that consumers, workers, and the wider community are all 'stakeholders' in companies and states. 'Inclusion' is a key buzz term.
>
> **Ethical (or Christian) socialism:** hardly a new idea but a revival of a strand of thought which was particularly important in Labour's early years. The ethical basis of Labour thinking has been reaffirmed. Within the modern Labour Party there is a flourishing Christian Socialist Movement. (Members include the late John Smith and Blair.) Yet in the context of a modern multi-faith and multi-cultural Britain more emphasis has been placed on a broader 'faith politics'.
>
> **The third way:** again, an old idea given some new substance, particularly by Anthony Giddens (1998), although it has been very variously interpreted and much criticised. Giddens treats the third way as an updating of social democracy. It has also been seen as a middle way between the command economy of old socialism and the unrestrained free market of neo-liberalism.

linked with liberalism on the European continent. Just as individuals should be freed from tyrannical governments, national communities should be freed from foreign rule. Later in the 19th century nationalism became more associated with the right of the political spectrum, as governments realised the value of a state-sponsored nationalism in securing popular support and legitimacy. In the early 20th century fascists adopted an extreme form of nationalism resting on racist assumptions. In the latter half of the 20th century nationalism became more commonly associated with the left and anti-colonial nationalism, or modern separation nationalism. Nationalism is thus something of chameleon ideology. Its fundamental idea is very simple but it takes colour from the political context in which it develops.

In Britain nationalist assumptions and rhetoric were absorbed into the mainstream ideologies, but particularly into conservatism, which exploited national symbols and sentiment. It was widely assumed in the 19th century and for most of the 20th century also that Britain was itself a nation-state. In so far as nationalism was seen as a doctrine with practical political implications, these were seen to be applicable to other countries – a free and united Greece, Italy, Poland and so on, aspirations which British liberals in particular supported. The British were less keen to apply the doctrine of national self-determination to the non-European peoples of the British Empire, or to Ireland. Irish nationalism led ultimately to the Easter Rising of 1916 and the establishment of a separate Irish state, covering most of Ireland. Such separatist nationalism has since developed elsewhere within the United Kingdom. By the 1970s a growing minority of the population of Northern Ireland, Scotland and Wales also sought independence.

It is difficult to define a nation. Nations may be bound together by a sense of a common history or culture, a common language or religion. Yet ultimately nations exist in the minds of their members – they are 'imagined communities'. It follows that a sense of national identity may change over time. Something of the sort seems to have happened in Britain. Surveys indicate that fewer people now see themselves as British, rather more as Scots, Welsh or English (see Chapter 2). This clearly could have implications for the long-term future of the British state. Of course, allegiances are not necessarily exclusive. Some acknowledge a dual allegiance, for example to Scotland and Britain. Devolution may succeed in satisfying Scottish and Welsh national sentiment and their desire for more self-government, although for the Scottish National Party and Plaid Cymru, nothing short of full independence and national sovereignty will suffice.

Beyond the politics of nationalism there are wider questions of political identity and allegiance. In the modern interdependent world of multi-level governance, narrow and exclusive national loyalties

BOX 4.5
Comparative politics: 'separation nationalism'

'Separation nationalism' is hardly unique to Britain. Two of the states founded to satisfy national self-determination after the First World War, Czechoslovakia and Yugoslavia, have broken up into smaller national groupings. Basque nationalists seek independence from Spain. An Italian political party wants to reverse the unification of Italy achieved in the mid-19th century by establishing a state of 'Padania' in the north. The collapse of the Soviet Union has led to the emergence or re-emergence of new 'nation-states.' Partly these movements reflect familiar concerns over national culture, but they also may be fed by economic interests – peripheral parts of a territory may feel they are neglected or discriminated against, but sometimes (as in the case of north Italy) more prosperous regions may prefer to cast off relatively backward areas which they feel they are subsidising. One possible reaction to devolution in the United Kingdom is an 'English backlash' against perceived subsidies to other parts of the UK.

appear outdated, and the idea of multiple allegiances seems to make sense, particularly within the context of the European Union. Thus it could be argued that it is not necessary for people in Britain to choose between UK and European citizenship; they can have both. Migration has also complicated people's sense of identity. In the USA the concept of Irish Americans or Polish Americans has become familiar. In Britain it is hardly surprising that immigrant communities may maintain a loyalty towards their country of origin as well as the country of which they have become full citizens. (However, discrimination and prejudice may reinforce a sense of a different political identity by members of minority communities.)

Globalization, it could be argued, has rendered the independent nation-state and the whole concept of national sovereignty increasingly obsolete. Yet globalization has also, paradoxically, fuelled nationalist sentiment. Faced with a fast-changing world in which traditional cultures and allegiances seem under threat, some people react by clinging more desperately to what they know. Predictions of the demise of nationalism seem premature at the least.

Racism

Racism, as a political doctrine, assumes that humankind is naturally divided into races, which have different characteristics. For racists it is their 'race' that defines them, and transcends other identities and loyalties (e.g. class, religion, language). At one time such ideas seemed to be buttressed by science, and a 'scientific' theory of racism became the official orthodoxy of the Nazi Third Reich, taught in schools, and practised to the extent of the mass genocide of the Holocaust. It is now recognised that the whole concept of race is a bogus scientific category, and biological racism should thus be discredited totally. Indeed, some argue that the very term 'race' is meaningless, and its continued use, even in the context of improving 'race relations', legitimises a concept with no scientific validity (Miles, 1989). It is suggested that 'scientific' racism has been replaced by a 'new racism' linked to notions of culture rather than biology, although in practice the language of culture provides a thin veneer for discrimination and prejudice based on observable physical differences (principally colour). Racism is often manifested in a narrow exclusive form of nationalism which, in the case of Britain, denies that blacks and Asians can be British.

In Britain today racism is officially beyond the pale. Mainstream politicians repudiate racism, overtly racist political parties generally attract minimal support, and the practice of discrimination and the expression of prejudice are officially outlawed. All this would suggest that racism is hardly worth discussing. Yet there is abundant evidence that racism is important in British politics. Thirty-two per cent of Britons surveyed have described themselves as 'very or quite racist' (Parekh, 2000: 119). For most members of minority ethnic communities racism is part of their everyday lives, as they continue to suffer substantial discrimination and prejudice. Increasingly it is recognised that key British

BOX 4.6
Institutional racism: the Macpherson Inquiry's definition, 1999

The Macpherson Report defined institutional racism as 'The collective failure of an organisation to provide an appropriate and professional service to people because of their colour, culture, or ethnic origin. It can be seen or detected in processes, attitudes and behaviour which amount to discrimination through unwitting prejudice, ignorance, thoughtlessness and racist stereotyping which disadvantage minority ethnic people.'
(Macpherson, 1999: 28)

organisations, such as the Metropolitan Police, are 'institutionally racist'.

Racism is sometimes linked with the assumptions of racial superiority arising from the legacy of imperialism, slavery and white power. However, racism is not directed exclusively against blacks and Asians from former colonies, but against Jews, Irish and eastern European asylum seekers. It is also not exclusively practised by whites, as there is evidence of prejudice within and between ethnic minorities both in Britain and elsewhere. Rather more persuasively, racism has been associated with economic deprivation. Racism in Britain has become most obviously manifest in relatively deprived urban areas (such as Bradford or Oldham) where black and Asian ethnic minorities appear to be in competition for jobs, houses and services with poor white workers. Differences are exacerbated by residential, occupational and educational segregation. Yet economic deprivation cannot explain all racism. Anti-Semitism, for example, has been evident among the old aristocracy and the middle classes as well as the poor.

More recently, particularly since the attack on the World Trade Center on 11 September 2001, religious differences have fuelled racist suspicions and fears. Thus in Britain as in many other western countries the term 'Islamophobia' has been employed to describe hostility to Muslims. Here ignorance heightens fear. It is too readily assumed that Asians are Muslims, when many are Hindu, Sikh or Christian, and that all Muslims are 'fundamentalists'. Most Britons are unaware of the differences within Islam, which are at least as great as those among Christians. Islamophobia has been exploited by parties such as the BNP. The religious and cultural practices of minorities can present some difficulties when they run up against the deeply held convictions of the majority, or even against the law of the land or international human rights, but such instances are relatively few and can generally be resolved.

Feminism

Feminism is unlike most other ideologies discussed in this chapter in that it is not associated with a political party. This might imply that the implications of feminism for politics are relatively marginal, but this is far from the case. Feminism has transformed the way in which people think about politics. Indeed it has changed the way politics is defined.

Feminism is conventionally described in terms of two historical periods or 'waves'. The main objective of the 'first wave' of feminism was attainment of political and legal equality for women. This movement developed during the 19th century, drawing inspiration from such texts as Mary Wollstonecraft's *Vindication of the Rights of Woman* (1792) and John Stuart Mill's *The Subjection of Women* (1869). Wollstonecraft argued that the revolutionary rights of man should be extended to women also, while Mill campaigned for not only legal and political rights for women, but the opening of occupations and professions monopolised by men. This liberal feminism was the dominant strand down to the late 1960s, by which time it included among its achievements votes for women (in Britain in 1918 and 1928), equal education opportunities, equal pay legislation, and legal prohibitions on discrimination on grounds of gender, particularly in employment (Bryson, 1992).

Some concluded that the battle for women's rights had been won. Yet a 'second wave' of feminism from the late 1960s onwards drew attention to the continuing severe disadvantages suffered by women despite their formal political and legal equality. Socialist and radical feminists argued that the liberals had failed to address the root causes of women's exploitation and oppression.

BOX 4.7
Comparative politics: fascism and racism

Racism is often linked with fascism, unsurprising as the Nazi version of fascism involved the most extreme and horrific racist practices, culminating in the Holocaust. Yet racism is not dependent on fascism. It existed before fascism and has survived the defeat of fascism in 1945. Fascism as originally advanced by Mussolini was profoundly anti-liberal and anti-democratic but not notably racist. It was associated with other interests and values – nationalism, militarism, totalitarianism, authoritarianism, corporatism and economic self-sufficiency. Fascism has attracted negligible support in Britain. In so far as fascist or quasi-fascist parties have secured any support it is not because of the broader fascist ideology espoused by their leaders but primarily because of their racism. Parties such as Mosley's British Union of Fascists, the National Front and most recently the BNP have exploited feeling against Jews, immigrants, asylum seekers and Moslems. The rest of their political programme, whether overtly or covertly fascist, has never really mattered.

Socialist feminists (both Marxist and others) focused on the continued exploitation of women in the family and the labour market: at home, women provided unwaged labour in the form of housework and child care; at work they were still to be found disproportionately in the lowest paid, most insecure jobs. Despite equal pay and equal opportunities legislation there appeared to be a 'glass ceiling' which it was difficult for women to rise above. For Marxist feminists in particular, women's inequality derived from capitalist property relations. Thus women's liberation could only come about through the overthrow of capitalism and the abolition of the bourgeois family associated with capitalism. Yet one implication was that class relations were more important than gender relations; it was class rather than gender that was the primary source of oppression.

This was denied by radical feminists, such as Eva

Figes, Kate Millett, Germaine Greer and Shulamith Firestone. For them the reason why women are exploited and oppressed is, quite simply, men. For the radicals, gender – not class, race or nation – was the most important social division. Patriarchy – literally, the rule of the father – was the key radical feminist concept, and patriarchal attitudes were all-pervasive. Gender differences – meaning superior male and subordinate female roles – were the consequence of a lengthy and deep-rooted process of social conditioning, which had to be challenged successfully if women were to achieve liberation. For the radicals much of women's oppression takes place in the private sphere – in the family and in personal and sexual relationships. A particular concern of radicals was violence against women, especially rape (including rape within marriage). One target was pornography, perceived to exploit women, emphasise their subordinate role and incite male abuse. Hence radical feminists have sought to break down the traditional division in political thought between the public and private spheres, arguing that 'the personal is political'. For them the two spheres cannot be separated, since women are at the receiving end of male-dominated power relationships throughout all areas of life.

Radical feminists have certainly had a major impact on gender relations in Britain, and cumulatively the women's movement (including all variants of feminism) has achieved a great deal. Feminists would argue there is still much to be done. Men continue to dominate the political process; even now less than one-fifth of MPs are women, despite the significant increase in the number of women elected in 1997 (which fell slightly in 2001). Although women now constitute half the paid labour force and a few women have spectacularly broken through the 'glass ceiling' to succeed in what was formerly an almost exclusively male world, company boardrooms, the judges' bench, and the highest levels of the civil service are still very largely male, and average female pay remains well below that of men, despite equal pay and equal opportunities legislation. Violence against women continues to destroy the lives of some and inhibit the freedom of females generally (Lovenduski and Randall, 1993).

Yet feminism is perhaps now more diffuse and in some ways more divided than it was. Women may

---

> **Definitions: types of feminism**
>
> **Liberal feminism** applied liberal assumptions to the position of women, and traditionally focused on the achievement of formal political and legal equality and freedom for women.
>
> **Marxist feminism** relates the oppression of women to capitalism, and assumes women's liberation entails the overthrow of capitalism and the abolition of the bourgeois family. Marxist feminists have emphasised equality in the workplace, and the need for support for working women.
>
> **Radical feminists** regard the oppression of women by men as a near universal feature of human society. The liberation of women and the overthrow of patriarchy (or male rule) must depend on women's own efforts. Practical concerns include violence against women and their exploitation within the family and domestic sphere – hence 'the personal is political'.

---

experience very different kinds of oppression depending on their position in society. The radical feminist agenda has sometimes been identified with the situation of middle class women, rather than the problems and needs of working class women. Similarly, it has been argued that white feminists have downplayed the importance of racial discrimination in the oppression suffered by black women. There are theoretical differences also. Some feminists (sometimes called 'eco-feminists) have shown strong sympathies with Green ideas, and others have re-emphasised motherhood and the female role in the care of children.

This has rekindled a debate over male and female 'nature'. While many feminists, through from Wollstonecraft to many modern radicals, have sought to minimise the effect of biological differences, arguing that gender differences are socially constructed rather than innate, some modern feminists are more prepared to assert that women do think and behave differently, and these differences are related to their biological roles. Whatever their position on the 'same–difference' debate, more feminists now acknowledge that women cannot ignore 'the problem of men' (Bryson, 1999, 2000).

Green thinking

No account of ideologies in British politics would be complete without some reference to Green thinking (sometimes termed environmentalism or ecologism). Although all mainstream political parties would argue that they have taken on board green ideas, they have not prioritised the environment in the way that Greens demand. All other ideologies focus on the interests and needs of humankind in general or a particular section of humanity – class, nation, race or gender. The green slogan 'Earth First!' subordinates the future of humankind to the future of the planet, although of course Greens would argue that the futures of both are bound up together.

While mainstream parties and ideologies welcome economic growth as a means of satisfying conflicting interests and demands without necessarily making anyone worse off, Greens insist there are limits to growth. Many of the resources on which our current standard of living depends are non-renewable and thus finite. Unless renewable energy resources are utilised to replace the dwindling stocks of fossil fuels, humans will ultimately exhaust those supplies. Pollution is also causing irreversible damage to the environment, destroying flora and fauna and threatening climate changes which could prove catastrophic. The relentless pursuit of growth to satisfy the needs of a still fast-expanding human population threatens not only other species but future generations of humanity.

Greens' predictions for the distant future are contentious. Some scientists as well as some politicians are more optimistic about the prospects for technological solutions to resource depletion. Some Greens have also perhaps exaggerated the more immediate threats and thus damaged their case by crying 'Wolf!' too soon. Most people would prefer to believe the more optimistic scenarios, particularly if the recommended solution to the darker predictions is what is perceived as a lower standard of living, particularly in the richer countries, like Britain. Politicians generally promise to make us better off, yet Greens are seeking to make us worse off, which is an intrinsically difficult message to sell. Yet few would dispute that there is a significant problem of resource depletion and pollution, even if there is room for argument over the precise details and the timescale for finding a solution. The real difficulty for the Greens is that conventional politics is concerned with short-term problems. Current political institutions and processes are equipped to help reconcile the conflicting needs and demands of the interest of the present generation of human adults (albeit often imperfectly). What they are not equipped to do is take into account the needs of future generations, let alone other species. Thus the greatest problem for Greens is devising a strategy that has some realistic prospect of achieving the greener planet which they seek.

Globalization and the 'end of ideology'

The end of the cold war, combined with intensifying globalization, has assisted in the revival of a debate over the 'end of ideology', a concept once popularised by Bell (1960) and reformulated in rather different terms by Fukuyama (1992). In Britain this broader debate about world politics has been echoed by a similar theme in a minor key, the post-war ideological consensus and its presumed return, in somewhat altered guise, in contemporary British politics.

As we have already noted, ideological consensus does not necessarily entail the end of ideology, but rather the dominance of a particular set of ideas or assumptions. The conventional wisdom suggests that British politics in the decades after the Second World War involved widespread acceptance of a set of common values, including the mixed economy, state welfare, planning, Keynesian economic theory, and conciliation in industrial relations. This political consensus was shattered by the rise of the New Right and Thatcherism on the one hand, and the revival of left-wing socialism in the Labour Party on the other. Since then, it is argued, there has been a return to a new consensus, tentatively under Major, more markedly under Blair, with 'New Labour' and the 'third way', although there has been considerable argument over the precise nature of this 'Blairite consensus' and the explanations for it.

One explanation is that New Labour and the 'third way' simply involve the continuation of Thatcherism – free market economics and business-friendly policies clothed in slightly altered rhetoric. Yet Blair's government has many policies quite different from its immediate predecessors: devolution, the national minimum wage, substantial increases in spending on public services.

More plausibly perhaps, Blair's government has involved a return to the pragmatism of traditional 'One Nation' Conservatism of the 1950s and 1960s and Harold Wilson's pragmatic interpretation of socialism. 'What matters is what works.' Consistent with this flexible approach to doctrine is the electoral imperative to occupy the middle ground and appeal to middle England. This of course applies as much to the Conservative opposition as to Labour. On this interpretation the Conservative Party's embrace of the New Right in the 1980s was only successful because Labour too then abandoned the middle ground. Labour's return to moderation has forced the Conservatives to follow suit, abandoning the free market and traditional family values for a commitment to public services and an inclusive tolerance of new lifestyles.

Yet ultimately globalization and external constraints make it more difficult for parties and governments to pursue distinctive policies in isolation from developments in wider world trends. Thatcherism was in part a model for others to follow, in part a reflection of the world. Privatisation and marketisation have been pursued by governments around the world of all political hues, which suggests global influences and constraints. Similarly, Blair's government has imitated some initiatives from elsewhere and also furnished a model for others to copy. The mood had changed from the ebullient enthusiasm for free market forces of the Thatcher years. While the difficulty of 'bucking the market' is widely appreciated, some of the problems of unrestrained market forces have also been painfully rediscovered. Thus Blair's search for an elusive 'third way' between free market capitalism and centralised state socialism is hardly new, but is today replicated in one form or another in many other countries.

Further reading

McLellan (1995) has written a good brief introduction to the contentious concept of ideology. For a fuller analysis see Seliger (1976) and Freeden (1996). Definitions of key terms and brief accounts of important thinkers can be found in specialist dictionaries of political thought (e.g. Williams, 1976; Bullock and Stalybrass, 1977; Scruton, 1996; Bottomore, 1991).

There are now many useful books on political ideologies in general, such as Heywood (1997). Leach (2002) relates ideologies specifically to British politics, as does Adams (1998). More substantial and difficult interpretations of British political thinking can be found in Beer (1982a), Greenleaf (1983) and Freeden (1996). The literature on specific ideologies is massive. Among useful readers are Eccleshall (1986) on liberalism, Eccleshall (1990) on conservatism, Wright (1983) on British socialism and Dobson (1995) on Green thinking. Readable interpretations of specific ideologies include Gray (1986) on liberalism, Davies on the ideas of the Labour and Conservative Parties (1996a, 1996b). Dobson (1995) can be recommended on Green politics and Bryson (1992) on feminism.

Although there is a very extensive literature on nationalism in general there are relatively few books that relate nationalism to British politics, but Marr (1992) is useful for an overview of Scottish nationalism, and Nairn (2000) provides a provocative nationalist perspective. The last chapter of Davies (2000) is good on both recent history and analysis. Bulmer and Solomos (1999) and Back and Solomos (2000) have edited useful readers on racism, on which see also Rex (1986), Miles (1989, 1993), Mac an Ghaill (1999) and Parekh (2000).

On more recent developments in mainstream ideologies, it is difficult to select one or two titles from the daunting literature on Thatcherism and the New Right. Gamble (1994) and Kavanagh (1990) are among the more readable. Ideas in the post-Thatcher Conservative Party are discussed in Ludlam and Smith (1996), and Gilmour and Garnett (1997). The literature on New Labour already almost rivals that on Thatcherism – see especially Blair's own collection of speeches (1996), Driver and Martell (1998), Ludlam and Smith (2001). On the third way see Giddens (1998). For the most recent expression of party policy and ideas see the main party websites (listed at the end of Chapter 8).

Part II

PARTICIPATING IN POLITICS

In this part we examine the political process in Britain, with particular reference to the opportunities people have for participating in politics and influencing policy. We begin in Chapter 5 with an overview of the range and extent of popular participation in politics, and the reasons for non-participation in general, and declining electoral turnout in particular. Various explanations for social exclusion and alienation are explored.

Free and fair elections are commonly regarded as a necessary condition for modern representative democracy. Chapter 6 examines how the British voting system for the Westminster Parliament operates in practice, and reviews alternatives. We go on to examine the impact of the different electoral systems for the European Parliament and for devolved parliaments and assemblies within the UK, as well as the scope for a more direct form of democracy through the increased use of referendums. Chapter 7 switches to voting behaviour, and the decline in the two-party system, examining the correlation between voting and class, gender, age and ethnic divisions within the population. We explore a range of explanations for the way people vote as they do, using recent British elections for illustration.

It is arguable that voting provides only an occasional and limited form of political participation. Chapters 8 and 9 examine other opportunities for involvement in the political process. Chapter 8 focuses on the parties that contest elections, examining how far modern British parties remain mass parties, their organisation at various levels, and the distribution of power and scope for internal democracy within parties. Chapter 9 turns to pressure groups as a supplement or alternative to participation through the ballot box and parties. Pressure group methods are explored, with reference to recent case studies. The chapter concludes with a review of the power and influence of groups, and their role within a democratic system.

The modern mass media provide a potentially crucial channel of communication between rulers and ruled. In Chapter 10 alternative perspectives on the role of the mass media in British politics are explored and illustrated through a range of examples, which assess the scope of the media to influence party allegiance and political opinions on specific issues.

Chapter **5**

Ways of participating in politics

Political participation	75
Who participates?	76
Why participate?	78
Do individuals need to vote?	79
Public opinion and participation	79
Political competence and participation	80
A changing political culture?	81
Political socialisation	83
Citizenship entitlements	85

This chapter examines political participation and political culture. We ask, what are the main forms of political participation, what proportion of the population may be considered active in politics, and who are the active participants? Are the patterns of political participation changing? What are the causes of falling participation rates in the most basic form of political behaviour – voting – and how might this trend be reversed? We then turn to the beliefs and attitudes shaping political behaviour. We ask, what is political culture and more specifically, what are the main characteristics of the British political culture and how have these changed? Finally, we examine the controversial political debate concerning both the nature and meaning of citizenship in contemporary Britain.

Political participation

Political participation is central to democracy. However, political theorists have argued about the extent of participation that is necessary for a healthy democracy. On the one hand it has been argued that individuals should participate to the maximum in politics, but also should participate in family decision making, and in college/school and workplace decisions. In other words, participation and democracy should form a way of life rather than just a narrow form of political behaviour. On the other hand it has been argued that a high level of participation from every individual is not a realistic expectation in a modern industrial society. In fact, it is only totalitarian societies that have required such exclusive political involvement and allegiance from their members. Apathy marks the limits of politics and should, in this sense, be recognised as a democratic value. Since a fully participatory democracy is not feasible in contemporary Britain or any other liberal democracy, it is more realistic to accept that political decision making is done by a political elite. The role of the masses is periodically to elect an elite to represent them. Democratic participation is safeguarded by 'rules' or 'procedures' such as free speech, periodic elections, two or more elites competing for office and the right to a secret vote.

The most basic form of participation in a democracy is voting in elections. Voting in British general elections averaged 76.5 per cent between 1950 and 1997, but the overall trend has become one of decline, from a general election average of over 80 per cent in the 1950s to 74.6 per cent in the 1990s. The decline has been particularly dramatic in recent years, from 77.7 per cent in 1992 to 71.5 per cent in 1997 and only 59 per cent in 2001. Voting turnout is lower at all other types of election, including referendums, and is especially low in European elections and local elections (see Table 5.1).

A rather higher level of political commitment than voting is registered by joining a political party or a cause group. Figures for individual membership of political parties are notoriously unreliable (and generally inflated) but it is clear that membership of all parties has declined

---

Definition
Political participation: citizen involvement in politics through for example voting, group and party activity aimed at influencing government and public policy.

Table 5.1 Recent levels of turnout

General election 1997	72%
Scottish Parliament 1999	58%
Welsh Assembly 1999	46%
European Parliament (UK) 1999	24%
Local government 1999 (average)	26%
Mayor of London 2000	34%
General election 2001	59%
Referendum on mayor for Lewisham 2001	18%

substantially from a high point of several million after the Second World War to well below a million more recently. The combined membership of the two major parties was about 700,000 in 1997. By 2002 the corresponding figure was only 610,000. Membership of pressure groups numbers many millions and far exceeds membership of parties (see Table 5.2).

Is the declining membership of so-called mass political parties causally linked to the rising participation in pressure groups? Figure 5.1 divides the population into three main types of participant: a small number of *activists*; the majority – *just voters* – whose participation in politics is limited to voting in elections; and the *almost inactive*, who scarcely participate at all. The British Political Participation Survey (BPPS) (Parry, Moyser and Day, 1992), from which these categories are taken, further subdivided political activists into five groups:

- contacting activists (7.7 per cent), who were politically involved through contacting officials

Table 5.2 Membership of parties and pressure groups (based on figures for 2001 and 2002)

Conservative Party	330,000
Labour Party	280,000
Liberal Democrats	76,023
Green Party	5,000
Amnesty International	154,000
Greenpeace	193,500
Friends of the Earth	110,200
RSPB	1,190,000
RSPCA	49,760
National Trust	2,800,000

and politicians by for example, phoning or writing a letter
- collective activists (8.7 per cent), who participated as members of pressure groups
- direct activists (3.1 per cent), who were protesters characterised mainly by the frequency of their direct action
- party campaigners (2.2 per cent), who were principally engaged in fund-raising, canvassing and clerical work and attending rallies
- complete activists (1.5 per cent), a tiny minority, involved in a wide variety of political activities, encompassing voting, party campaigning, group activity, contacting and numerous kinds of protest.

On this basis, it was estimated that real activists (the last-mentioned category) number about 625,000 in an adult population of about 41.6 million (Parry and Moyser, 1990: 150). However, political activity over such a wide field may be regarded as too 'heroic' a requirement for the active citizen. Perhaps it would be more reasonable to consider involvement on a fairly regular basis in any of the activities beyond voting and petition signing as an indicator of a politically active individual. On this less stringent criterion, a significant minority of Britons (between one-fifth and one-quarter) may be regarded as active citizens. Even so, the political participation of the vast majority is either minimal (voting in elections) or virtually non-existent.

Who participates?

Political activists are far from a microcosm of the nation, being found disproportionately among the well-educated middle class and those with stronger than average political opinions. The BPPS found that the salariat, those in professional or managerial occupations, were more likely than other social groups to be active politically. The reason is that the salariat possesses greater political resources in terms of wealth and education. Graduates were among the top 12 per cent on the overall participation scale, whereas those without formal qualifications had on average performed little in the way of political activity beyond

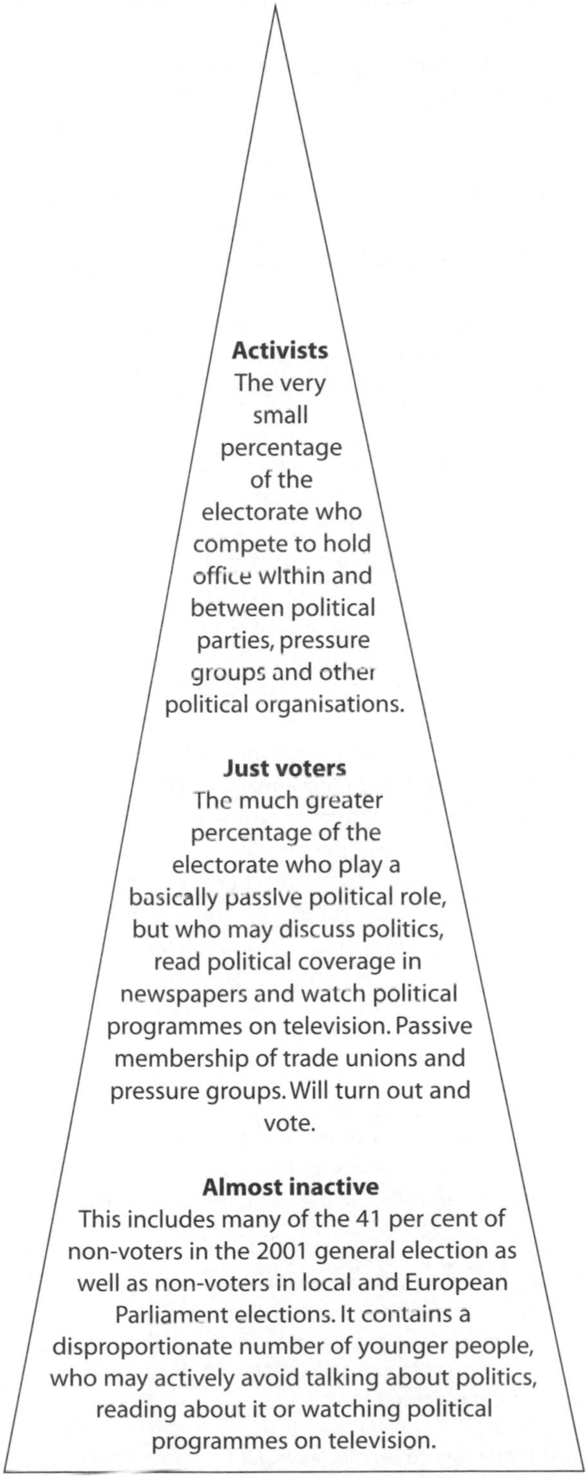

Activists
The very small percentage of the electorate who compete to hold office within and between political parties, pressure groups and other political organisations.

Just voters
The much greater percentage of the electorate who play a basically passive political role, but who may discuss politics, read political coverage in newspapers and watch political programmes on television. Passive membership of trade unions and pressure groups. Will turn out and vote.

Almost inactive
This includes many of the 41 per cent of non-voters in the 2001 general election as well as non-voters in local and European Parliament elections. It contains a disproportionate number of younger people, who may actively avoid talking about politics, reading about it or watching political programmes on television.

Figure 5.1 A hierarchy of political participation
Source: adapted from Milbrath, 1965: 16–22.

voting and petitioning. Participation thus seemed to increase with education. According to the *British Social Attitudes* (*BSA*) survey, graduates are more likely to have contacted an MP, signed a petition and gone on a demonstration than those with lower-level qualifications, who themselves are more likely to have engaged in such activities than those with no qualifications (Parry and Moyser, 1990: 155; Jowell *et al.*, 1987: 65). Education builds self-confidence, increases political knowledge and provides literary skills, all of which are necessary for significant political participation. The BPPS also found that gender differences in political participation, once significant, have largely disappeared. Women are as well represented as men among the politically active, although not at elite level (Parry and Moyser, 1993: 21). In Norris's words, the traditional view that women participate in politics less than men 'is no longer valid today as women and men are remarkably similar in their mass behaviour and attitudes across all modes of participation' (Norris, 1991: 74).

Second, higher than average political participation is related to political values. Those holding strong or extreme political views tend to participate well above average, with overall participation highest on the extreme left. By contrast, the moderate centre tends to under-participate. In this sphere, political values associated with the 'new' or 'post-materialist' politics of environmentalism, peace and feminism are also linked to higher than average participation. But whereas holders of strong/extreme views on the traditional left–right spectrum are very active in all fields of political activity, strong adherents of the 'new' politics express their ideological commitments through collective and direct action far more than through more conventional forms of participation (Parry *et al.*, 1992: 216). Much of the new concern for the environment is expressed at the local level by people who have been described as 'sporadic interventionists' – individuals protesting about a threat to their own backyards, who withdraw from the public arena once their purpose has been achieved. To the extent that Green, internationalist, lifestyle and feminist issues continue to rise in political significance, it may be expected that political activism too will increase.

Why participate?

Two basic approaches offer an answer to this difficult question. The first explanation is based on a rational assessment that the benefits of participation will be worth the effort involved. In other words, individuals each calculate that their chances of making changes in ways that favour them or promote their interests will be successful; and that such benefits will outweigh the personal costs involved. If, on the other hand, they calculate that their chances of success are poor, or that the small gains to be won are not worth the effort, then they will choose not to participate. (See Box 5.1.)

The second explanation is that individuals are socialised into developing civic attitudes and thus see participation as a 'duty' which will benefit their community. Robert Putnam has developed a complex theory to explain falling levels of political participation in general and electoral turnout in particular. His widely discussed and cited book *Bowling Alone* (2000) takes its name from the way in which bowling, which was once a major group activity in the USA, is increasingly becoming a solo pastime. Social capital is a key yet complex concept in his argument, through which he draws out the relationship between social interaction and political participation.

It should be noted that not all political scientists support the idea of a fully participatory democracy at either local or national levels. Amitai Etzioni, well known for his communitarian ideas, once

> *Definition*
> **Social capital** is a measure of the extent to which individuals interact with each other face to face as neighbours, members of clubs and other forms of association. A result of high levels of interaction is the development of civic attitudes which include the likelihood of voting in elections. The more individuals play passive roles in society, such as staying at home being fully occupied watching television and videos, the more likely they are to withdraw from public activities such as voting.

argued for the development of an 'active society'. His critics felt that Israel, a highly militarised society, most closely reflected his ideas. It could also be argued that society in Northern Ireland shows high levels of social capital, yet that society is scarred by sectarian hatred and associated violence.

Politicians showed great concern over recent poor turnouts and a discussion began concerning ways in which the trend might be reversed (see Table 5.3). Experiments in local government elections might be extended to general elections; should there be more mobile polling stations? Would modern electronic touch-screen voting, text-voting and e-voting attract potential voters? Should there be more postal voting? Should 'election day' be extended over a longer three-day period? Should those people who turn out and vote be eligible to win lottery prizes?

Table 5.3 Falling electoral turnouts

The cause?	The cure?
The electorate is losing interest in 'low-tech' voting with pencils in inconveniently located polling stations. Busier lifestyles demand more convenient ways of voting.	Reform voting methods by developing safe Internet voting, 'supermarket' voting and greater use of postal voting. Consider text voting from mobile phones.
The electorate is disillusioned by the limited choice available under first-past-the-post. Where opportunities exist for tactical voting, it remains a negative form of political behaviour.	Reform the electoral system. Although already reformed systems have not produced high turnouts, general elections are seen in a different light. PR could return general elections to greater significance in the eyes of the electorate.
The electorate is disillusioned by party politics, perhaps even alienated by the meaninglessness of representative democracy.	Further developments in 'new politics' and forms of participation other than voting. Reforms in measuring electoral opinion scientifically through polling techniques.

Or, as Labour minister Peter Hain argued, should voting be made compulsory?

Do individuals need to vote?

- Could marketing techniques replace voter democracy? As the electorate turns out to vote less and less, will policy makers rely increasingly on means other than the ballot box to find out what people want?
- Will the increased use of marketing techniques enhance democracy by helping policy makers to be more responsive to people's preferences? Indeed, has the position already been reached where some tools used by advertising agencies are superior to democratic methods?

Participation by citizens in politics is customarily seen principally in terms of voting, as well as a minority participating through their membership of parties and pressure groups. More recently, new forms of consultation are being seen as capable of performing the same function as voting in terms of communicating between government and the governed. For example, New Labour consults a 5000 strong 'People's Panel' in order to find out the public's likely response to policy initiatives.

Focus groups

Public opinion polls are an aspect of quantitative research in which a large number of people, usually over 1000, are asked a small number of questions. In contrast focus groups are an aspect of qualitative inquiry in which a small number of people, usually between six and twelve, are asked a large number of questions. Compared with opinion polls, focus groups are quick and cheap to organise.

Watching a focus group at work looks like 'organised pub chat', with people discussing topics introduced by the researcher in a relaxed and open-ended manner. Once the group has finished its discussions a great deal of work has to be done analysing and interpreting what has been said. Labour made great use of focus groups in order to rebrand the party as New Labour. Party researchers did not expect the focus groups to come up with ideas for New Labour's policies, but wanted them

to discuss ideas that new Labour was developing. In particular, the differences between Labour and Conservative policies were explained, with the focus group then discussing which words and phrases they liked best to define Labour's new policies.

Citizens' juries

Citizens' juries, sometimes called citizens' panels, are used by local government and health authorities as a means of consulting public opinion. Juries are carefully selected so that they socially represent the local community in terms of age, gender, ethnicity and class. A typical jury will contain 16 people, which is generally bigger than a focus group. The same jury members may meet time after time to discuss a variety of issues. Their discussions last much longer than those of a focus group, with jury members sometimes returning for a second full day to complete their discussions. Finally, the discussions of jury members are more directed around specific topics than the more loosely organised and sometimes vague discussions of focus group members.

Critics of citizens' juries argue that ordinary people are incapable of having useful views on complex issues. Sometimes elected councillors oppose citizens' juries because they feel that they threaten their representative role. Supporters argue that ordinary people may not be experts but nevertheless they can make considered judgements on complex issues. The term 'juries' is used because the legal system works on the assumption that 12 ordinary people who are non-specialists can reach a verdict at the end of a complex trial. Of course the verdict reached by a citizens' jury is not legally binding in any way, and the local council or health authority that has organised the jury is free to ignore its advice. On the other hand, however, there have been occasions when local policy makers have taken the feelings of a citizens' jury into account when making decisions.

Public opinion and participation

The ideal for radical democrats such as John Stuart Mill is the active citizen, the person who is not only politically well informed but who also plays a vigorous part in the affairs of the community. To what extent, however, do people today wish for a greater political role? How widespread are participatory values?

The BPPS tested the desire for more participation by asking respondents whether they thought:

- that ordinary citizens should have more say in the decisions made by government or whether those decisions were best left to elected representatives such as MPs or local councillors
- whether the public should be given more access to government documents even if it made the government's job more difficult
- whether workers and employees should have more say in how the places where they work are run.

These questions probed public opinion not only on political participation but also upon more open government, which may be seen as a prerequisite of a more participatory society, and on workplace democracy.

Only in the sphere of work did an overwhelming majority (four-fifths) express a wish for greater participation. This seems to be an issue that has steadily gained in public favour since the 1970s. According to the British Election Studies, the proportion of respondents agreeing that 'workers should be given more say in running the places where they work' rose from 56 per cent in 1974 to 80 per cent in 1986 (Jowell *et al.*, 1987: 58). With regard to political participation, however, the majority – although a small one – favoured leaving decision making to elected representatives. On the other hand, there was a majority (nearly three-fifths, 58.3 per cent) in support of more open government. These findings suggest a widespread desire for greater involvement and autonomy at work, combined with rather less widespread but still majority support for reforms that would bring about a more politically informed society. A sizeable minority (47.6 per cent) would like to play a greater role in government decision making at local and/or national level.

To what extent do those who believe strongly in a more participatory society act on their principles by themselves participating politically more than the average? It has already been noticed that people who are strongly committed to a particular ideology tend to participate above the norm. The BPPS

also found that a firm belief in the value of participation provided an impetus to greater activism, although a 'relatively modest' one. However, this generalisation requires careful analysis. A belief in greater participation did not increase participation in such matters as voting, contacting and party campaigning. Only with regard to collective action and, especially, direct action was there a strong link between holding participatory beliefs and greater political activism. Committed participationists were involved in direct action (e.g. strikes, demonstrations, road blocks) to a degree second only to the far left and higher than the most fervent supporters of feminism, environmentalism and the peace movement (Parry *et al.*, 1992: 218, 221–3).

Political competence and participation

Traditionally, citizen efficacy or competence – the belief by individuals that they are able to influence government decisions – has been seen as a vital element in an effective democratic society. How able to wield political influence do British citizens feel today, by what means would they seek to do so, and how many of them have actually tried to act on their beliefs?

There are several measures of citizen competence or, put another way, individual political efficacy. The main ones are:

- people's perceptions of the efficacy of their votes in general, local and other elections
- their perceptions of their ability acting both as individuals and in groups to influence members of Parliament (MPs)
- their notions of their capacity through individual and collective action to change an unjust law.

The British Political Participation Study found that about three-quarters of the sample believed that their individual votes could make a difference in elections. However, only about one-third believed that people like themselves as individuals could have any influence over MPs. But when asked what influence over MPs they might possess when acting in a group, people gave more optimistic responses, approximately two-thirds considering that in those circumstances they would be able to exercise some influence. This study concluded that 'feelings of political efficacy are fairly widely held in the population at large' (Parry *et al.*, 1992: 174).

As already noticed, actual involvement in politics beyond voting is confined to a small minority – under one-quarter – of the adult population. However, judging from responses to the question what respondents *would* do if they considered it necessary, potential for action is higher than actual involvement. Both the BPPS and the BSA surveys showed that an even larger proportion of people than actually participate feel confident in their ability to influence the political process if necessary, and also believe that effective mechanisms exist for them to do so (Jowell *et al.*, 1987: 56; Parry *et al.*, 1992: 423). All this suggests that despite the political passivity of the majority, participation potential and a sense of political efficacy are relatively widespread.

Research published in the mid-1990s indicated that participation potential or propensity to protest against an unjust law may actually be increasing. The conclusion of the survey's authors was that over the 11 years between 1983 and 1994 there had been a 'fairly general' increase in the public's propensity to protest. On average, a larger proportion of the population at the later date would take some action against an unjust law; a larger proportion would undertake more actions than before; and a larger proportion would engage in unconventional political action, such as going on a protest march or a demonstration (Curtice and Jowell, 1995: 154–5).

A changing political culture?

Has the often-remarked increasing resort to violence in British society in the 1980s and early 1990s, with regard to rising levels of recorded crime, sectarian street violence in Northern Ireland, and urban rioting in Bradford, Burnley and Oldham and elsewhere, spilled over into the political culture? At least since the 18th century, Britain has been widely regarded as possessing a 'moderate' political culture, in which the norms of Parliamentary government, an unwritten constitution based on tacit understandings, and the rule of law have enjoyed wide public endorsement. Even under the severe social strains and ideological pressures of the 1930s, there was no

> *Definition*
> A **political culture** is the pattern of understandings, feelings and attitudes that disposes people towards behaving in a particular way politically. It is the collective expression of the political outlooks and values of the individuals who make up society. All societies possess a political culture.

descent by more than a tiny minority into illegal or violent forms of protest. How far has this relatively mild political culture survived the impact of rapid and far-reaching post-war social change?

Poll evidence suggests that public dissatisfaction with British political institutions and its unwritten constitution increased in the 1980s and 1990s. Other signs of change in the political culture also became apparent in the mid-1990s. For example, asked whether people should obey the law without exception or whether there are exceptional occasions in which people should follow their consciences even if it means breaking the law, a larger proportion than formerly opted for conscience over law. Also, a dual trend occurred in public attitudes to different forms of protest. Support for conventional kinds of protest activity such as organising protest meetings, marches and demonstrations declined, while support for unconventional forms of protest such as organising nationwide strikes and occupying government offices increased.

There remains widespread public support for orderly, peaceful methods of political protest, and absolutely negligible positive support for protest activities involving violence against persons and property. But willingness to engage in more threatening forms of direct action such as strikes, refusals to pay rent and taxes and blocking roads appears to have increased. Civil disobedience strategies have been most evident in animal rights, anti-poll tax and anti-roads and other environmental protests in the 1990s.

Thus, the conclusion reached by the BPPS that the only form of protest to have increased down to the mid-1980s was the signing of petitions (Parry *et al.*, 1992: 420) certainly requires modification in the light of the widespread discontent and protest generated against the poll tax (1989 to 1992), new roads (from 1991), exports of live animals, and fuel

BOX 5.1

The new politics of participation

In September 1999 militant French road hauliers blocked fuel supplies in a protest against the rising cost of diesel. This encouraged British farmers, initially organised by Farmers for Action, lorry drivers, taxi drivers and in some places fishermen, to take similar action with blockades at oil refineries and fuel distribution depots. The Opposition leader described the blockade as a 'taxpayers' rebellion' which appeared to be supported by 95 per cent of public opinion. It was estimated that only 2000 individuals were involved directly in the fuel blockade, yet within days the country was plunged into crisis. Panic buying by the public left garages without fuel, and food shortages in some supermarkets. The government was clearly taken surprise by both the speed at which Britain was plunged into crisis and the freefall in the Government's popularity with the public.

Interpretations of the crisis

- **A Poujadist protest?** Pierre Poujade was prominent in French politics during the mid-1950s at a time when France was going through political and economic difficulties. At that time there was no well-organised, successful, moderate 'conservative' party to gather the support of right-wing voters. Many gave their support to the Poujadist movement which comprised 2.5 million French voters. Typical Poujadist supporters were tradespeople, craftspeople, and owners

of small or family firms. Poujadists disliked taxation, government and Paris politics, and big business.

- **A right-wing mass movement?** Some suspected that the petrol blockade was little more than the 'Countryside Alliance on wheels'. It was argued that the crisis mobilised individuals who had grievances against Labour, but who normally felt powerless in influencing government. Encouraged by the right-wing press, they felt that they had at last found an effective weapon. Labour supporters argued that the fuel protest was simply 'the forces of conservatism' using the global oil shortage as an excuse to organise action against Labour.

- **Phobic political participation?** The term 'phobic' was first used in political science in 1968 to describe the over-reaction of some individuals to what was seen as an exaggerated fear of communism. Phobic political behaviour can be understood as abnormal or erratic political behaviour resulting from fear or anxiety. What evidence was there of phobic behaviour? The opinion polls reflected abnormally huge shifts in opinion, with the Conservatives overtaking Labour. Within days of the crisis being resolved, however, Labour's lead was back to its 'normal' lead of 11 points ahead of the Conservatives. Arguably, such unusual behaviour appears phobic in nature.

protests. The Anti-Poll Tax Movement employed a wide range of methods of protest, including lobbying of MPs and councillors, petitions and demonstrations; on occasion, it was involved in violent disturbances such as the riot in March 1990 at Trafalgar Square which ended with over 140 being injured. More significant still, its massive campaign of non-payment 'tapped into' a long tradition of civil disobedience in Britain. In the first six months of 1992 alone, nearly 4 million people were summonsed for failing to pay the tax. This popular

non-cooperation 'fuelled by an admittedly rare combination of moral outrage and material self-interest' forced the government to back down and withdraw the tax.

Anti-roads protest was coordinated from 1991 by Alarm UK, an umbrella organisation for 250 groups. Peaceful direct action against a large number of road schemes, including extensions to the M3, M11 and A30, involved 'eco-warriors' in a large variety of obstructive activities on new road sites, including occupation of houses and treehouses, barricading themselves in tunnels, chaining themselves to concrete lock-ins and occupying offices of construction companies. Protests against the export of live animals in 1995, involving demonstrations and obstruction, succeeded in reducing the number of ferry companies and ports handling the trade, but protesters were far from satisfied with the new EU rules on the live transport of animals agreed in July 1995. In February 1998 the Countryside Alliance mobilised over 280,000 in London on a protest march which, while mainly against a ban on foxhunting, also expressed concern against other threats to the rural way of life. A second march in 2002, organized around the theme of 'Liberty and Livelihood', brought 400,000 supporters of the Countryside Alliance out onto the streets of London (see Box 9.1 on page 140).

The fuel protesters showed how, using the new technologies of communication, relatively few activists could create disproportional national disruption. At one extreme, the suicide attacks by al-Qaeda terrorists on the World Trade Center and the Pentagon in the USA in September 2001 highlighted the potentially deadly consequences of this in an age of globalization of direct action.

Political socialisation

The process by which people come to understand and mentally absorb the culture of their society is referred to as socialisation, and the process by which they acquire knowledge of their political culture is known as political socialisation. The notion of political socialisation holds that people's political knowledge,

---

BOX 5.2

Greenpeace: can direct action be justified in a liberal democracy?

Greenpeace activists were found not guilty of causing criminal damage when they dug up GM crops on a Norfolk farm. Greenpeace argued that, because of the risks of cross-pollination to neighbouring crops, they had a lawful excuse to remove the GM plants. This stimulated a debate about society's attitudes towards direct action politics.

Against direct action: It was argued that Greenpeace's direct action was not justified because Britain is a liberal democracy which offers citizens other, more peaceful, means of exerting influence on decision makers. Direct action is only justified in repressive and authoritarian regimes where alternative means of political participation do not exist. By 'getting away' with damaging private property, Greenpeace's example will encourage criminally-minded individuals to take similar action to get what they want. The result will be mob rule. Also, by resorting to direct action Greenpeace risks increasing the level of violence in political life. If there is another protest by more right-wing activists, such as the fuel protesters, will Greenpeace be tempted into launching counter physical attacks?

Finally, it was argued that Greenpeace's direct action was anti scientific progress. Unless there are experiments with GM crops the truth will never be known about their possible benefits and dangers.

For direct action: It was argued that direct action was legitimate because neighbouring farmers had no say in whether or not the GM experiment should take place near their farms, There was an urgent need to take action because if cross-pollination took place then not only would neighbouring farmers' crops be contaminated and worthless, but further cross-pollination could affect all future crops. Other means of exerting influence, such as lobbying parliament, take time and are rarely effective. Direct action is a form of direct democracy. Futhermore, direct action need not be violent, as shown by Greenpeace's example. All Greenpeace activists accepted the rule of law, were willing to appear in court for their actions, and would accept whatever verdict was reached.

Greenpeace's direct action was to defend moral principles. Here there is a contrast with the fuel protesters whose direct action was to defend their self-interests.

> *Definition*
> **Political socialisation:** the process by which
> political beliefs and attitudes are learned or
> acquired by experience and are transmitted
> from one generation to the next.

values, attitudes and beliefs are informally learned in a process that begins in childhood and continues throughout their adult lives. Although political socialisation is best seen as continuous, certain phases seem to be particularly important. Because of the malleability of the young and their greater exposure and susceptibility to influences, it is generally held that the pre-adult years are of critical significance to political socialisation, even though political orientations learned when young may be modified or changed as a result of later experiences and pressures.

The sources that influence the political learning of an individual are called the agencies of political socialisation. These agencies supply a range of political information, values and attitudes which individuals may absorb both consciously and subconsciously. The most influential agencies are the family, education, peer groups and the media. Inevitably, they reflect a changing political context. The manner in which these agencies combine, and which one of them becomes the major influence, vary, of course, for each individual. Often, because of the depth and intensity of the emotional relationships it involves, the family is the predominating influence. It passes on an ethnic, religious and class identity, which normally is associated with a particular set of political orientations, and it powerfully shapes a child's attitude to authority, to gender roles, and to values (individualistic/cooperative, authoritarian/democratic, tough-minded/tender-minded) which have clear implications for political behaviour. But no influence, however powerful, is totally determinative of political outlooks. Even in the case of the family, people may rebel as teenagers or gradually grow away from its values as adults. Often the political 'messages' emitted by the various agencies of political socialisation overlap and mutually reinforce each other. They may be all the more influential as a result. But sometimes – from books, films or television, from friends or at work – an individual receives and has to accommodate a 'message' that conflicts with the overall view of the world derived from the

other agencies. If it cannot be reconciled with the existing cultural perspective, it may bring about change within it.

The main agencies of political socialisation are themselves continually evolving. The considerable increase in recent decades of divorce and birth outside marriage may be weakening the family, thereby undermining its effectiveness as a mechanism for transmitting the political culture. In recent decades also, the proportion of the population with qualifications at all levels has risen steadily, and in the longer term an educated population may be expected to be a more participatory one. However, the young are more likely to participate in unconventional ways (protest politics) than conventional ones (voting in general elections). Significant mobilisers of youth in the 1990s have been the animal rights and environmental movements, together with the civil rights issues involved in the Criminal Justice and Public Order Act (1994) (Evans, in Dunleavy *et al.*, 1997: 112–13).

Changes in the media may also be expected to have an impact on the political socialisation process. The period since the 1970s has been characterised by the growing predominance of television as the major source of public information about politics, and by an increasing pro-Conservative bias in the press, which may, however, have been halted at the 1997 General Election.

Finally, an important theory of social change is the generation theory: that the political outlook of each generation is powerfully shaped by the dominant ideas and institutions of the age into which it is born. Table 5.4 illustrates the changes – and the continuities – in the political contexts of people growing up over the last four decades. In seeking to understand political attitudes and behaviour, it makes sense to consider the often sharply contrasting experiences of political 'generations', and whether these are moulded respectively by the carnage of the First World War, the 1930s Depression, the post-1945 welfare state, the 'permissive society' of the 1960s, the Thatcherite era of free markets and the 'enterprise culture', and the 'lifestyle' politics of the 1990s.

Anthony Heath and Alison Park tested this theory with reference to the 'Thatcher generation' of the 1980s, comparing it with three previous generations socialised in the 1920s/1930s, the 1940s/1950s and

Table 5.4 Political 'generations' and the political culture, 1960s–1990s

Political generation	Political context
1960s	Consensus over interventionist role of the state. Two-party domination and prevalence of traditional left–right issues. 'Permissive society' reforms: liberalisation of laws on abortion, divorce, homosexuality and capital punishment. Abroad: cold war, USA in Vietnam.
1970s	Erosion of consensus. Two-party politics but rapid growth of third parties: nationalists, Liberals. Emergence of new issues: Europe, feminism, environmentalism, peace, nationalism. Union militancy leading to 'ungovernability' debate. Northern Ireland issue again: IRA terrorism. Abroad: cold war, USA pulls out of Vietnam
1980s	Thatcherite conviction politics; rejection of consensus. Sharply polarised politics as major parties move left and right; formation of Liberal-Social Democratic Alliance and strong electoral performance by centre. Continuing IRA terrorism. Falklands War. Abroad: intensification of nuclear rivalry between two major powers followed by disintegration of USSR, break-up of its East European empire and end of cold war.
1990s	Conservative political domination undermined by economic failure (Britain's ejection from ERM, 1992) and 'sleaze' issue culminating in victory for New Labour in 1997 general election. New consensus based on Thatcherite economics and 'stakeholder' social values. Emergence of 'lifestyle' politics and growing prominence of environmental issues. Abroad: only one major power remaining (USA); Gulf War (1991) and disintegration of the former Yugoslavia after civil war.

the 1960s/1970s respectively. They found that, while there was no evidence that Thatcherite values had had a formative effect on the 1980s generation, there were real differences between the generations in attitudes towards traditional British institutions and Britain's place in the world. Thus, the generation socialised in the 1980s was less likely to identify with the Conservatives than any previous generation, and there was little evidence to support the notion that it was more materialistic in its economic attitudes than its predecessors. However, the authors did find a generation effect with regard to the monarchy and Europe. Support for the monarchy fell through each successive generation, reaching its lowest support with the youngest age group, while the generations growing up in the 1960s and 1980s were more likely than those growing up before or just after the Second World War to favour a closer relationship with Europe. Other political differences, in Heath and Park's view, were more likely to reflect life-cycle than generational differences. Thus, they attribute the greater apathy about traditional politics of those growing up in the 1980s than earlier generations not to 'a fundamental generation gap' but rather to the stage in the life-cycle of this group. In other words, 'political interest increases with age', and is likely to do so for the 1980s generation too (Heath and Park, in Jowell *et al.*, 1997: 4, 6, 7, 9, 16, 18).

Heath and Park concluded that their study substantiated other findings that the Thatcherite crusade for a fundamental change in values had failed. For example, despite the Thatcherite attack on statism, support for state welfare provision remained undiminished among the general public and among the young in the late 1980s and the 1990s. Opinion polls showed consistent public support for socialised values over more individualistic ones: in a MORI poll in March 1989, respondents by a massive five to one ratio endorsed a society in which 'caring for others' was more highly rewarded than 'the creation of wealth' (cited in Crewe, 1996: 406).

Citizenship entitlements

The concept of citizenship does not have a straightforward definition. Citizenship is a loosely defined concept which includes elements such as a common civic identity, a core of shared values, generally agreed rights and responsibilities, including an entitlement to participate in the nation's affairs. Citizenship is traditionally linked to nationality; however 'there are few states where citizenship/nationality is quite as complex as the United Kingdom's' (Greenwood and Robins, 2002: 511) (see Box 5.3).

The impact of Britain's EU membership, the consequences of devolution, especially in Scotland, the prospects of reunification in Ireland, the issue of asylum seekers and economic migrants, internal disturbances involving alienated youth from the ethnic minorities, and the consequences of 11 September 2001, have revived the issue of citizenship in British political debate. Various think tanks concerned primarily with promoting constitutional change have also called for a renewal of the concept of citizenship in a political climate increasingly sensitive to human rights and equal opportunities.

British citizenship is characterised by ambiguity and contradiction. For example, the British Nationality Act of 1981 defined five different categories of nationality entitlements resulting from Britain's colonial legacy. In other words, some British citizens had more rights than others. In fact, the only common

---

BOX 5.3
The confused British citizen

It is, of course, recognised that citizenship in an era of globalization, racial and cultural diversity, gender politics, supranational and multi-level governance, and generally increasing concern about human rights, has become an increasingly contested concept in many parts of the world. However …
citizenship in a British context is a far from simple concept. Significantly, a MORI poll in 1998 within Great Britain (it did not extend to Northern Ireland) found that a majority of citizens (51%) identified with their respective country within the UK. Surprisingly, 40% identified with Great Britain which (unlike the UK) is not a sovereign state, or nation, but a geographical entity. These findings confirm the confused state of citizenship within the UK.

(Greenwood and Robins, 2002: 514)

---

bond linking these citizens was their allegiance to the Crown. This, of course, means that technically the British are not citizens at all: they are subjects.

Margaret Thatcher saw the right to own property and the working of the free market as best protecting the rights of individuals. 'Big government' was a threat to individual liberty and ideally the state should be confined to performing minimalist functions of providing internal order and external defence. Welfare entitlements were not part of the Thatcherite view of citizenship. Concern over increasing social disintegration led some One Nation Tories such as the Home Secretary, Douglas Hurd, to argue that those who had benefited from the free market economy had a moral duty to become 'active citizens' and volunteer help to their local communities. Civic participation was, therefore, seen as the responsibility of the affluent, largely middle class, citizens.

The conception of citizens as consumers in the marketplace was developed by John Major's Conservative governments. The Citizen's Charter was concerned with the delivery of public services to the consumer citizen. Increasing numbers of league tables were published on the performance of public services as a means of informing consumer choice, a practice extended by Labour.

New Labour's view of citizenship involved cultural engineering to end social exclusion with a new pay-off between rights and duties. Described by some commentators as a 'tough love' formula, the state would provide resources for community development. Parenting classes, homework clubs, child-care facilities would be resourced in exchange for a reduction in youth crime, higher educational attainment, and improved employment prospects. Poor parents who allowed or encouraged their children to truant would be punished.

The shock to Labour's designs for constructing new citizenship values came in the prolonged rioting in Bradford, Burnley and Oldham, and the apparent rejection of British society by significant numbers of young Muslim males. Various reports, Denham and Cantle (2001) in particular, revealed an absence of common values that might unite Britain's diverse population. It was feared that some were excluding themselves from citizenship through choice rather than circumstance. The immediate political response, discussed in Chapter 24, was a set of proposals for requirements to speak English, citizenship tests and an oath of allegiance. In schools, citizenship education has already become a compulsory part of the school curriculum.

Further reading

On political participation, the major work is Parry, Moyser and Day (1992). For a useful discussion of changes in the 1990s, see Evans (in Dunleavy *et al.*, 1997). An equivalent American study is Milbrath (1965). See also Putnam (2000) and Etzioni (1968). On political culture, the classic work is Almond and Verba (1965).

The *British Social Attitudes* surveys, produced annually since 1983, provide essential analyses of changes in British political culture: see, in particular, Curtice and Jowell (1995). For a discussion of citizenship and education, see Greenwood and Robins (2002).

Chapter 6

Election systems and electoral reform

Electoral statistics   88
Turnout and outcomes   89
Proportionality in general elections   90
Tactical voting   90
Electoral systems   91
Electoral reform in Britain   94
Referendums   96

Elections play an important and complex role in most political systems. Even undemocratic societies hold elections in order to legitimise the existing political order. In democratic societies elections help resolve political conflict in a non-violent way, for even the losers may accept that their defeat was fair. Because elections are held regularly there is always the chance that the losers will do better next time, especially if the winners do poorly in government. In this way, elections help hold government accountable to the people. Generally, elections offer people a choice in who is to represent them, which then gives the winning candidates a mandate to govern. But the way in which the people's votes are translated into winning seats – the electoral system – influences who will win and who will lose. This chapter examines electoral behaviour as well as electoral systems used in Britain. There is much debate in Britain about the need for further electoral reform regarding general and local elections. The chapter concludes by exploring the referendum as an alternative means of expressing opinion.

Electoral statistics

British elections have produced some results which, at face value, appear perplexing. Some of these 'strange but true' electoral facts include the following:

- Labour won a larger share of the popular vote in the 1955 and 1959 general elections than it did in its record landslide victory 1997, but it lost these earlier elections to the Conservatives.

- In 1983 the Labour Party received 27.6 per cent of the popular vote and won 209 seats. The recently formed Liberal-SDP Alliance were close behind with 25.4 per cent of the popular vote, yet won only 23 seats. Labour was rewarded with one MP for every 40,000 votes it won, while the Alliance gained an MP for every 338,000 votes.

- In 1997 the Liberal Democrats' popular vote fell by over 700,000 from 1992, yet they won an additional 26 seats.

- In 1992 John Major's party won a record 14,091,891 votes which gave the Conservatives a 21-seat majority in the Commons. In 1997 Tony Blair won 13,516,632 votes which gave new Labour the largest post-war majority of 179 seats.

- The number of viewers who voted in the final night of Channel Four's *Big Brother* television programme in 2001 was greater than the combined Labour, Conservative and Liberal Democrat vote in the general election of that year.

Of course all of these apparently contradictory 'facts' can be explained. The strength of third party intervention can vary from one election to another, making it either easier or harder for the 'favourite' party to win. In tightly fought contests a third party might encourage tactical voting which results in the defeat of the favourite party, or a fourth party might draw a small yet critical amount of support from the favourite party, which again contributes to its defeat. The pattern of party support – the spread of votes – is also important in understanding election results. While piling up votes in safe constituencies will increase a party's share of the popular vote, it may not win it any extra seats. On the other hand, if a party's support is spread too thinly across the constituencies it risks coming second everywhere and not winning any seats. The level of turnout can be an important factor, particularly in marginal seats. And in all cases, the fate of the parties depended in great part on the

> Definition
> **Popular vote** is the percentage of Britain's voters that supports each party, regardless of constituency boundaries or seats.

first-past-the-post electoral system. Had another system been in place, election results would have differed; the chances of one party dominating government for long periods might be reduced while the chances of parties having to form coalitions in order to govern might be increased. Some recent examples, from a variety of elections, will help unravel some of these complexities.

Turnout and outcomes

In terms of winning popular support and gaining seats, the 1997 general election was a disaster for the Conservatives: not since the 1830s had they been so unpopular, and not since the Liberal landslide in 1906 had they won so few seats. What factors might explain this and other recent results?

The first contrast, shown in Table 6.1, is in the drop in turnout between the 1992 and 1997 general elections. Labour gained around 2 million additional votes, but the Conservatives lost over 4.5 million votes. Some commentators argued that the 1997 general election could be explained in large part by the 2 million Conservatives who abstained, the 1.5 million former Conservatives who switched to Labour, and the million or so who switched to the Liberal Democrats or voted for the Referendum Party.

The problem with this simple explanation is that the pattern of turnout varies a great deal geographically – from a low of 52 per cent in Liverpool

Riverside to a high of 82 per cent in Brecon and Radnor. Furthermore, as David Denver argued, the fall in turnout was smaller in Conservative-held seats (–6 per cent on average) than in those that were Labour-held (–8 per cent). Moreover, 'the decline was greatest in typically Labour-supporting areas....This is a sobering counter to the euphoria generated by Labour's landslide victory. The landslide was won on the lowest turnout since the war and it was lowest of all, and fell most sharply, in Labour areas' (Denver, 1997: 8).

The statistics concerning the 2001 general election are very similar to those of 1997 with the exception of the turnout level, which was at an historic low. Not since 1918, when the demobilisation of troops disrupted the election, had turnout been so low. Political scientists argued that actual turnout was even lower that the shocking official figure of 59.2 per cent. If turnout is recalculated taking into account the 4 million people omitted from the electoral register, 'then turnout was more like 54 per cent' (Whitely *et al.*, 2001: 776).

As in other recent elections, turnout levels varied considerably. It was lowest amongst young people; for example, while 79 per cent of electors aged 64+ turned out, only 38 per cent of 18–24 year olds voted. As before, turnout in 2001 varied from constituency to constituency. At opposite extremes were Winchester with 72.3 per cent turnout and, again, Liverpool Riverside with 34.1 per cent.

Even fewer turned out to vote in the elections to the European Parliament. For example, in the 1994 elections 36 per cent of the British electorate voted but in 1999 only 24 per cent voted, the lowest figure to date. Elections in other EU countries had significantly higher turnouts (47 per cent in France and 45 per cent in Germany). Some political scientists

Table 6.1 The 1992, 1997 and 2001 general elections									
	1992			1997			2001		
	Votes %	Seats No.	Seats %	Votes %	Seats No.	Seats %	Votes %	Seats No.	Seats %
Conservative	43	336	53	31	165	26	33	166	26
Labour	35	271	43	44	419	65	42	413	64
Liberal Democrat	18	20	3	17	46	7	19	52	8
Others	4	7	1	7	11	2	6	10	2
Turnout	78%			72%			59%		

explained Britain's position at the bottom of the 'EU turnout league table' in terms of 'voter fatigue'. For within a short period of time prior to the European elections, various members of the electorate had been involved in a general election, local elections, elections to the Welsh Assembly and Scottish Parliament, not to mention a number of referendums. Others put down low turnout to the parties' weak Euro campaigns, and the fact that the European elections are 'second order' elections which do not result in changes of government. Understandably, therefore, these elections resulted in much apathy.

Proportionality in general elections

First-past-the-post elections tend to exaggerate the lead of the winning party when translating votes into seats. Table 6.1 shows that the parties that won the 1992, 1997 and 2001 general elections received a greater share of seats than their share of votes. In its first landslide in 1997 Labour won 128 more seats more than the total 'deserved' by its share of votes, and 144 more seats in its second landslide of 2001.

Some argue that first-past-the-post over-represents both the leading parties – Labour and Conservative – whilst under-representing the Liberal Democrats. Table 6.1 shows that in 1992 both Labour and Conservative were over-rewarded in terms of the number of seats they won. In 1997, however, the Conservatives received a smaller share of seats than their share of votes. A proportional share would have meant another 39 MPs on the Conservative backbenches in 1997 and another 37 in 2001. The Liberal Democrats were less penalised by first-past-the-post in 1997 than in 1992, but strict proportionality would have resulted in 112 MPs rather than 46. In 2001, strict proportionality would have rewarded the Liberal Democrats with 122 MPs rather than 52. However, some commentators have pointed to the anomalous result for the Liberal Democrats in Scotland (see Chapter 7). Although both the Liberal Democrats and Conservatives won 16 per cent of the popular vote, Liberal Democrats were rewarded with 10 MPs and the Conservatives with only one.

In the past, psephologists calculated the impact of the electoral system in exaggerating the lead of the winning party in terms of the cube law: 'if votes

> *Definitions*
> **Psephology** is the study of elections and voting behaviour.
> **Psephologists** are people who specialise in this field of research.

are in the ratio a:b then the electoral system will convert this into the ratio $a^3:b^3$ in terms of seats' (Denver, 1997: 8). The cube law has for over 30 years been of declining usefulness in calculating the lead of the winning party. However, in 1997 and 2001 the exaggeration of Labour's lead was almost as large as predicted by it.

Some psephologists argued that biases in the electoral system, which used to work in favour of the Conservatives, now favour Labour. Factors such as the distribution of each party's vote (71 per cent of Conservative support is concentrated in the south) and constituency boundary changes favour Labour. It has even been calculated that if the Conservatives had won the same share of the vote as Labour in 2001, they would have still won over 100 fewer seats than Labour. To form the government after the next general election the Conservatives need a massive 12.4 per cent swing, which is even greater than Labour's record swing of 10.2 per cent that swept the party into office in 1997.

Tactical voting

The electorate appears to be using the electoral system in an increasingly sophisticated way in order to register its political preferences. By-elections, for example, have long seen safe seats for the party of government overturned by disgruntled voters wanting to 'send a message to Number Ten'. The impact of the Liberal-SDP Alliance in 1983 showed that the electorate was prepared to vote tactically in a general election. Labour's first 'landslide' victory shown in Table 6.1 might be explained in large part by the ability of both Labour and the Liberal Democrats to win seats outside their list of target marginals. There is evidence that this occurred because of tactical voting against the government on an 'unprecedented scale' in 1997 (Norris, 1997: 521). Although it is difficult to measure the exact extent of tactical voting,

> *Definition*
> **Tactical voting**: this involves voting for a second choice party which has a better chance of winning than the first choice party, in order to defeat the party most disliked.

Pippa Norris found that the electorate behaved differently according to the type of local contest:

> In Conservative seats where Labour was in second place in 1992, Labour's share of the vote went up by 13 per cent on average, while the Liberal Democrat share declined by about three per cent. In sharp contrast, in marginal seats where the Liberal Democrats were in second place in 1992, the Liberal Democrat vote increased by about two to three per cent, while the Labour share rose by less than average.
>
> (Norris, 1997: 521)

Tactical voting occurred in 2001, but to a lesser extent. A notable case won Dorset South for Labour by the slender majority of 153 votes. Veteran pop singer Billy Bragg organised a 'vote swap' on the Internet; although the Conservative vote increased by 5 per cent, Labour's rose by 6 per cent, as many swapped from Liberal Democrat (down 11 per cent) to Labour.

Electoral systems

Should so many of Britain's electorate have to resort to tactical voting in order to get the electoral system to produce a result that is acceptable? Is it preferable to have an electoral system that enables the electorate to vote 'strategically' by targeting their votes on their main choices, rather than having to make complex 'tactical' voting decisions on the best way of defeating the party they dislike most?

There are a considerable number of electoral systems; some differ only in terms of detail, others differ in terms of fundamental characteristics. A main characteristic that distinguishes electoral systems is the electoral formula of how votes are translated into seats. Giovanni Sartori distinguishes between majoritarian and proportional systems; 'in majoritarian systems the voter's choice is funnelled and

> *Definitions*
> **Electoral system:** an electoral system is the means by which voters elect candidates to political office.
> An **absolute majority** means more than half: in the case of elections, 50 per cent plus at least one additional vote.
> A **plurality** is simply the largest share in relation to other parties in a contest.

ultimately narrowed into one alternative; in proportional systems voters are not forced into concentrating their vote and their range of choice might be quite extensive' (Sartori, 1994: 3).

Majoritarian electoral systems

When people talk about a 'majority', they sometimes mean an absolute majority of more than half of all votes cast; often though the term is used to refer to a simple plurality, with the winner just being the candidate with the highest vote. In a tightly contested election of three or more candidates, the winner will receive well under 50 per cent of votes cast. Sartori describes Britain's first-past-the-post as a 'one-shot plurality' system. To become truly majoritarian there would need to be a second ballot in all seats that were not won with 50 per cent of all votes or more. Only the two front-runners would appear in the second ballot, ensuring that the final winner would receive over half the votes cast (See Box 6.1).

Proportional electoral systems

Systems of proportional representation may be more or less proportional in nature, ranging from a perfect correspondence between votes cast and seats won to a much looser approximation between votes and

> *Definition*
> **Proportional representation** (PR) involves an electoral system that produces a reasonably proportionate relationship between the percentage of the popular vote cast for each party and the percentage of seats gained in the parliament or assembly.

BOX 6.1
Types of majoritarian system

First-past-the-post (FPTP). Also known as 'simple majority' or 'single member simple plurality' (Farrell, 1997: 12). As well as in Britain, this system is used in the USA, Canada, India and, until recently, New Zealand. As David Farrell comments, three arguments are customarily made about the advantages of this 'winner takes all' system:

- Simplicity. The act of voting is simple, the system is straightforward and the results are easily understood.
- Stability. Because the system exaggerates the lead of the winning party, it does away with the need for parties to form coalitions in order to govern. In all post-war British general elections except those in 1964 and 1974, governments have been returned with workable, often large, Parliamentary majorities.
- Constituency representation: each MP represents a constituency. This is in contrast with some proportional systems where there is no simple constituency link between voters and their elected representatives. The main losers under this system are parties whose support is spread evenly but too thinly across the country; they may lose few deposits but win few seats. The winners are parties which can pile up their votes in particular parts of the country and so gain seats.

The **two-ballot or second ballot system**. The best known example of this is the French system. Should a candidate win more than 50 per cent of votes cast there is no need for a second ballot. Where this is not the case a second ballot is held, generally a week later, from which the least popular candidates have been eliminated. In practice, depending upon how many candidates qualify (by meeting rules which can vary) for the second ballot, it is possible that the winner of the second ballot may still not achieve a true majority. Sartori argues that the interval between the two ballots is important, because it allows voters to reconsider their voting intentions and 'reorient their choices on the basis of the returns of the first round' (Sartori, 1994: 11).

The alternative vote (AV). This is described by Sartori as a 'preferential' voting system within single-member constituencies, which requires every voter to number all candidates in order of preference: 'the candidates with fewest first preferences are eliminated and preferences are redistributed until an absolute majority winner emerges' (Sartori, 1994: 6). This system is associated with Australia. As Farrell states, at first glance the alternative vote system seems fairer than first-past-the-post: 'the candidate elected has more votes than all the other candidates combined.… This system also allows the voters a greater say over who they want to represent them: if it is not to be their first choice, then they can choose a second' (Farrell, 1997: 49). Farrell, unlike Sartori, sees the absence of second ballot as an advantage since it denies parties the opportunity to manipulate the electorate.

The supplementary vote. A Labour Party working party into electoral reform chaired by Lord Plant recommended this system. An elaboration of the alternative vote, the voter would have just two preference votes. Where no candidate receives at least 50 per cent of the vote 'then all but the top two candidates are eliminated and the second' preferences are redistributed (Farrell, 1997: 56). The winning candidate will have a majority of votes cast. This system was used to elect London's Mayor in May 2001 (turnout 33.6 per cent).

BOX 6.2
Types of proportional representation system

List systems. These are party-based rather than candidate-based, and are used in most European countries. There is great variation within the list systems, but the basic principle they all share is that 'each party draws up a list of candidates in each constituency. The size of the lists is based on the number of seats to be filled.... The proportion of votes each party receives determines the number of seats it can fill' (Farrell, 1997: 60). Had a list system been used in the 1997 general election, rather than enjoying a landslide Labour would have been the largest party but still 89 seats short of a majority. Liberal Democrats, with over 100 seats, would have been the obvious coalition partner. Lists may be open, with no rank ordering of candidates so that voters express their preferences, or lists may be closed, with the parties placing their senior candidates at the top of the list. In Israel, which treats the whole country as a single constituency, parties determine the rank ordering of candidates on the lists. Variations are based on establishing thresholds, calculating quotas and using unused votes to decide remaining seats. The d'Hondt system, used in Belgium, the Netherlands, Portugal and Spain, attempts to ensure 'that the average number of votes taken to elect any one candidate from a party is as nearly as possible equal to any other in that party. This is often called the "highest-average formula"' (Jones, 1994: 181). The Hagenbach-Bischoff system is a derivative of the d'Hondt using a different formula to calculate the quota, and is used in Greece. Finally, the Sainte-Lague system uses the highest average formula to translate votes into seats and is used, in modified form, in Sweden and Norway.

The single transferable vote system (STV). This is interesting insofar as some political scientists see it as a pure system of proportional representation, whereas others argue that in practice constituencies are too small and STV does not work proportionally. STV is based on multi-member constituencies, and electors rank candidates in order of preference. A quota is established as a threshold for winning a seat; in a five-member constituency, each party would need around 20 per cent of the vote to win a seat, 40 per cent to win two seats, and so on. The formula for calculating the quota varies; here the Droop formula is shown:

$$\frac{\text{total number of votes}}{\text{(total number of seats +1)}} + 1$$

Votes that a candidate wins surplus to the quota are redistributed according to second, third and fourth preferences, and so on. As the bottom candidates are successively eliminated, their preferences are also redistributed to remaining candidates. If STV is to be proportional, it requires more rather than fewer seats to be contested in large constituencies. STV is used in Ireland and for European Parliamentary and local elections in Northern Ireland. But, as Farrell recounts, STV as operated in Ireland includes an element of chance. Surplus votes happen to be the ones counted last before their preferences are redistributed. The preferences expressed in the winning pile of votes might be quite different. Some argue that STV is preferable to the list system since it retains constituency links with the electorate, with electors voting for candidates rather than parties, while retaining proportionality.

The additional member system. This is a combination of two other systems in order to get the advantages of local constituency links together with greater proportionality. Each voter has two votes – one for a constituency MP and the other for a party list. The constituency MP is voted in under the alternative vote or first-past-the-post system, with the other MPs getting elected from a regional or national list. The list seats are allocated so as to help compensate, or act as a corrective, for the disproportionality of the constituency vote. One disadvantage of this system is the creation of two classes of MPs.

Photograph: PA Photos.

IN FOCUS 6.1 Replacing the Conservatives?

Charles Kennedy, Leader of the Liberal Democrats, addresses his party conference in September 2002. The Liberal Democrats have benefited from proportional representation in elections for the European Parliament and for the devolved Parliament and Assembly in Scotland and Wales (where they share power with Labour). They aspire to replace the Conservatives as the main opposition party at Westminster where they already have more MPs at Westminster than any third party since 1929. Their chances would be substantially improved by a reform in the voting system for UK general elections.

seats. Some political scientists have argued that majoritarian systems tend to result in two-party systems as in the UK and USA, whereas proportional systems result in multi-party systems. So while proportional representation systems may be 'fairer', they may also result in greater governmental instability and the formation of coalition governments with policies based on compromise and negotiation which no electors voted for (see Box 6.2).

Electoral reform in Britain

The wisdom of electoral reform has been discussed since well into the last century, and in 1917 many believed that the campaign to introduce the single transferable vote system (STV) in some constituencies, and alternative vote (AV) in others, was as good as won. In the event Parliament rejected electoral reform, except for STV being used in a small number of (now abolished) university seats. For a variety of reasons public interest in electoral reform has intensified over recent decades. STV was introduced to some elections in Northern Ireland as a visibly 'fairer' system for representing the two traditions; the revival of the Liberals in the polls but not in the Commons portrayed the unfairness of first-past-the-post; feminists argued that proportional representation would result in women contesting more seats and with greater success; Britain's membership of the European Community/Union raised questions about reforming elections to the European Parlia-

ment; and finally electoral reform was seen as crucial for making elected local government more representative, through breaking up one-party domination and attendant problems of poor quality candidates and unacceptable standards of government.

The New Labour Government came to office in 1997 with a radical programme of constitutional change including consideration of electoral reform for general elections, as well as local government elections, elections to the European Parliament, and for electing the devolved assemblies it promised for Scotland and Wales. In addition to all this, it was committed to seeking approval for its reforms through referendums, giving these a much more prominent role in the overall electoral system of the UK. While many changes have subsequently been implemented, the system for UK general elections has remained unchanged (see Box 6.3).

Britain's electoral kaleidoscope

Britain has four basic electoral systems in operation: first-past-the-post (FPTP) in general elections and STV in Northern Ireland; regional closed lists in elections to the European Parliament and a hybrid list system to elect additional members to the Scottish Parliament and the Welsh Assembly.

The closed list system for the elections to the European Parliament was based on England being divided into nine regions, with Scotland, Wales and Northern Ireland each comprising a region (STV continued to be used in Northern Ireland).

BOX 6.3
The Jenkins Report

Resulting from pledges in Labour's 1997 election manifesto, a commission was set up to examine the issue of electoral reform. Lord Jenkins, once deputy leader of the Labour Party, President of the European Commission and leader of the SDP, chaired the five-member commission. With the exception of one member, the report recommended that the first-past-the post system should be replaced by AV-top up (sometimes also referred to as AV-plus). Jenkins recommended a hybrid electoral system based on the additional member system. The 'AV' component comprised electing between 80 and 85 per cent MPs to a slightly smaller Commons by the alternative vote. The 'top up' component for the remaining 15–20 per cent of MPs would be elected by a list system.

Some political commentators felt that Jenkins made modest proposals for reform in the hope that this would increase the chances of his recommendations being implemented. In the event, the report has 'disappeared' from the agenda of constitutional reform.

Voters simply chose a party from a ballot form similar to that in Figure 6.1. Seats were then awarded as a result of the d'Hondt system of counting (see above). In the past supporters had argued that proportional representation would result in raising turnout, but on this occasion it may have contributed to a further decline. Some argued that voting for a party rather than voting for a candidate increased the 'remoteness' of the Euro-elections.

Elections to Scotland's 129 member Parliament involved the election of 94 MSPs by FPTP and the remainder by 'top-up' regional lists. Table 6.2 shows that with 56 seats Labour was the largest party but was nine seats short of an overall majority. The Conservatives failed to win a single seat on the FPTP elections, with their 18 MSPs coming from the 'PR top-up' lists. The SNP emerged to become the official opposition party.

Table 6.3 shows that the Conservatives gained most from the PR element that elected additional members to the Welsh Assembly. Under FPTP only, Conservatives would have won only one seat. The only Labour candidate to benefit from the list element was Alun Michael, the then leader of the Welsh Labour Party. Some fear the risk of prejudice against the additional members elected from the lists because they could be seen as 'second class' representatives. If this view was to persist, it would be unfortunate that those elected by FPTP became seen as 'super MSPs' and 'super AMs' whilst those elected from the lists were assumed to be 'light-weight' representatives.

Although any conclusion has to be tentative, it appears that the PR element in the devolution elections has had the impact of destroying 'tribal

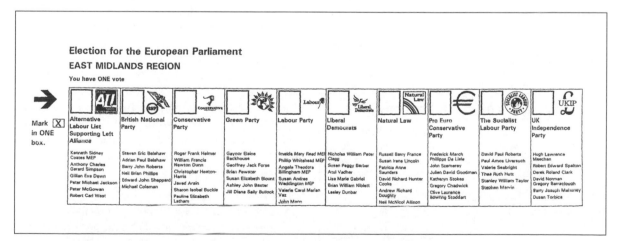

Figure 6.1 Ballot paper for European Parliament East Midlands region

Table 6.2 Elections to the Scottish Parliament, 1999

	First vote seats	First vote %	Second vote seats	Second vote %	Total seats
Labour	53	38.8	3	33.6	56
SNP	7	28.7	28	27.3	35
Conservative	0	15.5	18	15.4	18
Lib Dem	12	14.2	5	12.4	17
Others	1	2.7	2	11.3	3

Turnout 58%

politics' by forcing like-minded politicians into cooperating across party lines. In Scotland, and eventually in Wales, coalitions were formed between Labour and the Liberal Democrats. During the 1980s it was assumed that the intro-duction of PR nationally would benefit Labour at the expense of the Conservatives. The hard lesson for Labour supporters in the late 1990s was that PR in devolution hurt them and rewarded the Conservatives.

Referendums

In the past, Britain's politicians viewed referen-dums with much suspicion; Labour's post-war prime minister, Clement Attlee, described them as 'devices alien to our traditions'. Nevertheless, along with other EU members and the USA, Britain is resorting to increasing use of the referendum. Ref-erendums have been used on more than one occa-sion regarding the relationship of Northern Ireland, Scotland and Wales within the United

Table 6.3 Welsh Assembly Elections, 1999

	First vote seats	First vote %	Second vote seats	Second vote %	Total seats
Labour	27	38	1	36	28
Plaid Cymru	9	28	8	30	17
Conservative	1	16	8	16	9
Lib Dem	3	13	3	12	6

Turnout 46%

BOX 6.4

Comparative politics – elections in Germany – an AMS comparison

Members of the Bundestag are elected by a modified method of proportional representation – an additional member system – which is similar in principle to the system used to elect members to the Welsh Assembly and Scottish Parliament. In Germany, the level of support for the Social Democrats fell in 2002 from 41 per cent to 38 per cent of the popular vote. In terms of seats, they fell from 298 to 244. However, the Social Democrat leader Gerhard Schroder was able to claim victory in this knife-edge election because increased support for his Green coalition partners compensated for Social Democrat losses. Popular support for the Greens rose from just under 7 per cent to just under 9 per cent, giving the coalition a total of 306 seats.

Kingdom, with a nationwide referendum in 1975 on Britain's continued membership of the Euro-pean Community. All political parties are pledged to holding a referendum prior to Britain joining EMU and adopting the single currency. Britain's referendums have focused on seeking legitimacy for constitutional change, but other countries have held referendums to resolve moral issues or miscel-laneous debates such as whether smoking should be allowed in public places.

Referendums may differ in technical detail: a ref-erendum may be a 'top down' consultation exercise by government simply to find out the electorate's opinion on an issue, or it may be a 'bottom up' exercise in which the decision made by voters is binding. Thresholds may be introduced, as in the first devolution referendums in 1979, when at least 40 per cent of the electorate (not just voters) had to vote 'yes' before the new assemblies would be set

Definition
A **referendum** allows voters to register their opinions on specific questions regarding constitutional or policy issues.

up. Sometimes the term 'plebiscite' is used to refer to a referendum, and in the United States, particularly California, 'initiatives' are held, which are a form of referendum. Before an issue is put to the state's electorate, it must already have the support of a required number of voters who have signed the 'petition'.

Some support referendums as a means of achieving direct democracy; others feel that referendums have undesirable effects. (See Box 6.5.) It has been argued that a referendum polarises political opinion into two opposed camps rather than attempts to seek a compromise. Also the choice of voting 'yes'

or 'no' may be too simple for the complex issue being decided. For example, those opposed to holding a referendum on Britain entering the EMU argue that the decision may depend upon the rate at which sterling enters, or whether or not Britain is the only EU member not to join, and these conditions are not easily reduced to a 'yes/no' answer.

The difficulties in framing a satisfactory referendum question were illuminated in the run-up to the 1997 general election. The major parties were committed to holding a referendum prior to joining EMU but another party sponsored by the financier, the late Sir James Goldsmith, was committed to

---

BOX 6.5

The merits and disadvantages of initiatives and referendums

Many who exercise power are reluctant to opt for more direct democracy, and argue that while it may be appropriate for deciding local and state issues it has disadvantages in national politics. Conservatives tend to fear its use on key questions of defence and foreign affairs; liberals worry about the repercussions for minority groups. Many members of both categories feel safer with traditional methods of representative democracy.

In favour of votes on a single issue, it may be said that:

- They give people a chance to take decisions that affect their lives, whereas in a general election they can only offer a general verdict.
- They stimulate interest and involvement in public policy.
- They may exert pressure on the legislature to act responsibly, and in the public interest.
- They may help counter the special interests to which legislators can be beholden.
- They help overcome the obstructionism of out-of-touch legislators and therefore make reform more likely.

Against such consultation, it may be said that:

- Proposals can be ill thought-out and badly drafted.
- Campaigns can be expensive and therefore

to the advantage of well-funded groups; money is too dominant in the process, and business interests have far more scope to influence the outcome.

- There are too many issues for voters to handle, and many of them are too complex for popular understanding. The rash of tax-limitation measures and similar ones that starved schools and other essential public services (as in the USA) are ones where the mass of people are too ill-informed and apathetic to make a wise decision. They elect representatives to decide. This is what representative democracy is all about. If the voter dislikes the decisions made, he or she can turn against the controlling party in the next election.
- Initiatives and allied devices undermine political parties and therefore weaken the democratic process.
- They reflect an unwarranted mistrust of legislative bodies, and lessen their sense of responsibility for public policy.
- They encourage single-issue politics, rather than debate based on a conflict of broad principles.
- They can work to the disadvantage of minorities who can be persecuted by the majority – e.g. blacks and gays.

Source: adapted from Watts, 1997: 47.

letting the people answer a wider question. The Referendum Party campaigned for a referendum to be held on 'who should run Britain – Westminster or Brussels?' Sir James encountered problems when he attempted to flesh out the precise wording for his proposed referendum. He proposed that two questions be included: 'Do you want the United Kingdom to be part of a Federal Europe?' and 'Do you want the United Kingdom to return to an association of sovereign states that are part of a common trading market?' Critics argued that Sir James's questions were flawed. What, they asked, did he mean by 'Federal Europe'? They were unsure whether he had the EU of today in mind, or some hypothetical superstate not yet planned. (Although the Referendum Party failed to win a seat, some political analysts argued that its small share of the Euro-sceptic vote resulted in the defeat of 17 Conservative MPs.)

Similar difficulties were encountered by Euro-sceptic Conservative MP, Bill Cash, when he attempted to steer a referendum bill through Parliament. His proposed wording was:

Do you want the United Kingdom to propose and insist on irreversible changes in the treaty on European Union, so that the United Kingdom retains its powers of government and is not part of a federal Europe nor part of a European Monetary Union, including a single currency?

The advantages and disadvantages of holding referendums are summarised in Box 6.5. Mention is made that in the USA, initiatives have tended to become a political tool for wealthy interests to rally public support. An interesting development in Scottish politics reflected this linkage in rather an interesting parallel. In 2000 a struggle took place over the repeal of the controversial section 28 of the Local Government Act (or section 2a as it is sometimes known in Scotland). On the moral right was a coalition, which included Brian Souter, the wealthy businessman and evangelical Christian, opposed to repealing section 28. Supporters felt that 'lessons in homosexuality' will add yet another risk to young people who are already exposed to the dangers of drugs and crime. On the moral left was the Scottish Labour Party which felt that repealing section 28 was necessary to create a modern, more open society in Scotland.

Brian Souter privately financed what was variously referred to as a 'privately funded ballot', a 'private referendum' or an 'independent postal survey' on section 28. The results, based on a 34 per cent response rate, showed 87 per cent in favour of keeping section 28 and 13 per cent wanting to repeal it. Did this test of opinion show that there was a moral majority in Scotland that wanted to keep section 28? Or, taking into account the 66 per cent of Scottish people who could not be bothered to return their ballot papers, were supporters of section 28 in a moral minority?

Further reading

Denver (1997) includes analysis of the electoral system effect and the return of the 'cube' rule. Farrell (1997) is a detailed examination of alternatives which also considers historical origins. Jones (1994) is a comprehensive guide to the alternatives in current usage. Sartori (1994) is a controversial account of the workings of alternative electoral systems. See also Whitely *et al.* (2001). Also see Denver (2002) and Farrell (2001).

Chapter **7**

Voting behaviour

The decline of the two-party system   99
The primacy approach: the social basis of
    voting behaviour   101
Social class and voting behaviour   102
Gender and voting   103
Age and voting   104
Ethnicity and voting   105
The recency approach   105
The image of the party leader   107
Party images   108
Can issue preferences explain voting
    behaviour?   108
An econometric explanation of voting
    preference   109
The 2001 election: a campaign that
    changed nothing?   110
Measuring public opinion   113

This chapter moves on from electoral systems to examine why people vote as they do. In the late 1960s a political scientist could observe with considerable justification that in Britain 'class is the basis of British party politics; all else is embellishment and detail' (Pulzer, 1967: 98). Thirty years later social class appears to explain much less about variations in political behaviour, and today political scientists talk of 'class dealignment' as having taken place. But, as we shall see, there is much disagreement about the extent to which dealignment has occurred. Political scientists have developed various models to help explain the changes that have taken place in voting behaviour. Each model is useful in that it explains some aspect or other of voting, but none explains voting patterns entirely. How far do they help in analysing recent general elections? On the surface, in 1997 and again in 2001, Labour enjoyed landslide victories of historic proportions, but are there other explanations that put Tony Blair's successes into perspective? Finally, this chapter examines the reliability of opinion poll data on which political scientists base much of their research.

The decline of the two-party system

The electorate is not an unchanging entity, nor is it stable. Some changes occur because its composition is changing as young people attain voting age and become included, while others die. Other changes occur because of movements in attitudes, values and behaviour from one election to the next.

Thus there may be long-term and short-term changes that help explain voting trends. Although it is a basic point, it has to be remembered that when we compare the electorate of the 1950s with that of the 1990s, very different groups of voters are involved. Many voters in the 1950s would have remembered the Boer War as well as two World Wars; they might have experienced great economic hardship during the 1930s or been involved in the suffragette movement; they would certainly have witnessed the election of the Attlee government. None of these voters will have lived long enough to vote in the 1990s. In contrast, young voters in 2001 will have no real memories of the last Labour government which left office in 1979. But these young voters may well be aware of short-term changes in the political agenda on which elections have been fought; they may have noticed, for example, that the defence issue seemed to play a smaller role in the 2001 campaign than it did in 1987. The impact of these processes on voting behaviour has contributed to the decline of two-party voting. This can be seen in three closely related developments which have occurred during the last 40 years.

First, there has been a more or less steady decline in the percentage of the total vote won in general elections by the Conservative and Labour parties. For example, in 1951 nearly 97 per cent of voters supported either Labour or Conservative. After touching a low point of 72 per cent in 1983, the percentage rose to 78 per cent in 1992, and fell back to 74 per cent in 1997 and 75 per cent in 2001, all far below the 1951 level.

Table 7.1 When the voting decision was made in 1997 (per cent)

Question: When did you make up your mind how you would vote today?

	Conser-vative	Labour	Lib Dem	All
Before election was called	58	65	34	57
Since election was called	18	15	25	18
Within the last week	12	10	25	14
On voting day itself	11	9	16	11

Source: adapted from Kellner, 1997b: 619.

Second, one of the major causes for this decline has been the weakening of party identification. In other words, the links between voters and parties have grown weaker and weaker as fewer and fewer voters identified with particular political parties. As party loyalties have weakened, so electoral volatility has increased. Because an increasing number of voters do not have such strong emotional ties to particular parties, they find it easier to switch their vote to another party or decide not to vote at all. In recent elections this was reflected in two particular behaviours:

• Evidence since 1979 shows that an increasing number of voters are prepared to support different parties in local and general elections. In 1997 around half Britain's electors had the opportunity of voting in both elections on 1 May, and a Mori poll found that at least 10 per cent of Conservative and Labour general election supporters intended to vote Liberal Democrat in the local elections. 'Split ticket' voting accounted for the Liberal Democrat vote being 'seven per cent higher than the party's general election vote, with the Conservatives down by four per cent and Labour by five' (Rallings and Thrasher, 1997: 687). Despite their sound defeat in the 2001 general election, Conservatives enjoyed gains in the local government elections that were held on the same day, making a net gain of 120 seats.
• Table 7.1 shows that typically three out of ten Labour voters and four out of ten Conservative

voters decided which party to support as late as during the 1997 election campaign. Two-thirds of Liberal Democrat support came from 'late deciders'. This compares with the elections of 1983 and 1987, when only one in five of all voters decided during the last two or three weeks of the campaigns. In 1992 the equivalent figure rose to one in four.

Third, there has been a decline in class-based voting during the post-war years. In the 1950s approximately two-thirds of the working class voted Labour, and four-fifths of the middle-class voted Conservative (see Figure 7.1).

Since those early post-war years the links between class and party have weakened. Political scientists refer to this process as **dealignment.** What processes have been at work to cause the weakening of class and party links, voter and party links, resulting in greater volatility with a quarter of voters switching their support away from the two major parties? As might be expected of such a complex question, no single theory can explain adequately all the changes that have occurred in recent decades. Various explanations, however, can be grouped into two main types – those sharing the primacy approach and those sharing the recency approach.

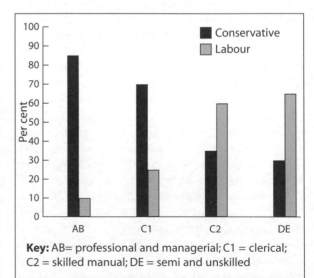

Figure 7.1 Class percentages voting Labour and Conservative, 1945–58

Source: data from Tapper and Bowles, 1982: 175.

The primacy approach: the social basis of voting behaviour

Much human behaviour reflects social divisions. For example, in terms of leisure and cultural behaviour patterns, almost all those attending a rave will be young people; far more elderly than young will spend a night at bingo. Only the more affluent in society will be found picnicking at Glyndebourne opera house. Many more men than women go fishing. Can voting behaviour be explained in this way by social divisions – such as age, gender, ethnicity, and class? How far are the very different experiences of individuals living in society reflected in their voting behaviour?

If the way in which individuals vote is an expression of their position in the social structure, then voting would tend to be stable. This is because an individual's sex, ethnicity, and so on are fixed. Of course an individual's voting habits might well change from time to time, but such changes that occur do so within an overall pattern of stability. It might be argued, for example, that this stability in voting behaviour was shown in practice by the long period of Conservative government from 1979 to 1997 being achieved on around 42 per cent of the vote in four consecutive election victories.

In their analysis of *The Loyalties of Voters*, Richard Rose and Ian McAllister (1990) devised a theoretical framework for exploring how a lifetime of learning steadily shapes how an individual might vote. A modified version of their framework is shown in Figure 7.2. The process begins with childhood political socialisation, since young children develop attitudes towards authority based on their own experience within the family. Some children will learn about authority in a strict authoritarian family where they are punished if they disobey the rules, whereas others will learn in a more open or democratic family where they may even be involved in making family decisions. Each

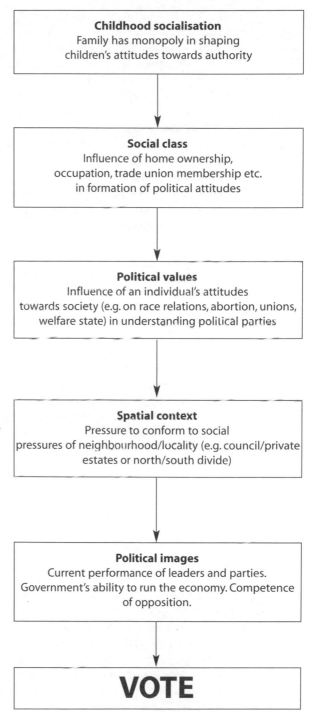

Figure 7.2 A framework for analysis of voting behaviour

Source: adapted from Rose and McAllister, 1990.

individual's family is located in the class structure, and so provides a social class identity and value system. All the learning experiences shown in the framework might influence one particular voter, while another voter might only be influenced by one or two of the experiences. The framework does not attempt to analyse voting loyalty in terms of one explanation only, but is flexible enough for new findings to be 'hung' on the framework in order to build up a fuller understanding of voting behaviour. A well-known American book, *The American Voter* (1960), influenced political scientists into believing that long-term factors in an individual's life were the most important in influencing his or her vote. The authors, Angus Campbell, Philip E. Converse, Warren E. Miller and Donald E. Stokes, set out a framework similar in principle to Rose and McAllister's but referred to theirs as the 'funnel of causality'.

Social class and voting behaviour

Of all the social divisions – such as age, gender, ethnicity, and the urban–rural split – it is social class that has preoccupied political scientists. As Figure 7.1 indicates, in the early post-war years there was a fairly positive relationship between social class membership and voting behaviour. Political scientists of the time were more interested in the 'class defectors' – the middle class socialists and the working class Tories – than they were in the majorities of voters who supported their 'natural' class party. Most research focused on the working class Tories since this was the most extensive of the deviant behaviour. Did a third of the working class vote Tory because they were deferential and preferred being governed by their social superiors? Was society – in the form of the mass media and education – undermining working class consciousness and thereby confusing a minority of working people as to which political party they ought to support? Had other social processes, such as slum clearance, the decline of occupational communities and the decline in workplace contacts brought about by increasing automation, resulted in weakening the ties for some between class and party? Or, finally, were some workers motivated more than others by affluence, and voting Tory on pragmatic or instrumental grounds because they

believed they would be better off in material terms under a Conservative government? These were the sort of questions that political scientists posed and set about answering.

During the 1960s and particularly during the 1970s the relationship between class and party weakened. This process of class dealignment was reflected in a reduction in Conservative support from the professional and managerial classes and a reduction in Labour support from the working classes. Figure 7.3 indicates the voting behaviour of social classes in the 2001 general election.

It can be seen that new Labour's appeal to what journalists dubbed 'middle Britain' continued to be very successful. Labour increased its support across all social classes in 1997, to the point where Pippa Norris described it as a 'catch-all' party, with Tony Blair's New Labour doing much better in constituencies with a high concentration of professional and managerial workers than Neil Kinnock's Labour Party in 1992: 'Labour has triumphed by maintaining its traditional base and yet simultaneously widening its appeal to middle England' (Norris, 1997: 523).

The most notable feature of the 2001 general election was the solid Labour gain in winning

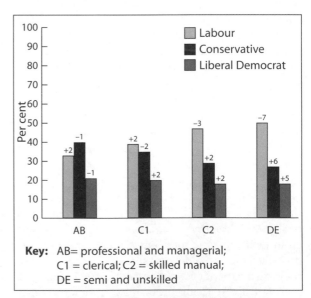

Key: AB= professional and managerial;
C1 = clerical; C2 = skilled manual;
DE = semi and unskilled

Figure 7.3 Class voting in the 2001 general election (change since 1997 at head of each column)

Source: data from P. Kellner, *Observer*, 10 June 2001.

middle class support and Conservative gain in winning working class support. As Peter Kellner's analysis (Figure 7.3) showed, the ABC1 classes swung by 2 per cent to Labour, consolidating the party's advances in winning the support of 'middle Britain'. It has to be remembered that only ten years previously in the 1992 general election, the Conservatives had a 32 per cent lead over Labour in middle class support. By 2001 the Conservative lead had been reduced to 7 per cent among social classes AB, and overturned into being 4 per cent behind Labour with class C1.

Compared with 1997 the Conservatives won increased support from the working classes in 2001, particularly social class DE. But this is still far below the levels of working class support enjoyed by the Conservatives in previous elections. For example during Margaret Thatcher's leadership of the party, Conservatives won the support of 42 per cent of class C2 and 30 per cent of class DE.

The analysis of electoral trends during the 1980s resulted in many political scientists believing that Labour was becoming a northern rather than national party, and in terminal decline. Much research effort was put into analysing Labour's shrinking core vote which, after affluent workers increasingly defected to Thatcherism, typically comprised that part of the Scottish and northern working class who lived in council houses and had joined a trade union. However, after 1997 journalists speculated whether it was the Conservatives who were now in near-terminal decline, having won their lowest share of the vote since 1832 and the smallest number of MPs since 1906. Labour won 1997 with almost double the largest swing any party had received in post-war general elections. And despite their slight drop in the popular vote, Liberal Democrats returned their biggest number of MPs since 1929. The questions about the future of Labour, crucial in the 1980s, seemed redundant after 1997 and 2001.

Gender and voting

The pattern of gender and voting has changed considerably over recent years. In 1967 it was possible to argue that 'there is overwhelming evidence that women are more Conservatively inclined than men'

(Pulzer, 1967: 107). There appeared to be sound reasons for this situation. Some argued that since women stayed at home more than men, it was natural that their attitudes should be shaped by the traditional values of the family. It was likely that women were more religious and more deferential than men. Also, not having a job meant that such women never experienced industrial conflict at the workplace and so did not value the role of trade unions. All these factors were believed to produce a political outlook among women that was more inclined towards supporting the Conservatives.

From 1979 onwards the gender gap narrowed until it disappeared in 1987 (see Table 7.2). The great mystery is why it returned in such a marked way in 1992, for Labour campaigned hard in order to win female support, and many of the issues at the top of its political agenda were 'women's issues'. Part of the answer may lie in the different ways different age groups of women voted. In a survey conducted between 1986 and 1988 David Denver and Gordon Hands (1992) revealed that a gender gap existed among young people, but it represented a reversal of the traditional picture. Boys gave more support (50 per cent) to the Conservatives than girls (35 per cent). It appeared that young males were attracted by Margaret Thatcher's 'macho' image whereas young females were attracted more by Labour's 'caring' image on health and education. (Surprisingly, attitudes on 'women's issues', such as abortion and divorce, accounted for little difference.) In 1997 the gender gap closed as

Table 7.2 Sex and party choice in general elections, 1987–97 (per cent)

		Conser-vative	Labour	Liberal Democrat
1987	Men	44	33	25
	Women	44	31	25
1992	Men	38	36	19
	Women	44	34	16
1997	Men	31	44	17
	Women	32	44	17
2001	Men	33	42	18
	Women	33	42	20

Sources: *Guardian*, 15 June 1987; *Daily Telegraph*, 14 April 1992; *Sunday Times*, 4 May 1997; *Observer*, 10 June 2001.

in 1987, but with women showing a 10 per cent swing to Labour compared with 6 per cent for men.

Joni Lovenduski's analyses of the 1997 and 2001 campaigns drew a useful distinction between women's issues (which mainly affect women) and women's perspectives (which are women's views on all political issues). An example of the former is party policy on nursery school provision; an example of the latter is policy towards the EU, where men focus on issues of sovereignty and the single currency while women are more concerned with social rights. Although women do not represent a solid voting bloc whose support is either to be won or lost, all the major parties made some attempt to develop policies for women, but it was Labour that 'made a sustained effort to convince women voters' (Lovenduski, 1997: 715). But by other measures women played a low profile in the campaign: the presidential nature of the campaigning focused on men; the party manifestos did not feature women's issues to the same extent as such issues had featured in party debates during the years prior to 1997; and a study of television coverage during a week of the campaign found that male politicians made 169 appearances compared with eight for females. The result, however, was a triumph for women with a record 120 female MPs entering the Commons.

Joni Lovenduski argued that 2001 was a particularly masculine campaign in which the 'wives/partners of party leaders generally received more national media attention than women politicians.… In 2001, despite the availability of many senior women politicians, women were even less visible in the national campaigns' (Lovenduski, 2001: 743). She continued to make the point that no major party really embraced women's perspectives, with the exception of Labour which produced what some might describe as a condescending women's version of the party manifesto. Even women's issues were overrun by what were seen as more pressing items with, in the case of the Conservatives, the 'save the pound' campaign stifling issues such as child care and the married couples' tax allowance.

Only a fifth of all candidates standing for election in 2001 were female. Labour fielded most women (149) with Liberal Democrats having 132 and the Conservatives 94. There were 118 successful in winning seats, with 95 returned as Labour MPs, 14

as Conservatives and 5 as Liberal Democrats. As in 1997, there was no gender gap in voting behaviour in 2001 (see Table 7.2). However, it has been argued by some political scientists that the raw statistics contained in the table 'average away' important gender differences in voting behaviour. In 1997 for example, when no gender gap was visible, younger women were actually voting Labour more than young men. Also older women were supporting the Conservatives more than older men.

Age and voting

There is a long-recognised association between increasing age and Conservative support. Why should age be an influence on voting behaviour? It has been argued that for most people property and wealth increase as they grow older, and as their families grow up, so aspects of the welfare state become less important to them, resulting in a more Conservative outlook. Others have suggested that age is an influence on voting in terms of 'political generations' passing through the electorate. Each generation forms its views and votes for the first time in a distinct political climate.

Figure 7.4 confirms the generalization, with the 65 year olds and over, being the only age group giving the Conservatives more support than

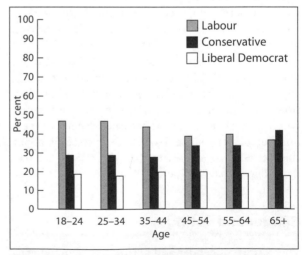

Figure 7.4 Party support by age in the 2001 general election

Source: P. Kellner, *Observer*, 10 June 2001.

Labour. However, the Conservative lead among 'grey' voters fell between the 1997 and 2001 general elections. In 1997 Conservatives enjoyed a 10 point lead over Labour whereas in 2001 it had shrunk to 5 points. Nevertheless, from 18 year olds, voting for the first time, to individuals who have retired or are on the verge of retirement at 64, Labour is the most popular party. Furthermore, the younger people are, the more likely they are to vote Labour.

Ethnicity and voting

In his book *Immigration and 'Race' Politics in Post-War Britain* (1992), Zig Layton-Henry made the point that participation by the ethnic minorities in elections can be used as a measure of political integration and support for democratic politics. At the same time, discrimination against ethnic minorities could result in political responses such as apathy, alienation or even rebellion. Others examine the ethnic minority vote in terms of its potential impact on election results. One in 20 Britons comes from an ethnic minority, but their votes are concentrated in a limited number of urban, mainly inner-city, constituencies. Some estimates suggested that in as many as 100 seats the majority of the sitting MP was less than the local ethnic minority vote (*Guardian*, 21 May 2001).

Race was pushed up the political agenda prior to the general election. In 1997 an 'Election Compact' was signed up to by party leaders in which they committed their parties to a 'clean' campaign which did not exploit the race issue. In 2001 the Commission for Racial Equality asked all MPs to sign up individually, and some Conservatives refused. The Conservative leader, William Hague, campaigned against creeping Euro-federalism and adopted a tough stance on 'bogus' asylum seekers. Encouraged by the tabloid press, these issues tapped into xenophobic, intolerant and racist sentiments. In the fraught circumstances of inevitable electoral defeat, Hague's attack on Labour's Europeanism turning Britain into 'a foreign land' was immediately interpreted as the race card being played in desperation to rally last-minute support.

Sixty-four members of the ethnic minorities stood for election, with 12 winning seats (all Labour). Although the ethnic minorities do not vote as a cohesive block, the vast majority support Labour (see Table 7.3). However, Afro-Caribbeans gave Labour considerably greater support than did Asians.

The recency approach

This approach challenges the ideas behind the explanations of voting behaviour that fall within the primacy approach. In other words, the argument that long-term factors influence voting is largely dismissed, and much greater stress is put on the importance of recent events as explanations of voting behaviour. In terms of Figure 7.2 the recency approach would focus on perceptions of parties, leaders, issues, the campaign, and the government's ability to run the economy. These perceptions can, of course, change quite quickly. A new party leader, a fall in the interest rate or a period of poor industrial relations can result in large swings of support from one party to another. Unlike the primacy approach which embraces life-long characteristics, such as gender, class and ethnicity, and so focuses on the relative stability of voting behaviour, the recency approach emphasises the volatility of voting behaviour which can result from relatively minor events that occur in politics.

The resounding electoral victory of New Labour in 1997, with its new constitution, new policies and new leader, sweeping to power on a 10 per cent national swing, suggests that primacy explanations of voting behaviour are no longer particularly useful. However, it is counter-argued that Labour's victory was not the result of an electoral tidal wave of changed voting – only one in three of the electorate

Table 7.3 Black and Asian voting in the 2001 general election (per cent)

	Black	Asian
Conservative	9	11
Labour	76	69
Liberal Democrat	4	4
Other	1	2
Refused an answer	10	14

Source: courtesy of Operation Black Vote.

voted Labour – but the result of tactical voting and the electoral system effect which gave Labour a landslide in seats. The primacy approach continues to make the point that Conservative governments throughout the 1980s and 1992 were elected on a stable 42 per cent of the popular vote. Furthermore, Labour's victories in 1997 and 2001 were expected, since opinion polls had been reflecting a prolonged and stable period of popularity beginning in 1992.

These arguments are dismissed by political scientists who support the recency approach. Neither the similar levels of support won by the Conservatives in 1979, 1983, 1987 and 1992 nor Labour's current electoral dominance reflects stable voting behaviour, for neither the Conservatives nor Labour had the same people voting for them at each election. A great deal of 'churn' takes place which is not revealed in simple statistics. Figure 7.5 illustrates the degree of churn that can normally be expected in changing voting intentions during a typical election campaign.

'Churn' is a useful metaphor for this phenomenon because, like the surface of a peaceful stretch or river, there will be many currents and flows of water beneath the surface. While opinion polls measure the superficial levels of party support, there will be large numbers of electors changing their minds on which party to support. Some might join the 'don't

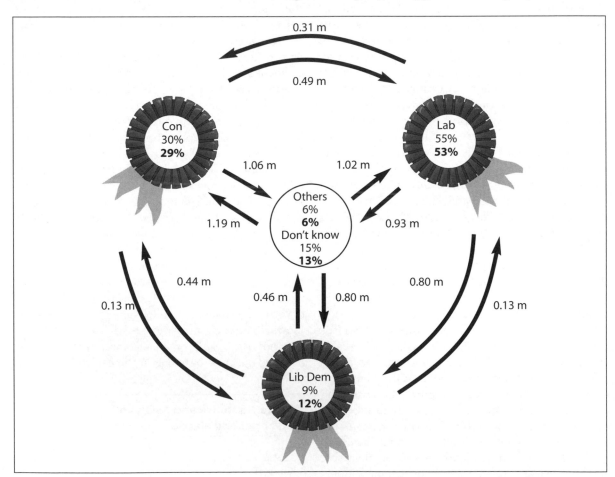

Figure 7.5 Electoral churn

The level of each party's support measured by opinion polls obscures the 'swaps' or 'shifts' made by millions of people in what is referred to as 'churn'. It was estimated that 8.5 million individuals changed their minds about whether or not to vote and which party they would vote for in the last three weeks of the 1997 campaign. The degree of churn was thought to be considerably less in 2001.

IN FOCUS 7.1 Leaders under fire

Former Conservative Party leader William Hague (right) with his successor Iain Duncan Smith at the Party conference in Blackpool, September 2001. It is widely reckoned that their recent choice of leaders has done the Conservative Party no favours. Iain Duncan Smith, who decisively defeated Ken Clarke in a poll of party members, initially failed to make much impression in Parliament or with the public.

Photograph: PA Photos.

knows', or decide to abstain. Also some who were previously 'don't knows' will have made up their mind about which party to support.

As many as a quarter of all voters normally make up their minds on which party to support in the final week of the campaign or on election day itself. In doing so, they are influenced by many last-minute developments or events. Unlike the primacy approach which exaggerates electoral stability, the recency approach stresses a volatile balance of support between the major parties, with support swinging from one party to another in response to economic events, personalities, political images and so on.

The image of the party leader

With the growth in the importance of television in political communication, and the emphasis on 'spin control' by the parties in order to project the most favourable image, are voters now influenced principally by their judgements on party leaders? Was there a 'Blair effect' in 1997 whereby a vote for Labour really meant a vote for Tony Blair as prime minister? In other words, was the 1997 general election in reality a presidential battle fought between Major, Blair and Ashdown? Could the same be said of the 2001 contest between Blair, Hague and Kennedy?

Some political commentators do not believe that the image of the party leader is so crucial in influencing voters. Only if there is not much to choose between the parties in terms of policies will the qualities of their respective leaders become more important to voters. Also, they argue, the experience of past elections shows that unpopular leaders can win. For example, in 1970 Labour Prime Minister Harold Wilson with a 51 per cent approval rating was far more popular than Conservative leader Edward Heath with only 28 per cent approval. Yet Heath won the 1970 general election.

William Hague, the Conservative leader, did not confound opinion poll predictions. Although a competent Parliamentary performer, he failed to gain the confidence of the wider electorate. His personal rating ('Who do you think would make the better prime minister?') stood at only 18 points at the beginning of the campaign. His somewhat erratic leadership contributed to the impression that the Conservative campaign was collapsing or had collapsed, with his party facing the prospect of meltdown at the polls. Towards the end of the campaign, his rating had fallen to 12 points, only one above Charles Kennedy. In contrast Tony Blair's rating stood at a commanding 45 per cent. It is hard to escape the conclusion that William Hague was an electoral liability for the Conservatives, and that his unpopularity contributed to the size of the party's defeat.

Party images

An internal post mortem into why the Conservatives were soundly defeated in a second successive election concluded that the party suffered from an unflattering image. It was seen as nasty, racist, narrow, intolerant, anti-women and homophobic. Although xenophobia and intolerance may be attitudes found in the ageing party membership in the country, they were not the attitudes on which election victories could be won in a progressive society. Some political commentators drew unflattering contrasts between the middle class, mostly male and all white body of Conservative MPs and the composition of wider society. Conservative MP John Townend praised Enoch Powell and lamented the passing of Britain's homogenous Anglo-Saxon society (*Guardian*, 29 March 2001). Such views were common amongst the Conservative grassroots and further contributed to the party's negative image.

In contrast, Labour's image was generally positive. Although there was disappointment about Labour's failure to deliver on numerous policies, especially health and education, the government was given the benefit of doubt. Labour's inclusive policies included elements of compulsion, but they set a sharp contrast to the social authoritarianism of the Opposition. In this and other ways, Labour's image connected with the public mood far more successfully than did the Conservatives'. Radical Thatcherism successfully connected with the public mood during the 1980s, whilst Labour's image made it unelectable as it 'lurched to the left'. In the 2000s, however, it was Labour's image that was congruent with people's aspirations.

Can issue preferences explain voting behaviour?

New issues can arise on the political agenda which do not fit into the traditional class interests of the parties, and can therefore blur the lines linking party and voter. For example, advocates and opponents of nuclear power development cross party lines, causing divisions among trade unionists in particular. The miners have an interest in closing existing nuclear power stations, while workers in the nuclear power industry support its expansion. The issue of Britain's role inside the European Union has caused deep divisions within and between the major parties as well as within public opinion at large. Moral issues, such as the abortion issue or health education, can become salient issues which have little relation to party positions and are better understood in terms of authoritarian or libertarian orientations.

With the weakening of class influences on voting and the emergence of new issues that did not fit traditional partisan splits, some political scientists argued that an increasing number of the electorate were voting on the basis of issue preferences. Mark Franklin found, for example, that the effect of voters deciding which party to vote for according to issue preferences more than doubled between 1964 and 1983 (Franklin, 1985). Some political scientists argued that Labour's electoral defeats between 1979 and 1992 were accounted for in part because its policies were no longer popular, even with its long-standing supporters. For example, Ivor Crewe considered that trends in public opinion revealed a quite exceptional movement of opinion away from Labour's traditional positions amongst Labour supporters over the past 20 or 30 years. There has been a spectacular decline in support for the 'collectivist trinity' of public ownership, trade union power and social welfare.

A 'consumer model' of voting behaviour has been constructed by H. Himmelweit and colleagues (1984) which is derived from an issue-based theory of voting. Voters 'shop around' to find the party with a programme of policies that offers the closest fit to their own policy preferences. Of course, voters may not have perfect information about various parties' policies, and even when they do have the relevant information, they may suspect that a party, if elected to office, would not implement its manifesto proposals. Although past studies showed that party support could be predicted with 80 per cent accuracy from consumer preferences, the 1987 general election raised some doubts about seeing voters as analogous to shoppers in the political marketplace. As Ivor Crewe commented in the *Guardian*, 'Labour's poor performance remains a puzzle because its campaign did succeed in placing its favourable issues much further up the agenda than in 1983.... Had electors voted solely on the main issues Labour would have won' (*Guardian*, 16 June 1987).

However, the 1992 general election once again raised the possibility that issue voting was an important factor which explained aspects of voting behaviour such as party choice and volatility. Although Labour succeeded in pushing some of its campaign issues – such as health, pensions and transport – well up among those the electorate saw as important, the top issues were inflation and taxation which lay at the heart of the Conservative's 'double whammy' propaganda drive.

In the 1997 campaign, Labour neutralised any repeat of the Conservatives' 'double whammy' by stating that a future Labour government would accept Conservative spending limits and not raise income tax. Indeed, after their tax-raising government it was now the Conservatives who were vulnerable on the tax issue. According to Mori, the top six important issues in the minds of electors were health care (68 per cent), education (61 per cent), law and order (51 per cent), unemployment (49 per cent), pensions (39 per cent), and taxation (33 per cent). On all but law and order where Conservatives enjoyed a small lead, and taxation, the sixth issue, Labour had substantial leads. Labour was successful in ensuring that its traditional issues were among the most important election issues, and had big leads on four of the six biggest issues. Unlike the situation Ivor Crewe described in 1983, had electors voted on the main issues in 1997 then this would help explain Labour's victory in the popular vote.

To what extent did the 'consumer' or 'supermarket' model explain voting behaviour in the 2001 general election? The Conservative campaign focused most heavily on the issues of asylum seekers and the euro. Although these issues were important to Conservative core voters, they were not seen as priority issues by the wider electorate (see Figure 7.6). The result was that the Conservatives failed to attract support from the 'middle ground' of British politics, and failed to win back support from the supposed 6 million voters who had abandoned it since 1992. In contrast, Labour campaigned on issues that had high priority in the minds of voters. Partly as a result, 28 per cent more of the electorate thought that Labour was best to handle the NHS; 26 per cent more thought that Labour was best on education. Only on the least important issue of asylum seekers did the Conservatives have a clear 10 point lead over Labour.

An econometric explanation of voting preference

Relatively minor events, such as a public sector strike or movements in inflation and interest rates, will have an undue influence on a volatile electorate. In the language of journalists, such events will cause the electorate to either 'feel good' or 'feel bad'. David Sanders analysed the relationship between public support for the government and changes in the key 'feel good' economic factors. He found that there was a time lag of three to four months between voters experiencing improved economic conditions and a decision to change the party they were supporting. Using past patterns of the 'feel good' factor and government support as well as economic forecasts, Sanders predicted in August 1991 an outcome that was very close to the actual result in April 1992.

It can be argued that John Major lost the 1997 general election on 16 September 1992 when, after an international loss of confidence in sterling, Britain was forced to withdraw from the ERM. It might also be argued that since Conservative popularity had never been restored, 'Black Wednesday' also denied William Hague victory. Public perceptions of the Conservatives' competence to manage the economy were dented and never recovered sufficiently to deliver a fifth or sixth consecutive election victory. Sanders's statistical analysis

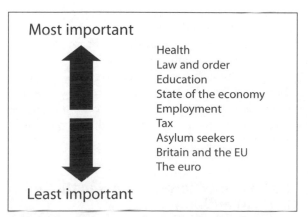

Most important

Health
Law and order
Education
State of the economy
Employment
Tax
Asylum seekers
Britain and the EU
The euro

Least important

Figure 7.6 The most important issues to the electorate, 2001

showed that after the ERM crisis 'the competence graph plunges downwards and continues to trend downwards thereafter' (Sanders, 1995: 161).

Withdrawal from the straitjacket of the ERM resulted in a sustained economic recovery. By January 1997 regular monthly falls in unemployment figures brought the total below 2 million, inflation was at 2.7 per cent, and interest rates had fallen to 6 per cent. Conventional political wisdom would have predicted that a grateful electorate, now 'feeling good', would have rewarded John Major's government with another term in office. However, this was not to be the case. As Gavin and Sanders explain, the government was forced to drop all the arguments in favour of Britain being in the ERM in order to get low inflation and economic growth, since Britain was now enjoying these conditions outside the ERM. Indeed, it was the countries remaining in the ERM that were suffering from rising unemployment, public spending cuts and slow growth:

> Indeed in the wake of Black Wednesday, the government was obliged to argue that economic growth could best be achieved by Britain's remaining outside the ERM. Such a policy U-turn, without a plausible story to justify it, engendered a loss of public confidence in the government's managerial capabilities.
>
> (Gavin and Sanders, 1997: 633)

The Labour Chancellor, Gordon Brown, had won a reputation for economic competence. He was 'prudent' regarding public spending while overseeing economic growth, falling unemployment, low inflation and low interest rates. Increases in taxation remained largely hidden, appearing on neither wage slips nor price tags. To all intents, Labour's campaign slogan could have echoed Macmillan's boast of 1958 that 'you've never had it so good'.

There were numerous parallels between Labour's economic performance and that of its Conservative predecessor, but public perceptions of each greatly differed. Yet there 'was no simple equation in the 1992–2001 period, in which the Conservatives were punished for poor macroeconomic performance between 1992 and 1997 by electoral defeat, whereas Labour was rewarded for sound macroeconomic performance between 1997 and 2001 by electoral victory' (Sanders et al., 2001: 793–4).

While actual performances in managing the economy by Conservative and Labour may have been similar, what differed was the electorate's subjective perceptions about the economy, which did influence voting behaviour. Recent Labour governments, led by Harold Wilson and James Callaghan, were not remembered by voters for their economic competence, whereas New Labour's success in managing the economy changed perceptions, and voters were willing to continue supporting Labour in 2001.

Straightforward evidence that an individual's economic perceptions are related to voting intentions is contained in Table 7.4. Here 'three-quarters of voters who thought Labour was best at handling Britain's economic difficulties voted Labour. A similar proportion of those who thought the Conservatives were best voted Conservative.' Even when other variables were taken into account 'economic perceptions exerted powerful effects on voters' choices in the 2001 election' (Sanders et al., 2001: 799–800).

The 2001 election: a campaign that changed nothing?

The date of the 2001 general election was delayed for a month because much of rural Britain was suf-

---

Table 7.4 Voting intentions and perceived economic management competence, May–June 2001 (per cent)

'If Britain were in economic difficulties, which party could handle the situation best?'

Supporters of:	Labour best	Conservative best	Neither/ don't know
Conservative	3	76	22
Labour	74	9	30
Liberal Democrat	18	12	34
Other	4	3	14

Source: Sanders et al., 2001: 799.

fering from an outbreak of foot and mouth disease. There was little enthusiasm from either the electorate or the media once the parties swung into action and the campaign began. This was reflected not only in the poor level of turnout but also in the lowest viewing figures for election night coverage on television. An ITV poll found that 70 per cent of viewers expressed little or no interest in coverage of the results.

It has been argued that the processes of class dealignment and reduced partisan attachment have left much of the electorate vulnerable to influence from short-term factors, many of which will be communicated during the campaign. Yet the summary of opinion polls showed that support for the parties remained stable during the weeks of the campaign. Support for both Labour and the Conservatives in Figure 7.7 is seen to be 'flat-lining' in the sense that there were no major gains or losses

for either party, with the campaign appearing to have had little impact on voters. The exception was support for the Liberal Democrats, which showed a modest increase.

Labour's historic victory

For the first time in the party's history, Labour was re-elected for a second term in office with a three-figure majority. The levels of support changed relatively little during the campaign, and following election day, very few seats changed hands. Overall there was a national swing of 1.6 per cent from Labour to Conservative, which resulted in the Conservatives winning one extra seat and Labour losing six. This reduced Labour's Parliamentary majority from 179 to 167. The Liberal Democrats enjoyed considerable success, winning 52 seats (6 more than in 1997) to become the largest third party since 1929.

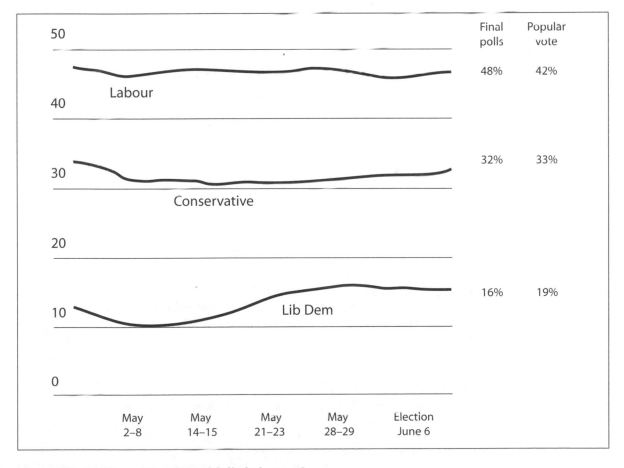

Figure 7.7 2001: a campaign with little impact?

Table 7.5 The 2001 general election results for Great Britain

	Seats won	Change since 1997	Total votes cast	% share of popular vote	% share of seats
Labour	413	–6	10,740,168	42	64
Conservative	166	+1	8,352,845	33	26
Liberal Democrat	52	+6	4,815,249	19	8
Other	10	0	688,693	6	2

Turnout 59% (–13)

The meaning of the campaign

Some political scientists sought to explain factors such as the electorate's lack of interest in the campaign and the low level of turnout in terms of the special nature of the 2001 election. In other words, did the 2001 general election have distinctive features which made it an almost 'one-off' election? Some argued that 2001 was not a conventional general election in which parties competed for support on manifesto issues, but a unique election because it really comprised three combined referendums. Certainly a significant effort was made by the Conservatives to convert the unpopularity of the euro into support for the Conservatives with a 'save the pound' campaign. However, the strategy failed for, although the euro was unpopular with the electorate, it was an issue of low importance in most voters' thinking. Also the electorate knew that all parties were committed to holding a future referendum on the euro, so attempts to turn the 2001 campaign into another referendum did not make sense. Therefore, it is not plausible to argue that in effect the general election was for most voters a referendum on the euro.

The second hypothesis was that the general election in Northern Ireland assumed the nature of a referendum on the Good Friday Agreement. It was certainly the case that in the campaigning, issues concerned with the Good Friday Agreement such as the release of prisoners and the decommissioning of weapons were prominent. Furthermore, there was a significant swing towards parties that most opposed the Good Friday Agreement. In other words, unionist and nationalist voters swung towards supporting their respective political extremes.

Large gains were made by the 'hardline' Democratic Unionist Party (DUP) over the 'moderate' Ulster

Unionist Party (UUP) both in terms of seats won and share of the vote. These results provide evidence that the DUP is becoming the most powerful force within Unionism. Similarly, 'hardline' Sinn Fein overtook the 'moderate' Social Democratic and Labour Party (SDLP) both in terms of seats won and share of the vote. Given the importance of the peace process in the campaign, and given the increasing polarisation in voting behaviour, there is some credibility in arguing that the 2001 general election took on much of the nature of a referendum on the Good Friday Agreement.

Finally, was the general election in Scotland an opportunity to vote on the issue of independence? Although the issue of Scottish independence was raised, other issues featured more strongly in the campaign. Support for the SNP wilted and the party lost a seat. Labour, the 'devolution party', remained the dominant party in Scottish politics, and the 'unionist' Conservative Party regained a Parliamentary presence in Scotland with one MP. These results provide little evidence to support the notion that 2001 was a surrogate referendum.

Table 7.6 The 2001 general election: results for Northern Ireland (changes since 1997 shown in brackets)

	Seats won		Share of the vote %	
Ulster Unionist Party	6	(–4)	27	(–6)
Democratic Unionist Party	5	(+3)	22	(+9)
Sinn Fein	4	(+2)	22	(+6)
Social Democratic and Labour Party	3	(0)	21	(–3)
UKU	0	(–1)	6	(–5)

Measuring public opinion

Many politicians believe that they can measure public opinion informally by reading newspapers, talking to party workers or listening to the views of their constituents. There are also more 'scientific' methods which are used by party managers who measure the response of the public to numerous aspects of their party's image. In terms of measuring the level of public support a party enjoys, local election (and local by-election) results can provide a guide. Opinion polls provide greater flexibility in measuring public attitudes since they can be conducted any time. Newspapers and television sponsor pollsters such as Mori, Gallup, NOP, ICM and Harris to carry out research. Many published findings report on the general level of support for each of the main parties based on answers from a representative sample of around 1000 people. The sample, balanced in terms of social class, sex, age and region to represent the electorate as a whole, is asked which party it would vote for if there was an election.

In some countries, opinion polls have been banned in the last days of the election campaign on the grounds that they interfere with the way people vote. The effects of polls can vary according to particular circumstances, but a 'bandwagon effect' can result from more and more people supporting a party because they want to see its support increase still further. Or if one party has a large lead in the polls there can be a 'boomerang effect' on election day, as overconfident voters stay at home because the polls have convinced them their party is going to win.

Predicting how the whole electorate will vote from the responses of a small sample of electors is bound to include a margin of error. This is usually estimated at 3 per cent plus or minus the published finding. Occasionally a 'rogue' poll may be published which may be based on faulty fieldwork and is far out of line with the results from other polls. In any election the most accurate poll is likely to be an 'exit' poll on election day, which asks voters which way they actually voted rather than which way they intend to vote.

During the 1992 general election campaign pollsters consistently predicted that the outcome would be a hung parliament, with most predicting that Labour would be the largest party. The fact

Table 7.7 The 2001 general election: results for Scotland (changes since 1997 shown in brackets)

	Seats won	Share of the vote %
Labour	56 (0)	44 (–2)
Scottish Nationalist Party	5 (–1)	20 (–2)
Liberal Democrat	10 (0)	16 (+3)
Conservative	1 (+1)	16 (–2)

that the Conservatives won with a respectable majority was the cause of considerable embarrassment for the polling organisations. Inquests into 'Why did the pollsters get it wrong?' revealed a number of possible problems both in the fieldwork stage of collecting people's opinions and later in interpreting the results. An enquiry by the polling organisations into why they had failed to forecast a Conservative victory found:

- The sampling quotas did not match the composition of the electorate since they contained too few middle class interviewees. Those organisations that used quotas, such as Mori and ICM, drew up more sophisticated quotas in order to better reflect the stratification of the electorate.
- Older Conservative supporters appeared more reluctant than their Labour counterparts to disclose their voting intentions face to face to an interviewer. ICM attempted to overcome this by experimenting with respondents completing a secret mock ballot form not seen by the interviewer. Later ICM, along with Gallup, adopted random telephone polling. Respondents are more likely to be candid to an unseen interviewer than during a face to face interview.
- There was a late swing to the Conservatives in 1992 which most pollsters missed.

Pollsters also adjusted their findings in order to increase their accuracy. Respondents were asked to recall how they voted in the last general election, and the whole sample was adjusted to match the actual vote. Pollsters have done much to repair the damage done to their reputation by their poor performance in 1992, but there is still a tendency to overestimate the Labour vote and underestimate the Conservative vote.

Although the pollsters celebrated their improved performance in 1997, some critics pointed out that they still had problems with their methods. Using average errors during the campaign, one poll still overestimated Labour's lead by 9 per cent; 44 polls published during the campaign predicted that Labour would win by a bigger margin than it did; had the 1997 general election been a closer contest, the pollsters would have got it wrong again. Finally, because of increased variation in constituency swings and greater tactical voting, it was argued that pollsters must pay greater attention to converting the 'popular support' percentages into Parliamentary seats.

Fewer opinion polls were published in 2001 than in previous elections. Partly as a result of this 'they figured less conspicuously in the media and they appeared to exert less influence in the campaign' (Crewe, 2001: 650). Labour enjoyed a substantial margin of victory over the Conservatives, so it was not difficult for the polls to predict a Labour victory. However, their measures of Labour's victory 'varied from ICM/Guardian's and Rasmussen/Independent's 11-point lead to the 17-point leads of NOP/Sunday Times and Gallup/Daily Telegraph'

(Crewe, 2001: 660). Ivor Crewe argued that despite their revised methodologies, pollsters still overestimated Labour support and underestimated Conservative support. He also argued that there was no evidence to provide pollsters with an excuse for their errors – in 2001 there was no late tactical switching to the Liberal Democrats and no late swing to the Conservatives. The causes of polling inaccuracies were located in methodology and sampling design.

Further reading

Cowling (1997) is a stimulating journalistic account of the 1997 general election. Curtice (1997) is an academic account of Labour's victory. Denver (2002) gives a comprehensive account of the theory of voting used to explain election outcomes, and Denver (1997) is an academic account which summarises the main lessons to be drawn from the 1997 general election. Useful accounts of the 2001 general election are to be found in Crewe (2001), Sanders *et al.* (2001), Saggar (2001), Lovenduski (2001) and Kellner (2001). For a comprehensive account see Butler and Kavanagh (2002).

Chapter 8

Political parties

Why parties? 115
Party systems 115
Types of party – cadre and mass parties 118
Ideological and pragmatic parties 118
Parties and interests 119
Party cohesion – factions and tendencies 120
The organisation of parties – power and
  decision making 121
The leadership 122
Parliamentary parties 126
Party conferences and the national
  organisation of the parties 128
The party membership and constituency
  parties 130
Power within the parties – the modern
  party and its membership 131
The finance of political parties 133
The future of the British party system 134

Politics for many people today means purely and simply 'party politics', a specialist and rather unsavoury activity undertaken by party politicians. This very narrow interpretation of politics is odd when one considers that organised political parties competing for power are a relatively recent phenomenon, the product of the last two or three centuries in western political systems, and more recent still elsewhere. Yet although the confusion of 'politics' with 'party politics' is misguided and misleading, it does underline how important parties have become in modern politics.

The ideologies of major British parties and some of their policy implications have already been discussed in Chapter 4. This chapter explores briefly why parties are necessary, and goes on to review the rather unusual party system in Britain. It explores some conventional distinctions between different types of parties, as a prelude to an analysis of the organisation and distribution of power in major British parties, and some of the issues involved. The topical problem of party finance is considered in a separate section. The chapter concludes with an examination of the future of mass parties, and more specifically of the British party system.

Why parties?

It is not immediately obvious why political parties are necessary in a modern democratic political system. Why could not voters just choose the best men and women for the job? Parties may seem to bring more divisiveness than is necessary to politics. Often it is suggested that a certain issue should be 'taken out' of party politics, or that party politics should play no part in, for example, local government. Could we not do without parties altogether?

The answer to that question is, almost certainly, no. Parties have developed in just about every political system involving representative democracy, which suggests that they are necessary for the operation of the system. What functions then do political parties serve?

Party systems

Competition for power between political parties has become almost a defining condition of modern western democracy. The British party system, like the party system in the United States and some other countries, has been traditionally characterised as a two-party system. Abundant evidence seems to support the description.

- Only two parties have formed governments since 1945. Labour has governed from 1945–51, 1964–70, 1974–9 and 1997 to the time of writing. The Conservatives have governed from 1951–64, 1970–4, and 1979–97.
- Through most of British history over the last 200 years there has appeared to be a two-party duopoly – Whigs and Tories, then Liberals and

BOX 8.1

Main functions of political parties

Political choice. Parties are the principal means by which voters are given an effective choice between different teams of leaders, and between policy programmes and ideas. Without parties it would be very difficult for voters as a whole to have much influence on the shape of the government to emerge or the policies to be pursued.

Political recruitment. Parties recruit and train people for political office and government. Virtually all MPs and most councillors are first nominated by political parties, which also recommend individuals for appointment to other posts such as school governors or Justices of the Peace.

Political participation. Belonging and taking an active role in political parties is one way in which ordinary citizens can participate in the political process besides voting. As party members they can help to choose candidates for public office, join in the election of party leaders and other party positions, and influence party policy, both directly through party conferences and policy forums and indirectly through other channels of communication with the party leadership.

Reconciling and aggregating interests. Parties involve coalitions of interests. They bring together various sectional interests in society, and assist in transforming a mass of demands into a coherent programme which can be placed before voters at election times. They resolve conflicting interests arising from the many issues with which governments are confronted.

Communication. Parties provide a two-way channel of communication between political leaders and their supporters. The party leadership use various channels of communication (e.g. speeches, party conferences and other meetings, websites, party publications) to persuade members and voters they are doing their best to meet their needs and aspirations, while members and supporters seek to channel their concerns to the leaders (representations to MPs and councillors, resolutions to party conferences, opportunities to voice views in meetings, surveys, focus groups etc.).

Accountability and control. Parties effectively take control of government, which in Britain normally means single-party government at Westminster and commonly but by no means always on local councils. Thus it is through parties that the governments of the country and other elected bodies can be held accountable for their performance at subsequent elections. Through parties, voters can clearly identify who is in charge, and either reward them by giving them another term in office or 'throw the rascals out' by preferring another party.

Conservatives, more recently Labour and Conservatives.

- Most of the seats in the House of Commons (and sometimes nearly all of them) have belonged to the two major parties since 1945.
- The whole British system of government seems to reflect the confrontation between two parties. There is a government and Opposition, a Cabinet and a shadow cabinet, a House of Commons with two sets of benches confronting each other (compared with semi-circular assemblies elsewhere).

Yet some would point out:

- Our two-party system is in part a product of the electoral system which severely penalises third parties, particularly those (like the Liberal Democrats) whose support is not concentrated in particular areas.
- The two-party share of the vote has declined marked from a high point (96 per cent) in 1951. The main third-party grouping has averaged around a fifth of the vote in elections since 1974.
- There have been several historical periods when

three or more parties have been significant – e.g. the 1850s, the late 19th century, and before and after the First World War.

- Particular parts of the United Kingdom such as Northern Ireland and Scotland do not involve a conflict between two major parties. In general elections in the 1980s the main choice over much of the south of England appeared to be between Conservatives and Liberal Democrats, with Labour a poor third in many constituencies.

- In local government there are virtual one-party systems (e.g. much of South Yorkshire and the North East), dominant party systems (e.g. Labour in Leeds), two-party systems (e.g Bradford), multi-party systems (e.g. Stockport, Calderdale) and even no-party systems (e.g. rural Wales, Lincolnshire, parts of North Yorkshire).

- In the new devolved political systems in Scotland, Wales and Northern Ireland there is a multi-party system, with (to date) fairly stable

---

BOX 8.2
Comparative politics: party systems in other countries

No-party systems. Now relatively rare and confined largely to traditional autocracies dominated by a ruling family (e.g. Saudi Arabia).

One-party systems. In most former Communist states only one party was permitted. In some former colonial states a nationalist party associated with the struggle for liberation from colonial rule achieved a virtual monopoly of political life. In both cases there is no competition between parties, although there may be competition between candidates within parties.

Dominant-party systems. In some states more than one party may contest elections, but one party dominates membership of the legislature and government, and there seems little real prospect for a change in power (in the short term at least). This was the position for many years in post-independence India, where the Congress Party dominated, and in Japan until recently, where the Liberal Democratic Party seemed to be permanently in power.

Two-party systems. In these two parties win most of the seats in the legislature and alternate in government, as with competition between Democrats and Republicans in the USA. (Note that third-party groups or candidates have sometimes challenged in US elections, but have not succeeded in changing the two party duopoly.)

Two and a half party systems. There are two major parties but normally neither can govern alone without the support of a smaller third party. This was the position in Germany for several decades. The Christian Democrats (CDU/CSU) and Social Democrats (SPD) are the two major parties who relied on the smaller Free Democrats (FDP) for support in coalition governments (note more recently the SPD/Green coalition, however).

Stable multi-party systems. Although many parties are represented and normally none can command a majority in the legislature, it is relatively easy to form stable coalition governments between parties, perhaps because ideological differences are not too deep. Until recently, both the Netherlands and France under the Fifth Republic might be included in this category.

Unstable multi-party systems. It is difficult to form coalition governments, and once formed such governments often prove short-lived. (Examples include France under the Fourth Republic, Italy and Israel.) One problem may be the existence of substantial anti-system parties which are excluded from coalition building (e.g. Communists and Gaullists under the Fourth French Republic, Communists and extreme right parties in Italy, until recently).

Note: an important question is how far a party system is the product of a particular electoral system (e.g. first-past-the-post elections leading to a two-party system, and proportional representation leading to a multi-party system), and how far they are products of significant divisions or cleavages in society.

coalition government in Scotland and Wales, and a rather unstable coalition in Northern Ireland (where the DUP which is opposed to the peace process is a substantial anti-system party). Significantly, all three are products of a more proportional system of representation than is used for Westminster.

Types of party – cadre and mass parties

In the analysis of political parties a distinction is often made between 'cadre' parties, based around loose groups of MPs and local notables, and mass parties, with an extensive active party membership in the country (Duverger, 1954). In many western countries early parties were of the cadre type, while subsequently socialist and social democratic parties were organised as mass parties. Many (but not all) older parties then acquired their own mass organisation.

In Britain the 18th-century Whigs and Tories essentially began as cadre parties based on Parliament, with only rudimentary organisation in the country. The growth of the franchise and the development of a mass electorate in the 19th century made it far more important for the major parties (now called Liberals and Conservatives) to recruit and identify supporters and ensure those eligible were registered to vote. Good constituency organisation became far more important. Both the existing major parties set up a national organisation to look after their new mass membership. So the Liberal and Conservative Parties became, in effect, mass parties. But the parties in the country only existed to serve the interests of the parties in Parliament. Power and authority remained with the Parliamentary leadership.

By contrast, the Labour Party was actually founded outside Parliament (as the Labour Representation Committee in 1900). The party outside Parliament thus existed before the Parliamentary party. The Parliamentary Labour Party (PLP) and the Leader of the PLP were supposed to serve the Labour Party as a whole, not the other way round. Under the Labour Party Constitution supreme power was vested in the Labour Party Conference, and in between conferences in the National Executive Committee (NEC) elected by the Party Conference. Thus the party began as a mass party, with

ultimate power resting with the mass membership. (However, the reality of power within the Labour Party did not closely match these constitutional provisions – see below.)

Yet although the Labour Party had a radically different constitution which reversed the customary relationship in Britain between the Parliamentary party and the mass party in the country, in practice Labour increasingly behaved like the older parties, and real power seemed to lie with the Parliamentary party and its leaders and officials rather than the grass roots (McKenzie, 1955). This was partly because the Labour Party operated within the same overall UK political system as the established parties and was constrained by its rules and conventions. Perhaps it was more because mass political parties are inevitably big organisations; as Robert Michels (1911) has argued, 'Who says organisation says oligarchy.' In other words, power in all large organisations tends to gravitate towards the few rather than the many – towards full-time leaders and permanent officials rather than the rank and file, even if the latter are supposed to be in control.

Ideological and pragmatic parties

Another distinction is sometimes drawn between ideological (or programmatic) and pragmatic parties. Thus a party may be closely linked with a particular ideology, with an associated political programme. This might be stated in the party's name, formal objectives and constitution. Such a party will try to convert voters to its own ideology and programme. Some other parties may appear more flexible, less tied to particular ideological assumptions, and concerned with the pursuit of office rather than the promotion of a particular political programme, prepared to adjust policies to the perceived preferences of voters. Indeed, one influential interpretation of party competition is that in order to maximise votes, parties need to seek the middle ground, and must carry any ideological baggage lightly (Downs, 1957). Such parties seeking to maximise electoral support are sometimes termed 'catch-all' parties.

This analysis was sometimes applied to British political parties. Thus while the Labour Party was seen as an ideological party, with its socialist objectives defined in the old Clause Four of its constitution, the Conservative Party was perceived as an essentially pragmatic party, or even a catch-all party, mainly interested in winning and holding on to power, and thus avoiding ideology and theory, seeking to appeal to a broad range of interests. There is (or was) something in the distinction. Yet as we have seen (see Chapter 4) the Conservative Party has always involved some ideological assumptions, while the Labour Party was always more flexible and pragmatic than its apparent commitment to the 'common ownership of the means of production, distribution and exchange' implied. Indeed McKenzie's (1955) celebrated study of British political parties argued that they were similar not only in organisational terms but also in their approach to policy, although another influential book which first appeared a decade later in 1965 (Beer's *Modern British Politics,* see Beer, 1982a) reasserted the distinctive ideological traditions of the two main parties.

The subsequent history of the two parties has blurred the distinction further, or possibly even led to a dramatic reversal of roles. Thus it is commonly argued that Mrs Thatcher purposefully transformed the Conservative Party into an ideological party with a clear commitment to the free market, while Blair's conversion of his party into New Labour, with a deliberate pitch for the votes of 'middle England' and for the support of business, has involved the embrace of pragmatism. The symbolic rewriting of Clause Four, and the adoption of a 'third way', coupled with the use of marketing techniques and focus groups, suggest that Labour has become a 'catch-all' party, aiming to sweep as many as possible into Blair's 'big tent'. Again, there is something in the analysis, but it should not be pushed too far. 'Thatcherism' always involved a substantial dose of traditional Conservative pragmatism, while the Conservative Party since Thatcher has shown some flexibility in reinterpreting its message. Blair's New Labour involves some significant shifts of emphasis, but its vocabulary and policies are not so very different from those of the traditional Labour movement (see Chapter 4).

Indeed, the distinction between ideological and pragmatic parties is not ultimately very helpful. Parties can hardly avoid ideological assumptions. More positively, they need ideals and a message to enthuse their supporters. They also need to show some consistency if they are to be taken seriously. Their ideas may have to evolve and change with the times, but too many sharp reversals of position in pursuit of votes cause confusion and mistrust. Even Downs (1957), whose theory assumes parties are in business to maximise votes, recognises that ideologies have their uses, as they enable voters to cut their information costs – in other words they do not need to find out where a party stands on every issue, because this can be inferred from the party's ideology. But if parties are inevitably ideological, if they are to succeed they have to interpret their ideology flexibly, and adapt to changed circumstances or face permanent exclusion from power and thus lose the opportunity to implement any of their ideas and policies. There are numerous instances of British parties behaving pragmatically – Labour ditching its previous commitments to leave Europe and renationalise privatised industries, the Conservatives abandoning their previous opposition to devolution and the minimum wage after 1997. Similar instances of policy reversals can be found throughout the history of British parties.

Parties and interests

Distinctions are commonly drawn between political parties and interest groups. Parties seek power through the pursuit of Parliamentary representation and formal occupation of government posts, while groups seek influence. Moreover, while groups commonly represent a single interest, parties, if they are to be successful, must involve coalitions of interests. Thus, to use the jargon, groups articulate interests while parties aggregate interests. Once more the distinction is hardly watertight. Some parties seem more concerned with protest than power, and some are linked closely with a particular interest (such as the Peasant Parties or Agrarian Parties found in some political systems). By contrast, some interest groups may put up candidates at elections, but often more to win publicity than with the expectation of winning (although a representative of one local group very unusually won a seat in the 2001 British general election).

Again the British Labour Party is sometimes singled out for its close relationship with a particular interest – trade unions, or the interests of labour, identified largely with the manual working class. Indeed, an unusual feature of the Labour Party is its federal constitution, representing other affiliated organisations, mainly trade unions. It was not even possible until 1918 to become an individual member of the Labour Party. Before then, people joined the Labour Party by joining an affiliated organisation. Critical to the early finance and membership of the Labour Party were the trade unions. Thus in the words of trade union leader and subsequently Labour minister Ernest Bevin, the Labour Party emerged 'from the bowels of the Trade Union movement'. The relationship between Labour and the trade unions has been a key issue ever since (see Minkin, 1992). While the relationship was arguably a source of considerable strength to Labour, it also provided ammunition for Labour's opponents, who argued that the unions controlled the party and its policies and rendered Labour unsympathetic to other interests (such as the middle classes, or business). The unpopularity of unions, particularly in the 1970s, the reduction in size and the fragmentation of the old manual working class, and the decline in union membership rendered the trade union connection and the identification of the party with the interest of the working class a fast depreciating asset. The process of making Labour electable from 1983 onwards involved reaching out to other social groups and areas of the country ('middle England'), wooing business, and distancing the party from the unions, to the extent that some unions have increasingly questioned the value of the Labour Party link. Modernisers within the party argued that these changes were essential if Labour was ever to regain power, and the argument has been to an extent vindicated by the 1997 and 2001 election results. Yet the contrast between old and new Labour should not be over-dramatised. The party has never in practice sought to appeal solely to its trade union and working class base. Labour's 1945 landslide depended on winning Parliamentary seats far from Labour's industrial heartlands.

Indeed other British parties have been linked with particular interests – the Conservatives with the landed interest and subsequently business

interests, and more broadly the middle classes. Such interests provided the party with much of its finance and active membership. Yet had the party allowed itself to become too closely associated with these interests it would never have won power and dominated government as it did for most of the 20th century. If Labour needs to reach out beyond its class base to win and retain power, this was even more obviously true for the Conservatives, as the interests with which they were popularly linked involved a far smaller proportion of the electorate. To win power the Conservatives needed to appeal to at least a sizeable minority of the working class, including trade union members, and they did, with considerable success.

Party cohesion – factions and tendencies

Any successful party arguably needs to involve a broad coalition of ideas and interests. Too narrow a focus will restrict its appeal and limit its chances of winning support. This is particularly the case in Britain where the electoral system heavily penalises smaller parties. Thus as we have seen (above and Chapter 4) the main British parties involve a wide range of interests and ideas. While perceived party unity is important for electoral success – divided parties are a turn-off for voters – the range of interests and ideological perspectives within a single party can be a constant source of tension, with the periodic threat of open dissent, rebellion and even a fundamental party split. Maintaining some semblance of unity and cohesion is not easy when there are so many pressures threatening to blow a party apart.

There are thus significant divisions within all major British parties – sometimes around leading personalities (e.g. Blair and Brown in the Labour Party), sometimes around particular issues (e.g. Europe in the Conservative Party), sometimes over party tactics and strategies (e.g. Liberal Democrat divisions over coalition with Labour or equidistance between the major parties), or over ideology (e.g. socialists and social democrats in the Labour Party, or the conflict between free market and 'one nation' Conservatives).

Each party contains factions or tendencies within it. Factions within the Conservative Party have

> *Definitions*
> A **party tendency** is sometimes defined as a loose and informal group within a party sharing a particular ideological perspective or policy stance.
> A **party faction** is a more stable, enduring group, sometimes with a constitution and formal organisation and membership.

included the Thatcherite No Turning Back group, the moderate Bow, One Nation and Tory Reform groups and the Euro-sceptic Fresh Start group. An old influential faction within the Labour Party was the left-wing Tribune Group. A faction that becomes too disciplined and strong may become almost a party within the party. Thus the Bevanites were accused of constituting a party within the Labour Party in the 1950s. Moreover the Labour Party in particular has been periodically concerned about the dangers of infiltration or 'entryism' by groups or tendencies that do not share the party's commitment to parliamentarism and its own moderate interpretation of socialism. Thus from the 1920s onwards the party was concerned to resist Communist infiltration, while from the 1960s it has been rather more concerned about Trotskyism, culminating in the very public denunciation at the Labour Party Conference by the Labour leader Neil Kinnock of the virtual takeover by the Militant Tendency of some Labour constituency parties and councils. Apart from the internal divisions and conflict caused by such groups, the perception that a party has been infiltrated by 'extremists' can be electorally damaging. Although the Labour Party has suffered most from association with extremists ('reds under the bed'), instances of former BNP and National Front activists working within the Conservative Party have sometimes undermined its recent attempts to appear more inclusive and welcoming towards ethnic minorities.

If the internal tensions and divisions within a party develop, a split may result. Needless to say these can be very damaging, perhaps leading to the demise of the party as a serious political force. One cause of the rapid decline of the old Liberal Party was a series of damaging divisions, in 1886, 1916–18 and 1931–2. Labour's internal divisions, long a source of electoral weakness, led to a major split in 1981 when some leading Labour 'moderates' left the party to form the Social Democratic Party (Crewe and King, 1995), and some commentators concluded that the Labour Party was effectively finished as a credible party of government. More recently, divisions within the Conservative Party severely weakened John Major's government and led to the party's debacle in 1997. Although there was no major split, some Conservative MPs 'crossed the floor' to Labour or the Liberal Democrats (see Table 8.1), a few former Conservatives switched to the Referendum Party or the UK Independence Party, and some former Conservative MEPs fought the 1999 European Parliament elections as a separate party. Although the bulk of pro-Europe Conservatives have remained within the party, they have increasingly appeared an embattled minority.

The organisation of parties – power and decision making

The above analysis suggests it is very important for a party to manage internal divisions and maintain an appearance of unity and cohesion. One of the

Table 8.1 'Crossing the Floor': recent changes of party by sitting MPs

Date	Name	From (party)	To (party)
1995	Alan Howarth	Conservative	Labour
1996	Emma Nicholson	Conservative	Liberal Democrat
	Peter Thurnham	Conservative	Liberal Democrat
1997	Sir George Gardiner	Conservative	Referendum
1998	Peter Temple-Morris	Conservative	Labour
1999	Shaun Woodward	Conservative	Labour
2001	Paul Marsden	Labour	Liberal Democrat

problems here is that modern political parties are extremely complex organisations which operate at a number of levels. The main elements of their organisation are:

- A clearly identified party **leadership**, including a single acknowledged leader who has considerable prestige and authority, and commonly a deputy leader, surrounded by a team (of ministers or shadow ministers or party spokespersons) which together constitute the collective party leadership.
- A **Parliamentary party** (presuming it has Parliamentary representation) with appropriate organisation for its effective functioning – including party committees and a whip system to maintain party unity and discipline.
- A permanent **party bureaucracy** to serve the party and provide it with administrative, promotional and often research support.
- A **mass membership** in the country (which for the major parties is organised into regions, constituencies and wards).

Key questions arise over the inter-relationship between these various parts of a modern political party.

The leadership

The leader of a major party normally has substantial prestige and authority, particularly when the leader is also prime minister. The leader of the Conservative Party has normally also been prime minister, and head of government, or has gone on to become prime minister. In the 20th century the only Conservative leaders never to hold the post of prime minister at some time were Austen Chamberlain and William Hague. Five Labour leaders have served as prime minister (MacDonald, Attlee, Wilson, Callaghan and Blair), although others have enjoyed the position and salary of leader of the Opposition. Leaders of the Liberal Party, and more recently the Liberal Democrats, have not commanded the same prestige, formal recognition and media coverage, although they normally exercise considerable authority over their own party and influence over party supporters and voters.

Photograph: Robert Leach.

IN FOCUS 8.1 Competing for power

The election manifestos of the main parties in 2001. In view of the importance attached to leadership in modern party competition it may be considered significant that while both Labour and the Liberal Democrats featured their leaders prominently on the front page for this election, the Conservatives did not (a reversal of previous practice). In theory, these rival party programmes should be a key element in the contest to win votes. In practice, few voters read them, an indication perhaps of falling interest in party politics, although they may be influenced by the (often highly selective) interpretation of the media.

Because the position of party leader has become so important (both in itself and because major party leaders are also, actually or potentially, prime ministers) the way in which these leaders are chosen or elected is of considerable importance. The selection or election of leaders has always been controversial, and the major parties have all changed their rules, in some cases several times.

In the 19th century the leaders of parties were not formally elected. Constitutionally it was the monarch who asked a member of Parliament (from either the Commons or the Lords) to form a

BOX 8.3

The authority of Labour and Conservative leaders compared

Labour leaders have appeared weaker in theory than their Conservative counterparts – because they have less often also been prime minister.

- They are bound by Conference decisions according to the Labour Party constitution.
- They are constrained by the National Executive Committee (NEC) between conferences, and have not always enjoyed a majority on the NEC.
- They do not control the appointment of their own deputy who is separately elected.
- They can not even choose their own shadow cabinet in opposition, which is formed from a Parliamentary committee elected by a vote of the Parliamentary Labour Party.
- They do not fully control the party bureaucracy.

However, in practice Labour leaders have generally enjoyed considerable power over their parties – at times ignoring conference decisions. When Labour leaders have also been prime minister they have enjoyed all the considerable constitutional powers associated with that office and have had as much authority as their Conservative counterparts. Historically it has proved more difficult to challenge a Labour than a Conservative leader.

government and serve as prime minister. However, the monarch had only a small and diminishing discretion in the choice of prime minister, and was constrained to send for at least a prominent figure and normally the acknowledged leader of a party (or combination of parties) that could command a majority in the House of Commons. Thus such was Gladstone's ascendancy over the Liberal Party that Queen Victoria felt bound to send for him four times to become Prime Minister, although she increasingly detested him. Leaders of opposition parties were not formally elected or officially recognised, although often a politician was sufficiently prominent (perhaps as a former prime minister) to be the acknowledged party leader.

For most of the 20th century the MPs who constituted the Parliamentary Labour Party elected their own leader and (subsequently) a deputy leader also. Where there were more than two candidates a series of ballots was held, with the bottom candidate dropping out, until one candidate emerged with an overall majority. Some of these elections were very closely contested. Thus when Harold Wilson resigned as Prime Minister in 1976 there were six candidates to succeed him, and James Callaghan eventually emerged as leader in the third ballot after Michael Foot had led on the first ballot.

The Conservative Party did not have a formal system for electing its leader until 1965. In the early 20th century when the party was in opposition there were separate leaders in the Commons and the Lords and there was no single officially recognised leader of the Conservative and Unionist Party. More normally the party was in government, and when a prime minister resigned other than because of an election defeat, a new prime minister was sent for by the monarch, normally after consultation with a few leading Conservatives. This informal system operated without significant difficulties until Harold Macmillan suddenly announced his resignation as Prime Minister on the eve of the Conservative Party Conference. The resulting frantic competition for support by candidates for the succession and a highly flawed process of consultation led eventually to the emergence of Sir Alec Douglas-Home as Prime Minister and Leader – and the refusal of two prominent Conservatives to serve in his government in protest against his appointment. This shambles reflected badly on the party, which in opposition moved to a system of formal election by MPs, as in the Labour Party, although with rather different rules.

This system was first used when Edward Heath was elected as Leader in 1965. In 1975 Heath was challenged by Margaret Thatcher, who surprisingly emerged as the leading candidate but without a sufficient majority on the first ballot. For the second ballot Heath withdrew and other candidates entered the contest, but Thatcher won an overall majority of the votes cast, so no third ballot was necessary.

BOX 8.4

How the Conservative Party elected its leader, 1965–98

First ballot: Winner needed an overall majority of Conservative MPs plus a 15 per cent lead over the nearest rival. If not achieved by any candidate, the contest went to a second ballot.

Second ballot: New candidates could now stand. Original candidates could continue or withdraw. The winner required an overall majority. If this was not achieved, candidates were allowed 24 hours to withdraw, and if a third ballot was required only the top two names went forward.

Third ballot: In the event of a tie, a fourth ballot was to be held unless the candidates could 'resolve the matter between themselves'.

Margaret Thatcher's was the first formal challenge to a sitting Conservative leader, and it was to be followed by others. She in turn was challenged in 1989 by a little known 'stalking horse' candidate (Sir Anthony Meyer), and then more seriously in 1990 by Michael Heseltine, who had dramatically resigned from her Cabinet over the Westland affair in 1986. Although Thatcher won more votes than Heseltine in the first ballot, she narrowly failed to secure the simple majority plus 15 per cent votes required in the party rules and was persuaded to stand down in the second ballot, when John Major and Douglas Hurd entered the contest, leading to a decisive victory for Major. Major was subsequently obliged to submit himself to re-election after he formally resigned the leadership, challenging his critics to 'put up or shut up'. John Redwood took up the challenge, and, although he lost, secured enough votes (89) and abstentions (20) to further damage Major's weakening position.

The last time this system was used was in 1997, after Major resigned as Leader following the Conservative defeat at the general election. Five candidates contested the first ballot, in which none came close to a majority. The two lowest placed candidates withdrew for the second ballot, in which Kenneth Clarke retained a narrow lead over William Hague, with John Redwood a distant third. With Redwood eliminated, William Hague secured a clear victory with 92 votes against Clarke's 70.

By this time the other parties had moved to a system of election involving the wider party membership. The Liberal Party was the first to broaden its election process. In 1975 David Steel was elected in a postal vote of Liberal Party members voting in constituency associations. The short-lived Social Democratic Party (SDP) began in 1980 with a collective leadership, but then moved to a postal ballot of individual members in which Roy Jenkins defeated David Owen to become leader in 1982. (David Owen succeeded unchallenged after Jenkins resigned in 1983.) When the Liberals and the SDP merged to form (ultimately) the Liberal Democrats, Paddy Ashdown was elected as Leader in a postal ballot of members in 1988. Following Ashdown's resignation as Leader in 1999, Charles Kennedy defeated Simon Hughes in a similar election.

Michael Foot was the last Labour Leader to be elected by the Parliamentary Labour Party in 1980. Following considerable pressure for more internal party democracy, a new system of choosing the Labour Leader was adopted after a special conference held at Wembley in 1981. One problem for Labour was that the party remained a federal body, with affiliated organisations (mainly trade unions) whose own members were thus affiliated members of the Labour Party. There were also individual members attached to Parliamentary constituencies. The rather clumsy solution was an electoral college in which originally trade unions had 40 per cent of the votes, constituency parties 30 per cent and the Parliamentary Labour Party 30 per cent. The system was first used in a contest for the deputy leadership in September 1981, when Denis Healey very narrowly defeated Tony Benn. It was subsequently used when Neil Kinnock and Roy Hattersley were elected Leader and Deputy Leader in 1983, and again in 1988, when they were unsuccessfully challenged. Using the same system, John Smith and Margaret Beckett were elected Leader and Deputy Leader in 1992.

After the 1993 Labour Party Conference the system of election was further modified. The proportions in the electoral college were adjusted, to give one-third of the votes to each of the constituent elements (Parliamentary Labour Party, constituency associations, unions). More significantly, unions and constituency parties were obliged to ballot members

Table 8.2 Labour leadership election 1994 (first and only ballot)

	Trade unions %	Con-stituen-cies %	MPs %	Total %
Tony Blair	52.3	58.2	60.5	57.0
John Prescott	28.4	24.4	19.6	24.1
Margaret Beckett	19.3	17.4	19.9	18.9

individually and divide their votes accordingly, thus meeting the demand for 'one member, one vote'. Using this modified system Tony Blair and John Prescott achieved a clear majority in the 1994 elections for Leader and Deputy Leader in each category as well as overall.

Thus the Conservative Party, which had been slow to introduce a formal system of electing its leader by MPs in 1965, became the only major party restricting its choice of leader to MPs alone after 1981. As part of a process of party reform aimed at giving more power and influence to ordinary members, William Hague introduced a new method of election which gave them the final decision on the leadership. Under the system then introduced, party members vote for two leading candidates chosen by the Parliamentary Party after a series of ballots. This method was put into practice for the first time after Hague resigned following the 2001 general election. Conservative MPs voted on five candidates in the first ballot, reduced to three in the second ballot after the bottom two

candidates, who had tied, dropped out. In that final ballot of Conservative MPs Kenneth Clarke led, with Iain Duncan Smith second and Michael Portillo in third place, and eliminated from the final election by party members, which was won convincingly by Iain Duncan Smith.

Clearly the method of election makes a difference. Duncan Smith would almost certainly not have won had the old method of electing party leaders still been in force – he was not the first choice of MPs, and it seems unlikely that enough Portillo supporters would have backed him a in a final ballot of MPs to beat Clarke. Ironically, had the election of leaders been thrown open to party members earlier, Clarke might well have won in 1997, and Thatcher (who was still very popular with ordinary party members) would almost certainly have retained the leadership in 1990. Yet there may be problems in giving party members the final say. As active party members may be atypical of ordinary voters, they may prefer a candidate with less broad electoral appeal. Opinion polls suggested that Clarke was the preferred choice of voters in 2001, and perhaps a better electoral prospect for the Conservatives.

Another interesting point is that whereas the Labour leader is in theory subject to annual re-election, in practice there has only been one (unsuccessful) challenge to a sitting Labour leader under the electoral college system in the last 20 years, while since 1975 there have been four challenges (two successful) to sitting Conservative leaders, despite the apparently greater deference to the authority of the leadership in that party, for which it

Table 8.3 How the parties choose their leaders

Conservatives	Labour	Liberal Democrats
A leadership contest can be triggered by a vacancy caused by death or resignation, or a successful no-confidence motion among Conservative MPs. Candidates face a series of ballots by Conservative MPs, with the bottom candidate eliminated after each round. Party members choose by ballot between the two leading candidates chosen by MPs.	When a sitting leader or deputy leader is challenged, or a vacancy is created by death or resignation, the choice is made through an electoral college: • a third of the votes are by Labour MPs • a third by the affiliated trade unions • a third by individual party members.	Leader is chosen by a ballot of all members.

was once claimed that loyalty was its secret weapon. A possible explanation is that the expensive and cumbersome complexity of Labour's electoral college systems deters challenges, and the new method of choosing the Conservative leader may prove to have a similar effect. However, the Conservatives, who are (or were) more accustomed to electoral success, may therefore be more ruthless in rejecting failed or failing leaders.

It also should not be forgotten that while most of the media attention is focused on the individual who is party leader, he or she is normally surrounded by other politicians with their own positions, power bases and popularity within the party, who together constitute a more collective leadership. The leader has to try to satisfy the political ambitions of those who may be real or potential rivals, but also needs to draw on their talents so as to present a credible and effective leadership of actual or potential ministers, and convince the voters of their collective competence. Within the leadership group, some politicians may come to seem indispensable, as Whitelaw was to Thatcher and Heseltine became to Major. Both these were disappointed candidates for the leadership who gave full loyalty to the victors. In Blair's government, Gordon Brown, who was reluctantly persuaded to forgo his own leadership hopes in 1994, evidently retained ambitions to lead the party in which he remained a hugely important figure, with real power in his own right.

Parliamentary parties

While most of the media and public attention is focused on the party leadership (both individual and collective), it should not be forgotten that parties began in Britain in Parliament, and these Parliamentary parties flourished long before any formal party leadership roles were acknowledged. Although it is sometimes suggested that modern Parliamentary parties are mere lobby fodder, coerced to troop through the division lobbies at the behest of their powerful leaders, they still retain a crucial role at the very centre of the modern party system. The most gifted politicians are powerless without a significant Parliamentary party behind them. Lloyd George, perhaps the ablest orator and administrator in 20th century British politics, was effectively forced out of office in 1922, at the height of his powers, never to return, because he did not have a united Parliamentary party with a majority behind him. His position depended on the support of the Conservatives, a party not his own, and this was withdrawn once Conservative backbenchers voted to fight the election as a separate party, against the advice of most of their leaders, who wanted to maintain the Lloyd George coalition. The power of ordinary Conservative backbenchers, revealed then, was subsequently formally recognised with the establishment of the 1922 Committee, which consists of backbenchers when the party is in government, and whose elected officers remain figures of real status and influence within the party. It is the 1922 Committee that acts as the sounding board for ordinary Conservative MPs, alerts the leadership to the concerns of the backbenchers, and organises leadership elections.

The Parliamentary Labour Party (PLP) continues to form a similar function within the Labour Party. When the Labour Party is in opposition the PLP elects a Parliamentary Committee, which becomes in effect the shadow cabinet. The leader is obliged to offer shadow posts to all those elected, although others who are not elected may be given a front bench role as well. When the Labour Party is in government, the leader chooses his or her own Cabinet (although he or she is normally constrained initially to offer Cabinet posts to former elected shadow cabinet members), and the PLP chooses a small Parliamentary Liaison Committee to provide a link between the Parliamentary party and the government.

Both the Labour and Conservative parties have their own system of specialist party committees covering a range of government functions, and these allow MPs to use and develop specialist interests and expertise. These party committees provide an additional channel of influence as well as a pool of more experienced MPs who may become members of key all-party Parliamentary select committees, or gain reputations that may earn them a government post when the party is in office.

Party cohesion and discipline is promoted by the party whips, who play a key role in the modern Parliamentary party, although the name and post date back to the 18th century. Today both major parties have a whip's office, led by a chief whip assisted by junior whips. Today they may use a combination of threats, bribes and cajolery to keep members of their party in line. An MP who dissents may risk losing some valued perks of the job – for example trips abroad on Parliamentary delegations. More seriously, a disaffected MP may be warned that he or she risks losing the prospect of promotion or a title, or membership of a prestigious Parliamentary committee. In more extreme circumstances, the whips may threaten to communicate their displeasure to an MP's constituency association (which could lead to his or her deselection as party candidate at the next election), or to withdraw the party whip, so that the MP is no longer considered a member of the Parliamentary party.

Yet such weapons are not always effective, particularly against MPs who have no further political ambitions or no realistic expectations of promotion. Even the withdrawal of the whip may not prove too damaging to an MP who retains the support of his or her constituency party. In 1994 the whip was withdrawn from eight Euro-sceptic Conservative MPs who had consistently refrained from voting with the party on European issues (they were joined by one sympathiser who voluntarily resigned the whip). These 'whipless nine' continued to constitute a separate Parliamentary grouping until the whip was restored without promises of future good behaviour a year later. Indeed former rebels in both major parties have sometimes gone on to become leaders or senior figures. Examples include Winston Churchill and Harold Macmillan and a Maastricht Euro-sceptic rebel (but not one of the 'whipless nine') Iain Duncan Smith among Conservatives, and Stafford Cripps, Nye Bevan and Michael Foot on the Labour side.

Altogether the power of the party whips should not be exaggerated. Indeed much of party discipline is self-discipline, as the futures of individual MPs and the party are closely bound up together. Party splits are perceived as damaging to a party's electoral prospects and hence to the prospects for re-election of individual MPs, who normally owe their position almost completely to party endorsement. Whips will use such arguments to help persuade MPs to support the party despite any reservations they may feel on a particular issue, but

normally such persuasion is superfluous as MPs are already well aware of the dangers of apparent division. Party splits spelt disaster for Labour in 1983 and for the Conservatives in 1997 and 2001. Thus MPs may often reluctantly toe the party line to prevent the appearance of damaging media stories of splits. However, some argue that the degree of party discipline evident in the post-war years has broken down or at least weakened of late, culminating in the record rebellion of 139 Labour MPs against Blair's Iraq policy on 18 March 2003. It is sometimes suggested that large majorities can be bad for party discipline; there is no fear of a government defeat, while it is more difficult to satisfy the political ambitions of increased numbers of MPs, who may consequently become more restive. Yet despite their substantial majorities, Thatcher and more recently Blair – at least until the Iraq crisis – dominated their Parliamentary parties. By contrast Major's small majority after 1992 did not seem to encourage party discipline and unity – quite the reverse.

Yet the power of ordinary backbench MPs is not to be measured by the size and frequency of rebellions. Much of their influence springs from the leaders and whips anticipating what the backbenchers will not stand for, and altering course accordingly. A celebrated example was when Wilson's Labour government backed down from its proposed trade union reforms after the chief whip informed the Cabinet that he could not get the reforms through the Parliamentary party. Similarly, Jim Callaghan swallowed his own reservations on introducing child benefit following backbench pressure, while Blair was persuaded to honour the commitment to legislate on the 'right to roam', providing access to the countryside for walkers, after inclining to a voluntary agreement with landowners. While most MPs want their party to succeed and want to remain loyal, they all have a 'bottom line', issues of principle on which they are not prepared to budge, as the party whips well realise. Indeed the whips' job is not just to persuade or coerce recalcitrant backbenchers, but often, more importantly, to convey backbench feeling to the party leaders, and warn them against proceeding (or sometimes failing to proceed) with policies or decisions in the teeth of substantial opposition from their own MPs.

Party conferences and the national organisation of the parties

Each party holds an annual conference for a week in the autumn, and these have been regarded as important events in the political calendar. In theory there is a massive difference between the role of the Labour Party Conference as the party's own 'parliament', supreme over party policy, and that of the conference in the Conservative Party with no constitutional power. Indeed one past Conservative Prime Minister, Balfour, said he would rather take advice from his valet than the party conference. In practice there was rather less difference than the contrasting constitutional position suggested (McKenzie, 1955). Labour leaders could, and effectively did, disregard conference decisions they opposed, while the Conservative leadership was sometimes influenced by strong expressions of conference opinion. One famous instance was when the Conservative leadership was bounced into a commitment to build 300,000 houses a year in 1951; another, rather more damaging to the party, was when the enthusiasm of the conference for the poll tax persuaded the government not to phase it in gradually (which had been the original intention) but to substitute it fully and immediately for the old domestic rates, a decision that proved disastrous for government and party.

Yet if the Labour Conference was never as powerful as the party constitution suggests, and the Conservative Conference more influential than its formal lack of power implied, there were still considerable differences in the way in which the conferences were conducted. Indeed, at one time Labour Party Conferences involved furious rows and party splits. The party leadership lacked effective control of proceedings. It did not control the agenda, or who could speak (even leading Cabinet ministers had no right to speak). One celebrated example was in 1960 when the leader Hugh Gaitskell defiantly declared he would 'fight and fight and fight again' to reverse a Labour Conference decision in favour of unilateral nuclear disarmament, to the jeers of the audience. Another came in 1985, when Neil Kinnock denounced Labour's (Militant-dominated) Liverpool Council to a mixture of cheers and boos. All this made for dramatic television, but also

reflected badly on a divided party. By contrast, Conservative annual conferences were generally carefully stage-managed and docile. Contentious motions and issues were kept off the conference agenda. Essentially they were viewed as rallies of the party faithful, rewarding loyal members with an opportunity to meet their leaders in a friendly social setting, and more importantly, allowing leading politicians to display some effective platform oratory and secure abundant valuable free publicity for the party.

More recently there has been some reversal of party roles. Labour Conferences have become more stage-managed and docile, while Conservative Conferences have sometimes involved serious embarrassment for the party leadership. Thus Anne Widdecombe (then shadowing the Home Office) secured a rapturous reception from the party faithful for her hard line on drugs at the 2000 conference, while alarming her own shadow cabinet colleagues who publicly distanced themselves from her views, leading to the kind of damaging media stories of party splits once more common in the Labour Party.

Altogether conferences in both major parties now seem to be more about public relations than policy. This is also true of the Liberal Democrats, who have problems in securing publicity, and for whom the annual conference is a substantial opportunity to get their politicians and policies across to the public. A successful conference for any party can result in a significant (if often only temporary) boost in its poll ratings. Yet television no longer provides saturation coverage of the autumn conference season, which no longer commands the same attention.

As political parties grew and acquired mass memberships they required more complex organisational structures to manage the relationship between the Parliamentary leadership and the extra-Parliamentary party, operating at various levels in the country. Major parties now require substantial permanent bureaucracies to meet their needs. This has meant employing increasing numbers of paid staff – particularly at the centre, but also in the regions and in constituencies – as well as using large numbers of unpaid voluntary party activists. Professional expertise is required for a range of purposes: raising money and controlling spending, marketing and advertising, policy-oriented research, legal advice, party management and administration. All major parties retain paid permanent agents in marginal constituencies, and these play a crucial role in maintaining the party organisation at constituency level, and maximising the party's vote at election times.

At national level the Conservatives' headquarters have long been at Conservative Central Office, founded in 1870. The party's chair is directly appointed by the leader, and Central Office has been described as 'the personal machine of the leader'. Its main tasks are money-raising, the organisation of election campaigns, assistance with the selection of candidates, research and political education. While Central Office has enjoyed substantial power and prestige in the past, it has become increasingly subject to criticism following poor election results and other evidence of the party's decline. Some party activists (e.g. in the Charter movement) would like to see Central Office become more accountable and subject to democratic control. Pressure for reform and more internal democracy in the party following the landslide defeat in 1997 led William Hague to introduce a range of changes (the Fresh Future).

The organisation of the Labour Party nationally has been subject to extensive change in recent years. Labour headquarters were long located at Transport House, in part of the central offices of the Transport and General Workers' Union, symbolising the close links of Labour with the trade unions. The party's organisation was not always efficient. Back in 1955, Harold Wilson famously described the Labour Party machine as a rusty penny-farthing bicycle in the era of the jet plane, in one of a series of critical reports (Pimlott, 1992: 194). In 1980 the party moved to its own modest headquarters in Walworth Road (subsequently renamed John Smith House after the death of the leader in 1994), but the criticisms of inefficient organisation persisted, until a substantial reorganisation started under Kinnock's leadership (Minkin, 1992, ch. 19). From 1995 key staff moved to the new campaign and media centre at Millbank Tower, which came to symbolise New Labour's slick public relations and 'spin doctoring.' Both the expense and the (increasingly unfavourable) image of Millbank led in 2002 to another move, to more modest but central premises in the heart of Westminster at Old Queen Street.

Labour leaders in the past have not had the control over party organisation enjoyed by Conservative leaders. This was partly because the party's official governing body (in between conferences) is not the Cabinet or shadow cabinet or even the Parliamentary Labour Party, but the National Executive Committee (NEC), which in the past was dominated by the trade unions, and, to a lesser degree, largely left-wingers chosen by constituency associations. Particularly in the 1970s and early 1980s there was often an NEC majority hostile to the party leadership. As the NEC had to approve the party manifesto and controlled key appointments in the Labour Party, including the post of general secretary, there was often division at the top.

In 1997 there was a significant reorganisation of the party's central machinery. The membership of the NEC was overhauled. The unions retained 12 seats, but on an NEC increased from 29 to 32 members. Party members could vote for six constituency party members, who could no longer be MPs (MPs and government ministers are represented separately). Separate women's representatives were abolished and instead there were new rules requiring a minimum number of women in different categories of NEC members.

There have been other important shifts in power within Labour's organisation. While Conference remains officially 'the supreme policy making body', the key institutions in reality are now the Joint Policy Committee, chaired by the prime minister and composed of equal numbers of the NEC and government, and a body that this body directs, an expanded National Policy Forum, with representatives from all members of the party, which reviews all party policy on a two-year rolling programme. Another important change was the appointment by the Prime Minister in 2001 of a Cabinet minister, Charles Clarke, as Party Chair (succeeded by John Reid in 2002). This brings Labour closer in line with past practice in the Conservative Party, where Cabinet and party heavy-weights were often appointed as high-profile party chairs (past Conservative Party Chairs have included Cecil Parkinson, Norman Tebbitt, Chris Patten and Brian Mawhinney).

Table 8.4 The new National Executive Committee of the Labour Party

No.	Who?	How selected?	Women?
3	Leader, deputy leader, treasurer	Ex officio; treasurer elected by Party Conference	
12	Trade union members	Elected at Annual Conference	at least 6 women
6	Constituency Party members	Elected by all members Cannot be MPs	at least 3 women
3	Government ministers	Chosen by Cabinet	
3	MPs/MEPs	Elected at Annual Conference	at least 1 woman
2	Labour councillors	Elected from Association of Labour Councillors	at least 1 woman
1	Young Labour representative	Elected at youth conference	
1	Representative of socialist societies	Elected at Annual Conference	
1	Leader of the European Parliamentary Labour Party	Elected by Labour MEPs	

Source: adapted from official Labour Party material.

Whereas the Labour Party national organisation in the past often appeared divided and shambolic, while the Conservative organisation seemed ruthlessly united and efficient, the image of the two parties has almost reversed, with the Conservative organisation becoming subject to growing criticism, and the party seeking to imitate aspects of Labour's successful electoral machine. Yet Labour has paid a price for its new-found organisational unity and efficiency. The Labour leadership is accused of acting like 'control freaks', seeking to manipulate all key roles in the party (as in the efforts to exclude Livingstone as Labour candidate for London mayor). Perhaps more damagingly, the party's slick public relations has become identified increasingly with manipulation and 'spin'.

The party membership and constituency parties

Organisation counts for little if there are few members to organise. Membership of all parties has declined since the war. Estimates suggest that Conservative Party membership is down from a million and a half in 1979, to 750,000 in 1987, to around 300,000 in 2001. The decline is particularly marked at the younger end. Once there was a thriving Young Conservative membership. Now the average age of members is 67. Comparisons with Labour are complicated by the question of affiliated organisations in the Labour Party. However, affiliated membership has declined with trade union membership from the 1980s onwards. After a long decline in the post-war era, individual membership rose slightly to 420,000 in the period leading up to the 1997 election. Since then numbers have fallen below 270,000 as some of these new members failed to renew their subscriptions. The Liberal Democrats have fewer than 100,000 members.

The problem is perhaps worse than the bald (but still probably inflated) membership figures suggest. All parties depend on extensive voluntary work from members, in maintaining constituency and ward-level party organisation, raising money, campaigning and fighting elections. Yet only a relatively small proportion of the members are active, while many do nothing beyond paying their annual subscription by banker's order. Local political meetings are commonly too poorly attended to be worth the time and expense of organising, and social events are not well supported. Increasingly members are involved with the party, if at all, in postal ballots, and the party leadership communicates with them directly. Some constituency parties are effectively run by a handful of members. Indeed, it may be questioned whether parties are in any sense still 'mass parties'.

Ironically, all major parties have been seeking (ostensibly at least) to give more power and influence to ordinary members. Party members have always had one very significant power – to choose party candidates for local and general elections. Although in certain circumstances the national party may seek to influence the choice of Parliamentary candidate, and exceptionally may block the selection of a particular candidate, in general it is the members voting at constituency level who choose. Moreover, particularly in the Labour Party, members have sometimes exercised powers to deselect sitting MPs with whom they have become dissatisfied. Beyond that, as we have seen (above), all major parties over the last 30 years or so have sought to involve party members in the choice of the party leader, and have made some show of involving them more in the policy making process.

Internal party democracy may not necessarily help a party to win elections, however, and can be positively detrimental, particularly as active members become fewer and less representative of potential party voters. Most people who vote for a party are not party members. The major parties have around 30 or more voters at general elections for every individual party member. Joining a political party has become very much a minority hobby. Active party members almost by definition are unusual creatures with views and preferences that may be similarly atypical. Thus the problem for parties is that they serve two very different political 'markets'. Pleasing the active membership may not involve policies that appeal to ordinary voters. Labour Party members in the 1980s wanted left-wing policies (including more nationalisation and unilateral nuclear disarmament) which the electorate rejected. Today, Labour's constituency activists and candidates are increasingly middle class professionals, out of touch with some of their traditional core working class voters in northern urban housing estates.

The problem for the Conservatives may be worse. Both William Hague and Iain Duncan Smith have argued for a broader, more inclusive party. However, its existing dwindling membership is elderly, overwhelmingly white and middle class, and although a good proportion of activists are female, many hold traditional views on gender relations. While the leadership would welcome more women and ethnic minority candidates, that seems unlikely to happen while unrepresentative constituency parties control the selection process. Moreover, the policies that appeal to them (such as zero tolerance on drugs, a hard line on asylum seekers, and support for 'family values') alienate some of the new target voters the party is trying to attract, including ethnic minorities, unconventional families, gays, and young people generally.

All main parties seem to have a problem recruiting and keeping younger members. Recent research suggests that Liberal Democrat activists are predominantly male, middle class with an average age in the late 50s. Perhaps the real problem is that older forms of political activity no longer appeal. Increasingly the parties are pursuing other methods of communicating with their members through postal surveys and interactive websites. Yet it seems most unlikely that the long-term decline in active party membership will be reversed.

Power within the parties – the modern party and its membership

Political parties remain crucial to the functioning of Parliamentary democracy. From the late 19th century onwards, mass political parties appeared increasingly important as a means of participation by ordinary citizens in the political process, and potentially as a bridge between the political mass and the political elite, particularly as they became more open and inclusive. More internal democracy within parties made sense at a number of levels. It was compatible with democratic assumptions within the political system generally. It gave ordinary members some return in terms of influence for the money and voluntary labour they supplied. It gave leaders a wider source of ideas, interests and policies that would help make the party more in touch with the electorate's concerns.

As long ago as 1911 Robert Michels argued that power in political parties (including even those that strongly proclaim their attachment to democracy) naturally gravitates to the Parliamentary leadership and permanent bureaucracy. There are many who would agree that the 'grass roots' or 'rank and file' are marginalised in modern parties, although, as we have seen, British parties have ostensibly decentralised power to their members. This may be because large organisations are inevitably oligarchies (the argument of Michels), or because British parties operate within a centralised political system, or because of media focus on leading personalities, or perhaps because leaders betray (or more subtly manipulate) their followers.

The last argument has been most commonly heard within the Labour Party. 'Betrayal' has been a familiar theme since Ramsay MacDonald ignored his own party and formed a National Government with the Conservatives in 1931. Much of the argument over organisational reforms in the 1980s barely concealed a battle for power between the 'moderate' Parliamentary leadership and a left-wing active membership. Giving power to the members was interpreted to mean giving power to activists who turned up to meetings, rather than those whose involvement was largely confined to paying their subscription. However, subsequent reforms since 1987 and more particularly under Blair have been interpreted (Webb, in Dunleavy *et al.*, 2002: 158) as 'motivated by the desire to enhance the autonomy of the leadership (at the expense of backbenchers and grassroots activists)'. In particular, critics point to the development of 'plebiscitary democracy' within the party which bypasses party activists and 'empowers' the 'ordinary members' who are perceived as 'more docile and more likely to endorse the policies (and candidates) proposed by the party leadership' (Mair, in Katz and Mair, 1994). Those voting by post will be influenced by the (business dominated) mass media rather than the debate within the party. While there is something in the argument, the problem is that members (let alone activists) constitute only a tiny minority of actual and potential voters. Because many constituency parties are now effectively run by a handful of activists there is even the danger (illustrated by the success of the Militant Tendency in the early 1980s) that a small unrepresentative group opposed to some of the party's core principles could take over locally and even perhaps nationally.

Yet modern political parties still rest on the assumption of an active mass membership. Parties continue to need members for all sorts of reasons – cynically for money and unpaid labour, but also for their genuine enthusiasm and commitment, and as an important source of ideas and opinions – hence the increasingly desperate drives to recruit new members and widen the increasingly narrow base of all parties. One reason that there has been an attempt to give an enhanced role to ordinary members in all the major British parties over recent years is because this was assumed to increase the attractiveness of party membership. Yet it may be questioned whether more grass roots power would or could attract people to join political parties in sufficient numbers to re-establish them as genuine 'mass parties'.

One pessimistic answer is that people are not interested in more participation in politics, full stop. There are more interesting and diverting ways for people to spend their leisure time in a modern consumer society. Another possible answer is that in so far as people have the energy and inclination to participate in politics, it is increasingly in single-issue pressure groups rather than political parties. Parties, involving coalitions of interests, inevitably require compromises, and the modification of ideals to meet practical realities. Those whose ideals motivate them to become involved in politics may be turned off by the messy and sometimes grubby processes of accommodation within mainstream parties. For them, political parties are part of the problem rather than the solution, contributing to the alienation of ordinary people from the political process rather than offering an opportunity for involvement.

Whatever the explanation, the UK political system depends to a degree on competition between mass political parties, which hardly any longer exist. It is not a problem confined to the UK, as a decline in party membership seems to be an almost universal problem in modern western democracies, affecting parties across the political spectrum, from communist and socialist parties on the left to Christian democrat parties on the right. Increased electoral volatility and the decline of old established parties has led to a new instability in politics in some countries, involving the appearance of fresh party formations with different agendas – Greens, separatists, and even racist and neo-fascist groups. British party politics has as yet been less affected, although there have been some straws in the wind – the growing support for nationalists in Scotland and Wales, for Green candidates, for assorted independents, and even for the BNP. If alienation from the established parties increases, there is the potential for a similar drastic reordering of the shape of the UK party system as has happened in countries such as Italy, France and the Netherlands.

The finance of political parties

The financing of political parties has become such an important and controversial issue that it requires a separate section. Parties need money for many purposes, for example, servicing their permanent organisation, paying administrators and agents, commissioning policy research, financing elections, political advertising and market research. There are three main possible sources of finance: subscriptions from ordinary members, donations from organisations and individuals, and state funding.

Ideally perhaps, money should be found by party members, through ordinary party subscriptions, but it is virtually impossible for a dwindling membership to provide the funds required. Much higher membership fees would deter potential recruits at a time when all parties are desperately seeking to encourage a larger and wider membership. Many 'unwaged' members (e.g. the large number who are retired) do not pay the full membership rates.

Thus additional sources of finance are solicited, from individual donors, from business organisations, trade unions, and other friendly bodies. Yet this can cause problems for parties, as has been only too evident in recent years. How far are contributors to party finances effectively buying influence or status? There is a long history of allegations of the award of honours in return for donations to political parties. Lloyd George, the Liberal Prime Minister, sold honours almost openly. More recently there have been charges that knighthoods and peerages have been given by Conservative governments to individual donors and directors of companies that have made donations to the Conservative Party.

More damaging are allegations of influence on policy. The Conservative Party received contributions from particular sectors of business, such as brewers, tobacco companies and construction companies, and there were suggestions they were particularly open to influence in these areas as a result. Particularly controversial were contributions from wealthy foreign businessmen (whose business methods sometimes appeared questionable). A particular problem was that most large donations to the Conservatives were until Hague's leadership secret – so there were allegations of hidden influence. Labour had long openly depended financially on contributions from trade unions, and Conservatives countered allegations of business influence on their own party with arguments that Labour was effectively run by the unions. More recently Labour has courted business, and Blair's Labour government was embarrassed by a large donation from Bernie Ecclestone, the Formula One boss, in 1997. The exemption of F1 events from bans on tobacco advertising was thought to reflect influence. The problems surrounding party donations were among the issues considered by the Neill Committee, which reported on the subject in 1998 (see Box 8.5).

Labour hoped that more transparency would end allegations of sleaze. Instead, the publication of donations has made it easier for journalists to allege some connection between gifts and a possible impact on policy. Publicity given to some donors has also sometimes upset party members. Thus in 2002 the revelation that the new owner of the Express group of newspapers had given the Labour Party £120,000 aroused anger from party members (including some ministers) that the party had accepted money from an individual who also owned a number of pornographic publications.

Such scandals have led to renewed interest in another possible source of party funding – state funding, ultimately out of taxation. Some countries already use such state funding. In fact, in the UK there is already some limited state financial help for opposition parties to fund policy research. While the government of the day can rely largely on the work of the regular civil service, paid special advisers and appointed commissions and committees of enquiry, opposition parties formerly had to rely largely on their own party resources and sympathetic independent research bodies. Either way, research costs money. The consequences of underfinanced and possibly ill-thought out research in opposition may be manifesto commitments which

Recommendations of the Neill Committee on party funding, 1998

- Public disclosure of donations to parties of more than £5000 (or more than £1000 to parties locally).
- A £20 million cap on parties' general election campaign spending.
- An end to blind trusts.
- A ban on foreign donations by non-citizens.
- A ban on anonymous donations to political parties of more than £50.
- Scrutiny of nominations for honours where nominees have donated more than £5000 to party within the last five years.
- An independent and impartial Election Commission to monitor the new regulations.
- More public money to finance political parties in Parliament (see below).

prove unworkable if the party exchanges opposition for government. This problem was addressed in 1975 by the then Labour government, which introduced payments to opposition parties to enable them to carry out their Parliamentary role more effectively.

More controversial is the notion of state funding for party election expenditure and party propaganda generally (which is already provided in some countries). Particularly with the current emphasis on image and marketing, it may be argued that the best-financed parties have a distinct advantage. In the past the Conservative Party regularly outspent the Labour Party, but these two far exceeded the financial resources of other parties. In 1997 Labour almost matched Conservative spending (£25.7 million to £28.3 million), while the Liberal Democrats spent just £2.3 million. In the 2001 general election, under the new rules administered by the Electoral Commission set up following legislation in 2000, the Conservatives spent £12,751,813, Labour £10,945,119, and the Liberal Democrats only £1,361,377, which was less than double the £693,274 of the tiny UK Independence Party (see Figure 8.1).

The future of the British party system

1997 already seems to mark a landmark election which has redrawn the British political map, in ways that were seemingly confirmed in 2001. A long period of Conservative Party dominance has given place to what could prove a similar or longer period of Labour dominance. The Conservative Party still appears in total disarray, seemingly unable to present a credible challenge. Of course, politics can change quickly as a result of unforeseeable events. The September 2000 fuel protest showed the volatility of public opinion and the potential vulnerability of the government in a crisis. The 'war against terror' could split party and government, resulting in an extensive party realignment, from which perhaps the Liberal Democrats could benefit.

A less dramatic but insidious threat to current Labour dominance could be provided by the ongoing devolution process. Labour in the past has depended on Scottish and Welsh seats to give it an overall majority (although Blair unusually won a majority of English seats). If devolution does ultimately lead to the break-up of the United Kingdom, this would damage severely Labour's longer-term prospects, not only because of the direct loss of Scottish and perhaps Welsh seats, but because of the intellectual impoverishment of the rump English Labour Party which in the past has been so much dependent on the inspiration and leadership of its Welsh and Scottish politicians. Yet even if devolution does not result in separation it

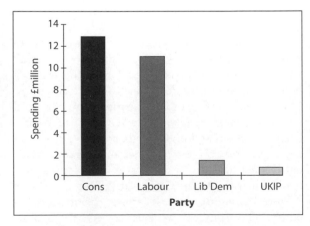

Figure 8.1 Spending by parties, 2001 general election

will lead directly to the loss of some seats in Scotland (as the result of the recommendations of the Scottish Boundary Commission). More seriously it has already weakened the cohesion and unity of the Labour Party in Britain, and provoked some serious rifts particularly between the UK leadership and the Welsh and London Labour parties (see Chapter 17). It seems more likely than not that differences between UK Labour, and Labour in devolved national and perhaps regional politics, will grow, if only because of the dictates of electoral self-preservation, as parties nationally and regionally try to distance themselves from UK policies that are perceived to be unpopular.

Devolution has been accompanied by electoral reform, which has also been introduced for elections to the European Parliament. The consequence has been increased representation for nationalist parties and smaller groups such as independent socialists, Greens and the UK Independence Party. Ironically, a major beneficiary of devolution and electoral reform has been the Conservative Party which strenuously opposed both, but has been rewarded by significant representation in 1999 in Edinburgh and Cardiff following its wipe out in the general election of 1997 in both Scotland and Wales (just one Scottish seat was won back in 2001). Electoral reform for elections to Westminster has been placed on the back burner since the report of the Jenkins Commission (see Chapter 6), but if it is ever reactivated it could transform the UK party system, as it has already transformed the Scottish and Welsh party system. Consequences could include the end of the traditional UK two-party system and the emergence of coalition government as the norm rather than the exception, as is already the case over much of the European continent. Within a more proportional electoral system and a multi-party system, smaller parties such as the Greens might find increased space to operate.

However, it is also possible that other minority parties, including extreme-right parties such as the British National Party (BNP), might gain a stronger role in a more fragmented party system.

Further reading

Useful and reasonably up-to-date books on British political parties include Garner and Kelly (1998) and Ingle (2000). The chapter by Baston in Seldon (2001) provides a review of the British party system in the light of Blair's first term, and several chapters in Dunleavy et al. (2002) touch on developments since 1997 and the second Labour landslide in 2001.

More specialist books include a dissection of Conservative Party members *True Blues* (1994) by Whiteley, Seyd and Richardson, Lewis Minkin's monumental study of the *Contentious Alliance* between the Unions and Labour (1992), and Eric Shaw's analysis of *The Labour Party since 1945* (1996). An extensive literature on Thatcherism and post-Thatcherism on the one hand and New Labour on the other has already been referred to in Chapter 4. Useful sources for updating include journals such as the *Political Quarterly*, *Politics Review* and *Talking Politics*. Party websites can also be consulted, including <www.conservative-party.org.uk>, <www.labour.org.uk> and <www.libdems.org.uk>.

For comparative analysis on parties see relevant chapters in books such as Hague and Harrop (2001). Lane and Ersson (1999) provide a sophisticated classification and analysis of European parties. This chapter has also included some reference to older literature that has influenced thinking on parties including Michels (1911, but with numerous editions since), Duverger (1954), McKenzie (1955 and subsequent editions), Downs (1957) and Beer (1982a and subsequent editions).

Chapter 9

Pressure groups

What are pressure groups?	**136**
Pressure groups and the political system:	
history and trends	**138**
New social movements	**141**
Pressure group targets	**144**
Pressure group influence	**148**
Pressure groups and democracy	**151**

Pressure groups are important institutions in modern democratic societies. They cover a broad spectrum, from the large business in high-level contacts at national government and European level to the smallest local group, and embrace an equally wide range of activities, from the secret, behind-the-scenes lobbying to highly visible protest. More people belong to pressure groups than to political parties. Study of the groups and their influence is therefore vital to an understanding of how the political system works. Starting with a definition and some leading examples of pressure groups, this chapter analyses their role in the political system and considers key recent trends in their activities, as well as the emergence of new social movements, before moving to a consideration of their targets for influence and the factors on which that influence depends. There follows a discussion of the debate on 'pressure groups and democracy' and the importance of authentic political representation through pressure group politics.

What are pressure groups?

Pressure groups, like parties, are informal political institutions that seek to influence the making and implementation of public policy. However, pressure groups are unlike parties in (at least) three important respects. First, they do not normally contest elections. Second, when they do stand for election, they do not do so with the aim of forming a government or part of a government (like the nationwide parties) or even of changing the constitution (like the nationalist parties) but to make a political point, by indicating the level of public concern on an issue (e.g. the environment) or by drawing support away from the government on a key issue, like Sir James Goldsmith's Referendum Party. Third, pressure groups typically have narrower concerns than parties. They generally contribute selectively to the political debate from a particular standpoint or in a specific field of concern; they do not adopt a comprehensive programme which seeks to cover the whole field of politics, as parties do.

Although they do not normally aim to exercise power directly or adopt an all-embracing perspective, pressure groups do share some characteristics with parties. In particular, they are agencies of *representation* and *participation*: they are mechanisms for the expression of people's interests and opinions and for popular involvement in politics. Also, even though they are not elected to it, they often play an important role in government, wielding influence through hundreds of regulatory and supervisory bodies which depend on the groups' cooperation to function at all. Finally, pressure groups can sometimes overlap with parties in important ways: for example, by providing funds, sponsoring candidates and enjoying a large amount of constitutionally sanctioned influence in shaping their policies: as, for example, the trade unions do in the Labour Party.

Types of pressure group

There are two main approaches to characterising pressure groups: the first describes groups in terms of what they represent, the second in terms of their strategies and relations with government. The first approach distinguishes two main types of pressure group: (1) sectional (or interest) groups; and (2) cause (or promotional) groups.

> *Definitions*
> **Sectional groups** are based on the performance of an economic function whereas **cause groups** are based on shared attitudes or values.

Sectional groups arise out of the performance of an economic function: they exist to further the interests of people as engaged in certain professions, trades and occupations – as, for example, teachers, shopkeepers, miners and company directors. Examples of sectional groups are the Confederation of British Industry, the Trades Union Congress, the British Medical Association, the Law Society and the National Union of Teachers.

Cause groups in contrast come into existence to promote some belief, attitude or principle. They are also referred to as attitude, ideological or preference groups. Examples are Greenpeace, the Child Poverty Action Group, Amnesty International, Shelter and Charter 88.

There are two main differences between the two types of group. First, whereas membership of a sectional group is limited to those with a shared background, membership of a cause group is open to all those sharing the same values. Second, whereas the purpose of the sectional group is to protect the interests of its own members, the aim of the cause group is generally to advance the public welfare as perceived by its members.

Although largely valid, the distinction between sectional and cause groups is not an absolute one. First, sectional groups may pursue causes: the British Medical Association, for example, as well as acting as a sectional professional interest on behalf of the terms and conditions of service of doctors, also campaigns on more general health issues such as drinking, smoking and the safety of boxing. Second, while in terms of their overall goals and motives many groups are clearly cause groups, such groups also often have material interests to defend. A charity such as Oxfam, for example, owns property, employs professional staff with careers to advance, and, although as a charity is precluded from engaging in overt political activity, needs to ensure that changes in the

tax law do not impede its fundraising activities. Finally, some groups are difficult to classify as either sectional or cause: protest groups, for instance, often have some features of each, local nimby (not in my backyard) groups being both altruistic and protective of an interest.

Despite these complications, the straightforward classification of groups into sectional and cause remains important, valuable and widely used. However, increasingly employed instead or in addition to this typology are the categories 'insider' and 'outsider', which Wyn Grant has developed (Grant, 2000: 19). The original typology is shown in Figure 9.1.

One important virtue of this typology is that it sets groups firmly within a relationship with government. It refers both to the strategy pursued by a group – whether or not it seeks acceptance by government – and to the status achieved or not achieved as a result of its efforts. This classification cuts across the sectional/cause distinction. Whilst it is probable that most insiders are sectional groups, it is also the case that not all sectional groups will be insiders. Also, cause groups can gain insider status: for example, Mencap and the Howard League for Penal Reform. The line between 'insider' and 'outsider' status is not an unchanging one, and in practice is often crossed. This is, first, because classic insider groups such as the British Medical Association do not hesitate to campaign publicly when occasion demands – that is, they adopt a combination of insider and outsider tactics. Second, groups move into and out of insider status: Grant cites the National Federation of Retirement Pensions Associations as a group that has lost insider status.

Finally, the distinction needs to be made between *primary groups* whose only reason for existence is political lobbying and *secondary groups* which are not primarily political. Exam-

> *Definitions*
> **Insider groups** are consulted on a regular basis by government, while **outsider groups** either do not want to become closely involved with government or are unable to gain government recognition.

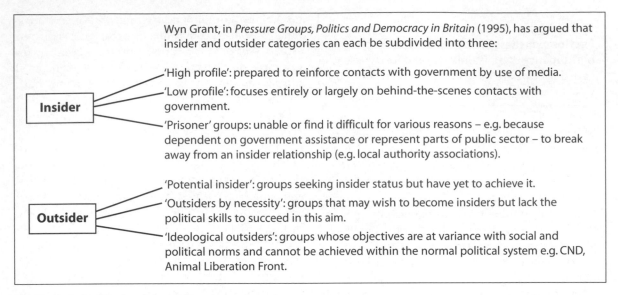

Wyn Grant, in *Pressure Groups, Politics and Democracy in Britain* (1995), has argued that insider and outsider categories can each be subdivided into three:

Insider

'High profile': prepared to reinforce contacts with government by use of media.

'Low profile': focuses entirely or largely on behind-the-scenes contacts with government.

'Prisoner' groups: unable or find it difficult for various reasons – e.g. because dependent on government assistance or represent parts of public sector – to break away from an insider relationship (e.g. local authority associations).

Outsider

'Potential insider': groups seeking insider status but have yet to achieve it.

'Outsiders by necessity': groups that may wish to become insiders but lack the political skills to succeed in this aim.

'Ideological outsiders': groups whose objectives are at variance with social and political norms and cannot be achieved within the normal political system e.g. CND, Animal Liberation Front.

Figure 9.1 Insider and outsider groups

ples of primary groups include professional lobbying companies, national cause groups such as Charter 88, specific issue groups such as Doctors for Tobacco Law (against television advertising), one-off national campaigns such as the Campaign to save Radio 4 Longwave, and local amenity and nimby groups. Secondary groups include the churches, the universities, trade unions, the motoring organisations and charities. Their main purposes are respectively religious, educational, economic, motoring and charitable, but they all from time to time make political representations on behalf of their members.

Pressure groups and the political system: history and trends

This section deals first with the analytical models that help us understand the role of pressure groups in politics and second, with the changes in politics that have helped to shape that role. Before 1939, although a large number of well-organised sectional groups already existed, it was relatively uncommon for groups to develop close relations with government. However, the wartime needs of the state, especially for higher production in industry and agriculture and for an emergency hospital service, made it dependent on group

cooperation, and close government–group relations developed in a number of fields (Smith, 1995: 31–3). The impact of post-1979 governments on pressure group activity is assessed principally in terms of the Thatcher and Blair administrations' willingness to involve groups in the policy process.

1979–97: Conservative Governments – the impact of Thatcherism

Thatcherite Conservatism was hostile to pressure groups, with ministers in this period referring to them variously as 'strangling serpents' (Douglas Hurd), and as being as essential to democracy as the 'sewage system' in any big city (Michael Portillo). Accordingly, important changes were bought about in government-pressure group relations by the Thatcher governments, changes which broadly continued under the premiership of John Major.

- The ending of neo-corporatism. Perceiving neo-corporatism as a major cause of Britain's economic decline, the Conservative government abruptly broke with this system after 1979. First, it ended the system of 'tripartite' consultation in economic policy making by moving to an arm's length relationship with business and trade unions, and by downgrading and then abolishing (1992) the

> *Definition*
> **Neo-corporatism**: a weak variant of
> corporatism which appeared in Britain in the
> 1960s and 1970s. It denotes the practice of
> close consultation between government,
> business and trade unions over economic
> policy and in particular the making of bargains,
> e.g. over prices and incomes restraint, which
> the producer groups were required to keep by
> ensuring the compliance of their members
> (also referred to as **tripartism**).

main tripartite forum, the National Economic Development Council (NEDC). Second, it severely curtailed trade union powers by legislation (Acts of 1980, 1982, 1984, 1988, 1990, 1992, 1993) and by engaging in and winning major industrial confrontations, e.g. the 1984–5 miners' strike. Third, it pursued economic policies that gave higher priority to curbing inflation than to containing unemployment, which was allowed to increase rapidly.

- The challenging of a range of intermediate institutions, professional bodies and welfare cause groups. The Conservative governments saw institutions such as local government, the universities and the BBC, and more broadly the welfare state, as in need of radical reform, and were not prepared to allow representatives of the affected organisations and causes to deflect their aims. Accordingly, local government associations, professional groups such as doctors and teachers, and the cause groups involved in the poverty lobby lost influence in this period.
- The fostering of 'sympathetic' interests. The Conservatives were not hostile to all pressure groups, and some groups increased their influence in the 1980s. These included, first, groups that supported New Right aims such as the Institute of Directors, financial institutions in the City and right-wing think-tanks, and second, groups that could assist in the implementation of Conservative policies such as independent schools, private health providers and housing associations.

Although important changes occurred, it should not be assumed that relations between the executive and pressure groups broke down during these years. Even where relations with ministers were reduced or discontinued, groups often retained contact with civil servants. There was much continuity – as well as significant discontinuities – between the Thatcher government and its predecessors in terms of government–group relations. As one researcher has pointed out, 'in a large proportion of cases the relations between groups and the executive neither improved nor deteriorated' (Baggott, 1995: 123).

Post-1997: the Blair approach

New Labour in government has shown greater willingness to listen to the views of pressure groups than its predecessors, but this is not to say that pressure groups necessarily wield greater influence. Part of New Labour's approach to governing is that many interests and voices are included in the 'big tent', including pressure groups. An early clue to Labour's inclusive philosophy was the contact made with previous outsiders who had been kept at arm's length by unsympathetic governments of the 1980s. For example, the director of the gay rights organisation Stonewall stated that there had been a sea-change in governmental attitudes, with representatives being able to talk directly to Labour ministers and their civil servants.

The advent of Labour governments has shifted the balance of advantage among causes and interests, as indicated by the fierce conflicts generated over the proposed ban on tobacco advertising, greater freedom for people to explore the countryside, and a free vote on a ban on foxhunting. First, Labour's exemption of Formula One (F1) motor racing from its tobacco advertising ban in November 1997 led to a public furore after it simultaneously leaked out that the party had received a pre-election gift of £1 million from the F1 chief, Bernie Ecclestone. Ecclestone had had talks with Blair a few weeks before the decision was announced. F1 argued that tobacco sponsorship was vital to the sport, and proceeding with the ban would lead to the loss to Britain of 50,000 full time jobs and £900,000 a year in exports, as well as the possible removal of F1 to Asia. Against this, the anti-smoking lobby, which included

ASH (Action on Smoking and Health), the BMA and several charities, countered that the association of tobacco advertising with motor racing glamourised smoking and helped make it attractive to young people. The key political issues involved the suspicion of party favours on policy in return for funding, and the power of powerful commercial interests to sway government decisions by behind-the-scenes lobbying. Labour was particularly vulnerable to such allegations in view of its pre-election attacks on Conservative sleaze and its criticisms of Conservative governments for failing to cut teenage smoking by banning tobacco advertising and receipt of large contributions to party funds from the tobacco industry. In retreating from the ban, Labour argued that it had not been the victim of insider lobbying but rather

had been won over by the strength of the argument that the global nature of the sport made a ban counter-productive. The upshot of the affair was that, on the advice of the chairman of the Committee on Standards and Privileges, the party returned the money to Bernie Ecclestone. The EU directive on sports advertising exempted Formula One from its ban until 2006.

Second, as anticipated from Labour's modernising of the party, links with the trade unions have weakened at all levels. Despite the introduction of a minimum wage and increased public spending on education and health, some unions have become increasingly critical of New Labour and voted to reduce their financial contributions to the party. A period of tension between the party and the trade union movement has been

---

BOX 9.1

The Countryside Alliance, September 2002

Political parties are no longer such an important means of political participation. In Britain, only 1.6 per cent of the electorate are members of political parties. It seems that many people now realise that local party members participate very little in political debate and policy making. Individuals who want to influence policy are now turning to single-cause special interest groups (such as the Snowdrop Campaign against gun ownership), to new social movements (such as feminists or environmentalists), or to popular protest (such as anti-motorway direct action).

Some of these newer means of political participation comprise very loosely organised movements, such as the women's movement, while others are more formally organised and structured. The Countryside Alliance, which organised its first rally in London in 1998, provides an example of the latter. Around 280,000 people from rural Britain marched to draw attention to countryside concerns as diverse as opposition to any measures that outlawed hunting, farmers' grievances about BSE and falling farm incomes, the loss of countryside to urban development, and

declining rural services such as transport, schools and shops. Reflecting this, the Countryside Alliance was supported by organisations such as the British Field Sports Society, the National Farmers' Union, the Clay Pigeon Association, the British Horse Society, the Country Landowners' Association, Timber Growers' Association, and the Trout and Salmon Association. A second 'Liberty and Livelihood' march in 2002 was supported by over 400,000 people. This demonstration of support may have been a factor in the government's partial retreat on fox hunting, which no longer would be unconditionally outlawed in principle, in a compromise that is unlikely to satisfy supporters or opponents of hunting.

Some dismiss the Countryside Alliance, saying that it has no clear message because it stands for so many issues. Some argue that Labour can ignore this rural vote, since it won a little over a quarter of the vote in the most rural seats and has only a dozen MPs from agricultural constituencies. Others have condemned the Countryside Alliance's demonstrations as another example of 'mobocracy' relying on street protests rather than rational argument.

Photograph: PA Photos.

IN FOCUS 9.1 The country comes to town

The Liberty and Livelihood march organised by the Countryside Alliance passes through central London to show its opposition to the proposed ban on hunting with dogs and its concerns for other rural issues. It was estimated that as many as 400,000 people took part, perhaps the largest demonstration for over a century. Within a year, however, twice as many demonstrated against Britain waging war against Iraq.

backbench anti-foxhunting bill which had received a large majority at its second reading and which, if it were to gain the backing of the government, looked like having a strong chance of success. The aim of the first demonstration was to pressurise the government not to make Parliamentary time for the bill, and in addition to express a variety of other discontents including the impact of the BSE crisis on the beef industry, the government's recent ban on sales of beef on the bone, cheap meat imports, the threat of legislation on the right to roam, possible further restrictions on shooting, the likelihood of more housing on rural land, and the steady erosion of rural schools, hospitals, public transport and village shops. The Countryside Alliance argued that what was at stake was the right of a minority to pursue its way of life without infringement by the majority, and that a ban on foxhunting would destroy large numbers of jobs in an already imperilled countryside. Critics claimed that the march was essentially a pro-hunting lobby, that public and Parliamentary opinion favoured a ban, and that the majority of those marching were Conservative voters who would not have marched against a Conservative government even though most of the matters complained of (apart from the possible hunting ban) had taken place over several decades under Conservative governments. The Labour government, however, responded with concessions, which included more financial help for beef farmers, soft-pedalling with a 'third way' option to allow controlled fox hunting, and softening its position on the right to roam by allowing landowners two years to reach voluntary agreements giving more access to the open countryside.

New social movements

Wyn Grant has observed that there is an 'increasing use of various forms of direct action' in British politics, with the Countryside Alliance march of 1998 (Box 9.1) and the fuel protest of 2000 (Box 5.1) as important examples (Grant, 2001: 337). Pressure groups and protest campaigns can be loosely connected through pursuit of common goals, and in some cases the resulting coalition make take the form of a new social movement.

predicted by some commentators, following the election of more left-wing leaders who have promised greater militancy in pursuit of their members' interests.

Finally, rural interests joined in massive marches through London organised by the Countryside Alliance early in spring 1998 and again in 2002 (see Box 9.1). The major focus of rural alarm was a

As noted above, it is customary to define a pressure group as an organisation that aims to influence policy by seeking to persuade decision makers by lobbying rather than by standing for election and holding office. Paul Byrne described a new social movement as something that is relatively disorganised (Byrne, 1997). Where a pressure group is a formal organisation which has *members*, a social movement may be an informal and loosely organised network, with *supporters* rather than members. On the other hand, a new social movement differs from direct action or a protest campaign. A new social movement exists for longer than a single protest, is wider in scope than a single issue campaign, and is national or global rather than local in terms of the scope of change it is trying to achieve. However, a new social movement could include a protest campaign as part of its activities, but as part and parcel of seeking greater change in society. For example, anti-motorway protest such as that mounted by the 'Dongas' at Winchester can be seen as contributing to a wider new social movement of environmentalists. Many motorway protesters may identify themselves as being 'green', but the environmental movement has many more goals than just ending motorway construction (see Figure 9.2).

Generalisations about groups of individuals can easily result in misleading images or even crude stereotypes. With this in mind, it can be argued that members of pressure groups can often be distinguished from campaign supporters and

BOX 9.2

Comparative politics: left and right social movements in the UK and USA

It is interesting to note that in Britain new social movements tend to be associated with the political left. The pacifists of the 1960s and 1970s, the 'second wave' of feminists, and environmentalists are more likely to be located towards the left of the political spectrum than the right. This was the case with 'old' social movements, such as the trade union movement. However, in the USA social movements are just as likely to be on the political right, such as the Moral Majority or Born Again Christian movement. The right in Britain is more likely to be found at the level of protest campaigns, such as the Countryside Alliance.

those in a social movement. Although they want changes to particular policies, pressure group members are likely to support the existing political and social order – the status quo – which is based on dominant values. Social movement supporters are more likely to support alternative ways of organising politics and society, and thus want changes that will fundamentally change the existing order. Where pressure group members are likely to support Parliamentary parties, social

Pressure groups e.g. Greenpeace and Friends of the Earth, seeking to influence policy	The Green Party seeking political representation in order to influence policy	Protest and direct action to prevent policy implementation, e.g. the Dongas

A **new social movement** such as environmentalists, including a wide variety of ecologists, conservationists, eco-warriors, concerned with changing society's values regarding the environment

Figure 9.2 New social movements: typical composition

movement supporters are more likely to reject Parliamentary parties and lead their own private lives in ways shaped by their alternative values and ideologies. In other words, members of pressure groups are likely to recognise government by a Parliamentary elite as legitimate and simply attempt to influence decisions made by the elite. In contrast, supporters of a social movement are likely to challenge the values of the governing elite, question its authority and replace 'conventional' politics with the 'new' politics of direct action.

The anti-capitalist social movement

Anti-capitalist protests and direct action against multi-national companies have become increasingly frequent in recent years. This type of new social movement has no established leaders, no organisation in the sense of having a headquarters staffed by office workers, but forms an international network linked by the Internet. It has been described as a 'global, anarchic and chaotic' body, but nevertheless has become a significant political force. Much campaigning takes place against the 'iron triangle' of global capitalism: the World Trade Organisation, the International Monetary Fund and the World Bank. Much additional 'grass roots' campaigning takes place against multinational companies such as McDonald's, Coca-Cola, Nike, Texaco, Shell, Microsoft, Disney and Gap. The protesters' causes range through anti-consumerism, environmentalism, anti-slavery and the promotion of human rights. Some oppose successfully advertised junk food replacing locally produced real food. Some oppose the use of 'sweatshop labour' by women and children in the Third World to produce expensive designer-label products in the west.

May Day 'anti-capitalist' or 'anti-globalization' demonstrations in London as well as similar events in Seattle and Quebec in 1999 are seen as 'pro-democracy' protests by many participants. Naomi Klein, for example, has criticised newspaper journalists for describing these events in terms of violence and extremism, whereas really they should be seen as a healthy part of democracy (Klein, 2001). Another example is a consumer boycott organised against Esso in 2001 in order to persuade the oil company to change its attitude towards global warming. Esso had suggested that there was no actual proof that global warming is caused by burning fossil fuels, and those scientists who have made the link are scare-mongers. The Stop Esso campaign noted that Esso provided George W. Bush with more than $1 million towards his presidential election campaign, and appeared to be repaid when the new president pulled the USA out of the Kyoto Agreement (see Chapter 25).

Pressure groups and the EU

The growing integration of Britain in the European Union has brought a considerable increase in lobbying at European level by British pressure groups. According to one estimate, the number of pressure group employees in Brussels doubled from 5000 to 10,000 between the late 1980s and 1994 (Grant, 1995: 98). The Single European Act (1986) and the Treaty of Maastricht (1993) gave considerable encouragement to this trend by increasing the number of policy areas in which decisions are made at European level, by extending the use of qualified majority voting, and by giving additional legislative powers to the European Parliament (see Chapter 16). Business and farming interests, trade unions, professional associations such as the BMA and the Law Society, and environmental groups all lobby at European Union level. Groups may lobby directly – many have offices in Brussels, with business groups predominating, by employing consultancy firms and through Europe-wide groups such as UNICE (Union of Industrial and Employers' Confederations of Europe), ETUC (European Trade Union Confederation), COPA (Committee of Professional Agricultural Organisations), BEUC (European Bureau of Consumers' Associations) and EEB (European Environmental Bureau).

Pressure groups target European institutions in this order: the European Commission, the Council of Ministers, the European Parliament, and the European Court of Justice. Grant comments that 'Lobbying activity is focused on particular directorates-general within the Commission. For some interests, their influence is closely bound up with one directorate-general: DGV (social affairs) for trade unions; DG VI (agriculture) for farmers' (Grant, 2000: 113). However, if 'the decision making process in the Commission is highly political at the highest levels, it is generally relatively technical at the lower levels, giving pressure groups opportunities' (Grant, 2000). Yet, for all their 'apparent dependence on groups, Commission officials retain considerable discretion and autonomy' (Grant, 2000: 114).

Since groups rarely exert direct pressure on the Council of Ministers but must rely on their own government to protect their interests, they frequently combine lobbying their own ministers with a 'Brussels strategy'; indeed, some political scientists now argue that the Brussels route is increasingly being taken. This tendency was reinforced after 1993 by a reduction of the influence of national governments following the extension of qualified majority voting (QMV), which made it even more imperative for groups to develop contacts with the Commission. Nevertheless, an important focus for pressure groups is the Committee of Permanent Representatives (COREPER) (see Chapter 16), since it and its working parties resolve most issues before the relevant ministers meet. Groups lobby respective national governments, and subsequent negotiations settle all but the most sensitive or contentious political issues, which are decided by relevant ministers. Grant concludes that 'each individual Council has its own particular atmosphere. Those Councils which meet more frequently may develop their own "club like" atmosphere.... Each Council may approach its task in a particular way which may make it more sympathetic to some lobbies and less so to others' (Grant, 2000: 116).

Although far less significant than the Commission as a focus of lobbying activity, the European Parliament's increased legislative powers following the Single European Act (ACT) and Maastricht enhanced its attractiveness to pressure groups, especially to those representing consumer, environmental and animal welfare interests. As might be assumed by the absence of business interests from this list, access to members of the European Parliament is something of a consolation prize for those relatively without influence elsewhere within the EU. Groups may be listened to readily, but not necessarily able to wield discernible influence.

It is worth stressing that since the passing of the

SEA and the Maastricht Treaty which extended the scope of EU policy, powerful pressure groups have established offices in Brussels. This enables them to lobby the Commission as well as lobby their own national governments in order to obtain influence in the Council of Ministers. Since the powers of the European Parliament have been increased, many groups now lobby MEPs. Grant comments that the 'unofficial groupings of MEPs from different parties and member states known as Intergroups have also become lobbying targets. There are around sixty of these groups covering subjects such as financial services, pharmaceuticals, defence industries and small and medium-sized enterprises' (Grant, 2000: 118).

Some pressure groups come together for the purposes of lobbying within the EU to form a Eurogroup. This has advantages and disadvantages. Obviously the Eurogroup can claim to represent more members than a single group working alone. For example, COPA (Committee of Agricultural Organisations in the EU) can claim greater representation than the UK National Farmers' Union (NFU), and ETUC (European Trade Union Confederation) represents more workers than the TUC. The disadvantage is that Eurogroups sometimes find it hard to agree on policy because of national differences. For example, the Committee on Common Market Automobile Constructors collapsed in 1990 because its members could not agree on policy issues.

The European Court of Justice has been used by groups both to force the UK government to implement EU legislation, for instance over the quality of drinking water, and to challenge domestic measures, such as pit closures by the miners' union (1992) and the proposed legal aid regulations by the Law Society (1993).

Pressure group targets

At which points in the political system do pressure groups seek to exert influence? British pressure groups have five main target areas: the 'core executive' – government ministers (including the prime minister) and civil servants (Whitehall); Parliament (both Houses); public opinion (mainly through the media); local institutions, including local government; and the European Union. As already noted above, the terms 'insider' and 'outsider' usefully refer both to the status of groups – insiders acceptable to government, outsiders not so – and to strategy – whether a group seeks acceptance at core executive level or, through necessity or choice, remains an outsider. Research suggests that many groups – sectional and cause – pursue multiple strategies, seeking to exercise influence – as resources permit – at a variety of points in the system. Thus, Baggott's (1995) study of a cross-section of pressure groups at national level (both sectional and cause) found that while insider groups had more frequent contacts with the political system at all points than outsider groups, a relatively large number of outsider groups were in quite frequent contact with the executive to junior civil servant level. This finding fits in well with Grant's further subdivision of insider and outsider groups, in which only two of the six sub-categories – insider 'prisoner' groups and 'ideological' outsiders – never cross the insider/outsider boundary line. In fact, this line is often crossed – first because, as already mentioned, groups adopt more than one strategy; second, because insider status can be lost as well as gained.

Pressure groups and government

The concentration of power in the executive makes government the main target for pressure groups in Britain. A well-established system of formal and informal contacts links insider groups with government. Increasingly, formal contacts have become institutionalised through pressure group membership of a wide variety of government-established committees; through the circulation of government consultative documents; and through widespread consultation with groups over the contents of delegated legislation (statutory instruments).

Even though formal consultation between government and groups is very extensive, the great majority of contacts are informal and typically occur at quite a low level of the civil service (see Table 9.1). Indeed, much business is done informally by telephone and face-to-face discussions between civil servants and representatives of the groups.

Two major features of insider groups' relationship of regular consultation and negotiation with government departments invite comment. First, the acceptability of a group to government – its recognition as an insider – depends upon its credibility. This rests upon such factors as:

- a group's representativeness – its genuine capacity to speak for a large number of people in its section of society
- the reasonableness of its demands and their compatibility with the aims of government – realism, moderation, responsibility and negotiability are the watchwords
- the reliability and quality of its advice – past track record and the extent of government need can both be important
- its ability to 'talk the same language' as government – i.e. its familiarity with government procedures
- economic leverage and veto power – diminished for some groups in the 1980s, e.g. TUC, but still can be a factor, e.g. the boycott of Standard Assessment Tests by the teachers' unions in 1993.

Conversely, characteristics which make for a group's unacceptability to government (thereby ensuring that it remains an outsider) include:

- incompatibility – possessing aims incompatible with those of government, e.g. the Marxist-inspired Radical Alternatives to Prison (RAP), which calls for the abolition of prison; and
- contentiousness – the likelihood that a group will be opposed by other groups, e.g. the Abortion Law Reform Association (ALRA) by the Society for the Protection of the Unborn Child (SPUC).

Second, there is the extent to which pressure groups in their linkages with government departments form *policy networks*, a concept that expresses a variety of relationships on a continuum between policy communities and issue networks. In a policy community, relationships between a group or groups and a government department are close, relatively exclusive, consensual and cooperative. The best example of a policy community in the post-war period is agriculture, where a close and generally harmonious relationship existed between the two main parties involved, the then Ministry of Agriculture, Food and Fisheries (MAFF) and the NFU. Health and transport are two further examples in which policy is made in semi-autonomous, segmented communities between departments and groups with privileged access. In policy communities, ministers, permanent officials and groups share an interest in increasing the resources devoted to a given policy area, and departments often identify closely with group viewpoints. The Department of Transport, for example, has often been cited as being both pro-road and pro-lorry, the former Department of Energy tended to side with energy producers against energy users, while MAFF invariably supported the interests of producers of food against its consumers, although this cosy relationship weakened as the result of a series of crises in British agriculture, culminating in the foot-and-mouth epidemic of 2001. Concerns over food safety, following BSE and other scandals, were among factors which led to the replacement of MAFF by the new Department of the Environment, Food and Rural Affairs (DEFRA) after the 2001 general election.

Issue networks are less stable than policy communities, and contain a larger number of participants – often several ministries as well as numerous pressure groups – who often find it difficult to agree on policy. The numerous departments – Treasury, Home Office, Employment, Education, Social Security – and pressure groups involved in inner-city policy in the 1980s provide an example of an issue network (Smith, 1995: 28).

In return for regular consultation by government, for being taken into the confidence of officials and allowed to state their case and conceivably gain concessions, groups are expected to conform to certain patterns of behaviour. They are expected at all times to be discreet about discussions in Whitehall and to refrain, even where they feel aggrieved, from 'going public', and especially from criticising ministers. They may also be expected to sell the policy to their members. Occasionally, this cosy, symbiotic relationship will break down and a group will attack its governmental 'patron': this happened in 1992 when the Engineering Employers' Federation

publicly called for 'a more effective and committed champion' than Michael Heseltine at the Department of Trade and Industry.

The benefits to government of this system of group representation include:

- up-to-date, often technical and highly specialised advice
- 'market' information in the various sectors
- compliance with their policies by the main interests in each specific field
- assistance in the administration of projects (where required).

In return, groups get:

- a hearing for their case (at the least)
- the chance to influence policy (including legislation) and decisions in their formative, early stages
- the possibility of gaining an executive role alongside government in the implementation of policy
- funds from government: studies have shown that government is an important source of funds for large numbers of groups in the environmental and poverty lobbies.

Pressure groups and Parliament

Survey evidence suggests the increased importance of Parliament as a target for pressure group lobbying in recent years. In the Study of Parliament Group Survey, 75 per cent of groups claimed to be in regular or frequent contact with MPs, and 59 per cent of groups claimed regular or frequent dealings with peers (Rush, 1990: 14). Factors facilitating the growing use of Parliament by groups included the discernible increase in backbench independence; the establishment of the new select committees after 1979, which provided another channel of potential influence; the growth of specialist political influence; the increased number of political consultancy firms; the distancing of government from pressure groups by Conservative governments after 1979; and the large majorities enjoyed by Conservative governments in the 1980s, which directed attention to Conservative backbenchers and the House of

Lords as the main obstacles to legislation. However, groups remain realistic in their perceptions of where power lies in the political system, ranking Parliament below government departments/civil servants, ministers and the media as influences upon public policy (Table 9.1).

Nonetheless, because Parliament is perceived as a policy-influencer, no pressure group can ignore it. Indeed, an important conclusion of the Study of Parliament Group Survey is that, 'contrary to what might be expected', more of the attention received by Parliament 'comes from insider than outsider, and more from sectional than promotional groups' (Rush, 1990: 277; see also Table 9.1).

Groups seek contact with Parliament for three main purposes:

- to amend legislation – or change policy – in often slight but, for the affected interest or cause, significant ways
- to sponsor legislation
- to influence the climate of public opinion by gaining additional publicity and support for an issue first raised or raised concurrently outside Parliament.

Characteristic activities of groups concerned about legislation include circularising MPs, wining and dining them to encourage sympathy for the group's viewpoint, requesting an MP to arrange a meeting with the minister responsible for a bill, asking an MP to speak in a second reading debate, and asking an MP to propose an amendment during the committee or report stages of a bill. In the Lords, too, peers regularly put down questions, speak in debates and

Table 9.1 Groups' ranking of influences on public policy

Civil servants/government departments	1
Ministers	2
The media	3
Parliament	4
Particular sections of public opinion	5
Public opinion generally	6
Other pressure groups	7
Political parties generally	8
One political party in particular	9

Source: Rush, 1990: 272.

table legislative amendments on behalf of groups. By prompting MPs or peers to act along such lines, groups can hope to persuade ministers to adopt a favourable amendment, back down on a controversial detail, clarify an ambiguous point, or give an assurance on the interpretation of a particular clause.

The time allocated to private members' legislation (although small – under 5 per cent) gives groups an opportunity to promote change rather than simply react to it. In the 1960s, sympathetic MPs sponsored much social legislation, liberalising the law on divorce, abortion, homosexuality, theatre censorship and capital punishment. Finally, groups can use Parliament in a broader way – often in combination with other strategies – to publicise their cause and shape public policy in their interest over a longer time-span. Such mechanisms include working through party committees, all-party committees and select committees, prompting Parliamentary questions and gaining the maximum number of signatures to an Early Day Motion.

The benefits derived by groups from their contacts with Parliament range over a spectrum from the very considerable to the quite modest to the minimal and negligible. At the former end are the occasional sponsorship of Private Members' bills together with such events as the successful campaigns waged against the Shops Bill (1986) by the shopworkers' union, the churches and various voluntary organisations, and by the large brewers against the DTI plan which would have forced owners of more than 2000 public houses to sell their 'surplus' outlets. In the middle of the range are the amendments to legislation, which groups quite frequently obtain, such as the amendment achieved by gay pressure groups to the Criminal Justice and Public Order Bill (1994) which reduced the age of consent for homosexuals from 21 to 18. Many groups, however, derive much less from their lobbying activities. When questioned by the Study of Parliament Group, just under 39 per cent of groups saw themselves as 'not very successful' at influencing legislation, and just under 6 per cent as 'unsuccessful'. In contrast, over 55 per cent claimed to be 'very' successful (7.2 per cent) or 'quite' successful (48.3 per cent). In return, the input by groups to the legislative process gives MPs a 'critical capacity' they would otherwise lack,

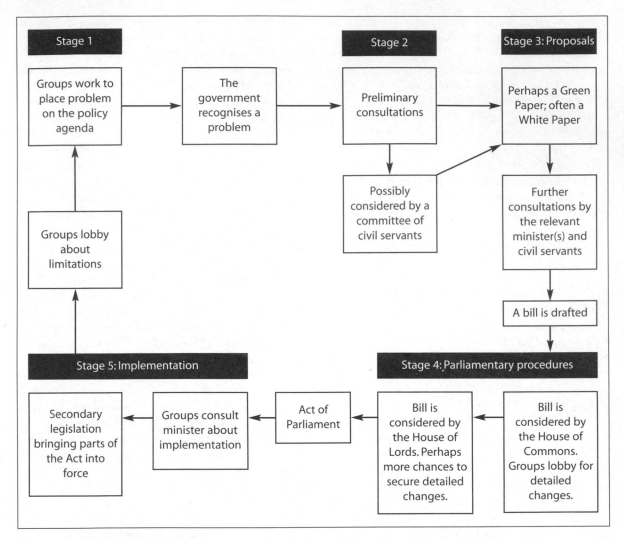

Figure 9.3 Pressure group influence on Whitehall and Westminster: the main stages

Source: adapted from Grant, 1995: 48.

and in addition it increases the legitimacy of measures by securing wider consent to them than would otherwise be achieved (Norton, 1990: 193, 196–7).

Pressure group influence

Influence on Whitehall and Westminster

Figure 9.3 sums up in diagrammatic form the stages at which groups may seek to influence policy and legislation. Summarised schematically, these are:

- agenda-setting: getting an item on to the policy agenda
- policy formation: helping to shape policy/legislation at the consultation and (for Acts of Parliament) drafting stages
- passage through Parliament (Commons and Lords) including Statutory Instruments
- implementation: groups help identify flaws in the policy/legislation and suggest remedies.

Whether and how far pressure groups succeed in influencing political decision making depends upon several factors including their resources, strategies and social and economic leverage.

Beyond Whitehall and Westminster

Because power in Britain is concentrated at the centre, most pressure group activity is directed at government and Parliament. None the less, a good deal of group activity takes place outside Westminster and Whitehall, with pressure groups running public campaigns and seeking influence in political parties, through the courts and at local level.

Public campaigns

Many groups seek to increase public awareness of their causes by running national campaigns. These include long-term educational campaigns designed to produce significant shifts in public opinion, such as the Campaign for Lead Free Air (CLEAR), and short-term 'fire brigade' campaigns warning about and seeking to avert a specific threat, such as the National Union of Mineworkers' (NUM) campaign against pit closures in 1992. Whilst public campaigning remains the leading strategy of outsider groups, insiders – and sectional groups – increasingly employ public campaigns in combination with Parliamentary and Whitehall strategies. Gaining media attention – for example, through a well-researched press release, letters to the quality newspapers or sometimes a carefully-staged 'event' – is central to the success of a public campaigning strategy. Groups can also seek to raise public awareness of an issue by various forms of protest and direct action. These include legal and non-violent methods such as marches and demonstrations – such as the massive London demonstrations organised by the Countryside Alliance against the anti-fox hunting bill and other perceived threats to rural life in 1998 and 2000 (see Box 9.1); the anti-racism demonstrations organised by the Anti-Nazi League; and consumer boycotts, such as that organised against South African goods by the anti-apartheid campaign. But they also include the illegal but non-violent non-payment tactics used by the Anti-Poll Tax Federation, the sit-ins employed by anti-roads protesters and the disruptive methods deployed by hunt saboteurs and anti-whalers, as well as the violent and illegal methods employed by, for example, some animal rights groups, such as the Animal Liberation Front, which break into laboratories, release animals and destroy equipment; and anti-capitalism and anti-globalization May Day riots in London, Seattle and Quebec involving groups such as Class War, Reclaim the Streets, Critical Mass, and Anti-Capitalist Convergence.

Political parties

Groups may also attempt to bring pressure on political parties. They may do this in a number of ways. The most obvious way is to make donations to political parties, as do both the trade unions (to Labour) and business (to the Conservatives). In the 1990s, trade union contributions to the Labour Party declined (from three-quarters to half its total funds, 1986–96) whilst business contributions have grown. At the same time, business contributions to the Conservatives declined sharply in the 1990s. Another method is to sponsor candidates, as the trade unions did before 1995 in the Labour Party. Some cause groups – such as the anti-hunting and anti-abortion lobbies – try to influence parties' choice of Parliamentary candidates. Others again attempt to persuade parties to place detailed commitments in their manifestos. In return for influence, such groups campaign for the party supporting their cause. Sometimes group and party membership overlaps, and this may help the groups achieve a favourable reception from parties. For example, most of the 418 Labour MPs elected in 1997 belong to trade unions (Butler and Kavanagh, 1997: 206). In addition, the Labour Party also contains many members of campaigning organisations such as CND, Greenpeace and Friends of the Earth, and of local community action, tenants' and women's groups (Seyd and Whiteley, 1992: 91–2). In late 1997 New Labour's simultaneous receptiveness to certain cause group demands, combined with its desire to attract business funds, produced embarrassment for the party over its exemption of Formula One from its proposed tobacco advertising ban.

Local groups

A wide variety of groups are active at local level, including economic (trade unions and chambers of commerce), community (tenants' associations, ethnic groupings), cause groups and social movements (Friends of the Earth, anti-hunting, women's groups) and the voluntary sector (Rural Community Councils, Age Concern, the churches, MIND). Many seek insider status at local level, the pattern of their representation in local government reflecting the political complexion of councils: thus, farming and landowning interests are well established in Conservative rural areas, local business interests and amenity and middle class residents' groups predominate in suburban areas with Conservative councils, while trade unions, community and ethnic minority representatives are influential in left-wing Labour urban authorities (Stoker, 1991: 133–4). Local areas are also the scene of well-publicised campaigns by nimby (not in my backyard) groups against such matters as unwanted schemes (e.g. the Channel Tunnel rail link, new roads, asylum centres, the construction of greenfield superstores, the dumping of toxic waste) and by local residents against the closure of schools, hospitals and playing fields.

Resources

Resources include finances, organisation, staffing, membership, expertise and leadership. It is generally believed that sectional groups possess an advantage over cause groups in terms of resources, and this is both normally the case and affords such groups a considerable bargaining advantage. Business groups such as the motor industry, weapons manufacturers, and the tobacco and brewing industries have far greater resources than consumers and pensioners, for example. However, well-resourced campaigns by major sectional groups have sometimes failed – such as the very expensive anti-nationalisation campaigns run by business between 1945 and 1979, and also the campaign against pit closures by the NUM in 1984–5, which was undermined by poor leadership and inadequate strategy. By contrast, groups representing single parents, the disabled, the unemployed and the elderly deployed much more

modest resources between 1965 and 1985, but made important gains through 'painstaking and persistent lobbying' (Whiteley and Winyard, 1987: 138). Again, some environmental groups are now as well-resourced as the larger sectional groups: for example, Greenpeace spent £350,000 on television equipment for its Brent Spar campaign, running a 24-hour news operation, equipped with its own film crews, editing suites and satellite technology (*Guardian*, 28 August 1995). However, lack of resources undoubtedly handicapped the anti-nuclear lobby in its protest against the Conservatives' extensive nuclear energy programme, which had the backing of the major forces in the energy industry, including the Central Electricity Generating Board, the Atomic Energy Authority, large national firms such as the General Electric Company (GEC) and big multinationals like Westinghouse and Rio Tinto Zinc.

Resources – whether slender or considerable – need to be deployed expertly if a group is to achieve its aims. The quality of the information it provides to government guarantees Amnesty International 'insider' status. Environmental groups such as Friends of the Earth have focused increasingly on providing reliable information to policy makers but may suffer loss of credibility if their test figures turn out to be mistaken and their solutions contested, as happened to Greenpeace in the wake of its successful campaign to avert the deep-sea dumping of the redundant Brent Spar oil rig. Parliamentary know-how is essential if groups are to influence legislation at the standing committee stage, but much of the briefing material they provide for MPs is over-long, too generalised and too late to be effective. Consumer groups, local government associations and certain trade unions possess such expertise, but City institutions demonstrated ignorance of such procedure over the Financial Services Bill (1986) (Norton, 1990: 194–6). Its knowledge of Parliamentary procedure enabled the pro-abortion lobby first to liberalise the abortion law and then to resist the campaign by anti-abortion groups to amend it between 1967 and 1975. Pro-abortionists attribute the failure of the pro-life lobby to reduce the abortion limit to the counter-productive tactics adopted by the Society for the Protection of the Unborn Child (SPUC), which sent a plastic foetus to every MP.

With regard to pressure group membership, size, density, solidarity, and quality have to be considered. Sometimes, as in the case of demonstrations, absolute numbers can be important, to show that a group is as well supported as its proponents – or as poorly supported as its opponents – respectively claim. For example, the potential influence of the Countryside Alliance march was strengthened by its being able to claim a turnout of over 400,000. Just as often, it is important to a group to show that it represents a high proportion of potential members. Thus, trade associations are strengthened by being able to claim – as they often can – that they represent over 90 per cent of an industry, whereas the authority of the CBI is undermined by its inability to speak for a wide range of diverse interests, and trade unionism is weakened by the fact that only a third of workers are members of trade unions. Finally, quality of membership matters, with cause groups often offsetting the handicap of small size by the dedication, enthusiasm and knowledge of their memberships.

Strategy

Adoption of an appropriate strategy can be a vital ingredient in group success. The way in which a group allocates its efforts between government departments, Parliament and public campaigns depends upon the nature of the group, its cause and the congruence (or lack of congruence) of its goals with public opinion. The degree of choice is often more limited than this suggests: thus, trade associations generally have little option but to adopt an 'insider' strategy, whereas 'ideological' groups like CND or oppositional movements like the Anti-Poll Tax Federation are forced by necessity into 'outsider' strategies. Within the field of law reform, a respectable group such as the Howard League for Penal Reform, which directs its efforts for liberal reforms within an acceptance of the legitimacy of the criminal law, has achieved 'insider' status with the Home Office to which the left-inspired Radical Alternatives to Prison (RAP) and Preservation of the Rights of Prisoners (PROP) can never aspire. Some sectional groups pursue 'insider' and 'outsider' strategies simultaneously: for example, the TUC continued its

institutionalised relationship with Whitehall while running effective national campaigns, involving Parliamentary, legal and mass action, against industrial relations legislation in the late 1960s and early 1970s. Congruence with public opinion also affects a group's choice of strategy: workers enjoying widespread public sympathy such as firefighters and nurses were able to run public campaigns over pay in the 1980s, but other industrial groups and the TUC had to take into account the likelihood of lukewarm, indifferent or even hostile public reactions when considering public campaigns.

Sanctions

A group's capacity to employ sanctions in pursuit of its goals depends upon its general importance in the national economy, and more specifically, its capacity to disrupt government plans by resistance and/or non-compliance. With regard to economic leverage and veto power, sectional groups are generally considered more powerful than promotional groups because they possess stronger weapons. While largely true, this needs to be treated with caution. Generally, the more powerful a group and the more essential its policy-compliance is to government, the less overt its threat of sanctions need be: the City, for instance, with its ability to talk down the pound, often gains decisions in its favour without any overt lobbying at all. However, the power of sectional interests can fluctuate, in large part because of shifts in government needs and changing political circumstances, as shown by the declining influence of farming, manufacturing and professional groups in the 1980s. At the same time, campaigns of non-compliance, delay and disruption can be formidable weapons in the hands of promotional groups, as demonstrated by the anti-poll-tax non-payment campaign, the physical obstruction of anti-roads protesters and the spoiling tactics of hunt saboteurs.

Pressure groups and democracy

There are two main arguments to consider; first, can pressure groups ever be internally democratic organisations, and second, do pressure groups enhance or distort democratic politics?

Robert Michels once argued that there was an 'iron law of oligarchy' at work in politics which resulted in radical left-wing parties always being led by much more moderate leaders. Does the iron law of oligarchy also operate to some extent inside pressure groups, resulting in the leadership being politically out of step with the membership? Two recent case studies bring some light to bear on this question through illuminating the nature of internal pressure group democracy.

Representation of the disabled

In lobbying government, disabled people are represented by numerous voluntary sector charities and agencies. These are very fragmented, and there is no single influential voice but rather many competing forces. Even so, these groups have greater resources and access to government than 'newer groups led by disabled people themselves' (Drake, 2002: 373). A crucial issue for disabled people is how far a voluntary body for the disabled should be staffed by people who are not disabled. Robert Drake has pointed out the

---

BOX 9.3
The National Farmers' Union (NFU)

The foot and mouth disease crisis which struck British agriculture in 2001 led to much conflict within the NFU. Many farmers were distressed by the government's policy of slaughtering animals to stop the spread of the disease. Often this meant killing healthy animals which were not infected as a precaution. Farmers wanted to have these healthy animals vaccinated against foot-and-mouth disease rather than slaughtered. The NFU argued that there was no satisfactory alternative to the slaughter policy. The NFU leadership was accused by many farmers of representing the interests of big farmers and agribusinesses, and not the interests of small stock farmers. It was argued that 60,000 farmers were members of the NFU, most of

them small farmers, yet it was the minority of big farmers who most influenced official policy (see Figure 9.4).

Small farmers complained that the NFU had never consulted them to find out their views, and consequently the union was not representing them in a democratic manner. Resulting from this, a number of small farmers left the NFU because other rival agricultural organisations represented their interests more accurately. A dilemma for large interest groups such as the NFU is that its membership is diverse. In the case of the NFU it speaks for big farmers and small farmers, arable farmers and livestock farmers, and they each have different interests and priorities, and want different policies.

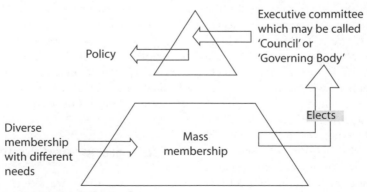

Figure 9.4 Pressure group power structure

BOX 9.4
The Royal Society for the Prevention of Cruelty to Animals (RSPCA)

During the 1980s the Labour Party experienced what was called 'entryism': individuals of a left-wing organisation, Militant Tendency, would join Labour constituency parties with a view to influencing the selection of local Labour councillors and the constituency MP. They would then hope to control local town councils if there was a Labour majority, as well as gaining a voice inside the PLP and at Labour's Annual Conference. It can be argued that all pressure groups are vulnerable to a similar form of entryism, as was claimed of the RSPCA in 2000.

The RSPCA is the world's oldest animal charity, which for the past 25 years has had a policy of opposing blood sports, such as fox hunting. The pro-hunting Countryside Animal Welfare Group, which is linked to the Countryside Alliance, has attempted to change the RSPCA's policy from within. The large Countryside Animal Welfare Group realised that if its members joined the RSPCA, they could use internal democracy to vote pro-hunting individuals on to the RSPCA's council (see Figure 9.4). Once there was a majority of pro-hunting members on the council, they could reverse the RSPCA's opposition to fox hunting. A bitter struggle took place within the RSPCA between the 'animal welfare' lobby (pro-hunting) and the 'animal rights' lobby (anti-hunting), resulting in the expulsion of the leader of the pro-hunting lobby, Richard Meade, an Olympic showjumper. Was the pro-hunting lobby acting democratically in its efforts to change the policy of the RSPCA, or was it guilty of entryism and trying to alter the very purpose of the RSPCA?

difficult problems of representation which exist: for example, some charities are almost as concerned with helping the families and relatives of disabled people as with helping disabled people themselves. In other words, the interests of the carers and the disabled become combined, yet what serves the best interests of relatives might not be in the best interests of the disabled themselves. Furthermore, some charities provide services based on their professional judgements rather than on the needs expressed by disabled people. In this respect, disabled people become more like clients or customers, benefiting only from the services charities decide to offer. The problem might be resolved if disabled people held positions in charities for the disabled, but in reality disabled people have found it very difficult to get established and hold positions in the most powerful charities.

Drake also argued that governments 'hear only what they want to hear', making the point that 'if a government opens a policy discussion to all comers it will receive many shades of opinion, both sympathetic and antagonistic to its own standpoint. In constructing a narrower filter, a government may exclude certain strands of opinion' (Drake, 2002). In other words, government may consult pressure groups but still control the type of advice it is likely to receive. Large traditional charities are always likely to be included but smaller groups, especially if they are radical and out of line with government thinking, are more likely to be excluded. However since disabled people are more likely to be involved in the latter type of group, they tend to be excluded from the political process. This results in the political agenda concerning disability being controlled more by professionals such as social workers and therapists than the disabled.

Pressure groups and power

Do the activities of pressure groups make the political system more democratic, or do pressure groups simply increase the power of the already advantaged? Does pressure group politics simply reflect the power differences found in wider society, with some interests having more influence than others? Or do pressure group activities reinforce these power differences in society, making the already powerful even more powerful? The main arguments are summarised in Table 9.2.

Table 9.2 Pressure groups and democracy: for and against

For	*Against*
• **Participation and political access.** PGs increase participation and access to the political system, thereby enhancing the quality of democracy. They complement and supplement electoral democracy in two main ways: first, by providing an important mechanism by which citizens can influence government between elections, and second, by enabling the intensity of feeling on issues to be considered, opinions to be weighed as well as counted.	• **Sectionalism and selfishness.** PGs improve participation, but unequally, benefiting the well organised but disadvantaging the weakly organised. In this sense, they work against – not in favour of – the public interest.
• **Improvement of government.** Consultation with affected groups is the rational way to make decisions in a free society. It makes government more efficient by enhancing the quality of the decision making process: the information and advice provided by groups help to improve the quality of government policy and legislation.	• **Anti-parliamentary democracy.** Groups and government form policy networks and policy communities, engaging in secret behind-the-scenes consultation: the resulting covert 'deals' detract from both open government and the authority of elected legislators in Parliament. Also, many groups are not themselves democratic organisations as they offer their members little opportunity for effective participation.
• **Pluralism.** PGs are a product of freedom of association, which is a fundamental principle of liberal democracy: its obverse is autocratic or tyrannical suppression of interests. Freely operating pressure groups are essential to the effective functioning of liberal democracy in three main ways: (1) they serve as vital intermediary institutions between government and society; (2) they assist in the dispersal of political power; and (3) they provide important counterweights to undue concentration of power.	• **Elitism.** Group system only apparently functions on a 'level playing field'; in practice, it reinforces the existing class and power structure – 'in the pluralist heaven the heavenly choir sings with a strong upper class accent' (Schnattschneider, 1960, cited in Grant, 1995: 33).
• **Social progress.** PGs enable new concerns and issues to reach the political agenda, thereby facilitating social progress and preventing social stagnation: e.g. the women's and environmentalist movements.	• **Pluralistic stagnation.** Group opposition can slow down or block desirable changes, thereby contributing to social immobilism.
• **Social cohesion.** PGs increase social cohesion and political stability by providing a 'safety-valve' outlet for individual and collective grievances and demands.	• **Social disharmony and dislocation.** Inegalitarian operation of groups increases social discontent and political instability by intensifying the sense of social frustration and injustice felt by disadvantaged and excluded sections of the population.
• **Opposition.** PGs assist surveillance of government by exposing information it would rather keep secret, thereby reinforcing and complementing work of opposition through political parties. PGs thereby improve the accountability of decision makers to electorates.	• **Failure of opposition.** True in theory but only to a limited extent in practice: in Britain's secretive political system, groups and parties combined are unable to mount effective opposition to government policies because they generally lack adequate information.

Further reading

Good recent texts on pressure groups in Britain are those by Baggott (1995), Grant (1995, 2000), Byrne (1997) and Coxall (2001). Jordan and Richardson (1987) and March and Rhodes (1992) are classic expositions of the policy networks approach, and Smith (1995) is a more recent one. Mazey and Richardson (1993) provides valuable insights into the developing world of Euro-lobbying, while Richardson (1993) affords a useful comparative perspective. See also Grant (2001). For 'new' politics and case-studies mentioned in the chapter, see Klein (2000, 2001), Younge (2000) and Evans and Hencke (2001).

Chapter 10

The mass media and politics

The mass media and society   156
The 'media as part of democracy' viewpoint   157
The 'media as a tool of the ruling class'
  viewpoint   159
Television politics   162
The 'tabloidisation' of the mass media   163
Tabloid television   164
Newspaper readership   165
The political impact of the mass media   166
More media, less politics?   169

The communication of political information is an important process in the political system, and the mass media play a central role in this activity. The mass media provide most of the electorate with a framework for understanding past, present and future events. Yet there is extensive debate about both the extent and the character of the impact of the mass media on politics. Some theorists believe that the mass media in Britain facilitate democracy by allowing a wide variety of views to be expressed. Some believe that the media are anti-democratic because of their power to manipulate the way people think about politics at home and abroad. Others are more concerned with discovering the meaning of media content through analysing interaction between media messages and the culture of specific audiences. Many critics have accused the mass media of trivialising politics. Because different television channels and newspapers find that they are competing for a limited number of viewers and readers, there is the tendency to make the news more attractive by treating it as entertainment rather than as a serious business. The chapter concludes by considering likely impacts of election television and newspaper reporting in an age of media diversity.

The mass media and society

Only a small proportion of Britain's population is actively engaged in politics and therefore learns about political affairs from first-hand experience. What the majority knows about politics is made up principally from what they learn from the mass media. In other words, for those individuals who do not participate directly in politics the mass media define their 'real' world of politics. Peter Golding has argued that 'The media are central in the provision of ideas and images which people use to interpret and understand a great deal of their everyday experience' (Golding, 1974: 178). This, of course, gives the mass media enormous potential power, since they can either set people's minds against the political system or help to generate popular support for it.

The mass media are still developing, to include not only newspapers, magazines, cinema, video, advertising hoardings, radio and terrestrial television, but also more recently multi-channel satellite, cable and digital television, the Internet and other embryonic modes such as mass texting. This growth implies greater choice for the individual but also a globalization of mass communication.

For example, cable and satellite television may expose British viewers to programmes that do not reflect 'typical' British values. Also the Internet, a linked network of electronic networks, has created an 'information super-highway' which provides an individual living in the remotest part of Britain with access to a world wide web. In so doing it provides the potential for that person to link up with other like-minded individuals anywhere in the world to create a 'virtual' organisation through which they can pursue political goals.

> *Definition*
> The **mass media** refers to all those forms of communication where large numbers of people are exposed to an identical message. The mass media provide the ideas and images which help most people to understand the world they live in and their place in that world.

The 'media as part of democracy' viewpoint

There are two basic viewpoints concerning the relationship between the mass media and society. First, there is the view that *the media are part of democracy* since they are themselves a 'free' institution. The media assist the working of a democratic system through facilitating free speech and unrestricted public debate. In Britain, there is no state control of either the press or broadcasting, although the latter is regulated so that it always serves the interests of the community as a whole. This results in a great variety of political opinions being given an airing, and many of them are hostile to the government of the day.

Broadcasting is bound by law to be 'impartial'. For example the Independent Broadcasting Authority is legally required to ensure that all news is presented accurately and that 'due impartiality is preserved on the part of persons providing the programmes as respects matters of political or industrial controversy or relating to current public policy'. During times of national emergency the government may extend greater control over broadcasting as part of its strategy for coping. John Whale has pointed out that the laws relating to both the BBC and ITA make it clear that ministers can instruct them to broadcast or withhold whatever the government wants. He added, 'That particular cannon has seldom been fired. It is not much use to party politicians: it was meant to guard the interests of the state (especially in wartime), not of any one political party' (Whale, 1977: 12). Direct intervention in broadcasting by the government is rare, but we shall see that governments can be extremely sensitive about what is broadcast.

The government has no substantial role in the newspaper business. There is no censorship apart from D (Defence) Notices. Thus, unlike broadcasting, there is no obligation for newspapers to be politically impartial. The press provide what can be seen as a 'marketplace for ideas' in which a wide spectrum of political opinion is made available to the public. As might be expected, some newspapers will be bought more than others, with the popular papers providing the public with what they want to read. In terms of a free market, these papers will

---

BOX 10.1

Media values: anti-Semitism and pro-Israeli bias in reporting Middle Eastern affairs?

There has been a long tradition of anti-Semitism in Western culture, culminating in the horrors of the Holocaust. But how far is genuine criticism of contemporary Israeli foreign policy really an excuse to revive an anti-Semitism that has never really gone away?

The liberal press, including the *Guardian, Independent, New Statesman* and *The Times* (and the BBC) have been accused of stirring up anti-Semitism because of the way in which they have reported events in the Middle East. In particular, a bitter controversy surrounded the actions of Israeli troops in the spring of 2002 when they entered a refugee camp in the West Bank town of Jenin.

Journalists were not allowed into the camp until the end of the military operation. Newspaper reports carried accounts provided by Palestinian survivors which pieced together into a horror story. What emerged was at worst a massacre, and at best a violent bloodbath resulting from Israeli disproportionate use of military force.

Accounts of the event in the American press were far more low key with, for example, the *Washington Post* finding no evidence to support Palestinian allegations of summary executions or a massacre. Israeli sources justified the attack on Jenin, the 'capital of suicide bombers'. Palestinians were dismissed as liars. The refugee camp, it was argued, was no ordinary camp but in reality an armed camp of Hamas fighters.

A complex debate took place in the British press, in which it became increasingly difficult to disentangle anti-Semitism from anti-Zionism or indeed opposition to the Israeli leader Ariel Sharon. Detecting media bias is a difficult task since objectivity is a difficult measure to apply. This is particularly the case in reporting Middle East events. On the one hand, brutal Israeli actions may have provided an opportunity for the expression of latent anti-Semitism in some parts of the British media; on the other, pro-Israeli journalists may have used claims of anti-Semitism in the hope of moderating critical reporting of the Sharon government.

thrive, while unpopular and unread papers will struggle and eventually cease being published. The fact that until recently the majority of British newspapers have generally supported the Conservative Party does not undermine this democratic view of the press; indeed, it provides crucial evidence that Britain did have a politically representative press during periods when Conservatives were supported by public opinion.

The bias in the press towards parties that support the status quo of a free enterprise system is inevitable since the newspaper industry is under private control and is part of the free enterprise system. In the past the interests of free enterprise were pursued most strongly by the Conservative Party, and for this reason it followed that the press was predominantly Conservative in its sympathies. In 1997, however, newspapers that had traditionally supported the Conservatives either reduced their enthusiasm for recommending that their readers vote Tory or switched to recommending Labour. Some commentators argued that the political sympathies of newspapers had changed less than appeared on the surface, since 'new' Labour was in fact a conservative, free-market supporting party. Having said this, the press plays an important 'watchdog' role for democracy, and has not shied away from criticising the Conservative Party and Conservative governments in the past or Labour today.

The media's 'watchdog' role can, as might be expected, be the source of tension between journalists and the government. This is because government in Britain has grown accustomed to operating in a climate of greater secrecy than some other Western governments, notably the US administration. As a consequence there can be much greater political embarrassment when investigative journalism unearths information that might threaten the government's standing. Governments in the past have frequently tried to suppress such information. For example, Labour and Conservative governments alike have been very sensitive about documentary television programmes which probe beyond the 'bombs and bullets' level of news reporting on Northern Ireland. The biggest uproar came in response to Thames Television's *Death on the Rock*. This programme explored the circumstances surrounding the killing of three IRA (Irish Republican Army) terrorists in Gibraltar by the SAS (Special Air Service). Roger Bolton, Series Director for *Death on the Rock,* defined the media's watchdog role:

> We, on the other hand, did not see ourselves as agents of the State. Our job was to ask what, why and how, to give the public in a democracy the information to which it is entitled. Put another way our job was not to further government policy but to report the facts, to get the truth.
>
> (Bolton, 1990: 41)

John Major's Conservative government was embarrassed by a series of media disclosures regarding sleaze; most publicity was devoted to the *Guardian*'s accusations that ex-minister Neil Hamilton had received 'cash for questions' from Harrods' owner Mohammed Al Fayed. Tony Blair's governments have been embarrassed by press scrutiny of 'influence for cash' suspicions, the first being when, after making an exception of Formula One motor racing from a ban on the tobacco sponsorship of sport, it was revealed that Formula One boss, Bernie Ecclestone, made a million pound pre-election donation to Labour. Other Labour links have since come under media scrutiny, such as those with Lakshmi Mittall over the purchase of a steel plant, the Hinduja brothers over a passport application, and with the soft-porn publisher, Richard Desmond, over his purchase of the *Daily Express*. Even the business dealings of the Prime Minister's wife, Cherie Booth, became subject to hostile press investigation when the convicted fraudster, Peter Foster, was involved in her purchase of two flats.

Finally, the mass media play an important role in the democratic process by helping to set the political agenda. Along with politicians, the public, parties and other organisations, the media play a crucial role in structuring and widening political debate in Britain so that issues such as the environment, law and order, or the state of the public services receive attention and are addressed by government. Yet there may not always be a correspondence between 'the order of importance in the media given to issues and the order of significance attached to the same issues by the public and politicians' (McQuail, 1987: 275). Sometimes the agenda set in the media is for the media, and far removed from the concerns of the electorate; other times not.

Through these functions the media, it has been argued, enhance and strengthen the quality of democracy in Britain. It can also be argued, however, that recent advances in media technology have increased opportunities for more specialised individual political participation. For example, the move from analogue to digital has reshaped television in ways similar to the impact of coaxial on telephone usage. Through the 'compression' of broadcast signals, many more channels have been, and are still being, made available. An expansion of sub-genre themed interactive channels has replaced what was once a choice from only a few national or regional channels. In other words, 'narrowcasting' allows transmission of political and other content to 'niche or even individualised consumer segments' of the public audience (Cornford and Robins, in Stokes and Reading, 1999: 109). Some political scientists have speculated that driven by this technological change, the world of media conglomerates (see Table 10.1) will be replaced by 'a perfect marketplace of ideas' leading to a massive growth in decentralised, grass roots politics. In this new media world, some have argued, any individual with media access would have the same potential political power as the *Sun*. Add to this the mobilising impact of the Internet for bringing together individuals who share political values, and it is possible to argue that technological change in the media could result in a new, more democratic, political order.

The 'media as a tool of the ruling class' viewpoint

An alternative view of the mass media in relation to society sees the media playing a much more creative role in shaping people's ideas, attitudes, beliefs and actions. In other words, the mass media do not simply reflect public opinion so much as help to mould it in the first place.

The mass media structure the complexities of the social world and make it understandable to readers, viewers and listeners in ways that are to the advantage of media owners. For example, journalists invariably use a consensus view of society as a framework that is imposed on their reporting in order to explain or make sense of events. In doing this, the media tend to give authority to certain

institutions – such as Parliament – while making those who advocate non-Parliamentary or direct political action appear as extremists or irresponsible fanatics. Journalists frequently consult or interview 'experts' for their opinions on issues; and these experts are invariably powerful people in society and naturally support the system which gives them power. Although experts may be seen to disagree with each other on specific issues, they are unlikely ever to challenge the consensus view of society in a fundamental way. The personal network that has built up between media personnel and politicians is also a source of creating 'a consensual or bi-partisan system' through inviting 'both government and opposition politicians' to appear on programmes. Before each appearance 'there are phone calls, brief discussions, and tacit bargaining. This continuing contact becomes a self-adjusting mechanism' (Tunstall and Machin, 1999: 92).

Whilst there was 'spectrum scarcity' in terms of a limited amount of airwave space, there was an argument for the strict regulation of broadcasting. However, technological advances have provided an abundance of airwave space, yet politicians remain stuck in the habit of demanding strict controls over broadcasting. Both the BBC and ITV are self-regulated in terms of implementing various codes and guidelines which are interpreted by the Broadcasting Standards Commission and the Independent Television Commission as well as by some 50 Acts of Parliament, including various Broadcasting Acts, the Contempt of Court Act and the Police and Criminal Evidence Act (Goodwin, in Stokes and Reading, 1999: 130). Whilst newspapers are portrayed as bastions of free speech, they are in fact tightly controlled. Regulation does not come, however, in the form of control by the Press Complaints Commission, which is a relatively weak form of self-regulation, but from a bank of controls including D Notices, considerations regarding contempt of court, prevention of terrorism, defamation, blasphemy as well as the exercising of 'prior constraint', a form of pre-publication self-censorship (Petley, in Stokes and Reading, 1999: 143).

The mass media cannot be neutral or impartial since they are a product of Britain's culture, a culture that is biased like any other culture, with assumptions and prejudices of its own. The imposition of this cultural framework is seen in what is referred to as the 'social manufacture' or 'social production' of the news. News does not 'just happen', rather 'it is made'. News programmes and newspapers have a number of predefined categories to be filled by 'the news': sport, human interest, politics, economics, and so on. For television especially, visually interesting material is more likely to become 'news' than are abstract developments. Agenda-setting is important politically because of the consequences of an issue being placed on the agenda. If industrial strikes are put on the agenda rather than industrial accidents, it will lead to demands for tighter trade union legislation rather than stricter factory regulations. News about 'social security scroungers' will stir up different feelings about society than news about 'tax evaders'. Sometimes there is an over-reaction to what is seen as a threat to society, and this is referred to as a 'moral panic'. During the 1970s there was a feeling that mugging was a new, violent and increasingly common street crime. The reaction was out of all proportion to the threat, which was not new, but nevertheless demands for more policing and tougher penalties were fed into the political system. Twenty years later, there are similar panics over asylum seekers looking for sanctuary in Britain.

The leading stories in national newspapers influence the choice of issues covered by television and radio later in the day. In other words, the agenda set by television, which people see as being 'objective', takes its lead from stories in the national press. Invariably, since they come from a generally pro-capitalist press which supports the existing political order, there is a marked tendency to attack any 'threatening' or disruptive counter-culture such as that presented by feminists, pacifists, militant environmentalists or animal rights protesters, and activist members of ethnic minorities, including asylum seekers.

Newspapers and much of television and radio are commercial enterprises concerned with making a profit for their shareholders. Put simply, they form part of the capitalist system, and this shapes the values they promote. Referring to newspapers in Britain, Colin Sparks argued that they were 'first and foremost businesses. They do not exist to report the news, to act as watchdogs for the public, to be a check on the doings of government, to defend the ordinary citizenry against abuses of power, to unearth scandals or do any of the other

fine and noble things that are sometimes claimed for the press. They exist to make money, just as any other business does' (Sparks, in Stokes and Reading, 1999: 46). Indeed, the mass media are very big business. Six leading newspaper publishers account for some 80 per cent of all daily, Sunday and local newspaper sales. Most of these concerns are conglomerates which have financial interests in other sectors of the communication industry as well as in non-media interests (see Table 10.1). This pattern of ownership can represent a threat to democracy.

First, concentration limits the range and diversity of views and opinions that are able to find public expression. More significantly, it is those views and opinions representing the least powerful social groups that are systematically excluded by the process of concentration. Second, concentration of control over the media into the hands of large conglomerates emphasises production for maximum profit at the necessary expense of other social goals that should be a vital aspect of communication media. Third, such concentration is undemocratic in two senses. It removes the media from public surveillance and accountability: that is, it renders them externally undemocratic (Murdoch and Golding, 1977: 105–6)

Forthcoming communications legislation promises to reduce regulation of Britain's television services through further liberalising of the market. Existing legislation (the 1996 Broadcasting Act) contains the so-called 'Murdoch amendment' designed to keep his media empire from owning a British terrestrial television channel. No company that owns more than 20 per cent of the UK newspaper market may also own a terrestrial television company. However, according to press reports, the Labour government appears to be opening the door for a Murdoch take-over of ailing Channel Five.

Some politicians are fearful of Rupert Murdoch's media dominance and the wider implications of further expansion for future decision making on issues like the euro. Already small British companies such as British Satellite Broadcasting and ITV Digital have collapsed, unable to compete with Murdoch's media empire.

Early commentators on the mass media, such as John Whale, were considerably less worried about the effects of ownership on communication. At

Newspapers	Total market share %	Group	Executive control	Other media interests
Sun The Times Sunday Times News of the World	34.5	News International	Rupert Murdoch	Extensive world press interests, satellite and digital TV, radio, cinema, books etc.
Daily Mirror Sunday Mirror People Scottish Daily Record	19	Trinity Mirror	Victor Blank	Local and regional press, magazines
Daily Mail Mail on Sunday	19	Daily Mail and General Trust	Lord Rothermere	
Daily Express Daily Star Sunday Express	12	Northern and Shell	Richard Desmond	Magazine interests (soft porn)
Daily Telegraph Sunday Telegraph	7.5	Hollinger	Conrad Black	Extensive N. American press interests
Guardian Observer	3.5	Guardian Media Group	The Scott Trust	Local and regional papers
Financial Times	3	Pearson	The Pearson Board	Publishing interests
Independent Independent on Sunday	1.5	Independent Newspapers	Tony O'Reilly	Local newspapers

Table 10.1 Newspaper ownership and wider media interests

the time Whale was writing, the 'press baron' who owned papers and who personally dictated editorial policy had disappeared. There were no proprietors like Lord Beaverbrook or Lord North-cliffe, who used to instruct their editors what to put in the *Daily Express* and *Daily Mail* respec-tively. Contents and policy were determined by professional staff journalists who decided what items to cover, and what items to comment about. However, events were to overtake this argument, with the emergence of a new generation of press barons such as Rupert Murdoch and the late Robert Maxwell. There was concern that not only were these new proprietors so powerful that they could intervene in the same ways as the old press barons, but also that they did not usually have to intervene, since editorial staff anticipated and

wrote what they knew would find the approval of their respective proprietors.

However, issues of ownership and control have made a dramatic impact upon the press. The case of the *Sun* shows how a newspaper can be redi-rected away from the political views of its estab-lished readership. Rupert Murdoch purchased the broadsheet *Sun*, which developed from the pro-Labour *Daily Herald*. Murdoch had a reputation for moving his newspapers to the right, and in 1974 this was to happen to the *Sun* 'in opposition to the opinion of its readers', the majority of whom supported Labour (Curran and Seaton, 1990: 81). Thus in a little over a decade, Labour had lost the support of a mass circulation daily paper and the Conservatives gained yet another supporter in Fleet Street, which a further decade

BOX 10.2

Do the British public's Euro-sceptic attitudes result from press hostility to the EU?

The European Commission has produced a report which criticised both jingoistic reporting and the reporting of untrue stories which are usually about European harmonisation (such as fishermen's hairnets, straight bananas, one-size condoms, and banning British lavatories). The Commission accused British newspapers of suffering from 'mythomania'. The report continued to criticise British newspapers for not printing corrections when such stories were proved to be false. Finally, the report criticised some newspapers for finding the EU 'guilty' by associating it with Europe's Nazi past.

Paul Whiteley has argued that attitudes towards the EU are clearly linked to reading certain newspapers. For example, with Euro-sceptic papers, only 10 per cent of *Daily Mail* readers, 16 per cent of *Sun* readers and 29 per cent of *Times* readers wanted Britain to join the euro. In contrast, 51 per cent of *Guardian* readers favoured Britain joining the euro. The exception to this apparently clear-cut pattern was the Euro-sceptic *Daily Telegraph*, with two-thirds of its readers either in favour of Britain joining the euro or preferring to 'wait and see' before deciding.

later was to be the most ardent champion of Thatcherism. The values of groups such as the ethnic minorities, unions, feminists and others beyond the Conservative domain are marginalised by the media and remain unrepresented. Even the major opposition party, Labour, was generally portrayed as a dangerous and unpatriotic enemy within. Only when 'new' Labour endorsed the Thatcherite agenda and accepted free-market economics did the *Sun* change sides.

For some media commentators, issues of ownership and control within the media have assumed a greater importance as the result of globalization. The so-called 'special relationship' in foreign policy

between the USA and the UK is reflected in the world of mass media communication. With foreign news, for example, most of video news 'shown on the world's TV screens comes from two video agencies – one British-owned [Reuters], one US-owned [APTN] – both based in London' (Tunstall and Machin, 1999: 81). The result of this Anglo-American duopoly is that Reuters and Associated Press 'bestride the news agendas and news flows of the world'. They are 'wielders of a unique political force – the "power of news" around the world' (ibid.: 88).

Resulting from the internationalisation of media ownership, 78 per cent of non-tabloid national newspapers sold each day in Britain are owned by foreign concerns: 'The two sales leaders in the elite (broadsheet and up-market) national category – *The Times* and *Daily Telegraph* and their Sunday versions – were controlled by Murdoch and Black (Tunstall and Machin, 1999: 140). While the political implications of a largely foreign-owned press are rarely debated in public, Tunstall and Machin noted that these papers 'sided with the anti-Major, anti-European faction of the Conservative party', resulting in the unusual situation of a British Conservative prime minister being opposed by the bulk of the national press on his most important policies (ibid.: 146–7).

Television politics

Most people rely on television as their main source of information. As long ago as 1962 a BBC survey showed that 58 per cent of the sample learned the news primarily from television, whereas only 33 per cent learned it mainly from newspapers. Another study ten years later revealed that 85 per cent named television as their main source of information. There is a tendency for people to believe what they 'see' on television but to be sceptical about what they read in the press. Nearly 70 per cent think that television is the 'most trustworthy' news source, while only 6 per cent are prepared to rank newspapers so highly.

Since television is perceived by so many as providing a source of objective political information, it is not surprising that there are tensions between politicians and personnel in the media. Examples

BOX 10.3

Comparative politics: the 'watchdog' role of the British and American press

There is no comparison between the relatively sycophantic British press at national and local level and the US press which scrutinises Republican and Democrat administrations with equal rigour on behalf of American citizens. In this sense, therefore, the British media fails miserably in performing its 'watchdog' role. Indeed, even the reformed 'lobby system' is an expression of the cosy relationship between the media and the government, with the former depending on the latter for the supply of 'news' items. This dependency relationship between journalists and politicians is in sharp contrast to the American tradition of investigative journalism.

have been provided above of specific programmes in which the government of the day did not feel it was being treated fairly. Politicians have also complained about the aggressive questioning they receive on Radio Four's *Today* programme.

It is not only specific programmes that have interested politicians but the general 'tone' of a network which has, from time to time, been examined by a 'bias monitoring unit'. Some commentators felt that during the period when the last Conservative government was deciding the future of the BBC – whether its Royal Charter should be renewed or whether it should be privatised – broadcasters were so anxious not to upset the government that their reporting of government policies was noticeably uncritical. In a rather similar way it has been argued that the independent television companies are 'controlled' by the periodic franchise renewal process.

Government ministers sometimes come to see policy failure in terms of poor presentation in the media. In other words, rather than recognising that the policies in question are ill thought-out, inappropriate or not working, it is argued that for some reason 'the message is not getting across'. This logic places the blame with the media for communicating poorly rather than with ministers for governing poorly. In order to receive favourable treatment, politicians and their parties will attempt to manipulate the media in a number of ways. First, accusing television journalists of being biased may produce positive results:

> A party can try to bias television in its favour by alleging that the broadcasters are biased against them. If that produces any response at all it may encourage the broadcasters to alter the balance in its favour. Even if the broadcasters do nothing it may encourage the viewers to regard television as biased against the party and to make allowances for that when they watch.
> (Miller *et al.*, 1990: 72)

Second, parties will attempt to manipulate the media, particularly television, by what is known as 'spin'. This involves dealing with events, particularly potentially damaging ones, in order to get them interpreted in a favourable way by journalists. Labour came to power with a reputation for skilful spin, but in office found that news management could 'spin out of control'. The most extreme example was provided by the leaking of an e-mail from a senior Labour adviser, Jo Moore, suggesting that it could be a good day to publish and 'bury' departmental bad news within minutes of the first tower of the New York Trade Center being hit on 11 September 2001. The incident contributed to the resignation of two advisers and a minister, but critics argued that what Jo Moore did was no more than a logical extension of the type of spin practised by Number Ten.

The 'tabloidisation' of the mass media

It has been argued that western culture is in a crisis. Some have identified a process in the mass media that involves reducing the intellectual demands made on viewers, listeners or readers; Americans call it 'dumbing down'. It is argued that film-makers, television producers and newspaper editors reduce standards in order to increase their share of the market; within ITV, for example, 'there are undoubtedly pressures to reduce and popularise news output' (Crisell, in Stokes and Reading, 1999: 69).

Some political commentators are convinced that the dumbing-down process has affected the quality broadsheet newspapers as well as the tabloids.

Photograph: PA Photos.

IN FOCUS 10.1 The master of spin?

Alastair Campbell, then prime minister's official spokesperson (later of the Communications and Strategy Unit) and architect of the lobby reforms, leaving Downing Street after a special political Cabinet meeting called by Prime Minister Tony Blair to approve Labour's General Election manifesto. It is an indication of the importance attached to presentation and communication that Campbell has become more recognisable (and reportedly more influential) than many Cabinet Ministers. After the election he withdrew from his direct role in press briefing to become the Director of Communications and Strategy in the Prime Minister's Office, but he remained a controversial figure.

They argue that 20 or 30 years ago, quality broadsheets like *The Times,* the *Guardian* and the *Telegraph* made much greater demands on readers by assuming a higher level of knowledge and greater concentration. It is argued that in the last ten years or so, quality broadsheet newspapers have become more like the tabloids. Anthony Sampson has argued that 'the frontier between the qualities and popular papers has virtually disappeared'. He noted that the amount of foreign news, Parliamentary reporting and serious investigative reporting has declined. The quality broadsheets

now include stories about celebrities – the Beckhams, the Gallagher brothers, or Kylie Minogue – in a way they used not to.

It is argued that today's quality press are trivialising the news, which deadens intellect and harms critical thought, which is not good for democracy. An example of this is found in the way serious newspapers devoted much space to covering Tony Blair's changed hairstyle, including computer graphics of his appearance at various stages of baldness. Is this just 'a bit of fun' or does it trivialise politics and put serious political debate at risk? At the same time, it is also argued that the tabloid papers have become more tabloid. For example, during the 1960s the middle-market papers – the *Daily Mail* and the *Daily Express* – had as much written text on their front pages as today's broadsheets. The reporting was serious: the *Daily Mirror* devoted considerable space to foreign affairs, once giving 15 pages to cover the political crisis in Cambodia. Finally, it is noted that even regional and local newspapers are going tabloid, mixing gossip with news coverage.

Others have lamented a decline in political news reporting, which extends beyond the *Sun* into all newspapers. Compared with the recent past, newspapers contain many more features, lifestyle and travel articles and interviews with celebrities, and much less hard political news. Nick Cohen argued that in the 1960s a third of all journalists from national newspapers were based outside London, either in the regions or overseas where they reported on events. Now nearly 90 per cent of all journalists on national newspapers work in London, and write stories on material which comes to them through press agencies. In addition, he continued, newspapers now employed inexpensive young journalists on temporary contracts, and this has led to a decline in the number of experienced journalists who have developed a specialism in politics. He was concerned that if television was expected to take the place of newspapers in reporting politics, there are problems since it cannot offer the same depth or scope as a serious newspaper.

Tabloid television

It is argued that serious television programmes are also influenced by tabloid values. This is because news programmes have become seen as 'entertainment' rather than 'education'. As a result, programmes focus on 'human interest' stories at the expense of more complex or abstract news items. Many political commentators were surprised when the tabloid papers' obsession with the Princess of Wales appeared to be shared by the BBC's flagship documentary programme, *Panorama*, which devoted a programme-long interview to exploring her problems and ambitions.

Why are media values now tabloid values?

- Circulation battles: quality broadsheets are locked into a bitter struggle to win readers. There are fears that because of a declining market, one of the quality newspapers will disappear in the near future. Hence they are all attempting to maximise their sales, which means moving 'downmarket'. Similar arguments might be applied to television.
- Newspapers are trying to get younger readers. Therefore papers now use snappier headlines and shorter sentences to report 'soundbite' politics. Others argue that such techniques are an insult to the young, because editors are treating them as if they really are dumb.
- The influence of Rupert Murdoch's style on journalism on the mass media. An example may be useful to convey the new media culture associated with Murdoch. When Elvis Presley died in 1977, no *Times* reporter was sent to Memphis to cover the funeral, since it was decided that it was not an appropriate story for a serious newspaper. Murdoch bought *The Times* in 1981, and two journalists were sent to Jamaica to cover the death of Bob Marley. *The Times* then introduced its own style of bingo game, again unthinkable under its previous owner.
- The influence of greater competition in the electronic media from satellite and cable television. Their impact has resulted in pressures to lower standards.

Newspaper readership

More than a thousand newspaper titles are published in Britain, more than half being 'free papers' which depend on advertising for revenue. The ten papers that comprise the national daily press account for roughly 13 million of the 19 million in circulation each day. The *Sun* enjoys the biggest circulation, and the *Financial Times* the smallest. The circulation of some newspapers has declined markedly: for example, in 2002 the *Daily Express* is selling less than a million copies a day for the first time since 1924, and the *Daily Mirror* is experiencing its lowest sales since 1946 (Stanyer, 2002: 378). Reflecting Britain's centralised administration, the national press remains concentrated in London, with 69 per cent of all daily papers in circulation being edited in London. Local and regional newspapers, therefore, account for only a minority of daily circulation. (Sparks, 1999: 42). Alongside newspapers there are approximately 10,000 magazines published in Britain, with publication dominated by IPC and EMAP (Stokes, 1999: 20).

The rack of papers seen outside any newsagent symbolises the British class system. The quality broadsheet press titles (*The Times*, the *Daily Telegraph*, the *Guardian*, the *Independent* and the *Financial Times*) are read overwhelmingly by the higher socio-economic groups. There are two papers (the *Daily Mail* and the *Daily Express*) competing in the mid-market area for the middle and lower middle class readers, while the mass-circulation *Sun*, *Mirror* and *Star* have predominantly working class readers. There is relatively little crossover in readership between these different titles. (Sparks, in Stokes and Reading, 1999: 47). In a comparison of the social profile of the readers of *The Times* and the *Sun* it was revealed that 'the readership of these two kinds of newspapers is centred on different social groups ... the readership of the quality press is predominantly upper and middle class, while the readership of the popular press is predominantly working class' (ibid.: 50).

Treatment of the news varies enormously between papers. The quality papers contain much more of what might be described as 'hard news' in addition to comment and editorial. The mass circulation papers more closely resemble adult comics, and are designed for 'looking at' rather than 'reading', containing 'soft news' features which have interest but not immediate newsworthiness. Much space is taken up with photographs and large-print headlines. Where the quality press focuses on international events and city news, the mass circulation papers rarely fail to devote considerable space to 'scandal' of one sort or another.

Only 21 per cent of the adult male population reads a quality broadsheet newspaper, and only 12 per cent of adult females do so. Not only has the tabloid press become more tabloid in nature over recent years, but the press has generally undergone political change: 'national newspapers became markedly more partisan from 1974 onwards. This was partly in response to the growing polarisation of British politics. But it also reflected the cumulative impact of a new generation of partisan, interventionist proprietors' (Curran and Seaton, 1990: 80). It was once assumed that such changes would have little impact upon the political behaviour of the electorate, but some have challenged this assumption (see Box 10.5).

The political impact of the mass media

There is a view that the mass media can actually create news by 'setting up' newsworthy events that otherwise could not have taken place. Some think that the mere presence of television cameras at a demonstration increases the risks that it will develop into a riot. Some may argue that if such a riot is shown on the television news, this can create 'copycat' riots in other areas. Another view is that the mass media may enhance or reduce the importance of events, but those events cannot be created by the media. Doris Grabler has argued that assessing the impact of particular media content is difficult because audiences already possess a fund of knowledge and attitudes that they bring to bear on new information; because 'researchers rarely know precisely what this information is, or the rules by which it is combined with incoming information, they cannot pinpoint the exact contribution that particular mass media stories have made to an individual's cognitions, feelings, and actions (Grabler, 1997: 15). She continued to make the point that factors such as personnel and context are important in any assessment of media impact. For example, an item in a newspaper or on television that influences a politician or activist is likely to have greater impact than an item that shapes the perceptions of someone who is politically passive. Reading about the potential of space-based laser weapons in a

Reader's Digest article is claimed to have been the critical factor behind President Reagan's 'Star Wars' initiative which, in turn, many believe was influential in causing the collapse of the Soviet Union. Such an impact would be unlikely no matter how many ordinary Americans read and were impressed by the same article.

Furthermore, the context of media influence is an important consideration. For example, media coverage of blood sports resulting in a 5 per cent swing in public opinion against fox hunting will have less immediate political impact than general election campaign coverage that results in a 5 per cent electoral swing. Colin Seymour-Ure, on the other hand, argued that the political impact of any communication will be influenced by its timing, frequency and intensity (Seymour-Ure, 1974: 36).

Frequency

The constant repetition of messages over a period of time may make an impact on the political climate. Colin Seymour-Ure argues that the habit of the mass media in presenting a 'Westminster' view of British politics can mislead the public:

> The construction regularly put upon the nature of British politics by the mass media stresses heavily the 'Westminster' as opposed to the 'Whitehall' elements. The power of Parliament, and the extent to which it figures in political processes at all, are arguably emphasised more than they should be if an accurate impression of events is to be given. If that is so, the frequency of media coverage has much to do with it.
>
> (Seymour-Ure, 1974: 36)

Intensity

When one story dominates all others, it is said to be communicated more intensely. An unexpected or urgent event can be turned into a crisis by the intensity of media coverage, such as the untimely death of the Princess of Wales. The Falklands War of 1982 is another interesting example of a high-intensity media event. The Gulf War, in which Saddam Hussein's Iraqi invasion of Kuwait was reversed by an alliance of American, British and Arab forces,

BOX 10.4

The importance of timing in media political influence: the Zinoviev letter

One of the most interesting examples of political impact resulting from the timing of news took place during the general election campaign of 1924 with the publication of the Zinoviev letter. The letter, now very widely believed to have been a fake, was marked 'Very Secret' and was supposedly sent from the Third Communist International in Moscow to the Central Committee of the British Communist Party. It urged the need to stir the British working class into revolutionary action and form them into a British Red Army. The letter was published in the Press on 25 October and dominated the campaign until polling day on 29 October. The *Daily Mail* gave the letter the most sensational treatment, and of the remaining papers only the *Herald* declared it to be a forgery. Some argue that the 'Red Scare' resulting from the Zinoviev letter lost Labour the election. In other words, had the news of this letter, which had been known for some considerable period, been released at a different time, then Labour might have won the general election.

dominated the world's news media in January 1991. The intensity of reporting in Britain was reflected in the first round-the-clock BBC radio channel being devoted to reporting the conflict.

Television and press coverage of elections

Despite the extraordinary outcome of the 1997 general election, coverage of events on television fell flat. Some commentators concluded that in 1997, 'British election television news was voluminous, substantive, and more detailed than in many other countries. Nevertheless ... the news was more negative in 1997 than in previous campaigns, and this process may turn voters off' (Semetko *et al.*, 1997: 614). Politicians launched attacks on their opponents on a daily basis, faithfully reported by television journalists, and the 'balance requirement'

of the Representation of the People Act 'despite all its good intentions, often resulted in regimented soundbites and negative conflict that may in fact have conspired against understanding' (ibid.: 615).

Labour enjoyed its greatest level of endorsement by the daily and Sunday national press in the 1997 general election campaign:

- In 1945, when Labour's Parliamentary landslide was won on 48 per cent of the popular vote, it was supported by daily national papers that had a combined 35 per cent of all newspaper circulation.
- In 1964, when Labour was returned to power on 44 per cent of the popular vote, it had the support of three national dailies which together had 42 per cent of all newspaper circulation.
- In 1983, Labour won only 28 per cent of the popular vote, and was supported only by the loyal *Daily Mirror*, which accounted for 22 per cent of newspaper circulation.
- In Labour's 1997 Parliamentary landslide, achieved on 44 per cent of the popular vote, the party was supported by six dailies which represented 62 per cent of all newspaper circulation.
  (Source: Seymour-Ure, 1995: 588)

Labour's leader, Tony Blair, had carefully established good relations with Rupert Murdoch's News International and it was not a surprise when the *Sun* changed sides (Box 10.5). The *Sun* had been a Thatcherite rather than pro-Conservative paper, and in changing its allegiance it became pro-Blair rather than pro-Labour. Another press baron, Lord Rothermere, whose publishing empire included the *Daily Mail* and London's *Evening Standard*, also announced his conversion to New Labour. The second Labour government has retained a high level of press approval, with only the most traditional Conservative-supporting newspapers offering sustained criticism. As indicated above, the testing time for Labour's new relationship with the press is likely to focus on its policy towards the euro (see Box 10.2).

Declining advertising revenue has placed much of Britain's media industry in financial crisis, and in the competitive struggle to win circulation and audiences, this had an impact on coverage of the 2001 general election. Since public apathy towards the election was at a high level, newspaper editors

BOX 10.5

Looking back to 1992 and 1997: did the *Sun* win it?

The influence of tabloid newspapers, the *Sun* in particular, on voting behaviour in the 1992 general election is still discussed by political scientists. The day following the election the *Sun* headline told readers 'It's the Sun Wot Won It', and some journalists agreed that the claim was largely justified. Poll data indicated that during the last week of the campaign, the anti-Labour blitz in the Tory tabloids had produced swings to the Conservatives of 4 per cent among *Sun* readers and 2 per cent among *Daily Mail* readers. Paul Whiteley, a political scientist, argued that the *Sun* was more effective in getting marginal Conservative voters to the polling stations (who might otherwise have abstained) than in converting potential Labour voters into actual Tory voters. He calculated that the *Sun* effect in 1997 of supporting Tony Blair was to reduce the size of the Conservative vote by *Sun* readers by 16 per cent, instead of the 8 per cent it would have dropped if the paper had continued to support the Tories.

did not want to 'inflict' unwanted political coverage on uninterested readers. During the campaign, only a quarter of tabloid front pages referred to the forthcoming election. On television 'there were fewer slots on the main terrestrial news bulletins for the additional stories and analysis that characterised coverage of previous campaigns. Instead, much of the additional news coverage was partially "ghettoised", broadcast on the less-watched new digital 24-hour news channels' (Stanyer, 2002: 380).

Backbench exposure: Parliament or the media?

Relations between government and the media have a turbulent history, particularly during periods of political crisis. Routine day-to-day relations between government and journalists were also controversial under the old and somewhat discredited 'lobby system' whereby 'cooperative' reporters were

treated on a favoured basis (see Box 10.6). Relations between the media and Parliament have also been contentious. Some politicians opposed television cameras entering the Lords and then the Commons because they thought that televising proceedings would 'devalue' Parliament in the eyes of the electorate. Oddly enough television has reduced the importance of Parliament in some ways, but not so much in the eyes of the public as in the actions of politicians. Close to Parliament are the television and radio studios at 4 Millbank. Which venue, the Commons or Millbank, is the more important for a backbench MP who wants publicity for his or her views?

- Many MPs find that it is much easier to get a hearing at Millbank than it is in the Commons. This is particularly true for maverick backbenchers who frequently have a controversial view they want to communicate to the public, yet rarely have the opportunity of being called to speak in Commons debates.
- There are now many more opportunities for MPs to appear on television and radio than existed in the past. The number of political programmes, such as those broadcast at lunchtime on Sunday, has increased during the last 20 years.
- MPs reach a wider audience more quickly by

BOX 10.6

The lobby system

The Westminster lobby system of twice-daily briefings for political correspondents in Number Ten has been criticised for a number of reasons. First, during periods of tense relations with the press, governments have suspended lobby briefings. Second, when briefings were 'off the record', government spokespersons could abuse the confidentiality surrounding what they said. Some newspapers used to boycott such briefings, and welcomed the changes in 1997 in which all briefings were 'on the record'. Third, the lobby system tends to be dominated by a small number of 'privileged' journalists. Changes will involve the presence of more journalists, including representatives of the foreign press.

appearing on television or radio than by speaking in a Commons debate. Many ministers feel that a 12-second 'soundbite' on Radio 4's *Today* programme or the television news is more effective than a lengthy speech in Parliament.

- Newspapers now monitor television and radio more closely than they follow proceedings in Parliament. In recent years there has been a sharp decline in the reporting of Parliamentary debates in the quality broadsheet newspapers. A consequence of this is that the press follows up television and radio news items in the next day's papers. Hence MPs are more likely to push their concerns on to the political agenda through appearing in the television and radio studios at Millbank than on the floor of the House of Commons.

- Finally, MPs gain greater recognition through appearing on television and radio than through debating in the Commons. This may be because television and radio stresses the 'entertainment' or 'soap opera' ingredients of politics – conflict between individuals, clashes of personality, and aspects of scandal – whereas the focus of Parliament is on the more routine legislative process. In short, politicians on television and radio come across as colourful personalities who capture the attention of viewers and listeners, whereas in the Commons they are more 'grey' and much less attractive.

More media, less politics?

Newspapers contain less 'politics' than in the past, and in any case their circulations are generally in decline. Political television also appears to be losing popularity. This may result from television becoming increasingly based on market principles. If this is the case, as many commentators believe, the old Reithian concept of public service broadcasting is coming to an end. What then is the future of politics and the media?

While British culture may have reached the point of 'media saturation', does this mean that more political information is being disseminated throughout the population? For the increased diversity within the media now means that one person's consumption of media diet may differ greatly from another's. For example, a member of the 'chattering classes' may regularly read the political press, watch Paxman on *Newsnight*, catch specialist programmes on Radio Four and even contact a government website for information. The same media diversity would enable another person to watch a great deal of television that has no political content, read specialist non-political publications such as 'fanzines', and pursue personal interests on the Net without ever being exposed to any political content. The growth of interactive cable, TV and the Internet offers opportunities both for greater 'connectivity' between like-minded individuals interested in bringing about political change and for total insulation for individuals from the world of politics. The former scenario promises a modified, perhaps greatly modified, political order in which power is redistributed towards ordinary citizens and democracy undergoes a revival; the latter scenario promises a rich diet of niche, 'dumbed-down' entertainments provided by globalized media giants to increasingly apolitical publics. Or finally, will the conventional broadcast and press mass media lose their political function and retreat to providing only entertainment, because citizens turn to the Internet for what little political information they require?

Further reading

Curran and Seaton (1990) and Seymour-Ure (1974) both provide interesting discussions of the position of the media in society. Whale (1977) provides a comprehensive discussion of the political context within which the media operates and which it influences. Stokes and Reading (1999) reviews a range of empirical and analytical material concerning media studies. Tunstall and Machin (1999) analyses Britain's partnership with the USA and subservient media roles, and Anderson (1997) provides an interesting case-study of the environment and the media.

Part III

BRITISH GOVERNMENT: WESTMINSTER AND WHITEHALL

Part II of this book was concerned with the political process. Part III shifts the focus to the process and institutions of government. We have chosen to begin with the traditional heart of British government in Westminster and Whitehall. At one time this would have needed no defence, as that was almost all that seemed to matter, apart from a strictly subordinate local government system. UK membership of the European Union, and more recently devolution within Britain, mean this is now no longer the case. The contrasted pressures of globalization, and for delegation and decentralisation, have combined to create a fast-developing system of multi-level governance within and alongside the old British centralised state. New institutions imply new values and assumptions which challenge some of the most fundamental values associated with the old British constitution. However, traditional institutions and principles have not been rejected and replaced, but continue to coexist, somewhat awkwardly, with the new. Some of the consequent tensions and contradictions at the heart of British government remain unresolved. To describe and explain British government now is to try to hit a moving target, for the likely end-result of this constitutional revolution is still far from clear.

We therefore focus in Part III on the traditional centre of the British governmental system in Whitehall and Westminster, while fully acknowledging the extensive implications of internal reforms and external pressures on long-established features and principles of British government at the centre. The emerging new world of multi-level governance, involving a more complex and contentious state, is left for a closer examination and analysis in Part IV.

Chapter 11 begins with the key features and principles of Britain's unwritten (or more accurately uncodified) constitution, but goes on to question how far these remain valid in the face of on-going reform. Chapter 12 focuses on what is often now rather awkwardly described as the 'core executive in Britain' (Smith, 1999): the prime minister and Cabinet system, with senior civil servants and advisers. There are old questions here about prime ministerial power, but also about the capacity of the core executive (however defined) for effective action. Chapter 13 switches to the great departments of state, arguments about relations between elected ministers and civil servants, and the impact of management reforms on traditional civil service values. Chapter 14 is devoted to Parliament and the legislative process. The functions and effectiveness of the House of Commons and the on-going reform of the Upper House are discussed fully, as are the implications for the Westminster Parliament of other parliaments and assembles – in Strasbourg, Edinburgh, Cardiff and Stormont. Finally, Chapter 15 looks at the law and the judicial process, and the sometimes awkward relations between judges and politicians, along with a discussion of rights and the redress of citizen grievances. The chapter ends with a brief analysis of the implications of the 1999 Human Rights Act.

Chapter **11**

The evolving British Constitution

What is a constitution?	173
The classification of constitutions	174
The evolution of the British Constitution	175
The main characteristics of the British Constitution	177
Representative democracy	180
The rule of law	180
Ideological perceptions of the British Constitution	181
The movement for constitutional reform	183
Labour and the constitution: a government of radical reform?	184

The British system of government is in the midst of radical change, which could lead eventually to the most extensive transformation of the way in which Britain is governed for 300 years. The changes not only affect specific institutions and processes, but have implications for long-entrenched constitutional principles. Textbooks on British government (including this one) must be rewritten extensively. All this needs saying at the outset, because it is insufficiently appreciated. This is partly because constitutional reform does not seem to excite the public, nor win elections. However it also partly reflects the Labour government's rather low-key and fragmented approach to its own reform programme. A series of radical initiatives have been pursued almost in isolation from each other, and, critics suggest, uninformed by any overall vision. Thus the full significance of the reforms and their potential implications for the British Constitution have not generally been grasped.

Any examination of the British system of government and ongoing constitutional reform needs to be set in context. This chapter begins with a discussion of constitutions in general, and how much they tell us about particular systems of government, and the effectiveness (or otherwise) of the safeguards they provide against abuse of power or the infringement of fundamental rights.

We will then examine the sources of the British Constitution and its underlying principles. Because of the lack of an authoritative document, key constitutional principles have generally been inferred from political practice. They have long been open to diverse interpretations from different ideological perspectives, and some have become decidedly contentious, partly as a result of recent changes. Thus, finally, we examine the constitutional reform movement which began in the late 1980s, and analyse the extensive programme of constitutional reform already undertaken by the Labour government, as well as further reforms in the pipeline and prospects for the future. Among the alternative scenarios here and in subsequent chapters is the break-up of Britain.

What is a constitution?

Political science has sometimes neglected the study of constitutions. This is for two main reasons. First, formal constitutions are imperfect guides to political reality – to the actual as compared with the supposed distribution of power within a state. For example, many constitutions either omit or scarcely mention the roles in the political process of such important institutions as parties, pressure groups and public bureaucracies. In fact, the structure and number of parties are so influential upon the way political systems work that some leading political scientists see these factors as the major determinants of the whole nature of political regimes. Clearly, much important political behaviour occurs outside the formal legal framework. Second, formal constitutions have been frequently and easily flouted and overthrown. The constant demolition of allegedly binding constitutions since 1918 appears to mock the 19th-century belief in the capacity of written codes of rules to mould political actions. The tearings-up of written constitutions by dictators are merely dramatic examples of this process.

Yet while formal constitutions are *incomplete* as guides to political practice, as no single document could ever define and describe a country's political system in its complex entirety, they do matter for a number of reasons. They commonly include the most important procedural rules of a political system. They frequently also contain statements of key political principles, and commitments to basic rights and freedoms. Alongside moral codes and cultural norms, they provide a means of restraint on politicians and civil servants. Finally, they are the major way of giving legitimacy to a particular system of government, to a particular way of organising the distribution of power within a state. The US Constitution, for example, remains immensely important for an understanding of American politics and government. Books on US politics commonly include the text of the original constitution with all subsequent constitutional amendments. Even though some of its provisions do not operate entirely as its founding fathers intended, the constitution continues to be treated with reverence by politicians and citizens. It is a constant reference point when major disputes over government arise.

However, while constitutions may be treated with great reverence, they are not 'above politics' but *about* politics and *in* politics. Constitutions are *about* politics because they provide the framework of rules that shape political behaviour – the main 'rules of the game'. Second, constitutions are *in* politics because as bodies of the most important rules in a country they are subject to pressure from the competing individuals, groups and classes they affect. Constitutions at any given moment are always more or less advantageous to some and disadvantageous to others. For example, the single-member, simple

majority electoral system for the Westminster Parliament benefits the major parties but operates against the Liberal Democrats. A constitution, therefore, is something that politicians and political activists are always seeking to change, radically modify, keep the same or, if they are revolutionaries, overthrow.

The classification of constitutions

It is customary to classify constitutions according to whether they are

- written or unwritten
- flexible or inflexible
- unitary or federal.

Written and unwritten constitutions

Britain's Constitution is widely described as unwritten in the sense that it is not contained in a single authoritative document, although substantial parts are in fact written (for example, in various Acts of Parliament), so it is better described as 'uncodified'. Even so, this is distinctly unusual in the modern world. While at one time virtually all systems of government were unwritten, today nearly all other countries incorporate their major constitutional rules into a single document. Newly independent states, or countries that have experienced a revolution or fundamental regime change, invariably draw up a set of rules for the practice of government, just as any newly constituted club or society usually draws up a 'constitution'. Britain has not done so, partly because its system of government has evolved over time, and has not been subject to sharp regime changes since the 17th century. Its system of government seemed to work, and indeed some features were admired and copied by other countries. On the principle 'If it ain't broke, don't fix it', a written constitution has not seemed necessary. However, some constitutional reformers have argued the need for a written constitution, and it is possible that some of the constitutional reforms now in process may eventually require codification of Britain's rules of government.

Definition
A **constitution** is simply a set of rules and conventions that lays down the powers and functions of state institutions and their relationship with each other.

Flexible and inflexible constitutions

This distinction relates to the ease with which a constitution can be changed. A flexible constitution may enable a system of government to evolve with the times, but could appear more vulnerable to ill-considered change, or subversion. A constitution that is too rigid and inflexible may lack the capacity to adapt to new pressures and altered circumstances, perhaps of a kind its original designers could hardly anticipate.

A common characteristic of 'written' or 'codified' constitutions is that the constitutional law they embody has the status of a higher form of law. For example, Article VI, Clause 2 of the US Constitution states: 'This Constitution ... shall be the supreme law of the land.' Whereas written constitutions are normally only alterable by special procedures, an uncodified constitution like Britain's can be amended by the same process as the ordinary law, or even by changes over time in unwritten conventions. However, although all written constitutions lay down set procedures for constitutional change, they differ in flexibility. In some countries a majority of two-thirds or more is required in each house of parliament, and the proposed change may additionally require support in a referendum and/or by each state in a federal system. In other countries, constitutional reform proposals face fewer obstacles. However, changing judicial interpretation can lead to significant change even in countries with an apparently 'rigid' constitution. Thus the American Supreme Court has allowed its interpretation of the constitution to evolve with the times, with for example considerable implications for racial segregation and civil rights.

Unitary and federal systems

While some states have a federal constitution in which the powers of government are divided between different levels, other states continue to emphasise their unity (see Box 11.1). Thus the French Fifth Republic is 'one and indivisible'. This does not preclude other levels of government (regional and local), but these are legally subordinate to the sovereign state.

Britain (like France) is a unitary state, at least in legal form. The United Kingdom of Great Britain and Northern Ireland is a political union of several

> **Definition**
> **Sovereignty** means supreme power. Within a state it refers to the ultimate source of legal authority. When used of states in their external relations, sovereignty means a state's ability to function as an independent entity – as a sovereign state.

countries, each with a different constitutional status. Legally, it consists of the Kingdoms of England and Scotland, the Principality of Wales and two-thirds of the province of Ulster (Northern Ireland), which remained loyal to the British Crown in 1922 when the rest of Ireland split away to form what eventually became the Republic of Ireland (1949). The third edition (1998) of this book firmly insisted that the UK remains a unitary state, but this now appears more questionable. While the on-going process of devolution, in theory, does not affect the unity of the United Kingdom or the sovereignty of the Westminster Parliament, political realities begin to suggest otherwise, and perhaps foreshadow the development of a quasi-federal, or ultimately fully federal, system of British government, or alternatively the break-up of Britain. (See pages 184–6 and Chapter 17 for a fuller discussion of the constitutional implications of devolution.)

The evolution of the British Constitution

Britain's piecemeal approach to radical constitutional change is perhaps characteristic of the style of British politics. Britain has not had a revolution for over 300 years (and even the 1688 revolution was more a *coup d'état*, which emphasised continuity rather than change). Britain has not experienced the sharp regime changes which have characterised French government and politics for over two centuries. Change is evolutionary rather than revolutionary. Reforms, sometimes quite fundamental, have been grafted onto traditional institutions. The new is painlessly absorbed into the old and familiar, as if to reassure the faint-hearted that nothing has really changed.

Because constitutions are inherently political, they have to be seen in a dynamic rather than a static way. The British Constitution is the product

BOX 11.1

Comparative politics: federalism in the USA and other countries

The founding fathers of the United States of America virtually invented federalism. Political thinkers like Thomas Hobbes had earlier declared that sovereignty (or supreme power) could not be divided. Under a federal system sovereignty is deliberately divided between two (or conceivably more) levels of government. Each is sovereign (or supreme) in its own sphere. This was important for the American founding fathers, seeking to reconcile the rights of the original 13 states with the need for some overall coordination of (especially) defence, foreign policy and inter-state trade. Thus powers were effectively divided between the federal government and state governments. This solution was attractive to other countries where there was a similar need to accommodate both unity and diversity, particularly where different ethnic, cultural and national groups are located within the same territories. Thus today there are many federal states, including the USA, Canada, Switzerland, Australia, Germany, India and Belgium (Hague and Harrop, 2001: 202–6).

A federal state virtually demands a written constitution. If each level of government is supreme in its own sphere, there has to be some authoritative document determining those spheres, laying out the functions of the federal and state governments. This could involve listing the functions of each (perhaps with some powers exercised 'concurrently'), or merely listing the powers of one level, and ascribing all other powers to the other level. Thus the US Constitution details the powers of the federal government, reserving all other powers to the states. Inevitably this does not preclude tensions between the levels of government. A major theme of the history of American government has been the alleged encroachment of the federal power on states' rights. However, without some authoritative allocation of responsibilities there would be chaos. Thus if Britain is evolving towards a federal system, at some stage or other a written constitution will be required.

of history. Its provisions reflect a continually changing balance of power between classes, groups and interests. This balance and those constitutional provisions have been changed as a result of political action by 'new' groups using such means as demonstrating, lobbying and marching in order to bring about concessions from the established order. Thus the aristocratic 'balanced' constitution of the 18th century became the middle class liberal constitution of the 19th century which in turn – as a consequence particularly of the franchise extensions of 1918 and 1928 – became the liberal democratic constitution of the 20th century.

These changes have involved major shifts of power between the leading national institutions. By the mid-19th century the monarchy and the House of Lords had been supplanted as dominant bodies by the House of Commons which – 100 years later – had itself been in part displaced from the centre of the constitutional scene by a large bureaucracy and a vast web of outside interests. Clearly rules that have changed so often and so dramatically over the past two centuries will change again, and change considerably.

One point is worth stressing about the process of constitutional change and about the nature of the constitutional 'settlement' that results from any period of intense constitutional activity. The process itself always consists of a kind of dialogue between (crudely) the forces of conservation and the forces of transformation, and the upshot – the constitution at any particular moment – represents in essentials a compromise between them. In that sense, the constitution represents the terms, the arrangements, on which a country can be ruled.

In this quite abstract but very important sense, constitution making is about engineering consent to government. Thus, in Britain agitation by the middle and working classes and by women broke the constitutional settlements prevailing respectively in the early 19th, late 19th and early 20th centuries. At each point in time, public consent to the constitution was no longer possible on the old terms; change was a condition of political stability. In essence, the nature of constitutions is to express the conditions under which people will consent to be governed.

BOX 11.2
The major sources of the British Constitution

The British Constitution is best described as partly written, but uncodified: that is, not set down in a single document. However there is, of course, a British constitution in the sense of a set of 'rules, customs and understandings empowering and limiting government'. It is a constitution that, as we have seen, 'was never invented or designed but just grew, so that political facts became constitutional rules' (Madgwick and Woodhouse, 1995: 11, 18).

- Statute law – law passed by Parliament, some of which is of a constitutional nature – e.g. Acts determining the composition of the electorate and the conduct of elections, and Acts laying down the powers and composition of the House of Lords.
- Common law – theoretically the immemorial law of the people, in practice the law as determined by decisions of courts. The remaining prerogative powers of the crown (now exercised by the government of the day) derive from common law.
- Conventions – unwritten rules of constitutional behaviour which are widely accepted and observed, largely because of the political difficulties which would follow if they were not. Most of the powers relating to the prime minister depend on convention. Conventions may evolve over time, and may be difficult to date precisely

(e.g. the convention that a prime minister must sit in the House of Commons).
- The law and custom of Parliament – many of the rules relating to the functions, procedures, privileges and immunities of each house are contained in resolutions of both houses, conventions and informal understandings. These have been definitively listed and described in Erskine May's treatise on the *Law, Privileges, Proceedings and Usages of Parliament*.
- Works of authority – in the absence of other authoritative written sources, works by eminent experts on the British constitution are consulted – e.g. Walter Bagehot, *The English Constitution* (1867), Edward Dicey, *The Law of the Constitution*, and Sir Ivor Jennings, *The Law and the Constitution* (1933).
- European Union law. Since the UK joined what was then the European Community in 1973, EC/EU law has been binding on the UK and applied by British courts. This has implications for the constitutional principle of Parliamentary sovereignty. Additionally, some specific EU rules are of a constitutional nature.
- The European Convention on Human Rights. This was (in effect) incorporated into UK law by the 1998 Human Rights Act, which came into force in 2000.

The main characteristics of the British Constitution

As well as being flexible and partly written but uncodified, and unitary rather than federal (see discussion above), the British constitution displays the following characteristics:

- constitutional monarchy
- Parliamentary sovereignty
- representative democracy
- the rule of law.

All of these characteristics require some further explanation and discussion. Some are increasingly contentious.

Constitutional monarchy

The United Kingdom, as the name implies, remains a monarchy, but a limited or constitutional monarchy. Thus it is generally reckoned that the Queen 'reigns but does not rule' and has little or no political power. The personal political power of the monarch has been eroded gradually over the centuries and is now vestigial. Constitutional experts used to debate the monarch's discretion in the choice of prime minister, or to refuse a requested dissolution of Parliament, but the circumstances in which there might be scope for discretion now seem remote or far-fetched. The Queen, in the words of Walter Bagehot, the 19th-century authority on the constitution, retains the right to be consulted, the right to encourage and the right to warn. The prime minister still has regular meetings with the sovereign, and it is possible that the present Queen's experience of successive governments and prime ministers from Churchill onwards might sometimes make her advice worth listening to.

However, if the power of the monarch is too negligible to be a live political issue, the institution of the crown and the issue of the royal prerogative are more contentious. Ministers, members of the armed forces and civil servants are officially servants of the crown rather than the public or 'the state'. Official communications are 'On Her Majesty's Service'. This may seem a quaint archaism, but it serves a negative function: there is no positive injunction to serve the public interest. Indeed civil servants who have leaked information that they considered ought to be made public in the public interest have been prosecuted. Until recently it was not even possible to sue the crown or servants of the crown. Moreover some of the powers of the sovereign, which are no longer exercised by the Queen, have not been abolished but transferred, mainly to the prime minister. Thus it is the prime minister who exercises the former 'royal prerogative' powers to declare wars, make treaties and dissolve Parliament. A prime minister can involve Britain in war without seeking ratification from Parliament – although politically it would be suicidal to take such a step without the assurance of Parliamentary and public support.

Until recently the future of the monarchy has rarely been a political issue, but it is now more openly debated. Criticism of the monarchy as an institution in Britain, and increased debate over its financial costs and benefits, has been exacerbated by the perceived personal shortcomings of some members of the royal family. Moreover, the removal of the principle of heredity from the second chamber (although as yet incomplete) may be thought to have implications for a hereditary monarchy. However, the funeral of the Queen Mother, followed

soon afterwards by the royal golden jubilee celebrations (both in 2002), seemed to boost public support for the monarchy, and for a short while took the wind out of republican sails, until the collapse of the high-profile trial of Princess Diana's former butler on charges over the alleged unauthorised removal of some of the late princess's belongings. Those who argue for the retention of the monarchy claim that the practical alternatives are worse: see Box 11.3.

Parliamentary sovereignty

Parliamentary sovereignty is the 'dominating characteristic' of the British Constitution, declared Vernon Bogdanor in 1988 (p. 55). What Parliamentary sovereignty means in practice is that, in formal terms, Parliamentary authority in the United Kingdom is unlimited: Parliament can make or unmake law on any subject whatso-

---

BOX 11.3

Comparative politics: constitutional monarchies and republics

The retention of the monarchy is rare although not unique among countries with a reasonable claim to democracy. Belgium, the Netherlands, Sweden, Denmark and Spain are among examples in Europe of democratic states that retain a hereditary monarch, who in all cases has negligible personal political power. In addition, several Commonwealth countries still acknowledge the Queen as their head of state (although the issue has become politically very controversial in Australia). However in France, the USA and most other countries that are regarded as democratic, republicanism is regarded as the natural corollary of democracy, and the retention of the principle of heredity for filling the post of head of state appears incompatible with democratic values. The US President is both head of state and head of government. More commonly, there is a separate formal head of state with little effective power, either directly elected by the people, or indirectly elected by Parliament.

ever; and it can do so retrospectively. The classic statement of its omnicompetence derives from William Blackstone, the 18th-century jurist, who declared that Parliament 'can do everything that is not naturally impossible'. No person may question its legislative competence, and the courts must give effect to its legislation. It may be noted that the constitutional principle of Parliamentary sovereignty does not mean that Parliament is particularly powerful in practice. Indeed the decline in the power and effective influence of Parliament is widely lamented (see Chapter 14). However, it may be questioned how far even the constitutional principle remains valid.

First, how far has Parliamentary sovereignty been impaired by membership of the European Union (EU)? The European Communities Act (1972) gave the force of law in the United Kingdom to obligations arising under the EC treaties; it gave EC law general and binding authority within the United Kingdom; it provided that Community law should take precedence over all inconsistent UK law; and it precluded the UK Parliament from legislating on matters within EC competence where the Community had formulated rules. It might be argued that Parliamentary sovereignty is not impaired, because membership of the EU has not broken the principle that Parliament cannot bind its future action. Thus, the European Communities Act could be repealed, and indeed had the 1975 referendum on continuing membership of the EC gone the other way, the United Kingdom would probably have withdrawn from the Community.

However, while Britain remains a member of the EU it does appear that Parliamentary sovereignty has been impaired. Britain's legal subordination to Brussels was underlined by an important legal case in 1991, R. v. Secretary of State for Transport *ex parte* Factortame Ltd no 2. (the Factortame case). The European Court of Justice in effect quashed sections of a British Act of Parliament (the Merchant Shipping Act 1988) which provided that UK-registered boats must be 75 per cent British-owned and have 75 per cent of crew resident in the UK. The Act had been designed to prevent boats from Spain and other EC countries 'quota-hopping' by registering under the British flag and using the UK's EC fishing quotas. British legislation had been over-

turned before by the Court but no earlier case had provoked such an outcry.

In effect, the UK Parliament has bound itself procedurally by the 1972 European Communities Act so that in areas of EU legislative competence, EU law is supreme and the British courts will give it precedence over national UK law where the two conflict. Thus, since 1973, Britain has possessed 'dual constitutional arrangements, as an independent state and as a member of the European Community (Union)'. Since then, it has had, and still has, 'a parallel constitution' (Madgwick and Woodhouse, 1995: 42).

It may also be questioned whether devolution will ultimately destroy the sovereignty of the Westminster Parliament. The official answer here is clear. Devolution is not the same as federalism. Power devolved is power retained, because sovereignty or supreme power is unaffected, and thus any functions that are devolved can be called back. Devolution itself may be reversed. The third edition (1998) of this book strongly supported this argument, citing the suspension of the Stormont Parliament in 1972 and the resumption of direct rule of Northern Ireland after 50 years of devolved government. Since then the new Northern Ireland Assembly and Executive has been suspended more than once, reinforcing the point. Moreover, in strict legal terms the argument remains valid. Yet political realities suggest otherwise. Northern Ireland is a special case, but it now seems scarcely conceivable that devolution in Scotland and Wales is reversible, unless the Scots and Welsh become convinced that devolution was a mistake. All the pressures seem to be the other way – to concede more powers to the Scottish Parliament and Welsh Assembly. Thus it is arguable that Britain is evolving towards a quasi-federal system of government which entails the end of UK Parliamentary sovereignty. (These points are discussed further later in this chapter and in more detail in Chapter 17.)

This may be seen as an illustration of the obvious point that the UK Parliament is subject to political constraints on what it can actually – as opposed to what it may legally – do. Whereas Parliament is the legal sovereign (or possesses constitutional supremacy), the electorate is the political sovereign. Governments must therefore pay some regard to pressure group views and to the opinion polls.

Definitions
Parliamentary sovereignty means that Parliament has supreme power.
Popular sovereignty means that supreme power rests with the people.
There is clearly potential for tension or open conflict between these two doctrines. The views of the elected representatives of the people clearly may not always coincide with the views of the people themselves.

Acts of Parliament with the full force of law can become a dead letter. Trade union resistance wrecked the 1971 Trade Union Act and widespread popular revolt helped destroy the poll tax. The prohibition of alcoholic liquor would be as unpopular in Britain as it was for a brief spell in the USA, and no government has ever tried it.

Representative democracy

Tension between Parliamentary sovereignty and popular sovereignty suggests that Parliamentary sovereignty does not necessarily entail democracy, which is another widely assumed and much-prized characteristic of the British system of government, even if it is less discussed by constitutional lawyers. It is a mark of the evolutionary nature of the British system of government that it is difficult to pin down precisely when Britain became a democracy (and radical critics would deny that it is, in some important respects, even now). While a series of Acts extended the vote to a wider proportion of the population until a full adult franchise was virtually achieved by 1928, this was necessarily accompanied by a gradual acceptance of democratic principles over time, which in turn prompted the emergence of new conventions embodying the spirit of democracy. Thus it came to be established that the peers should not frustrate the will of the democratically elected House of Commons, particularly on issues which had been submitted to the people in a manifesto by the governing party. Similarly, it became an unwritten rule that the prime minister and head of government should be a member of the House of Commons, and normally the elected leader of the majority party.

Of course, British democracy involves representative (or Parliamentary) democracy rather than direct democracy (see Chapter 1). It is elected representatives of the people rather than the people themselves who decide. Thus Parliament can legislate to abolish capital punishment even when opinion polls suggest public support for it. (However, it is worth mentioning that British governments have made more use of referendums recently on essentially constitutional issues.) How far the British government and Parliament are truly representative of the people remains to a degree contentious. They are representative to the extent that they are elected, yet we have already seen that the seats political parties secure in the Westminster Parliament and local council chambers do not closely reflect the proportion of votes cast in general and local elections (see Chapter 6). Blair's government, like Thatcher's government, enjoys a substantial Parliamentary majority secured on around 43% per cent of the votes cast and a much smaller proportion of the total electorate. Nor is Parliament or government a microcosm of the nation. Women, ethnic minorities and manual workers are all significantly under-represented compared with their proportions in the population. (The ways in which Parliament can be said to represent the people are explored in more detail in Chapter 14.)

The rule of law

The fundamental principle is that people are subject to the rule of law, not to the arbitrary will of their governors. No one is above the law. Ministers and public authorities are bound by the law. Actions without the authority of law can be challenged in the courts. Citizens should have redress for illegal or arbitrary acts by public authorities, through the ordinary courts, administrative tribunals or other special machinery, such as complaints to the various 'ombudsmen' over what is termed 'maladministration' (see Chapter 15).

The leading jurist A. V. Dicey (1835–1922) saw the rule of law as a fundamental characteristic of the British Constitution, viewing it as of equal importance to the doctrine of Parliamentary sovereignty. Although in strict constitutional terms, the rule of law is subordinate to Parliamentary sovereignty which could be used to remove the rights it entails, the rule of law remains of key significance. In particular, it underpins the very important constitutional principle of the partial separation of powers, whereby although executive and legislative branches are 'fused', the judicial branch is largely independent and separate, and can check the executive. In addition, the rule of law enshrines principles such as natural justice, fairness and reasonableness which can be applied by the courts. (For further discussion of the rule of law, see Chapter 15.)

Ideological perceptions of the British Constitution

After a period of intense controversy over constitutional issues within and between British parties in the years leading up to the First World War, there appeared to be a broad consensus over the system of government lasting up until the 1970s. Even so, this apparent agreement concealed some very different assumptions on the constitution. These different ideological assumptions help to explain the marked differences in attitude to constitutional reform which subsequently emerged between the parties in the last quarter of the 20th century.

Conservatives and the constitution

Conservative governments and Conservative-dominated governments have sometimes been responsible for developments with considerable constitutional implications – for example, the 1867 Reform Act, the 1921 Irish Treaty, Britain's entry to the European Community, 1973, and some of the measures introduced by the Thatcher government, particularly Executive Agencies from 1988 onwards. Even so, Conservatives have generally been more concerned to conserve the existing constitution rather than promote constitutional reform, although they have generally not sought to reverse reforms carried through by their opponents.

Although the Conservative Party came to accept a form of Tory democracy by the end of the 19th century, it was always a version of democracy that placed a continuing emphasis on the need for leadership. Conservatives see authority as flowing from above: they traditionally emphasise strong government and accord popular participation a minimal role. So government, backed by a loyal party, governs; and the electorate, through Parliament, consents to this firm leadership. Conservatives regard (or used to regard) loyalty to the party leader as a primary political virtue, and party as a socially integrative force, enabling people of ability to bind the nation together by drawing support for their policies from all classes and groups.

By tradition and instinct, Conservatives were committed to the preservation of the Union. Following their alliance with Liberal Unionists opposed to Irish Home Rule, the party was commonly known as 'Unionist', and although reluctantly obliged to concede the establishment of the Irish Free State, the Conservative and Unionist Party continued to uphold the union with Ulster, and subsequently oppose devolution to Scotland and Wales. Thus the Conservatives opposed Labour's devolution proposals from 1974–9, and in the 1992 and 1997 elections John Major warned the electorate that the Union was in danger.

The Conservatives' position in the 1997 general election blended support for small-scale evolutionary change with opposition to Labour's radical programme. Their 1997 manifesto maintained that Conservative governments had taken 'significant steps' towards open, accountable government, had decentralised government, strengthened Parliament and adopted measures that recognised national diversity within the Union. However, they strongly opposed the other parties' proposals for radical constitutional reform which included a Bill of Rights, a new electoral system, devolution to Scotland, Wales and the English regions, and reform of the House of Lords.

However, after their landslide defeat in the 1997 election, and as Labour's constitutional reforms proceeded, the Conservatives were forced to adopt a more pragmatic position on certain reforms. Thus once the referendums in Scotland and Wales secured support for Labour's devolution proposals, the Conservative Party put forward its own candidates for election for the Scottish Parliament and Welsh Assembly, and accepted devolution as an accomplished fact. Similarly it refrained from defence of the hereditary peerage, while attacking increased prime ministerial patronage over the House of Lords, proposing a larger proportion of elected members than the government was prepared to concede.

Liberal and Liberal Democrat support for constitution reform

While Conservatives have strongly defended the existing constitution, Liberals and more recently Liberal Democrats have placed radical constitutional reform at the centre of their programme, seeing it as the major precondition of social and economic progress. Thus in the 19th century Liberals supported Parliamentary reform, and from 1886 onwards Irish Home Rule and subsequently 'Home Rule all round'. In the early 20th century the Liberal government took on and defeated the House of Lords. After the Second World War the Liberal Party was the first to support entry into the European Economic Community, and it continued to support devolution to Scotland and Wales as well as English regional government. It has sought to defend civil liberties and individual rights, and to strengthen the role of Parliament. Unsurprisingly, it has campaigned consistently for electoral reform, as the 'first past the post' system has particularly penalised it.

The Liberal Democrats under Ashdown and Kennedy have maintained this radical approach to the constitution. In 1997, they advocated a far-reaching programme of constitutional reform including proportional representation, a Bill of Rights, the strengthening of Parliament, and large-scale devolution and decentralisation of power away from Westminster and Whitehall. Since then they have supported much of the Labour reform programme, accepting seats on a Labour Cabinet Committee on the constitution in 1997, and entering coalition with Labour in the Scottish executive from 1999 and in the Welsh executive from 2000. Yet the Liberal Democrats have not been content to act as junior partners in a Labour project, and they have continued to criticise aspects and perceived shortcomings in Labour's programme – particularly the failure to proceed with the commitment to a referendum on electoral reform, the delays over elected assemblies for the English regions, and Labour's initial modest proposals for Lords reform. The Liberal Democrats remain the most enthusiastic supporters of both decentralisation and closer European integration, with considerable implications for the British Constitution.

The Labour Party and the constitution

For much of its history the Labour Party was less interested in radical constitutional reform than might be expected, although it intermittently pursued Lords reform, and occasionally toyed with other constitutional changes. Labour wished to capture and control the state rather than reform it. Its priorities were social and economic reform, and it was assumed that this could be achieved through the existing state apparatus. Thus Labour endorsed the strong executive embodied in British constitutional arrangements, but for a different reason from the Conservatives. It perceived the Labour Party as a vehicle for the Parliamentary representation of the working class and argued that, once having gained an electoral majority for its programme, the party had a mandate to enact it without check or hindrance. In addition to these ideological reasons, Labour had some self-interest in maintaining the constitutional status quo. Favourable features included an electoral system that both protected the two major parties from third-party competition and helped to hold them together; executive control of Parliament which ensured the passage of party programmes; strong central control over subordinate levels of government; and virtual freedom from judicial interference (Dunleavy *et al.*, 1997: 130).

In the 1970s the advances of the nationalists and the threat this presented to Labour support in Scotland and Wales were among the factors in tipping the party towards devolution. Labour's internal divisions over Europe provoked another constitutional innovation in 1975, a referendum on Britain's continued membership of the European Community, before referendums were also held (and lost) on Labour's devolution plans for Scotland and Wales. Yet although these initiatives had significant constitutional implications, they were pragmatic responses to the party's problems rather than part of an overall reform programme.

It was only in the 1990s that Labour took up the cause of radical constitutional reform. While Labour had not previously been in the vanguard of the drive for constitutional reform, its conversion was crucial because without the commitment of a major party reform would not have happened. For the Labour Party, experience of the long Conservative dominance from 1979 to 1997 raised concerns over civil liberties and minority rights, as well as provoking more interest in electoral reform. If the consequence was coalition, that increasingly seemed preferable to permanent exclusion from power. Blair inherited a reaffirmed commitment to devolution from his predecessor as Labour leader, John Smith, but he had reasons of his own for a more general commitment to constitutional reform. He was keen to promote cooperation and perhaps coalition with the Liberal Democrats, and wished to lay claim to the progressive reforming Liberal tradition of the early 20th century. Indeed, it has been argued that 'the fundamental case for devolution ... is that of diversity, and diversity is more of a liberal value than a socialist one' (Bogdanor, in Seldon, 2001: 154). Yet Labour's old state-centred collectivism no longer appeared either feasible or electorally appealing. Blair's New Labour was thus cautious on the economy and radical on the constitution, a reversal of Labour's former priorities. Labour entered the 1997 election with an ambitious programme of constitutional change with momentous implications for the future government of Britain.

The movement for constitutional reform

Constitutional reform was a cause that had become increasingly fashionable from the late 1980s onwards. Compared with the earlier period of constitutional concern in the 1960s and 1970s, which had been limited to specific issues, this new phase was about fundamentals, and produced radical proposals for reform. An important step was the formation of the influential pressure group, Charter 88, symbolically 300 years on from the Revolution of 1688 (see Box 11.4).

Much of the interest in constitutional change came from the centre and left of the political spectrum (Barnett, 1997), but there was also some support from elements of the right, such as the neo-liberal think tank the Institute of Economic Affairs, and individuals such as a former head of Margaret

> **BOX 11.4**
> ## The main demands of Charter 88
>
> - A Bill of Rights to ensure key civil rights
> - Freedom of information and open government
> - A fair electoral system based on proportional representation
> - A reformed democratic, non-hereditary second chamber
> - The subordination of the executive to a 'democratically renewed Parliament'
> - An independent, reformed judiciary
> - 'An equitable distribution of power between local, regional and national government'
> - A written constitution.

Thatcher's Political Unit, Ferdinand Mount (1992). In March 1997 the two centre-left parties, Labour and the Liberal Democrats, which had already been cooperating closely in the Scottish Constitutional Convention, produced an agreed raft of proposals for constitutional reform.

The reforming mood also gained some endorsement by public opinion. A 'State of the Nation' poll commissioned by the Joseph Rowntree Trust in 1995 found that the proportion of people believing the system of government works well had

> **BOX 11.5**
> ## Constitutional reform: the Labour–Liberal Democrat proposals, 1997
>
> - Select committee on modernisation of House of Commons
> - Abolition of hereditary peers
> - Scottish Parliament and Welsh Assembly elected by proportion representation
> - Referendums on creation of an elected London authority and elected English regional assemblies
> - Incorporation of European Convention of Human Rights into UK law
> - Electoral commission to recommend alternative to present voting system
> - Freedom of Information Act.

dropped to a mere 22 per cent, while 81 per cent were in favour of a Freedom of Information Act, and 79 per cent wanted a Bill of Rights and a written constitution. There was strong support also for greater use of referendums, the enforcement of the MPs' code of conduct by the courts, civil or criminal, and the investigation of ministerial misconduct by people other than politicians. The last points indicated increased concern over 'sleaze' in the final years of the Major government and diminished public confidence in the conduct of British government and politics.

Labour and the constitution: a government of radical reform?

By the end of first term the Labour government had enacted a substantial part of its ambitious constitutional reform programme (see Box 11.6).

By any standard this amounts to a formidable catalogue of constitutional reform measures, which have already had massive implications for Britain's system of government (further details are discussed in subsequent chapters). In terms of achievement it compares favourably with the efforts of previous Labour governments. Thus the Wilson government was forced to abandon its plans to reform the Lords in 1969, while the Wilson/Callaghan administrations of 1974–9 failed to implement their devolution proposals. The relative ease of implementation of the Blair government reforms may partly be attributed to the size of its majority, although Labour also learned from its previous failures. Holding referendums first effectively settled the substantive issue of devolution, leaving Parliament only to decide the details. Similarly, the two-stage model adopted for reforming the Lords meant that abolition of the hereditary principle was decided and substantially implemented before Parliament became bogged down in arguments over the composition of the new second chamber.

Two 1997 manifesto pledges were not delivered by the election in 2001. The government has recently recommitted itself to one of these, to hold referendums on elected assemblies for the English regions. The other, to hold a referendum on a reformed electoral system for the Westminster Parliament, has so far been ignored. While the government did fulfil its

promise to appoint a commission to recommend a new voting system, Lord Jenkins's report has been effectively shelved. However, the government's adoption of a variety of electoral systems for devolved assemblies and the European Parliament has initiated a debate and begun a process of reform which may not be easily halted (see Chapter 6). Besides

---

BOX 11.6

The Labour government's legislation on constitutional reform

- Referendums on devolution in Scotland (1997), Wales (1997), and Ireland (1998)
- The establishment of Regional Development Agencies for the English regions (1998)
- A referendum on a directly elected mayor for London, with a strategic authority for governing London (1998)
- A Parliament for Scotland with legislative powers, elected by the additional member system (1998)
- An Assembly for Wales, with executive powers, elected by the additional member system (1998)
- An Assembly for Northern Ireland elected by the single transferable vote system and a partnership executive representing both the Unionist and Nationalist communities (1998)
- A new electoral system (a regional list system) for the European Parliament (1999)
- A directly elected mayor for London, elected by the supplementary vote, and a Greater London Authority elected by the additional member system (1999)
- A Human Rights Act allowing judges to declare that legislation is incompatible with the European Convention on European Rights.
- The removal of all but 92 hereditary members from the House of Lords (1999)
- A Freedom of Information Act (1999)
- Limits on election campaign spending (Elections, Political Parties and Referendums Act, 2000)
- A separate executive for local authorities, involving either a local cabinet system or a directly elected mayor.

these failures to deliver manifesto commitments there were some other omissions in Labour's first-term programme to which critics have drawn attention, including failures to strengthen the role of Parliament (beyond marginal reforms to Parliamentary procedures), to strengthen significantly the role of local government, or to reform the civil service.

Not all the reforms implemented have appeared completely successful or met all the demands of critics. The future of devolution and the peace process in Northern Ireland remains precarious, although this largely reflects the scale of the problem, and the intransigence of the two communities rather than any particular failure of the British government. Welsh devolution has been extensively criticised for not going far enough, and there have been similar criticisms of the relative impotence of the London mayor and authority. The timidity of the government's proposals for Lords reform and the shortcomings of the Freedom of Information Act have been extensively criticised. Yet in each case, almost no one seems to want to return to the pre-reform position; rather, the consensus favours taking reform further.

Beyond these specific criticisms there is a more general criticism that Labour's various initiatives do not seem to be related to any overall vision (Peele, in Dunleavy et al., 2002: 75), that the reforms are insufficiently 'joined up' (to use New Labour terminology). Indeed, what is striking is the sheer diversity and absence of pattern in the reforms – the different electoral systems employed for different institutions; the dissimilar mechanics of devolution in Scotland, Wales and Northern Ireland (Hazell, 2000: 269–71) the apparent failure to relate Lords reform to other constitutional change, particularly devolution. It is as if each reform was considered in isolation. Moreover, there appears to be no clear sense of direction, nor even any realisation of the implication for established constitutional principles, such as Parliamentary sovereignty and the unitary state (see Box 11.7).

One obvious consequence of devolution is increasing diversity within the 'United Kingdom' as devolved executives increasingly exercise their devolved powers in different ways. At the moment this diversity may be relatively limited, as Labour rules at Westminster and is the dominant coalition partner in Edinburgh and Cardiff. However, if

---

BOX 11.7

The end of Parliamentary sovereignty and the unitary state?

The established orthodoxy is that Parliamentary sovereignty and the unitary state remain unaffected by recent constitutional change, although some argue that it has already been eroded by UK membership of the European Union. Vernon Bogdanor (in Seldon, 2001) claims that it has further reduced by at least three developments:

- The employment of referendums. As these are advisory rather than binding, formally the sovereignty of the parliament is unaffected. But Bogdanor argues that 'a referendum which yields a clear outcome on a reasonable turnout binds Parliament'. Thus the sovereignty of the people is substituted for the sovereignty of Parliament.
- The Human Rights Act, which does not give judges power to reject Westminster legislation, but 'nevertheless alters very considerably the balance between Parliament and the judiciary' so that Parliament will feel obliged to respond to a judicial decisions that a statute is incompatible with the European Convention of Human Rights.
- Devolution, particularly Scottish devolution. While the sovereignty of the Westminster Parliament is theoretically unaffected, in practice English MPs have lost responsibility for legislation on devolved functions

Bogdanor (in Seldon, 2001: 151) argues that the Human Rights Act and the Scotland Act 'have the characteristic of fundamental laws. They in practice limit the rights of Westminster as a sovereign Parliament, and provide for a constitution which is quasi-federal in nature.'

different parties take control of the various governments within the UK there could be increased scope for disagreements and perhaps serious demarcation disputes between different levels of government. This may ultimately necessitate some kind of written constitution, with provision perhaps for judicial arbitration over disputes. A written constitution is part of the Charter 88 package of proposals that Labour has so far ignored or rejected, but it may prove the logical culmination of reforms already implemented. A written constitution, particularly if it contained safeguards against hasty amendment by a bare Commons majority, would effectively mean the end of Parliamentary sovereignty, and in so far as it spelled out the respective functions of different levels of government, would also involve the end of the unitary state.

A federal Britain is, however, only one possible longer-term outcome of the constitutional reform process. For Irish, Scottish and Welsh nationalists, devolution and federalism are only stages on the road to separation and the break-up of Britain. Some who have opposed devolution all along (including many Conservatives and some Labour critics, like Tam Dalyell) have feared that it is a slippery slope on the road to independence, as indeed nationalists wish. By contrast, Labour and the Liberal Democrats hope that devolution will satisfy the legitimate demands of many in Scotland and Wales to have a greater say in decisions that affect them, and that devolution will ultimately strengthen rather than weaken the British state. It is impossible to know now who is right and what the eventual outcome will be. The various peoples of the United Kingdom have embarked on a journey in which the final destination is unknown.

Further reading

Britain's Constitution and constitutional reform has become a difficult and fast-changing topic. A useful overall account of the British Constitution before the Blair government's reform programme is provided by Madgwick and Woodhouse (1995). Thoughtful reflections on the principles and practice of the traditional British Constitution have been provided by Johnson (1977) and Mount (1992). A more comprehensive account is provided by de Smith and Brazier (1994), and the more recent Hood-Phillips, Jackson and Leopold (2001). Chapter 12 on constitutions in Hague and Harrop (2001) provides some useful comparative background against which the very unusual British Constitution can be assessed.

On constitutional reform see the publications of the pressure group Charter 88 and its website www.charter88.org.uk. Holme and Eliot (1988) provides the background to its formation and programme. For academic commentary on the reforms, see works by Robert Hazel and the Constitution Unit, especially *Constitutional Futures* (1999), reviewing prospects for reform after the election of the Labour government, and *The State and the Nations* (2000) on the early record on devolution. There is a useful review by Vernon Bogdanor in Seldon (2001) of constitutional reform in Labour's first term, and much relevant material in various chapters, especially those by Gamble and Bogdanor, in Dunleavy *et al.* (2003). Articles in journals such as *Politics Review* and *Talking Politics* provide useful updating on recent developments, but government, party and newspaper websites are the best sources for keeping abreast of current issues.

Chapter **12**

Prime Minister and Cabinet

The prime minister   187
The role of the prime minister   189
The Prime Minister's Office   194
The Cabinet   195
The Cabinet Office   197
Prime ministerial government?   198
A 'Blair presidency'?   200
Constraints on prime ministerial
  government   200
Prime ministerial power: an irrelevant
  debate?   203
Criticism of the British core executive   203

The powers of the state are conventionally classified as executive, legislative and judicial, which can be related in many countries to distinctive institutions, whose functions are kept separate. In Britain there is no clear separation of powers, particularly between the executive and the legislature. Moreover, even the definition of the executive in Britain is somewhat problematic.

In this chapter and the next we consider the institutions that make up the core executive in Britain. This complex of offices and institutions at the pinnacle of the central decision making process goes beyond the prime minister and Cabinet to include both their support institutions (the Prime Minister's Office and the Cabinet Office) and, in addition, the departments themselves, headed by ministers assisted by a small number of senior civil servants. The focus this chapter is on the prime minister and Cabinet system. We

> **Definitions**
> The **executive** is the institution charged with the day to day government of the country, responsible for making policies and administering laws.
> The **legislature** is the institution responsible for making laws.
> The **judiciary** is the institution responsible for adjudicating on the law and legal disputes.

> **Definition**
> **Core executive**: The term 'core executive' refers to the key institutions at the centre of government. It covers the prime minister, Cabinet and its committees, the Prime Minister's Office and the Cabinet Office, coordinating departments such as the Treasury, the government's law officers and the security and intelligence services.

describe its principal features, consider the controversy over prime ministerial or Cabinet government, and conclude with an examination of its strengths and weaknesses, and proposals for reform.

The prime minister

The modern office of prime minister embodies a formidable concentration of power. In summary, the prime minister is responsible for forming a government; for directing and coordinating its work; and for general supervision of the civil service. The prime minister takes particular interest in – and exercises strong influence over – decisions on the economy (as first lord of the Treasury) and on defence and foreign affairs; the prime minister also has special responsibilities in the sphere of national security. The prime minister decides upon the date for a general election (normally after consultation with senior colleagues) and, subject to the formality of royal assent, dissolves Parliament. Finally, the prime minister is the national leader, as evidenced by his or her role in representing the country at international conferences and meetings, signing treaties and playing host to leaders of other states.

> **Definition**
> The **prime minister**: a head of government whose power normally derives in Britain from leadership of the largest party in the legislature.

IN FOCUS 12.1 Where are they now?

Only four members of Tony Blair's first Cabinet appointed in May 1997 were still in the same post by January 2003. Six others occupied different posts within the Cabinet.

Photograph: COI.

Table 12.1 Cabinets compared

Person	1997 office	January 2003
Tony Blair	Prime Minister	Still in post
John Prescott	Environment, Transport and the Regions and Deputy PM	Still Deputy Prime Minister but ministry split up 2001
Gordon Brown	Chancellor of the Exchequer	Still in post
Robin Cook	Foreign Secretary	President of the Council and Leader of the Commons Resigned over Iraq, 17 March 2003
Lord Irvine	Lord Chancellor	Still in post
Jack Straw	Home Secretary	Foreign Secretary
David Blunkett	Education and Employment	Home Secretary
Margaret Beckett	Trade and Industry	Environment, Food and Rural Affairs
Jack Cunningham	Agriculture, Fisheries and Food	No longer in government. Still Labour MP.
Donald Dewar	Scotland	Died 2000 (Scotland's First Minister 1999–2000)
George Robertson	Defence	No longer in government. Secretary General NATO and life peer.
Frank Dobson	Health	No longer in government. Still Labour MP. Was Labour candidate for London Mayor, 2000.
Ann Taylor	President of the Council and Leader of the Commons	No longer in government. Still Labour MP.
Chris Smith	National Heritage	No longer in government. Still Labour MP.
Harriet Harman	Social Security	Dropped in reshuffle 1998. Returned to government 2001 as Solicitor General (not in Cabinet).
Marjorie Mowlam	Northern Ireland	Not in government or Parliament after 2001
Ron Davies	Wales	No longer Westminster MP. Member, Welsh Assembly.
Clare Short	International Development	Still in post
Lord Richard	Lord Privy Seal and Leader of the Lords	No longer in government. Still Labour peer.
David Clark	Chancellor of the Duchy of Lancaster	No longer in government. Made life peer 2001.
Gavin Strang	Transport	No longer in government. Still Labour MP.
Alistair Darling	Chief Secretary to Treasury	Transport

The role of the prime minister

Patronage

The most important element of prime ministerial patronage is the power to select the 100 or so politicians – drawn mainly from the House of Commons but also from the House of Lords – who at any given moment form the government. The prime minister appoints not just the Cabinet of normally 20–23 members but also ministers of state, under-secretaries of state, whips and law officers such as the attorney-general and solicitor-general. Between one-third and one-quarter (depending on the number of seats won) of the victorious party at a general election can realistically expect office. By no means all politicians seek ministerial office, but most probably do. The continuing power to 'hire and fire' is a formidable source of control for the prime minister. Ministerial changes – by forced or deliberate reshuffle – occur quite frequently. For example, only half of Tony Blair's first Cabinet after the 1997 general election remained in the Cabinet after the 2001 election four years later. Of those only three, besides Blair himself, remained in the same post: Gordon Brown, Lord Irvine and Clare Short. Some departments have seen three or four different ministers in five years (e.g. Transport, Trade and Industry, Northern Ireland).

The prime minister also plays a key role in the selection of individuals to fill a wide variety of other leading posts in national life. This influence extends over the creation of peers as well as over the appointment of top civil servants at the permanent secretary and deputy secretary levels, the heads of the security services and the chairs of royal commissions. In addition, the prime minister has ultimate responsibility for recommendations of honours in the various New Year, Queen's Birthday and special honours lists.

Direction and organisation of the government

The prime minister is responsible for directing and organising the work of the government at the highest level (see Box 12.1). The prime minister must steer the government: colleagues expect such leadership and governments tend to drift without

---

BOX 12.1

The role of the prime minister: key aspects

- **Elected by the people**: authority of PM derives from being leader of the party which gains a Parliamentary majority in a general election.
- **Appoints government** (and others to leading roles): the PM 'hires and fires'.
- **Steers government**: the PM directs and coordinates government policy and strategy, chairs Cabinet, and has a special interest in key policy areas.
- **Organises government**: including setting up, reorganising and abolishing departments of state, and overseeing organisation of the civil service and other parts of government.
- **Requests dissolution of Parliament from monarch**, effectively determining the date of elections.
- **Controls the House of Commons**, through leadership of a disciplined majority party (normally).
- **Gives leadership to nation**, particularly in time of national crisis (e.g. war), but has high political profile always, and represents country at home and abroad.

---

it. This involves setting broad policy objectives (within the framework of party ideology and the party manifesto) and devising short-term and long-term strategies for attaining these goals. The leadership, of course, is always in a collective context: the prime minister is not a single executive like the US president. Within that framework, there are clearly differences in style. Margaret Thatcher is well known for having led from the front. Harold Wilson, on the other hand, although a good short-term tactician, was generally more concerned to conjure consensus from his colleagues than to lead them in a particular direction (Madgwick, 1991: 140–1). Unless he or she specifically exempts them, the prime minister expects ministerial colleagues to support government policy according to the convention of collective responsibility (see below).

The steering role means that the prime minister

IN FOCUS 12.2 The Cabinet, October 2002

Photograph: Imagemakers London Ltd.

1.	Tony Blair	Prime Minister, First Lord of the Treasury, Minister for the Civil Service
2.	John Prescott	Deputy Prime Minister
3.	Gordon Brown	Chancellor of the Exchequer
4.	Robin Cook	President of the Council and Leader of the House of Commons (resigned 17 March 2003)
5.	Lord Irvine of Lairg	Lord Chancellor
6.	Jack Straw	Secretary of State for Foreign and Commonwealth Affairs
7.	David Blunkett	Secretary of State for the Home Department
8.	Margaret Beckett	Secretary of State for Environment, Food and Rural Affairs
9.	Clare Short	Secretary of State for International Development
10.	Alistair Darling	Secretary of State for Transport
11.	Alan Milburn	Secretary of State for Health
12.	Geoff Hoon	Secretary of State for Defence
13.	Andrew Smith	Secretary of State for Work and Pensions
14.	Helen Liddell	Secretary of State for Scotland
15.	Paul Murphy	Secretary of State for Northern Ireland
16.	Peter Hain	Secretary of State for Wales
17.	Lord Williams of Mostyn	Leader of the House of Lords
18.	Patricia Hewitt	Secretary of State for Trade and Industry
19.	Charles Clarke	Secretary of State for Education and Skills
20.	Tessa Jowell	Secretary of State for Culture, Media and Sport
21.	Hilary Armstrong	Parliamentary Secretary, Treasury, and Chief Whip
22.	John Reid	Minister without Portfolio and Party Chair
23.	Paul Boateng	Chief Secretary to the Treasury
24.	Lord Grocott	Lords Chief Whip and Captain of the Gentlemen of Arms
25.	Nick Brown	Minister of State for Work
26.	Sir Andrew Turnbull	Secretary of the Cabinet and Head of the Home Civil Service

with his or her top advisers must decide upon the allocation of work between the Cabinet, its committees, ministerial groups, and bilateral meetings and consultations. Structuring the framework of decision making involves the prime minister in drawing up the Cabinet agenda, and in deciding the composition, terms of reference and chairship of Cabinet committees. The special status of the prime minister is also evident in his or her special responsibility for and strong personal involvement in certain key policy areas.

Thus, the prime minister can play a decisive role in the determination of economic policy in consultation with the chancellor of the exchequer and the Treasury, and of important foreign policy and defence matters in concert with the foreign secretary and defence secretary respectively. The prime minister alone is ultimately responsible for matters of national security that never go before Cabinet.

Finally, issues may arise over the whole field of governmental concern in which the prime minister either has to get involved or chooses to take a particular interest. Thus, prime ministers in the 1960s and 1970s were unavoidably involved in industrial, trade union and pay policies; prime ministers have consistently taken leading roles in the development of initiatives in Northern Ireland. They may choose to become involved in any area that attracts their interest, although they risk upsetting the departmental minister concerned: thus James Callaghan intervened in the fields of education, hospitals, personal tax reform, nuclear policy and aircraft purchasing policy, while Margaret Thatcher on her own initiative cancelled a research programme on the transmission of Aids, pushed for more British history in the National Curriculum, insisted on the introduction of market principles into the NHS (National Health Service), and put her weight behind the poll tax and a national identity card scheme to curb football hooliganism (Donoughue, 1987: 5–6; Young, 1990: 548–9). Similarly Tony Blair has taken a particular interest in foreign policy, education, health, and law and order.

As well as playing a key part in deciding the nature, timing and ordering of issues reaching the Cabinet agenda, the prime minister chairs Cabinet meetings. Prime ministerial 'styles' of chairmanship have varied considerably. Whatever their particular style, the chairmanship gives prime ministers the capacity to shape the direction and result of policy discussions, for example by making their views known before and during the meeting, by their handling of Cabinet (who is called to speak and in what order) and by their summing up of 'the sense of the meeting' at the end. In the process, they may deploy various manipulative 'arts' of chairmanship including delay, obfuscation of the issue, verbosity, deliberate ambiguity, adjournment (followed by 'arm-twisting'), briskness (sometimes Cabinets have complained of being 'bounced' into decisions), sheer persistence and authority. For all these wiles, they may not always succeed, and examples abound of premiers failing to get their way (see pp. 201–2). Votes are rarely taken in Cabinet: they encourage division, dilute collective responsibility, and are vulnerable to 'leaks' and misleading reports in the media. But it is the task of the prime minister to summarise the decisions reached, taking into account the weight of opinion for or against a course of action as well as the numerical balance of opinion,

and sometimes concluding against what appears to be the majority view. After the meeting, Cabinet conclusions are recorded by the Cabinet secretary in consultation with the prime minister.

The prime minister also makes decisions about the structure of the government, involving in particular the allocation of duties between the departments of state. The fluctuations in the number of departments – 30 in 1951, 21 in 1983, 19 in 1993 – and the changes in their functions are evidence of considerable prime ministerial activity in this sphere. Tony Blair as Premier continued this departmental restructuring, creating a new super-ministry of Transport, Environment and the Regions for his deputy, John Prescott and a new Department of International Development in 1997. After the 2001 election Blair replaced the old Ministry of Agriculture, Fisheries and Food (MAFF) with a Department of the Environment, Food and Rural Affairs, while John Prescott's empire was broken up.

Finally in this regard, the prime minister has overall responsibility for the work of the civil service (the Cabinet secretary is head of the civil service). This power has three main aspects – appointments, organisation, and practices. Developments since 1979 have seen a significant strengthening of the prime minister's position in relation to Whitehall. On top appointments, prime ministers are frequently willing simply to endorse the recommendations of the Senior Appointments Selection Committee, although on occasion they have taken a more proactive role. But on organisation and tasks, the Thatcher–Major era saw large-scale change launched and carried through, with a series of reforms initiated and supervised by advisers and personnel at the centre of government. Thus the massive reorganisation of the civil service involved by the Next Steps programme was proposed by Thatcher's Efficiency Unit, a group within the Prime Minister's Office, while under John Major the package of reforms involving the Citizens' Charters and the market testing or contracting out of some civil service functions to the private sector were carried out by a unit within the Cabinet Office (Burch, 1995: 131).

The power of dissolution

The prime minister has the exclusive right to recommend to the monarch the timing of the dissolution of

Parliament within a five-year period. While not an important power in relation to Cabinet and the prime minister's own party, the ability to call for a dissolution undoubtedly strengthens a prime minister's hand against the opposition parties. However, it is a weapon that may backfire, since misjudgements, like those of Edward Heath in calling a general election in February 1974, and of James Callaghan in failing to call one in autumn 1978, can contribute to a party's electoral defeat, and lose many MPs their seats. Normally, the PM consults with senior ministers, including the chief whip, before making a decision about an election date and then informing Cabinet of the final choice. A dramatic illustration of the way in which the prime minister decides the date of the election was provided in 2001. Blair and his party had planned for an election on 3 May, and preparations were already at an advanced stage when the foot-and-mouth disease crisis intervened and there were calls for postponement. Most of the Cabinet and party were keen to go ahead in May. Blair himself became increasingly convinced that a May election would appear insensitive, and on his own initiative decided on a delay until June (Rawnsley, 2001: 473–9).

National leadership

The prime minister occupies a special role in the life of the country which quite distinguishes the occupant of the office from other Cabinet members – as national leader. This is always the case but becomes especially apparent at times of national crisis such as war: for example Churchill's role in 1940–5, Thatcher's in the Falklands War (1982), Major's during the Gulf War (1991), Blair's during the Kosovo (1999) and Afghanistan wars (2001). But the public spotlight focuses upon the PM at other times, too – during general elections, at times of political difficulty (e.g. during the fuel crisis in September 2000 or the foot-and-mouth crisis in spring 2001), and when key decisions affecting the nation's future are being made (e.g. during EU inter-governmental negotiations). Prime ministers must please more than their close associates and their parties if they are to succeed. Ultimately they are judged by their success in providing effective national leadership by opponents and neutrals as well as friends. Failure in key areas of policy

destroyed the premierships of Heath, Callaghan and Thatcher.

The prime minister's relations with party, Parliament and the media are often closely linked to the authority with which prime ministers are able to carry out their executive and national leadership roles. It is as the leader of the party that has gained a Parliamentary majority in a general election that a prime minister gains office in the first place; it is the continuing regular support of that party in Parliament that maintains the prime minister's authority to govern. Relationships with the party, therefore, are of the greatest significance, and these are two-way. The prime minister seeks to maximise control of the party, while the party strives for influence over the prime minister. The long-running battle between John Major and the Conservative Euro dissidents, first over the ratification of the Maastricht Treaty and then over the European single currency, with the Prime Minister constantly appealing for party unity and the rebels demanding concessions, well illustrates this point.

Faced by recalcitrant backbenchers, the PM can appeal to personal ambition (the power of patronage is a potent weapon) and party loyalty (a general desire to do nothing to assist the 'other side'). In general, prime ministers are strongest in their relations with their parties in the months following victory in a general election or leadership election. Such 'honeymoon' periods may be very brief indeed, as John Major's experience in 1992 showed. In April, the fact that he enjoyed much greater popularity than Neil Kinnock made an important contribution to the Conservatives' election victory, but by early November he had become the most unpopular prime minister since records began. Blair, by contrast, remained well ahead in the opinion polls from his election victory in 1997 until the unexpected fuel protests of September 2000, by which time the Prime Minister had enjoyed a 'honeymoon' of over three years. Prime ministers are at their weakest when government policies seem not to be working and provoke popular hostility and opposition. It was Thatcher's mounting unpopularity as a result of high interest rates, a stagnant economy and the poll tax, that led the party to revolt against her in November 1990.

The prime minister's performance in Parliament is always the subject of close scrutiny. Every

Wednesday for half an hour the premier appears in the House of Commons to answer 'prime minister's questions'. (This was the result of a change introduced by Blair; formerly it was two 15-minute sessions a week). 'Question Time' is by far the most common prime ministerial activity in Parliament. Prime ministers can expect to answer about 1000 questions per Parliamentary session, a large proportion of them on economic and foreign affairs. Many of the questions appear as supplementaries which are more difficult to prepare for. Question Time is a testing ordeal, therefore, at which much is at stake, including personal reputation, command of party, and the authority of the government.

While Parliament is sitting, premiers may expect to be constantly preoccupied with it in other ways too. Their concerns include the progress of government legislation, set-piece speeches in full-dress Parliamentary debates, and more generally the state of party morale. 'Parliamentary business' is always an item on the Cabinet agenda. A recent study has suggested that, whereas before 1940 prime ministers were often 'multi-faceted Parliamentary performers who would, for example, both make a speech in a debate and then intervene subsequently', in the period after 1940 they have tended to attend the Commons 'only for a set and specific purpose, especially the effectively mandatory prime minister's question time' (Dunleavy, Jones and O'Leary, 1990; see Box 12.2).

Contemporary prime ministers need to pay particular attention to the way they and their governments are presented in the media. They inevitably spend much of their lives in public – being interviewed on television, briefing lobby correspondents, making speeches at this or that public function, responding impromptu in the street or airport lounge or on the doorstep to queries about the latest crisis, scandal or leak. If they succeed in presenting a decisive image, they will be given credit for their handling – or, more pejoratively, for their 'manipulation' – of the media; if they are tripped up, fluff their lines, or in any way give a less than positive impression, not only their own reputation but the government's too will suffer. In other words, self-presentation through newspapers, radio and television has become another vital prime ministerial concern. Tony Blair has been rarely out of the headlines since 1997.

BOX 12.2
Prime ministers and Parliament

- Answering questions at question time is far more common than any other prime ministerial activity, and often features on main television news. (Blair has substituted one half-hour session a week for two 15-minute sessions.)
- Statements to the House by prime ministers (less common from the Thatcher premiership onwards).
- Speeches have become much rarer – Blair 'led for the government in only three debates' in the first two sessions of the 1997 Parliament (Norton, in Seldon, 2001: 54).
- Interventions in debates in a spontaneous, unscripted way have 'completely withered and died'.
- Voting – Blair's voting record is 'the worst of any modern prime minister – voting in less than one in ten divisions in the first two sessions of the 1997 Parliament' (Norton in Seldon, 2001: 54).
- Decline in prime minister's accountability to Parliament – Norton, Hennessy and others have argued that this has become particularly noticeable under Blair, although this seems just an extension of an already marked trend.

Sources: Dunleavy and Jones, 1993; Hennessy, 2000; Norton, in Seldon, 2001.

Prime ministers need also to be concerned about their personal standing in the opinion polls. The polling organisations sound out public opinion on such matters as the moral qualities (toughness, integrity, truthfulness and compassion), leadership style (dictatorial/consensual) and policy achievements of the prime minister. They compare the premier's political standing with that of his or her main rivals, and then often compare these ratings with party support. These relative positions – prime ministers compared with other leaders; party leaders compared with their parties – fluctuate continually during the lifetime of a Parliament.

The Prime Minister's Office

Although the prime minister wields extensive powers, and normally dominates the entire governmental system, he or she does not head a large department but is directly served by a Prime Minister's Office of around 100 people, of whom around one-third are senior officials and advisers. It was only in 1974 that a policy unit was established within the Prime Minister's Office at Number Ten to give the prime minister an independent source of policy advice. John Major's policy unit had just eight special advisers, while Tony Blair initially had 12 (Hennessy, 2000: 487). Reflecting the importance New Labour attached to news management, the Blair government also introduced a new Strategic Communications Unit in November 1997 to coordinate press relations of the various departments and ministers, and ensure everyone was 'on message', leading to some tension between the Labour Party's 'spin doctors' and the permanent civil servants responsible for government information.

Further changes were introduced after the 2001 election. Before the election the Prime Minister's Office, headed by Blair's chief of staff, Jonathan Powell, included the Private Office, the Political Office, the Policy Unit, the Press Office, the Strategic Communications Unit, and a number of special advisers. After the election Jonathan Powell remained in overall charge of the substantially reorganised Prime Minister's Office in which the Private Office and Policy Unit were merged to form a new Policy Directorate. In addition Alastair Campbell, formerly the Prime Minister's official spokesperson, became head of a new Directorate of Communications and Strategy, dealing with press relations, political communications, policy presentation and strategic planning, while a new Directorate of Government Relations was set up to deal with relations with ministers, departments and the new devolved governments (Holliday, in Dunleavy *et al.*, 2002: 94–5).

A prime minister's department?

It used to be argued that the prime minister was at a disadvantage compared to his leading colleagues as he or she lacked a department of his or her own, and some critics have urged the need for a larger and more powerful prime minister's department at

> **BOX 12.3**
> ## The 'kitchen cabinet'
>
> Most prime ministers have had a purely unofficial 'kitchen cabinet' of close confidants, a circle of 'friends' to whom they can look for personal support. Some of these may hold no official position. However, Margaret Thatcher's most trusted aides came from the Prime Minister's Office, in fact, and included Charles Powell, a foreign affairs adviser in her Private Office, Bernard Ingham, her chief press secretary, and – over a much shorter period of time – her Parliamentary Private Secretary, Ian Gow. Tony Blair's close circle of trusted advisers has varied over time but in the early years included Jonathan Powell; Alastair Campbell, his press secretary until 2001; David Miliband, head of the Policy Unit; Charlie Falconer and Philip Gould (Hennessy, 2000: 493–500). Peter Mandelson's influence seems to have fluctuated, declining after his two resignations, although he is widely reckoned still to have Blair's ear.

the centre of British government. However, others claim that the expansion of the Prime Minister's Office, which has continued further under Blair, makes the argument redundant. 'Do we need a Prime Minister's Department? It's largely an academic debate now because we already have one' (source close to Blair, quoted in Hennessy, 2000: 485). Holliday (in Dunleavy *et al.*, 2002: 94–6) has also emphasised the increased integration and coordination of the Prime Minister's Office and the Cabinet Office under Blair, which he claims 'makes them, in effect, a single executive office' (see p. 199, and Figure 12.1). By contrast, Riddell (in Seldon, 2001: 31–2), while acknowledging 'that the changes introduced since June 1997 have significantly changed the scale and scope of the Downing Street operation' inclines to scepticism over a prime minister's department. He points out that 'the Number 10 operation is still small by comparison with the executive offices in presidential systems, such as the United States and Germany, and even in prime ministerial systems such as Australia and Canada'.

The Cabinet

The Cabinet is the country's top executive committee. It usually consists of between 20 and 23 members. In October 2002 the Labour Cabinet contained 23 members (see In Focus 12.2), 21 from the House of Commons and two from the House of Lords (Lords Irvine and Williams), both with duties specifically related to the upper house. Six Cabinet ministers were women (there had been seven before the resignation of Estelle Morris as Secretary of State for Education and Skills). This marks a considerable advance on the recent past. Harold Wilson's 1974 Labour Cabinet included only two women. Conservative Cabinets between 1979 and 1990 generally contained just one, the Prime Minister, Margaret Thatcher. John Major's first Cabinet was all male. However, it may be noted that while Blair's Cabinets have contained a substantially larger female membership, none have yet occupied the most senior and prestigious posts. Status within the Cabinet is not equal, and most Cabinets divide into a small circle of ministers who may expect to be frequently consulted by the prime minister and an outer circle who count for less. The 'plum' jobs are the chancellorship of the Exchequer and the foreign and home secretaryships, which a victorious party's leading few politicians may expect to occupy.

On occasion, and notably in times of war, a small inner Cabinet has been formed, as in the Falklands War, for example. Thus, although the decision to commit the Task Force in 1981 was taken by full Cabinet, Margaret Thatcher formed a small War

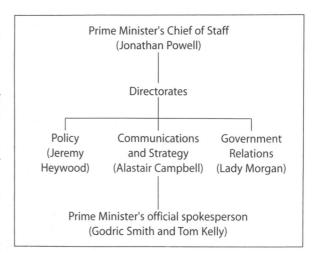

Figure 12.1 Prime Minister's Office, as reorganised following the 2001 election

Cabinet of five to run the war on a day-to-day basis. Blair similarly formed what was effectively a smaller war cabinet over Kosovo in 1999, although there were regular reports to the full Cabinet (Hennessy, 2000: 504–5).

Cabinet business

Cabinet meetings became more numerous throughout the 20th century down to the 1960s but declined thereafter, slowly at first but then dramatically under Thatcher to a much lower level which was continued by Major and Blair. The full Cabinet normally now meets once a week when Parliament is sitting, although in times of crisis it may meet more frequently. Under Blair the length of Cabinet meetings has also noticeably shortened, commonly to an hour or less (Hennessy, 2000: 481).

Very few decisions in the modern Cabinet system are actually made by Cabinet, although virtually all the major policy issues come before it in some form. Its agenda over a period of time consists predominantly of three kinds of matter: routine items such as forthcoming Parliamentary business, reports on foreign affairs and major economic decisions, such as the Budget and interest rate changes; from the 1980s regular slots have been found for EU matters and home affairs; disagreements referred upwards for Cabinet arbitration, for example from Cabinet committees or from a departmental minister in

---

BOX 12.4
The role of the Cabinet

- Formal approval of decisions taken elsewhere.
- Final court of appeal for disagreements referred from below.
- Crisis management of emergencies and issues of major political controversy.
- Debating forum and sounding board for leading ministers.
- Legitimiser conferring full legitimate authority upon government decisions.
- Symbol of collective executive rather than single-person executive in Britain.

IN FOCUS 12.3 The Cabinet in session

Prime Minister Tony Blair (seated centre left) chairs a special Cabinet meeting in 10 Downing Street in October 2001 to discuss the development of military action against Afghanistan following the attack on the World Trade Center in New York in September.

Photograph: PA Photos.

dispute; and important contemporary concerns – a broad range, including national crises such as a war, issues of major controversy such as a large-scale strike, and matters of considerable political sensitivity, such as pit closures in 1992. The Cabinet itself does not make many of the major policy decisions, nor does it generally initiate policy. In the 1990s, under John Major, more extensive use was made of political Cabinets, where the Cabinet secretariat withdraws and the party chair joins the meeting (Seldon and Kavanagh, 1994: 165). Box 12.4 summarises the role of the modern Cabinet.

Cabinet committees

Because of the sheer volume and complexity of modern governmental business, the bulk of decisions within the Cabinet system are taken by Cabinet committees (either ministerial standing committees or ministerial ad hoc committees). Cabinet committees either take decisions themselves or prepare matters for higher-level decision, possibly at Cabinet. Official committees (of civil servants) shadow ministerial committees and prepare papers for their consideration (Burch and Holliday, 1996: 44). Cabinet committee decisions have the status of Cabinet decisions, and only when they are unable to reach agreement is a matter referred to full Cabinet. The prime minister and senior members of the Cabinet chair the most important Cabinet committees. The committee chair must agree any request to take a dispute to full Cabinet, but in general such appeals

are strongly discouraged. Treasury ministers however, in 1975 gained the right of automatic appeal to Cabinet if defeated on public spending in committee (James, 1992: 69).

The establishment, composition, terms of reference and chairmanship of Cabinet committees are the responsibility of the prime minister. Before 1992 their structure was supposedly a secret, although they did gradually come to light from the 1970s as a result of ministerial memoirs and partial statements by the prime minister. After the 1992 general election John Major decided to make public the entire system of Cabinet standing committees and the subjects with which they deal.

Cabinet committees have become central to decision making in the post-war period, even though in recent years their number and frequency of meeting have fallen. Thus Margaret Thatcher reduced the number of committees, establishing a mere 30–35 standing committees and 120 ad hoc committees in six and a half years between 1979 and 1987. She also reduced the frequency of Cabinet committee meetings, with the result that by 1990 the average annual frequency of meeting was only just over half that registered in the late 1970s. This trend continued under Major, who however tended to use ministerial standing committees more, and ministerial ad hoc committees less, than his predecessor. The consequence of the fall in the number of committees and in the frequency of their meetings has been 'a more regularised and streamlined Cabinet committee system' (Burch and Holliday, 1996: 45).

Under Tony Blair, although the number of committees was increased, they have been used rather more erratically. Key Cabinet committees met regularly to process devolution legislation and discuss the Iraq, Kosovo and Afghanistan military operations, but 'on a range of other issues, however, Mr Blair has not used Cabinet committees and has either worked through ad hoc groups, like previous Prime Ministers have done, or bilaterally with relevant departmental ministers' (Riddell, in Seldon, 2001: 32–3). (See Box 12.5.)

The Cabinet Office

The Cabinet Office is another institution at the heart of the core executive which has developed in response to the large growth in the volume of government business. Dating from 1916, its most important component so far as central government is concerned is the Cabinet Secretariat, a group of some 30 senior civil servants on secondment from other departments working under the direction of the Cabinet Secretary.

After the 2001 election the Cabinet Office was placed under the control of the deputy prime minister, and a number of new special offices and units were brought within it. Among these were the Office of Public Service Reform (to oversee the implementation of the government's reform programme), the Delivery Unit (to monitor and improve policy delivery) and the Forward Strategy Unit. In addition a number of more specialised units covering policy issues that cut across departmental boundaries have been housed within the Cabinet Office from 1997 onwards. These include the Social Exclusion Unit, the Performance and Innovation Unit, the Women's Unit and the UK Anti-Drugs Co-ordination Unit.

Following the appointment of Sir Andrew Turnbull as the new Cabinet Secretary in 2002 a further reorganisation brought together these reform and delivery units and other units that started in the Cabinet Office into a single integrated structure. The reorganised Cabinet Office was to focus its work on four key objectives:

- to support the prime minister in leading the government

> **BOX 12.5**
> ## Some important Cabinet committees in Blair's government
>
> - Defence and Overseas Policy (DOP)
> - Constitutional Reform Policy (CRP)
> - Nations and Regions (CNR)
> - Domestic Affairs (DA)
> - Economic Affairs, Productivity and Competitiveness (EAPC)
> - Public Services and Public Expenditure (PSX)
> - The Environment (ENV)
> - Welfare Reform (WR)
> - The Legislative Programme (LP).

- to support the Cabinet in transacting its business
- to lead and support the reform and delivery programme, and
- to coordinate security and intelligence.

Like the office of prime minister, the Cabinet lacks formal constitutional existence. Both institutions are creations of convention. The document *A Code of Conduct and Guidance on Procedure for Ministers* (1997, previously *Questions of Procedure for Ministers*) is the first Cabinet paper a new minister is handed, and has been described as the nearest thing to a written constitution for Cabinet government in Britain. An important concern is the collective responsibility of ministers. Thus the document declares, 'Decisions reached by the cabinet or ministerial committees are binding on all members of the government', that is, not just on members of the Cabinet. The doctrine of collective responsibility, which holds that all ministers accept responsibility collectively for decisions made in Cabinet and its committees, is the main convention influencing the operation of the Cabinet.

The doctrine of collective responsibility is clearly of value to the prime minister in the control of Cabinet colleagues. On the other hand, it does lay reciprocal obligations on the prime minister: first, not to leak decisions, and second, to run the government in a collegial way, making sure that ministers have reasonable opportunities to discuss issues. One problem for ministers is the often limited part they have played in making the decisions to which they are required to assent. This latter point has implications not only for the conduct of Cabinet itself but also for the composition of Cabinet committees which – if they are to take authoritative decisions in the name of the Cabinet – must be representative of the Cabinet as a whole (James, 1992: 9).

There are only two occasions when the principle of collective responsibility has been formally suspended; in 1932 when there was an 'agreement to differ' over tariffs among members of the National Government, and in 1975 when members of Wilson's Labour government were allowed to campaign on both sides of the referendum on whether the United Kingdom should remain in the EEC. There have been other occasions when individual ministers have 'sailed close to the wind' in allowing disagreements with government policy to become public; for example Tony Benn in the 1974–9 Labour government, and Clare Short in Blair's Cabinet. It has also been argued that leaks of confidential information by ministers, including the prime minister, and the publication of diaries by former Cabinet ministers such as Richard Crossman, Barbara Castle and Tony Benn have breached conventions of collective responsibility and secrecy.

Cabinet minutes

Cabinet minutes – which are the responsibility of the Cabinet Secretariat – aim not to record every shift and turn of Cabinet debate but simply to reflect, in the words of a former Cabinet Secretary, Sir John Hunt, 'as much agreement as is there'. Controversy has occurred over the extent of prime ministerial involvement in the process, with certain members of Labour Cabinets suggesting that this could be considerable (Castle, 1980: 252). But the then Prime Minister, Harold Wilson, denied it, maintaining at the time (1970) that only 'very, very occasionally' was he consulted about the minutes before issue. He later stated that 'the writing of the

---

> **Definition**
> **Collective responsibility:** the convention of Cabinet government that requires all ministers to support publicly decisions of Cabinet and its committees, or resign.

---

conclusions is the unique responsibility of the Secretary of the Cabinet.... The conclusions are circulated very promptly after Cabinet, and up to that that time no minister, certainly not the prime minister, sees them, asks to see them or conditions them in any way' (cited in King, 1985: 40). This later statement is widely accepted now as a correct account of routine procedure (Seldon, 1990).

Prime ministerial government?

Some commentators have argued that the British system of government has evolved towards prime ministerial government (Crossman, 1964; Benn, 1980) or even 'presidential' government (Foley, 1993; Hennessy, 2000) in the post-war period. The premierships of Margaret Thatcher, and more recently Tony Blair, have been seen as validating this thesis. Briefly, these writers argue that a considerable concentration of power in the premiership has occurred, resulting in 'a system of personal rule in the very heart of our Parliamentary democracy' (Benn, 1980). The prime minister's powers of appointment and dismissal of ministers, control over government business, special responsibilities in the spheres of strategic economic matters, defence, foreign policy and security, command over government information and publicity, and constitutional capacity to request a dissolution of Parliament are considered to have elevated the premiership at the expense of the Cabinet.

By making decisions through informal ministerial groups and bilateral meetings with a minister and officials, the prime minister can bypass – and downgrade – Cabinet. The prime minister has a direct relationship with all ministers and expects to be informed about all new policy initiatives, which makes it possible to kill off those he or she dislikes. Whereas if he or she wishes, a prime minister can intervene selectively over the entire field of policy making, the cabinet can deal only with the material which is put before it. Recently there have been fewer and shorter meetings of Cabinet and fewer Cabinet papers. Under Blair, meetings have 'rarely lasted more than an hour' (Hennessy, 2000: 481). The prime minister's position at the centre of the Cabinet committee system enhances his or her power. After identifying eight main policy networks

BOX 12.6

The practical implications of collective Cabinet responsibility

- **Cabinet solidarity.** Ministers may disagree until a decision is made, but are expected then to support it publicly or, at least, not express their lack of support for it. If they feel they must dissent publicly, they are expected to resign, as Robin Cook did in March 2003 over the decision to invade Iraq without a second UN Security Council resolution. A dissenting minister who fails to resign normally faces dismissal, although Clare Short initially survived public criticism of Blair's Iraq policy.
- **Cabinet secrecy.** A precondition of Cabinet solidarity is that Cabinet discussion is secret. Ministers need to feel free to speak their minds secure in the knowledge that their views will not be divulged to the media. Ministers who are known to disagree with a policy may be expected to have little commitment to it: well-publicised disagreements, therefore, have potentially damaging consequences for public confidence in government.
- **Cabinet resignation** if defeated on a Commons vote of confidence. The convention requires that the Cabinet – and therefore the entire government – should resign if defeated on a vote of confidence in the House of Commons. This aspect of the convention still operates unambiguously: when the Labour government elected in October 1974 was defeated on a vote of confidence on 28 March 1979, the Prime Minister James Callaghan immediately requested a dissolution. However, it rarely happens because the circumstances of a government lacking an overall majority are so infrequent.

in the British Cabinet system (such as domestic policy, overseas policy and European Union policy), Burch and Holliday found the prime minister to be 'a core member of seven networks' and also that the prime minister's power potential 'has been increased in all networks of which he or she is core' (Burch and Holliday, 1996: 105–6).

The expansion and increased status of the Prime Minister's Office since the 1970s, especially the formation of the Prime Minister's Policy Unit, has increased the prime minister's capacity 'to oversee government strategy, to monitor departmental work and to initiate policy from the centre'. Contemporary prime ministers are better informed about what is happening across the whole range of government, and there is an increased tendency for business to flow to the Prime Minister's Office and for ministers to consult Number Ten before launching policy initiatives (Burch and Holliday, 1996: 45). Some argue that the Prime Minister's Office under Blair is virtually already a prime minister's department of the kind that some centralising reformers have argued for in the past (Hennessy, 2000:. 485–6).

The impact of British membership of the EU on top decision making has strengthened the prime minister's hand and weakened Cabinet. As the leading British negotiator in EU treaty-making the PM has to be given considerable latitude to make deals in Britain's interests, and when other ministers are involved in European policy making, to assent to any changes in negotiating positions. This point extends beyond Europe to the general enhancement of the PM's position by the impact of international summit meetings, such as Group of Eight (G8) meetings (James, in Rhodes and Dunleavy, 1995: 75; Lee, 1995: 214–15).

More intense media focus on the prime minister has increased the need for the prime minister constantly to demonstrate leadership, control of party, a political vision, and personal charisma. The premiers' ability to do all these things is vital to the success of their parties (and to their own continuance in office); hence their emphasis on presentation of their policies and relationships with the media, and the key role in their premierships of the Downing Street press officers and their ability to put a favourable 'spin' or gloss on events (Burch and Holliday, 1996: 100–2; Seymour-Ure, 1995:

197). This was developed further by Blair, under whom 'Party campaigning has been transplanted into Whitehall, with many of the same personnel and the same methods' (Scammell, in Dunleavy *et al.*, 2002: 180–3).

A 'Blair presidency'?

Some commentators have proposed an extreme version of the prime ministerial power thesis to suggest that Blair is effectively Britain's president, while others have taken a contrasting view (see Box 12.7).

The quotations from Riddell is interesting in that he had in the early days of New Labour himself written an article arguing that it was 'Goodbye Cabinet Government. Welcome the Blair Presidency' (*The Times*, 1 August 1997). The notion of a presidency always implied a greater shift from past practice than has actually occurred. Admittedly, Cabinet meetings are fewer and shorter, the prime minister's attendance at Parliament more sporadic, the Prime Minister's Office a little larger and perhaps more effective. But Blair has only continued developments already well under way; there has been no sharp break with the past. If Blair appears more presidential than some of his predecessors, Major or Douglas-Home, perhaps the contrast is less obvious with Lloyd George, Churchill or Thatcher. Moreover there are differences within, as well as between, premierships. Harold Wilson (1979: 17) told the Parliamentary Labour Party on returning to power in 1974 he would be 'a deep-lying centre half' rather than having to 'occupy almost every position on the field, goalkeeper, defence, attack' when he first became Prime Minister in 1964. Circumstances matter. Prime ministers seem stronger when things are going well, more presidential in periods of war or national emergency. Significantly, it was at the end of the Balkans War in 1999 that one 'senior Whitehall figure' observed that Blair 'bestrides the world like a Colossus' while another commented 'Because of the war, presidential government is more extreme than ever now' (reported in Hennessy, 2000: 507).

BOX 12.7
President Blair? Two contrasting perspectives

In Britain's unwritten constitution a Prime Minister is *primus inter pares*, first among equals. Tony Blair recognised no equal in his Cabinet, and only his Chancellor was sufficiently strong to challenge that supremacy. This Prime Minister planned to be *primus*. From the beginning it was designed to be a presidential premiership.

(Andrew Rawnsley, 2001: 50)

So far from being a dominant presidential figure, Mr Blair emerges as a more cautious leader – sharing power with his Chancellor on many issues, keen to set a broad strategic direction except when his personal involvement is needed, reluctant to take risks, and frustrated by the difficulty of achieving change.

(Peter Riddell, in Seldon, 2001: 37)

Constraints on prime ministerial government

However, despite the comprehensive assertion of the powers of the PM's office by Margaret Thatcher and Tony Blair, it remains inappropriate to describe the British system as 'prime ministerial government'. In practice, prime ministerial power can vary considerably according to the disposition of the individual prime minister to exploit the capacities of the office and political circumstances such as size of Parliamentary majority, and simply how 'events' fall out. Constitutional, political, administrative and personal constraints prevent the prime minister from achieving the degree of predominance suggested by the prime ministerial government thesis.

Constitutional constraints

Britain's top decision making body remains a collective not a single executive, and the prime

BOX 12.8

Comparative politics: prime ministers and presidents

- The implied comparison, in the notion of 'President Blair'; is with an American president. The US president is (effectively) directly elected by the American people and combines the role of head of government with head of state. He is the acknowledged head of the armed forces, and the focus of national loyalty.
- Yet as head of government the US president may often have less control of policy than a British prime minister, particularly if he does not have a majority in Congress, which is not uncommon. The main reason that a UK prime minister often appears more powerful is because of the fusion of the executive and legislature in Britain compared with the constitutionally separate executive and legislature in the USA.
- However, the US president is a rather unusual type of president. Many other 'presidents' around the world are formal heads of state, not heads of government, with little political power (for example the presidents of Germany, Italy, Ireland). Most are not subject to direct popular election.
- The French Fifth Republic comes somewhere between the US and German models. It is sometimes characterised as a 'dual executive' because it has both a directly elected president with significant powers, particularly in foreign affairs, and a prime minister (who has to command a majority in the French Assembly) largely responsible for domestic policy.
- Interestingly, the post-1997 Labour government has been compared with the French political system, with Blair as a Fifth Republic-type president dominating foreign affairs, and Brown as a French-model prime minister controlling not only the economy but large areas of domestic policy (Hennessy, 2000: 513).

minister's role therefore is to provide leadership within a Cabinet context in which collective responsibility remains the rule. In the final analysis, the 'mortal wound' to Margaret Thatcher was struck by the Cabinet, which 'rejected her' (Jones, in Rhodes and Dunleavy, 1995: 87).

Political constraints

Appointment and dismissals: constitutionally the prime minister has a free hand in the making of government appointments, but politically selection is constrained by the pool of talent within a particular party, by party standing and by the need to please sections of the party (left and right, 'wets' and 'dries', Euro-enthusiasts and Euro-sceptics). This means in practice that Cabinets contain individuals whom the PM would rather be without and also that many Cabinets contain one or two politicians of the highest calibre and with a following in the party who may be rivals for the party leadership: 'these are people whom the Prime Minister needs as much, or maybe more sometimes, than they need the Prime Minister' (Roy Jenkins, cited in James, 1992: 133). Political considerations also constrain the PM's power of dismissal and demotion: Macmillan in dismissing seven Cabinet ministers and nine ministers outside the Cabinet in July 1962 (the so-called 'Night of the Long Knives') damaged his own standing, as the brutality of the sackings caused resentment in the party and gave the appearance of panic to the country. Thatcher's big Cabinet reshuffle of July 1989 which included the demotion of the reluctant Sir Geoffrey Howe from the post of foreign secretary also had very damaging consequences (Young, 1990: 555–7). John Major, in an unguarded moment, revealed to an interviewer that he would not sack unfriendly Cabinet colleagues because of adverse political consequences. 'You and I can think of ex-ministers who are causing all sorts of trouble. Do we want three more of the bastards out there?' (Major, 1999: 343; the 'bastards' were widely reckoned to be Lilley, Redwood and Portillo). While Major had problems with a dwindling majority, even Blair faces significant constraints. Thus although Mowlam (2002) has argued that he should remove Brown from the Exchequer because of the alleged 'poison' in their relationship at the centre of government, it was generally considered that this was politically difficult and virtually impossible.

Policy: the prime minister heads an executive whose collective task is to implement the party manifesto, in which inevitably individual ministers play key roles. Often party considerations constrain policy. A good illustration of this is policy towards Europe which has caused a series of prime ministers from Macmillan to Blair often acute problems of party management. Wilson suspended collective responsibility and held a referendum to avoid splitting Labour, and Major resigned the party leadership in 1995 in an attempt to put to rest incessant Cabinet and party dissension over Europe. While Blair was reportedly keen to push forward entry to the euro sooner rather than later, it was clear that his chancellor wielded an effective veto on a referendum until his five economic tests had been met.

Tenure: ultimately the party may remove a sitting prime minister, but this is a rare event, having been the fate of just four of the 17 prime ministers in the 20th century: in addition to the recent case of Thatcher in 1990, Asquith (1916), Lloyd George (1922) and Chamberlain (1940) all resigned after losing the support of senior colleagues and a sizeable section of the majority Parliamentary party. The very unusual combination of circumstances that led to the downfall of Thatcher included the availability of a strong prime ministerial candidate outside the Cabinet (Heseltine), the recent resignations of two Cabinet 'heavyweights' (Lawson and Howe), with Howe giving a particularly wounding resignation speech, a by-election disaster at a normally safe Conservative seat (Eastbourne), adverse economic indicators, public anger at the poll tax for which Thatcher was generally blamed, and the considerable unpopularity of the prime minister and the party she led in the opinion polls.

Administrative constraints

The major institutional constraint upon a prime minister is the Cabinet. However great their powers of manipulation, prime ministers have often suffered defeats in Cabinet, as did Wilson on trade union reform (1969), Callaghan on his wish to declare a state of emergency during the 'Winter of

Discontent' (1979) and Margaret Thatcher on a number of issues, including the decision to enter the ERM (1990), which was pushed through against her resistance. On crucial issues, prime ministers are usually careful to bind the whole Cabinet to a decision: on the sending of the Task Force to the Falklands, Thatcher asked every member of the Cabinet individually to indicate a view. John Major, especially in his first two years before acquiring a personal mandate in 1992, was careful to take decisions collectively in order to bind his colleagues to the final outcome.

The prime minister can also be restrained in a number of ways by the departments and the civil service. Government departments are 'the key policy-making institutions in British politics' and the PM/'Core executive' 'does not play a decisive role in all, or even in most of, the stages of the policy process' (Smith, Marsh and Richards, in Rhodes and Dunleavy, 1995: 38). Characteristically, in relation to the departments, the prime minister is in ' the position of a bargainer rather than of a leader enjoying a significant power of command' (Burch, 1995: 136). Policy tends to arrive at the PM at such a late stage that effective challenge becomes difficult. The prime minister may be able to squash ministerial policy initiatives but would find it hard to impose a policy on a minister.

Personal constraints

Finally, there are personal limits upon the power of the prime minister – the limits of any single individual's ability, energy, resources and time, together with the (very considerable) extent to which decisions are shaped by circumstances beyond any individual's ability to control. A survey of the prime minister's 'diary' during the 1970s has shown how stretched a single individual is to fulfil such a punishing schedule of consultations, meetings, appointments, conferences, receptions and visits: according to this estimate – assuming a 13-hour day, a five-day Whitehall week and a Cabinet year of 44 weeks – only about one day per week is available to the PM for 'the Cabinet role', rising to over one and a half days when time spent with civil servants is taken into account; the rest of the time is spent on party matters, Parliament, and hosting and visiting (Donoughue, 1988). Moreover, the PM's special concerns (foreign affairs, the economy and security) are particularly vulnerable to setbacks which rebound swiftly on the popularity and even credibility of the premier. A prime minister who takes personal charge of a crisis, as Blair did on foot-and-mouth disease in 2001, puts his own position on the line if he fails.

To summarise: the British prime minister has very considerable powers – and these have been stretched to the limit by a dynamic prime minister such as Thatcher and more recently by Blair also. But the constraints upon the premier make 'prime ministerial government' an inappropriate description. Is 'Cabinet government' a more apt one? Our earlier discussion suggested that the Cabinet itself neither originates policy nor takes more than a small proportion of major decisions. Most policy decisions in British government are taken by the departments. However, the Cabinet retains what may be described as 'a residual and irreducible' authority; it has not sunk into merely 'dignified' status (Madgwick, 1991: 259). It remains strong enough to help depose a dominant prime minister and also to provide a collective shield to protect both a prime minister and his or her leading ministers when they get into political difficulties. The British system of decision making at the top has grown more complex, diffuse, and extensive, but arguably it is still a collective executive in which the prime minister provides leadership within a Cabinet system.

Prime ministerial power: an irrelevant debate?

Although the argument over whether Britain has Cabinet or prime ministerial or perhaps even presidential government has rumbled on for at least 40 years, some modern academics consider that it is largely irrelevant to the understanding of political and governmental power in modern Britain (see e.g. Smith, 1999, ch. 4 and Smith in Holliday et al., 1999: 109–18).

- In assuming a bipolar struggle between prime minister and Cabinet the traditional debate oversimplifies the complexity of Britain's core executive, and the role of other players within

that core executive, including the Treasury, senior permanent civil servants, advisers and Cabinet committees.
- It fails to distinguish sufficiently between the power of Cabinet ministers as heads of departments with real resources at their disposal and interests behind them, and the power of the Cabinet as a collective body.
- It focuses too much on the traditional centre of British government in Whitehall and Westminster, ignoring the shift towards multi-level governance, in which the prime minister and Cabinet are only operating at one level.
- In focusing on the power of institutions it underestimates the importance of relationships between key players and the resources they can deploy in bargaining – resources that may shift significantly over time.
- It underestimates the importance of the context in which conflicts within government are fought out. Factors such as the size of a government's majority, the governing party's discipline and cohesion, and the poll standing of the prime minister and leading rivals are not minor incidental features, but crucial to power relationships.
- In focusing on actual and potential conflicts within the British core executive it substantially ignores the far more important external constraints on UK government policy making. While there were clearly differences within the British government on a wide range of recent major policies (e.g. the Falklands task force, the poll tax, the decision to join and then leave the ERM) the outcome in most cases was not substantially determined by internal debates and power struggles.

Criticism of the British core executive

Besides the debate over where power lies in practice within the British core executive, there is another argument over where, ideally, it ought to lie and over the effectiveness of the executive. Before the advent of the Blair government, some political commentators lamented that a single executive capable of providing policy leadership and coherence had not emerged (Burch, 1995: 33). There was 'a hole in the centre of government' (Bogdanor,

---

Table 12.2 Prime ministerial power and constraints on prime ministerial power: a brief summary

Prime ministerial power	Constraints on prime ministerial power
• PM's power of patronage – to 'hire and fire'	• Political constraints on exercise of patronage
• PM's position as majority party leader (normally)	• PM faced with powerful rivals in government and potential alternative leaders
• PM's position as chair of Cabinet – heading whole machinery of government	• PM can be outvoted in Cabinet
• PM's control over civil service	• PM has limited power over civil service, which has strong tradition of political neutrality
• PM's effective control of Parliament	• PM may face revolt in Parliamentary party
• PM's power to dissolve Parliament and choose election date	• PM has limited freedom of manoeuvre in setting election date
• PM's power to intervene personally in any area of government	• Opportunity cost to PM's intervention in any policy area – cannot intervene everywhere
• PM represents country abroad	• PM is not a president – there is a separate head of state
• PM's standing in country as head of government and party – enhanced by mass media	

Guardian, 4 June 1997). It was argued that policy remained largely the preserve of the departments, thereby – in default of a corrective mechanism – undermining collective decision making and accountability. One of the most frequent criticisms of the operation of modern Cabinet government was the weakness of coordination and strategic direction at the top. Many reform proposals therefore focused on strengthening the capacity of prime minister and/or Cabinet to provide improved policy making coordination and better long-term strategic direction. Reformers argue that there is a crying need to overcome the 'short-termism' seemingly endemic in post-war British government, which has had especially damaging consequences in the fields of foreign and economic policy. Some continued to argue for a smaller inner Cabinet charged with the overall coordination and steering of government business, others for a prime minister's department.

Some argued almost the opposite. The problem with the British executive, they maintained, was that it was too powerful and too secretive. Suggested reforms included limiting the premier's political and other patronage, decentralising power, making the executive more accountable to Parliament and public, and making government more open through a Freedom of Information Act.

In some respects the Blair government seemed to respond, after some fashion, to both these diametrically opposed criticisms. As we have seen, central institutions such as the Prime Minister's Office and the Cabinet Office were overhauled and strengthened, and generally New Labour has placed considerable emphasis on coordination, or 'joined-up government'. At the same it has ostensibly pursued a policy of decentralisation, through devolution, regional development agencies, modernising local government and devolving power in the NHS, while introducing more open government, including a Freedom of Information Act. Yet critics argue that the dominant narrative of the Blair government has been of central command and control rather than real decentralisation.

Further reading

On the prime minister, the main source is now Hennessy (2000). Dennis Kavanagh and Peter Riddell provide thoughtful complementary analyses of Blair as prime minister in Anthony Seldon's *The Blair Effect* (2001). Older useful sources include King (1985), Jones (1990) and Foley (1993). A brief updated summary of the continuing debate on 'prime ministerial government' is provided by Neil McNaughton in *Talking Politics* (2002).

On the Cabinet and the central executive

generally see Rhodes and Dunleavy (1995), Burch and Holliday (1996), and Smith (1999). Useful brief discussions can be found in Smith (in Holliday *et al.*, 1999), and particularly for developments since the 2001 election, the chapters by Martin Smith and Patrick Dunleavy in *Developments in British Politics 7* (Dunleavy *et al.*, 2003).

Websites

10 Downing Street: <www.number-10.gov.uk>/
Cabinet Office:
Office of the Deputy Prime Minister:

Chapter 13

Ministers, departments and the civil service

The organisation of British central
  government   206
The internal organisation of central
  government departments – politicians
  and civil servants   208
The civil service – size and distribution   209
The British civil service – three major features 210
Recruitment of the higher civil service –
  issues of expertise and bias   210
From old public administration to new
  public management?   213
The Conservative reforms: a revolution in
  government?   213
The Blair government and the civil service   216
Standards in public life   217
Ministerial responsibility revisited   218
Where does power lie? Decision making
  within departments   222
The resurgence of the traditional model: do
  ministers decide after all?   224

In the last chapter the focus was on the central direction and coordination of policy in Britain by the core executive, with particular reference to the prime minister and the Cabinet. However, the proportion of departmental decisions that are either sufficiently important or controversial to be taken to Cabinet has become very small indeed, and the vast majority of governmental decisions are made in departments. Not only do departments take the bulk of decisions – from the relatively minor to the undeniably major – it is no accident that they do so. For whenever new responsibilities are created by legislation, Parliament confers them squarely upon departments. New powers developed by statute are given to ministers, not to the Cabinet or the prime minister. The political and administrative importance of departments stems directly from their legal-constitutional pre-eminence. How decisions are taken within

departments is consequently of vital significance in British government. To what extent are ministers the real decision makers, or to put the question in another way, how far does the real power lie with civil servants? Thus this chapter continues our examination of the 'core executive' by considering the major departments of state, and the respective roles of the ministers who head them and the civil servants who staff them. We explore the radical changes in the civil service introduced by the Conservatives between 1979 and 1997, and subsequently maintained by Labour, together with the implications of these and other developments on the traditional civil service principles of permanence, neutrality and anonymity. We examine issues of accountability and responsibility which have arisen in the relationship between elected politicians and civil servants, and conclude with a discussion of the distribution of power and influence within government.

The organisation of British central government

The central government of the United Kingdom is organised into a number of government departments of varying size and importance. Ministries or departments have emerged rather haphazardly over the last few centuries, and particularly over the last century, as the responsibilities of government have expanded. There have also been frequent reorganisations under which the functions of government have been reallocated between departments, which have been renamed frequently as a consequence, and sometimes renamed when there has been no substantial change in responsibilities. All this can be very confusing, particularly as departments are frequently referred to by their acronyms, which change with the names.

Is there any coherent rationale behind these

departmental reorganisations? Back in 1918 the Haldane Report into the machinery of government reckoned that there were two main principles under which the tasks of government might be grouped: by function or service (e.g. education, health, transport) or by client group (children, pensioners, the disabled, the unemployed). Haldane came down in favour of the functional principle. Since then, it has been argued that there are two other ways in which tasks might be allocated: by area, or by work process (e.g. departments of architecture or accounting).

It should be clear that the actual organisation of British central government does not completely follow any one of these principles entirely. While most departments follow Haldane's service model, there are also others that deal with particular areas of the United Kingdom – Scotland, Wales and Northern Ireland. Moreover, particular ministers have sometimes been given specific responsibilities for part of England. In addition, ministers (if not departments) have sometimes been appointed for particular client groups. Thus we have had ministers for the disabled, and a minister for women. Organisation by work process has rarely been used explicitly in central government (although it was once common in local government, with for example departments of Engineering, Surveying and Architecture).

Administrative fashion has sometimes influenced organisational change. In the 1960s and 1970s there was a general presumption in favour of large-scale organisation in both the private and public sectors. 'Big was beautiful' because it was argued, it could yield economies of scale, and lead to better coordination of policy. Thus a number of 'giant departments' were created which merged previously separate ministries, for example the Department of Trade and Industry (DTI), the Department of Health and Social Security (DHSS), and the Department of the Environment (DOE). Subsequently there was a reaction against 'big government', and also against large departments, which were held to produce problems for effective management, and thus diseconomies rather than economies of scale. Thus the DHSS, and for a time the DTI, were redivided, while a separate Transport Department was hived off from the DOE. After 1988, disaggregation went further with the introduction of executive agencies (see below).

More often, organisational change seems to have reflected political factors rather than administrative

theory. Thus the creation of a new department may be intended to signal the importance the government attaches to a particular responsibility, sometimes in response to public pressure – hence the creation by Harold Wilson's government of the Ministry of Technology and by Edward Heath of the Department of the Environment. Occasionally a new department has been created to accommodate a particular politician.

BOX 13.1
Departmental reorganisation under the Blair government

A mixture of administrative, political and personal factors seems to have driven some of the Blair government's departmental reorganisation. Thus part of the rationale behind the monster Department of the Environment, Transport and the Regions in 1997 was to create an important job for the Deputy Prime Minister, John Prescott, although it also no doubt was intended to show the importance Blair's Labour government attached to these responsibilities. Four years later, after the 2001 election, Prescott became head of the Office of the Deputy Prime Minister, based in the Cabinet Office, but retained overall responsibility for regional devolution. His old department was briefly replaced by the Department for Transport, Local Government and the Regions (DTLR). The environment was separated from transport and linked with food and rural affairs in a new department (DEFRA). This was partly to answer criticism that the Blair government was unresponsive to the countryside and rural issues, and in the process to scrap the old unpopular Ministry of Agriculture, Fisheries and Food, associated with policy failures over BSE and foot-and-mouth disease, and linked in the past with producer rather than consumer interests. In May 2002, following the resignation of Stephen Byers (see pp. 219–20), Transport became a separate department under Alistair Darling, and the regional and local government responsibilities of the DTLR were transferred to the Office of the Deputy Prime Minister.

The internal organisation of central government departments – politicians and civil servants

Departments are officially directed and run by politicians drawn mainly from the House of Commons. Today virtually all the ministers who head departments are of Cabinet rank, and most of these now hold the title of secretary of state. Below the secretary of state each ministry frequently contains at least one minister of state and two or more Parliamentary under-secretaries of state: these junior ministerial appointments are the route by which aspiring politicians gain experience of government, and often but not invariably lead in time to promotion to full ministerial rank. The Department for Education and Skills – a large department – has a Cabinet minister at its head assisted by three ministers of state and three Parliamentary under-secretaries of state. By contrast, a very small ministry like the Welsh Office has one Cabinet minister and two Parliamentary under-secretaries of state. Junior ministers (ministers of state and Parliamentary under-secretaries) normally assume responsibility for specific tasks: in the Department for Education and Skills, for example, they cover employment and disability rights, further and higher education, school standards, life-long learning and welfare to work.

Ministers are the political and constitutional heads of departments. Departments, however, are largely composed of permanent officials. Below

> *Definition*
> **The civil service**: Civil servants are 'Servants of the Crown, other than holders of political or judicial offices, who are employed in a civil capacity and whose remuneration is paid wholly and directly out of moneys voted by Parliament' (Tomlin Commission, 1931). It includes all those directly employed by government departments and executive agencies.

the ministerial 'team' there is a body of civil servants headed by the permanent secretary, the most senior official in the departmental hierarchy. In addition to acting as the minister's top policy adviser, the permanent secretary is in charge of the daily work of the department, is responsible for its staffing and organisation, and is also its accounting officer. Below the permanent secretary, in order of rank, are the deputy secretaries, under-secretaries and three other grades down to principal. Broadly speaking, each department is normally divided up, first into several areas of policy, each the responsibility of a deputy secretary, and then into a number of functional units (or branches), each with an under-secretary in charge. (Figure 13.1 brings together the points made so far about departmental structure in diagrammatic form, while Figure 13.2 provides a specific example.)

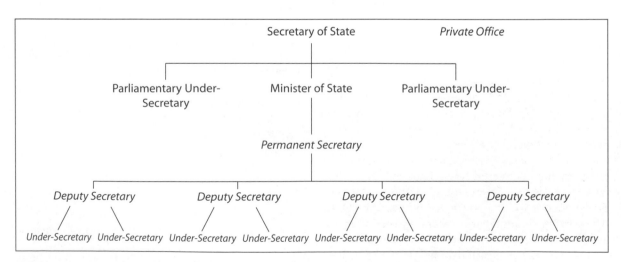

Figure 13.1 Structure of a typical department of state (civil servants italicised)

Secretary of State for Education and Skills
(The Right Hon Charles Clarke, MP)

Minister of State (Schools)
(David Miliband, MP)

Minister of State (Universities & Life-long Learning)
(Margaret Hodge, MP)

Parliamentary Under- Secretary
(Baroness Ashton of Upholland)

Parliamentary Under- Secretary
(Ivan Lewis, MP)

Parliamentary Under-Secretary
(Steven Twigg, MP)

Figure 13.2 Ministers in the Department for Education and Skills, 2002

The civil service – size and distribution

The civil service covered some 480,000 individuals by 2002. Their numbers had declined from 735,000 in 1979 as a result of a deliberate policy designed to prune the bureaucracy carried out by Conservative governments between 1979 and 1997. However, these figures somewhat exaggerate the reduction in bureaucracy as some of these workers continued to be employed elsewhere in the public sector. The civil service only constitutes about 10 per cent of all public sector employees (others are employed in local government, the health service, the armed forces and public corporations). Within the civil service the proportion of industrial civil servants – i.e. those employed as 'blue collar' manual workers in factories and workshops – has declined from 53 per cent of the total in 1939 to 6 per cent by 2001. Thus non-industrial 'white collar' civil servants now constitute 94 per cent of the total service.

Although the civil service is still widely associated with London, and more specifically Whitehall (see In Focus 13.1), it is increasingly geographically dispersed. Of the non-industrial civil servants, one-fifth (21 per cent) work in London; just under one-seventh (15 per cent) work in the rest of the South East whilst the remaining two-thirds work in the provinces. However, it remains true that the majority of the most senior civil servants remain London-based.

Perhaps more significant than geographical decentralisation is the increasing managerial decentralisation of the modern civil service. Most executive functions of the civil service are now carried out by executive agencies which have been established under the Next Steps programme (1988) to

Photograph: Lynton Robins.

IN FOCUS 13.1 Whitehall

Whitehall is still the centre of British government where leading civil servants work, despite increased geographical decentralisation and managerial delegation to executive agencies. The term 'Whitehall village' has been coined to describe the small intimate world in which leading government officials meet in face to face formal and informal relations with each other and with ministers.

> **Definition**
> **Executive agencies** (often referred to as 'Next Steps' agencies) are organisations with some managerial autonomy within the civil service which are responsible for a specific function or service.

improve management in government and the delivery of services. By 2002, over 73 per cent of the civil service were working in 93 Next Steps agencies or on Next Steps lines. Each agency is headed by a chief executive who generally reports to a minister. The minister sets the chief executive output, financial and quality of service targets for each year.

This chapter is primarily concerned with a tiny fraction of the non-industrial civil service – the top policy-making grades who mostly work in London and who since April 1996 have been banded together as the senior civil service (SCS). The SCS also includes senior diplomatic personnel and a number of other staff at a similar level. It constitutes less than 1 per cent of the entire non-industrial civil service (453,700). Members of this group form the administrative elite who, in cooperation with their ministerial superiors, 'run the country'.

The British civil service – three major features

British constitutional theory makes a clear distinction between the political role of ministers and the administrative role of civil servants. Ministers are in charge of departments and responsible to Parliament for running them, while civil servants advise ministers on policy and implement government decisions. Three major features of civil servants are linked to this distinction: permanence, political neutrality and anonymity (see Box 13.2).

These general points are valuable as guidelines but also need to be handled with care. For example, civil servants, although not allowed to play a formal (party) political role, are much more involved in the political process than the description of their work in terms of 'administration' suggests. They are obviously heavily involved in the politics of bargaining for influence within departments, between

BOX 13.2
Features of the British civil service

- **Permanence.** Unlike the position in the USA (see Box 13.3), where large numbers of administrative posts change hands when the political complexion of the government changes, in Britain civil servants are career officials prepared to serve governments of any party.
- **Political neutrality.** British civil servants are required to be politically impartial, not allowing their own political opinions to influence their actions and loyally carrying out decisions whether they agree with them or not; they must not engage in any partisan political activity.
- **Anonymity.** It is the function of ministers to be politically answerable for their departments to Parliament and public, whereas it is the role of civil servants to offer confidential advice in secret. If civil servants became public figures, this might compromise their neutrality since they would become associated in the public mind with a particular policy; it also might undermine the frankness of the advice offered to ministers.

departments, with outside interests and in their relations with ministers. They are centrally concerned with policy advice to ministers. This inherently political (and problematic) aspect of the role of civil servants will become amply evident in the discussion of decision making within departments in the next section. Moreover, in the post-war period, and with increasing rapidity in the 1980s and 1990s, traditional features of the civil service have been eroded to a significant degree, especially its neutrality and anonymity, and this is examined in the final section.

Recruitment of the higher civil service – issues of expertise and bias

For much of the 19th century civil servants were recruited by a system of patronage, by who they knew rather than what they knew, which was hardly likely to promote efficient government. Following the 1854 Northcote–Trevelyan report, competitive examinations were introduced, with the aim of recruiting the best and brightest graduates into the higher civil service. This aim was substantially achieved. In the 20th century the British higher civil servants generally had outstanding academic records, with first class degrees from the older and more prestigious universities. However in the latter part of the 20th century there was increasing criticism of top British civil servants on two main grounds; their lack of relevant skills and expertise, and their narrow and unrepresentative social and educational background.

While there was little doubt that the senior civil servants recruited by the rigorous selection process were in general exceedingly able, critics argued that they usually lacked relevant subject knowledge of the services they were called on to administer, and managerial skills and training. Nor were these deficiencies systematically addressed through in-service training. Moreover, as most were recruited straight from university, they had little direct experience of the outside world, particularly commerce and industry. The professional and technical expertise of British senior civil servants was compared unfavourably with their French equivalents (see Box 13.3).

The Fulton Report (1968) called for changes in civil service recruitment, promotion and training, recommending preference to be given to graduates with more relevant degrees, a considerable expansion of late entry in order to enable people from many walks of life to bring in their experience, and the widening of the social and educational base from which top civil servants were recruited. The idea of demanding 'relevance' was rejected, but although expansion of late entry had disappointing results, from the mid-1980s there was a significant programme of two-way temporary secondments between Whitehall and industry, commerce and other institutions (Hennessy, 1990: 523–4). By 1996 there had been a dramatic increase in recruitment from the private sector, with a quarter of the 63 posts advertised in the senior civil service going to private sector applicants. Secondments outside Whitehall had also increased, with 1500 civil servants on medium to long-term attachments in

BOX 13.3

Comparative politics – public bureaucracies in the USA and France, compared with Britain

USA. The American public bureaucracy is highly complex, fragmented and at higher levels more politicised than the British. The complexity partly reflects the US federal system and division of powers. Bureaucracies exist at federal, state and local levels, but there is also a bewildering proliferation of departments, bureaux and agencies, often with overlapping responsibilities. However, in Britain devolution, the growth of executive agencies, policy units and quangos involves more complexity and fragmentation than in the past, and the civil service has lost its uniformity. Whereas British higher civil servants are expected to be politically neutral, many senior posts in the USA change hands when control of government changes (the 'spoils system'). American public officials do not generally enjoy the same prestigious status as their British or French equivalents.

France. A strong, technocratic and highly prestigious bureaucracy serves the French 'one and indivisible' Republic. While senior British civil servants had the reputation of being able generalists without much specialist background or training, senior French public officials tend to be specialists with technical expertise. However, the French public service is not necessarily a career service on the lines of the British civil service. Although leading bureaucrats are recruited from the elite *Ecole Nationale d'Administration*, whose graduates are referred to as *Enarques*, some subsequently move into politics, and others transfer into the private sector, and sometimes back into the state service. This more specialist education combined with a greater breadth of experience may help to account for the role of French officials in modernising the economy and implementing prestigious projects.

1996. The Blair government established a new group headed by the Cabinet secretary and the president of the CBI to oversee the development of shorter, more flexible secondments from the civil service into industry, especially of junior-level civil servants from outside London.

A rather different criticism was that the senior civil service were socially and educationally unrepresentative of the public they served. To an extent it was almost inevitable that the aim to recruit the best brains would result in an unrepresentative civil service, but a persistent bias in favour of recruitment of Oxbridge graduates did tend to reinforce the rather exclusive and distinctly unusual social and educational background of senior servants. Broadening the base of recruitment away from Oxbridge-educated arts graduates has occurred very gradually, although canvassing for recruits at 'redbrick' and 'new' universities intensified from 1991. Another concern has been the gender and ethnic bias. Although women make up just over half of the total number of civil servants, they are heavily concentrated at the junior levels, and only just over a fifth of the senior civil service are female (see Figure 13.3). Similarly, while 6 per cent of civil servants come from ethnic minorities (closely corresponding to their proportion in the economically active population), a significantly lower percentage is employed in the senior civil service (2.4 per cent) or at the senior or higher executive officer level (3.7 per cent), although this partly reflects the younger age structure of the ethnic minority population.

As senior civil servants advise ministers and influence policy making, it is a matter of some continuing concern that important sectors of the community are under-represented in their ranks. While they may strive to give disinterested and impartial advice, their attitudes will inevitably reflect their own educational and social background, and their ignorance of very different environments. If relatively few top civil servants have had direct experience of state schools or universities other than Oxbridge they may be less competent to advise on education. If relatively few have had to juggle the demands of their professional work with domestic work, child care or care of the elderly and infirm, which remain disproportionately female responsibilities in British society, they will have little direct insight into the problems of working women. If they have never felt at first hand the prejudice and

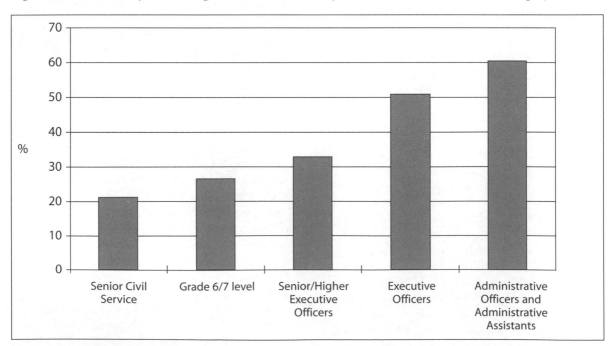

Figure 13.3 Women employed in the civil service by grade, 2001

Source: civil service statistics.

discrimination which is the routine experience of most blacks and Asians, they can scarcely appreciate the attitudes and behaviour of ethnic minority communities and the problems of living in modern multi-cultural Britain.

As should be clear, civil service statistics have been monitored and analysed extensively, and some efforts have been made to correct the imbalance in recruitment to, and promotion within, the civil service of women, members of ethnic minorities and those classified as disabled. The civil service is slowly becoming more representative of the public it serves. Yet the composition of the highest ranks in a career service inevitably reflects patterns of recruitment 20 or 30 years ago from a society that was different in important respects, and it will take time before change is perceptible among the permanent secretaries, deputy secretaries and under-secretaries who constitute the highest levels within the service.

From old public administration to new public management?

The term 'new public management' (NPM) is often applied to the extensive changes introduced into managing public services, not only in Britain, but in many other countries, particularly in the western world. Indeed, many of the theoretical assumptions behind NPM, and many key initiatives, originated elsewhere, particularly in the USA. In Britain it is argued that NPM has increasingly displaced the values and processes associated with traditional public administration, not just in the civil service but in other parts of the public sector such as local government and the National Health Service. Although there are differences in interpretation and emphasis across varieties of organisations and services, NPM involves a number of generally recognisable features. (See Box 13.4).

The Conservative reforms: a revolution in government?

The Conservative reforms between 1979 and 1997 constituted the most radical change in the civil service since the Northcote–Trevelyan reforms of

---

BOX 13.4
Features of new public management

- A managerial culture that reflects private sector norms and practices rather than those of traditional public administration.
- The promotion of competition, markets and quasi-markets within the public sector.
- More managerial delegation, decentralisation and organisational disaggregation.
- An emphasis on economy, efficiency and effectiveness (the three Es).
- Performance measurement, standards and targets.
- Flexibility of pay and conditions (sometimes including performance-related pay).
- A greater emphasis on customer choice and service quality.
- The contracting out of some service provision to the private sector, with the separation of purchaser and provider (or client and contractor) roles.
- Privatisation of some former public services – with state regulation rather than state control.

1854. Reforms initially proceeded piecemeal in line with the manifesto commitment to reduce 'waste, bureaucracy and over-government' but gathered speed after the 1988 Next Steps Report which led to the introduction of executive agencies.

Reduction in size

The Conservatives achieved a very large reduction in civil service numbers (735,000 to 494,300) between April 1979 and April 1996, a drop of over 32 per cent. The lower personnel targets were attained by a combination of natural wastage, early retirement, the non-filling of vacant posts, the transfer of civil service functions to appointed public sector boards, and privatisation. Much larger cuts were achieved in the industrial civil service, which fell by 132,000 from 168,000 to 36,000 (80 per cent) in this period, than in the non-industrial civil service, where numbers dropped by 110,000 from 568,000 to 458,000 (19 per cent). Under the Labour government the numbers of the non-industrial civil service have changed little (454,000 in 2001), while the industrial civil service has declined further (to 29,000).

Curtailment of privileges

The Thatcher government 'de-privileged' the civil service by setting aside the settlement of pay based on the system of 'fair comparison' and then offering relatively low increases related to 'market forces' and introducing performance-related pay; holding out successfully against the 21-week strike by civil service unions in support of their pay claim (1981); banning trade union membership at the Government Communications Headquarters (GCHQ), which had been shut down for a short period in 1981 as a result of the strike action; and abolishing the Civil Service Department (1981), which Thatcher regarded as too much the champion of the civil service and as insufficiently supportive of the government's efforts to defeat the civil service strike. Its responsibility for civil service pay, conditions of service and staffing was transferred to the Treasury, and the Cabinet secretary became the official head of the civil service.

Improving efficiency – the Rayner scrutinies

The quest for greater efficiency and the elimination of 'waste' in government began in 1979 with the establishment in the Cabinet Office of a small Efficiency Unit headed by Sir Derek (later Lord) Rayner, who was then the joint managing director of Marks and Spencer. Rayner initiated a series of scrutinies of departments with the aim of reducing costs and streamlining procedure. The scrutinies led to substantial savings, amounting to £1.5 billion by 1993. Rayner also launched an attack on unnecessary paperwork which led to the scrapping of 27,000 forms and the redesigning of 41,000 more.

Improving efficiency – the Financial Management Initiative (FMI)

Begun in 1982, the FMI sought to improve financial management in all departments by laying down three principles. Managers at all levels were to have: (1) a clear view of their objectives and the means to assess and, wherever possible, measure outputs of performance in relation to those objectives; (2) well-defined responsibility for making the best use of their resources, including a critical scrutiny of output and value for money; and (3) the information (particularly about costs), the training and the access to expert advice that they need to exercise their responsibilities effectively.

A variety of management information systems designed to enable ministers to discover 'who does what, why and at what cost?' in their departments were developed under the Rayner and FMI approaches, such as MINIS (Management Information System for Ministers) at the Department of Environment (DOE) and Activity and Resource Management (ARM) at the Department of Trade and Industry (DTI). MINIS-style systems soon spread throughout Whitehall. The overall aim was to transform civil service culture along business lines, to enhance the role of civil servants as managers of people and resources, and to downgrade their role as policy advisers. The reforms reflected the Thatcherite ethos that the task of the civil service was to manage resources with maximum effectiveness in pursuit of policy goals set by ministers.

Improving efficiency – the 'Next Steps' programme (1988)

This programme originated in a certain disappointment at the slow progress of the FMI and other 'managerial' reforms, as a result of which the Efficiency Unit – now headed by Sir Robin Ibbs, a former Imperial Chemical Industries (ICI) executive – produced a report focusing on the obstacles to further improvement in civil service management. Entitled *Improving Management in Government: The Next Steps*, it argued that there had been insufficient focus on the delivery of services, even though the vast majority of civil servants (95 per cent) were in service delivery or executive rather than policy advice roles. Believing that the civil service was too large and diverse to be run as a single entity, the report advocated its division into (1) a small 'core' engaged in supporting ministers with policy advice within

---

BOX 13.5

Example of an executive agency: the Driver and Vehicle Licensing Agency (set up 1990)

- Sets itself clear targets (e.g. to reduce average waiting time for driving tests, and to reduce delays in issuing driving licences).
- Has shown considerable enthusiasm for marketing, e.g. customised number-plates.
- Has cut costs by putting provision of security and cleaning services out to private tender.

---

the traditional departments; and (2) a wide range of executive agencies responsible for the delivery of services, each headed by a chief executive. Departments would set the policy and budgetary objectives and monitor the work of the agencies, but within that framework, agencies would have considerable managerial independence, with chief executives controlling the recruitment, grading, organisation and pay of their staffs. It is argued that the new agencies have improved service delivery, increased cost-effectiveness and produced significant savings.

Another advantage claimed for the transfer of activities to executive agencies was a reduction in ministerial overload, although critics have argued it has also further weakened ministerial accountability and effective political control, particularly in politically controversial areas such as the Prison Service or the Child Support Agency.

By April 1996 huge progress had been made on the Next Steps programme: altogether, with 102 agencies already established in the Home Civil Service, nearly 71 per cent of the civil service (350,000) was working in Next Steps agencies or along Next Steps lines. The Blair government has since maintained and indeed slightly expanded this proportion to over 73 per cent. Some Next Steps agencies – such as the massive Benefits Agency (71,000) – considerably reduced the size of their 'parent' departments. Most of them, however, are small or medium-sized: for example, the Vehicle Inspectorate (1471), the Royal Mint (997), the Public Record Office (455) and the Teachers' Pensions Agency (370).

Increasing efficiency – market-testing (1991)

During the 1980s, compulsory competitive tendering (CCT) had been introduced in local government and the NHS. Following a White Paper *Competing for Quality* (1991), CCT or market-testing was extended to the civil service. The first part of a rolling programme of market testing (November 1992) put out nearly £1.5 billion of civil service work to competitive tender, requiring over 44,000 civil servants to compete with outsiders for their jobs. By January 1995, when ministers were claiming that market testing had brought savings of £400 million a year over the previous two years, over £1 billion of work had been transferred to the private sector. Half of the work had been put out to the private sector without any competing in-house bid, but in-house teams had won 73 per cent of the contracts they were allowed to tender for. A further £1.1 billion worth of work was to be tendered and competed for over the following year (Theakston, 1995: 150–1). Privatisation of some agencies had been envisaged by the Ibbs Report from the outset. Part of the 'prior options' tests applied within departments included the contracting out or privatisation of a part of their activities. Thus, the initial presumption that most civil service activities would remain within the public sector seems to have been reversed from autumn 1992, although only eight small central government organisations were transferred to the private sector between 1992 and 1995.

The Citizen's Charter (1991)

The Citizen's Charter was the 'big idea' of John Major, and essentially consisted of a campaign to raise standards in the public services. It applied to public services generally and included, for example, health and education as well as services delivered by the civil service. Each service was required to publish performance targets and results against set targets, and there were to be well-publicised and readily available complaints and redress procedures. The aim was to improve standards of service without injecting extra resources. By 1995, nine agencies had published individual charters specifying standards that customers and clients were entitled to expect, such as the Jobseekers' Charter published by the Employment Service Agency.

BOX 13.6

The impact of reform on key attributes of the traditional civil service

- **Permanence.** Traditionally, the civil service has been a single hierarchical organisation, characterised by security of tenure and a common system of pay and promotion. The permanence of the civil service underpinned its public service ethos and commitment to impartial service of the government of the day. This permanent and unified civil service has been undermined in the last two decades by several developments, notably the appointment of increasing numbers of outside political advisers to ministers; the hiving off of the majority of civil servants into executive agencies; the introduction of market testing and contracting out; and the transfer of responsibility for most recruitment and pay to departments and agencies. Approximately one-quarter of agency chief executives and some top civil servants were appointed from outside. By the mid-1990s a unified, career civil service no longer existed.

- **Neutrality.** In traditional theory, the role of a top civil servant was to give ministers honest and impartial advice. A leading criticism, supported by some survey evidence, of the Thatcher–Major years was that the civil service was 'politicised'. Thus, a MORI poll for the First Division Association showed that most senior civil servants believed that being open and frank with ministers was a barrier to promotion and that they have to toe the line if they want to get on (*Guardian*, 13 July 1995). A second worry is the use of the civil service for party political purposes. The Major and Blair governments have both been accused of involving permanent civil servants in the promotion of policies for partisan objectives. However, it is arguable that top-level civil servants are necessarily politicised by engaging in 'the devising, promotion, execution and defence of policies and strategies rooted in adversarial partisan politics' (Madgwick and Woodhouse, 1995: 148).

- **Anonymity.** The anonymity of civil servants – an important corollary of ministerial responsibility – has been seriously eroded. As ministerial willingness to assume responsibility for the mistakes of officials has declined, so the practice has grown of naming and blaming individual bureaucrats. Some of the chief executives who head the more controversial Next Steps agencies have attracted considerable media attention and sometimes serious personal criticism. They are also more directly accountable to Parliament. After an initial struggle, the Major government agreed to publish replies of agency chief executives to Parliamentary questions in Hansard.

The Blair government and the civil service

Rhodes (in Seldon, 2001: 97) asserts 'New Labour was slow to get under way in modernising the civil service', suggesting it was 'not a priority'. He goes on to argue that although 'the easy assessment is that government policy was pragmatic and we got more of the same ... the drip, drip, drip style of reform obscured an important shift of emphasis from markets to networks.'

Labour accepted most of the Conservative reform programme, including privatisation, marketisation, managerialism, regulation, the Citizen's Charter and administrative decentralisation through executive agencies. One particular problem identified by Labour was fragmentation and lack of coordination (*Modernising Government* White Paper, 1999). Government was insufficiently 'joined-up'. 'Departmentalism' is a familiar difficulty of government. Moreover, the Conservative Next Steps programme had substantially weakened civil service unity, which had been a counter-acting tendency. Labour's devolution programme took the process somewhat further, although the staff of the new Scottish Executive are still formally part of a unified civil service.

Labour has pursued 'joined-up government' by establishing a plethora of cross-departmental units and action zones. However, to an extent the new coordinating machinery has increased the sheer complexity and, ironically, even the fragmentation of government. Responsibility and accountability are blurred, and delivery rendered more difficult. Moreover some have argued that there is a continuing tension between the New Labour 'third way' approach to management, emphasising networks, mutual trust and cooperation, and the earlier New Right-inspired emphasis on markets, competition and regulation. Cooperative networking and diplomacy have not replaced competitive market relations in British public administration, and the two approaches do not combine easily.

Standards in public life

The reform programme in the 1980s was about improving the efficiency of government. The probity of government was more often taken for granted. However a series of scandals in the 1990s reawakened older concerns over ethical standards among politicians and office holders. Some of the concerns were over the conduct of MPs (see Chapter 14) but several ministers were forced to resign, some for personal or sexual misconduct which had little to do with their government duties, but others in circumstances with wider implications. Beyond these scandals there were also concerns over the rules and principles covering those who held public office, whether as ministers or civil servants, and the relations between them. Thus Prime Minister John Major set up the Nolan Committee on Standards in Public Life in October 1994. Nolan's terms of reference were to examine current concerns about standards of conduct in public office holders and to make recommendations as to any changes required to ensure the highest standards of propriety in public life. His brief covered Parliament (see Chapter 14), ministerial appointments to quangos (see Chapter 19), and central government. Nolan responded (Nolan, 1995) by laying down the 'seven principles of public life'.

The Nolan Report made a number of more specific recommendations regarding the conduct of ministers and civil servants which were largely

> **BOX 13.7**
> ## The Nolan Report, 1995: the seven principles of public life
>
> - **Selflessness.** Holders of public office should take decisions solely in the public interest. They should not do so in order to gain financial or other material benefits for their family or their friends.
> - **Integrity.** Holders of public office should not place themselves under any financial or other obligation to outside individuals or organisations that might influence them in the performance of their official duties.
> - **Objectivity.** In carrying out public business, including making public appointments, awarding contracts, or recommending individuals for rewards and benefits, holders of public office should make their choices on merit.
> - **Accountability.** Holders of public office are accountable for their decisions and actions to the public and must submit themselves to whatever scrutiny is appropriate to their office.
> - **Openness.** Holders of public office should be as open as possible about all the decisions and actions that they take. They should give reasons for their decisions and restrict information only when the wider public interest clearly demands.
> - **Honesty.** Holders of public office have a duty to declare any private interests relating to their public duties, and to take steps to resolve any conflicts arising in a way that protects the public interest.
> - **Leadership.** Holders of public office should promote and support these principles by leadership and example.

accepted and incorporated into a non-statutory Civil Service Code (1996) and a revised Code of Conduct for Ministers (1997).

Critics argue that the emphasis on collective Cabinet responsibility (reaffirmed in the guidance to ministers) considerably limits the apparent commitment to more open government and accountability. Furthermore, the new guidance has

BOX 13.8

Extracts from *Cabinet Practice: A Code of Conduct and Guidance on Procedure for Ministers*

This paper (Cabinet Office, July, 1997) lays down guidelines to ministers and civil servants in the operation of Cabinet government. It requires ministers:

- To uphold the practice of collective responsibility.
- To account to and be held to account by Parliament for the policies, decisions and actions of their departments and Next Steps agencies.
- To give accurate and truthful information to Parliament, correcting any inadvertent error at the earliest possible opportunity; ministers who knowingly mislead Parliament are expected to offer their resignations to the prime minister.
- To be as open as possible with Parliament and the public, refusing to provide information only when disclosure would not be in the public interest.
- To require civil servants who give evidence before Parliamentary committees on their behalf or under their direction to provide accurate, truthful and full information in accordance with the duties set out in the Civil Service Code.
- Not to use resources for party political purposes; to uphold the political impartiality of the Civil Service and not to ask civil servants to act in any way which would conflict with the Civil Service Code.

not really changed the doctrine laid down in the 1983 Armstrong Memorandum which asserted that the civil service has '*no constitutional personality or responsibility separate from the duly elected government of the day*' and stressed that the duty of the civil servant was first and foremost to the ministerial head of department. Thus, although civil servants are supposed to be politically impartial, their first loyalty is to the (party) government of the day, which almost inevitably involves some tensions for their impartiality.

Ministerial responsibility revisited

The convention of individual ministerial responsibility governs relations between ministers, civil servants and Parliament. It means that ministers – and ministers alone – are responsible to Parliament for the actions of their departments. Individual ministerial responsibility is the major form of constitutional accountability, forms the basis of the relationships between ministers, civil service and Parliament, and involves ministers in several levels of responsibility.

The delegation of managerial responsibility which is a key aspect of executive agencies clearly implies some reduction of direct ministerial responsibility. Of course ministers remain in charge of policy, but the difficulty of dividing responsibility neatly between 'policy' and 'operations' (for which chief executives are responsible) was illustrated in the sacking of Derek Lewis, the Director-General of the Prisons Agency, in 1995, following the Parkhurst prison escapes. Lewis took the blame for failures in the prisons service, despite the extent to which policy and operations issues merge and despite the extent to which intervention by the Home Secretary, Michael Howard, compromised Lewis's operational independence in practice (Barberis, 1996: 19). An authoritative study concludes that the ability of ministers to evade their responsibilities stems mainly from executive dominance over Parliament but also derives from the lack of precision in the definition of accountability (Woodhouse, 1994: 284–5).

Ministerial responsibility means that ministers are required to inform Parliament about the conduct of their departments, and explain their own and their departments' actions. Individual ministers constantly explain and defend depart-

Definition
Individual ministerial responsibility: the constitutional convention by which each minister is responsible to Parliament for the activities of his or her department and 'carries the can' for failure.

mental policy before Parliament – at Question Time, during the committee stage of legislation, before select committees and privately to MPs. Ministerial answers to political questions are not always entirely full or satisfactory, and sometimes they are downright evasive. None the less, individual ministerial responsibility in its first meaning of 'answerability' or 'explanatory accountability' still applies. The doctrine of individual ministerial responsibility also requires that ministers should make amends for their own or their departments' errors and ultimately in certain circumstances resign. Resignation may be for personal misconduct, political misjudgment, departmental fault in which the minister is involved, and policy differences with the government. This section examines the contemporary validity of this convention.

Ministerial resignations for personal misconduct

Over the last 40 years most ministerial resignations have been because of personal misconduct, commonly for some sexual impropriety. John Major's 1992–7 government suffered a spate of resignations arising out of sexual misconduct and financial impropriety, against a background of intense media publicity over sexual and financial 'sleaze', particularly after the prime minister's 'back to basics' campaign. Ministers who resigned for sexual misconduct were later surprised to discover that John Major himself had conducted a clandestine affair with his colleague Edwina Currie for four years before he became Prime Minister. It is a moot point how far such personal issues affect the performance of public duties and should entail resignation. There have clearly been some changes in the moral climate. Only a few years ago revelations of homosexual relationship spelled ruin for a politician. Until 1967 such relationships were illegal, and for some years afterwards were sufficiently damaging still to invite blackmail. Since then there have been openly gay Cabinet ministers. The consequences of heterosexual extramarital affairs are less predictable. While some ministers have been forced out, others, such as the Conservative ministers Alan Clark or Steve Norris, have indulged in serial and highly publicised adulteries without damaging (and perhaps even enhancing) their political fortunes.

Ministerial resignations for political misjudgements and mistakes

Several ministerial resignations fall into this category.

- In the Westland affair (1986), Leon Brittan, the Trade and Industry Secretary, resigned after severe pressure from Conservative backbenchers over the role of his department in leaking to the press a select passage in a letter from the Solicitor-General to the Defence Secretary, Michael Heseltine, who was embroiled in a row with Brittan, and less directly with Margaret Thatcher, over the future of Westland helicopters. The affair had led to Heseltine walking out of the Cabinet and it threatened to engulf the Prime Minister. Conservative backbenchers demanded a ministerial sacrifice, and Brittan resigned.
- Edwina Currie, the Parliamentary Under-Secretary of State for Health, resigned after making the statement that 'most of the egg production of this country, sadly, is now infected with salmonella', which caused public alarm and aroused the fury of egg producers and Conservative backbenchers (although her observation may have been substantially true).
- Both Peter Mandelson's resignations may be attributed to political misjudgements, his first when his secret £373,000 home loan from fellow minister Geoffrey Robinson was made public in December 1998. It could have led to a conflict of interest and in any case should have been declared. The second resignation in 2001, following his failure to give a coherent account of his involvement in the fast-track passport application by the Indian businessman S. P. Hinduja, was more questionable. While his own initial recollections appeared somewhat confused, it is not clear that he did anything improper, and he might well have survived had he not had 'form'. Neither resignations were remotely connected with his departmental responsibilities at the Department of Trade and Industry or the Northern Ireland Office; indeed he was reckoned to be a success as a minister.
- The resignation of Stephen Byers in 2002 might be ascribed primarily to political misjudgements and mistakes. The principal problems on the railways arose either before he

became Secretary of State for Transport in 2001, or could be attributed to earlier decisions. Although his decision to put Railtrack into liquidation in 2001 was criticised by shareholders and elements in the media and opposition, it was welcomed by the governing party. The misjudgement that set in train the events that culminated in his resignation was his failure to accept or insist on the resignation of his adviser Jo Moore for her notorious e-mail suggesting that the attack on the World Trade Center on 11 September 2001 provided an opportunity to 'bury bad news', which came to symbolise the government's alleged obsession with 'spin'. The initial misjudgement was compounded by subsequent internal rows within his department, and a hostile media campaign which suggested that Byers' accounts of events had been misleading.

- The resignation of Estelle Morris as Education Secretary in October 2002 was unusual in that she frankly confessed in her resignation letter to the Prime Minister, 'I have not felt I have been as effective as I should be or as effective as you need me to be.' Blair himself, most of her Labour Party colleagues, many teachers' representatives and others who had worked with her, strenuously rejected this verdict and regretted her departure, which was blamed on a hostile media and opposition campaign, while the opposition claimed that the fault lay with the government's education policy rather than the minister. Her resignation, however, followed a series of embarrassing failures in the service and department over which she presided, including the failure to ensure completion of background checks on all new teachers on which the department had insisted, leading to a delayed start of term for many pupils, and culminating in the A level marking scandal, where it was alleged that thousands of students had been given the wrong grade. Criticism of her handling of crises for which she was not initially personally responsible may have been less than fair, but it seems that the resignation is best categorised as arising from political misjudgements and mistakes (*Guardian,* 24 October 2002, 25 October 2002).

Resignations for policy errors

Perhaps the most obvious example of ministerial resignation for policy errors or failure was when the invasion of the Falklands in 1982 led to the resignations of the entire Foreign Office team headed by Lord Carrington. The reason Lord Carrington gave for his resignation was his failure to foresee and to take steps to prevent the Argentinian invasion, which he later called 'a humiliating affront to this country'. However, John Nott, the Defence Secretary, who was criticised for the weakness of the Falkland Islands' defences and, more realistically, for signalling an apparently diminished British commitment to the retention of the islands by a proposal to withdraw HMS *Endurance*, remained in office. On this occasion, because of the seriousness of the situation and the intensity of Parliamentary and public disquiet, collective responsibility could not save the Foreign Office ministers. In order to minimise damage to the credibility of a government a considerable sacrifice was called for, but not so great as to endanger the government's survival. So Carrington and his subordinates went, but Nott stayed.

However, ministers do not normally resign if associated with a failed policy. In such circumstances, the prime minister and Cabinet usually come to the aid of a beleaguered colleague, expressing support in public, whatever may be said privately. In other words, individual ministers in

---

BOX 13.9

The politics of individual and collective responsibility

In cases involving government failure and criticism:

- A matter of **collective responsibility** may be treated as a matter of **individual responsibility** in order to minimise loss of public confidence in the government; however
- A matter of **individual responsibility** is sometimes transformed into a case of **collective responsibility** in order to shield a particular minister.

political difficulties are shielded by the convention of collective responsibility. There are numerous examples of non-resignation after serious failures of policy, in several of which – Suez, the spy scandals of the early 1960s, Concorde, and Britain's departure from the ERM – the close involvement of the prime minister was probably conclusive in 'saving' the minister concerned.

These cases suggest that, while Parliamentary criticism over failed policies can certainly damage a minister and can sometimes prompt policy changes, it cannot force resignation if the minister wishes to remain in office and has the support of prime minister and party.

Ministerial resignations for official errors

It is even more unusual for ministers to accept vicarious responsibility for their officials and resign after mistakes within their departments have been brought to light. The assumption by ministers of personal accountability for all that happens in their departments has been undermined, it is often said, by the sheer size and complexity of modern Whitehall departments and the consequent impossibility of one person being able to keep informed of all that goes on in them. Numerous cases in the post-war period suggest the reluctance of ministers to shoulder the blame for civil servants when things go wrong.

The resignation of Sir Thomas Dugdale in the Crichel Down affair (1954) used to be regarded as an example of a minister resigning for the mistakes of his officials. Dugdale, it was said, accepted full responsibility for the negligence of his civil servants in a dispute over the compulsory purchase of land. Yet it now appears that Dugdale was personally involved in the maladministration which led to his downfall. Moreover, hounding by his own backbenchers played a key part in the resignation (Hennessy, 1990: 503; Brazier, 1988: 139).

Today, ministers are not normally held responsible for decisions made in their name but of which they could have had no knowledge. No post-war case, Geoffrey Marshall has observed, has involved the assumption that 'a ministerial head must roll for civil service error' (Marshall, 1989: 130).

BOX 13.10
The Scott Report (1996) – a case study in the refusal to admit responsibility?

Controversy blew up in November 1992 over sales of British arms to Iraq in the late 1980s. The opposition parties alleged that the government secretly relaxed its own guidelines on the sale of arms to Iraq in 1988, that numerous government ministers over the following years told Parliament that this was not the case, and that leading officials in the Foreign Office and DTI assisted ministers in the misleading of Parliament. The incident had come to light accidentally during the prosecution by Customs and Excise of three businessmen of the Matrix Churchill company for illegally exporting arms for Iraq. Denying charges of deception, the Prime Minister, John Major set up an inquiry into the affair under Lord Justice Scott, whose 1806 page, five-volume report was published in February 1996. The report provided the most comprehensive examination of the inner workings of British government ever undertaken; in the words of one academic commentator, it was 'the longest, most thorough, most revealing and most damaging public inquiry into the heart of central government ever seen' (Tomkins, 1996: 349). Its main findings were that the shift in arms sale policy was deliberately concealed from Parliament, that the criminal prosecution by HM Customs and Excise of the three businessmen was wrong, and that the government had wrongly used its powers to block the release of government information that would have helped their defence.

The report had serious constitutional implications. It revealed that ministers had seriously misled Parliament over government policy and that they had been assisted by civil servants in doing so. However, the government managed to limit the political damage that might have been expected to follow such a critical report, and won the Commons vote on the report by one vote (320 to 319). No minister resigned and only one civil servant resigned – for reasons of conscience because he could not put up with the deceit and hypocrisy, not because he was pushed into it by his superiors.

Where does power lie? Decision making within departments

Much of the discussion so far has not directly addressed vital questions over power and influence at the centre of British government. Where does power lie between politicians and bureaucrats, between ministers and leading civil servants? Five models of the minister–civil servant relationship are considered here:

- The traditional public administration model, which reflects the constitutional orthodoxy that ministers decide, while civil servants offer advice, and then loyally and impartially implement the decisions of ministers.
- The liberal-bureaucratic model, which implies an adversarial relationship between politicians and public officials, where the latter hold most advantages, and thus are normally the real decision makers.
- The 'Whitehall village' model (originally advanced by Heclo and Wildavsky, 1974) which suggests that ministers and leading civil servants inhabit a small closed world in which relationships are more complex and not necessarily conflictual.
- The 'power bloc' model, a radical left-wing perspective which suggests that the civil service reflects establishment values and uses its expertise and permanency to thwart radical policies.
- The 'bureaucratic over-supply' model, a New Right perspective, which uses neo-liberal economic assumptions to argue that the civil service pursues its own interest rather than the public interest to expand public services and public spending.

The traditional public administration model

The traditional public administration model expresses the perception of minister–civil servant relations that is embedded in formal constitutional theory. It is the orthodox account according to which ministers take policy decisions and defend them publicly, whilst civil servants brief ministers, processing information so that their political superiors can choose between options in an informed way, then unquestioningly implement ministerial decisions. In this view ministers always have the final say, while civil servants are impartial advisers.

This model assumes a clear dividing line between political decision making, which is what ministers do, and administration, which is the job of civil servants in tendering advice and carrying out decisions. This is not only the traditional textbook view but also predominates within the civil service itself and among ministers. It is the model reaffirmed by the Cabinet Secretary, Sir Robert Armstrong in his *Note of Guidance on the Duties and Responsibilities of Civil Servants in Relation to Ministers* (1985). A new version of the memorandum issued after the Westland affair in 1987 also stated the traditional view that ministers are responsible to Parliament for the conduct of their departments, while civil servants are answerable to ministers.

The liberal-bureaucratic model

Many observers believe that the traditional model simply describes the norm to which participants in government aspire, but ignores the political realities of a situation in which the 'departmental view' often prevails. The liberal-bureaucratic model best expresses the fact of civil service power in a context in which lip-service is still paid to the textbook theory of ministerial–civil servant relations. This approach portrays the relationship in adversarial terms as a constant power struggle in which civil servants often obstruct and sabotage ministerial policy instructions (Theakston, 1995a: 47). This interpretation became widely accepted as a consequence of the popular comedy television series *Yes, Minister* and *Yes, Prime Minister* (based on some inside knowledge). While the model does not exclude the possibility that a minister can dominate a department, it suggests that a variety of factors often tilt the balance of power in a department away from the minister and towards the permanent officials (Box 13.11).

The 'Whitehall village' model

The 'Whitehall village' model draws attention to aspects of the minister–civil servant relationship largely ignored by the other models. It was first developed by two American academics, Hugh

BOX 13.11
Constraints on the effective power of ministers

- **Numbers.** Ministers are outnumbered by officials: there are roughly six leading civil servants to every minister.
- **Permanence.** Civil servants are permanent while ministers are 'birds of passage' who change jobs frequently. The average tenure of ministerial office since 1945 is just over two years: there were 12 Trade and Industry Secretaries between 1979 and 1997. It takes ministers a lengthy period to master the business of their departments (according to Crossman about 18 months) and during this time they are largely dependent on official briefing.
- **Weak preparation for office.** Few ministers on taking office have specialised knowledge of their departments, and frequent moves to do not help them acquire expertise. Ministers rarely come to office with clearly defined policies, priorities or objectives. Unexpected situations that arise during their terms of office further increase their dependence upon officials (James, 1992: 39).
- **Ministerial workload.** Ministers face multiple demands upon their time – from Cabinet, Parliament, constituency, media and increasingly from the EU in addition to their departments. On average they spend about two-thirds of their working week on other than departmental matters.
- **Control of information.** Top civil servants control the information going before ministers, the way in which it is presented and its timing, all of which gives them a formidable capacity to shape decisions. They can also influence public opinion by the secret briefing of known opponents of their minister's policy or by 'leaking' to the media.
- **Coordinating role.** Both formally through official committees and through informal contacts with their opposite numbers in other departments, top civil servants prepare and to a varying extent predetermine the work of ministers. Crossman (1976: 616) argued that the system of official committees was 'the key to the control by the Civil Service over the politicians'. Civil servants can also use their contacts with officials in other departments to resist the policies of their own minister.
- **Implementation.** Civil servants can employ a variety of tactics to thwart implementation of policy, including delay, and finding practical difficulties.

Heclo and Aaron Wildavsky, in their book *The Private Government of Public Money* (1974). The model was applied by them to public expenditure decision making, but its relevance to virtually all areas of Whitehall was soon realised. The village analogy suggests that leading politicians and civil servants inhabit a relatively small, enclosed Whitehall world of face-to-face relationships which are much more complex than implied by notions of simple domination by either elected politician or official. In practice, relationships between ministers and leading officials are cooperative as well as conflictual. Ministers and higher civil servants today often come from a similar social and educational background and share many values, interests and aspirations. Often a minister and permanent secretary of a spending department will be on the same side, sometimes in conflict with other departments and the Treasury. Yet civil servants have their own networks of informal contacts and official committees which operate across departments, just as politicians have similar informal and formal networks.

The power-bloc model

According to the power-bloc model, the civil service functions as an establishment veto group. Important advocates of this radical left version of the liberal-bureaucratic model are Ralph Miliband in *The State in Capitalist Society* (1973), Brian Sedgemore in *The Secret Constitution* (1980) and

Tony Benn (1982). Miliband argued that the civil service comprises an administrative cadre whose conservative bias reflects the interests of the privileged sections of capitalist society from which it is largely recruited. Sedgemore and Benn drew on an interpretation of the problems of the 1964–70 and 1974–9 Labour governments (of which Benn was a member) to argue that the civil service was able to deploys its administrative expertise, its permanency of tenure, and its formal and informal co-ordinating networks to thwart radical policy initiatives by left-wing ministers like Benn.

The bureaucratic over-supply model

The bureaucratic over-supply model came to the fore in the 1970s and is mainly but not exclusively linked with the New Right critique of government and civil service growth in previous decades. It drew on the analysis of public or rational choice theory advanced by William Niskanen and others. Niskanen applied classical liberal economic assumptions of the pursuit of self-interest to the public sector. In the absence of market constraints and the profit motive, public sector bureaucrats would thus seek to maximise the size of their own 'bureau' or department and its spending, because this would favour their own pay, promotion prospects, conditions of service and status. Such growth would involve the supply of more public services, more public spending and a bloated, inefficient and wasteful bureaucracy (bureaucratic over-supply). Niskanen's analysis provided some theoretical support for the New Right view in the 1970s and 1980s that the civil service was wedded to the social democratic consensus and believed in interventionist government and big public spending. Thus the Thatcherite right were as suspicious of the civil service as the Bennite left, but for very different reasons. More significantly, this New Right analysis was not just descriptive but prescriptive, and pointed to its own solutions: both the bureaucracy and 'big government' needed 'cutting down to size', through transferring some activities to the private sector and subjecting others to competition. Thus the bureaucratic over-supply model provided much of the theoretical underpinning for the Thatcher government's programme of civil service reform.

The resurgence of the traditional model: do ministers decide after all?

In the latter 1970s and 1980s the liberal-bureaucratic, power-bloc and bureaucratic over-supply theories held the field, while the traditional public administration model of the civil service was in eclipse. By the late 1990s, as a result of the changes in Whitehall produced by the Conservative governments between 1979 and 1997, this situation had been largely reversed.

The radical left power-bloc model has become less fashionable. While it remains broadly true that the higher civil service is largely recruited from socially privileged groups, it does not follow that it will refuse to carry out the radical policies of left and right politicians and governments. Arguably, the two most radical governments since 1945 have been the Labour administrations of 1945–51 and the Conservative administrations of 1979–97, yet the civil service can scarcely be said to have blocked either the Keynesian, welfare and nationalisation policies of the one or the monetarist, anti-welfare and privatisation policies of the other. Tony Benn's radical plans for nationalisation and planning agreements in the 1974 Labour government were arguably thwarted by the opposition of the Prime Minister and most of his Cabinet colleagues rather the civil service. The evidence scarcely suggests a monolithic civil service steadfastly obstructing the radical reforms of politicians. Instead, 'Whitehall is a seething mass of discrete departmental interests', in which departments – each with its own distinctive 'view' and 'ethos' – continually bargain and compete with each other for, amongst other things, larger shares of public expenditure and a place in the Parliamentary legislative timetable (Drewry and Butcher, 1991: 84–5). Thus, the lines of conflict are not usually between ministers and civil servants within a department but between departments, with each department's ministers and civil servants combining to advance and defend departmental interests against ministers and officials in other departments combining to do the same.

The bureaucratic over-supply model has been far more influential. It was the inspiration for a sustained, successful attack on the power, prestige and privileges of the civil service by Conservative governments after 1979. It provided the political and ideological thrust for the Conservative reforms of the civil service in the 1980s and 1990s. Margaret Thatcher came to power in 1979 convinced that the civil service was too big, too expensive, too negative and too consensual. She believed it had become an overblown bureaucracy, wasteful and inefficient, more adapted to finding problems in new initiatives that to solving them, and compromised by the failures of post-war British governments. The reform process she launched in the 1980s – which continues today – aimed at curtailing the privileges, increasing the efficiency and transforming the culture of the civil service. Yet the substantial implementation of this radical reform programme rather undermines its underlying assumptions of inherent expansionism among public sector bureaucrats. New Right Conservative politicians found willing allies and collaborators among the permanent civil servants in their search for efficiency savings and in developing competition.

Although this bureaucratic expansionism model was politically influential, it hardly seems to explain the actual behaviour of senior civil servants. The key Whitehall departments have always been – and remain – small departments such as the Treasury. One influential study (Dunleavy, 1991) has applied public choice assumptions to argue that bureaucrats will engage in bureau shaping rather than bureau maximising. While competition and market testing has often adversely affected the pay and conditions of service of routine manual and clerical workers, it has generally involved increased opportunities and more managerial autonomy for senior officials. In pursuit of their own self-interest, they do not necessarily want or need 'big government'.

Indeed the unimpeded implementation of the Conservative government's civil service reform programme has not only somewhat undermined the bureaucratic oversupply model which provided much of its rationale, but also the more general assumption of official dominance. Ironically, at the very time when the notion of bureaucratic manipulation of naïve politicians was widely popularised by the programme *Yes, Minister*, political practice indicated otherwise. Not only the civil service reforms, but other policy initiatives, such as the trade union reforms, the privatisation programme and ill-fated poll tax, suggested that it was ministers who were deciding policy after all, a point reinforced

by some of the significant changes in direction made by the Blair government after 1997.

Moreover, some of the arguments advanced against the traditional public administration model no longer look quite so persuasive. Thus the gap in expertise between ministers and permanent officials can be exaggerated. Many ministers have good or outstanding academic records, similar to those of higher civil servants. If they lack specialist knowledge of the subject matter of their department and managerial skills, the same has been widely alleged of British civil servants, whose non-relevant education, lack of management training and lack of experience of the outside world have been compared unfavourably with French elite bureaucrats. In addition, ministers are now far less dependent on civil service expertise and advice. They could always tap party research groups and independent think tanks, but the increasing numbers of special advisers means they have sympathetic alternative sources of advice regularly on hand within their own departments. Labour brought in 38 such advisers between 1974 and 1979, the Conservatives had 42 special advisers in 1993, and Labour immediately moved 58 special advisers into place in 1997, 37 of them into the departments. It has been suggested that political advisers 'have added an extra dimension to the support that officials provide ministers, keeping in touch with the party and generating alternative ideas on policy within a framework of political values shared with the minister' (Theakston, 1995: 15).

There is also some evidence that civil servants actually prefer strong ministers who have minds of their own, partly because the system depends on knowing the minister's mind and acting accordingly, partly because strong ministers are more likely to protect the interests of their department and service, and partly simply because they are more interesting and exciting to work under. Thus as Hugo Young has argued, 'The constitutional textbooks are truer now than they have been for some time' (cited in Theakston, 1991–2: 94).

The resurgence of the traditional public administration model does not mean, of course, that policy making is totally the preserve of ministers while civil servants are limited to a purely administrative role. During the Scott Inquiry, ministers (including two prime ministers) admitted that they could not possibly see every paper passing through their offices and hence had to rely on officials to filter the paperwork (Madgwick and Woodhouse, 1995: 147). In fact, ministers actually see only a tiny fraction (under 1 per cent, according to one estimate) of their departments' work. Thus, their influence is primarily in terms of making the very small number of top departmental decisions together with 'setting the climate' of policy making so that officials can predict their intentions and make policy accordingly. The liberal-bureaucratic model remains relevant in situations in which weak ministers are 'captured' by their officials, thus emphasising that minister–civil service relations are a matter of balance rather than automatically accepted authority (as the traditional theory holds).

The Whitehall village model usefully draws attention to the inner life of the political administrative community at the centre of British government. Its emphases – on cooperation between ministers and mandarins within departments and on the role of inter-departmental collaboration between civil servants in the preparation of decisions – capture much of the reality of top-level policy making. There is a sense in which a single 'government community' exists, characterised by agreement on the rules of the game and the desirability of excluding outsiders. But this model has been justly criticised as inherently too limited in focus to capture that reality in its entirety. For example, in focusing on life in the 'Whitehall village', it largely ignores that 'community's' external relationships, both in terms of policy inputs from pressure groups, ideological think tanks, party manifestos and so on, and in terms of the way in which ministers' need to defend policies before Parliament and public actually helps to shape the policies themselves (Pliatzky, 1982: 35, 37; Theakston, in Pyper and Robins, 1995: 52). The shaping effect of party and ideological influences on ministerial–civil servant relations may be gauged from the fact that no department concerned with domestic policy had a 'departmental view' at odds with Thatcherism by the early 1990s (G. K. Wilson, 1991; cited by Theakston, in Pyper and Robins, 1995: 19).

Further reading

For extracts from a wide range of sources, including some key public documents, see Barberis (1996). Among broad surveys see Pyper (1995) and Drewry and Butcher (1991). On the post-war history, Hennessy (1990) and Theakston (1995) should be consulted. On relations between minister and civil servants, see Theakston (in Pyper and Robins, 1995) and Smith, Marsh and Richards (in Rhodes and Dunleavy, 1995). For analysis of the role and power of senior civil servants see Theakston (1999).

On ministerial responsibility, see Woodhouse (1994), Marshall, (1989, 1991), Pyper (1991, 1994) and Gray (1996/7), who provide authoritative analyses.

On civil service reform since 1979, see Hood and James (in Dunleavy et al., 1997) and Butcher (in Pyper and Robins, 1995). There is relatively little on civil service reform since 1997, perhaps because there is relatively little yet to report (at least compared with radical changes elsewhere). Thus Gavin Drewry in Blackburn and Plant (1999) and in Jowell and Oliver (2000), Andrew Massey in Savage and Atkinson (2001) and Rod Rhodes in Seldon (2001) devote more space to discussing New Labour's 'administrative inheritance' and speculating about the future than analysing substantive reforms. The White Paper *Modernising Government* (1999) may also be consulted.

Websites

Home Office: <http://www.homeoffice.gov.uk/>
Foreign Office: <http://www.fco.gov.uk/>
Health: <http://www.open.gov.uk/index/../doh/dhhome.htm>
Education: <http://www.open.gov.uk/index/../dfee/ dfee-home.htm>
Scotland: <http://www.Scotland.gov.uk/>
Wales: <http://www.cymru.gov.uk/>
Northern Ireland: <http://www.alexandra14nio.gov.uk/>

Chapter **14**

Parliament and the legislative process

The functions of the House of Commons   228
Representation   228
Legislation   233
Scrutiny and influence of the executive   238
Forum for national debate   240
Recruitment of a government   241
Executive dominance of Parliament   242
Reform of the House of Commons   243
The upper chamber   244
Powers and functions of the upper chamber   244
Composition of the upper chamber   246
Reform of the upper chamber   246
The Westminster Parliament and other
    parliaments   249

We now turn from government to Parliament and from the executive to the legislative process in the British political system. Britain's Parliament at Westminster is very old, dating back to 1265. It began as an English Parliament, adding Welsh, Scottish and Irish representatives with successive Acts of Union, and losing most of its Irish representatives with the establishment of a separate Irish state in 1922. The Houses of Parliament provide a visual symbol of the heart of British government, the very centre of political power. Indeed, the sovereignty of Parliament has long been regarded as the key principle of the British Constitution. Yet some argue that despite its venerable age and prestige, Britain's Parliament is no longer very powerful, but is dominated by the executive which largely controls the legislative process which is nominally Parliament's main reason for existence. The House of Commons does not fulfil its functions particularly effectively, while the composition of the House of Lords has long been so indefensible as to render it incapable of exercising much effective power. Moreover, the Westminster Parliament is no longer the only representative assembly elected by British citizens, but is now just one among a number of levels of representative bodies, with considerable implications for its future.

In this chapter we examine critically the composition and functions of both chambers of the Westminster Parliament. We begin with the House of

---

IN FOCUS 14.1 Mother of Parliaments?

Aerial view of the Houses of Parliament (centre of picture), Parliament Square and Westminster Abbey (right foreground), with the river Thames in the background. Parliament and Big Ben, widely recognisable the world over, symbolise the centre of British politics. Critics however allege that Parliament is neither powerful nor effective. It is no longer the only representative assembly to which UK citizens send members. The photograph gives some idea of the extent of the Palace of Westminster, which contains not only the two Houses of Parliament, but Westminster Hall, the Speaker's house, libraries, committee rooms, members' offices, dining rooms, tea rooms and numerous bars.

Photograph: PA Photos.

Commons, which is much the most important, critically examining how far and in what sense it represents the British people, and how effectively if fulfils its main functions, particularly its role in the legislative process and its scrutiny of the executive, together with proposals for reform. We then turn to the linked issues of the composition and powers of the upper chamber within the context of the ongoing House of Lords reform process. We conclude with a discussion of the future of the Westminster Parliament in a multi-level system of representative bodies.

The functions of the House of Commons

The House of Commons has five main functions:

- representation
- legislation
- scrutiny
- forum for national debate
- recruitment of a government.

The essence of Parliament, its primary role in the political system, is legitimation. In other words, it authorises the actions of rulers, thereby justifying their acceptance by the ruled. And it can fulfil this purpose because of its historic status, constantly renewed, as a unique forum for national representation, law-making, political criticism, debate and leadership recruitment.

Representation

The representative character of the House of Commons underpins its other roles. The House of Commons has long been held to represent the common people of Britain, and this claim was strengthened by the extension of the franchise to the whole adult population in the course of the 19th and early 20th centuries. Thus the Commons represents the people of Britain because it has been elected by them. Its representative and democratic character are now closely interlinked.

Yet while the House of Commons represents the people it is not typical of the wider population, and does not represent them in the sense of being a social microcosm of the nation, MPs being predominantly white, male, middle-aged and middle class. (See Box 14.1.) Does it matter that MPs are socially unrepresentative of the nation? It can be argued that electors want representatives with the skills to perform their roles effectively, and these skills are unequally distributed through the nation. It is thus perhaps no accident that occupations with an emphasis on communication skills (law, education, journalism) are well represented in the House of Commons. On the other hand, a parliament which is significantly unrepresentative of society may lack the range of experience necessary for informed deliberation and legislation. If women are under-represented there is a risk that a woman's perspective will be insufficiently taken into account, not only on what may be traditionally thought of as 'women's issues' (such as child care, abortion, violence against women) but on the whole range of economic and social policy. If ethnic minorities and non-Christian faiths are under-represented, the reality of racial and religious discrimination routinely experienced by minorities will not inform debate on these issues. If relatively few MPs have shared the kind of education, housing and employment of most of their constituents, there is almost bound to be some gap in the comprehension of their problems. Beyond that, there is a deeper concern that parts of the electorate are becoming increasingly disenchanted with and alienated from the politicians who are there to represent them.

While the House of Commons collectively represents the whole people, each individual MP also represents a particular geographical area or Parliamentary constituency, while groups of MPs also represent particular sections of the national community, in particular political parties, and interest groups. These more specific forms of representation are sufficiently important to require more detailed consideration.

The representation of constituencies

The House of Commons consists of 659 MPs, elected by single-member Parliamentary constituencies. Candidates for Parliament may stand as representatives of a party, but once elected, each MP is expected to represent the interests of the constituency as a whole and to be at the service of all constituents. In this way, as members for particular constituencies, MPs collectively may be said to represent the entire

BOX 14.1
Unrepresentative MPs

- Women remain considerably under-represented, despite a significant advance in 1997 (60 women MPs in 1992, 120 in 1997, 118 in 2001 (18 per cent of the total)). The main reason for the recent increase in women MPs was the two Labour landslide majorities, as the Labour Party has made some efforts to increase the proportion of women candidates. A reversal of party electoral fortunes could see a significant fall in the number of women MPs, unless the Conservative Party in particular chooses more women candidates.
- Ethnic minorities are still under-represented, although in 2001 the highest number ever, 12, of black/Asian MPs was elected (but still under 2 per cent of all MPs).
- The middle-aged are over-represented. 70 per cent are aged between 40 and 59.
- MPs are better educated than the average – over two-thirds are graduates. However while 64 per cent of Conservative MPs elected in 2001 had attended an independent (or 'public') school, this was true of only 17 per cent of Labour MPs and 35 per cent of Liberal Democrats.
- Over four-fifths of MPs have a professional or business background. A large number of MPs have a background in education or law, reflecting some convergence in the composition of the main parties, although most Labour professionals came from the public sector – teaching, civil service, local government. However, while 36 per cent of Conservative MPs have a business background, this is true of only 8 per cent of Labour MPs.
- The working class is under-represented. Only a small and declining number (51, 12 per cent) of Labour MPs were previously manual workers, and almost none from other parties.

country, which would not be true of their roles as party and group representatives.

Yet if each MP represents a particular constituency, that does not necessarily mean that he or she has to act and vote according to the wishes of his or her constituents, at least according to an influential theory of representation derived from the 18th-century Whig politician and thinker Edmund Burke. 'Your representative owes you, not his industry only, but his judgement; and he betrays, instead of serving you, if he sacrifices it to your opinion' (speech to his electors at Bristol, 1774). Parliament in this view is 'a deliberative assembly of one nation rather than a congress of ambassadors': in other words it should lead public opinion rather than simply reflect it. But there is also the delegate theory of representation – part of the ideology of radical democracy – in which the elected representatives are considered to be the agents of, and directly accountable to, their constituents.

Most MPs take their constituency responsibilities very seriously, and the burden of work can be considerable. MPs' constituency work falls into two main categories. First, there is the local welfare officer/social worker role, dealing with a wide variety of problems (e.g. housing, health and social security) on behalf of individual constituents. MPs tackle the problems at the appropriate level, conducting a voluminous correspondence with ministers, departments, local authorities, quangos, local Department of Social Security (DSS) offices and so on. Also MPs can raise constituents' grievances through the medium of Parliamentary questions and debate, and if all these means fail they can refer cases of alleged public maladministration to the Ombudsman (see Chapter 15).

Second, MPs act as promoters of local interests, working to further the interests of the constituency as a whole by, for example, working to get orders for local industries, to attract new commercial and industrial investment, to get roads built, to find solutions for local industrial disputes, and to prevent local factories, schools and hospitals closing. In a democratic society, this MP–constituency relationship is of profound practical and theoretical importance, serving as a barometer of public opinion for representatives and as both safety-valve and potential mechanism of grievance resolution for citizens.

The representation of parties

MPs are elected (almost always) as representatives of party, and party underpins their activities once in the House. Table 14.1 shows how party determines the composition of the House of Commons, structuring it decisively into a party of government (Labour) and a party of official opposition (Conservative), flanked by a sizeable third party (Liberal Democrat) and several much smaller opposition parties. However, although MPs clearly represent parties, the actual distribution of seats does not reflect the distribution of support for parties in general elections (see Chapter 6). Nor do MPs necessarily closely mirror the opinions of party members and activists who selected them as candidates, although MPs with markedly different views from those of their constituency party may face criticism and ultimately perhaps deselection (see Chapter 8). Alternatively, MPs who become unhappy with their party may leave it and seek to join another party. This is called 'crossing the floor', as an MP who moves from the governing party to opposition (or vice versa) crosses the floor of the House of Commons to take a seat on the other side (as Winston Churchill did in 1904, from Conservative to Liberal, or Paul Marsden in 2001, from Labour to Liberal Democrat).

Government is party government. All British governments since 1945 have been recruited from a single party which normally has a clear majority in the House of Commons, and it is that party that supplies a team of leading politicians to fill ministerial posts (Chapter 12). It is the party that initially provides a government with a programme based on its election manifesto, which forms the basis of the legislation it puts before the Commons. Subsequently it is crucial for governments to retain their Parliamentary majority by maintaining the support of their Parliamentary party (and preferably the party in the country).

Party also underpins the activities of the official opposition, sustaining its two main constitutional functions of providing an alternative programme and team of leaders with which to replace the government, and regular criticism of the government of the day. Discipline and cohesion are almost as important for the opposition as for the government, and increasingly important for the Liberal Democrats and other smaller parties if they are to have Parliamentary and electoral credibility.

Thus it is vital for parties to remain united, especially in their formal activities such as voting in Parliament. Open divisions are damaging to a party and encouraging to its rivals. For a government they may jeopardise the passing of legislation, and for an opposition, destroy any chance to embarrass or defeat the government. The worst eventuality is that a party will split, and as may happen as a result, suffer electoral defeat – as Labour did in 1983 and 1987 after splitting in 1981. MPs are subject to three influences conducive to party loyalty before any formal mechanisms might begin to operate. These are, first, their natural sympathy for the causes and purposes their party represents; second, their desire (especially if they are ambitious) not to alienate the leadership; and, third, their concern to keep on good terms with their local parties which tend to dislike rebellions against party policy. Party discipline and cohesion is further maintained by various elements of party organisation in the House of Commons: Cabinets and shadow cabinets, the whip system, party meetings and party committees (see Box 14.2).

Party, then, dominates Parliament, but the reverse is also true. Parliament equally clearly dominates party. Thus virtually all UK parties accept the legitimacy of Parliament, and have as their major aim the winning of seats in the House of Commons. Although all the major parties now involve their

---

Table 14.1 Party composition of the House of Commons after the 1997 and 2001 general elections

	Seats 1997	Seats 2001
Labour	418	412
Conservative	165	166
Liberal Democrat	46	52
Ulster Unionist	10	6
Scottish National Party	6	5
Democratic Unionist Party	2	5
Plaid Cymru (Welsh Nationalist)	4	4
Sinn Fein	2	4
Social Democratic & Labour Party	3	3
Independent	1	1
Speaker	1	1

BOX 14.2

Maintaining party cohesion and discipline in the House of Commons

- **Cabinets and shadow cabinets.** The Cabinet is normally drawn entirely from one party with a majority in the Commons, and thus provides a collective leadership for the party. Indeed the inclusion of ambitious potential rival leaders in the Cabinet renders a dangerous backbench revolt less likely and reinforces party unity. 'Shadow' cabinets provide collective leadership for the official opposition party. The Conservative shadow cabinet is chosen by the leader. When Labour is in opposition its shadow cabinet is elected by the Parliamentary Labour Party, although the leader allocates shadow cabinet portfolios and appoints additional members of 'shadow' teams.

- **The whip system.** Whips play a central role in linking the party leaderships with the backbenchers. It is the whips who advise leaders on what the party will or will not stand; who offer ideas to leaders on how to head off backbench rebellion; and who indicate to disaffected backbenchers the likely consequences of their actions. The whips try to ensure that backbenchers support party policy in divisions (or votes) of the House of Commons. Party MPs are sent a weekly outline of Parliamentary business with items underlined once, twice, or three times, depending on whether an MP's attendance is merely requested (a one-line whip), expected (a two-line whip), or regarded as essential (a three-line whip). Defiance of a three-line whip constitutes a serious breach of party rules. Yet whips are personnel managers rather than disciplinarians. They rely mainly on persuasion (which may sometimes include veiled inducements and hints of honours or promotion). The ultimate sanction against a party rebel – withdrawal of the party whip (i.e. expulsion from the Parliamentary party) – is rarely used, and can prove counter-productive, as the Major

government discovered when the whip was withdrawn from eight Conservatives in 1994, only to be subsequently restored in 1995 (Alderman, 1995: 9–10; Ludlam in Ludlam and Smith, 1996: 118–19).

- **Party meetings.** Meetings of the Parliamentary party provide an important channel of communication between party leaders and backbenchers, allowing the airing of grievances and concerns. The Conservative Party meets weekly in the 1922 Committee when Parliament is sitting. When the party is in government, only backbenchers attend; when it is in opposition, the Committee includes all Conservative MPs except the leader. Its chair, who enjoys direct access to the leader, is an important figure and the '1922' plays a key role in the party, especially in times of controversy and crisis. When in opposition, the Labour Party meets as the PLP (Parliamentary Labour Party), in meetings attended by members of the shadow cabinet. When the party is in government, Labour ministers attend meetings of the PLP when the work of their departments is under discussion; communication between the government and its backbenchers is maintained by the Parliamentary Committee whose members include the leader and deputy leader, the chief whip, four ministers (three from the Commons) and six backbenchers.

- **Specialist party committees.** Each major party also forms a large number of specialist committees, which may enable backbenchers to influence party policy on specific subjects. These purely party committees should not be confused with all-party committees, such as the increasingly important departmental select committees (see Table 14.4), which may lead to a cross-party consensus which could erode discipline and cohesion within parties.

ordinary members in the selection of leaders, these virtually have to come from the ranks of MPs, and need to perform effectively in the Parliamentary arena. It is generally Parliamentary parties that have the major influence on party policies (Adonis, 1993: 40–1). In addition, Parliament provides the main arena for the party battle between elections. The continuing conflict in the House of Commons between government and opposition does influence public opinion on the reputation of the rival parties, through television, radio and the quality press.

The representation of interests

MPs not only represent parties: they also, less formally (and sometimes less openly), represent a range of interests. Some of this arises naturally from their past (and sometimes continuing) occupations, their membership of a range of organisations, their personal and family connections and leisure pursuits. It is only to be expected that a former teacher or miner will retain some concern for that occupation, and indeed some useful experience and expertise to contribute to debates on the subject. Similarly, MPs who are keen churchgoers, fox hunters or ramblers have an interest which they will naturally seek to defend and promote where relevant. They may indeed have some purely honorary or perhaps more responsible position in an outside organisation, which gives them an additional obligation to look after its interests. They have families and friends who may involve them with other interests. Much of this is relatively uncontroversial, and indeed may enrich the deliberations of Parliament. However, some representation of interests by MPs has raised rather more concern (see Box 14.3).

Since 1975 Parliament has kept an annual register of interests. However, doubts remained about the adequacy of existing public information about MPs' financial interests. Public concern about the apparently declining ethical standards of MPs increased in the 1990s. Newspaper allegations that some MPs were asking 'cash for questions' were upheld, and two Conservative backbenchers were reprimanded by the Commons, and suspended without pay for 20 and 10 days respectively. Soon afterwards, the Committee on Standards in Public Life, initially under the chairmanship of Lord

---

BOX 14.3

MPs and the representation of interests – some areas of concern

- Sponsorship of election candidates through a particular party, such as Labour Party candidates by trade unions. This practice ended in 1995. Unions could not instruct MPs how to speak or vote as that would be a breach of Parliamentary privilege, but they have expected MPs to watch over their interests.

- Payment of fees to MPs to serve as advisers, consultants or directors: the Nolan Committee (1995) found that 168 MPs, consisting of 145 Conservatives, 15 Labour and 6 Liberal Democrats, shared 356 consultancies.

- Access to the Commons as MPs' research assistants and aides. The use of House of Commons photo-identity passes by organisations as a cover for commercial lobbying activities in return for services to the MP concerned first became evident in the late 1980s.

- Lobbying of MPs by professional consultancy firms. This kind of lobbying developed into a multi-million pound industry during the 1980s, with the total fee income earned by 50 consultancy firms estimated at over £10 million a year in 1991.

- Direct lobbying of Parliament by all types of group. A study in 1992 of the 129 all-party Parliamentary groups that specialised in subjects rather than international ties revealed that a large number were financed by individual businesses, groups of companies, trade associations, lobbying firms and charities.

- Specialised assistance on an ad hoc unpaid basis. A wide range of groups provide information and support for MPs' Parliamentary activities, such as select committees and Private Members' bills.

- MPs' pursuit of outside occupations. Outside interests are represented in the House of Commons through MPs' part-time engagement in outside occupations such as, for example, journalists, lecturers, lawyers and company directors.

Nolan, was appointed (see page 217). Lord Neill became Chair in 1997, and Sir Nigel Wicks in 2001 <www.public-standards.gov.uk>.

The recommendations of the Nolan Committee (May 1995) were substantially implemented. The key moves were the banning of paid advocacy, the adoption of a new Code of Conduct and the appointment of a Parliamentary Commissioner for Standards. An early task for the first Parliamentary Commissioner for Standards, Sir Gordon Downey was to investigate charges against Conservative MP Neil Hamilton concerning financial improprieties, including failing to declare receipt of hospitality and failing to register cash payments. The commissioner, in a 900-page report published after the general election in July 1997, found 'compelling' evidence that Hamilton had taken up to £25,000 in cash from Mohammed Al Fayed, the owner of Harrods, to ask Parliamentary questions. The Commons Standards and Privileges Committee accepted this report, criticising Hamilton for standards that 'fell seriously and persistently below' what was expected of an MP. The Nolan restrictions on paid advocacy contributed to a 66 per cent drop in the number of consultancies declared by MPs in the 1997 Register of Members' Interests (from 240 to 80).

Legislation

Parliament is not only a legislative assembly, but Parliamentary law in the UK is still regarded as sovereign (see page 253). This is now questionable with regard to European law (and, perhaps also, international law). However, law passed by the Westminster Parliament remains supreme over other forms of British law, such as common law (law declared in courts by judges on specific cases). This suggests that law making is the most important function of Parliament, and indeed Parliament still spends a great deal of its time considering legislation. Even so, it may be questioned whether Parliament effectively makes the law. Westminster legislation today is substantially an executive function. Government dominates the legislative process from start to finish. Although ordinary backbench MPs retain some limited opportunities to initiate legislation, they normally have little

chance of converting their draft bills into law. Most of the time devoted by Parliament to the scrutiny of legislation is spent on government bills, and it is almost entirely government bills that are ultimately successful in passing through all their stages to become Acts. Parliament's effective influence on the principles and even the details of government legislation is usually limited. Although significant amendment, and very occasionally even defeat, of a government bill remains a possibility, the government's (generally disciplined) party majority ensures that its legislation normally emerges from its passage through Parliament more or less in the form intended.

Parliament, it may be said, legitimates rather than legislates. Although it is government rather than Parliament that substantially makes law, Parliament's assent remains vital to the establishment of the legitimacy of that legislation. Thus the formal Parliamentary stages of legislation remain important (they are outlined in Table 14.2). Yet they do not tell us very much about how law is

---

Definitions of Parliamentary legislation

Bill: a bill is a draft Act of Parliament. It remains a bill until it has passed all its stages (see Table 14.2).

Act: an Act of Parliament (also known as a statute) is a bill that has passed though all its stages and received the royal assent.

Public bill/Act: a public bill or Act is one that affects the whole country. It may be introduced by the government (government bill) or an ordinary backbencher or 'private member' (**Private Member's bill**) (see p. 238).

Private bill/Act: a bill or Act that affects only part of the country or community. (A local authority for example may seek to acquire special powers in its area through a private act.)

Delegated legislation (sometimes referred to as **secondary** or **subordinate legislation**). The technical name is Statutory Instruments. Many Acts are outline in form, giving authority to ministers or to other public bodies to make necessary orders or regulations under the authority of the parent Act. Thousands of Statutory Instruments are published every year.

really made in Britain. Where do the ideas for new laws come from? Who decides that legislation is necessary? Which interests influence the shape and content of legislation, and how? Is the formal completion of the Parliamentary stages with the royal assent really the end of the process? How are Acts implemented and adjudicated upon? How far are they successful in fulfilling the intentions of the legislators? To answer such questions it is important to go beyond the formal Parliamentary stages of legislation, to consider the crucial early formative pre-Parliamentary stages of the legislative process, the extra-Parliamentary influences on the formal Parliamentary stages, and the all important process of implementation, adjudication and review.

Where does the legislative process really start? Not normally in Parliament. The initial idea may come from a variety of sources, perhaps from a government department or an official report such as a Royal Commission, or possibly from a party manifesto or a pressure group or media campaign. Whatever the initial inspiration, the idea for legislation will not normally get far unless it wins government favour and eventually receives the backing of the Cabinet, and finds a place in the government's legislative programme.

Before a government decides to legislate it will normally consult widely across departments and other relevant public bodies, and often extensively with outside interests (see Chapter 9). This process of consultation not only provides the government with more information and expert opinion, but also may be crucial in winning the argument in Parliament and the country. If the government is able to claim that it has consulted widely with affected interests and secured their support, this reduces the scope for effective opposition. In some cases the government seeks not just the acquiescence of key interests but their active cooperation (for example, any reform of the National Health Service is likely to depend on the willing support of the medical professions for successful implementation).

Thus only after much initial consultation will the department principally concerned begin the process of drafting a bill using the services of expert Parliamentary law drafters, Parliamentary Counsel. Drafts with be circulated to other interested departments, and consultation with outside inter-

> *Definitions*
> A **Green Paper** is a consultative document, implying the government has not finally made up its mind.
> A **White Paper** normally involves a firmer statement of government intention.
> However, sometimes ministers may observe that a particular White Paper 'has green edges', indicating a readiness to listen to arguments and make changes.

ests will continue. It may take a year or two before the government feels ready to introduce a bill in Parliament. Thus normally much activity will have taken place before Parliament gets the opportunity to consider a government bill. Debates on the Queen's speech may provide some opportunity to comment on proposals to legislate, but unless Parliament is given the opportunity to discuss a Green or White Paper, the first time Parliament has any real opportunity to debate a bill is at the second reading.

Bills can be first introduced into either the Commons or the Lords, although more controversial measures are normally introduced in the Commons. The first reading of a bill is purely formal, with no debate. A dummy copy of the bill is placed on the Speaker's table, and a date announced for the second reading. Only after the first reading is the bill printed and circulated. The second reading normally involves a full debate on the principle of the bill, which can be defeated then, but this would be a most unusual fate for a government bill. If it passes its second reading the bill proceeds to the committee stage, normally taken by a standing committee, although a committee of the whole House may consider very important bills with constitutional implications, or at the other extreme, relatively simple and non-controversial bills.

During the committee stage the bill is considered in detail, line by line and clause by clause, and amendments may be proposed, either by the government, seeking to tidy up and improve the bill, or by government or opposition party MPs. The process of consultation with outside interests will continue throughout the committee stage. Friendly committee members may sometimes be prepared to introduce amendments drafted by such outside

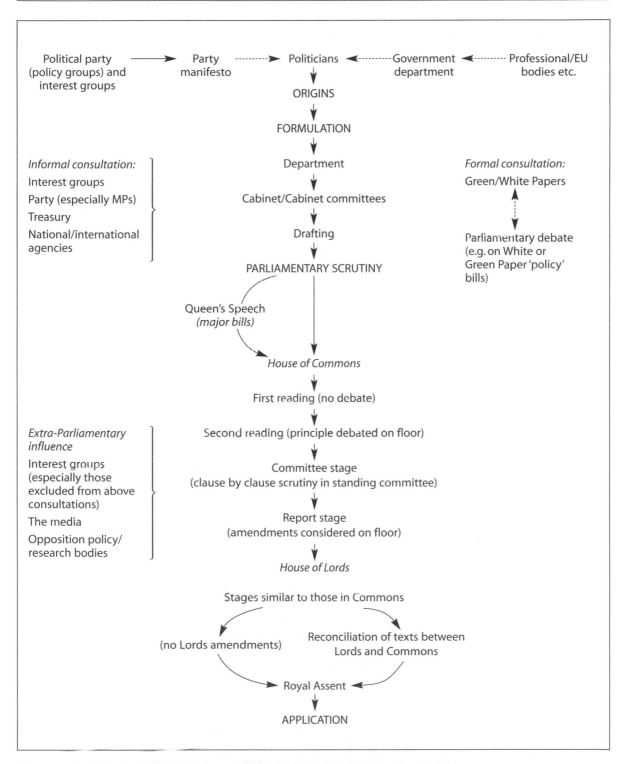

Figure 14.1 Principal stages in the legislative process for government bills

Source: Adapted from tables in Drewry, 1988: 124–5, and Adonis, 1993: 93.

Table 14.2 Parliamentary stages of legislation

Stage	Where taken	Comments
First reading	Floor of House of Commons (unless introduced in Lords first)	Purely formal – no debate
Second reading	Floor of House of Commons	Debate on principles – very unusual for a government bill to be defeated at this stage
Committee stage	Normally in standing committee, on which government normally has majority. Some bills may be taken in committee of the whole House.	Considered in detail, clause by clause – amendments can be made, but normally only those introduced by ministers have much chance of success. Can take weeks.
Report stage	Floor of House of Commons	Report on amended bill – further amendments can be made
Third reading	Floor of House of Commons	Debate (often short) on final text and approval of bill – generally a formality
House of Lords	Bill passes through similar stages in Lords (unless introduced first in Lords). Committee stage normally taken on floor of Lords not in standing committee.	Lords may amend bill (some further amendments may be introduced by government). If bill is amended it returns to the Commons for further consideration.
Consideration of Lords amendments	Floor of House of Commons	Lords amendments may be accepted, if not the Lords usually gives way. Otherwise, the bill can be reintroduced and passed next session without the Lords assent under the Parliament Act.
Royal Assent		Purely formal (last refused by Queen Anne). Bill then becomes an Act (or Statute).

groups. If the governing party has a substantial majority in the Commons as a whole, it will have a commensurate majority on all committees. Thus most of the amendments passed by the committee will be the government's own amendments, although it may accept amendments proposed by its own backbenchers, and occasionally even an opposition amendment. This process may help improve the legislation, closing loopholes, removing obstacles to successful implementation, and perhaps securing the goodwill of important interests whose full cooperation may be crucial to ensure that the Act achieves its intentions.

After the committee stage comes the report stage, when the amended bill is reported back to the House of Commons as a whole. Further amendments may be considered here, before the House proceeds immediately to a debate on the third reading. If the bill passes its third reading, it proceeds to the House of Lords (assuming the bill was initiated in the Commons) and follows similar stages there, with further opportunities for consultation and amendment. After a bill has passed all its stages in both Houses it goes to the monarch for the Royal Assent (last refused in the reign of Queen Anne, three centuries ago). It then becomes an Act, and the law of the land.

It sounds like a very thorough scrutiny, yet it is not

always as effective as it sounds. Governments normally seek to push a large and complex legislative programme through as quickly as possible without significant concessions. Thus MPs on the government side in standing committee often appear to have taken a vow of silence. By contrast, opposition MPs are only too voluble, speaking at length to numerous amendments – some essentially 'wrecking amendments' undermining the whole principle of the bill, to delay proceedings as long as possible. This may go on until the government loses patience and 'guillotines' debate through a timetabling measure. Often this can mean that important parts of a bill are never scrutinised in committee, although sometimes the omission is remedied in the Lords (see below).

While the Royal Assent may seem to mark the end of the legislative process, a new Act often requires extensive subsequent delegated legislation if it is to be successfully implemented. Thus the Act may confer on ministers or other public bodies the authority to lay detailed regulations and orders having the force of law before Parliament. Thousands of such Statutory Instruments are published annually. They are no longer regarded as a sinister threat to the power and sovereignty of Parliament, but as an essential adjunct to modern governance, allowing regulations to be amended with changing circumstances, and permitting useful experiments. Often they will involve further consultation with affected interests. For example, a change in the list of dangerous substances that cannot be sold over the counter might involve discussions with chemists, doctors and the police.

With or without the addition of delegated legislation, Acts still have to be implemented. Often implementation is not the responsibility of the central government but of other agencies, such as local authorities, who may proceed slowly and reluctantly, arising from their own opposition to a particular measure. Alternatively they may complain that they have been given statutory responsibilities without adequate resources. Or there may be political problems in the way of implementation. Thus some Acts are never fully implemented, and a few have never been implemented at all. On other Acts there may be considerable discretion given over methods of implementation.

Finally, Acts are open to interpretation and adjudication in courts of law. Although judges must

---

BOX 14.4
Comparative politics: the UK Parliament and the US Congress

The United States Congress is a legislature in the full meaning of the term. It makes laws. 'All legislative powers herein granted shall be vested in a Congress of the United States' (American Constitution). Both houses of Congress, the House of Representatives and the Senate, play an important role in the legislative process, and both have to agree before legislation can go forward for presidential approval. If the president declines to approve laws passed by Congress, this veto can be overridden by a two-thirds majority of both houses of Congress. Although the executive (the presidency) can propose laws, these may be modified substantially or rejected by Congress, which is quite often controlled by a different party from the president's party, as they are elected separately and for different terms. Thus neither the executive nor the legislature substantially controls the policy making process. The system is one of 'checks and balances', deriving from the separation of powers in the US constitution.

By contrast, the executive dominates the legislative process in the UK Parliament. Virtually all government bills are passed, while most bills introduced by ordinary MPs fail, and these can normally only succeed if the government does not oppose them. The subordinate role of the British Parliament stems from the fusion of executive and legislative powers in the Westminster system, compared with the separation of powers in the US constitution. Thus, the British Parliament is controlled by the government by means of its (usually) disciplined majority in the House of Commons. The unelected upper house has a minor role in the process: it may improve the scrutiny of government bills, but effectively lacks the power to reject them. The British Parliament, like most in western Europe, is essentially a reactive, policy-influencing assembly that may modify or even (very exceptionally) reject government legislative proposals, but has negligible opportunities to initiate legislation. Unlike the US Congress, it is not a legislature in the full meaning of the term.

accept an Act of Parliament, they may sometimes interpret it very narrowly and restrictively. In such judicial interpretation only the wording of the Act will be taken into account, not the pronouncements of governments or speeches in Parliament.

Thus the legislative process in Britain is executive-dominated from start to finish. Parliament has a negligible role in the origination and formulation of legislation (with the exception of Private Members' bills – see below), and no role in implementation beyond its generally inadequate scrutiny of delegated legislation. On the Parliamentary stages of legislation, government backbenchers generally have more influence than the opposition, for the simple reason that the opposition cannot normally threaten the government's majority, while dissent in its own ranks can. Thus governments may be prepared to make some concessions to critics on its own side. Beyond that, governments can expect to carry most of their legislative proposals substantially unchanged.

Private members' legislation

The only partial exceptions to the generalisations above are Private Members' bills. These can be introduced under various procedures, but the only method that normally stands any chance of success is through the annual ballot under which up to 20 backbenchers secure the right to introduce bills on a number of Friday sittings set aside for private members' measures. Yet there are a number of practical limitations on Private Members' bills.

Only a very small proportion of private members' legislation reaches the statute book. Even so, some Acts introduced by private members have been important, transformed lives, and changed attitudes. Thus private members' legislation changed the law on capital punishment, homosexuality, divorce and abortion in the 1960s, outlawed video 'nasties', compelled front-seat passengers to wear seat belts, restricted advertising on cigarettes in the 1980s and banned cruelty to wild animals (although not fox hunting) in the mid-1990s. Such controversial social issues with a strong moral dimension often cut across normal party lines, thus both government and opposition parties find it more convenient to leave such potentially difficult questions to a free vote.

BOX 14.5

Limitations on Private Members' bills

- They are not supposed to entail the expenditure of public money (which requires a money resolution).
- Lack of time is the crucial constraint. Ordinary backbenchers effectively lack the procedural devices used by the government to curtail debate, and thus most bills run out of time. Normally, only the first half dozen or so of the 20 bills introduced have a chance of passing all their stages and becoming law.
- Bills are unlikely to make progress if the government is opposed, because the government with its majority can use the whip system to destroy a bill. (In practice, some Private Members' bills may be government measures in disguise, with the government offering its own facilities and benevolent support for a backbencher sponsoring a bill that the government favours but has no time for in its own legislative programme).
- Even if the government is not opposed, a bill that arouses strong animosities among a minority of MPs may often be effectively blocked. It may be 'talked out' by opponents 'filibustering', and thus run out of time, or 'counted out' because too few MPs can be persuaded to attend on Fridays (in the absence of pressure from party whips).

Scrutiny and influence of the executive

Governments are accountable to Parliament, and through Parliament to the people. Thus it is in Parliament (primarily in the House of Commons) that the government must explain and defend its actions. Major opportunities for scrutinising and influencing the government through the procedures of the House of Commons are Parliamentary questions, general, adjournment and emergency debates, early day motions, select committees, and correspondence with ministers (Table 14.3).

An old and important select committee is the

Public Accounts Committee (PAC), which has a central role in the Commons' scrutiny of government expenditure. It has 15 members, and is chaired by a senior member of the opposition. It is particularly concerned to ensure the taxpayer gets value for money from public spending. Since 1983 it has been powerfully assisted by the National Audit Office, an independent body directed by the Comptroller and Auditor-General (CAG) with a staff of 900, which produces around 50 Value for Money reports every year. Reports of both the PAC and the CAG are often extremely critical of government departments. The 'economy, efficiency and effectiveness' audits of the PAC and the CAG have thus produced some hard-hitting reports. However, PAC reports are rarely debated by the House, and when they are, the debates are poorly attended and receive little public attention. None the less, the scrutiny of government expenditure by Parliamentary officers has improved considerably in the last decade; what remains inadequate is Parliament's own ability to deploy to maximum effect the information provided (see further, Liddell, 1994: 46–50).

Parliamentary reformers from the 1960s advocated the greater use of departmental select committees (DSCs) to improve scrutiny of the executive, and their case was reaffirmed by the Select Committee on Procedure (1978) which recommended the establishment of a new system of select committees to provide regular scrutiny of the work of every government department. These proposals were implemented in 1979. Some existing select committees were abolished; those retained included the Public Accounts Committee, and committees overseeing the work of the Parliamentary Commissioner (or Ombudsman), Statutory Instruments and European legislation. The new departure was the introduction of 14 (now 16) new DSCs to scrutinise the work of government departments. Their task is 'to examine the expenditure, administration and policy in the principal government departments ... and associated bodies' and to make reports with recommendations. In conducting their investigations, they can send for 'persons, papers and records'.

DSCs have been hailed by a Conservative former Cabinet minister Michael Jopling as 'the most important development in parliamentary procedure in my thirty years in the House. Select Committees are giving backbenchers teeth with

Table 14.3 Main methods of Commons' scrutiny of the executive

Procedure	Function
Questions	Backbenchers may submit oral and written questions to ministers.
	Written questions and replies are recorded in Hansard.
	Ministers reply to oral questions daily, Monday to Thursday, 2.35–3.30 p.m.
	Prime Minister's Question Time 3.00–3.30 p.m. Wednesday (n.b. MPs may ask one (unscripted) supplementary question).
Debates	General – on Queen's Speech, no-confidence motions (rare) and motions tabled by government and opposition.
	Adjournment debates – opportunity to raise general or constituency issues.
	Private Members' motions – 11 days per session allocated to these.
	Emergency debates – can be demanded but rarely conceded by Speaker.
Early day motions	Proposing and signing early day motions enables MPs to express their views – gains publicity, but no debate follows
Select committees	Able to scrutinise executive away from the floor of the Commons.
	Powers to send for 'persons, papers and records' and can interrogate ministers.
	Includes 16 departmental select committees and many others (e.g. Public Accounts, Public Administration, European Legislation, Statutory Instruments, Standards and Privileges, Modernisation of the House of Commons).
	Party balance on select committees reflects that of the House as a whole. (Unanimity difficult as contentious select committees may divide on party lines.)
Correspondence with ministers	Main way in which MPs pursue cases and issues raised by constituents.

which to tackle the executive' (*Guardian*, 22 March 1997). They undoubtedly constitute a marked improvement on the Commons machinery to scrutinise the executive available before 1979. However critics point out that, despite the frequent excellence of their reports and the occasional publicity achieved by their investigative sessions, they lack real clout. Their occasional effectiveness is offset by their more frequent lack of impact. They are the product of 'an executive-dominated system and lack the resources or prestige to sustain the kind of inquisitorial role that US congressional committees have long enjoyed' (*Guardian*, 22 March 1995). Some of the advantages and limitations of DSCs are listed in Table 14.4.

Forum for national debate

Parliament commands attention as the focus of national debate on all kinds of occasion, in a manner no other institution can match. Such occasions include Prime Minister's Question Time; the beginning and end of major debates in normal circumstances; more heated moments such as the Westland affair (1986) when a government's, a prime minister's or a leading Cabinet minister's reputation is at stake, with even a whiff of resignation in the air; and lastly, the great historic occasions when the House of Commons

has sometimes appeared to rise above party conflict. Thus the Conservative Leo Amery famously called out to Labour's Arthur Greenwood 'Speak for England, Arthur' in the celebrated 1940 Norway debate which was to bring down Neville Chamberlain and make Churchill head of a coalition government. On this occasion a debate in Parliament had momentous consequences, which decisively transformed the conduct of the war and perhaps materially changed the course of history. Yet critics suggest that such occasions are very much the exception. More commonly, debates take the form of relatively narrow, almost ritualistic combat between rival teams of party gladiators urged on by compact stage armies of supporters. Thus the proceedings in Parliament often seem to amount to little more than episodes in a continual election campaign, rather than offering a more open and wide-ranging forum of national debate.

Indeed, Parliament is not always even given the opportunity to debate issues of national importance. Parliament is not in session for substantial periods of the year, including some three months in the summer. While events may lead to demands for a recall of Parliament, this is rarely conceded. Even when Parliament is in session it is not easy to organise an extensive debate on some unanticipated development. Much of the Parliamentary timetable is determined well in advance. While emergency debates may be demanded, they

---

Table 14.4 Benefits and limitations of departmental select committees (DSCs)

Positive benefits of DSCs	*Limitations of DSCs*
Powers to send for 'persons, papers and records' improve scrutiny and accountability of executive.	Party whips' influence on membership of DSCs compromises independence and effectiveness.
Coverage of proceedings aids open government.	Many members of DSCs lack necessary motivation, knowledge and skills.
DSCs may have pre-emptive or deterrent effect – deterring ministers and civil servants from behaviour that they might be unable to justify before committee.	Most DSCs lack the staff and budgets for substantial independent research.
Committee investigation and reports may ultimately persuade government to change course.	Limited powers: ministers normally attend when requested, but are not obliged to answer questions. Civil servants may withhold information in the interests of 'good government' or national security.
Committee membership helps develop specialisation and expertise – and committee can seek outside advice and assistance.	Lack of influence: few DSC reports are debated on the floor of the House of Commons, and ministers can (and generally do) ignore them.

are rarely conceded by the Speaker. Explicit Parliamentary approval is not required for some of the most momentous decisions a government can take. The British prime minister has inherited most of the old prerogative powers of the crown, and does not need express Parliamentary sanction for such crucial and potentially far-reaching acts as signing treaties and even declaring war (see Chapter 12). As Hennessy (2000: 89) has observed, 'here, the royal prerogative is all. Unless primary legislation is required, Parliament does not have to be routinely involved at all.'

In practice, a wise prime minister will normally try to involve Parliament as much as possible. Churchill during his wartime premiership treated the Commons with 'high respect', addressing numerous 'secret sessions' which gave MPs 'a sense of being privy to special knowledge' (Jenkins, 2001: 622). Eden, by contrast, failed to carry Parliament with him over Suez in 1956, refused a request for the recall of Parliament from the Leader of the Opposition (Hennessy, 2000: 245), and (it is now clear) lied to the House of Commons on the crucial issue of foreknowledge of Israeli plans. Thatcher wisely agreed to an exceptional Commons debate on a Saturday over the Falklands crisis, and this perhaps helped her to maintain a level of bipartisan support for the subsequent task force. Blair, often criticised for his neglect of Parliament, took the precaution of seeking explicit Parliamentary sanction for military operations against Iraq in 1998 (Hennessy, 2000: 503). After some apparent initial reluctance, he also agreed to the emergency recall of Parliament in September 2002, and addressed the house of Commons in a debate on the Iraq crisis.

However, Parliament does not always seem to provide an effective forum for national debate. Even if Parliament is generally given the opportunity to debate issues of national importance, it no longer appears to be at the centre of national debate. The proceedings of Parliament are now much less reported even in the quality press. Although the Commons reluctantly let in the television cameras after a long delay, and it is now possible for members of the public to follow Parliamentary proceedings on minority channels, the main BBC and commercial news and current affairs programmes devote only cursory treatment to Parliament.

Indeed, much of the real national debate now seems to take place through the media.

Recruitment of a government

Anyone seeking high office in government must normally first seek election to the House of Commons, and gain recognition there. Although in Britain it is taken for granted that ministers are drawn from Parliament, and predominantly from the House of Commons, it is not necessarily the case in other democratic states. Indeed, in some countries where there is a stricter separation of executive and legislative powers, government ministers are not even allowed to serve as members of the legislative assembly. Elsewhere it is more common than in Britain for some ministers to be drawn from the worlds of business, finance or academia, without serving as elected representatives. Even in Britain prime ministers have sometimes sought to recruit ministers from outside Parliament, but such ministers have been obliged by convention to obtain a seat in the Commons (through a Parliamentary by-election) or in the House of Lords. However, such appointments have been few, and not always successful. Businessmen and trade unionists without prior experience of Parliament have often found it difficult or frustrating to cope with Parliamentary conventions and procedures.

The importance of prior entry to the House of Commons for an ambitious aspiring politician can be illustrated simply. In 1983 a young married couple both sought to become prospective Labour candidates at the forthcoming general election, and agreed to support the political career of whoever was first successful. Both had qualified as barristers, although the wife was considered the more outstanding, and had the additional advantage of coming from a strong Labour family. However, it was the husband who, at the eleventh hour, finally and rather unexpectedly landed the nomination for a safe Labour seat at Sedgefield, and was duly elected as the youngest member of the Parliamentary Labour Party. He rapidly made his mark in the much depleted Labour ranks, and was promoted to its front bench in 1984. By 1994 his reputation had risen sufficiently to become Leader of the Labour Party in 1994, and Prime Minister in 1997

(Rentoul, 2001). The story may be now only too well known, but the point is that without his prior selection for a winnable Labour seat, Tony Blair would never have been able to pursue a significant political career, let alone become Prime Minister. Indeed it is possible that had Cherie Booth won the race for a seat, it would now be her husband playing the loyal supporting role to his wife's political career.

Election to, and successful performance in, the House of Commons are thus the main criteria for political advancement, and promotion into government in the British political system. It is in the Commons that ambitious politicians first attempt to make, and then as ministers try to sustain, their reputations. Yet the skills of Parliamentary debate are widely acknowledged to be no real preparation for running a department, and the two kinds of ability are not invariably present in the same person. Outstanding Parliamentary orators do not necessarily make good ministers. Conversely it is possible, indeed likely, that some potentially outstanding ministers are not discovered though the British system of recruiting and training for government office.

Executive dominance of Parliament

In Britain over the last century or so, but particularly since the Second World War, governments have normally dominated Parliament for the reasons summarised in Box 14.6. It is virtually impossible in normal circumstances (that is, government possession of a working majority) to bring a government down, and in practice very difficult to engineer any defeat in the House of Commons. Executive dominance of Parliament is thus the general rule.

Of course, an opposition can make life awkward for a government in a number of ways, which include harassment of ministers in debates and at Question Time, motions of censure, the frequent use of delaying tactics and the suspension of pairing arrangements. Censure motions ('That this House has no confidence in Her Majesty's Government') are normally rare in periods of sizeable government majorities, but more frequent when the opposite situation prevails: there were three between 1976 and 1979, the final one – in March 1979 – resulting in defeat for the Labour govern-

BOX 14.6
Reasons for government control of the House of Commons

Government control of the House of Commons rests on four main factors:

- **Possession in normal circumstances of a majority, allied with the habit of loyal voting by its own supporters.** Out of 16 general elections between 1945 and 2001, only in February 1974 did one party fail to win an overall majority of seats, although in three other elections (1950, 1964, October 1974) the governing party only enjoyed single-figure majorities. Far more commonly, governments have enjoyed comfortable majorities, coupled with generally strong party discipline.
- **Power to determine the parliamentary timetable.** Although a significant proportion of Commons business is initiated by the opposition and backbenchers, some three-quarters of Commons time is devoted to the consideration of government business.
- **Ability to curtail debate.** The government can restrict debate by employing the closure and the guillotine. The closure – the request 'that the question be now put', stopping debate if successful – is rarely used now to restrict debate on government business. The guillotine – an 'allocation of time' motion regulating the amount of time to be spent on a bill – is normally used when the government considers that progress on a major piece of legislation is unsatisfactory at committee stage. In recent years, guillotine motions have been used more frequently.
- **Control over the drafting of legislation.** As we have seen (above), legislation from initiation to completion is dominated by the Cabinet, Cabinet committees and the departments, and is essentially now a function of the executive.

ment. In February 1997, a Labour censure motion on the beef crisis was narrowly defeated. Oppositions can delay the passage of government measures by stalling ploys at the committee stage of bills, and by calls for frequent divisions at the second and third reading stages. Finally, oppositions can harass minority governments or those lacking a majority by breaking off pairing arrangements, as Tony Blair did in December 1996, thereby putting pressure to turn up and vote on sick MPs or even those out of the country.

In fact, notwithstanding its adversarial context, much government business is conducted by mutual agreement between government and opposition, and obstruction does not arise. Indeed, for much of the time a consensual model is more appropriate to the House of Commons than an adversarial model. This consensual aspect of the House arises for several reasons. First, much government legislation – notably that of a technical or administrative kind – is uncontroversial. Second, the opposition may have its own motives for not pressing resistance too far: in addition to recognising the difficulties of governing, it wants to avoid being stigmatised as merely factious, provoking similar treatment when the roles of government and opposition are reversed, and to avoid opposing legislation that is popular or for which there is a mandate.

Governments may have less to fear from opposition parties than from their own backbenchers, for when they enjoy a secure party majority, they can only be defeated when some of their own backbenchers join forces with the opposition parties. A particular combination of circumstances is required for a government to be defeated in the House of Commons, including a small majority, a certain level of rebelliousness among its own backbenchers, and a disciplined opposition. Between 1945 and 1970, no government was defeated in the House of Commons as a result of a revolt by its own backbenchers, but from 1970 there has been increasing backbench dissent. This has not normally seriously threatened governments with secure Parliamentary majorities. However, Conservative rebellions presented a serious threat to John Major's small and declining majority after 1992. By contrast Blair's government with its massive majority could survive a record rebellion by 139 Labour MPs over Iraq in March 2003.

Reform of the House of Commons

For a variety of reasons, including Parliament's declining public reputation and its weaknesses in relation to the executive and the scrutiny of European legislation, reform of Parliament came to the fore in the 1990s. Some progress was made before 1997, particularly in strengthening safeguards against corruption and 'sleaze' following the Nolan Report, and improving Commons procedures (the Jopling reforms of 1994). The Blair government was committed by its election manifesto to a reform of Prime Minister's Questions and the appointment of a Commons select committee to review its own procedures.

Blair swiftly changed Prime Minister's Question Time from a twice-a-week quarter of an hour event on Tuesdays and Thursdays to one taking place once a week for half an hour on Wednesdays. The aim of the reform was ostensibly to transform the nature of PMQT from its 'bearpit', conflictual atmosphere to one involving more considered and reflective exchanges between the prime minister and the leader of the opposition, although it is highly questionable whether it was noticeably effective in this respect. The confrontations between Blair and Hague between 1997 and 2001 were markedly adversarial. Some critics considered the reduction in the number of sessions weakened the prime minister's accountability to Parliament (even though the time devoted to them remained the same), and Blair has been more generally criticised for devoting 'less time to parliamentary activity than his predecessors' (Norton in Seldon, 2001: 54). Partly in answer to such criticisms, Blair inaugurated in 2002 regular prime ministerial appearances before the Liaison Committee of the House of Commons, mainly composed of chairs of select committees.

The promised Select Committee on the Modernisation of the House of Commons was appointed in 1997, and proceeded to recommend in a series of reports a number of reforms, mostly to be tried initially on an experimental basis. Some of these have been implemented. Westminster Hall has been utilised as a 'parallel chamber' for debates not involving votes, enabling more MPs to participate in Commons debates. Some changes in the scrutiny of legislation were introduced, for example, enabling the scrutiny of legislation to be carried over between Parliamentary sessions, and improvements were made to the scrutiny of European business (Cowley, in Dunleavy *et al.*, 2000; Norton, in Seldon, 2001). When the reform-minded Robin Cook became Leader of the House after the 2001 election, there was some further impetus for change. In October 2002 the Commons finally voted for a revised Parliamentary day, starting in the morning and finishing in the early evening, and for a shorter summer recess, changes which were implemented from January 2003 and which should make the House more amenable to the increased number of women MPs as well as some of their more family-minded male colleagues.

Yet this overhaul of the Commons timetable has not substantially affected the earlier verdict of Philip Norton (in Seldon, 2001: 48) on the reform process: 'the changes appeared limited and failed to change significantly the relationship between the legislature and the executive', leading to the conclusion that Parliament had 'if anything, been further marginalised'. Thus the government rejected 'modest' proposals for the reform of the appointment and scrutiny of select committees. However, this was perhaps unsurprising. Few governments would readily acquiesce in reforms that might significantly increase Parliament's effective scrutiny of their work, or impede their own ability to get their business through. Thus it seems unlikely that any major transformation of executive dominance of Parliament will be achieved while governments retain secure Parliamentary majorities backed by party discipline.

Philip Cowley (in Dunleavy *et al.*, 2000: 120) argues that 'the greatest of the reforms to the UK Parliament ... will be the indirect reforms, those that occur as a result of Labour's other constitutional policies'. Cowley goes on to cite the Human Rights Act (see Chapter 15) and devolution (see Chapter 17). However, the most significant development of all could be the new voting systems introduced for the European Parliament and devolved assemblies. Although Blair's government has deferred reform of elections for the Westminster Parliament, voting reform is now on the political agenda. A change in the voting system in the direction of more proportional representation (see Chapter 6) is perhaps the only reform that might fundamentally alter executive–legislative relations in Britain.

The upper chamber

However, if reform of the lower chamber under the Blair government has so far been relatively modest and (for some) disappointing, radical reform of the upper chamber is already well under way (although highly controversial and as yet incomplete), and it is this to which we must now turn,

The British Parliament, like most legislatures around the world, is bicameral; in other words it has two chambers or houses. In many other countries the second chamber has a significant role. The US Senate is actually rather more powerful and prestigious than the US lower house, the House of Representatives. However, the British upper house, the House of Lords, because of its bizarre composition (until recently composed largely of hereditary peers), has long been of marginal significance to British government and politics. One indication of its declining role is that while in the 19th century many prime ministers and other leading ministers came from the House of Lords, since 1902 no serving prime ministers have sat in the Lords. The Lords only has the power to delay legislation for up to a year, and its undemocratic composition has generally inhibited their lordships from exercising even this limited power too often.

Powers and functions of the upper chamber

The main functions of the upper chamber are as follows:

- **Legislation:** revision of House of Commons bills, giving ministers the opportunity for second thoughts; initiation of non-controversial legislation, including government bills, bills by individual peers, private bills (promoted by bodies outside Parliament, e.g. local authorities), and consideration of delegated legislation.
- **Deliberation:** the provision of a forum for debates on matters of current interest.
- **Scrutiny:** the upper chamber subjects government policy and administration to scrutiny through questions and through the work of its select committees (e.g. European Communities, Science and Technology).
- **Supreme court of appeal:** the upper chamber is

the ultimate court of appeal in the United Kingdom.

Legislation

Constitutionally, despite its reduced powers, the upper house remains an essential part of the legislative process, and spends rather over half its time on legislation. By the Parliament Act of 1911, the Lords completely lost its power to delay or amend money bills, which receive the Royal Assent one month after leaving the House of Commons, whether approved by the Lords or not. But it retained the power to delay non-money bills for up to two successive sessions (reduced to one session only by the Parliament Act of 1949). The present powers of the House of Lords – as defined by the Parliament Acts of 1911 and 1949 – are as follows:

- to delay non-money bills for up to one year
- to veto (a) bills to prolong the life of Parliament beyond the statutory five-year period; (b) private bills (not to be confused with Private Members' bills); and (c) delegated legislation.

In practice the Lords has accepted further limitations on its own power of delay. The main guiding rule – firmly established by Conservative opposition peers in the immediate post-war period – is that the upper house does not oppose measures included in the governing party's manifesto at the previous election (the Salisbury/Addison doctrine). In addition, the Lords rarely press an amendment or delay a measure to the point where the Parliament Acts have to be invoked. Of more importance, however, are those cases where the Lords have passed adverse amendments on government legislation, thereby causing delay.

The House of Lords can cause political embarrassment to the government of the day, but no more. The upper house has on numerous occasions impeded government legislation and forced concessions, although generally on minor issues, but it is far from being a severe constitutional obstacle to the party in power. Nor can it be said to treat the legislation of both parties impartially, being much more severe on Labour legislation than on Conservative. Its relatively greater 'independence' dates from the failure of the Parliament (no. 2) Bill (1969) which would have reduced its delaying power to six months

and eliminated the voting rights of hereditary peers. The failure of this reform attempt boosted its morale by prompting the realisation that it had a valuable role to fulfil after all. From 1979, when large government majorities and weak oppositions prevailed in the House of Commons, the Lords did become one of the main sources of resistance to government, but only in a minor key.

Another significant trend in recent decades has been the greater use made of the Lords by governments to revise and generally tidy up their legislation. The extent of this change may be gauged from the fact that between 1987 and 1990 the upper house made 7868 amendments to government bills compared with 2854 amendments to government legislation between 1970 and 1973. Most of these changes are introduced by ministers. Because much of this tidying-up process has to be done hurriedly at the end of sessions, one peer has described the upper chamber as 'a gilded dustpan and brush'. Suggested causes for this development include inadequate consultation, government indecisiveness, and poor drafting in the early stages of legislation, but whatever the reasons, it has made the House of Lords an increasingly attractive target for pressure groups (Shell, 1992: 165–6).

Deliberation and scrutiny

The House of Lords – which devotes approximately one day per week to general debate – is often praised for the overall quality of its debates, but their overall impact is questionable. Its exercise of its scrutiny functions (through questions and select committees) is of greater consequence. Thus, Conservative governments after 1979 were embarrassed by ad hoc select committee reports on *Unemployment* (1979–82) and *Trade and Industry* (1984–5) and by the Science and Industry Select Committee's criticisms of cuts in the government's budget for scientific research (1991). In addition, the House of Lords Select Committee on the European Communities, which considers initiatives proposed by the EC Commission, is well staffed, able to consider EC proposals on their merits, and expert; it produces over 20 reports a year which, like other Lords select committee reports but unlike their equivalents in the Commons, are all debated. Overall, however, the

House of Lords has made no attempt to establish through its select committees a mechanism for consistent, comprehensive scrutiny of government, but has rather used them to fill gaps left by the Commons select committee system.

Supreme Court of Appeal

The House of Lords not only contributes to making the law, but adjudicates on the law in its role as the United Kingdom's supreme court of appeal, which in most other countries would be considered a dangerous confusion of functions that should be constitutionally separate. Specialist law lords were appointed from the 19th century to assist the Lords to fulfil its function as a supreme court, and by convention only those suitably qualified take an active part in this judicial role. However, some critics are now arguing that the dual role of the upper chamber in making and adjudicating on laws is difficult to defend, and a separate supreme court is needed.

Composition of the upper chamber

If the powers of the Lords have been controversial, the traditional composition of the upper chamber has come to be regarded as unsustainable in a modern democratic era. The House of Lords long consisted of lords temporal (holders of hereditary titles) and lords spiritual (the archbishops and senior bishops of the Church of England). In the 19th century specialist law lords, appointed for life, were added to assist the Upper Chamber in its judicial capacity as the highest court in the land (see above). The composition of the House of Lords was more significantly affected by the Life Peerages Act 1958, which empowered the Crown to create life peers and peeresses, and the Peerages Act 1963, which allowed hereditary peers to disclaim their titles and admitted hereditary peeresses into the House of Lords in their own right. These two Acts had the incidental effect of introducing a small proportion of women (7.0 per cent) to what had been an all-male chamber. Rather more significantly, the upper chamber was transformed over a period from an almost entirely hereditary chamber to a chamber in which appointed life peers commonly outnumbered hereditary peers in its work, because whereas most of the hereditary peers

did not attend regularly, many of the life peers were 'working peers' who constituted the bulk of the active membership. However, the hereditary peers retained a nominal majority, which could become effective when a subject dear to their hearts (such as hunting) was debated.

However, the composition remained bizarre, and not only because the majority of members still claimed their seats from an accident of birth. The only religion represented as of right is the established Church of England, which hardly seems appropriate in what has become a multi-faith Britain. Moreover, while appointment may constitute an advance on heredity as a qualification for membership, the life peers owe their appointments to prime ministerial patronage (although the prime minister normally accepts recommendations from the leaders of opposition parties), which hardly seems much more democratic. In practice, retired ministers and long-serving MPs are among those commonly offered peerages. Thus debates in the Lords often feature elderly politicians, who were once household names but are now largely forgotten, giving substance to a quip of the former Liberal leader, Jo Grimond, that the House of Lords proves there is life after death.

A final objection to the composition of the upper chamber was its unbalanced representation of political parties. Although a substantial minority of peers are crossbenchers who are independent of party allegiance, among those who took a party whip Conservative peers outnumbered Labour peers by 300, before the Labour government reform process started. Although the built-in Conservative advantage was less than these figures imply because Conservative peers were less regular attenders than Labour or Liberal Democrat peers, even in the 'working house' the Conservatives remained by far the largest party. Moreover, this built-in Conservative advantage has had a marked effect on the Lords' function as revising chamber. On average, whereas the Lords inflicted 70 defeats a year on Labour governments between 1974 and 1979, it defeated Conservative administrations only 13 times a year between 1979 and 1997.

Reform of the upper chamber

While it has long been recognised that the hereditary second chamber is indefensible in a democratic era, reform of the Lords has proved difficult. As Robert Hazell (1999: 114) has observed, 'it is impossible to decide a satisfactory system for Lords' membership without first deciding what interests peers are there to represent'. This is not easy in Britain. The key function a second chamber performs in a federal state is to represent the interests of the states, as the Senate does in the USA or the Bundesrat in Germany. It is more difficult to establish such a clear function in a unitary state, as the UK remains, at least in theory. The government's proposals for reforming the Lords have sometimes been criticised for being insufficiently related to other ongoing constitutional changes, particularly devolution. However, the final outcome of the devolution process as yet remains unclear. It might be easier to devise a logical role for a second chamber if British government continues to evolve towards a quasi-federal or ultimately perhaps a fully federal system. In one sense Lords reform is long overdue, and some would argue that it has come a century late, but in the immediate context it is arguably a little premature.

One solution to the Lords reform dilemma is simply abolition. Unicameral legislatures have become more common (112 of the world's 178 parliaments), as some mature democracies have abolished their second chamber while many new and post-Communist states only have one chamber (Hague and Harrop, 2001: 219). Yet this solution has never found much favour in Britain, although Labour proposed it for a time. It is commonly argued that a second chamber provides an opportunity for second thoughts on over-hasty legislation from the lower house. If it is accepted that some kind of revising chamber is necessary or desirable, it is then a question of deciding how that chamber should be composed. While many favour a wholly or largely elected second chamber, a problem here is that such a democratically elected body could challenge the legitimacy and primacy of the House of Commons.

Because previous reform proposals had foundered on the failure to agree on the composition and powers of the second chamber, Blair's Labour government opted for a two-stage model of reform. Stage one was to involve simply removing the hereditary peers; stage two a more long term and comprehensive reform. The government moved quickly towards the abolition of the right of hereditary peers to sit in the

BOX 14.7

Old and interim reformed composition of the House of Lords, after House of Lords Act 1999

	Old composition	Interim new House
Spiritual peers (archbishops and senior bishops of Church of England)	26	26
Hereditary peers	777	92
Law lords	27	27
Life peers	525	525
Total	1355	670

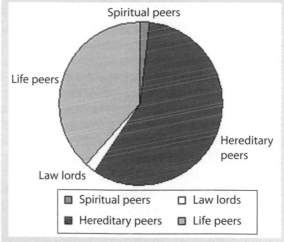

Unreformed House of Lords (pre 1999)

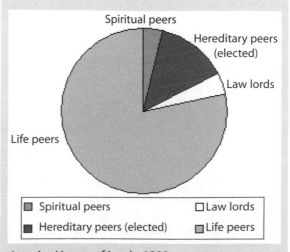

Interim House of Lords, 1999

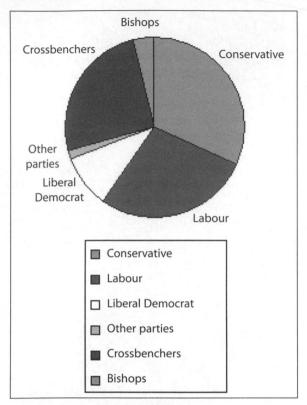

- ■ Conservative
- ■ Labour
- □ Liberal Democrat
- ▨ Other parties
- ■ Crossbenchers
- ▨ Bishops

Figure 14.2 Party affiliations of members of upper house, 2001

Lords, but faced with the prospects of a prolonged battle with the upper house, instead reached a compromise allowing the hereditary peers to elect 92 of their number to remain as members of the transitional House pending a more fundamental final reform. After the 92 peers were chosen, the rest of the hereditary peers lost their powers to speak and vote in the Lords. (The interim composition of the half-reformed House of Lords, compared with its former composition, is indicated in Box 14.7.)

By 2002 the party affiliations of the interim upper chamber were as indicated in Figure 14.2, with 217 Conservatives, 188 Labour, 66 Liberal Democrat and 177 crossbenchers, plus 24 bishops (source: Joint Committee Report, 2002). Thus the Conservatives remain somewhat over-represented, although they now lack even a theoretical majority. Ironically, however, this partially reformed upper chamber has caused rather more problems for the Labour government than the old House of Lords. The reform has also slightly improved the percent-

age of women members. There are now 105 women, including 100 life peers and five of the elected hereditary peers.

The second stage of Lords reform has proved far more difficult. The government adopted a time-honoured device for dealing with politically awkward questions, appointing an independent Royal Commission chaired by Lord Wakeham, a former Conservative minister. Wakeham's commission reported in January 2000, and recommended no radical change in the functions of the upper chamber; the Commons was to remain the dominant body and the Lords' judicial role was to continue. On composition, the report argued that at least 30 per cent of members should be female (a substantially higher proportion than the 16 per cent in the present Lords, or 18 per cent in the Commons), ethnic minorities and different faiths should be fairly represented, but no political party should have an overall majority and at least 20 per cent of the whole house should be crossbenchers. However, the crucial proposal was that the chamber would largely be appointed, with only a minority of peers elected. The government largely endorsed the Wakeham Report. Lord Irvine, the Lord Chancellor, drafted a White Paper in November 2001, which proposed a small elected element (20 per cent), with a further 20 per cent appointed by an independent Appointments Commission and 60 per cent appointed by party patronage.

These government proposals met with very wide-ranging opposition from the Liberal Democrats (who, like the constitutional pressure group Charter 88, want a fully elected second chamber), from the Conservatives who had defended the hereditary element but now had switched to support an 80 per cent elected chamber, and from many Labour backbenchers who wanted a larger elected element (*Talking Politics*, April 2002; *Guardian*, 14 May 2002). The Commons all-party select committee, chaired by Labour MP Tony Wright, reported in favour of a 60 per cent elected house, with law lords and spiritual peers abolished. Responses to the government's White Paper indicated a strong preference for a mainly elected chamber. The government thus accepted there was no consensus in support of its own proposals, and established an independent joint committee of both houses to undertake widespread consultation and issue a report on options for reform.

The Joint Committee reported in December 2002. The report identified five desirable qualities in a revising chamber: legitimacy, representativeness, independence, expertise, and the absence of domination by any one party. It considered some 600 members should sit for a 12-year term. Yet it did not propose a clear recommendation on the detailed composition of the revised upper chamber, instead presenting seven options, ranging from a wholly appointed to a wholly elected house. Both houses are to vote on the options in January 2003. Clearly there is considerable disagreement among members of both houses, and between and within parties, and a compromise seems likely, with perhaps 50 per cent or 60 per cent of the new chamber being elected and the rest appointed. Whatever the outcome it seems likely that it will be some years before the stage two of Lord reform is completed and a reformed upper chamber finally established.

The Westminster Parliament and other parliaments

Although the Westminster Parliament remains at the centre of British politics, formally at least, in the sense that its sovereignty remains a key principle of the unwritten (or uncodified) British Constitution, it is no longer the only parliament with which British politics is concerned. UK membership of the European Union has meant that representatives are also elected to the European Parliament. While this used to be dismissed as a mere talking shop, its influence on European Union decision making, and hence on decisions that affect Britain, has grown steadily in recent years (see Chapter 16). Indeed, some would argue that it has become a more effective policy-influencing body than the Westminster Parliament. Additionally, since 1999 the Westminster Parliament now coexists with a Scottish Parliament with legislative powers, and assemblies for Wales and Northern Ireland. There is also a new Greater London Assembly and the prospect of elected assemblies for the English regions (see Chapter 17). Thus the Westminster Parliament may increasingly appear one of many representative assemblies in the evolving British system of governance. The exis-

tence of these other parliaments and assemblies has considerable and potentially increasing implications for the role and functions of the Westminster Parliament, and the parliaments require considerable liaison and coordination.

UK membership of the European Union already has considerable if contentious implications for the sovereignty of the Westminster Parliament. Under the Treaty of Rome and subsequent treaties, European Union law is binding on member states. Parliamentary sovereignty seems increasingly circumscribed, despite attempts to improve the legislative accountability of the European Union to national parliaments. With an increasing proportion of legislation emanating from the European Union, Westminster surveillance of European directives and regulations is a matter of some importance. The task involves both Houses of Parliament. In the Commons, the system was strengthened in 1991 by the addition of two standing committees of 13 members each to the already-existing Select Committee on European Legislation (the 'Scrutiny Committee'). The Scrutiny Committee refers EU legislation that it sees as requiring further scrutiny and debate to one of the two standing committees that have the power (1) to question ministers and officials, (2) debate the merits of the issues at stake on a substantive motion, and (3) refer documents for debate on the floor of the House, subject to the agreement of the leader of the House. However, debate by the House as a whole can lead not to amendment but only to a 'take note' motion, in the hope that the government will modify its position. The House of Lords also has a scrutiny committee, the Select Committee on the European Communities (1974), whose task is to decide which of the hundreds of EU documents deposited with it each month require scrutiny because they raise important questions of policy or principle or for other reasons. The scrutiny work is then carried out by six sub-committees whose reports are normally debated by the House.

The Maastricht Treaty stipulated that national parliaments should receive Commission legislative proposals in good time for information or possible examination. However, in its highly critical 24th Report (1995), the Commons Scrutiny Committee asserted that this declaration had proved to be 'a sham' and that EU law 'increasingly seemed to be made in a private club', with the Brussels Commission routinely requiring ministers to endorse laws for which there is no formal or official text. The Select Committee warned that if future practice did not conform to basic democratic procedures, it would consider a boycott. It listed over 40 examples of proposed laws that it had had to consider without being able to read a formal text or after a decision had been taken by the Council of Ministers.

While the EU remains a hybrid political system in which institutions representing member states continue to play a major or preponderant role, the scrutiny of European legislation seems likely to remain a dual function of the European Parliament and the parliaments of member states. That being so, there is clearly a need for improved cooperation between national parliaments and the European Parliament. In the case of the UK, this may be facilitated by formal and informal party links between MPs and MEPs. From a party perspective there is however a possibility of some divergence of interests between a party's national and European representatives, especially as the latter are part of wider European parties (see Chapter 16).

The longer-term implications of the devolution of power to the Scottish Parliament and Welsh and Northern Ireland Assemblies will also have a profound effect on the role and perhaps ultimately composition of the Westminster Parliament. Much of the law passed at Westminster will now be English (or English and Welsh) law rather than UK law, while law passed in the devolved assemblies may have knock-on implications for Westminster. At the very least there is a need for considerable liaison between the various parliaments and assemblies. Initially the potential for serious conflict between parliaments was somewhat lessened by Labour or Labour-dominated governments in Westminster, Edinburgh and Cardiff. More problems are predicted if a future Conservative majority at Westminster faces Labour-controlled bodies in Scotland and Wales, or if a Labour UK government confronts an SNP-dominated Scottish Parliament.

Some of the implications of these developments for long-established British constitutional principles, particularly the sovereignty of the Westminster Parliament and the unity of the United Kingdom, are discussed in the next chapter (15) and in Part 4.

Further reading

Adonis (1993), can be recommended as an introduction, while Griffith and Ryle (1989) is an authoritative longer study. Ridley and Rush (1995) contains valuable essays on aspects of Parliament, and Rush (1990) considers the relationship between Parliament and pressure groups. Shell (1998) should be consulted on the upper house. Judge (1993) is an advanced work locating Parliament at the centre of an analysis of the UK state. For recent developments under the Blair government see the chapters by Blackburn and by Ryle in Blackburn and Plant (1999), by Cowley in Dunleavy *et al.* (2000), by Oliver in Jowell and Oliver (2000) and by Norton in Seldon (2001). The first stages of Lords reform are discussed in Richard and Welfare (1999).

On specific aspects of Parliament, the following articles can be recommended: Norton (1994, 1995a, 1995b), Alderman (1995), Berrington, (1995), Wright (1997) and Wakeham (2000).

Websites

Parliament (links to House of Commons and House of Lords): <www.Parliament.uk>./
Committee on Standards in Public Life: <www.public-standards.gov.uk>.

Chapter **15**

The law, politics and the judicial process

The rule of law	251
Law in England, Scotland and Europe	253
The courts	253
The judiciary	254
The police and policing	256
Human rights and civil liberties	258
Administrative law: protecting civil liberties and redressing grievances	259
Judicial review	260
Administrative tribunals	261
Statutory inquiries	262
The ombudsman system	263
The European Convention on Human Rights and the Human Rights Act	264

As we have seen (Chapter 11), the main functions or powers of the state are classified as legislative, executive and judicial. Thus the state is involved in law making (Chapter 14), executing the law through its ministers and public officials (Chapters 12 and 13), and adjudicating on the law when disputes arise between private citizens, or between the state and its citizens (this chapter). While some political theorists argued that these functions and the personnel exercising these functions should be kept strictly separate, and this separation of powers has been enforced as far as practicable in some constitutions (notably the US Constitution), this has not been the case in Britain. Yet if there is no clear separation of powers in the British system of government, the legal and judicial system is often considered to lie somehow outside and beyond politics.

Even so, in this chapter we argue that inevitably (and particularly in Britain) the law and politics are closely intertwined. The language of the law, and legal concepts and precepts, permeate the theory and practice of politics. Lawyers play a leading role in government and Parliament, and figure prominently in public bureaucracies and business. Court judgments can have significant political consequences, affecting both governments and the lives

of ordinary people. Judges themselves continue to wield massive power and influence, not just through the courts but in politics and government generally, and questions can and should be asked about their social and educational background, and their personal and political views. These are among the issues that we seek to address in this chapter. Questions can be also asked about the efficiency and effectiveness of the judicial system in Britain. Does it deliver justice, fairly, quickly and reasonably economically? How might it be improved? There are also important issues surrounding the enforcement of law and the pursuit of prosecutions by the police. Finally there are other vital questions about the protection of human rights and civil liberties in Britain, and the effectiveness of the various channels for securing redress of grievances against the state and public authorities.

The rule of law

The rule of law has long been considered one of the fundamental principles of the unwritten (or uncodified) British Constitution. It has, however, been variously interpreted from the time of the 19th century jurist, Dicey. Today, the rule of law involves a number of assumptions, although each of these involves some qualification or raises some questions.

- Everyone is bound by the law. No one is above the law. Ministers and public officials are subject to the law and have no authority to act beyond the powers conferred on them by law (the *ultra vires* principle). *However*, British ministers are usually in a strong position to change the law

---

Definition
The rule of law: the framework of legal rules guiding and restraining political behaviour in a liberal democratic society.

---

because of executive dominance of the Parliamentary legislative process, coupled with the doctrine of Parliamentary sovereignty and the supremacy of statute law.

- All persons are equal before the law. All citizens have legal rights and can have recourse to the law, and the law is supposed to treat all citizens on an equal basis. *However*, there are some doubts over equality before the law in practice. 'The law, like the Ritz Hotel is open to all.' Legal proceedings can be expensive, and although there is legal aid for those with limited means, it is restricted (e.g. it is not available for libel cases). Some would argue that the law in practice has systematically favoured property owners and established interests.

- Law and order must be maintained through the officials and institutional machinery of the state, which has a monopoly of the legitimate use of force within the state's borders. Thus citizens should be protected from violence and disorder, but should be forcibly restrained from taking the law into their own hands and acting as private vigilantes. *However*, the maintenance of law and order may sometimes lead to restrictions on individual liberty and human rights, such as restrictions on freedom of movement, and detention of suspects without trial. The maintenance of law and order became a key issue for Conservative governments after 1979 (Benyon and Edwards, in Dunleavy *et al.*, 1997: 328–35). More recently, the war against terror has been used to justify restrictions on civil liberties under the Blair government from 2001.

- Legal redress is provided for those with complaints against other individuals, organisations or the state. *However*, doubts are still expressed over the effectiveness of some of these remedies (see below).

- The law and legal processes and personnel should be independent and free from political interference. The courts are generally reckoned to be free from political pressures in practice. *However*, 'The most remarkable fact about the appointment of judges is that it is wholly in the hands of politicians' (Griffith, 1997). Labour proposals to create an independent Judicial Appointments and Training Commission (Brazier, in Blackburn and Plant, 1999) have yet to be implemented, and most

---

BOX 15.1

Types of law

Law is conventionally subdivided into a number of categories, such as criminal, civil and administrative.

Criminal law provides standards of conduct as well as machinery (police, courts system) for dealing with those who commit crimes. Crimes are normally classified as (1) against the state (treason, public order), (2) against the person (murder, assault, rape), and (3) against property (robbery, malicious damage). A successful *prosecution* in a criminal case leads to a *sentence* (e.g. fine, imprisonment, community service, probation).

Civil law is concerned with the legal relations between persons. Normally, proceedings in a civil court depend upon a *plaintiff* pursuing an action against a *defendant*, and they generally result in some *remedy*, such as damages, specific performance (where the defendant has to keep his or her side of the bargain), or a 'declaration' of the plaintiff's legal rights. Cases in criminal law have to be proved 'beyond reasonable doubt'; actions in civil law are decided on the 'balance of probabilities'.

Administrative law is 'the body of general principles which govern the exercise of powers and duties by public authorities' (Wade, 1988). Administrative law is more systematically developed on the European continent than in Britain. However, this sphere of law has grown considerably in Britain over the last century, as the state through legislation has intervened in aspects of social life hitherto untouched. Administrative law is concerned with the legal restraints that surround the activities of those who apply policy decisions. It is a key example of the interconnectedness of politics and law, with a variety of judicial and quasi-judicial institutions (the ordinary courts, tribunals, the ombudsman) supplying and applying a framework of rules within which public authorities act. It is centrally involved in the question of citizen rights and redress of grievances (see pp. 259–66).

judicial appointments remain the responsibility of the lord chancellor, who is a key member of the executive and legislature, as well as being head of the judiciary. As we have seen (Chapter 11) there is no strict separation of powers in Britain, and there are also strong links between politics and the law generally (see above).

Law in England, Scotland and Europe

It is difficult to summarise briefly the legal and judicial system in the United Kingdom, because there are marked differences within the state, particularly between English and Scottish law and their respective judicial systems. The English law and judicial system differs markedly from that prevailing over most of the European continent. While continental law is generally based on written codes deriving ultimately from Roman law, English law is based on common law, assumed to be the immemorial but uncodified law of the English people, and declared by judges in court cases. Thus the law is essentially contained in decisions on past cases which are binding on subsequent cases of a similar nature. Although judges are theoretically only declaring the law, in effect, particularly when new circumstances arise, they are in effect making new law. However, as we have already seen (Chapter 14), statute law is supreme over common law, so the law made by Parliament (and effectively by the government) overrides judge-made case law.

Scottish law is influenced by Roman law, in contrast with English law and like continental European law, and involves distinctive principles and practice and a separate system of administration. Although Scottish law, like English law, remains bound by the theoretical sovereignty of the Westminster Parliament, the devolution of legislative powers to the new Scottish Parliament has already led to some further significant divergences between English and Scottish law, and these differences seem likely to become more marked over time.

However, besides these difference between legal principles and practice within Britain, law in Britain is subject to growing supranational influence and control. Thus the British government ratified the European Convention on Human Rights in 1951, allowed individual petitions from 1966,

allowing British citizens to take their case to the court at Strasbourg, and finally passed a Human Rights Act allowing judges to declare that legislation is incompatible with the European Convention on Human Rights (see below). From 1973 the United Kingdom has been a member of the European Community (now Union), so that it is subject to EU law, and to the decisions of the European Court of Justice at Luxembourg (not to be confused with the European Court of Human Rights at Strasbourg, which formally is nothing to do with the European Union). Naturally European Union law is strongly influenced by the mainstream European continental legal tradition, and this in turn has had some impact on English law, particularly perhaps in the growth of judicial review (pp. 260–1). On top of this, the United Kingdom is increasingly influenced by international law and international conventions. It seems likely that over a period of time these international and cross-national influences will lead to more convergence between legal principles and systems

The courts

The UK system of courts is complicated. Scotland and Northern Ireland have their own rather different court systems. Most of what follows applies particularly to England and Wales (see Figure 15.1). Minor criminal cases are tried without a jury in magistrates courts, by legally qualified, full-time stipendiary (paid) magistrates in the cities, and by part-time lay magistrates advised by legally trained clerks elsewhere. More serious criminal cases for 'indictable' offences and appeals from the magistrates court are heard in the Crown Court before a judge and jury (unless the defendant pleads guilty, which is commonly the case, when a jury is not required). Appeals from conviction in the Crown Court are usually to the Criminal Division of the Court of Appeal. The Court of Appeal consists of Lords Justices of Appeal and other judges who are members ex officio. A further appeal on a point of law may be allowed to the House of Lords, sitting as a court composed of the lord chancellor and law lords.

A few minor civil cases are heard in magistrates courts but most minor cases are heard by county

courts, presided over by circuit judges. More important cases are heard in the High Court, which is split
into three divisions – Queen's Bench Division, dealing with common law, Chancery Division, dealing
with equity, and the Family Division, dealing with
domestic cases. Appeals from lower courts are heard
in the appropriate division of the High Court.
Appeals from the High Court can be made to the

Civil Division of the Court of Appeal, and from there
to the House of Lords, the final court of appeal.

The judiciary

Heading the judicial system are the lord chancellor
and other law officers, who are political appointments

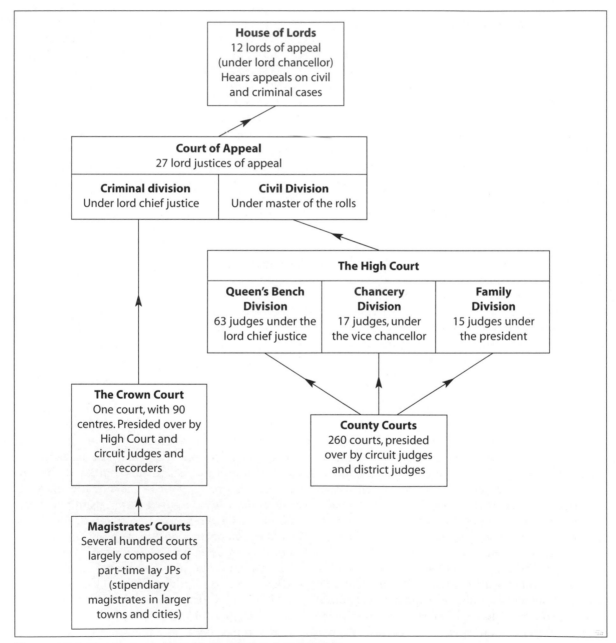

Figure 15.1 The system of courts in England and Wales

Definition
Judicial independence: the constitutional
principle that in order to protect individual
freedom the judiciary should be independent
from the other branches of government, the
executive and the legislature.

---

and members of the UK government or Scottish
executive. As they are appointed by the governing
party these law officers are often politically controversial figures. Below them are the law lords, the
Lords of Appeal in Ordinary, appointed by the Crown
on the advice of the prime minister, who remain
members of the Lords even if they relinquish their
judicial role. Some other senior judges are appointed
on the advice of the prime minister, while other High
Court judges, circuit judges and recorders are
appointed by the Crown on the advice of the lord
chancellor and drawn almost exclusively from the
ranks of senior barristers (Griffith, 1997). The division in the legal profession between the 4000 or so
barristers, who alone can plead cases in the higher
courts, and around 50,000 solicitors who deal directly
with the public, and among their other duties prepare
the cases for barristers to plead, is relatively unusual
in other countries. (Critics suggest it is a restrictive
practice which benefits lawyers rather than their
clients.) Once appointed, judges are virtually irre-
movable before the obligatory retirement age, which
was reduced from 75 to 70 in 1993, with the proviso
that the lord chancellor could authorise continuation
in office until 75 if it was 'in the public interest'
(Brazier, in Blackburn and Plant, 1999).

Judges are powerful and often controversial figures. They may become celebrated or notorious
public figures because of their sentences in criminal
cases, their comments during the course of a trial
and their observations in summing up (for which
they cannot be sued). Politicians and the media
have sometimes criticised judges for passing sentences that are considered too light. Judges in their
turn have been critical of mandatory sentences for
certain categories of crime, which reduce judicial
discretion. As law and order is an emotive political
issue, it is perhaps unsurprising that politicians and
judges are drawn into conflict. Because of their role
in declaring (and effectively making) the law, they
are inevitably helping to shape public policy and

influence public attitudes. In addition to their
judicial activities, judges because of their public
standing and legal expertise are often invited to
conduct or chair major enquiries into controversial
political areas (e.g. the Scott Inquiry on the arms to
Iraq scandal in 1996).

The orthodox view is that the judicial system is
impartial, symbolised by the blindfold figure of
Justice above the Central Criminal Court. Judges
balance the scales of justice fairly, without fear of
favour. The acknowledged impartiality of the judiciary legitimises the whole administration of justice in
the United Kingdom. Judges are moreover sometimes seen also as stout defenders of the rights and
freedoms of citizens against arbitrary and unjusti-
fied acts by governments and public authorities. The
growth of judicial review over the last 30 or 40 years
(see below) provides some support for this perspective. The 1998 Human Rights Act seems likely to
provide further opportunities for judicial intervention against government. Yet critics argue that
judges are almost inevitably biased in their attitudes
and decisions because of the kind of people they are.
Senior judges are drawn almost exclusively from the
ranks of the white male upper-middle class. (Table
15.1 demonstrates the continuing gender bias in the
higher levels of the judiciary.) Recruited normally
only after a long career at the bar and not obliged to
retire before 70, judges are also predominantly
elderly. While they may strive earnestly to appear
impartial, their own highly restricted and exclusive
social background is almost bound to affect their
assumptions and outlook, which is inevitably conservative with a small 'c' and, critics allege, generally
with a large 'C' also (Griffith, 1997). Indeed, some
judges almost seem to pride themselves in their
ignorance of mass culture and common language.

Table 15.1 Senior judges by gender, 1999

Level of judiciary	Male	Female
Lords of Appeal in Ordinary	12	0
Heads of Division	5	0
Lords Justices of Appeal	34	1
High Court Judges	89	8
Circuit Judges	522	36
Recorders	797	78

Source: Lord Chancellor's Department.

Photograph: PA Photos.

IN FOCUS 15.1 Cherie Booth

Prime Minister Tony Blair's wife Cherie Booth, seen here as she was sworn in as a QC in 1995, has pursued a successful career as a barrister, specialising in human rights cases. She reportedly has ambitions to be a High Court Judge, although these may have been adversely affected by her unwitting involvement at the end of 2002 with a former conman, engaged to help the purchase of a flat for the Blairs' eldest son at Bristol University.

More disquietingly, they sometimes appear more sympathetic to 'white collar' criminals than their working class counterparts, show marked leniency to men in rape cases, and send more blacks than whites to prison for longer periods for equivalent offences.

Trial by jury might afford some protection against the (perhaps largely unconscious) bias of the judiciary, but it is now used only in a minority of cases, and it is proposed to restrict it still further. It is an issue on which there are strong conflicting views. Jury trials are expensive and time-consuming (which, critics allege, is why some lawyers like them). It is also suggested that juries are not competent to decide on complex legal issues. Anecdotal evidence suggests that the deliberations of some juries may involve a muddled compromise between diametrically opposed gut reaction of individual jurors, even if most of the time they seem to follow the guidance of the judge. Yet juries can sometimes show an obstinate independence. A jury acquitted Clive Ponting, a civil servant at the Ministry of Defence, on a charge of breach of the Official Secrets Act in 1984, despite a very clear direction from the judge to convict. Ponting had leaked information to a Labour MP because he felt strongly that the Conservative government was deliberately misleading Parliament. However, in a not dissimilar case in November 2002 a jury found the former MI5 officer David Shayler guilty of breaches of the revised Official Secrets Act (1989), following a clear direction from the judge in the case (although the judge went on to impose a much lighter six-month sentence than the prosecution had demanded). Shayler had argued that he had broken the law in the public interest, to expose law-breaking by MI5, but there is no provision for such a 'public interest' defence in the terms of the Act. (See In Focus 19.1.)

The police and policing

All states require police to enforce the criminal law and prevent disorder. It is the most vulnerable members of society, such as the old, the young, women and minorities facing discrimination and prejudice who most need the protection of an efficient and impartial police force. Yet even more than judges, police appear to represent the coercive role of the state. Although a good police force is a requirement for any civilised nation, the police in many countries are feared and hated, while the chief of police has become a familiar figure of demonology. It says something for the British police that they long avoided this unenviable reputation. While fictional portrayals in novels, music hall, and early films and television occasionally showed police officers as bumbling, they were almost never portrayed as harsh or corrupt. Although this image of the friendly British bobby was perhaps somewhat idealised, it was not altogether a myth. Unusually, the ordinary police did not (and still do not) carry guns, indicating an uncommon degree of mutual trust between the police and the communities they served. This trust still survives in many parts of the country. However, confidence in the impartiality and efficiency of the police in Britain was never universal, and now appears lower than it used to be.

Just as there are issues over the possible bias of the judiciary, there are similar concerns over the police. This is not because the police are recruited from a very restricted social and educational elite (as could be said of judges). On the contrary, most police have been recruited from lower white collar and working class family backgrounds. In spite or perhaps even because of this, it is widely alleged that the police behave in a more deferential manner towards 'respectable' people. Many senior police officers are members of the secretive Freemasons, and socialise with the local elite. Moreover, it is suggested that they are less concerned, or less well equipped, to pursue 'white collar' crime.

Possible class bias has received rather less scrutiny of late than the alleged sexist, homophobic and racist attitudes of sections of the police. Women police officers (roughly one in six of the total force) do not fit easily into the rather 'macho' police culture, and have found it difficult to secure promotion to the highest levels in the force. This macho culture sometimes led in the past to the unsympathetic treatment of female victims of rape and male violence, with the police particularly reticent over intervention in 'domestic' issues, which was one factor in the reluctance of women to report rape and other crimes of violence. More recently, many police forces have made strenuous efforts to treat such crimes sympathetically and pursue them seriously. The same macho culture has sometimes contributed to a marked lack of sympathy and sometimes hostility towards homosexuals – with some forces energetically pursuing prosecutions of homosexuals, spying on activities in public lavatories and even acting as agents provocateurs in clubs. Again, attitudes are changing, perhaps more slowly, but sufficiently to allow a few police themselves to 'come out'.

Allegations of police racism have received considerable publicity in recent years. It has to be said that racism in the police largely reflects racism in wider society, although the problems have perhaps been more pronounced in some forces. Relatively few blacks and Asians have been recruited into the police (less than 2 per cent), and they have often found it difficult to obtain acceptance from their white colleagues and secure promotion. This has tended to reinforce the mutual suspicions, amounting sometimes to marked antipathy, between the police

and minority communities. There is substantial evidence in support of the long-standing allegation that members of ethnic minorities are far more likely to be stopped and searched than members of the majority white community. There is also evidence of routine racist abuse of blacks and Asians, and some cases of violent maltreatment of black suspects. Tragically there have also been high-profile police failures to secure convictions of those responsible for black victims of crimes of violence, most notably of Stephen Lawrence and Damiola Taylor. The Macpherson Inquiry into the handling of the murder of Stephen Lawrence led to acknowledgement that there was institutional racism in the Metropolitan Police and other police forces. (See Chapter 4 for a discussion of institutional racism, and Chapter 24 for policy to combat racism.)

The efficiency and effectiveness of the police have also been called into question by some high-profile miscarriages of justice and failures to solve crimes. Some miscarriages of justice were perhaps the consequence of intense media and public pressure on the police to secure convictions, leading to hasty and ill-prepared prosecutions, but in a few cases involving the extraction of dubious confessions from suspects and even the fabrication of evidence. Some former police officers have been jailed for corruption, undermining faith in the integrity of the police.

All this raises important concerns over the accountability and control of the police, an issue in many countries. It is considered important on the one hand that the police should be independent from direct control by party politicians, but on the other that they should be fully accountable to the public or their representatives. Squaring that circle is difficult and in Britain, police accountability and responsibility are somewhat blurred. The police used to be a local authority responsibility, but control by elected councillors, never very effective, particularly on operational issues, has progressively been weakened as a consequence of police force amalgamations and a reduced councillor element on police authorities. Today these are virtually quasi-autonomous local public bodies, often covering several local authorities, headed by chief constables with substantial operational control.

If local accountability is not particularly effective, what of accountability at the centre? Nationally, the minister in charge of crime and the police is the home secretary, but he only ever had direct responsibility for London's Metropolitan Police, and even this was transferred in 2000 to the Metropolitan Police Authority. Thus the home secretary is not answerable in the Commons for the conduct of police authorities and local police forces. Despite having overall responsibility for the police, successive home secretaries have found it difficult to pursue reorganisation and modernisation of the police. Most of the recommendations of the 1993 Sheehy Report have been resisted successfully by the police.

The machinery for handling complaints against the police has improved but remains controversial. Formerly, the investigation of complaints was wholly in the hands of the police themselves (although officers from another force might be brought it for serious cases). A Police Complaints Board was introduced to supervise the process in 1976. Following the 1984 Police and Criminal Evidence Act this was replaced by a beefed-up Police Complaints Authority, which supervises the investigation of serious complaints, although the actual investigation is still carried out by police officers, so it is still questioned whether this amounts to a genuinely independent inquiry.

Policing, together with law and order generally, can hardly be taken out of politics. Indeed it remains a hotly contested political issue, particularly so under Blair's Labour government, which has tried to counter the accusation that the party was 'soft on crime'. Blair first came to national prominence as shadow home secretary, with his sound bite that Labour would be 'tough on crime and tough on the causes of crime'. Labour's home secretaries – Jack Straw from 1997 and David Blunkett from 2001 – have been notably 'tough', and the Prime Minister has also made periodic interventions on law and order issues. Labour's claims of increased police recruitment and reduced crime rates have been criticised by the Conservative opposition. Statistics in such areas require careful interpretation. Increased reports of certain crimes may follow media publicity, yet there may also be substantial 'unreported crime' for a variety of reasons. Increases or decreases in police convictions may reflect changes in police activity. People's fears of some kinds of crime may be intensified by media campaigns or scare mongering, creating a 'moral panic'. Yet the fear of crime, and indeed the reality of crime, is sufficiently serious to blight lives. An impartial, efficient, well organised and accountable police service, trusted by the communities it seeks to protect, remains an obviously important objective for governments of any party.

Human rights and civil liberties

The hallmark of a liberal democratic state, it is often said, is the effectiveness with which a range of basic citizen rights or civil liberties is guaranteed. These rights or liberties have long been extolled by British people, and it is vital therefore to examine to what extent this confidence in the security of such rights is justified. Three points provide a context for this discussion:

- Virtually all British civil liberties stem from a fundamental principle: that people may do what they like so long as no law prevents them.
- Legal protections against infringements of this fundamental freedom in specific instances (e.g. freedom of expression, meeting, association and so on) have been established gradually throughout history and were not enshrined in any particular statute (until the Human Rights Act, which came into force in 2000).
- The question of citizen rights or liberties has both a positive and negative aspect: the right to do certain things and the right not to have certain things done to you.

Box 15.2 is concerned with the *civil rights* enshrined in the principle of classical liberal theory.

Definitions
Civil rights are rights to which individuals are entitled as citizens of a state. They may be embodied in a state's constitution.
Human rights are rights that it is assumed all human beings have by virtue of being human, and that should not be infringed.
Natural rights are similar to human rights. In political theory, natural rights are rights humans are assumed to possess in a state of nature and not through government. It is further assumed that governments are not entitled to deprive people of their natural rights.

BOX 15.2

Civil rights in the United Kingdom (and some limitations)

- **Political rights,** including the right to vote, guaranteed by Representation of the People Acts (1918, 1928, 1948, 1969).
- **Freedom of movement**, which includes the right to move freely within, and the right to leave, Britain (but note powers to detain suspected terrorists, and police powers to stop and search on suspicion).
- **Personal freedom**, including freedom from detention without charge (Magna Carta 1215, habeas corpus legislation in the 18th century – but note exceptions, especially detention without charge in Northern Ireland).
- **Freedom of conscience**, which includes the right to practice any religion, the right of parents to withdraw children from religious instruction in state schools, and the right of conscientious objection to conscription into the armed forces.
- **Freedom of expression**, which includes the right of individuals and the media to communicate information and express opinions; but note freedom of expression is limited by laws on treason, sedition, blasphemy, obscenity, libel, incitement to racial hatred, defamation, contempt of court and the Official Secrets Act.
- **Freedom of association and meeting**, which includes the right to meet, march and protest freely; but note some restrictions by the police and other public bodies on public order grounds, and restrictions on 'secondary picketing' in industrial disputes.
- **The right to property**, which includes the right to property and to use it, and not be deprived of it without due process; but note compulsory purchase orders, planning restrictions and the like.
- **The right to privacy:** a general right to privacy is contained in Article 8 of the European Convention of Human Rights, now incorporated into English law through the 1998 Human Rights Act; but note exceptions in the interests of state security, which are used to justify political surveillance, phone tapping and so on.
- **Rights at work**, including protection against unfair dismissal, the right to a satisfactory working environment, and freedom from racial and sexual discrimination (all embodied in a series of Acts of Parliament).
- **Social freedoms**, including freedom to marry and divorce, to practice contraception and seek abortions, and to practice homosexuality between consenting adults (contained in several post-war Acts of Parliament).

These rights have achieved gradual realisation in Britain, some from as long ago as Magna Carta (1215) but largely over the past two centuries (and they were given further protection in the Human Rights Act of 1998; see pp. 264–6).

Administrative law – protecting civil liberties and redressing grievances

How are the rights and freedoms set out in Box 15.2 in practice protected? What channels of redress do citizens, groups and organisations have if they feel they have been illegally, unfairly, unreasonably or arbitrarily treated by a public official or public authority? Of course, aggrieved citizens will commonly first pursue a complaint with the organisation directly concerned. They may ask to see the manager, or follow a publicised complaints procedure within the organisation. However there are a number of other recognised channels which may be taken to achieve a remedy.

Definition
Redress of grievances: the legitimate expectations by a citizen in a democratic society that complaints against public officials will be considered fairly and impartially, and that legal remedies for wrongs will be available should malpractice be found.

- contacting an elected representative – a member of Parliament or councillor
- appealing to the ordinary courts for judicial review and remedy
- appealing to an administrative tribunal
- providing evidence to a public inquiry
- complaining to an Ombudsman
- invoking the European Convention on Human Rights.

Judicial review

Recourse to the courts can often be expensive and time-consuming, and is normally only effective where a clear breach of the law is involved. Often citizens are complaining about the merits of a particular decision rather than a breach of the law. However, the ordinary courts have been interpreting more administrative behaviour as involving a breach of the law, and providing more effective remedies. While critics have often accused the judiciary of having a pro-establishment or pro-government bias (as perhaps in the Ponting case, see page 256), over the last 30 or 40 years the political role of the courts in scrutinising the actions of government and public officials has become steadily more important. In the opinion of one recent academic observer: 'the great success story of the past thirty years has been the remorseless march of administrative law calling governments to account in court' (Lee in Seldon and Kavanagh, 1994: 137).

The grounds on which an application for review can be made were summarised by Lord Diplock in the GCHQ case as illegality, procedural impropriety and irrationality, to which proportionality can now be added (Box 15.3).

There are however some significant limitations to judicial review in Britain.

- Judges work within the framework of Parliamentary sovereignty. Because Parliament is sovereign, judges cannot strike down legislation as unconsti-

---

> **Definition**
> **Judicial review:** the constitutional function exercised by the courts to review the legislation, regulations and acts of the legislative and executive branches of government.

---

tutional. Thus, in the UK 'judicial review' means preventing public authorities from doing anything which the ordinary law forbids or for which they have no statutory authority. By contrast, in codified constitutions such as the United States, the Supreme Court from the early days of the Republic assumed the role of striking down legislation deemed unconstitutional.

- Judges in Britain cannot pronounce on the merits of legislation – that is, they are not justified in substituting what they would have done for what Parliament enacted on a given occasion. Judges distinguish clearly between matters of policy, on which Parliament is the only authority, and matters concerning lawfulness, on which the courts may legitimately intervene. (However, judges can now declare that legislation appears incompatible with the European Convention on Human Rights: see pp. 264–6.)
- Judicial review can be subject to statutory exclusion.
- The courts themselves in particular types of case have imposed strict limitations on their own power to scrutinise executive action. These types of case relate to executive decisions made under the royal prerogative, and were defined by Lord Roskill in the GCHQ case (1985) to include the making of treaties, the defence of the realm, the prerogative of mercy, the grant of honours, the dissolution of Parliament and the appointment of ministers (Madgwick and Woodhouse, 1995: 88).

Judicial review has undergone considerable expansion in recent years. In 1974 there were 160 applications for review of administrative decisions by the courts; in 1980, 525; in 1984, 918; in 1991, 2089; and in 1996, about 3800. Leave to apply can be refused, and was granted in only a quarter of cases in 1996. There has also been an extension of the legal criteria judges are prepared to consider in helping them decide the legality of a particular decision. Before Pepper v. Hart (1992), the courts – for whatever reason – had observed a self-limiting rule not to refer to the records of Parliamentary debates in Hansard in order to clarify the meaning of an ambiguous statute, but in this case reference was made to a Parliamentary debate to establish the meaning of legislation (Loveland, 1993).

BOX 15.3
Grounds for judicial review

- **Illegality.** The principle here is that exercises of power by public authorities must have specific legal authority. The fundamental doctrine invoked by the courts is *ultra vires* (beyond their powers), which prevents public servants taking actions for which they have no statutory authority: in other words, acting illegally. When courts consider an administrative action under an enabling statute, they have a regard to whether the power in question was directly authorised by the statute or whether it may be construed as reasonably incidental to it. They can also consider whether a minister or other public authority abused power by using it for a purpose not intended by statute or whether, in exercising power, a decision maker took irrelevant factors into account or ignored relevant factors.
- **Procedural impropriety.** The courts also allow executive decisions to be challenged on the grounds that the procedures laid down by statute have not been followed. In reviewing administrative actions, the courts may also invoke the common law principles of natural justice. These are twofold: first, the rule against bias (no one to be a judge in his own cause); and second, the right to a fair hearing (hear the other side). Under the first

rule, administrators must not have any direct (including financial) interest in the outcome of proceedings; nor must they be reasonably suspected of being biased or of being likely to be biased. Justice must not only be done but manifestly must be seen to be done. The right to a fair hearing requires that no one should be penalised in any way without receiving notice of the case to be met and being given a fair chance to answer that case and put his or her own case.
- **Irrationality.** This ground for review dates back to a case in 1948 when the judge held that a decision made by an authority would be unreasonable if 'it were so unreasonable that no reasonable authority could have come to it'. Although the test of unreasonableness has been used since then to strike down local authority actions, its use is rare.
- **Proportionality.** The use of proportionality as a ground for judicial review in the 1990s reflects the increasing influence of European Union law on British judges, especially the European Court of Justice and the Treaty of Maastricht which contains within it the statement that 'Any action by the Community shall not go beyond what is necessary to achieve the objectives of the Treaty'.

Administrative tribunals

Appeal by an aggrieved citizen to an administrative tribunal may be more appropriate where a particular decision that does not involve a clear law is involved – for example the refusal of a grant, a pension or a license. Tribunals are a very important part of the British system of administrative justice. They are normally established by legislation and cover a wide range of functions, many of them in the field of welfare. There are tribunals for national insurance, pensions, housing, education, the National Health Service (NHS) and immigration. Claims arising out of injuries at work, industrial

disputes, unfair dismissal and redundancy are dealt with by industrial tribunals.

Tribunals are usually composed of a chairman with legal qualifications (often a solicitor) and two lay members representing interests related to the concerns of the particular tribunal. They are independent and not subject to political or administrative interference from the departments under whose aegis they usually work. Their functions may be described as quasi-judicial: to hear appeals against initial decisions of government agencies, or sometimes disputes between individuals and organisations. Their role is to establish the facts of each case and then apply the relevant legal rules to it; in the majority of instances, to decide what the statutory rights and entitlements of the aggrieved actually are. Except where the parties request privacy, tribunals hear cases in public. They provide simpler, cheaper, speedier, more expert and more accessible justice than the ordinary courts in their specific sphere of responsibility. It is possible to appeal against their decisions – normally to a superior court, tribunal or a minister. For a small number of tribunals, however, including the National Health Service Tribunal, the Social Security Commissioners and the Immigration Appeal Tribunal, no appeal is available.

The mode of operation of tribunals is determined by the Tribunals and Inquiries Act 1971. Under this Act, a Council on Tribunals has the functions of reporting on the tribunals under its supervision (to the lord chancellor and secretary of state for Scotland, and ultimately to Parliament); of hearing and investigating complaints against tribunals for members of the public; and of being consulted by the responsible minister before procedural rules for tribunals and inquiries are made. A second important provision of the Act concerns the giving of reasons for tribunals' decisions, another matter supervised by the Council on Tribunals. Most of the tribunals listed in the first schedule of the Act are required to supply oral or written reasons for their decisions (unless exempted by order of the chancellor after consultation with the Council). But tribunals are only required to give reasons if requested, and are not obliged to inform the parties of their right to request them.

The general trend of the last quarter of a century has been towards making the procedure of tribunals more judicial, but without forfeiting the advantages of tribunals over ordinary courts. These are greater informality, specialisation, capacity to conduct their own investigations and flexibility in terms of the formulation of reasonable standards in their own spheres. The Franks Committee on Administrative Tribunals and Inquiries (1957) recommended that tribunals move towards 'greater openness, fairness and impartiality'. Proceedings should be held in public and reasons for decisions should be given; the parties before tribunals should know in advance the case they had to meet, should have the chance to put their own case either personally or through representatives, and should be able to appeal against decisions; finally, proceedings should not only be impartial, through stronger safeguards regulating

their composition, but also be seen to be impartial by no longer being held on the premises of government departments. Under the supervision (since 1958) of the Council of Tribunals, the procedures of administrative tribunals have become both more uniform and more fair in many of the ways recommended by Franks, such as proper notice of hearings and of the case to be answered, rights to appeal and legal representation at hearings. Outstanding problems in the system relate primarily, although not solely, to the lack of appeal from certain tribunals (already noted); its limited extension (not all tribunals are included); and the particular condition (on request only) of the obligation to give reasons even if, in practice, tribunals do provide reasons.

Statutory inquiries

Often aggrieved citizens are concerned with some proposed rather than past action of a public authority – such as a new road, housing development or airport runway. The standard method for giving a hearing to objectors to a government proposal is the statutory inquiry. Virtually all legislation concerned with planning and land use makes provision for holding an inquiry. Most often, inquiries arise about new towns, housing, town and country planning, road, aviation and other transport developments, agriculture and health. Inquiries are usually held, then, within the context of government policy: notable examples are individual appeals against a compulsory purchase order for the acquisition of land for a specific purpose, or against the refusal of planning permission by a local authority. The procedure before, during and after the inquiry is regulated by rules laid down by the Tribunals and Inquiries Act 1971. Decisions of inquiries may be challenged on the grounds of either procedure or the substance of the decision in the High Court within six weeks of the decision. While affected third parties in land-use cases do not have legally enforceable rights, legislation governing planning usually protects their interests to a certain degree. Proposals have to be adequately publicised, for instance, and third parties have to be afforded the opportunity to state their cases before decisions are taken.

While realising the need not to impose unnecessary delays on inquiry procedure, the courts in hearing appeals from inquiry decisions have sought to safe-guard the rights of the public. For example, they have ruled that objectors at an inquiry should be able to take 'an active, intelligent and informed part in the decision-making process' (1977) and that they must be given 'a fair crack of the whip' (1976) in putting their case. The courts have received important support in this regard from the Council on Tribunals, which not only raises specific questions relating to inquiries with the chancellor, but also (as with tribunals) reports on their working, has the right to be consulted before procedural rules are made for them, and receives public complaints about them. How successful the courts and Council had been in bolstering the inquiry system as a bastion of democracy became a matter of increasing controversy during the 1980s, however, mainly as a result of disquiet about government handling of issues arising out of its proposals for the management of nuclear waste. Keen to avoid the delays and furore surrounding the 340-day inquiry into the Sizewell-B nuclear reactor (1985), the government in late 1985 proposed to limit the terms of reference to the Inquiry relating to the Dounreay fast-breeder reactor to the question of where to dump the waste, rather than to allow it to enter the debate about whether to dump or, as its critics preferred, store it. In 1994, after the government had given the go-ahead to the Thorp nuclear re-processing plant, the High Court rejected an attempt by environmentalists to force a public inquiry.

The ombudsman system

As well as legal rights, citizens have a more general right to a good standard of administration. The office of Parliamentary commissioner for administration (PCA) was established in 1967, after rising public concern that traditional Parliamentary channels were inadequate to protect the citizen against administrative abuse by government departments and agencies. The commissioner was commonly referred to as the 'Ombudsman', the term long used in Sweden, from where the idea came. His or her brief is to investigate, and if possible remedy, complaints by individuals and corporate bodies who feel that they have experienced 'injustice in consequence of maladministration' at the hands of central

government. Maladministration relates to the way in which decisions are made, and can include:

corruption, bias, unfair discrimination, harshness, misleading a member of the public as to his rights, failing to notify him properly of his rights or to explain the reasons for a decision, general high-handedness, using powers for a wrong purpose, failing to consider relevant materials, taking irrelevant material into account, losing or failing to reply to correspondence, delaying unreasonably before making a tax refund or presenting a tax demand or dealing with an application for a grant or license, and so on.

(de Smith and Brazier, 1990: 649)

Appointed by the Crown on the advice of the lord chancellor, the PCA enjoys an independent status similar to that of a High Court judge. His or her salary is fixed by statute and charged on the Consolidated Fund; he/she holds office 'during good behaviour' and can be removed on addresses from both Houses of Parliament. There is a staff of about 55 largely drawn from the civil service. During investigations, which are conducted in private, the PCA can call for the relevant files of the department concerned; as a matter of course, he or she informs the head of department, and any civil servant involved, of the investigation. The PCA possesses the powers to investigate a matter thoroughly: he or

---

Definition
Ombudsman is a term which originates from Scandinavia, and is used in Britain to denote an official (male or female) who is responsible for dealing with complaints against government (the Parliamentary Commissioner for Administration, local authorities (Local Commissioners of Administration) and the NHS (Health Service Commissioner). The Ombudsman can normally only deal with 'maladministration', meaning that there was something wrong in the way the decision was taken (neglect, bias, delay etc.). The term has sometimes officially or unofficially been extended to other complaints officers in both the public and even the private sectors.

she can administer oaths and compel the attendance of witnesses as well as the presence of documents.

Complainants have no right of direct access to the PCA, but must approach him or her through an MP. This was because MPs were concerned that the PCA should supplement rather than supplant their own historic role in securing redress of constituents' grievances. Normally only a small proportion of complaints are accepted for investigation – complaints are rejected if they do not involve maladministration, or if there is a right of appeal to a tribunal. However, the majority of complaints investigated are found to be justified. The PCA issues a report on each investigation to the referring MP, with a copy to the department involved. Where maladministration is found, a department is expected to correct it – for example, by issuing an apology or financial recompense to the aggrieved person – but the ombudsman has no power to compel it to do so. Where, as occasionally happens, the department refuses to correct an injustice, the PCA may first bring pressure to bear on it by means of the Commons Select Committee on the PCA, and if this fails, can lay a Special Report pointing out the unresolved injustice before both Houses of Parliament.

Initially limited to the investigation of maladministration in central government, the ombudsman system was later enlarged by the addition of ombudsmen for Northern Ireland (1969), the National Health Service (1973), and local government in England and Wales (1974) and Scotland (1976). Unlike the position with regard to the PCA, direct access to these ombudsmen is allowed (in the case of local government, only since 1988), and both the health and the local government commissioners receive a much larger volume of complaints than the PCA. As with the PCA, however, neither local nor health commissioners have any enforcement powers, although in Northern Ireland a complainant does have legal redress where a legitimate grievance is found, being able to apply to the county court for an appropriate remedy. If a local authority in mainland Britain chooses not to comply with an adverse report by a local ombudsman after various efforts have been made to persuade it, the ombudsman can require it to publicise the reasons for non-compliance (Thompson, 1993: 19–20).

Ombudsmen have made a less dramatic impact on British public administration than their early advocates hoped, because of lack of public awareness of the system, and inadequate powers of enforcement. The only powers of the ombudsmen against a recalcitrant public authority are those of publicity. However, most of their recommendations are accepted and implemented by the departments and authorities concerned, and they have secured on occasion substantial compensation for victims of maladministration. More usually small-scale payments in compensation follow a report, and sometimes just an apology.

The European Convention on Human Rights and the Human Rights Act

The European Court of Human Rights has long played a part in upholding and enlarging civil liberties in Britain, although between 1966 and 1997 it did so in a somewhat roundabout way. The UK ratified the European Convention on Human Rights in 1951 and allowed individuals to petition the Court from 1966. Although these were not legal rights in Britain and therefore not enforceable in British law, they turned out to be an important influence on civil rights. British courts could take note of the convention and presume Parliament did not intend to legislate inconsistently with it. Moreover, the UK government normally complied with judgments of the European Court. However, these rights were not enforceable in British law because, although Britain renewed its ratification of the convention every year, unlike the other countries who have signed the document it did not incorporate the convention into British law until 1998. Hence British citizens were not able to use the convention to appeal to British courts when their rights were infringed. They were able to appeal to the European Court at Strasbourg, but only after they had tried and failed to find remedies in the British courts. No legal aid was available, and the Court took a long time to reach its judgments – an average of five years for a case to move through the entire process. In all, down to 1997, the Court pronounced on 98 British cases and found violations of human rights in 50 of them. (The UK has lost more cases before the European

Court than any other signatory state.) The decisions of the European Court were not, strictly speaking, enforceable in the UK, but the UK government agreed to respect the decisions made by the court, and in practice its verdicts were observed, normally by changing British law accordingly. (Box 15.4 lists the rights available under the European Convention on Human Rights and its Protocols.)

Following its 1997 manifesto promise to incorporate the European Convention on Human Rights into British law, the Labour government passed a Human Rights Act in 1998, which came into force in 2000 (Wadham, in Blackburn and Plant, 1999; Lester, in Jowell and Oliver, 2000; Wadham and Mountfield, 2000). This means that British citizens who consider that their rights have been infringed are now able to take their cases to British courts rather than to the European Court of Human Rights in Strasbourg. The Act makes it illegal for public authorities, including the government, the

courts and public bodies discharging public functions, to act in a way incompatible with the European Convention on Human Rights (Box 15.4).

In theory, the Human Rights Act preserves Parliamentary sovereignty. Judges do not have the power to strike down Acts of Parliament (as they do in Canada, for example). Instead, they are able to declare a law 'incompatible with the Convention', which should prompt the government and Parliament to change the law through new fast-track procedures. However, Bogdanor (in Seldon, 2001: 146–8) argues that the Act 'alters considerably the balance between Parliament and the judiciary' and enables judges 'to interpret parliamentary legislation in terms of a higher law, the European Convention'. Thus 'the Human Right Act in effect makes the European Convention the fundamental law of the land'. The argument is contentious. Morris (also in Seldon, 2001: 378) seems sceptical of the argument that 'major social and political change will be driven

---

BOX 15.4

Rights under the European Convention on Human Rights and its Protocols (summarised)

Convention

2. Right to life.
3. Freedom from torture or inhuman or degrading treatment or punishment.
4. Freedom from slavery or forced labour.
5. Right to liberty and security of person.
6. Right to a fair trial by an impartial tribunal.
7. Freedom from punishment for an act which did not constitute a criminal offence under law when it was committed.
8. Right to respect for family and private life, home and correspondence.
9. Freedom of thought, conscience and religion.
10. Freedom of expression.
11. Freedom of peaceful assembly and association, including the right to join a trade union.
12. Right to marry and found a family.
13. Right to an effective remedy before a national authority (not included in Human Rights Act 1998).
14. Freedom from discrimination on grounds of sex, race, colour, language, religion etc.

Protocol No. 1

1. Right to peaceful enjoyment of possessions.
2. Right to education. Parental right to the education of their children in conformity with their own religious and philosophical convictions.
3. Right to free elections with a secret ballot.

Protocol No. 4

(not ratified by UK, nor in Human Rights Act 1998)

1. Freedom from imprisonment for debt.
2. Freedom of movement for persons.
3. Right to enter and remain in one's own country.
4. Freedom from collective expulsion.

There are other Protocols which are yet to be ratified by the UK and not included in the Human Rights Act (Wadham and Mountfield, 2000: 142–8). However, Protocol 6 (abolition of death penalty except in time of war) is included in the Human Rights Act 1998.

by judges rather than legislators', pointing out that 'there is little evidence of this in those countries in which the Convention has long been domestically incorporated'.

While it is perhaps too early to assess the longer term impact of the Human Rights Act on the British constitution and the relations between the judiciary and the legislature, it has certainly had some significant immediate implications for British politics and law. The European Court of Human Rights declared in 1998 that some provisions in the Representation of the People Act limiting election expenditure violated the convention, requiring the rewriting of UK legislation on political funding. In 2001 the Court upheld an action by residents in the Heathrow area which claimed that night flights involved an infringement of a basic human right (to sleep). Yet ironically the Human Rights Act has not prevented some British citizens from being deprived of what is generally regarded as a far more basic and important right. Following the attack on the World Trade Center on 11 September 2001, the British government introduced emergency legislation to deal with terrorism, including powers to hold terrorist suspects without trial, which would normally infringe article 5 of the convention – the right to liberty. However article 15 allows the suspension of rights in an emergency. How long the courts are prepared to countenance such drastic measures to combat the threat of global terrorism remains to be seen.

Further reading

On key themes covered by this chapter, including the rule of law, the executive and the courts and redress of grievances, see Madgwick and Woodhouse (1995), de Smith and Brazier (1994) and Hood-Phillips, Jackson and Leopold (2001).

On the judiciary, see Griffith (1997). On relations between the executive and the judiciary see articles by Woodhouse (1995, 1996, 1997) and Loveland (1997).

On rights, and the debate leading up to the Human Rights Act 1998, see Klug, Starmer and Weir (1996), the special issue of *Political Quarterly* (1997), and Freeman (1997). Contrasting views of the Human Rights Act can be found in the comments of Bogdanor and Morris in Seldon (2001). Further background and critical analysis in provided by the Director of Liberty, John Wadham (in Blackburn and Plant, 1999) and by Lester (in Jowell and Oliver, 2000). A more detailed account, including key texts, is provided in Wadham and Mountfield (2000).

Part **IV**

MULTI-LEVEL GOVERNANCE: GOVERNMENT AND POLITICS ABOVE AND BELOW WHITEHALL AND WESTMINSTER

Part III of this book has concentrated almost exclusively on British central government – government and politics around the world of Whitehall and Westminster. As far as older books on British government were concerned, this was almost all that mattered. After all, the United Kingdom was a unitary state, and the Westminster Parliament was deemed sovereign. Although there was local government, this was clearly subordinate, constitutionally and in reality, to central government. In terms of the constitution, and it appeared in terms of real power, there was little below Whitehall and Westminster and nothing above.

However today British government and politics appear far more fragmented, multi-layered and complex. Fragmentation in government and policy making has taken place across two dimensions, vertical and horizontal. First, there is now a substantial and increasing input into British government and politics from both above and below Westminster and Whitehall – most conspicuously from the European Union (Chapter 15) on the one hand and from devolved national and regional governance (Chapter 16) and local governance (Chapter 17) on the other. Policies that affect the people of Britain are now made at a number of levels, even if the UK level remains much the most important.

But besides this obvious vertical fragmentation of the policy making process, there is secondly also a horizontal fragmentation which cuts across each layer of this new multi-level governance. Government at each level no longer appears singular and monolithic (Whitehall or the council) but diverse and fragmented, with a mass of departments, quangos, executive agencies competing and cooperating. Increasingly the label 'governance' is preferred because it encompasses, not just government institutions, but the whole political process which surrounds decision making. Much of this process requires cooperation between various government departments and agencies, the private sector, voluntary bodies and community interests. Sometimes it involves formal public–private partnerships or elaborate policy networks. Moreover these levels of governance are overlapping and interdependent. It is generally impossible to divide up neatly services and policy areas and assign them exclusively to a particular level of government.

Today a new British state seems to be in the process of emerging, yet its final shape is far from clear. Nor has it altogether yet displaced the traditional framework of British government outlined in Part III. In Chapter 19 we explore the complexity that is modern British governance, and examine various ways in which this new emerging state might be characterised.

Chapter **16**

Britain and the European Union

The European ideal, 1945–58   269
Britain and Europe, 1945–73   270
The development of the European ideal:
  integration and enlargement   271
Britain and Europe from 1973 to the
  present   273
The European Union: superstate or inter-
  governmental organisation?   276
The institutions and processes of the
  European Union   277
The impact of the European Union on the
  British state and government   281
The impact of EU membership on
  British politics: parties, pressure groups
  and voters   283
The impact of the European Union on UK
  policies   285
The future of the European Union and
  the relationship between the UK and
  the EU   286

Among the other levels of government beyond Whitehall and Westminster that are now affecting the everyday lives of people living in Britain, the most important is the European Union, an organisation that did not exist even in embryo at the end of the Second World War, and which the United Kingdom only joined in 1973. Yet it should already be clear from the discussion of many topics in earlier chapters that the European Union has already had massive implications for British politics. It is now necessary to provide in this chapter some more detailed analysis of the European Union, its development, institutions and processes, in order to understand more fully the often problematic relationship between Britain and Europe, and the implications of UK membership of the EU for the British state, its politics and its policies. We will conclude with a brief examination of the future of the EU, and the UK's role within it.

The European ideal, 1945–58

The new Europe that emerged in the second half of the 20th century was driven by both politics and economics, but political considerations were paramount. Centuries of division and conflict within Europe, culminating in the death and destruction of the Second World War, had convinced many of the need to end old antagonisms and promote instead a new era of cooperation, peace and prosperity. The wastes of war were all too apparent in 1945. Most of Europe had suffered massively from a conflict which affected civilians as much as or more than the armed forces, and had endured the humiliation and privations of defeat and occupation. A substantial part of the industrial capacity and social fabric of Europe had been destroyed physically. Millions of refugees were left homeless and starving. Both those countries that were technically victors in 1945 and those that had clearly been vanquished faced an uncertain economic and political future.

The prospects for democracy in the new and restored states emerging from the ashes of war seemed precarious, particularly in the two countries that had been at the centre of the conflict. Although France had been accorded the status of a partner in final victory, this hardly obscured the reality of the military and political collapse of France in 1940, or the enduring problems of the French economy, or the continuing depth and bitterness of political and social divisions. Indeed many of these problems remained only too apparent throughout the brief and troubled existence of the Fourth French Republic which was established in the aftermath of war but never managed to secure legitimacy. Germany seemed in far worse shape, after 12 years of Nazi dictatorship, followed by military defeat and the destruction of its economy. The war's end involved occupation and division of a much reduced Germany which was additionally burdened by millions of German refugees from Poland, the Baltic states and Czechoslovakia.

It was partly because of the scale of the problems faced by Europe in general, and France and Germany in particular, that many sought Franco–German reconciliation and closer European integration, to prevent any recurrence of the scale of the disasters that had overwhelmed Europe twice in 30 years. Thus the prime motive of the architects of what is now the European Union was the prevention of war. While it was certainly hoped that closer European integration would help rebuild agricultural and industrial production, a principal objective was to lock the economies of France and Germany so closely together to render another war between them impossible, as Robert Schuman argued in introducing the Schuman Plan in 1950. This was a strong motive also for other European states (such as Belgium) that had suffered from Franco–German conflict.

Robert Schuman and Jean Monnet, the founding fathers of the new Europe, did not imagine that a closer European union could be established quickly or easily. Rather, they envisaged that an on-going process of integration of key policy areas would lead over time to closer union, as states and peoples experienced the practical benefits of cooperation. Thus the European Coal and Steel Community (ECSC) of 1952 established a supranational body, the High Authority (forerunner of the European Commission), with extensive powers to regulate the coal and steel industries in the member states. The same countries as formed the ECSC, France, Germany, Italy and the Benelux states, went on sign the Treaty of Rome in 1957, inaugurating the European Economic Community (EEC), which established a customs union with internal free trade and a common external tariff, and the European Atomic Energy Authority (Euratom). The most important common policy established in the early years was the Common Agricultural Policy (CAP), which initially absorbed three-quarters of the EEC budget, although subsequently increasing funds were devoted to social and regional policies.

Britain and Europe, 1945–73

British governments initially took no part in these developments. Geography and history have combined to keep Britain both part of, and apart from, Europe. While the Channel has continued to provide a physical and symbolic barrier, Britain has remained closely linked with western Europe in terms of its religion, culture, trade and politics. Despite growing global interests from the 16th century onwards, concerns over the balance of power on the continent and rivalry with other European states over trade and colonisation involved Britain periodically in coalitions and wars with its continental neighbours, culminating in the World Wars of the 20th century.

At the end of the Second World War, however, British concerns and interests appeared different from those of the rest of Europe. Britain retained the illusion of great power status, one of the 'big three' that had defeated Nazi Germany, with a still extensive overseas empire. Its political system was stable, its economic and financial interests remained world-wide. Not having experienced the miseries of defeat and occupation, British politicians and the British public generally saw no imperative need for closer economic and political integration with other European states. British politicians were certainly concerned about the future of Europe. However, Britain's Empire and Commonwealth, coupled with the transatlantic 'special relationship' with the USA, had strong conflicting influences on Britain in the period immediately after the Second World War (see Chapter 3). Although Winston Churchill called for 'a kind of United States of Europe' in a speech at Zurich in 1946, he went on to make it plain that Britain would be among the 'friends and sponsors of the new Europe' rather than an integral part of it. Thus although British governments took a generally benevolent interest in the moves towards closer European integration by their continental neighbours, they remained aloof from the establishment of the European Coal and Steel Community in 1952 and the European Economic Community in 1958 by France, Germany, Italy and the Benelux countries. Indeed, the UK government took the lead in establishing a rival trading block, the European Free Trade Association.

Political and economic developments combined to provoke a rapid reassessment of Britain's relations with Europe from the mid-1950s onwards. The rapid liquidation of the British Empire was one factor. The opposition of the USA and even some Commonwealth countries to the disastrous 1956 Anglo-French Suez expedition was a defining moment, which destroyed lingering illusions of Britain's world power status. Continuing economic problems evidenced by low growth, adverse trade balances and recurring sterling crises contrasted with the strong economic performance of the EEC countries. Thus Harold Macmillan's Conservative government sought entry in 1961. Diplomatic negotiations dragged on into 1963, when they were abruptly terminated with the veto of the French President, General de Gaulle. Wilson's Labour government met a similar rebuff when it tried to enter the EEC in 1967, and it was only the removal of de Gaulle from power that finally enabled Heath's Conservative government to join the EC, along with Ireland and Denmark, in 1973.

The development of the European ideal: integration and enlargement

The history of the European Union can be presented as a triumphal process towards ever deeper European integration and a steady expansion in membership, population and boundaries. Yet the progress has often been slow and uneven, while there has been some increasing tension between enlargement and integration, between widening and deepening the European Community/Union.

One indication of the success of any club is the enthusiasm of new members to join it. By that token the European Union has been very successful. There has been a progressive enlargement of what began as

the European Economic Community in 1958. The original six members were joined by three more in 1973, the United Kingdom, Ireland and Denmark. Greece joined in 1981, and Spain and Portugal in 1986. German reunion following the fall of the Berlin wall led to a significant increase in the size of the German state and the population of the EU. In 1995 Austria, Finland and Sweden joined, bringing the number of member states to 15.

Since then a number of other European states, many from the former Soviet-dominated Eastern Europe, have applied to join, and accession negotiations for a number of these are at an advanced stage, leading to the imminent prospect of a European Union of 25 states and subsequently up to 30 states. The enthusiasm of states to join the European Union may surprise British Euro-sceptics. However, for the original members European cooperation has largely delivered the peace and prosperity they had hoped for. The EU remains popular not only with the original six founding states, but among a substantial majority of the peoples of states who joined from 1973 onwards. Ireland has prospered economically. Greece, Spain and Portugal, previously politically isolated as a consequence of their dictatorial regimes, have acquired greater political stability as well as economic prosperity since becoming members of the European club. Many of the former Eastern European states, and new states established following the collapse of the USSR, similarly hope for increased political stability and economic growth from being locked into the western European political and economic system.

Table 16.1 Europe: what's in a name?

The European Coal and Steel Community (ECSC)	Precursor of EC/EU established in 1952 following Treaty of Paris
The European Economic Community (EEC)	Established 1958, along with Euratom (European Atomic Energy Community) after 1957 Treaty of Rome
The Common Market	Term used in Britain to describe the EEC in its early years. The Rome Treaty did involve a Common Market, but promised more.
The European Community (or the European Communities)	Technically resulted from merger of ECSC, EEC and Euratom in 1965
The European Union	Term adopted after the Treaty of the European Union (TEU or Maastricht Treaty) 1992

BOX 16.1
Enlargement of the European Community/Union, 1952–2003

Dates	Countries
1952, 1957 (Original members of ECSC and EEC	Belgium, France, Germany, Italy, Luxembourg, Netherlands
1973 (First enlargement)	Denmark, Ireland, United Kingdom
1981	Greece
1986 ('Southern enlargement' – with Greece)	Portugal, Spain
1995	Austria, Finland, Sweden
Applicant states as at January 2003	Bulgaria, Cyprus, Czech Republic, Estonia, Hungary, Latvia, Lithuania, Malta, Poland, Romania, Slovakia, Slovenia, Turkey

Current members as of December 2002

Applicant states

Source: adapted from Nugent, 2002.

Alongside the continuing enlargement of the European Community/Union there have also been some uneven but significant steps towards closer integration of the existing member states. However, progress was sometimes rendered more difficult by the unanimity rule – key developments require the full consent of all member states and can be prevented by the veto of any member. Thus after the early progress of the European Communities, the pace of European integration slowed in the 1970s and early 1980s. Crucially, non-tariff barriers to trade still impeded the development of a full European internal market. It was only in 1986, with agreement on the Single European Act, that a timetable was finally agreed for the elimination of non-tariff barriers to trade and competition by 1992.

The 1992 Maastricht Treaty or Treaty of the European Union (TEU) marked further progress towards closer integration, particularly a timetable towards monetary union and the adoption of a Social Chapter by 11 of the 12 member states. It also involved agreement on a common foreign and security policy, and cooperation on justice and home affairs. The new momentum towards closer integration was maintained with Treaties of Amsterdam (1997) and Nice (2000) and particularly with the formal inauguration of the common currency, the euro, in 1999, and the introduction of notes and coins to replace national currencies in 12 member states in 2002.

Yet there are some doubts on the capacity of the EU to absorb so many new states without impeding further progress towards closer integration. Each of the past enlargements shifted the balance of power and interests within the EC/EU, and each put some strain on existing institutions and policies. At the very least, this latest enlargement will require an extensive modification of existing institutions and procedures (see below), otherwise there could be total gridlock as each member state defends what it considers to be its own vital interests, if necessary by using the veto. Beyond that, some fundamental adjustments to existing policies appear necessary. The Common Agricultural Policy could not be extended in its present form to the largely poorer new applicant states without adding substantially to its already sizeable financial burden on the EU budget. A massive redirection of social and regional funds will be necessary to reduce the increased disparities between regions following

Photograph: Robert Leach.

IN FOCUS 16.1
Europe's new currency

Although the single European currency was officially launched in 1999 it did not become a reality for most Europeans until January 2002 when euro notes and coins replaced national currencies in 12 EU member states. Britons travelling to the Eurozone have become familiar with the new money, which is also now accepted in some large British shops. This greater familiarity with the euro did not initially persuade British public opinion that the time was ripe to give up the pound.

enlargement, and this is likely to have adverse effects on the regional aid currently directed to some of the poorer regions in existing member states, including Britain. As some of the new member states seem unlikely to qualify immediately for membership of the euro, it seems likely that a 'two speed' or 'variable geometry' Europe could be the consequence for some time to come.

Britain and Europe from 1973 to the present

British entry into the European club failed to settle the issue of UK relations with Europe, for the British conversion to the EC was never wholehearted, at either elite or mass level. In so far as Community membership was sold to the British public it was on the basis of presumed economic benefits – higher growth and living standards. The European

Community's political implications, evident from the pronouncements of its leading founding figures and in the Treaty of Rome, were largely ignored. This was not (as has sometimes been suggested) a deliberate conspiracy by British governments to keep people in the dark. It simply reflected a widespread British view that joining the European 'Common Market' (as it was then widely called in Britain) was essentially a 'bread and butter' issue – quite literally in the case of some opponents who made much of the effect of entry on the price of a standard loaf and a pound of butter.

Yet the economic benefits of UK entry were not immediately obvious. Partly this was because the UK joined too late to influence the shape and early development of the EC. Thus the UK had to sign up to rules designed by others to meet the economic needs of the original six member states. The British economy with its relatively tiny agricultural sector was unlikely to benefit significantly from the Common Agricultural Policy which then absorbed three-quarters of the EC budget. Moreover 1973, the year of UK entry, was also the year of the energy crisis that signalled the end of the post-war economic boom. While the original members of the Community had enjoyed huge growth rates and sharply rising living standards which ensured the continuing popularity of European integration, the early years of UK membership were accompanied by 'stagflation' rather than the promised sustained higher rates of growth. Britain had joined the party too late.

Thus Community membership remained politically controversial in Britain. The only mainstream political party consistently in favour were the Liberals, and subsequently Liberal Democrats (and even they have contained a few dissidents). The bulk of the Labour Party had opposed entry in 1973, and the return of a Labour government under Wilson in 1974 entailed a renegotiation of the terms of entry and a referendum in 1975, resulting in a two-thirds majority for staying in. Yet although the government officially recommended a Yes vote, a third of the Cabinet campaigned on the opposite side, and Labour remained deeply divided on the issue. On the British left the European Community was widely perceived as a rich man's capitalist club, providing the economic underpinning for NATO. By 1983, and back in opposition, Labour was pledged to withdrawal from Europe without even a prior referendum.

Most Conservatives were then far more enthusiastic about Europe. After all, Britain's membership of the EC was a Conservative achievement, supported in her early years by Margaret Thatcher who, although she had belligerently demanded and obtained a rebate from the EC budget, went on to sign and endorse the 1986 Single European Act. It was only towards the end of her premiership that Thatcher's own reservations on European integration and the threat it presented to Britain's national sovereignty became clearer.

To try and suppress nationhood and concentrate power at the centre of the European conglomerate would be highly damaging...We have not successfully rolled back the frontiers of the state in Britain only to see them reimposed at a European level with a European superstate exercising a new dominance from Brussels.

Margaret Thatcher, speech at Bruges, 1988

Even so, Thatcher (rather reluctantly) agreed to UK entry to the Exchange Rate Mechanism in October 1990, and it was only after her fall from power soon afterwards that her opposition to the whole European project intensified. John Major, her successor, seemed more enthusiastic about Europe:

My aim for Britain in the Community can be simply stated. I want us to be where we belong. At the very heart of Europe. Working with our partners in building the future.

John Major, speech, 1991

Definition
Euro-sceptics is a term commonly applied to those who are sceptical or hostile towards the UK's involvement in further European integration (including the single currency). Some Euro-sceptics are opposed to Britain's continuing membership of the EU. Those who positively support the UK's involvement with European Union are variously described as 'Europhiles', 'Euro-enthusiasts' or simply 'Europeans'.

However, the Maastricht Treaty was to mark further divisions with Britain's European partners, as John Major's government negotiated an opt-out from the 'Social Chapter' and monetary union (see below). Indeed, the problems that Major's government encountered over Britain's brief membership of the Exchange Rate Mechanism and the ensuing catastrophe of 'Black Wednesday' in 1992 (see Chapter 3) fuelled increasing Euro-scepticism on the Conservative benches, at the same time as the Labour Party was becoming more favourable to the European Union, and, in principle, towards European monetary integration. Thus the two major parties had apparently reversed their positions compared with 20 years previously.

Even so, although Blair came to power with an apparently more positive attitude to the European Union and his government quickly signed up to the Social Chapter, Britain remained on the sidelines when the euro was officially launched in 1999. While the Prime Minister made increasingly positive noises, suggesting his government was committed to joining the Euro in principle, his Chancellor sounded a more cautious note with his five economic tests, and entry was effectively ruled out for the first term. Following the second landslide election victory in 2001, over a Conservative Party fighting to 'Save the pound', there were predictions that Labour would seek entry early in the new Parliament. Yet the government continued to procrastinate, partly for economic reasons but perhaps more for political reasons – they were insufficiently confident that they could win a referendum on the issue in the face of public apathy and media hostility. Whatever the reasons, the fact remained that Britain was once more out of step with most of Europe, and

---

Table 16.2 Time chart: key dates in development of the EC/EU and in UK involvement

1950	The Schuman Declaration (or Schuman Plan)
1951	Treaty of Paris to establish the European Coal and Steel Community
1952	European Coal and Steel Community instituted
1957	Treaty of Rome to establish European Economic Community (EEC) and Euratom
1958	EEC and EURATOM initiated (France, Germany, Italy, Benelux countries)
1960	Rival European Free Trade Association (EFTA) established
1961	UK (Macmillan, Conservative Government), Ireland and Denmark apply to join EEC
1963	French veto (President de Gaulle) terminates entry negotiations
1967	Second UK attempt to join EEC under Labour government under Harold Wilson leads to renewed French veto
1970	Conservative government under Heath initiates third attempt to join EEC
1973	UK, Ireland and Denmark join the EEC. Membership enlarged from six to nine states
1974	Labour government (Wilson) begins renegotiation of terms of entry
1975	Labour government recommends 'Yes' vote in referendum on whether UK should stay in EC. Two-thirds of voters vote 'Yes'.
1979	First direct elections for European Parliament
1981	Greece joins the European Community
1983	Labour Party pledged to UK withdrawal from EC without a referendum
1986	Spain and Portugal join the EC, Single European Act signed.
1990	UK (Thatcher government) joins European Exchange Rate Mechanism (ERM)
1992	Maastricht Treaty (TEU). John Major secures opt-out from 'Social Chapter' and monetary integration. 'Black Wednesday': UK forced out of ERM
1995	Austria, Finland, Sweden join European Union
1997	Amsterdam Treaty (in force 1999). Labour government signs up to Social Chapter
1999	The euro becomes the official currency for 11 EU member states. European Commission resigns following fraud and corruption allegations
2000	Nice Treaty
2001	Conservatives (under Hague) fight election campaign to 'Save the Pound'
2002	Euro notes and coins replace national currencies in 12 EU member states

not part of what is perhaps the most significant move towards European integration since the Treaty of Rome was signed in 1957.

However it was not simply the euro that continued to divide the UK from Europe. Despite acceptance of the Social Chapter, the Blair government continued to champion flexible labour markets in the face of the more corporatist approach of the European Union and most other member states. It is sometimes suggested that New Labour prefers what has come to be called the Anglo-Saxon or American free market model of capitalism rather than the more interventionist Rhineland or European alternative.

More significant perhaps are the differences that have emerged over foreign policy since 11 September 2001, with Blair's Britain emerging as the closest ally of President Bush's global campaign against terrorism, in marked contrast to increasing European reservations over American policy in general, and towards Iraq and Israel in particular. This has reawakened doubts over Britain's European credentials. The old tensions between Britain's relationship with Europe and its 'special relationship' with the USA that have plagued previous governments have re-emerged. Thus the UK is still widely perceived as an awkward partner, at a time when the European Union is taking decisive steps towards closer integration and substantial enlargement.

Yet British reservations over the pace and extent of European integration have been sometimes shared by other European countries. France has at times also appeared an 'awkward partner' particularly under President de Gaulle, who feared that French national sovereignty and interests might be subordinated in a federal Europe. Since then France has often been slow to implement EU regulations. Voters in Denmark initially rejected the Maastricht Treaty, and in Ireland the Nice Treaty was similarly rejected. Both Denmark and Sweden, along with the UK, initially declined to join the euro, and even the Germans had considerable reservations over exchanging the strong and successful Deutschmark for the new and untried European currency. Germany and France are both currently resisting long overdue reforms of the Common Agricultural Policy, which must be completed. Even the Irish threatened to derail the Nice Treaty (together with EU enlargement) by voting to reject it in a referendum, a decision reversed by a second referendum in 2002. However, it is the British who are still largely perceived as the most reluctant Europeans.

The European Union: superstate or inter-governmental organisation?

The big issue remains the nature and scope of political union. From its beginning there has been controversy over the nature of the European Community/Union and the direction in which it is going. Some talked from the start of a United States of Europe, a 'USE', whose political and economic clout would match that of the USA. They had no reservations in proposing a federal system on US lines, in which supreme power or sovereignty would effectively be divided between two or more levels of government. Others envisaged a weaker form of association, sometimes termed a confederation rather than a federation. General de Gaulle, the former French President, talked of a *Europe des Patries* (a Europe of countries), essentially an inter-governmental association of sovereign nation states.

Much of continental Europe is untroubled by talk of federalism. Countries such as Germany, Belgium and Spain, already federal or quasi-federal countries themselves, see the European Union as just another tier in a system of multi-level governance. Sovereignty is not lost, but pooled. For a substantial body of opinion in Britain, federalism is the dreaded 'f word.' Euro-scepticism and euro-phobia have been fed by fears of the EU's political agenda and the threat

---

Definition
Federalism involves the division of sovereignty between two or more levels of government. In a federal system each level of government is, in theory, sovereign or supreme in its own sphere. The USA and Germany are examples of federal states. Whether the European Union is already or in the process of becoming a federal system is contentious. Devolution within the United Kingdom (see Chapter 17) is not deemed to involve federalism as in theory the sovereignty of the Westminster Parliament is unaffected, but it is sometimes argued that Britain is becoming a 'quasi-federal' state.

BOX 16.2
The principle of subsidiarity

The Community shall act within the limits of the powers conferred on it by this Treaty and of the objectives assigned to it therein.

In areas which do not fall within its exclusive competence, the Community shall take action, in accordance with the principle of subsidiarity, only if and in so far as the objectives of the proposed action cannot be sufficiently achieved by the Member States and can therefore, by reason of the scale or effects of the proposed action, be better achieved by the Community.

Any action by the Community shall not go beyond what is necessary to achieve the objectives of this Treaty.

Article 3b of the Treaty Establishing the European Union.

European monetary union now appears the most serious and immediate threat to those concerned over a potential loss of British national sovereignty and British (or English) national identity. Euro-sceptics see the national currency as a crucial symbol of national independence and a key element of national economic policy. The challenge has been further dramatised by the introduction of euro notes and coins among 12 member states. Yet if left outside 'Euroland' the UK could lose influence in a 'two-speed' Europe, in which Britain was 'left in the slow lane'.

The institutions and processes of the European Union

The controversy over the very nature of the European Union discussed in the last section is an essential preliminary to any appreciation of the issues surrounding its very complex institutions and processes. From the start there was a tension between the interests of EC/EU as a whole, and the interests of the separate member states, and this tension is fully reflected in EC/EU institutions. Those who wish to see and those who fear the development of a European 'superstate' or a federal United States of Europe can find in the supranational institutions all the elements of a sovereign state: an executive in the form of the European Commission, a legislature (at least potentially) in the shape of the European Parliament, and a judiciary in the European Court of Justice. (Other supranational bodies include the Economic and Social Committee, the Court of Auditors, the European Central Bank and the European Investment Bank.)

Yet alongside these institutions which are all supposed to serve the interests of the EC/EU as a whole there are others that look after the interests of member states: the Council of Ministers, consisting of national politicians served by their own national civil servants in the Committee of Permanent Representatives (COREPER), but increasingly more important than either, the European Council, involving regular meetings of the heads of government of member states. Each member state holds the presidency of the European Union for a six month period in rotation, and initial meetings are held at locations within the country holding the presidency. Even in

to the sovereignty of the Westminster Parliament and British independence. Indeed, as European Union law is supreme over the law of member states, the constitutional principle of Parliamentary sovereignty is now highly questionable (see Chapters 11 and 14).

It was fears of the growing power of EU institutions which led to the formal declaration at the Maastricht Treaty of the clumsily-named 'principle of subsidiarity'. Thus the Treaty requires the Community 'to take action … only if and insofar as the objective of the proposed action cannot be sufficiently achieved by the Member States' and can 'by reason of its scale and effects be better achieved by the Community'. This may be seen as an application of a wider principle that decisions ought to be taken at the lowest level consistent with efficiency. The implication here is that decisions might be devolved below the nation-state level to devolved regional government or local government. Indeed, the Maastricht Treaty gave some encouragement to such devolution of power, establishing a new Committee of the Regions to represent such subnational interests. The devolution of power to national executives and assemblies in the UK, and variable pressure for English regional government, fit into this agenda.

the early days when there were only six member states, decision making was not made easy in the Council of Ministers by the unanimity rule, which meant that any single member state government could prevent action by using its veto. In 1965 French ministers refused to attend the Council of Ministers, effectively preventing any decisions. The 'empty chair' crisis was eventually resolved by the 'Luxembourg compromise' under which the veto was retained for issues of great importance to member states, but a system of qualified majority voting (QMV) is used for other issues. Today some matters are decided by simple majority, others by qualified majority, but the veto is still jealously guarded. The on-going enlargement process makes the need for a reform of the voting system now more urgent, with the prospect of an EU with double the number of member states.

The on-going enlargement of the Union is bound to involve some considerable changes, particularly in the composition of institutions. Thus the Commission and the European Parliament are already arguably too large, and existing member states may have to surrender some of their rights to nominate Commissioners and Justices, and put up with fewer MEPs.

While some of these procedural issues are of mind-boggling complexity, the crucial point is not too difficult to grasp. The European Union involves a curious constitutional hybrid, part embryo state, part inter-governmental organisation. Throughout its history there has been a built-in tension between its quasi-federal and inter-governmental institutions and interests. Where the balance of power really lies is partly a matter of perception, but partly also may vary over time and particularly over policy areas. It is difficult to be definite over longer-term trends. Increased EU regulation and common policies fuel the fears of Euro-sceptics, but the obstinate and often successful defence of national interests particularly by the larger member states can make Euro-enthusiasts despair.

It is the European Commission that is commonly perceived as the essence and centre of the supranational authority of the European Union. Although it has not become the effective executive for a federal Europe envisaged by Jean Monnet, it retains a key role in the initiation of legislation and new regulations, and has detailed responsibility for the administration of the European Union. While Commissioners are nominated by member states (smaller states nominate one Commissioner each, the large ones two), the Commissioners are not supposed to look after the interests of their own country but have to swear an undertaking to serve the Union as a whole. They each take charge of at least one of the Commission's directorates (or departments) each responsible for a particular policy area or service. The president of the Commission is a key political figure. Past presidents include Britain's Roy Jenkins and the controversial French politician, Jacques Delors.

While Euro-sceptics lament the increasing power of the European Commission it is often suggested that this supra-national body has progressively lost its leadership role (Nugent, 2002, ch. 6; Cram, Dinan and Nugent, 1999: 44–61). From the start the Commission was relatively less dominant than the equivalent High Authority in the European Coal and Steel Community, and the Commission by itself proved unable to lead and develop further European integration in the face of French opposition under de Gaulle.

It was only intergovernmental conferences that finally succeeded in breaking the deadlock, and restoring some forward momentum to the European project. This reflected the reality of the power of the member states. Since then the Council of Ministers and the European Council (effectively a new supreme intergovernmental institution not envisaged by the founding fathers) have gained at the expense of the Commission. In 1984 the Secretary General of the European Commission complained of the 'institutional drift away from the spirit, and indeed the letter, of the Treaties of Rome', arguing that 'the Community system is gradually degenerating into intergovernmental negotiation', which he blamed on the unanimity rule and 'the constant intervention of the European Council'. More recently the Commission has also been obliged to pay more attention to the European Parliament (see below). The prestige of the Commission was further damaged by revelations of fraud and corruption which led to the resignation of the entire Commission in 1999 and the initiation of a reform programme led by the new President, Romano Prodi and Vice President, Neil Kinnock.

The European Court of Justice is the supreme judicial body in the European Union. One judge is

Table 16.3 The location, composition and functions of key European Union institutions

Institution	Location	Composition	Functions	Comments
European Commission	Brussels	2 Commissioners for large, 1 for smaller states Serve for 4 years	Propose laws Draft budget Administer laws and policies	Commissioners swear allegiance to EU, head Directorates
European Court of Justice	Luxembourg	16 judges, 1 from each member state plus 1 additional	Rules on EU law, adjudication in disputes	EU law supreme over state law
European Parliament	Strasbourg – committees may meet in Brussels	MEPs directly elected by voters in member states (by regional list system)	Largely consultative, but increasing role in legislation, budget	MEPs sit in European parties, not in national blocs
Economic and Social Committee	Brussels	Representatives of interests	Purely consultative	Marginalised in modern EU
Committee of the Regions	Brussels	Representatives of regions of EU	Consultative role, particularly on regional policy	Established after Maastricht Treaty
Council of Ministers	Largely in Brussels	Relevant ministers of member states	Major executive body and initiator of legislation; forum for defence of interests of member states	Unanimity still needed on major issues
COREPER Committee of Permanent Representatives	Brussels	Civil servants on secondment from member states	Bureaucracy serving Council of Ministers	Does initial work for Council of Ministers
European Council	Peripatetic (see above)	Heads of government	Forum for resolving key issues	From 1974, now crucial

nominated by each member state for a six-year period. The Court interprets and rules on European Union law and adjudicates in disputes between EU institutions and member states. European law overrides the national law of member states, and has to be implemented, although implementation has sometimes been delayed. The increasing workload of the European Court of Justice (ECJ) led to increasing delays in obtaining judgments, so that a subsidiary Court of First Instance was introduced to speed up the judicial process.

The European Parliament gained some additional authority and legitimacy following the introduction of direct elections in 1979, although consistently low turnouts by voters in Britain (23 per cent in 1999) and declining turnouts in most other member states suggest some lack of interest or lack of faith in democracy at the European level. Part of the problem is that these elections do not appear to decide very much. National elections in Britain, France, Germany and other countries may lead to the fall of governments and sometimes significant changes in policy, but elections for the European Parliament have little if any immediate impact on the government and decision making of the European Union, even though the European Parliament has gained additional powers from the Single European Act and Maastricht Treaty.

Each member state elects a number of MEPs (members of the European Parliament) roughly in proportion to the size of population, but allowing some over-representation of the smaller states (see Table 16.4). Until 1999 elections for the European Parliament in Britain were conducted under the first-past-the-post system, leading to wildly fluctuating party representation at Strasbourg. Other member states used some version of proportional representation, mostly a regional party list system, which Britain adopted in 1999.

In practice, elections for the European Parliament involve large remote electoral areas, generally little-known candidates, and predominantly national rather than European issues. In Britain, turnout is the lowest in the European Union – only one in four bothered to vote in 1999 – but the results are commonly treated as a verdict on the performance of the government and opposition nationally. Once elected, MEPs do not sit in national blocs but in European party groups. Thus British Labour MEPs form part of the European Socialists Group, and Conservative MEPs belong to the European Peoples Party and European Democrats, which are the two largest parties represented in the European Parliament. No party has an overall majority. The 1999 elections involved some gains for the centre/right parties at the expense of the left.

Much criticism has been directed at the alleged 'democratic deficit' – the apparent weakness of democratic control and accountability within Europe. There is something in these criticisms, but

Table 16.4 MEPs elected to European Parliament by country (after 1995 enlargement)

Country	Number of MEPs
Austria	21
Belgium	25
Denmark	16
Finland	16
France	87
Germany	99
Greece	25
Ireland	15
Italy	87
Luxembourg	6
Netherlands	31
Portugal	25
Spain	64
Sweden	22
United Kingdom	87

they are not entirely fair. While the European Parliament is often denounced as a mere talking shop with little real power, the same is widely alleged of many national parliaments, including the Westminster Parliament (see Chapter 14). Indeed, recent reforms have given the European Parliament more involvement in legislation, and the budget, and have increased the accountability of the European Commission following the 1999 crisis, so that in some respects MEPs now have rather more influence than backbench MPs at Westminster. The real problem for the European

Table 16.5 Votes and seats for UK parties in European Parliament elections, 1979–99

Party	1979 % votes	1979 seats	1984 % votes	1984 seats	1989 % votes	1989 seats	1994 % votes	1994 seats	1999 % votes	1999 seats
Conservative	48.4	60	38.7	45	33.0	32	26.8	18	35.8	36
Labour	31.6	17	34.8	32	38.9	45	42.6	62	28.0	29
Lib/Lib Dem	12.6	1	18.5	0	6.2	0	16.1	2	12.7	10
SNP	1.9	1	1.6	1	2.6	1	3.0	2	2.7	2
Plaid Cymru	0.6	0	0.7	0	0.7	0	1.0	0	1.9	2
UK Ind Party									7.0	3
Green Party			0.6	0	14.5	0	3.1	0	6.25	2
N I Parties*	3.3	3	3.8	3	2.6	3	2.8	3		3

Note: elections from 1979–94 under first-past-the-post system, 1999 regional party list system.

* Northern Ireland: distribution of seats determined by single transferable vote

Parliament is the hybrid nature of the European Union and the power of inter-governmental bodies such as the Council of Minister and the European Council. In so far as the governments of member states, accountable to national parliaments, often seem to take the crucial decisions, the influence of the European Parliament is likely to remain peripheral. Nor is it likely in these circumstances that voters will perceive European Parliament elections as important or meaningful. Yet there is an element of hypocrisy in some of the criticisms. Thus Euro-sceptics routinely condemn the 'democratic deficit' at Strasbourg and Brussels but generally resist proposals to give the European Parliament more powers. Enoch Powell was rather more honest when he roundly rejected the whole concept of a European Parliament:

> The European Assembly is not, in our sense of the term, a 'Parliament', and it is not the wish of the people of this country that it should ever be a Parliament in the sense of being the ultimate repository of the legislative and executive powers under which the people of the United Kingdom are to live.
>
> Enoch Powell, speech in House of Commons, 1986

The European Union is also widely criticised for its bureaucracy. In so far as bureaucracy implies regulation and 'red-tape', that is the essence of modern government and indeed modern organisation. If bureaucracy is taken to mean officialdom, there are obvious reasons the bureaucracy of the European Union should appear cumbersome. The institutional complexity of the EU requires a similarly complicated bureaucracy. Besides the bureaucracy serving the Commission (which is small by the standards of that of member states), there are the officials of COREPER on whom the Council of Ministers and European Council are dependent, and the administrative support services for the European Parliament and other EU organisations. Operating in three principal sites hardly helps. While MEPs attend plenary sessions of the European Parliament at Strasbourg and committee meetings in Brussels, their officials are based in Luxembourg. More important still, the number of languages now involved in the European Union requires a veritable army of translators and interpreters. Procedures are undoubtedly complex, as anyone can testify who has struggled to interpret the convoluted flow diagrams which are sometimes helpfully supplied to provide a simplified summary of the various procedures for approving new legislation or the annual budget. Some of this complexity arises from the necessity of consulting and winning the approval of member states, key institutions and major interests within the EU. The procedures are complicated by the requirements of democracy rather than bureaucracy.

Enlargement is sharpening the debate over the future of the European Union as a whole and of specific institutions. The former French President Valery Giscard d'Estaing has revealed the preliminary draft for an EU constitution which seeks (among other things) to define the powers of, and the relationship between, the various EU bodies. More controversial is a proposal for the appointment of a president of the European Council as opposed to the current six-moth rotating presidency. Particularly contentious for Britain is Giscard d'Estaing's suggestion that the EU might be renamed the United States of Europe, which to Euro-sceptics implies a federal superstate. However, the proposed Article 8 declares 'Any competence not conferred on the union by the constitution institutions rests with the member states', which is reassuring for those who maintain the primacy of the nation state (*Guardian*, 29 October 2002).

The impact of the European Union on the British state and government

The impact of membership of the European Union on the British state and system of government can be considered at various levels: first, its effect on the British constitution and long-established constitutional principles; second, its effect on the machinery of government, including the central executive and organisation of departments; and third, its impact on the day to day process of government.

Some initial discussion of the impact of EU membership on the British constitution has already been provided (e.g. in Chapter 11). Needless to say, the issue remains highly contentious. For Euro-sceptics, the European Union presents a continuing and increasing threat to British national sovereignty and the sovereignty of the Westminster Parliament. Those more well disposed toward the EU emphasise the gains resulting from pooled sovereignty (e.g. Cope in Savage and Atkinson, 2001). Indeed, it can be argued that even if the UK was outside the EU, the freedom of action of the British government would be constrained by the EU and its influence on world trade and investment, without its being able to influence EU policy. The European treaties signed by British governments are not so very different from other treaties: benefits are secured in exchange for undertakings which constrain future freedom of action.

Yet obligations arising from membership of the European Union do differ from the obligations imposed and freely accepted in other treaties and international associations both in scope and kind, particularly because of their major implications for a wide range of domestic policies. More specifically, the British government and the Westminster Parliament have had to accept the supremacy of EU law over UK law. It is true that the British government can influence the framing of EU law, and that there are procedures for consultation with the parliaments of member states as part of the EU, but it is difficult to deny that Parliamentary sovereignty has been affected. However, it is not just membership of the European Union that has undermined the principle of Parliamentary sovereignty. The use of referendums, the devolution Acts and the incorporation of the European Convention of Human Rights (incidentally unconnected with the European Union) all have damaging implications for Parliamentary sovereignty, even if the principle has been theoretically but tortuously upheld (see Bogdanor, in Seldon, 2001, and the discussion in Chapters 11, 15 and 17 of this book). Moreover some modern critics of the British constitution would argue that Parliamentary sovereignty is not a principle worth defending anyway (Mount, 1992, Hutton, 1995, 1996).

Membership of the European Union has had an impact on other aspects of the British system of government. The referendum was first introduced into Britain for a vote on whether the country should remain in the European Community, and has since become an accepted if irregular mechanism for settling controversial issues of a constitutional nature. EU membership contributed

significantly to the pressures for electoral reform in the UK, as Britain's first-past-the-post electoral system produced even more disproportionate results in elections for the European Parliament than it did for Westminster, and the UK system was markedly out of line with that used by other member states. Thus in 1999 the regional list system was used for British elections to the European Parliament, while the system of election used for the Scottish Parliament and Welsh Assembly (the additional member system) followed another model familiar on the European continent. Although some pressures for electoral reform existed prior to membership of the EC/EU, they were strengthened by European precedents. Much the same could be said of demands for devolution and regional government, which predated membership of the European Community, but were reinforced by the parallel pressures for more national and regional autonomy in other member states, and by the development of European regional policy and the establishment of the Committee of the Regions. European legal principles and procedures have also begun to influence British law.

The machinery of government has been less affected than might have been expected by EU membership – the British state has adjusted its institutions and procedures incrementally rather than radically (Bulmer and Burch, in Rhodes, 2000). Departmental organisation has been scarcely affected. There is no separate department for Europe nor a secretary of state for Europe in the Cabinet. As a consequence, there is also no Departmental Select Committee for Europe in the House of Commons, although there is a European Legislation Committee to examine (mainly) proposals for European legislation. There is now a European section of the Cabinet Secretariat, which signals the importance of Europe at the heart of British government. Even so, any one studying the changing formal structures of the Cabinet, departments and Parliament over the last 30 years or so would hardly conclude that they had been much affected by EU membership.

Yet if the formal structure of British government at the centre appears little altered, the change in the working practices of ministers and civil servants, and in the business content of British government, has been marked. 'On an administrative level, most senior British ministers and many senior civil servants spend many days each month commuting to Brussels for EU meetings. Much of the rest of their time back in Westminster and Whitehall is spent tackling questions relating to the EU agenda' (Hix, in Dunleavy *et al.*, 2002: 48). This reflects the extensive consequences of EU membership for so many areas of policy (see below).

The impact of EU membership on British politics: parties, pressure groups and voters

Membership of the European Union has had considerable implications for British parties and the party system. Both major parties have been split over Europe, which has been a cross-party issue regularly threatening party realignment. Labour was manifestly deeply divided on the issue from the 1960s onwards, and the European issue was a major factor in the SDP split from Labour in 1981 which nearly 'broke the mould' of British party politics, but in any event helped ensure Conservative dominance for 18 years. Conservative divisions over Europe date back at least as far as Labour's, but were initially less disastrous for the party, although it was on Europe that Powell broke from the Conservatives and recommended a vote for Labour in 1974, perhaps tipping a close election in Wilson's favour. Conflicting attitudes towards Europe caused tension within Thatcher's last administration, but became far more damaging under John Major, threatening the survival of his government,

and undermining any immediate prospects of a Conservative party recovery after the landslide defeat of 1997.

The Liberals and their Liberal Democrat successors perhaps profited from the divisions among their opponents, but otherwise their more consistent and united support for Europe has hardly profited them electorally, particularly in elections for the European Parliament, where the voting system gave them negligible representation until 1999. The European issue has also spawned new parties which have a minor but occasionally significant impact on the British political scene – the single issue Referendum Party which appeared a threat to the Conservatives in 1997, and the UK Independence Party which managed to pick up three seats on the new voting system introduced for elections for the European Parliament in 1999.

The need to organise for European elections, and subsequently the need to become part of European parties in the European Parliament, have had some knock-on effects for the major British parties. For Labour this was perhaps less of a problem as the party was a member of the Socialist International, and leading Labour politicians were used to fraternising with European socialists and social democrats. Thus they have been consistent members of the European Socialist party. The Conservatives found locating acceptable ideologically sympathetic partners in Europe rather more difficult. The ideas of Christian Democracy which were influential on the centre right on the continent involved too much state intervention and social partnership for a Thatcherite Conservative Party now convinced of the virtues of the free market, while Christian

Table 16.6 Party representation in the European Parliament, 1999

Party	Total size of party group	UK MEPs included in party group
European United Left/Nordic Green Left	42	
Party of European Socialists	180	30 (29 Lab, 1 SDLP)
Greens European Free Alliance	48	6 (Greens, SNP, PC)
The Europe of Democracies and Diversities Group	16	3 (UKIP)
European Liberal, Democratic and Reformist Group	50	10 (Liberal Democrats)
European People's Party and European Democrats	233	37 (36 Cons, I UUP)
The Union for a Union of Nations	31	
Technical Group of Independents	18	
Independents	8	1 (DUP)

Democrats found British Conservatives rather too right-wing. Thus for a time the Conservative MEPs were linked with a few Spanish and Danish MPs in the European Democratic Group, but they are now in the main centre-right European People's Party.

There is always the potential for tension and perhaps open conflict between the parties focused on Westminster and Strasbourg. One danger, particularly for the now more Euro-sceptic Conservatives, is that their MEPs might 'go native', becoming markedly more sympathetic to European institutions, processes and policies than the parent party back home. Indeed, the 1999 European Parliament elections did provoke an open split, although in the event the pro-European Conservatives did not secure much support. There is now a similar problem with the Scottish Parliament and Welsh Assembly, so the parties will simply have to learn to accommodate multi-level governance, and adjust their organisations accordingly.

How far closer involvement with other parties in Europe has influenced the political thinking of British parties is perhaps less clear. German and Swedish social democracy, and to a lesser extent perhaps French socialism, certainly helped influence the transformation of the Labour Party in the 1980s and 1990s. Labour's red rose symbol was borrowed from Francois Mitterrand's French social-ists. Germany's Gerhard Schroeder was for a time closely linked with Tony Blair over the third way or 'middle way'. Some of this might have happened outside the EU anyway, although it does seem that involvement with European socialists has contributed to the softening of Labour attitudes to Europe. British Conservatism seems to have been rather less susceptible to influence from its continental neighbours, although this may be changing as the party desperately seeks new ideas for running public services.

As the impact of the European Union on UK public policy has grown, Brussels has become increasingly a natural target for pressure group activity (Mazey and Richardson, 1993). Some of this has just involved British groups like the CBI or the NFU or British-based firms extending their range, acquiring their own offices in Brussels or employing professional lobbyists. However, many groups have sought to combine with comparable interests in other member states to establish Europe-wide groups, with potentially more muscle to influence EU policy. It is estimated that there are some 700 of these Europe-wide groups, of which nearly 70 per cent represent business, 20 per cent public interest groups, 10 per cent the professions and 3 per cent trade unions, consumers, environmentalists and other interests (Nugent, 2002: 304).

The European Commission is the main target of most groups, partly because of its powers and its readiness to consult with interests, especially Eurogroups. It is more difficult to lobby directly either the European Council or the Council of Ministers, so groups tend to seek to influence these bodies indirectly through national governments (Grant, 1993). The increase in the influence of the European Parliament on the legislative process and the EU budget has led to more intensive lobbying at Strasbourg. There is also the Economic and Social Committee, which is the European Union's own institution for representing group interests – yet most groups prefer to target more influential bodies directly rather than through the ESC (Nugent, 2002: 284).

It has proved much more difficult to persuade the British people to engage with Europe. There is continued evidence of widespread ignorance and confusion about the EU and over specific institutions and issues. Turnout levels for elections to the Euro-

Table 16.7 Examples of Europe-wide interest groups

Organisation	Acronym
Committee of Agricultural Organisations in the EU	COPA
Union of Industrial and Employers Confederation of Europe	UNICE
European Trade Union Confederation	ETUC
Association of European Automobile Constructors	ACEA
European Chemistry Industry Council	CEFIC
European Association of Manufacturers of Business Machines and Information Technology	EUROBIT
Council of European Municipalities and Regions	CEMR
The European Citizen Action Service (represents and lobbies for the voluntary and community sector)	ECAS

pean Parliament have generally been the lowest in Europe since the first elections in 1979 (see Table 16.8). Although the only referendum held on Europe resulted in a substantial majority in favour of remaining in the European Community in 1975, opinion surveys since then have indicated a pervasive if ill-informed Euro-scepticism, and more recently opposition to the single currency (Hix, in Dunleavy *et al.*, 2002: 53–8).

Curiously however, parties that have aligned themselves with what appeared to be public opinion on Europe have signally failed to profit electorally – Labour in 1983 and the Conservatives in 2001 both managed to lose disastrously, indicating that Europe is not a priority issue for voters. However, while Labour has proved it can win general elections despite being out of step with voters on Europe, winning a referendum on the single issue of joining the euro could prove much more difficult.

The impact of the European Union on UK policies

The actual impact of the EC/EU on UK policy has been increasingly significant but highly variable, depending on the policy area concerned. Fiscal policy has clearly been affected. UK entry to the EC involved the introduction of value added tax, and there are EU rules that constrain taxation and expenditure. Even so, pressures to harmonise taxation have generally been resisted. In so far as there are factors favouring greater convergence on, for example, duties on alcohol, these have more to do with the loss of revenue from smuggling than from EU regulations.

Yet Simon Hix (in Dunleavy *et al.*, 2002: 48) argues that while 'The British Government is still sovereign in deciding most of the main areas of public expenditure ... this is only one aspect of policy making. In the area of regulation, over 80% of rules governing the production, distribution and exchange of goods, services and capital in the British market are decided by the EU.' Hix goes on to argue that this severely constrains British economic policy, preventing the adoption of either neo-Keynesian demand-management and pump-priming or a Thatcherite deregulatory supply-side policy.

As far as specific policy areas are concerned, agriculture and fisheries policy have been affected most dramatically, as EC entry required a shift from farm income support policies (with low prices) towards price support policies. Both systems involved agricultural subsidy, although the Common Agricultural Policy notoriously led to periodic over-production, with 'butter mountains' and 'wine lakes'. Britain, with its relatively small agricultural sector, was always likely to be a net loser from the CAP. British farmers have, however, benefited substantially from EU subsidies. Persistent efforts to reform the CAP have partly been frustrated by the strength of farming interests in some member states. However, some British criticism of continental agriculture seems exaggerated or misplaced. The BSE and foot-and-mouth disease crises were substantially the consequence of British farming practices and British policy, and cannot be attributed to the EU.

The UK has gained rather more from the EC/EU regional and social policy. The net benefits to deprived regions have sometimes been less than they might have been, as British governments have sometimes seen EU funding as an alternative rather than addition to UK spending on economic regeneration, contrary to the intentions and sometimes the regulations of the European Commission.

Table 16.8 Turnout levels: elections for the European Parliament (excluding new member states in 1995)

Country	1979	1984	1989	1994	1999
Belgium	91.6	92.2	90.7	90.7	91.0
Denmark	47.1	52.3	46.1	52.5	50.5
France	60.7	56.7	48.7	53.5	46.7
Germany	65.0	56.8	62.4	58.0	45.2
Greece	78.6	77.2	79.9	71.1	75.3
Ireland	63.6	47.6	68.3	44.0	50.2
Italy	85.5	83.9	81.5	74.8	70.8
Luxembourg	88.9	87.0	87.4	90.0	87.3
Netherlands	57.8	50.5	47.2	35.6	30.0
Portugal	–	72.2	51.1	35.7	40.0
Spain	–	68.9	54.8	59.6	63.4
United Kingdom	31.6	32.6	36.2	36.2	23.1
Total EU	63.0	61.0	58.5	56.4	

Many other policy areas have been much less affected. The management and funding of health services differs markedly between the member states of the EU. Educational policy and social security payments and social services have been only relatively marginally affected by membership of the EU, although member states increasingly face common problems (e.g. over funding pensions) which may ultimately lead to increased convergence. Foreign and defence policy too was until recently affected only marginally. Early attempts by the original six members to develop a European Defence Community foundered in the 1950s, and defence and foreign policy has been shaped by the requirements of NATO. Attempts to develop a common foreign policy after Maastricht have not been conspicuously successful. It remains to be seen whether the European Rapid Reaction Force proves significant. The UK however has been accused of being more subject to American influence than working with its European partners.

The future of the European Union and the relationship between the UK and the EU

Prophecy is hazardous. The European Union is at a critical stage in its development. While it is too early to judge the success of monetary union, the introduction of the euro has been relatively smooth and trouble-free, and has been accepted widely. This could mark another crucial stage on progress towards economic and political integration. However, the ongoing substantial enlargement of the EU will inevitably widen the gap between rich and poor states and regions within it, requires major institutional reform and further reforms in agricultural and regional policy (liable to impact adversely on existing member states, including Britain), and could impede further European integration. EU policy towards the rest of the world, particularly the developing world, will also come under scrutiny. The continuation of high levels of agricultural protection could effectively cancel out efforts towards debt cancellation and improved aid. A large question mark remains over the potential for developing a coherent and distinctive European foreign and defence policy, but such a policy may appear increasingly necessary if European and US aims and priorities diverge significantly in the future.

The British role in all this also remains problematic. Successive British governments have found it difficult to forge alliances and make an impact in Europe. Partly this is because of conflicting pulls on policy, particularly the 'special relationship' with the USA which has markedly influenced both Conservative and Labour governments, and has

---

BOX 16.3

Arguments for and against Britain joining the single European currency

Arguments for	Arguments against
UK loss of influence in EU and world if outside Eurozone	Loss of national and Parliamentary sovereignty with loss of pound
Increased economic and monetary stability from single currency – less uncertainty	Interest rates fixed by European central bank; 'one size fits all'
Increased transparency of prices and more competition – leading to lower prices	UK government and Bank of England lose key policy instrument
Fears that London would lose out as world financial centre if outside Eurozone	Disastrous experience of ERM ('Black Wednesday' 1992) shows dangers of tying UK currency to Europe
Fears of less inward investment in UK if outside Eurozone	Relative success of UK economy outside Eurozone shows membership not vital
Benefits from elimination of currency exchange costs from joining euro	UK economy out of step with EU
	Complaints that the euro has led to higher prices in Euroland

often appeared to damage the country's European credentials with its EU partners. Many Britons seem to lack or positively reject a European identity, and may feel a closer affinity with the USA, because of a common language and a substantially shared culture. Yet the sometimes canvassed possibility of the UK exchanging EU membership for membership of the North American Free Trade Area, even if feasible, would substitute an unequal dependent relationship with a superpower, inevitably preoccupied first and foremost with the interests of the Americas, for a partnership between equals. Isolation appears dangerous in an era of intensifying globalization, and there seems little realistic alternative to continued if troubled engagement with the rest of Europe.

Here the key issue remains membership of the single European currency. The euro replaced national currencies in 12 member states in 2002, and is freely circulating. Already in Britain some stores are accepting euros. It now appears that the transition to the euro has been successful and it is here to stay. It seems unlikely that the UK can play a full part in the institutions and processes of the European Union if it remains outside the euro zone. However the economic benefits and disadvantages of UK membership in current circumstances remain clouded, while the political obstacles to the government winning a referendum on the issue are formidable.

Further reading

Pinder (2001) provides a useful introduction to *The European Union*. Nugent (2002) remains the best guide to European institutions and procedures. Cram, Dinan and Nugent (1999) have edited a useful collection of essays on recent *Developments in the European Union*. Detailed up to date information on all current developments can be obtained from the EU website: <http://europa.eu.int>.

On the troubled history of the UK's relationship with the European Union, Young (1998) provides a full and lively account from a the perspective of a Euro-enthusiast. The accounts of key protagonists such as Heath, Thatcher and Major can be consulted in their memoirs. There is a useful chapter on Blair's approach to Europe in J. Rentoul's (2001) biography. Simon Hix reviews the impact of the EU and the euro on British politics in Dunleavy *et al.* (2002), while Anne Deighton performs a similar task in Seldon (2001). Bulmer and Burch examine 'The Europeanisation of British central government' in Rhodes (2000).

Chapter 17

Devolution: the disunited kingdom

The British state   288
A confused national identity?   288
Northern Ireland and Irish nationalism   290
The troubles in Northern Ireland   291
The search for peace in Northern Ireland   294
Scottish nationalism and the pressure for
    devolution   297
The Scottish Parliament and government   298
Devolution in Wales   299
Asymmetrical devolution   302
The English question   303
English regional government   304
Devolution, federalism or separation?   305

The British state appears to be under pressure from both above and below. While some fear British national sovereignty is threatened by the growth of a European superstate (see Chapter 16), others suggest that it could disintegrate into smaller component parts in response to demands for further devolution and decentralisation. It cannot be assumed simply that the British state will go on for ever, in its present form with its current boundaries. In this chapter we review some of the pressures threatening the unity of the United Kingdom. We examine the variously expressed nationalist pressures in Northern Ireland, Scotland and Wales, culminating in very different forms of devolution for each area, with considerable but as yet unclear implications for the future of the British state and the majority nation, England. We conclude with a brief analysis of alternative scenarios.

The British state

Although its government and politics are often considered a model of longevity and stability, Britain has not escaped change. A 'British' state only really emerged following the Act of Union between England and Scotland in 1707, although there had been a 'union of crowns' since 1603. 1801 saw the Act of Union with Ireland, which created the United Kingdom of Great Britain and Ireland. In 1922 26 Irish counties seceded to form the Irish Free State (later, the Republic of Ireland), while the remaining six counties remained part of the United Kingdom of Great Britain and Northern Ireland. However, the border between the north and the south remained contested, while the Republic's constitution (until 1999) claimed that its national territory consisted of the whole island of Ireland. Change is more evident still if Britain's overseas colonies are considered. A British Empire emerged in the course of the 17th and 18th centuries, and reached the height of its power and prestige in the 19th century. Withdrawal from empire in the period after the Second World War reduced Britain's territorial responsibilities overseas, bringing change to both the structure and functions of the old British imperial state.

From 1998, the British state has already devolved some power to its national component parts, Scotland, Wales and Northern Ireland, and further devolution to the English regions remains on the agenda. It is possible that this devolution will satisfy the demands of the various parts of the United Kingdom for more control over their own affairs and ultimately strengthen the Union. It is also possible that more powers might be devolved until a federal Britain emerges, with a federal and state levels of government each supreme in their own sphere. Alternatively, the process of devolution could lead to the disintegration of the British state and its separation into new independent political units, each belonging, as sovereign nation states, to the European Union and the United Nations. The future is uncertain and the stakes are high.

A confused national identity?

In the end the British state is likely to last as long as the various peoples who live within its borders want it to last, and this will depend on issues of

> *Definition*
> **Devolution** involves the delegation or decentralisation of power. It is the term employed to describe the transfer of power in the UK downwards from central government to Scotland, Wales, Northern Ireland and perhaps ultimately the English regions. Devolution is distinguished from federalism (see Chapter 16) because it is does not, in theory, involve any transfer of sovereignty, which remains with the Westminster Parliament. Thus, nationalist critics argue, power devolved is power retained. Others suggest devolution is a half-way house on the road to a quasi-federal or fully federal system, or perhaps the break up of Britain.

political identity and allegiance. Yet these may change over time. In Chapter 2 Sir Ivor Jennings was quoted as claiming, back in 1941, 'Great Britain is a small island with a very homogeneous population. Few think of themselves as primarily English, Scots or Welsh.' His observation may have been substantially correct at the time of writing, in the midst of the Second World War. Today the population is less homogeneous, and the cultural identities and political allegiances of the various peoples living within the borders of the UK state have become particularly complex. Most of the Catholic community in Northern Ireland has long continued to regard itself as Irish rather than British, owing political allegiance to the Irish Republic, although the Unionist majority passionately insist on their British identity. Opinion polls indicate that an increasing proportion of those living in Scotland and Wales regard themselves as Scots or Welsh rather than British (see Chapter 2), which is one factor that helps to explain rising support for the Scottish and Welsh nationalist parties. England remains by far the largest part of this complex mosaic of nations and communities, and many of its inhabitants still refer to themselves as interchangeably 'English' or 'British' (to the annoyance of Scots and Welsh), although there has been some recent debate over 'Englishness' and its potential political implications (e.g. Paxman, 1998)

Post-war immigration has intensified and complicated ethnic divisions which cut across these old national communities and identities. Some of the ethnic minorities in many of Britain's large cities maintain a complex pattern of allegiances, often including strong cultural or religious links with other countries and communities, but commonly including a sometimes passionate identification with the country to which they now belong, unless they have become alienated by rejection and discrimination. However, many seem to find it easier to identify with Britain than with England on the one hand or Europe on the other.

Conflicting cultural influences resulting from the pressures of globalization have added additional dimensions to these confusions over identity and allegiance. Membership of the European Union (as well as the growth of package tour holidays to European destinations and increased sporting and cultural ties) should have helped to reinforce a sense of a common European cultural heritage. Yet the media reflect more the influence of the American and English speaking world, and weaken a sense of a pan-European identity. Not all citizens of the UK would, however, freely identify with Anglo-American, or western, or liberal capitalism, as the anti-globalization movements indicate (see Chapter 8). Nor clearly would they all any longer identify with Christian values and civilisation. A multi-faith Britain has created new tensions within the national community.

The historian Norman Davies (2000: 870) has asserted categorically, 'The United Kingdom is not, and never has been, a nation state.' A nation-state is a state that consists of a single nation – a community of people bound together by some common characteristic such as language, religion, culture or ethnicity, although in the last resort a nation exists in the minds of its members. By this criterion the United Kingdom is not a nation state. However, the same writer observes, 'Multiple identities are a natural feature of the human condition' as 'Everyone feels a sense of belonging to a complex network of communities, and there is no necessary tension between them.' Indeed, multiple identities fit comfortably with the notion of multi-level governance, suggesting that it is unnecessary to choose between being Glaswegian, Scottish, British or European.

Yet in some circumstances people may feel obliged to choose between rival identities and loyalties. Nationalism is a political doctrine that is normally associated with an exclusive allegiance to

BOX 17.1
The British state: core and periphery

Mainstream accounts of British history imply that the growth of the British state was a beneficial and largely voluntary process from which all Britain's peoples ultimately benefited. Thus, it could be claimed, Wales and Scotland prospered from being partners with England in a profitable commercial and imperial enterprise. There is something in the claim, particularly as far as Scotland is concerned. Scottish and Welsh nationalists of course tend to interpret history rather differently, arguing that their culture, and perhaps their economy, suffered as a consequence of English dominance.

Some political scientists have attempted to explain the inter-relationships between Britain's nations and regions in terms of 'core–periphery' theory. The 'core' of the British state is South East Britain, with an 'outer core' comprising East Anglia, the Midlands and Wessex. Beyond the core is an 'inner periphery' made up of the North of England, Wales and the South West, and an 'outer periphery' – Scotland. These areas correspond with arcs drawn around London at 80, 200 and 300 miles.

The core–periphery idea has been developed in terms of the colonial domination of the Celtic periphery by the English core. Michael Hechter (1975) has advanced a persuasive theory of internal colonialism whereby the advanced core areas dominate and exploit the less advanced peripheral areas. In other words, by much the same process as Britain colonised much of the wider world, so the area making up Britain's core colonised the areas on its periphery. Historically this process was marked by the statutes of 1536, 1707 and 1800 which brought Wales, Scotland and Ireland respectively into the English-dominated Union.

Relations between the core and periphery are complex and vary over time. Thus while the Second World War had an integrative affect on the whole of the United Kingdom (and even the communities in Northern Ireland were drawn closer together in the face of the common German enemy), the rapid liquidation of the British Empire after the war and Britain's relative economic decline increased the strains between the periphery and the core within the United Kingdom.

one national community and state (see Chapter 4). This has long been the case in Northern Ireland, where there is a sharp divide between 'Nationalists' owing allegiance to the Irish Republic, and 'Unionists' who retain a fanatical attachment to the United Kingdom and their British identity. It may one day become the case in Scotland, whose people may ultimately feel obliged to choose between a British or a Scots identity.

Northern Ireland and Irish nationalism

If Britain does break up as a political unit, 'John Bull's other island' – Ireland – began the process. It was the demand for Irish 'Home Rule' in the 19th century that provided the stimulus for the policy which the Gladstonian Liberal Party adopted of 'home rule all round' – the forerunner of devolution.

Irish nationalism and Irish separatism subsequently provided a precedent for Scottish and Welsh nationalism.

Ireland was always the least integrated part of the 'United' Kingdom. Its people had remained predominantly and obstinately Catholic while those in Great Britain were largely converted to varieties of Protestantism. What has come to be called the 'Irish problem' was really an 'Ulster' or 'British problem', resulting from 'the English, and their self-serving strategies of plantation and subordination begun in the seventeenth century' (Judd, 1996: 49). Protestants were deliberately settled in Northern Ireland. Hatreds stirred then remain alive today. Union with Ireland only came about in 1801 following the crushing of the revolt of the United Irishmen in 1798, and was never a success. The growth of British power and prosperity hardly impacted on the bulk of the Irish, who earned a bare subsistence from land rented from absentee landlords. The 1845 Irish potato famine and the failure of land reform fed a growing nationalist movement which eventually convinced the Liberal leader, William Gladstone, that home rule was the only solution to 'the Irish problem'. This led to a crisis in British politics, split the Liberal Party and led to a 20-year period of dominance by the Conservatives who supported the Union. The failure to concede home rule to moderate Nationalists before the First World War led to the Easter Rising of 1916 and its bitter aftermath, with the dominance of a new breed of nationalist who demanded full independence and was prepared to fight for it. The failure of repression led to the Irish Treaty of 1921 and the emergence of the 26-county Irish Free State, leaving the remaining six counties as a Northern Ireland statelet within the United Kingdom.

It is often said that Northern Ireland is 'a place apart'. The people of Northern Ireland live in a distinctive political culture, support different political parties (see Table 17.1), and face a unique constitutional problem yet to be resolved. The partition of Ireland in 1922, creating what was initially known as the Irish Free State to the south, did not solve the 'Irish problem', since a sizable Catholic and substantially Republican minority, now amounting to 40 per cent of the population, still lived in the North. In a sense, two minorities live side by side in Northern Ireland: the Catholic minority in Northern Ireland which feels threatened by the Protestant majority, and the Protestant minority which feels threatened by the Catholic majority should the North reunite with the South. The troubles in Northern Ireland arise from centuries of divisive historical experiences which have embittered relations between the communities to an extent which it is difficult to comprehend outside the province. Rulers and politicians long forgotten in Britain are celebrated in exotic murals. Quaint ceremonies, ritual marches, rival flags and symbols have become central to Northern Irish politics. Anyone seeking a solution to the Irish problem would prefer 'not to start from here'.

The troubles in Northern Ireland

However, although the roots of the Irish troubles lie in the distant past it is only comparatively recently that they re-erupted. The years following the end of the Second World War were relatively peaceful ones in Northern Ireland. It appeared that differences between the two communities might progressively be eroded by their shared interest in increasing affluence. Although Catholics remained discriminated against in terms of employment, welfare and political rights, they then appeared better off than their counterparts to the South. The Irish Republican Army (IRA) waged an unsuccessful campaign in the late 1950s, and this too was taken as evidence that Catholics now accepted the political status quo in return for improved living standards. The emergence of moderate Unionists, such as Terence O'Neill, who became Northern Ireland's Prime Minister in 1963, offered the prospect of further improvements in community relations. However, O'Neill's brand of progressive Unionism was opposed by many Ulster loyalists determined to resist change, and he was forced out of office. Serious rioting led to British troops being sent to restore order. Initially these troops were welcomed by Catholics, but inevitably their strong-arm role became identified with supporting the Protestant state rather than defending the Catholic minority. The political condition of Northern Ireland moved close to a state of revolution.

Violence against Catholics led them into accepting the more militant provisional wing of the IRA as their defence force. The position of the IRA was strengthened by the policy of internment, a practice sometimes referred to as the 'recruiting serjeant for the IRA', since it involved the imprisonment of suspected terrorists, including innocent Catholics. The troubles were to become yet more intense in January 1972 when, in controversial circumstances, British paratroopers appeared to over-react on the streets and killed 13 unarmed individuals in a tragedy which came to be known as 'Bloody Sunday'. British Prime Minister Edward Heath announced that the Parliament at Stormont was suspended. From April 1972 Northern Ireland came under direct rule from Westminster. A referendum on the future of the province in 1973 did little to clarify the position because of Catholic abstention. Some 57.5 per cent of Northern Ireland's electorate wanted to remain part of the United Kingdom, 0.6 per cent wanted Northern Ireland to unite with the Republic of Ireland outside the United Kingdom, but 41.9 per cent abstained.

Northern Ireland experienced a grim cycle of violence. Discrimination and repression won recruits into the Provisional IRA who regarded British soldiers and members of the (largely Protestant) Royal Ulster Constabulary as representative of an alien occupying power and thus legitimate targets. Loyalist paramilitaries attacked Catholics, particularly those suspected of IRA sympathies, and there were (almost certainly well-grounded) Nationalist suspicions of collusion between loyalist paramilitaries and the security forces. Much of the killing seemed more random: sometimes just the religious affiliation of the victim seemed to provide sufficient excuse for murder. The escalation of violence led to a rising cumulative total of death and serious injury in the province, besides the economic damage caused by the destruction of businesses and the deterrent to new investment. Social segregation was intensified as Catholics living in mainly Protestant areas and Protestants in mainly Catholic areas were forced out of their homes. In some parts of Belfast and Derry (or Londonderry to Unionists) virtual no-go areas were established, 'policed' by paramilitaries using punishment beatings and shootings to maintain internal discipline.

Periodically, violence was exported to the British mainland. Thus the Conservative MP, Airey Neave,

---

BOX 17.2
The roots of conflict in Northern Ireland: different perspectives

Religious struggle? Some see religion as central rather than incidental to the conflict. The struggle between Protestantism and Roman Catholicism, which began in 16th-century Europe as a life and death contest between rival ideologies, has survived in Ulster when antagonism has long softened elsewhere. Religious differences still keep the two communities apart. Church attendance remains high (contrary to trends on mainland Britain) and there are other institutions working to maintain the link between religion and politics, including the Orange Order, a semi-secret fraternal organisation with the support of around two-thirds of Protestant males, and segregated schooling, which provides the children of the Catholic community with an Irish identity.

Internal colonial struggle? Alternatively, the conflict in Northern Ireland might be understood as an internal colonial struggle between periphery and core, similar to the struggle of Algeria for independence from France in the 1950s. The argument runs as follows. Although the native populations enjoyed rising living standards under minority colonial rule, they still demanded full equality with the more privileged settlers (in the case of Northern Ireland, the descendants of the Scots Presbyterians settled in Ulster from the 17th century). The beleaguered settler population includes fundamentalists ('loyalists' in Ulster terminology) unwilling to compromise. There is a struggle, often bloody, between the native majority who have discovered nationalism and want independence, and a settler minority who want to maintain the power and privileges enjoyed under the colonial system of exploitation.

Class struggle? Finally, the conflict may be viewed as essentially a class struggle distorted by the labels of Ulster Protestantism and Irish Catholicism. This perspective suggests the dominant class has maintained its position of power by pursuing a policy of 'divide and rule', manipulating members of the working class into fighting each other. According to this analysis the Protestant working class 'have been duped into thinking they enjoy (economic) advantage' over Catholics (Bruce, 1986: 254). The advantage may be more illusory than real: the economic gap between members of the Protestant and Catholic working class in employment has diminished, and a common culture of poverty afflicts Protestants and Catholics alike who are without work and rely on welfare. However, because they believed that they were better off than Catholics, the Protestant working class remained loyal to the state and was unwilling to unite with the Catholic working class in order to advance their common class interests.

who had played a leading role in securing the Tory leadership for Margaret Thatcher, was murdered in 1979. In 1984 Margaret Thatcher herself narrowly escaped when an IRA bomb exploded at the Conservative Party Conference, killing five and seriously injuring two senior ministers, Norman Tebbitt and John Wakeham. John Major's Cabinet survived a mortar attack on Downing Street in 1991. There were other more random victims of IRA violence following pub bombings in Guildford and Birmingham. To the British government and the bulk of British public opinion the perpetrators were despicable terrorists and murderers. However, IRA volunteers who died in the course of the 'armed struggle' were treated as heroes and martyrs within their own community. Such divergent perspectives are not uncommon in similar conflicts, where particular communities totally reject the legitimacy of the state and its agents. (Examples include the Basque extremists in Spain, Tamil Tigers in Sri Lanka, and Kashmiri separatists in India.)

However, it became increasingly clear over time that neither side could win by the use of force. The British government could not defeat the IRA, and the IRA could not achieve its goal of a united Republican Ireland by the armed struggle.

Whatever the root cause of the conflict between the two communities (see Box 17.1), further divisions have developed within both, leading to a complex and confused party system. Northern Ireland parties were always distinctive. The main British parties refrained from contesting Northern Ireland elections. In the old Stormont Parliament and in representation at Westminster until the 1970s, the dominant (almost the only) party was Ulster Unionist, which was linked with the Conservatives. Sinn Fein commonly won a couple of mainly Catholic constituencies, but the victors refused to take their seats. The troubles from the late 1960s onwards led to a split in Unionism. Ian Paisley was elected as an independent Unionist against the official Unionist in 1970 and founded the Democratic Unionist Party in 1971, which now threatens to overtake its Ulster Unionist rivals. Meanwhile the Ulster Unionists (now separated from the Conservatives) have suffered from periodic splits and have become deeply divided over the ongoing 'peace process'. There are also smaller parties linked with loyalist paramilitaries. On the Catholic

Table 17.1 Some of the political parties in Northern Ireland

Party	Support and aims	Politicians
Ulster Unionist Party (UUP)	Protestant, supports union with Britain, has supported the peace process, but is increasingly divided	David Trimble, Rev. Martin Smyth, Jeffrey Donaldson
Democratic Unionist Party (DUP)	Protestant, supports union with Britain, opposed peace process and power sharing	Ian Paisley, Peter Robinson
Social Democratic and Labour Party (SDLP)	Catholic, republican and nationalist, but committed to constitutional methods. Supports peace process	Mark Durkan, Seamus Mallon, John Hume
Sinn Fein (SF)	Catholic, republican and nationalist, linked with IRA and 'armed struggle' but signed up to peace process	Gerry Adams, Martin McGuinness
Alliance Party of Northern Ireland (APNI)	Non-sectarian – seeks to bridge gap between two communities	John Alderdice, Sean Neeson
Progressive Unionist Party (PUP)	Protestant, Unionist, supports peace process	David Ervine
United Kingdom Unionist Party (UKUP)	Breakaway from Unionist party, opposed peace process, now divided	Robert McCartney

or nationalist side the most obvious division is between the peaceful constitutional nationalism of the Social Democratic and Labour Party (SDLP) and Sinn Fein (linked with the paramilitary IRA). However, the peace process has also opened up fissures in the Republican ranks, reportedly between the military leadership of the IRA and the political leadership of Sinn Fein, but more obviously between the main provisional IRA and splinter movements such as 'Continuity IRA' and the 'Real IRA' opposed to the Republican ceasefire. Attempting to bridge the community divide is the small Alliance Party.

The search for peace in Northern Ireland

A series of attempts to find a peaceful settlement were made in the 1970s and 1980s, although in all these attempts Sinn Fein was regarded as beyond the pale, while Paisley's DUP was effectively excluded also, for it regarded every new initiative as a sell-out. Instead, British governments tried to secure agreement between the moderate Nationalist SDLP and moderate Unionists.

The Sunningdale Agreement (1973–4)

Direct rule from Westminster was not seen by the British government as a long-term future for Northern Ireland. The ultimate goal of Heath's Conservative administration was the re-establishment of some form of devolved government in Northern Ireland, in the hope that this would find widespread acceptance in both communities. The Secretary of State, William Whitelaw, proposed the setting up of an assembly elected by proportional representation, with a power-sharing executive with Unionist and SDLP representatives which would gradually assume greater policy responsibilities. Also a Council of Ireland would be established with its membership drawn from the assembly as well as from the parliaments in Westminster and Dublin. This early attempt at power sharing split the Unionists and was effectively ended in 1974 by a general strike organised by the Ulster Workers Council which brought the province to a standstill. The 'Orange Card' had been played to great effect, and left some commen-

tators asking whether Ulster militants or the British state now governed Northern Ireland.

The Prior plan (1981–5)

A later Conservative Secretary of State in Thatcher's government, James Prior, conducted a rather similar experiment with 'rolling devolution'. Once again an assembly was to be elected which would in time gain greater and greater responsibility for policy making. As before, there was relatively little support for the idea, which was made unworkable in practice, and the assembly was dissolved after four years. Yet again the devolution experiment ended in failure.

The Anglo-Irish Agreement (1985)

A new agreement was signed by Margaret Thatcher and the Irish Premier. This involved provision for more cooperation between Britain and Ireland, including greater cross-border cooperation to defeat terrorism, with Dublin being consulted routinely on Northern Ireland affairs. Unionists were outraged by this provision which they saw as constitutionally unique – that is, a foreign government given the power to influence domestic policy in a part of the United Kingdom. 'Ulster Says No' was the slogan of the Unionist parties. Sinn Fein also, but for different reasons, opposed the agreement. The SDLP was in favour, as were the front benches of all Britain's major parties, although there was fierce opposition from some Conservative backbenchers.

The peace process (from 1993 onwards)

What differentiated the peace process that began in 1993 from earlier initiatives was that for the first time Sinn Fein (and effectively the IRA also) was party to the negotiations. The SDLP could support successive plans for peace but could not end the violence. Only the support of the IRA and Sinn Fein could do that. After 20 years of armed struggle it was clear that the IRA could not be defeated, nor could it achieve victory by force. A series of public and secret communications raised hopes of breaking the deadlock – talks between the SDLP's John Hume and the Sinn Fein leader Gerry Adams, secret messages from the Republican leadership to the British government, and finally talks between British Prime Minister John Major and Albert Reynolds (the Irish Taoiseach), which led to the Downing Street Declaration, which renounced any long-term British strategic interest in Northern Ireland and accepted the right of the peoples of north and south to unite at some time in the future. Sinn Fein would be able to join negotiations for a settlement if it renounced violence.

The Official Unionists, then led by James Molyneaux, responded to the Declaration in a cautious but positive way. In contrast, Ian Paisley condemned it as a 'sell-out'. Dramatic progress was made in August 1994 when the IRA announced a 'complete cessation of military operations'. This led in turn to the agreement on Joint Framework Documents by the British and Irish governments in 1995. These foreshadowed most of the details of the later Belfast Agreement of 1998. However, further progress in the peace process was put on hold by Unionist demands for prior IRA decommissioning of its weapons. John Major opted for pre-talks elections to a Northern Ireland forum, which Sinn Fein and the IRA regarded as a delaying tactic, and in February 1996 the IRA ended its ceasefire. In April 1996 elections went ahead in which both the Unionists and Sinn Fein did better than anticipated. Negotiations between the parties began in June, but serious progress remained effectively on hold, pending the UK election and a likely new Labour government.

The Labour election victory in 1997 effectively restarted the Northern Ireland peace process. The IRA announced a restoration of a ceasefire in July 1997, and after six weeks of non-violence the new Northern Ireland Secretary, Mo Mowlam, announced that Sinn Fein would be invited to participate in the peace talks, without any precondition of disarming. Ian Paisley's Democratic Unionists had already pulled out of the talks, but David Trimble's Ulster Unionists continued to participate. After a period of intense negotiations in which Mo Mowlam wooed the Republicans while Tony Blair reassured the fearful Unionists, a formal agreement was eventually reached on Good Friday, 1998. Most of the ideas in the Belfast Agreement 'were articulated or prefigured before Labour took office' (O'Leary, in Seldon, 2001: 449.) Key elements included:

- parallel referendums to be held on the agreement in both parts of Ireland

- a devolved assembly in Northern Ireland, elected by the single transferable vote system of proportional representation, with legislative and executive functions
- a first minister and deputy first minister to be elected together by parallel consent of parties representing a majority of unionists and of nationalists
- an executive consisting of ten ministers to be allocated by the d'Hondt procedures (to ensure proportionate power sharing
- a north–south Ministerial Council
- an inter-governmental 'British–Irish Council' (to provide a balancing east–west forum to balance the north–south body).

The agreement was popularly endorsed in May in by a referendum majority of 94 per cent in the Republic of Ireland and 71 per cent in the North, where nearly all Catholics and a more narrow majority of Unionists voted in favour. There was also important government backing. The US government provided substantial support for the peace process, which was effectively guaranteed by both the UK and Irish governments. The terms were incorporated in an international treaty, the

Table 17.2 The June 1998 elections to the Northern Ireland Assembly

Party/bloc	First preference vote %	Number of seats	% seats
Social Democratic and Labour Party	22.0	24	(22.2)
Sinn Fein	17.7	18	(16.7)
All Nationalists	**39.8**	**42**	**(38.9)**
Alliance Party of Northern Ireland	6.4	6	(5.5)
Women's Coalition	1.7	2	(1.8)
All 'others'	**9.4**	**8**	**(7.3)**
Ulster Unionist Party	21.0	28	(25.9)
Progressive Unionist Party	2.5	2	(1.8)
All 'Yes' Unionists	**25.0**	**30**	**(27.7)**
Democratic Unionist Party	18.0	20	(18.5)
UK Unionist Party	4.5	5	(4.6)
Independent 'No' Unionists	3.0	3	(2.8)
All 'No' Unionists	**25.5**	**28**	**(25.9)**

Source: adapted from O'Leary, in Seldon, 2001: 458.

British–Irish Agreement. However, one major problem was that the key issue of decommissioning remained unresolved. Here Blair gave assurances to Trimble which were to be a source of trouble later.

Implementation of the agreement has been predictably difficult, and its future still seems precarious. Elections to the new Northern Ireland Assembly in June 1998 produced a delicate balance on both the Nationalist and Unionist sides. Sinn Fein came closer to parity with the SDLP among the Nationalists, while the Ulster Unionists and their pro-agreement Unionist allies only just won more seats (and fewer first preference votes) than Paisley's DUP and other anti-agreement parties. The position was made more difficult by differences within Trimble's party. Even so, the assembly proceeded to elect David Trimble and the SDLP's Seamus Mallon as First and Deputy First Ministers in July. Further progress was stalled by wrangling over the north–south bodies, arms decommissioning and Chris Patten's report on the police body to replace the Royal Ulster Constabulary. Unionists feared they were making all the concessions without any guarantee that violence was over.

In October 1999 Mo Mowlam, who was unpopular with Unionists, was replaced as Northern Ireland Secretary by Peter Mandelson, to Unionist satisfaction. In November 1999 Trimble secured 58 per cent support from his party's Ulster Unionist Council for entry into government, promising to resign if there was no progress on decommissioning, and the Assembly proceeded to choose the ministers for the new Northern Ireland Executive – three UUP, three SDLP, two Sinn Fein (including Martin McGuinness, reportedly a former IRA commander, as Minister of Education) and two DUP (who were nominated but refused to participate in the Executive). In December the Republic of Ireland modified its constitutional claim to Northern Ireland, in a revised clause of its constitution which recognised that 'a united Ireland shall be brought about only by peaceful means with the consent of the majority of the people expressed, in both jurisdictions of the Ireland' thus 'copper-fastening the consent principle' to reassure Northern Ireland's Unionists (Wilford and Wilson, 2000: 90). In the same month the first meetings of the North–South Ministerial Council and the British–Irish Council were held.

While O'Leary (in Seldon, 2001: 471–5) per-

BOX 17.3

The Northern Ireland Executive at the time of suspension (October 2002)

This is shown in running order of party choice according to the d'Hondt mechanism. First and Deputy First Ministers are elected by parallel consent.

First Minister: David Trimble (UUP)
Deputy First Minister: Mark Durkan (SDLP)
Enterprise, Trade & Development: Sir Reg Empey (UUP)
Finance and Personnel: Sean Farren (SDLP)
Regional Development: Peter Robinson (DUP)
Education: Martin McGuinness (SF)
Environment: Sam Foster (UUP)
Employment and Learning: Carmel Hanna (SDLP)
Social Development: Nigel Dodds (DUP)
Culture, Arts & Leisure: Michael McGimpsey (DUP)
Health, Social Services & Public Safety: Bairbre de Bruin (SF)
Agriculture and Rural Development: Brid Rodgers (SDLP)

---

ceives the dual executive or premiership of Trimble and Mallon as a major institutional weakness of the Agreement which delayed the formation and impeded the functioning of the Executive, Wilford and Wilson (2000: 106) have seen the emergence of the Office of the First Minister and Deputy First Minister as 'the administrative answer to the centrifugal tendencies in the executive ... the hub, coordinating the work of the ministerial "team" in pursuit of wider strategic policy objectives' and effectively 'a government-within-a-government'.

It appeared that the main elements in the agreement were all now in place, but arms decommissioning remained a ticking timebomb under the peace process. In February 2000 Mandelson suspended the Assembly to stave off the resignation of Trimble on the decommissioning issue, to the fury of Nationalists. After further prolonged negotiations between the British and Irish governments and the main parties the IRA made a statement promising that it would eventually 'place its arms beyond use' in May 2000, and the Assembly and Executive was restored. IRA arms dumps were inspected by the international commissioners in June. John Reid replaced Mandelson as Secretary of State in January 2001 (as a result of allegations unconnected with Northern Ireland). Since then, in a symbolic gesture, small quantities of arms have been reported to have been put beyond use. However, the future of the agreement remains precarious. Revelations of a Sinn Fein spy scandal at Stormont in Autumn 2002 led to Trimble and the Unionists withdrawing from the Executive, the fourth suspension of the devolved institutions and the resumption of direct rule. Shortly afterwards, for reasons unconnected with the province, Paul Murphy replaced John Reid as Northern Ireland Secretary.

O'Leary (in Seldon, 2001: 404) concludes, 'If the Agreement does collapse then Blair and Mandelson will have to take a full measure of responsibility for their part in endangering what Blair and Mowlam helped put together.' He argues that Mandelson has made unjustifiable concessions to the Unionists on policing and the suspension of the Assembly. The Unionists themselves see the peace process rather differently, as a zero-sum game in which they have made all the concessions for few tangible benefits. The problem for any Northern Ireland secretary is that the peace process depends on maintaining majority support in both communities, and the precarious position of Trimble, who only barely enjoys a majority within his own party, gives the Unionists blackmail potential. A succession of previous Ulster Unionist leaders, some with past reputations as hardliners, have been forced out by their aggrieved followers when they made compromises. Trimble's support is crumbling and his party is losing ground to the uncompromising DUP. Thus the British government is obliged to conciliate the Unionists to keep Trimble and his divided party on board. Yet the Republicans also have their own (less publicised) internal differences, between their political and military leadership, and within the ranks of the military (as the persistence of minority anti-Agreement factions such as Continuity IRA indicates). To some, Gerry Adams has betrayed the Republican movement just as David Trimble is thought by rather more Unionists to have betrayed them. Political leaders in Northern Ireland who make concessions are thus routinely denounced for their 'sell-out' or 'surrender'.

The alternative to keeping Trimble and his Unionists on board the peace process is potentially dire. If past British governments failed to coerce the Nationalist minority and maintain order in the province, they are unlikely to succeed in coercing the Unionist majority. Peace in Northern Ireland remains deeply flawed and precarious, yet the level of violence has been substantially reduced, and life in the province has become more normalised. Ultimately, demographic trends seem likely to result in a Nationalist Northern Ireland and the Irish unification that neither the ballot nor the bullet could procure. In the meantime the diminishing Unionist majority need time to adjust and prepare for this altered political reality. There seems to be no other credible way forward.

Scottish nationalism and the pressure for devolution

Scotland provides a second interesting example of the failure of the United Kingdom to meet perfectly the nation-state ideal. Scotland had been an independent state for centuries when its king, James VI, succeeded to the English throne in 1603 as James I. This union of crowns became a full union of the two states and parliaments in 1707, but the inequalities in population, wealth and power ensured that England dominated. However Scotland retained its distinctive national identity, which in the 20th century was reflected in a separate legal system, education system and established church. Scottish affairs were handled by the Scottish Office, with a 'mini-parliament' of Scottish MPs meeting in the form of the Scottish Grand Committee.

Many Scots shared a wider British nationalism. Scots peopled the Empire, including the settlement of Scottish Presbyterians in Northern Ireland in the early years of the 17th century. Even as late as the 1945 general election, nationalist sentiment was weakly expressed, with the Scottish National Party winning only 1.3 per cent of the Scottish vote. The decline of Britain's Empire and world role, along with industrial decline which adversely affected the Scottish mining, shipbuilding and textiles, gave renewed significance to Scottish nationalism. The SNP began to win significant votes and seats in the 1970s. These successes worried the Labour Party which had come to dominate Scottish politics, and helped commit the 1974–9 Labour government to Scottish devolution.

The 1979 devolution referendum was lost because of a requirement of support from at least 40 per cent of the Scottish electorate (not just those who voted). In the event, although 32.5 per cent of the Scottish electorate voted 'yes', compared with 30.7 per cent who voted 'no', the largest proportion of the electorate (37.1 per cent) abstained. The failure of the referendum effectively brought down Callaghan's Labour government, and ushered in 18 years of Conservative rule, ending any immediate prospects for devolution. The SNP initially lost votes and seats, although nationalist feelings were aroused by Margaret Thatcher's strident expression of English nationalism, and by policies such as the poll tax (introduced in 1989 in Scotland, a year earlier than in England). One consequence was that the number of Conservative MPs returned to Scottish seats declined with each successive election, until none at all were elected in 1997.

Labour became strongly recommitted to devolution in the 1980s, and from 1988 to 1995 joined with the Liberal Democrats, Scottish trade unions, local authorities and other organisations in a Scottish Constitutional Convention, which hammered out an agreed programme for devolution that was to provide the basis for the 1998 Scotland Act. The SNP, committed to full independence, declined to join the Convention, while the Conservative government under John Major and the Conservative Party in Scotland maintained their opposition to devolution and support for the Union. Tony Blair upset some Scottish Labour supporters by announcing that there would be a referendum prior to any devolution, in which Scottish voters would be asked, first whether they wanted a Scottish parliament, and second, whether it should have tax-varying powers. The referendum held in September 1997 gave an overwhelming backing to a Scottish parliament (74.3 per cent) and a 63.5 per cent support for tax-varying powers. This conclusively settled the issue, rendering further Conservative opposition to the Parliament and what it had described as a 'tartan tax' fruitless. The party of the Union was obliged to accept a major constitutional change which it had previously argued would lead to the break-up of Britain.

The Scottish Parliament and government

Elections were held for the new Scottish Parliament in May 1999. The results were expected to be much closer than in Wales, as the SNP appeared to be making substantial inroads into Labour's vote. In the event, Labour maintained its position as the largest party in Scotland, but under the additional member voting system predictably failed to secure an overall majority. The results were as shown in Table 17.3.

The electoral system benefited both the nationalists and (ironically) the Conservatives, who had always opposed proportional representation. Labour moved immediately towards a coalition administration with the Liberal Democrats, with whom they had worked closely in the Constitutional Convention. A key sticking point in the negotiations between the two parties was student fees, which the Liberal Democrats had opposed, but a

---

Table 17.3 Elections for the Scottish Parliament, May 1999

Party	% constituency votes	No. constituency seats	% regional list votes	No. list seats	Total seats
Labour	38.8	53	33.6	3	56
SNP	28.7	7	27.3	28	35
Conservative	15.5	0	15.4	18	18
Lib Dem	14.2	12	12.4	5	17
Other*	2.7	1	11.3	2	3

*The successful members of the Scottish Parliament (MSPs) elected for other parties were Tommy Sheridan (Scottish Socialist Party), Denis Canavan (independent Labour) and Robin Harper (Green)

compromise was eventually agreed and the new coalition executive was formed with Labour's Donald Dewar as First Minister and the Liberal Democrat, Jim Wallace, as Deputy First Minister. Donald Dewar, widely respected and regarded as the 'father of the nation' and its new Parliament, did not live long to enjoy his new position. He died on 11 October 2000, and after a Labour Party election was succeeded by Henry MacLeish, who himself was obliged to resign following accusations over the funding of his private office, to be replaced by his rival in the earlier party election, Jack McConnell.

There has been some disappointment with the record to date of Scottish devolution, although the Parliament has been relatively successful compared with the Welsh and Northern Ireland Assemblies. Major political difficulties were caused by the early intra-coalition differences over student fees and proportional representation in local elections, and rows with pressure groups over the abolition of

hunting and the scrapping of the notorious 'Section 28' of the Local Government Act prohibiting local authorities from 'promoting' homosexuality. As far as the parties are concerned, Labour has been troubled by internal differences and allegations of sleaze, while the Liberal Democrats have struggled to assert their separate identity in the Labour-dominated coalition. However, the opposition parties seem in no better shape. The SNP has found it difficult to come to terms with the 'half-way house' of devolution, and has made less impact than might have been expected, which was perhaps a factor in their charismatic leader Alex Salmond surrendering the leadership, to be succeeded by John Swinney. The Conservatives have felt obliged to accept devolution as an accomplished fact, but although the new electoral system for the Scottish Parliament rescued them from political oblivion north of the border, they also have made little or no progress, narrowly winning back just one seat in the 2001 general election in Scotland after their wipe-out in 1997.

BOX 17.4
The Scottish Cabinet, June 2002

First Minister: Jack McConnell (Labour)
Deputy First Minister and Minister of Justice: Jim Wallace (Lib Dem)
Minister for Education and Young People: Cathy Jamieson (Labour)
Minister for Enterprise, Transport and Lifelong Learning: Iain Gray (Labour)
Minister for Environment and Rural Development: Ross Finnie (Lib Dem)
Minister for Tourism, Culture and Sport: Mike Watson (Labour)
Minister for Social Justice: Margaret Curran (Labour)
Minister for Finance and Public Services: Andy Kerr (Labour)
Minister for Health and Community Care: Malcolm Chisholm (Labour)
Minister for Parliamentary Business: Patricia Ferguson (Labour)
Lord Advocate: Colin Boyd (Labour)
Solicitor General: Elish Angliolini

(The Cabinet is supported in the Scottish Executive by 11 junior ministers.)

Devolution in Wales

In Wales, domination by the English 'core' resulted in the decline of Welsh culture, particularly the Welsh language. By the early 20th century 'English was taught as the language of advancement, and the use of Welsh was actively discouraged' (Madgwick and Rawkins, 1982: 67). Support for Welsh nationalism had more to do with preserving the Welsh culture and language from extinction than with Welsh self-government. Support for Plaid Cymru, the Welsh nationalist party, remained negligible until the late 1960s, and even after that was substantially confined to the Welsh speaking areas of north and central Wales. In the 1979 devolution referendum only 11.8 per cent of the Welsh electorate voted 'yes' to devolution, heavily crushed by the 46.5 per cent who voted 'no' and the complacent 41.7 per cent who did not bother to vote one way or the other. An even lower turnout marked the 1997 devolution referendum, and although the percentage voting 'yes' more than doubled and secured a wafer-thin majority for devolution, it still only represented one in four of the Welsh electorate. Welsh devolution was the product of the demand for Scottish devolution rather

BOX 17.5

Comparative politics – the future of Scotland: the Quebec scenario or the Slovak scenario?

Nationalist writer Tom Nairn (1981, 2000, 2001) has gleefully described the break-up of Britain as virtually accomplished, assuming it is only a question of time before Scotland becomes an independent state. Iain McLean (in Seldon, 2001: 444–6) has suggested two alternative future scenarios, based on comparisons with Quebec and Slovakia. Quebec is a French-speaking province of Canada where there has been persistent pressure from nationalists for an independent Quebec state. Yet voters, perhaps fearful of adverse economic consequences, have narrowly rejected the independence option in referendums. Thus Quebec for now remains part of Canada, in contrast with Slovakia, which having threatened separation from the former Czechoslovakia, suddenly found itself 'unexpectedly independent, to its short run disadvantage' (McLean, in Seldon, 2000: 444).

Will Scotland's future resemble the Quebec scenario (substantial home rule within a federal state) or the Slovak scenario of independence? Either seems possible, but two major linked issues may decide the outcome – the future of the Scottish economy, and the funding of Scottish public spending. The discovery of North Sea oil in the 1970s enabled the SNP to claim that an independent oil-rich Scotland would be better off. Declining revenues from the North Sea have damaged this argument, although Scottish nationalists now point to Ireland as an example of the economic growth that could follow independence. However the Scots could be worse off, if they lose the very generous funding they receive within the United Kingdom. Under the so-called Barnett formula, public spending per capita in Scotland is now reckoned to be 31 per cent above the GB average, while Scottish income is now close to the UK average, so that Scotland no longer appears particularly disadvantaged. McLean argues that the 'Slovak scenario' could result if the UK government attempts to reduce Scottish funding, perhaps in the face of political pressure from hard-pressed English regions – particularly if elected regional assemblies are introduced. A UK government squeeze on Scottish funding would create a strong reaction from opposition parties and voters in Scotland. The resulting political crisis could lead to separation on the Slovak model. McLean (in Seldon, 2000: 445–6) concludes that if the Quebec scenario unfolds, Blair 'will be hailed as the saviour of a new flexible union', whereas if the Slovak alternative scenario comes about, devolution will be seen as his 'biggest mistake'.

than the result of Welsh pressure. The relatively limited demands from the Welsh 'periphery' for autonomy from the 'core' were reflected in the relatively weak powers of the proposed new Welsh Assembly, with no tax-raising powers, and no right to pass primary legislation, especially when compared with those of the Scottish Parliament.

The bare majority on a low poll was enough to trigger the introduction of a Government of Wales bill in November 1997, which became an Act in July 1998. The executive powers of the Welsh Office were transferred to the Assembly, which however had only secondary legislative powers. Elections took place in May 1999, and surprised expectations by failing to produce an overall Labour majority (only 28 seats out of 60). While support for Plaid Cymru had been boosted by the devolution process, Labour had been weakened, first by the bizarre resignation of the Secretary of State for Wales and Welsh Labour leader, Ron Davies, after he was robbed on Wimbledon Common, and second by the manipulation of the party's internal electoral processes to secure the new leadership for the Blairite Alun Michael, who was 'widely perceived to be the choice of London rather than Wales' (Osmond, 2000: 39) instead of the more popular Rhodri Morgan. The election results were as shown in Table 17.4.

The use of the additional member electoral system not only significantly increased the representation of

Table 17.4 Welsh National Assembly: election results, May 1999

Party	% constituency votes	No. constituency seats	% regional list votes	No. list seats	Total seats
Labour	37.6	27	35.5	1	28
Plaid Cymru	28.4	9	30.6	8	17
Conservative	15.8	1	16.5	8	9
Liberal Democrats	13.5	3	12.5	3	6

the Welsh nationalists but also resurrected the political fortunes of the Conservative Party in Wales, which had won no seats in the 1992 and 1997 general elections. The Welsh Labour group initially formed a minority Cabinet with its leader Alun Michael as First Secretary. A minority administration seemed feasible as Labour remained much the largest party, and it appeared unlikely that the Conservatives would be able to combine with other opposition parties to provide a viable alternative. Yet Labour suffered some embarrassing defeats, culminating in a successful opposition vote of no confidence in Alun Michael in February 2000. Rhodri Morgan succeeded him, and initially governed with an informal understanding with Plaid Cymru, and subsequently with a full coalition with the Liberal Democrats.

Welsh devolution so far has hardly been an unqualified success. Labour's internal dissension got the Assembly off to a bad start, and there were rows over EU regional funding, free eye tests, teachers' pay, and particularly agriculture. Hazell (2001: 46) declares that the part of Labour's constitutional settlement 'which is clearly not working is the National Assembly for Wales'. Even so, it appears that support for devolution in Wales has strengthened rather than weakened (Osmond, in Hazell, 2000: 63–6). There is a widespread view that the Assembly has been given too few powers to be effective, and it seems likely that there will be increased pressure from all parties for primary legislative powers and more budgetary discretion. Rhodri Morgan has notably departed from the timid approach of his predecessor, Alun Michael, citing the Welsh national hero Owen Glyndwr:

> Owen Glyndwr wanted a country united in properly organised society with representation from all parts of Wales. He envisaged a Welsh future in a European context ... Six centuries later we are starting to think in those terms again.
>
> (Rhodri Morgan, *Western Mail*,
> 17 April 2000, quoted by Osmond, in Hazell,
> 2000: 41)

As Osmond notes, this is strikingly different language from that used by Alun Michael, but what is equally striking is that Welsh politicians are only just 'starting to think in those terms again' after the institution of the National Assembly. While the Scottish Parliament was the outcome of a long internal debate over devolution, the Welsh National Assembly seemingly had to be established

---

BOX 17.6
The Welsh Cabinet (June 2002)

First Minister: Rhodri Morgan (Labour)

Deputy First Minister and Minister for Rural Development and Wales Abroad: Michael German (Lib Dem)

Minister for Education and Life-Long Learning: Jane Davidson (Labour)

Minister for Economic Development: Andrew Davies (Labour)

Minister for the Environment: Sue Essex (Labour)

Minister for Finance, Local Government and the Communities: Edwina Hart (Labour)

Minister for Health and Social Services: Jane Hutt (Labour)

Minister for Open Government: Carwyn Jones (Labour)

Minster for Culture, Sport and the Welsh Language: Jenny Randerson (Lib Dem)

(Cabinet ministers are assisted in their work by deputy ministers.)

first to inaugurate debate on the form of political devolution that the people of Wales wanted.

Asymmetrical devolution

Although the devolution process in Wales, Scotland and Northern Ireland has run in parallel, with new assemblies and devolved governments established in each within a few months, what is striking is how different the pattern of devolution in each country has been. 'One's overall impression of Labour's constitutional design is its incoherence' to the extent that it must be 'incomprehensible to most citizens' (Ward, in Jowell and Oliver, 2000: 135). 'Each of the assemblies has a different size and composition, a different system of government, and a very different set of powers' (Hazell, 2000: 3). The divergence is more striking still if the new London government and progress towards English regional governance are included in the overall assessment of devolution, as they commonly are (Hazell, 2000, chs 5 and 9). Does this administrative untidiness matter? On the one hand it provides supporting evidence for the view that Labour's constitutional reforms lack any coherent overall vision; each initiative seemingly has been pursued in isolation, and some of the differences appear arbitrary. On the other hand it could be argued that most of the more obvious differences reflect very different histories, cultures and political problems. The legacy of inter-communal strife and hatred in Northern Ireland, and the whole history of the British engagement with Ireland as a whole and its contentious partition, mark off the province from the generally peaceful nationalist politics of Scotland and Wales. Thus an awkward collection of unique institutions with clumsy checks and balances designed to protect minorities and assuage the fears and suspicions of the majority was the minimum requirement for progress.

Scotland and Wales are more superficially similar. Yet whereas Wales was effectively colonised by England, the political union of England and Scotland (whatever Scottish nationalists may now claim) began as a more equal partnership with the willing assent of, and even some enthusiasm from, the Scottish establishment. Scotland moreover retained its own distinctive church, and legal and education systems, and substantially separate administration,

which could be readily transferred to a new Scottish government. Moreover, the demand for a Scottish Parliament was based on a distant historical precedent and a more recently established but fairly clear consensus in favour of devolution. Detailed plans has been drawn up in the Scottish Constitutional Convention, backed by a broad swathe of Scottish opinion, and only had to be implemented.

The situation was very different in Wales, where devolution had been rejected decisively only 20 years before, and where popular backing remained in doubt until the last minute. It is often argued that Welsh nationalism is more commonly expressed in terms of culture and language than political institutions. Welsh law and administration were closely integrated with that of England, there were fewer functions that could readily be transferred, and the case for legislative devolution appeared more questionable. It could be claimed that the Welsh voted uncertainly for devolution first, and only then began to consider what powers their new devolved institutions should have. Thus Osmond (in Hazell, 2000: 37) argues that the Welsh Assembly became in its first year 'a constitutional convention by other means'. It may be that Welsh devolution over time comes to resemble the Scottish pattern more closely, as more powers are demanded in imitation of Scottish precedents, but it is unsurprising that the Welsh Assembly began so markedly inferior in powers to its Scottish equivalent.

How far this administrative untidiness really matters is perhaps questionable. Most federal systems involve a considerable range in state populations, reflecting specific historical and cultural factors. Other countries that have pursued devolved government, such as Spain, have tackled the process incrementally like the UK, with considerable variations in powers and levels of autonomy for different areas. Yet it seems likely in such situations that regions with fewer powers will, over time, demand functions and resources comparable to those where devolution has been extended further. Thus Welsh politicians are already demanding similar powers to those exercised in Scotland, while English regional assemblies, if and when they are established, will also seek to imitate the perceived market leader in the devolution process.

For all these reasons, the devolution that has so far been implemented does not amount to a stable settlement. Ron Davies, the Welsh politician and

Table 17.5 Devolution in Scotland and Wales compared

Powers	Scotland	Wales
Executive functions devolved	Health, education, local government, social services, housing, economic development agriculture, fisheries, food, transport, tourism, environment, sport, arts	Health, education, local government, social services, housing, economic development, agriculture, fisheries, food, transport, tourism, environment, sport, arts
	Legal system, penal policy, policing	Welsh language
Legislative functions devolved	Primary legislative powers devolved for above functions	No devolution of primary legislative powers
Finance and taxation	Funded by block grant from UK Scottish Parliament can vary level of income tax by 3p in the pound	Funded by block grant from UK

former Secretary of State for Wales, who led the devolution campaign until his abrupt political demise in October 1998, has declared that devolution was 'a process not an event'. This was particularly true in Wales where the case for and extent of devolution continues to be debated, but it is also manifestly the case for the UK as a whole. The referendums of 1997 and 1998, the Acts establishing devolved parliaments and assemblies in 1998 and 1999, and the elections for those devolved bodies in 1999 have not marked the achievement of devolution, but stages in the devolution process, which remains unfinished. Where it will eventually lead is unclear, and may not be so for decades.

The English question

An obvious problem with devolution to date is that it is asymmetrical in another sense to that described in the section above. Devolution to Scotland, Wales and Northern Ireland together only involves a small minority of the United Kingdom. Of the 'four nations in one' England is much the largest in area and even more in population (see Chapter 2). Thus England remains a massive cuckoo in the devolution nest. The growth of nationalist politics and changing national identities and allegiances pose questions for members of the majority nation, accustomed to consider themselves interchangeably

English and British. Some fear a narrow and racist English nationalist backlash, while others more optimistically believe that devolution, and perhaps the ultimate break-up of Britain, could help the English rediscover their own national culture and identity. There has been a spate of books on what it means to be English (e.g. Paxman, 1998).

There are more pressing political and constitutional concerns arising out of devolution. One issue concerns the number and role of Scottish MPs in the Commons following devolution. Scotland remains over-represented at Westminster, which was always difficult to justify, but even more anomalous now Scotland is also represented by its own Parliament. If the 2002 recommendations of the Scottish Boundary Commission are implemented, Scotland will lose 13 (mainly Labour) seats in the Commons, and Scottish and English constituencies will then have a similar average electorate. This does not, however, resolve the issue of the post-devolution role of Scottish MPs at Westminster. The so-called 'West Lothian question', named after the old constituency of the dissident Labour MP, Tam Dalyell, who asked it, has yet to be answered (Dorey, 2002). As Tam Dalyell has pointed out, Scottish MPs cannot vote on, for example, Scottish education because that has been devolved to the Scottish Parliament, yet they can vote on education in England. This seems illogical. Thus Dalyell himself declared that he would not vote on English matters. The Conservative Party under William Hague's leadership demanded 'English votes on English laws', restricting involvement on legislation affecting only England, or England and Wales, to those MPs representing English, or English and Welsh, constituencies. This could involve the development of a two-tier House of Commons, with some MPs with considerably restricted responsibilities. It could also profoundly affect executive–legislative relations. A future UK government with an overall Commons majority could find itself in a minority on English matters, which might constitute the bulk of its work, particularly if further powers are devolved, in Wales as well as Scotland.

One apparently logical solution is the creation of a separate English Parliament in addition to the Westminster Parliament representing the whole of the United Kingdom. If the Scots, Welsh, and Northern Irish are entitled to home rule, why not the English also? Thus each 'nation' within the union would acquire its own devolved assembly (which could also provide the basis for the development of a federal Britain). This solution, however, has not yet attracted much support. One problem is the sheer preponderance of the population of England within the UK. An English Parliament would represent 83 per cent of the UK population. There would be damaging scope for duplication and conflict between the UK and English Parliaments.

English regional government

Another solution is the development of English regional government, particularly if the main aim of devolution is seen as bringing government closer to people, decentralising power and promoting regional economic development rather than satisfying nationalist aspirations. This would match initiatives in several other member states of the European Union, which itself established a Committee of the Regions as part of the Maastricht Treaty.

Under John Major's Conservative government some efforts were made to rationalise the untidy pattern of existing regional administration, bringing together previously separate regional offices of central departments into new integrated government offices for the regions (GORs). The Labour government went further with the introduction of appointed regional

---

BOX 17.7

The regional development agencies

Eastern	East of England Development Agency (EEDA)
East Midlands	East Midlands Development Agency (EMDA)
North East	One North East (ONE)
North West	Northwest Development Agency (NWDA)
South East	South East England Development Agency (SEEDA)
South West	South West of England Regional Development Agency (SWERDA)
West Midlands	Advantage West Midlands (AWM)
Yorkshire and the Humber	Yorkshire Forward (YF)

---

development agencies (RDAs: see Box 17.6) with very limited budgets and powers, and also promised referendums on elected regional assemblies, a promise not implemented in Labour's first term but reaffirmed in a White Paper, published by the Department of Transport, Local Government and the Regions in May 2002 (Cabinet Office/DTLR, 2002). However, referendums will only be held in a region when the government considers that there is 'sufficient public interest' in the idea of an elected regional assembly. This could lead to a rolling programme of devolution, under which some regions acquired assemblies before others.

If this plan for elected assemblies proceeds it could lead to a more balanced set of sub-UK national and regional bodies, with English regional assemblies serving populations comparable with those of the devolved Scottish Parliament (and larger than those served by the Welsh and Northern Ireland assemblies). Yet regional consciousness is variable, but generally low, in England, and the demand for regional government patchy (Tomaney, 2002: 728–9). In so far as it exists it appears in part as an English backlash against (particularly Scottish) devolution. Poorer regions of England, such as the North East, appear to be relatively disadvantaged in terms of funding, powers and political representation in comparison with Scotland, and are demanding a fairer distribution of resources.

Another problem is that the government 'is committed to a maximum three tiers of government', so that elected regional assemblies could not be superimposed over two tiers of elected local government. That means that 'any region allowed to move to a referendum will first need to go through a review of local government structure by the Boundary Committee' (Jeffery and Mawson, 2002: 718). This will be a significant hurdle to overcome. It will require voters to accept something like the unitary local authorities that were largely rejected in the consultation exercises conducted by the ill-fated Banham Commission under John Major's government (see Chapter 18, and Leach, 1998). In effect, voters may have to choose between new elected regional assemblies and the continuation of the old elected county councils, which fought a long and largely successful rearguard action against their threatened abolition in the 1990s. The old counties may make little sense as administrative areas in the 21st century, but they still score higher in terms of identity and allegiance than regions. Thus the traditional county interests could frustrate the pressure for further regional devolution. Moreover, some who have little love for counties see cities and their hinterlands as providing a more dynamic base for regional economic regeneration than the areas of the current GORs and RDAs.

Even if some regional assemblies are eventually created, probably initially in the North East, and possibly in the North West, Yorkshire and Humber, and the South West, their proposed powers and budgets will not be remotely comparable with those of devolved government in Scotland, or even Wales and Northern Ireland. Thus English regional assemblies, particularly if they are only instituted in a few regions, would only further emphasise the asymmetry of devolution.

Devolution, federalism or separation?

Some alternative future scenarios have already been touched upon. One possibility is that the process will not go much further. The present pattern of sub-UK national devolution will more or less continue within the current complex system of multi-level governance. Prospects for English regional devolution may recede (perhaps because a Labour government indefinitely postpones the issue, possibly resulting from a change in government, or possibly because of the rejection of elected assemblies in referendums). Extensive further powers may not be conceded to existing devolved bodies, and the sovereignty of the Westminster Parliament may appear unaffected (as indeed Blair's Labour government always insisted). However, for different reasons it seems most unlikely that the present arrangements for governing Wales and Northern Ireland can persist for long in their current form.

Even this minimalist scenario will involve (and to degree has already involved) considerable problems of liaison and coordination between the Westminster government and the various devolved administrations. As we have seen (Chapter 12), the Prime Minister's Office has already been reorganised to create a Directorate of Government Relations, with a particular concern for relations with the new devolved forms of government within the United Kingdom. Beyond the issue of the relations between central government and the devolved administrations there is the issue of the relationships of the latter with each other. This is particularly important for Unionists in Northern Ireland, who hope that the British–Irish Council promised in the Belfast Agreement will strengthen east–west links within the British Isles and balance the developing north–south links within Ireland of which they are apprehensive (see In Focus 17.1). Apart from this, however, the devolved administrations may learn from each other. Members of the Welsh Assembly looking for increased powers will certainly take a strong interest in Scottish institutions and processes. The devolved governments are hardly in competition with each other, and indeed may sometimes find it advantageous to combine together to extract concessions from the centre.

Inter-governmental relations ultimately may have to be more formalised. It is possible that the devolution process will be extended to create, over time, a quasi-federal or fully federal Britain (with or, more probably, without Northern Ireland). This, Ward (in Jowell and Oliver, 2000: 130)

Scottish First Minister Jack McConnell (left) meets Northern Ireland's First Minister David Trimble (centre) and Deputy First Minister Mark Durkan (right) at Edinburgh in June 2002, to strengthen ties between the two devolved administrations, and boost the east–west ties included in the Good Friday agreement to balance the north–south links between Northern Ireland and the Irish Republic.

Photograph: PA Photos.

argues, is the only logical way out of what he describes as the representation dilemma (or what has been termed the 'West Lothian' question). This would end the unitary status of the United Kingdom and the sovereignty of the Westminster Parliament. The Scottish and Welsh levels of government would no longer appear conditional and subordinate, but sovereign in their own sphere. This would almost certainly require a written constitution, if only to regulate the functions and inter-relationships of the various levels of government. How far the British system of government has already progressed in this direction is contentious. Bogdanor (in Seldon, 2001: 148–51) argues that Parliamentary sovereignty has already been virtually destroyed and a quasi-federal system established. O'Leary (in Seldon, 2001: 468–71) by contrast cites Mandelson's suspension of the Northern Ireland Assembly in February 2000 as evidence of the maintenance of Westminster sovereignty. He argues that it 'spells a blunt warning to the Scottish Parliament and Welsh Assembly.... Sovereignty remains indivisibly in Westminster's possession.'

A third possibility is that Northern Ireland could eventually unite with the south, and Scotland and perhaps Wales also could become independent sovereign states within the European Union. These areas of the present United Kingdom would cease to send representatives to the Westminster Parliament, which would become an English rather than a UK or British parliament. The 'Break-up of Britain'

predicted and advocated by nationalists like Tom Nairn would become an accomplished fact. The eventual separation of Northern Ireland from Britain seems only too plausible, if only because of demographic trends which may turn the current nationalist minority into a majority, perhaps within 20 years, although some joint sovereignty or consociation arrangements could survive as a viable alternative. The political circumstances that could lead to Scotland's separation have already been lightly indicated. It is certainly a highly plausible future scenario, although certainly not the only one (see Box 17.5 on the Quebec and Slovak scenarios). A sizeable minority of Scots (from a quarter to a third in recent years – see Curtis, in Hazell, 2000: 228) support independence, but it would need the settled support of a majority to succeed. Religious differences are a major factor inhibiting further nationalist advance, as the significant Catholic minority that has been the bedrock of the Scottish Labour vote has shown little interest to date in the SNP. Support for independence in Wales is currently much lower than in Scotland – around 10 per cent (Curtis, in Hazell, 2000: 238).

Whatever eventually happens will no doubt come to seem 'inevitable'. Yet at present the future seems uncertain, to be influenced by events, the successes and failures of politicians, and ultimately the decisions of peoples. States in a democratic era require popular legitimacy. The British state will survive as long as enough people in its constituent parts want it to survive. It will break up if national communities seek independence. Ultimately what matters is the political consciousness and identities of peoples rather than institutional machinery, although of course the perceived effectiveness of institutions may influence political attitudes.

Further reading

The ideology of nationalism is discussed very briefly in Chapter 4 of this book, and rather more in chapter 5 of Leach (2002). There is an extensive literature on nationalism in general, rather less on nationalism in Britain. Davies (2000) provides a stimulating history of the British Isles, which is a corrective to Anglo-centric accounts. Marr (1992) and Harvie (1994) both offer readable accounts of modern Scottish politics and the growth of nationalism, while Nairn (1981, 2000, 2001) provides a provocative nationalist perspective. There is rather more theoretical substance in Hechter (1975) and Bulpitt (1983). Paxman (1998) provides an engag-ing perspective on *The English*. Dorey (2002) illuminates 'The West Lothian question in British politics'.

Events are moving so fast on the devolution front that most textbooks are out of date almost as soon as published. The early stages of implementation are explored by various authors in Blackburn and Plant (1999), and by Ward (in Jowell and Oliver, 2000) and Hazell (2000). There are also substantial chapters by Iain Maclean on 'The national question' and Brendan O'Leary on 'The Belfast Agreement and the Labour government' in Seldon (2001). On the debate over devolution to the English regions there is a special issue of *Regional Studies* (**36** (7), October 2002), devoted to 'Devolution and the English question'. Journal articles, newspapers, and websites are essential for further updating – e.g. the official websites <www.wales.gov.uk> and <www.scotland.gov.uk>, and relevant departmental websites – e.g. the Department of Trade and Industry website for Regional Development Agencies, and the Office of the Deputy Prime Minister <www.odpm.gov.uk> for English regional devolution.

Chapter **18**

Local governance

From local government to local governance 308
Representing communities and securing
  accountability 311
The politics of local governance: local
  interests and parties 313
Decision making within organisations: local
  politicians, managers and professionals 314
Territory and community: the reorganis-
  ation of structure 316
The delivery of services 320
Reforming the finance of local governance 322
Central–local and inter-authority relations
  under multi-level governance 325

Local governance clearly fits into the framework of multi-level governance under which the European and devolved dimensions of British government have already been discussed (Chapters 16 and 17). Yet it may be questioned whether it belongs in a part of the book that is explicitly related to the developing modern British governmental system as opposed to the traditional Westminster model outlined in Part III. After all, some features of local government and politics are fairly old and familiar. A comprehensive system of local councils was in place before the end of the 19th century. Yet democratic local institutions have been subject to almost continuous change over the last 40 years, as their structure, functions, finance and internal workings have been radically and sometimes repeatedly reformed. Moreover, this chapter is not just concerned with elected local authorities, but with the whole range of (largely appointed) local public bodies that have grown up in recent years to form part of a local public sector which works extensively with the private sector in formal and informal partnerships and with the voluntary or third sector in policy networks.

Definitions
Local government: is conventionally understood to mean the government provided by elected local authorities (or local councils).
Local governance: includes appointed agencies and other local governing bodies besides elected local authorities but also emphasises the process of governing, rather than the institutions of government, and relations between organisations and sectors, and with the local community.

From local government to local governance

Although the old local councils never ran all local public services, they controlled most of them, and were thus effectively the local government for their areas. Not any more. Whole functions have been transferred while effective control of other has been significantly eroded, so that, as Blair himself (1998: 10) has observed, 'There are all sorts of players on the local pitch jostling for position where previously the local council was the main game in town.' Here the term 'governance' is particularly apt. What are involved are not just the formal institutions of local government but the whole process of delivering local services and governing communities through complex inter-relationships of public, private and voluntary bodies. Much of this fits with the changed emphasis on government 'steering' rather 'rowing' (Osborne and Gaebler, 1992), or 'enabling' rather than 'providing' (Clarke and Stewart, 1988; Brooke, 1989). It echoes much of the language of the new public management (see Chapter 13) on the one hand and New Labour's 'third way' on the other (see Chapter 8).

To most people local public services are important, and some sections of the community – the young, the old, and those who are disabled, sick or poor – are very heavily dependent on them. Among the services that are locally delivered are:

- schools
- health services
- social services
- public housing
- land use and planning
- roads and public transport
- environmental health (including refuse collection and disposal)
- vocational training
- local amenities (such as parks, libraries and sports facilities)
- public protection (police and fire services).

At one time nearly all these services were the responsibility of elected local councils, but this is no longer true. The provision of local health services is now the responsibility mainly of hospital trusts and primary care trusts (responsible for health care in the community). Police services are controlled by essentially independent police authorities (although these still contain some indirectly elected local authority members). Vocational training is controlled by learning and skills councils. Local public transport is operated by private bus and train companies, although it is partly regulated and often subsidised by local councils. Much remaining public or social housing is provided by voluntary housing associations.

> **BOX 18.1**
>
> ## Some of the appointed councils, authorities and trusts operating at local level, 2000
>
> | Organisation | No. |
> | --- | --- |
> | Learning and skills councils (replaced training and enterprise councils, 2000) | 47 |
> | Local enterprise and careers service councils (Scotland) | 39 |
> | Registered social landlords (housing associations) | 2421 |
> | Housing action trusts | 4 |
> | Police authorities | 49 |
> | Health authorities/boards | 114 |
> | Hospital trusts | 387 |
> | Primary care groups/trusts | 488 |
>
> Source: House of Commons Select Committee on Public Administration, *Fifth Report 2000/01: Mapping the Quango State*

> *Definition*
>
> **Compulsory competitive tendering (CCT)**
> placed statutory obligations (1980, 1983, 1988) on local authorities and health authorities to put certain services (e.g. cleaning, catering, laundry, ground maintenance, vehicle maintenance, refuse collection) out to public tender, allowing private firms to compete for their provision. As a consequence some services in some authorities were effectively privatised (although the authority retained statutory responsibility). Labour replaced CCT with 'Best Value' (1998) which retained the principle of competition, but allowed contracts to be awarded on the basis of other factors besides price.

Even where elected local authorities retain statutory responsibility for a service, it may be actually provided by another organisation – by a voluntary body largely funded by the council, by a private company, under contract, or by another public agency. Working with voluntary bodies, such as the Women's Royal Voluntary Service, goes back a long way, and is generally cheaper and often more effective than direct public provision. The voluntary or 'third' sector is popular with both the New Right who are critical of public bureaucracies, and with much of the centre and left keen to encourage more public participation in service provision. Partnership with the private sector has also always existed, particularly in urban redevelopment schemes and other major capital building projects. The recent increased involvement of the private sector in public service provision is however more controversial. It reflects New Right faith in competition and market forces as an antidote to the perceived waste and inefficiency of monopoly public providers, and a New Labour commitment to partnership with business and networks.

Thus the Thatcher government first encouraged and then obliged health authorities and local authorities to put certain services out to tender (compulsory competitive tendering, CCT). As a consequence some refuse collection, cleaning, ground maintenance, vehicle maintenance, catering and laundry services, and subsequently leisure services are now provided by private firms under contract, although the services are still publicly funded and regulated (Wilson and Game, 2002: 327–36).

Even where such services are retained in-house by councils, they are commonly run on commercial lines as quasi-autonomous units.

Another important development by the Thatcher government, substantially implemented under the Major government, was the introduction of more managerial delegation and competition within the public sector, for example through the local management of schools (LMS), under which the bulk of local education authority spending was delegated to school governing bodies, which henceforth had to manage their own budgets. Schools could also apply to 'opt out' of local authority control altogether and become 'grant maintained schools' with more power, and receiving funds direct from central government. In a similar move, hospitals could apply to become 'trusts' independent of the district health authority, and GP practices could apply to be fundholders, controlling their own budgets. These developments encouraged more competition between schools and between hospitals in 'internal markets'. School budgets were 'pupil related'. The more pupils successful schools attracted, the more money they obtained. Similarly, in the health service 'money followed patients' and hospitals could attract more finance by offering better services in a competitive environment. (However, lack of capacity often inevitably limited the scope for expansion.)

These extensive changes have resulted in the appearance of 'all sorts of players on the local pitch', to the extent that the provision of local public services seems increasingly fragmented. The proliferation of agencies presents particular problems for the 'wicked issues' which cut across agency and service boundaries and require a more coordinated approach (Leach and Percy-Smith, 2001, ch. 8). Governments have had to place increased emphasis on inter-agency collaboration. Thus the Conservative government promoted 'care in the community', involving the cooperation of health authorities, local authority social service departments and voluntary organisations. The Labour government has introduced a whole raft of new cross-agency initiatives in the interests of 'joined-up government.'

In this new world of local governance, elected local authorities increasingly were expected to play a new role as enablers rather than providers. Once, as 'the major game in town' they provided nearly all the local public services themselves. Some of those functions they have lost entirely, while for others they retain the ultimate responsibility, but no longer provide them directly, instead 'enabling' others to provide them. The new enabling role requires new skills, in drawing up and monitoring contracts, in inspecting and regulating. Where local councils are working with other agencies and the private and voluntary sectors in partnerships and networks, diplomatic cooperation is required, rather than the line management local government officials were used to in large hierarchical organisations. This is sometimes referred to as 'third way management'. Instead of the command and control management of old large and hierarchically structured public sector organisations or the competition and profit maximisation which drives the private sector, third way management emphasises leadership, diplomacy and collaborative joint working.

However, local councils retain some advantages in this fragmented jumble of local agencies and networks. They still have extensive statutory powers, control many key resources, remain multi-purpose bodies, and crucially are the only directly elected bodies that can claim to represent their local community. This gives them a legitimacy lacking in other public agencies, and in the business and voluntary sector, however public spirited these other bodies may claim to be. As the only bodies with some claim to represent the whole of their local communities, councils remain well-placed to take the lead on major local issues and projects that concern the community.

Blair's Labour government has not sought to reverse the fragmentation in the delivery of local public services brought about by its Conservative predecessors, although it has introduced some significant further changes, converting grant maintained schools into foundation schools, bringing fundholding GPs within its new primary care trusts, and replacing training and enterprise councils with local learning and skills councils. In general it has emphasised cooperation rather than competition, while retaining some aspects of the competitive regime. Thus in the interests of 'joined-up government' it has set up a number of inter-agency partnerships and policy networks to address issues such as drugs, social exclusion, crime and community safety.

As far as contracting out is concerned, Labour has relaxed the element of compulsion but still insists councils should seek 'best value', although not necessarily the lowest price, through competition. Labour has sought to encourage improved service

BOX 18.2

Some examples of 'joined-up' policy initiatives

Education action zones to encourage innovation and flexible approaches to learning in areas of high deprivation – involving clusters of schools, the local authority, learning and skills council, local business and community interests.

Employment zones to improve employment opportunities for the long-term unemployed in the poorest areas.

Health action zones to tackle ill-health and health inequalities to improve the health of local people – involving the NHS, local authorities, community groups, the voluntary sector and businesses.

Quality protects to improve the health and education of children being looked after by social services, and to improve opportunities for them when leaving care.

Sure start: local partnerships to bring together health, education and child care services to help young children and families in deprived areas to prepare for schooling and to prevent subsequent social problems (e.g. truancy, youth crime, drug abuse).

New deal for communities: local partnerships to develop and implement community-based plans to address the problems of 'the worst housing estates' including crime, drugs, unemployment, failing schools and community breakdown.

National strategy for neighbourhood renewal to deliver policies for poor neighbourhoods across a wide range of areas, including housing, education, jobs, skills, community development and shops.

Local Government Association's New Commitment to Regeneration involving 22 pathfinder local authorities working in partnership with the public, private, voluntary and community sectors to develop strategies for the long-term regeneration of the area.

Source: adapted from Leach and Percy-Smith, 2001: 202–3.

provision under the Beacon Council scheme, through which local authorities can apply to become Beacon Councils for particular services, and undertake to share best practice with other authorities (Leach and Percy-Smith, 2001: 206; Wilson and Game, 2002: 342–3). More recently, the Labour government has agreed local public service agreements (PSAs) with individual local authorities, under which the government provides additional grant in return for progress on agreed local objectives. The government has also promised a relaxation of central controls over high-performing councils (Wilson and Game, 2002: 344–9).

Representing communities and securing accountability

For many, local governance is not just about the efficient delivery of local public services, as the last section perhaps implied, but about local democracy and community self-government. The 19th-century French writer, Alexis de Tocqueville, declared that without local self-government people lacked the spirit of liberty. John Stuart Mill considered local representative bodies provided a crucial education in democracy. For these theorists representative democratic institutions at local and national level were mutually dependent. This assumption has been shared by most of those who have written on local government in Britain since their day. A recurrent lament in many recent books on the subject has been the erosion or bypassing of democratic local government by appointed agencies, or the 'new magistracy' or 'local quangocracy' (Cochrane, 1993; Skelcher, 1998; Wilson and Game, 2002).

Definition
New magistracy is a term sometimes used to describe the growth of unelected local government. In the 19th century unelected magistrates (Justices of the Peace) performed an administrative role in county government until 1888. Thus the renewed importance of appointed bodies today in the administration of local services is described as a 'new magistracy'. Other terms include 'appointed state' and 'local quangocracy' (see Chapter 19 for quangos).

BOX 18.3
The case for local democratic institutions

- **Choice** – elected local authorities offer local communities a degree of choice over local decisions and service levels, allowing them to satisfy different needs and preferences within a diverse United Kingdom.
- **Experimentation and variety** – a degree of autonomy for elected local authorities allows experimentation and the development of policies that may be copied elsewhere or become national policy.
- **Public participation** – elected local authorities provide more opportunities for participation in the political process, and a training ground for national politicians.
- **Dispersal of power** – local councils help to avoid central government wielding too much power.

There is much in the criticism of the 'democratic deficit' in current local governance. However, it should be acknowledged that not all is well with what remains of democratic local government in Britain:

- Turnout in local elections is very low: 30–40 per cent on average, but much lower in some inner city areas.
- The first-past-the post system, still used in local elections as in Westminster elections, distorts the representation of parties and interests in the community, and creates many virtually one-party councils where there is no effective opposition and no prospect of a change in control.
- Those who do vote in local elections vote overwhelming on national trends and issues, almost regardless of the record of the local council, thus undermining effective accountability.
- Very few participate in local government in any way beyond voting (e.g. attending council or party meetings, inspecting accounts, involvement in school governing bodies or council tenant bodies).
- Surveys reveal low public interest in, and extensive public ignorance of, the functions, personnel and issues of local government (which goes some way to explaining some points above).

- Elected members are not very socially representative of those they serve (predominantly elderly, white, male and middle class).
- There has been some criticism of the calibre of councillors, and the reluctance of people with relevant experience and expertise to stand for election to councils.
- There have been some scandals which have undermined public trust in local government (e.g. Doncaster).

Some of these points may be exaggerated – scandals are rare, and the general standard of conduct is reckoned to be high. There are elements of contradiction in other criticisms. Higher calibre councillors would almost certainly mean councillors who were less socially representative. Thus although it is sometimes lamented that not enough businesspeople become councillors, businesspeople are commonly over-represented compared with their numbers in the community. Moreover, it is still the case that elected multi-purpose bodies remain the simplest and most effective means of representing local communities. If local democratic institutions are not working as well as they might, this suggests a need for reform rather than their further erosion. A number of changes have been tried or canvassed:

- Making voting easier, e.g. by holding elections on Sundays or public holidays, improving the location of polling stations, making more use of postal votes, or using telephone or Internet voting.
- Reforming the electoral system, to make councils more representative, and make votes count more.
- Reorganising local government by relating local authorities to meaningful communities.
- Making local authority decision making more effective and transparent, e.g. by scrapping the committee system for a strong executive such as a local cabinet system or directly elected mayor.
- Taking local government to the people, decentralising power through areas committees and neighbourhood councils, and improving opportunities for citizen participation.

Some of these changes have already been tried, with varying success. Thus limited experiments in easier postal voting, telephone and electronic voting did increase turnout in 2002 (Lynch, 2002). Blair's

Labour government has also legislated to force through stronger executive leadership on councils. So far, there have been mixed results on referendums to introduce directly elected mayors, and whether this experiment will increase interest in local government remains to be seen (Wilson and Game, 2002: 360–6). While some are enthusiastic, the local government world and many academics are sceptical. Relating local authorities to meaningful communities was one of the objectives of the 1992–6 Banham Commission on local government reorganisation set up by John Major, which was generally accounted a failure (Leach, 1998). Reforming the local electoral system has yet to be tried, although it is on the agenda in Scotland. While it may reduce the number of 'wasted' votes (and thus increase the incentive to vote) and also reduce one-party councils, it has to be said that the introduction of proportional representation in other elections (e.g. to the European Parliament in 1999) has not increased interest or turnout. Decentralising power and increasing participation have been recurrent themes in experiments from the 1960s onwards, often with some immediate effect but with generally little longer-term impact. While it may be argued that much of the participation on offer is token rather than real, it is also the case that active participation requires interest, time, energy and long-term commitment, commodities that are generally in short supply.

The problems of local democracy, and of citizen involvement in local governance, cannot be divorced from the general problems of public apathy and alienation manifested in declining turnout in national elections in the UK and elsewhere (see Chapter 6), in declining participation in political parties (see Chapter 8), and declining interest in traditional forms of political communication (see Chapter 10). If democracy is to be meaningful, new ways of engaging with people may have to be developed.

If local authorities are imperfectly democratic, most of the other agencies involved in the delivery of local public services are hardly democratic at all. Some however contain directly or indirectly elected elements. Thus parent and staff governors of schools are elected. School governors also include members (commonly elected councillors themselves) nominated by the council, and such indirect representation is found on some other bodies. More commonly members are appointed, and research shows that such appointed members are generally much less socially representative of the local community than councillors. Many of these other local agencies are less open in their procedures than elected local authorities. Yet although more could be done to make some of this 'other local government' more open and accountable, there is more to be said for it than is admitted by critics:

- Some bodies enable service users and community representatives to become directly involved in service management and provision, aiding citizen participation (sometimes among the 'socially excluded') and arguably a more direct form of democracy. The ballot box is not the only way to give people a voice in decisions that affect them.
- Some more specialist agencies are able to tap community resources (e.g. voluntary labour, specialist expertise, money) which might be less easily available to large multi-purpose organisations.
- More complex partnerships and networks may be essential to accommodate multi-agency and cross-sector working.

The politics of local governance: local interests and parties

Politics is about power. Just as decisions by national governments create winners and losers, so do the processes of local governance. A decision to redevelop a city centre, close a school or hospital, build a new sports centre or high-speed tram system, give a grant to a youth club, transfer housing stock to a housing association, will inevitably impact on the local community, benefiting some and upsetting others. Rightly or wrongly, decisions may be perceived to benefit particular groups at the expense of others – middle class suburban dwellers, or ethnic minorities, or unmarried mothers. Those living in 'sink estates' may feel that 'they' never do anything for 'us'. Those concerned by their rising national and council taxes may feel too much money is 'squandered' on people who trash the expensive services and facilities lavished on them by 'do-gooders'. Some of those in authority may be seen as acting in a systematically biased way, destroying trust in institutions such as the police, or social services departments or schools. Such perceptions can even raise inter-community tensions to such an extent as to provoke riots and serious disorder. Even where such violent manifestations of conflicting interests are fortunately absent there may be a host of cross-cutting political differences – between motorists and public transport users, between inner city dwellers and suburbanites, between commercial and residential interests, between second home owners and rural workers, between those who favour developments that offer employment opportunities (such as a new airport, supermarket or factory) and those who wish to conserve the environment.

Some of these conflicts are manifested in local party politics. Most local authorities and virtually all of the major urban councils are run on party political lines, contested by the same parties that contest national elections (although independents still predominate in some more rural areas). While some critics suggest that party politics is unnecessary or positively harmful in local government, the same issues and interests that divide parties nationally are largely replicated at local level, so party involvement is inevitable and assists the democratic process for the same reasons as in national politics. In practice party politics involves more contested elections and voter choice, and party campaigning tends to increase interest and turnout.

Traditionally Labour dominates in the cities, particularly in the inner urban areas, while the Conservatives have controlled the more rural and suburban authorities, and Liberal Democrats, like lightning, can strike anywhere, including northern cities like Liverpool or Sheffield, prosperous commuter territory (e.g. some of the outer London boroughs, Harrogate in Yorkshire), or the Celtic fringe – the south west of England, rural Wales and Scotland. By and large, Labour-controlled authorities are more likely to favour spending on core public services, while Conservatives are keener to keep council tax low, although there are some important differences within both parties as well as between them, and the Liberal Democrats in particular may be associated with different interests in different areas, championing inner city interests sometimes taken for granted by Labour in some authorities, and competing with the Conservatives for suburban votes elsewhere. The relatively recent success of first Liberals and now Liberal Democrats in local government has led to more 'hung' or 'balanced' councils where no single party has overall control, leading in many cases to informal and often formal coalitions, most usually between Labour and the Liberal Democrats (as in the Scottish Parliament or Welsh Assembly), but sometimes between Conservatives and Liberal Democrats. Such coalition politics would undoubtedly increase further if proportional representation was ever introduced into local elections. As it is, some councils are virtually one-party.

Decision making within organisations: local politicians, managers and professionals

Just as in national politics there is some debate over the relative power of elected politicians and appointed bureaucrats (see Chapter 13), there is a similar debate over the influence of councillors and senior local government officers in local government. Officers have their own professional and departmental interests to defend, and have familiar advantages in terms of permanence, expertise and control over information. Some have concluded that it is officers who effectively rule rather than elected members. Yet it is members who have formal authority and thus legitimacy, and a party organisation behind them. Increasingly also, leading members of larger authorities are virtually full-time rather than part-time amateurs. Members can take effective control if they have the will, as is demonstrated by the record of some left-wing Labour councils and New Right-inspired Conservative councils. Moreover, as with ministers and civil servants, the relationship between members and officers may often be collaborative rather than competitive, sharing an interest in a particular department or service, and often supporting similar policies. This tendency is perhaps increased by the large number of different types of authority in which senior local government officers can choose to make their careers. Officers who have their own political opinions may thus gravitate towards authorities in which they feel more comfortable. Yet the local government professions also have their own interests to advance and defend.

The internal decision making processes of local councils have aroused much criticism in the past, particularly the delays involved in hierarchies of committees of elected members deciding on recommendations which are generally the consequence of a similarly (but less open) complex hierarchy of groups of officials. Moreover, the committee system obscured the realities of power in many councils, for the real debates and decisions took place behind closed doors in party group meetings, turning all-party committee meetings into a purely formal registering of decisions already taken by the ruling party group. All this, it was argued, was confusing to the public and hardly helped the cause of increased accountability, democratic governance and local participation.

One fashionable remedy, advocated by the Conservative politician Michael Heseltine among others, was directly elected mayors with real power, an idea borrowed from local government in France and some US cities. The incoming Labour government also saw merit in elected mayors. In 1998 the government issued a consultation paper *Modernising Local Government*, which argued for a stronger exec-utive, followed by a White Paper in the same year, with a strong steer towards elected mayors, although a local Cabinet system was another recommended option. Legislation followed in 2000, which obliged every council to consult the local community on plans for reform. It was hoped that prominent local figures outside conventional local party politics might be tempted to stand. From a Labour perspective the promotion of elected mayors got off to a bad start with the voters' choice of Ken Livingstone as Mayor of London (see Box 18.6 and In Focus 18.1) over the Conservative and official Labour candidate. Things have hardly improved since. Most local referendums held to date have rejected elected mayors, and there have been some surprising results in the few local authorities where mayoral elections have already taken place, including the choice of 'H'Angus the Monkey' (Stuart Drummond) as Mayor of Hartlepool on a platform which included free bananas for school children, a pledge apparently unfulfilled (Rathbone, 2002; Wilson, *New Statesman* 13 January 2003). It is too early to tell whether the introduction of directly elected mayors will transform local government deci-sion making, or increase interest and involvement in local government, but the record to date is not very encouraging (Wilson and Game, 2002: 100–7, 360–6).

Needless to say, there is politics involved also in the internal decision making of appointed bodies, although this may not involve overt party conflict (even if the parties may exert considerable influence

---

BOX 18. 4

Comparative politics – running US cities – mayors and city managers

American city government has provided some of the models for proposed reforms of UK local government, and particularly the introduction of elected mayors. There are four principal systems used in the USA:

- **Strong mayor and council** – there is a directly elected mayor who is the most powerful person in the city, and appoints all departmental heads, although an elected council debates and endorses local policy and legislation.
- **Weak mayor and council** – the mayor is directly elected but so are many departmental heads, so the power of the mayor is less (although may be strengthened by a disciplined party organisation).
- **City commission** – a small number of commissioners are elected to run the city on a city-wide ballot. (This system was introduced in the early 20th century to counteract corruption in city politics.)
- **Council-manager systems** – councillors (or commissioners) are elected by the city, but appoint a city manager to execute their policy. The city manager appoints heads of department and other employees. Although city managers effectively run cities, they are not elected, but are employees of the council and can be (and often are) sacked.

---

on appointments to some bodies). Thus there are conflicts between different professions and different specialisms in the health service, with some presti-gious areas (like surgery) often claiming a large share of scarce resources. These conflicts may mirror the differing priorities of national and local politicians. There is also sometimes a conflict between the appointed and largely part-time lay members of authorities and the full-time professional officers and managers, similar in some respects to the conflict between elected members and officers in local govern-ment, and a conflict between medical practitioners who insist on their professional autonomy and general managers or accountants seeking to reduce costs. The wider public may be less aware of these conflicts than those within elected local government as there is less accountability and publicity, but the conflicts may be just as sharp, with often major, if not generally appreciated, consequences to service users.

Both elected and appointed local agencies are subject to a wide range of pressure group interests (see Chapter 9), including groups of local residents or council tenants, parent–teacher associations (PTAs), groups concerned with particular diseases or medical conditions (e.g. dyslexia and Alzheimer's), leisure groups (e.g. allotment associations, sports clubs), producer interests (e.g. chambers of commerce representing business interests and trades federations representing workers and trade unions). These are generally engaged in the political process not entirely for altruistic reasons but to secure benefits for their members – policy decisions in their favour, new equipment or facilities, often financial support of some kind. Some groups, however, have something to offer local public bodies – information, expertise, even voluntary labour in the case of some established third-sector groups. Gerry Stoker (1991) concluded that the willingness of councils to respond to various types of pressure groups depended closely on their prevailing politics. Labour councils may be more prepared to listen to trade unions, tenants' groups, women's groups and ethnic minority associations, while Conservative councils may pay more attention to the local chamber of commerce and business interests generally, as well as professional interests and local residents' associations. Other groups may be relatively ignored.

Territory and community: the reorganisation of structure

Local governance, by definition, is about locality, but what kind of locality? How are the areas for the local governmental bodies drawn up? How large can they be (in area or population) and still be termed local? How small can they be and still fulfil their functions effectively? How far do they match the pattern of life and work in modern Britain, and how far do they match the local communities with which people actually identify?

> **BOX 18.5**
> **The community power debate**
>
> There has been a long academic debate among scholars in Britain, to an extent echoing similar debate in other countries such as the USA and France, over power in the local community. Pluralists who argue that power is widely distributed have often used urban politics to demonstrate this. They have cited evidence from decision making to demonstrate that there is no single local elite dominating the town and its policy processes. Others have cited different kinds of evidence to demonstrate the existence of urban elites. American radicals and French Marxists have argued that decision making systematically favours business interests. Much of this community power debate has been replicated in Britain, although it has been similarly inconclusive. Older case studies found evidence for a quasi-pluralist policy process in Birmingham (Newton, 1976), elite decision making in Kensington and Chelsea (Dearlove, 1973), and strong business influence in Lambeth (Cockburn, 1977) and Croydon (Saunders, 1980). Perhaps these merely confirmed the initial perspectives of some of the academics involved, although they do all illustrate the complexity of the conflicting interests involved in the governance of urban areas, and dramatise some of the issues involved in the distribution of power locally.

The reform of local government and governance has been obsessed with these question for 40 years or more, and they are no nearer a resolution than at the start. Behind theoretical discussions over efficiency and community there are often more covert concerns over power and influence. New boundaries may transform the balance between parties and interests. Most debate has taken place over the structure of Britain's elected local authorities, but there has also been a long-running argument over the optimum areas for administering health, and more recently on bodies concerned with specific functions such as police, or vocational training. Needless to say, different areas and boundaries for different agencies increase the problems of collaboration between them.

A common perception was that many of the ills of local government stemmed from a defective structure. Thus from the early 1960s onwards there have been a series of real and projected reorganisations of the size, boundaries and functions of elected authorities. Some of these reorganisations have been widespread, covering all or most of the country, such as the major upheavals of 1972–4, and the more recent reorganisations of Scottish and Welsh local authorities (1996) and English shire counties and districts (1992–6) under John Major's government. There have also been other changes restricted to particular parts of the country, such as the continuing saga of London government, under which a London-wide strategic authority was established by one Conservative government (Macmillan's) in 1963, abolished by another (Thatcher's) in 1986, to be re-established in rather different form by Blair's Labour government in 2000 (see Box 18.6). Abortive changes which were not implemented, largely because the governments sponsoring them lost power, include the radical Redcliffe–Maud report of 1969 (Wilson's Labour government) and 1979 plans to restore powers to the cities under Callaghan.

In retrospect, many of these reforms reflected prevailing fashion or current academic and political wisdom: for example, the faith that larger local authorities would result in economies of scale and improve efficiency in the 1960s, and the subsequent reaction against 'big government' in favour of more flexible units 'closer to the people' in the 1980s and 1990s. Similarly, there was a recurring debate between those advocating a two-tier system of local government, and those wanting all local government functions to be concentrated in the hands of one all-purpose or unitary authority. Particular models drifted in and out of fashion – the notion of 'city regions', based on cities and their hinterland, (which partially inspired Scottish reorganisation in 1974) or 'estuarine authorities', straddling both banks of river estuaries (Humberside, Teesside).

Whether all, or indeed any, of this frantic reorganisation produced the benefits anticipated is questionable. The direct and indirect costs of organisational change were certainly considerable, and the savings and improvements in efficiency substantially unquantifiable. It is difficult to

argue that local government is now less confusing to the public. On the contrary, periodic changes involving new unfamiliar names for redesigned authorities have had the opposite effect. Commonly reorganisation stirred up a hornet's nest, for although relatively few people know much about local government or can be sufficiently bothered to vote in local elections, a minority seem to care passionately about particular areas or authorities – fervently campaigning to save or restore Rutland, abolish Humberside, reinstitute the Yorkshire Ridings. The view of many of those who have followed the twists and turns of the reorganisation saga is that future governments would be well-advised to think twice before embarking on another attempt (e.g.

Photograph: PA Photos.

IN FOCUS 18.1 The Mayor of London

London's Mayor, Ken Livingstone (right) and Chair of the London Assembly Trevor Phillips walk with Queen Elizabeth II in her visit to open the new City Hall. Livingstone, the former Leader of the Greater London Council abolished by Margaret Thatcher's government, was denied the Labour nomination for the new post of directly elected mayor and won as an independent against all-party opposition in 2000.

BOX 18.6

The government of London: the London Mayor and Greater London Authority

The earlier Greater London Council, established by a Conservative government in 1963, was abolished in 1986 by the Thatcher government, which detested its left-wing Labour council and leader, Ken Livingstone. The new 1997 Labour government was pledged to restore a strategic authority for London. It proposed a smaller and less powerful Greater London Authority and a directly elected mayor. These proposals were endorsed by 72 per cent of voters (on a turnout of 34 per cent) in a referendum of Londoners in 1998.

The Labour Party was confident of winning the election in 2000 for the high-prestige post of mayor, but the Labour leadership was determined to block the candidacy of former GLC leader, Ken Livingstone (a maverick Labour MP since 1987). The former Health Secretary Frank Dobson very narrowly and controversially defeated Livingstone for the Labour nomination. The outcome was a severe embarrassment for Labour. Livingstone stood as an independent, defeating Steve Norris (who had replaced the disgraced Jeffrey Archer as Conservative candidate) under the

supplementary vote system, with Dobson a distant and eliminated third. The elections for the 25-strong GLA Assembly resulted in 9 Labour members, 9 Conservatives, 4 Liberal Democrats and 3 Greens. The GLA has strategic (but not operational) responsibilities for transport, policing, fire and emergency planning, economic development and planning, and is now housed close to Tower Bridge in a new building designed by Lord Foster.

Livingstone's position combines a high profile with relatively weak powers. He initially tried to run an all-party administration, although he and Steve Norris subsequently parted company, and he has relied largely on Labour within the GLA. He was engaged in a long-running battle with the Labour government over its public–private partnership for the modernisation of the London tube, which did little to heal his rift with the party. More damaging for his own popularity has been the introduction of congestion charges as a bold but controversial bid to alleviate London's traffic jams.

London	England			Scotland	Wales
	Provincial conurbations	**Rest of England**			
Two-tier	*Unitary*	*Mixed*		*Unitary*	*Unitary*
Greater London Authority & Mayor (1)	Metropolitan districts (36)	Unitary authorities (46)	County councils (34)	Unitary authorities (32)	Unitary authorities (22)
London boroughs (32)			District councils (238)		
	(parish or neighbourhood councils)				

Figure 18.1 The structure of elected local government in Britain

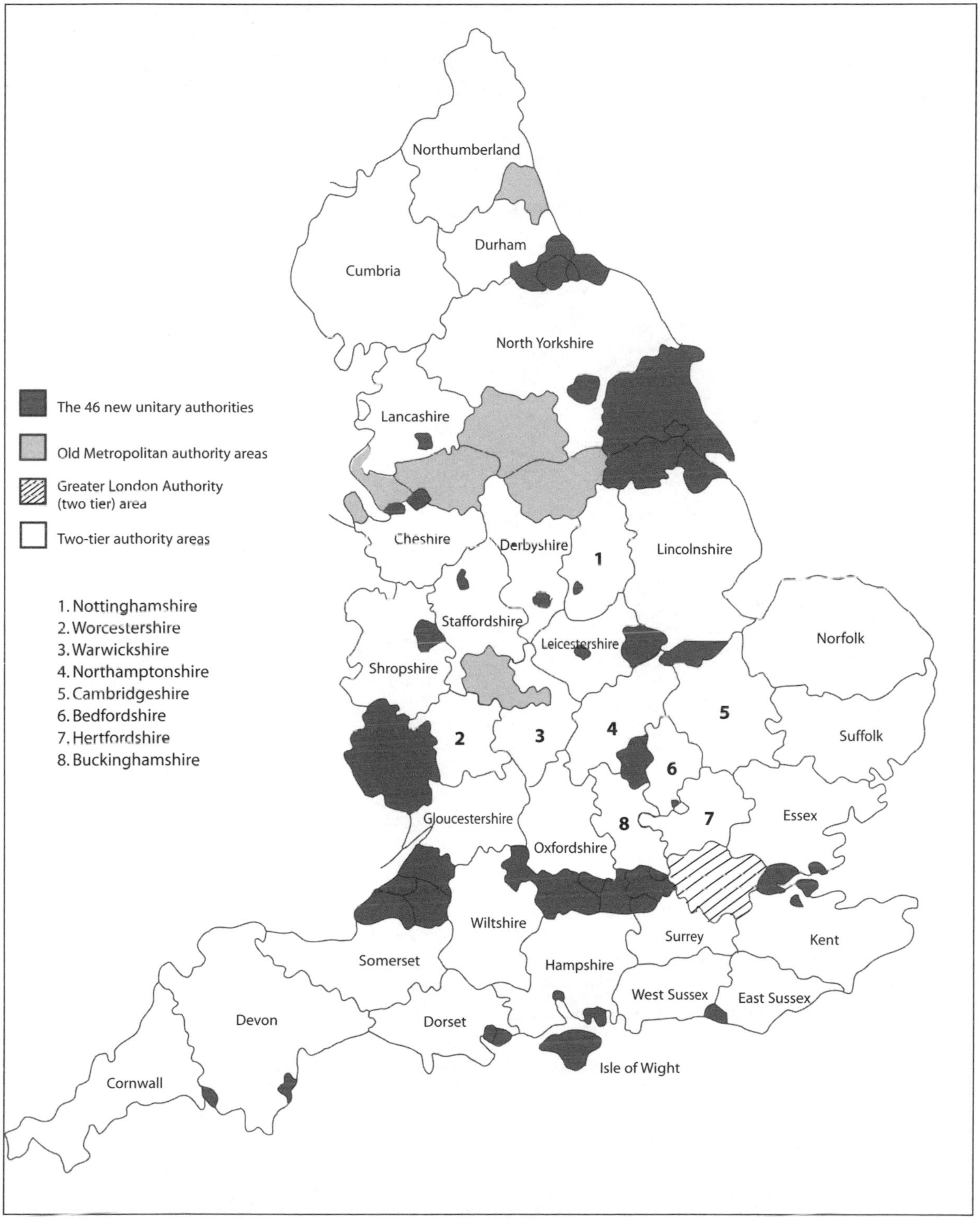
The 46 new unitary authorities
Old Metropolitan authority areas
Greater London Authority (two tier) area
Two-tier authority areas
1. Nottinghamshire
2. Worcestershire
3. Warwickshire
4. Northamptonshire
5. Cambridgeshire
6. Bedfordshire
7. Hertfordshire
8. Buckinghamshire
Northumberland
Durham
Cumbria
North Yorkshire
Lancashire
Cheshire
Derbyshire
Lincolnshire
Norfolk
Staffordshire
Leicestershire
Shropshire
Suffolk
Essex
Gloucestershire
Oxfordshire
Wiltshire
Surrey
Kent
Somerset
Hampshire
West Sussex
East Sussex
Devon
Dorset
Isle of Wight
Cornwall

Figure 18.2 The local authority map in England from 1998

Source: Based on Wilson and Game, 2002.

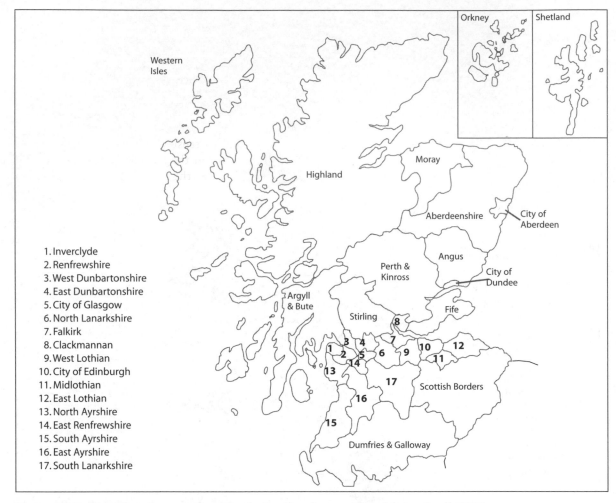

1. Inverclyde
2. Renfrewshire
3. West Dunbartonshire
4. East Dunbartonshire
5. City of Glasgow
6. North Lanarkshire
7. Falkirk
8. Clackmannan
9. West Lothian
10. City of Edinburgh
11. Midlothian
12. East Lothian
13. North Ayrshire
14. East Renfrewshire
15. South Ayrshire
16. East Ayrshire
17. South Lanarkshire

Figure 18.3 The 32 unitary authorities in Scotland operational from April 1996

Source: Based on Wilson and Game, 2002.

Leach, 1998). However, it is suggested that the introduction of a regional elected tier of government in England (see Chapter 17) would require further simplification of local government and the abolition of the two-tier system which remains in most of the shires.

The current local government map in Scotland and Wales (see Figures 18.3 and 18.4) is the result of the latest reorganisation imposed by the Major government. English local government (see map) is still partially shaped by county divisions going back a thousand years, overlaid by more recent tinkering, coupled with the cumulative consequences of successive reorganisations of urban government and lower-tier authorities.

There is now only one level of elected local government in Scotland, Wales and most of the larger cities and towns in England, and two levels (counties and districts) elsewhere.

The delivery of services

The division of the main functions between county and district councils is shown in Table 18.1. By and large, the most important and expensive services are run by the counties. As we have seen, London also now has two elected tiers (London boroughs and the Greater London Authority), but here it is the boroughs that have most effective control of the

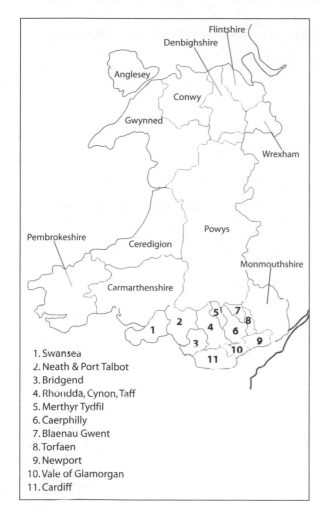

1. Swansea
2. Neath & Port Talbot
3. Bridgend
4. Rhondda, Cynon, Taff
5. Merthyr Tydfil
6. Caerphilly
7. Blaenau Gwent
8. Torfaen
9. Newport
10. Vale of Glamorgan
11. Cardiff

Figure 18.4 The 22 unitary authorities in Wales operational from April 1996

Source: Based on Wilson and Game, 2002.

delivery of local services. Unitary authorities (all those in Scotland and Wales, and in the metropolitan areas of England, plus a few new unitaries established by the latest local government reorganisation) combine county and district functions. To complicate matters further, some areas (mainly more rural areas) have flourishing small parish councils with few powers, and others have introduced largely consultative lower-tier neighbourhood or community councils.

The areas for administering local health services have generally been determined by the perceived functional requirements of the service rather than notions of community. Thus local health manage-

ment has been based generally on hospital catchment areas, although in the 1974 reorganisation area health authorities were devised to match the boundaries of local authority authorities responsible for social services. This never worked quite as intended, as the main operational tier consisted of health districts, and in 1982 the Thatcher government abolished the area tier. Although the Blair government is ostensibly driving through further decentralisation in the health service, the hospital trusts (including the proposed new foundation hospitals) and the primary care trusts will not generally cover the same areas as elected local authorities.

The same has been true of other single-purpose local agencies. Training, once a function of elected local authorities, was transferred first to training and enterprise councils, which have been abolished by the Blair government to make way for fewer and larger learning and skills councils. Police authorities have become increasingly autonomous from elected councils, and the operational requirements of the police force are generally held to require larger areas than many local authorities. While economic regeneration remains a major concern of elected local authorities, a plethora of initiatives from central government has involved the establishment of much more localised agencies (for example, the now defunct urban development corporations, mostly covering very limited inner city areas), as well as wider regional bodies (such as the new regional development agencies – see Chapter 17). For some functions, such as transport, there are on-going debates over the most appropriate level, regional or local, for sub-national planning and administration.

Many of these developments take local governance further away from the local communities with which people identify, but which are generally deemed too small for the efficient delivery of local government services. This tension between community self-government and functional efficiency has been a key theme of the debate over areas and structures for 40 years or more. The debate is no nearer resolution, although the general trend is still towards larger areas, despite the reaction against 'big government' (see above), and local governance which appears more remote and less comprehensible to many people.

Table 18.1 Who does what? English county councils and district councils (principal functions)

County council	District council
Education (most of budget now delegated to schools)	
Social services (largely community social workers – but councils regulate privately provided institutional care)	
	Housing (regulation and some provision – but much former council housing sold to tenants and transferred to other landlords, especially housing associations)
Planning (structure plans, environment and conservation, economic and tourism development)	**Planning** (local plans, development control, environment and conservation, economic development)
Highways and transportation (transportation planning, county road building & maintenance)	**Street cleansing and lighting**
Public protection (waste disposal, trading standards, fire services)	**Public protection** (refuse collection, food safety, pollution control)
Leisure and amenities (libraries, county parks, grants to village and community projects)	**Leisure and amenities** (allotments, museums, local parks, playing fields, swimming pools, sports centres)

Reforming the finance of local governance

On the finance of local governance (as of the finance of government nationally) an initial distinction should be drawn between capital spending (spending on long-term projects like hospitals or schools, or very expensive equipment expected to have a long life) and current or revenue spending (money needed for wages and salaries of staff, fuel, materials, interest payments on borrowing and so on). Capital spending by public bodies is usually financed by borrowing (which is the same way as most individuals finance much of their own purchases of houses and expensive longer-life items like cars). Formerly most of this money came from the issuing of government or local authority bonds. As this was part of the Public Sector Borrowing Requirement (PSBR) which successive governments have tried to keep under control to comply with dictates of prudence and international rules, public services have often been starved of capital investment. As a consequence, both the Major Conservative government and the Blair Labour government have sought

new sources of capital investment from the private sector under the private finance initiative, under which the private sector supposedly bears the risk, and undertakes responsibility for completion of projects on time (with penalties for under-performance) and the cost is transferred to the revenue budget. Generally, critics argue, this is a more expensive way of raising capital investment in the long run, but the advantage for government is that it is not part of the Public Sector Borrowing Requirement, while hospital trusts and local authorities may obtain new purpose-built hospitals and schools sooner rather than later.

As for current expenditure, the Chancellor's spending review of 2002 involved substantial increased spending on health and education, and more money for a range of other services (*Guardian*, 16 July 2002). Most of this money, although raised centrally through national taxation, will be spent locally, by schools, hospitals, primary care trusts, police authorities and other bodies. Local governance is thus big business, involving major spending. There is a delicate balance between central direction and local discretion over how this money is spent. All central governments tend to employ the rhetoric of decentralisation – of devolving more autonomy to those responsible for the actual delivery of services. Yet all governments are aware that they will be judged on the effectiveness of their spending and service delivery, so money is given with strings attached – including an increasing number of centrally determined targets that have to be met – otherwise, it is feared, increased spending might disappear into a 'black hole', with no perceptible improvement in public services. At the same time, governments are also aware that meeting their targets depends on the active cooperation of front-line agencies and workers on the ground, who have knowledge of specific local conditions and problems, and need to be given some discretion over management and spending.

There is no easy answer to this tension between central direction and local autonomy, which is particularly evident over spending, because for many services local governance relies substantially or almost entirely on income that the bodies involved do not raise themselves. Hospital trusts may raise some money from voluntary sources and from marginal activities like car parking fees, but this is an insignificant part of their income. The introduction of internal markets in health and education by the Conservative governments of Thatcher and Major gave hospital trusts, GP fundholders and school governing bodies some financial incentives to increase their activities. If money follows patients or pupils, hospitals and schools can increase their income by increasing the numbers of patients treated and pupils admitted, but of course additional patients and pupils also involve additional costs, so careful calculations of income and spending are required. In addition, the rules governing internal markets are determined by government and can be changed. The same goes for rewards for meeting government targets. Local institutions may distort their own priorities to secure additional funding, and then discover that the government's priorities and funding regime have changed.

Conceivably it would be better if local agencies had to raise money locally and justify their spending to the local community, but one obvious problem here is that some local communities are much better off than others. If the quality of local services depended largely or exclusively on the money that could be raised locally, the poorest areas with the greatest needs would have the least income for spending on public services. That is one reason that even elected local authorities that do have their own tax raising powers still rely on grants from the national exchequer for the bulk of their spending. The same goes for other service and agencies. If police authorities or hospital trusts or learning and skills councils had to rely mainly on some form of local taxation, the areas with the most acute law and order problems, health needs and training requirements would receive the least money. Thus almost inevitably local governance is substantially dependent on central funding in some form or other, and the old adage 'who pays the piper calls the tune' applies.

This is not to deny that there may be more scope for local funding and increased local accountability. This is an argument that has been applied particularly to elected local authorities. Commonly, the local council is the largest single employer in its area, and local authorities are responsible for more than a quarter of all public spending. Unsurprisingly, local government expenditure is politically controversial. Those opposed to big government and high public spending in general are critical of council spending and efficiency, and seek to reduce the size and scope of local government, while in contrast there are strong pressures from public sector unions, client groups and other specialised interests to improve service levels and spending.

Besides controversy over the size and scope of local spending, there are arguments over the sources of revenue to meet that expenditure. The bulk of the money spent by councils comes from sources over which they have little or no control, from central government grant (which governments of both parties have often manipulated to favour areas where their own party predominates) and from the now centrally determined business rates (national non-domestic rates or NNDR). Additionally councils derive some income from fees and charges, many of which are discretionary, and from their own council tax. Critics argue that this financial dependence on the national exchequer reflects excessive central dominance of local government, and also reduces effective local accountability, as councils are not responsible for raising most of the revenue they spend.

The council tax was introduced in 1993 (following the disaster of the poll tax, see Box 18.7). It is a tax on the capital value of domestic properties (houses or flats) divided into eight property bands, but with a 25 per cent rebate for one-person households. The actual tax levied will depend not only on the property band (and whether or not a rebate applies) but on the money needed by each local authority for its expenditure (plus the money needed by other authorities, such as police authorities (which 'precept' on the council) after all other receipts are taken into account (national non-domestic rate, central government grant and income derived from fees and charges). Thus levels of council tax depend on where householders live, the value of their property and the number of people in the household. The

BOX 18.7
The poll tax – a policy disaster

The poll tax was a local government tax that was only levied for three years, 1990–3, in England and Wales, and for four years in Scotland (1989–93). It was introduced to replace domestic rates, an ancient tax on property, unpopular for a variety of reasons. The rates were a highly visible form of taxation, unlike for example value added tax (VAT) which is 'hidden' within the price of goods. They were a regressive tax as poorer households paid a larger proportion of their income in rates than affluent households. They were not directly related to the use made of local authority services. Only householders paid rates, so other residents used local services without contributing directly to their cost. They were based on old rental values which few understood. However rates also had advantages from a local government perspective. They were easy to collect, cheap to administer, and difficult to avoid. They could be adjusted easily from year to year to meet a council's spending needs, and their yield could be predicted very accurately. The regressive element in rates was substantially compensated by the introduction of up to 100 per cent rate rebates for poorer householders.

The Conservative government decided to replace rates with a 'community charge'. The name was significant. It was supposed to be a *charge on consumers* for local government services, rather than a *tax* on local *citizens*. Yet it became known universally as the 'poll tax', a per capita tax similar to the poll tax that provoked the Peasants Revolt back in 1381. Almost all adult residents rather than just householders would pay, restoring the link between taxation and representation. The government hoped that this would deter high spending by local councils, who would be punished by voters through the ballot box for their higher poll tax.

Critics argued that the new tax was regressive and unfair because it was not linked to ability to pay. Most local voters found they were paying more, sometimes much more. It proved a bureaucratic nightmare, three times as expensive to collect as the old rates and subject to widespread evasion. Many councils were still chasing up defaulters years after the tax was abolished. It was also widely seen as a tax on voting. Those seeking to evade the new tax (including many students) avoided registering to vote. This also affected population figures used as a basis for government grant calculations. Poorer councils thus suffered twice over – from loss of revenue from defaulters, and loss of income from grants based on an assessment of needs from low population estimates.

Public reaction was very hostile. The tax provoked serious riots, led to major reverses for the Conservatives in Parliamentary by-elections and local elections, and contributed significantly to Margaret Thatcher's departure from Number Ten. The new Conservative government, under John Major, moved to scrap the poll tax, replacing it with a new council tax in 1993, a tax on domestic properties, like the old rates, but based on capital values rather than rental values, and with a simpler method of evaluation.

proportion of total revenue that councils derive from the council tax can vary considerably between authority and authority, as well as over time, but the average council in recent years has met around a quarter of it spending needs from the tax. Because income from other sources can fluctuate considerably from year to year, it does not necessarily follow that an above-inflation increase in council tax is the result of some commensurate increase in a council's spending, nor does a reduction in tax necessarily mean spending cuts. Because changes in council tax levels often bear little relation to changes in spending, effective accountability to the local electorate is reduced. It is difficult even for the tolerably well-informed local taxpayer to know who to blame (or to reward) for a tax bill.

Central–local and inter-authority relations under 'multi-level governance'

There has been a long academic debate over what used to be called 'central–local relations', perceived as the relationship between the government at Westminster and elected local authorities. Central–local relations implies that there are only two levels of government that matter, and is thus now a rather inadequate term to describe the still developing system of multi-level governance in Britain, with which local governance has to relate.

Thus the European Union has a large and growing impact on British local governance, both as a source of additional funding, chiefly through the European Regional Development Fund and the Social Fund, as well as specific funding for problems such as the decline of coal mining, and through the impact of EU legislation on local responsibilities for the environment, waste management, transport and planning. Local authorities are now among the most vigorous lobbyists in Brussels.

Among the various levels of government with which English local authorities have to relate, the most important by far remains the government at Westminster. Local authorities in Scotland, Wales and Northern Ireland have devolved national as well as the now more remote UK government to cope with, and even in England government offices for the regions, regional development agencies and

regional chambers constitute together a growing regional administrative tier with which local councils have to deal. Moreover, decentralisation of decision making to institutions like schools means that councils have to relate to an increasingly important level of government below them.

The position is complicated by the fragmentation of local governance. Local agencies have to deal 'horizontally' with each other, and the private and voluntary sectors locally, as well as 'vertically' with other levels of governance.

Central–local relations have commonly been illustrated in terms of various analogies or models. Thus some saw local government as the 'partner' of central government, which implies a degree of equality, while others perceived local government in a position of impotent dependence as the 'agent' of the centre. A third view uses the term 'steward' which emphasises the subordinate position of local government but suggests rather more discretion than the agent model. Finally, the 'power dependence' model suggests that both central and local government have resources that they can use in relationship with each other (Rhodes, 1981, 1988). These models can be adapted (if somewhat awkwardly) to meet the more complex relationships arising within multi-level and inter-authority governance. Thus if elected local authorities are too dependent on central government for their powers and finance to be regarded as 'partners', the same is even more true of other public agencies that do not have the legitimacy of election, or their own taxes. Yet knowledge of local conditions and responsibility for implementation of central policies can give local agencies of all kinds considerable leverage over decisions locally and policy outcomes. In practice there are significant differences between policies and service levels between local authorities, and similar differences were seen between various training and enterprise councils (TECs) and will presumably be evident in the local learning and skills councils which have replaced them. Similar points could be made about health authorities, hospital trusts and primary care trusts. The chances of patients receiving certain forms of treatment, their waiting times, and their survival rates from difficult operations depend to a significant degree on where they live. If such bodies were simply agents implementing national policy, these substantial differences would not exist.

It is the 'power dependence' model that can most usefully be adapted to inter-authority relations, and relations between the public, private and voluntary sectors (Rhodes, 1997). In partnerships and policy networks, for example, each participating organisation may bring in certain strengths or resources that will help to determine its influence in decision making. Thus in a public–private partnership, a local council may contribute significant statutory powers, finance, information and legitimacy arising from its election, while a private firm may offer additional finance, commercial enterprise and experience, and specific expertise. In a collaborative relationship between public agencies, such as between a local authority and health authorities over care in the community, each participant brings something that is useful to the other, and both may benefit from a fruitful cooperation (in a positive-sum rather than zero-sum game). Health authorities benefit from the transfer of some patients from expensive institutional care to cheaper community care, while cash-starved local authorities obtain some health service finance to improve levels of care. If the policy operates properly patients should benefit also, as many prefer to stay in their own homes or in sheltered accommodation rather than have to enter a long-stay hospital or local-authority-regulated care home to obtain the level of personal and nursing service they need (although in practice some of the burden of care is effectively transferred not to professional staff but to largely female relatives).

Optimists see the new world of local governance as offering many opportunities for the development of cooperative policy network in which organisations from the public, private and voluntary sectors work together, drawing on a wide range of resources, and encouraging the inclusion and participation of people from across the whole local community. Instead of the command and control relationships typical of old-fashioned public bureaucracies, or the competitive zero-sum relationships of the free market, such networks involve a collaborative positive-sum relationship between equals, involving diplomatic skills and different less authoritative forms of leadership, a true 'third way' in managing and delivering services to people (Rhodes, 1997).

Pessimists by contrast emphasise the fragmentation of government, the potential waste, duplication and inefficiency resulting from too many agencies with overlapping responsibilities. They are more cynical over the prospects for mutual cooperation between organisations in policy networks, assuming that each will follow its own self-interest, guided by its own organisational culture. Some formal partners will be only token participants and will offer few if any useful resources. The bulk of the local community will be bemused by the more complex and fast-changing institutional environment, and will become more apathetic and alienated rather than engaged participants. No one will be effectively in charge, and accountability will be weaker. Decisions will take longer and less will be achieved.

Further reading

The relevant chapters (mainly 5, 6 and 7) of Greenwood, Pyper and Wilson (2001) offer a very useful introduction. Wilson and Game (2002) provides a more thorough account of contemporary local government which focuses largely on elected local authorities, although it provides some coverage of non-elected local government. The most recent edition of an older textbook, Byrne (2000), can also still be recommended. Leach and Percy-Smith (2001) focuses on governance (including other public bodies, the private and voluntary sector) as well as traditional local government. Rhodes (1997) does not focus exclusively on local governance, but his analysis of policy networks is useful for understanding much of the governance literature.

Books covering more specific aspects of local governance include Gyford (1991), Stoker (1991) and Skelcher (1998). Butler, Adonis and Travers (1994) provides a detailed analysis of the poll tax story.

As always, websites provide important sources on recent and current developments, e.g. <www.local.gov.uk> and the Local Government Association's website <www.lga.gov.uk>. Many local authorities have their own websites. Newspapers and specialist academic journals (e.g. *Local Government Studies*) and professional journals (e.g. *Municipal Journal)* are other useful sources.

Chapter 19

The new British state: towards multi-level governance

Characterising the modern British state   327
The attack on government   329
Restructuring the state: quangos and
    agencies   329
Privatisation, contracting out and
    competition   332
New Labour and partnership with business
    and the voluntary sector   333
Steering, not rowing: the enabling state   335
The regulatory state   335
Open government and the secret state   338
The disintegration of the British state or
    towards multi-level governance?   341

In this final chapter in Part IV we seek to bring together some of the strands identified in previous chapters as well as some additional material, in an attempt to characterise the newly emerging British state. While it is clear that the British state has changed and will almost certainly be subject to further transformation, there is less agreement on the nature of the British state today. Here we will outline and evaluate some of the contrasting verdicts on modern British government, and in the process review concerns over non-elected government (quangos), the growth of regulation, and government secrecy. We examine the New Right criticism of government and the public sector, and New Labour's approach to governing, which has emphasised partnership with the private and voluntary sectors, policy networks, and 'joined-up government'. We conclude with a discussion of the role of the fast-changing British state within a system of multi-level governance.

Characterising the modern British state

There have always been conflicting characterisations of the British state. While admirers in the early 20th century lauded a free modern democratic state, critics abroad and at home saw a repressive, secretive, tradition-ridden imperialist state. Although Marxists regarded the British state as a capitalist state dominated by business interests, those in the centre of the political spectrum saw a welfare state with a mixed economy, while neo-liberal critics dubbed Britain a collectivist state. All this serves to emphasise the contentious and essentially subjective nature of such descriptions. How the British state is viewed, both in the past and today, inevitably reflects ideological assumptions.

While it is widely agreed that the British state and the processes of British government has changed massively over the last 25–35 years, there is less agreement over how that change should be characterised. Some would emphasise the extent to which reforms of institutions and processes have, over a period, transformed traditional constitutional principles such as Parliamentary sovereignty and the unity of the United Kingdom. Yet from another perspective the real changes seem to have more to do with the functions of the state than its constitution. Thus it was the Thatcher government's privatisation and contracting-out programme, in reaction against 'big government', that has led to the 'rolling back' or 'hollowing out' of the state (Rhodes, 1997, 2000).

By contrast, for some commentators Thatcherism involved a strong state rather than the minimal state lauded by neo-liberals (Gamble, 1994), and centralisation rather than the decentralisation to consumers and service users claimed in government rhetoric. The apparent contradiction was sometimes resolved by the suggestion that the government was seeking 'more control over less' (Rhodes, 2000: 156). While some, largely sympathetic, politicians and commentators emphasised the new enabling role of the state, under which government sought to enable others, including the private and voluntary sectors, to deliver public services, critics pointed to a massive increase in state regulation, and the creation of a regulatory rather than the old 'welfare' or 'control' state (Moran, 2000, 2001). Yet the Thatcher government claimed to be in the business of deregulation – relaxing planning controls and deregulating bus transport, as well as criticising the 'excessive regulation' emanating from Brussels.

Today the state appears more complex. The fashionable term 'governance' emphasises the process of governing rather than the institutions of government, and blurs the distinction between government and governed. Governance does not just include those who as ministers, civil servants, or elected councillors are part of 'government' but business and the voluntary sector, parties and pressure groups in so far as they contribute to the process of governance and the delivery of services to the community.

Governance necessarily involves collaboration between agencies and sectors, and partnership working rather than the clear lines of authority and responsibility found in more traditional management hierarchies. It draws on the agenda of the Americans Osborne and Gaebler in *Reinventing Government* (1992), some of the ideas of the new public management (see Chapter 13), together with strands of New Labour and third way thinking (Giddens, 1998, Newman, 2001), as well as the writings of some leading British political scientists, including Rhodes (1997) and Stoker (1999, 2000; Pierre and Stoker in Dunleavy *et al.*, 2002).

Another prominent theme has focused on the extent to which the British state has become more or less democratic. One trend, commonly lamented, has been the growth of appointed bodies or quangos, apparently at the expense of control by democratically elected politicians. Thus critics talk

> **Definition**
> **Quango** is an acronym for (originally) quasi-autonomous non-governmental organisation. Quangos are, however normally funded, appointed and ultimately controlled by the state (so part of government), but they have a degree of independence as they are not part of government departments nor directly accountable to ministers or elected politicians. National quangos are officially described as 'non-departmental public bodies' (NDPBs) and are thus distinguished from executive agencies (see Chapter 13) which have some managerial autonomy but are attached to departments.

of the 'appointed state', 'quangocracy' or the 'new magistracy', and lament a 'democratic deficit' as more decisions are apparently made by unaccountable appointed agencies or bureaucrats (Skelcher, 1998). The most obvious manifestation of this trend has been the erosion of powers and responsibilities of elected local authorities (see Chapter 18). Yet there are also now many more opportunities for citizens to cast votes than 30 or 40 years ago – for the European Parliament, for devolved assemblies, in national and local referendums, for school governing bodies and user councils, to the extent that declining electoral turnout and apathy is sometimes blamed on 'voter fatigue' or overload.

A closely allied debate has taken place over the issues of freedom of information and open government. While the Blair government has introduced a Freedom of Information Act and has emphasised open government, critics suggest this has more to do with rhetoric than reality, alleging that the British state remains a 'secret state'.

Table 19.1 From old government to new governance: the shifting focus

Old government	New governance
The state	The state and civil society
The public sector	Public, private and voluntary (or third) sectors
Institutions of government	Processes of governing
Organisational structures	Policies, outputs, outcomes
Providing ('rowing')	Enabling ('steering')
Commanding, controlling, directing	Leading, facilitating, collaborating, bargaining
Hierarchy and authority	Partnerships and networks

Source: adapted from Leach and Percy-Smith, 2001: 5.

Finally, and fundamentally, there is now considerable debate over how far the state is or can remain British. Doubts on the survival of a British state are relatively recent. Although there has sometimes been considerable controversy over the direction in which British government and politics was going, it is only in the last 30 years. and more particularly the last 10 years, that serious doubts have grown over the extent to which the state would remain British. Today it is sometimes argued that the independence and sovereignty of the British state has been eroded substantially, from above by the European Union and other supra-national bodies, as well as by the more intangible power of global capitalism, and from below by devolution, decentralisation and fragmentation. Perhaps more important than the institutional changes associated with these trends are issues of identity and allegiance. Thus devolution can be seen as a consequence rather than a cause of a declining British identity, and the fragmentation of personal allegiance. Yet at the same time it is also possible that UK citizens will be able to embrace multiple allegiances and identities within an evolving system of multi-level governance.

The attack on government

The last two centuries have seen a massive and unprecedented growth in the activities of the British state and the size of public spending. The growth has not been steady and continuous. Wars in general, and both 20th-century World Wars in particular, have provided a strong stimulus to increased government intervention and regulation while accustoming people to higher levels of taxation. Thus while peace involved a fall from previously high wartime expenditure, it did not involve a return to pre-war levels. After the Second World War, following an initial fall, public spending rose steadily, partly in response to demographic trends (including longer life expectancy), but more especially as a consequence of deliberate public policy. All parties were apparently committed to the welfare state and Keynesian demand policies. This meant the state accepted extensive responsibilities for the provision of health, housing and full employment, on top of a new system of social security from the 'cradle to the grave'.

By the mid-1970s there was a marked reaction against 'big government'. Partly this reflected opposition to rising levels of taxes to meet the bill for rising public spending, but it also reflected some disillusion with the results of state welfare provision and full employment policies. Thus it appeared that the welfare state had not succeeded in abolishing poverty, as the rediscovery of child poverty had made apparent. State housing and planning policies had produced some conspicuous disasters in the form of uninhabitable tower blocks and 'sink' estates. Keynesian demand management no longer appeared able to deliver full employment, growth and tolerable levels of inflation: instead Conservative and Labour governments alike presided over 'stagflation': economic stagnation with rising unemployment on the hand and accelerating inflation on the other, a combination that orthodox Keynesian economists had previously considered impossible.

Critics, particularly on the right of the political spectrum, but not just from the right, argued that the problem was not this or that specific government policy, but government in general. Government had grown too big. Public spending was absorbing dangerously high levels of total national income, crowding out private sector enterprise and investment. High marginal levels of taxation were destroying incentives to hard work and risk taking. Government organisations, it was argued, were inherently inefficient, as they were not subject to effective competition and the profit motive. The remedy was thus to cut public spending and roll back the state (Kavanagh, 1990). The attack on big government became the new orthodoxy, pursued with some reluctance by Callaghan's Labour government (1976–9), and then more enthusiastically by Thatcher's Conservative government.

Restructuring the state: quangos and agencies

The Thatcher government, as we have seen (Chapter 4) was ideologically committed to a revival of free market thinking which favoured a substantial reduction in the public sector coupled with policies to encourage competition and the private sector. Some of the cuts in public spending were real and painful enough to those who felt their effects, but the overall reduction in state expenditure was no more than marginal. That was because cuts in some services were matched by increases in others, sometimes as a result of deliberate policy (the government initially, but not later, increased spending on defence and law and order) but more substantially because of the steep rise in unemployment, with inevitable consequences for the social security budget. Moreover, some areas of the welfare state, such as especially the NHS, remained too popular to touch; thus Thatcher herself declared that the National Health Service was safe in her hands. The rhetoric of Thatcherism outran its performance. The state and public spending were restructured rather than drastically cut back. There were certainly cuts in some parts of the public sector, in the number of civil servants, and later in the size and spending of elected local authorities. However many of the activities involved were not abolished or transferred to the private sector, but reorganised within the public sector.

One aspect of this restructuring was the growth in number of quangos. A 'quango' is a rather ugly acronym, originally standing for 'quasi-autonomous non-governmental organisation', although 'non-governmental' is something of a misnomer, as most of the organisations dubbed 'quangos' are funded by the taxpayer, and indirectly appointed and controlled by government. Thus 'quango' is sometimes taken to stand for 'quasi-autonomous national governmental organisation', and another term 'qualgo' has been occasionally used to mean 'quasi-autonomous local government organisation'. A range of other names have been employed to describe these organisations – fringe bodies, non-departmental public bodies, appointed bodies, para-state organisations – but all these terms mean much the same. What all these organisations have in common, however, is that they are not controlled directly by national or local elected politicians.

There were always some good reasons for putting some government-sponsored or funded activities in the hands of an appointed body rather than elected politicians. In some cases it was particularly important that certain bodies were seen to be independent of the government of the day – examples include the BBC and ITA, the Equal Opportunities Commission and the Commission for Racial Equality. In other cases a key motive was to attract the services of relevant experts. While some of the quangos already mentioned are large executive bod-

ies with multi-million pound budgets, many other quangos are purely advisory, and experts often give their services for nothing. Indeed, it may often be much cheaper to establish a quango than run an activity as part of a government department.

The main criticisms of quangos are over the issues of patronage and accountability. Many positions on appointed bodies are effectively in the gift of ministers, and there has been considerable criticism of the criteria by which appointments are made. Under both Labour and Conservative administrations the partners and other relations of politicians have not infrequently been appointed. This may be more innocent than it sounds – there is pressure to appoint more women to such bodies, and the wives of politicians are a known quantity, and often well qualified to fill relevant posts – yet inevitably it appears they are chosen for their connections rather than themselves. In the past, Labour governments appointed leading trade unionists to many quangos, partly because of their expertise, and partly because some organisations needed representatives of 'labour' to balance business representatives. Conservative governments were sometimes accused of stuffing health authorities, training and enterprise councils and urban development corporations with business-people (often Conservative supporters), although they too could respond that such people brought essential expertise and commitment to running these organisations. It is difficult to evade accusations of political partisanship in appointments, as sometimes a particular organisation is seen as inherently party political. Even more clearly, many quangos are not very accountable to the public. Not only are they unelected, their proceedings are often held in secret, and even if reports and accounts are published, they receive little effective public scrutiny.

It would be inaccurate and unfair to link the growth of quangos too closely with Thatcherism. Quangos had been identified and criticised well before the advent of the Thatcher government. Indeed, initially quangos were part of the over-mighty state that New Right Conservatives railed against, and Margaret Thatcher promised a bonfire of quangos. Some indeed were abolished as the result of a report into 'non-departmental bodies' (Pliatzky, 1980). However, Conservative governments proceeded to establish a wide range of new appointed bodies, although they generally refused to accept that these were 'quangos' because of the term's pejorative associations. Many new quangos were created as the consequence of the government's determination to 'hive off' activities from the civil service and traditional local government. Indeed, some argued that the proliferation of quangos was part of a deliberate strategy to make the centre appear smaller – a somewhat cosmetic attack on 'big government'.

The creation of some new 'regulatory' quangos may be seen as a direct consequence of a shift away from the old welfare state, in which the state provided and controlled services, directly towards a 'regulatory state' in which other public, private and voluntary bodies provided the services subject to state regulation (see below). Naturally such bodies must inspire confidence in their neutrality and independence of direct government control, so almost inevitably they are controlled by appointed qualified experts rather than elected politicians. However, it has also been argued that the proliferation of appointed bodies reflected a purposeful bypassing of democratic institutions, particularly elected local government, in favour of a 'new magistracy' (after the appointed local magistrates who administered much of county government until 1888).

The transformation of most of the old unified civil

Table 19.2 Types and examples of quangos

Type	Examples
Executive	Arts Council, Regional Development Agencies
Advisory	White Fish Authority, Advisory Committee on Hazardous Substances
Quasi-judicial	Pensions Tribunal, Employment Tribunal, Disability Appeal Tribunals
Regulatory	Audit Commission, National Audit Office, Oftel, Ofwat, Ofgem, Ofsted, QAA, Food Standards Agency,
Cross-cutting	Social Exclusion Unit, Better Regulation Taskforce, New Deal Taskforce

service into a diverse collection of executive agencies with substantial managerial autonomy (following the introduction of the Next Steps programme from 1988 – see Chapter 13) has made British government more complex and diverse. Although some distinctions can be drawn between older non-departmental public bodies (or quangos) and the new executive agencies on issues of staffing and ministerial responsibility, variations within both types of organisation seem rather more significant than the differences between them, to the extent that even some leading participants appear confused over the formal status of their own organisation. In effect, the Next Steps programme has created many more public bodies with variable autonomy from direct ministerial control.

The Blair government has not significantly challenged the trend towards the proliferation of agencies and fragmentation of government. It has continued Next Steps agencies, and replaced some older quangos with newer quangos of its own. It has, however, placed rather more emphasis on collaboration and cooperation between agencies and sectors, and the creation of public–private partnerships and policy networks. To counteract some of the problems of co-ordination arising from increased institutional fragmentation it has established a number of cross-cutting units or task forces in the interests of 'joined-up government', such as the Social Exclusion Unit. Taylor (2000) has argued strongly that such

BOX 19.1
Executive agencies and quangos

Executive agencies are still part of the civil service, subject to civil service conditions and codes of practice. They are organised within government departments, and are subject to ministerially imposed policy objectives, budgets and performance targets. They are headed by chief executives and operate within framework documents which give them considerable operational autonomy. Examples include the Child Support Agency and the UK Passports Agency.
Quangos may be sponsored and financed by government departments but they are non-departmental public bodies, not normally staffed by civil servants. They have rather more autonomy than executive agencies, and are normally less accountable to ministers and Parliament, and less subject to ultimate ministerial control and policy directives.

developments do not involve the 'hollowing out' of the state, but rather 'filling in' the gaps between agencies in the interests of more effective government control over policy delivery. This is consistent with other characterisations of the Blair premiership as involving a stronger executive with increased control over the government machine (see Chapter 12).

Whether quangos involved more or less government and central control they remain an area of legitimate concern. Despite periodic attempts to reduce their number, they have proliferated over the last 30 years, for good, bad or mixed reasons. Once the only government bodies that seemed to count in the UK were government departments, staffed by civil servants, and (a long way behind) elected local authorities. Both old central departments and local councils have lost out increasingly to these other appointed public bodies. Government has become more complex, and less subject to direct ministerial control. It seems unlikely that the trend can now be reversed.

Privatisation, contracting out and competition

If the Thatcher and Major governments involved extensive restructuring to the state, they also saw a significant transfer of assets and activities from the public sector to the private sector. Most significant here was the privatisation of nearly all the former nationalised industries: the industries that the 1945–51 Labour government had transferred to state control (although some had previously been municipally owned and run). After a few relatively minor privatisations, gas, steel, telecommunications, water, electricity, coal and railways were sold off between 1984 and 1995. Most of the early share issues were oversubscribed following a massive public advertising campaign, so that shares rose immediately well above the launch price, enabling many subscribers to take a quick and substantial profit, but also provoking accusations that assets had been underpriced and sold off too cheaply. Subsequently shareholders in British Telecom, and more conspicuously Railtrack, found that shares could go down as well as up. The most obvious beneficiary of the sale of assets, however, was the Treasury, which was able to reduce substantially British public borrowing as a consequence. However, the impact on

Table 19.3 Some of the principal privatisations

Date	Company or undertaking
1981 onwards	British Aerospace
1984 onwards	British Telecom
1986	British Gas
1987	British Airways
1988	British Steel Corporation
1989	Water authorities
1990	Electricity distribution
1991	Electricity generation
1995	British Rail

current expenditure and taxation was less than might be expected. Some former nationalised industries broke even, and those that required massive exchequer subsidies, such as the former British Rail, still needed similar injections of cash following privatisation.

Of course the New Right argued that transfer to the private sector would also secure substantial gains in efficiency as a result of a more competitive environment. One problem here was that several of the former nationalised industries appeared to be natural monopolies with little scope for the injection of much competition. However elements of competition were introduced into electricity generation and supply, and British Telecom also faced competitive suppliers. In practice consumers were protected from the exploitation of monopoly power not so much as by competition as by regulation, and new regulatory bodies were introduced for each of the major privatised industries (see Box 19.3).

Perhaps the privatisation that had the most profound and far-reaching effects was none of those described briefly above, but the sale of council houses. This had been Conservative policy since the early 1950s, but the Thatcher government turned a vague aspiration into reality by passing legislation that obliged local authorities to sell houses to sitting tenants with substantial discounts for long occupancy. The policy was undoubtedly popular, enabling many former council house tenants to become home owners. There were 1.3 million houses sold in this way in ten years, involving a massive cumulative transfer in assets. Many of the buyers gained handsomely, sometimes selling on their houses at a substantial profit, although others who bought houses on large estates in more economically deprived areas sometimes found that the purchase was not a good investment. More recently some critics have suggested that the sale of council houses, particularly in the prosperous south east, has removed a substantial pool of cheap housing for relatively poorly paid workers, including many in the public sector like nurses or teachers, and caused a recruitment crisis in some areas where such workers could no longer afford to live.

Besides such massive transfers of assets, the Conservative governments from 1979–97 also attempted to introduce more competition into the provision of public services. One mechanism was the introduction of compulsory competitive tendering (CCT – already briefly described in Chapter 18) into parts of the National Health Service and local government. The deregulation of bus transport led to a substantial shift from publicly owned and controlled bus companies into the hands of private operators. Many services previously provided exclusively by public organisations are now undertaken by private firms for profit, although they remain the statutory responsibility of local or health authorities who lay down the terms of the contract and monitor its implementation (Walsh, 1995). In addition, in the last years of the Thatcher government and under the Major government further competition was introduced through the introduction of internal markets (or quasi-markets) into health and, to a lesser extent, education. As a consequence, health providers such as hospitals were competing to some extent for patients, and schools for pupils.

As we have seen (Chapter 13), more financial delegation and commercial practices were also introduced into the civil service in the 1980s. From 1988 the introduction of executive agencies involved more managerial autonomy, but also obliged civil servants to reach prescribed targets and operate in a more commercial manner. Some of these executive agencies have since been privatised. In 1991 market testing was introduced into the civil service, and certain government activities were put out to tender, and some privatised. The introduction of the Citizen's Charter in the same year emphasised higher standards in public service provision but also reaffirmed the importance of competition to achieve this goal.

Another important development was the introduction of the private finance initiative (PFI) in 1992. This allows public sector organisations to seek new capital investment from the private sector. Instead of the government having to borrow to pay for a large project, such as a new hospital, school or prison, the private sector funds the design, construction, maintenance and management of the project which is then leased back to the public sector. The advantage for the government is that it secures increased public investment without affecting the Public Sector Borrowing Requirement, although critics argue that the long-term costs are higher than through traditional borrowing. Although introduced under the Major government it has become an extremely controversial feature of the Labour government's public investment programme.

New Labour and partnership with business and the voluntary sector

The Labour Party in opposition strenuously opposed most of the Conservative privatisation programme, and initially promised renationalisation of some public undertakings. It also opposed compulsory competitive tendering and many of the changes introduced into the health and education services, including internal markets. However, the Blair government has generally proved unable or unwilling to put the clock back. The major Conservative privatisations have not been reversed (with the partial exception of the collapse of Railtrack in the autumn of 2001), and Labour has proceeded with the part-privatisation of air traffic control. Although CCT has been replaced by the more flexible 'best value' regime, the provision of key local government services is still subject to competition, and many remain privately provided. The Labour government has effectively endorsed greater managerial delegation and autonomy by continuing Next Steps agencies and proceeding to further significant decentralisation within the National Health Service.

New Labour has more particularly enthusiastically embraced partnership with the private sector, through PPPs (public–private partnerships) and, most controversially, through the private finance initiative (PFI). An extensive programme of new investment in the London Underground railway system is to be financed by a public–private partnership, despite the strong opposition of the directly

---

elected London Mayor, Ken Livingstone, and his transport adviser. Many new hospitals and schools are being built under PFI. More controversially still, some large private consortia have become deeply involved in the delivery of education services.

Although much of the ideological debate has been over the relative merits of public provision on the one hand, and private provision for profit on the other, there has been some focus also on a third way – provision by mutually owned or voluntary organisations. The most important example of 'mutuals' used to be the building societies, which were owned by the members and not run for profit. However, most of the largest building societies have become public limited companies with shareholders instead of members, who were generally happy to vote for the legal transfer of assets and pocket often substantial sums in recompense. The most significant example of voluntary provision of public services is now the housing associations, which were favoured as a 'third force' in the supply of rented accommodation by the Conservative government (the other two being the council and private landlords), and over time have become the main providers of rented 'social housing'. While most Labour councils opposed the sale of council houses in the 1980s, many voluntarily cooperated in the transfer of much of their remaining housing stock to housing associations.

Voluntary provision of public services is far from new in the UK. Indeed in the 19th century it was generally the preferred method of provision. Thus schools were provided by voluntary religious organisations, with increasing state subsidy, and many hospitals were initially established on a voluntary basis. For many Victorians suspicious of state intervention such an approach was more acceptable, and it remains more ideologically acceptable today both to free market advocates hostile to direct state provision and to many within the Labour party who retain an aversion to private provision of public services for profit.

BOX 19.2
From Railtrack to Network Rail

The Labour government took a politically controversial decision in 2001 to put Railtrack into receivership, and introduce a new not-for-profit body to administer Britain's rail infrastructure. Critics in the Conservative opposition and the city accused the government of back-door renationalisation and argued that the decision to pull the plug on Railtrack would undermine private sector investors' faith in public–private partnerships, and make it far more expensive for the government to borrow, because of the extra element of risk and uncertainty. By contrast the government argued that Railtrack was a failed and effectively bankrupt company which required huge additional public funds to bail it out, which it was unreasonable to expect taxpayers to provide – shareholders should realise that shares can go down as well as up. In the event a compromise deal was reached which involved some compensation for shareholders. It remains to be seen how Railtrack's successor body, Network Rail, will perform, and whether such a 'not-for-profit' organisation is a viable alternative to a public limited company.

Voluntary organisations conjure up images of small-scale operations by well meaning but inexpert amateurs. However, many voluntary associations today are big business, employing substantial numbers of well-paid professional staff. They may be relatively large and bureaucratic organisations. Although they are 'not for profit' they are run on commercial lines, and although they are not part of government, they rely substantially on state financial support. They thus inhabit a 'grey area' between the public and private sectors. Although they lack some of the disadvantages of each, they may also lack some of their advantages – less susceptible to the discipline of market competition of the private sector and less publicly accountable than mainstream government organisations. They may, however, seem increasingly attractive to a Labour government seeking a third or middle way between the state and the market.

Steering, not rowing: the enabling state

The cumulative impact of all these changes has transformed the character of the British state. While many services are still publicly funded, they are often no longer controlled and provided by centralised public sector organisations, but by the private sector, the voluntary sector or by decentralised quasi-autonomous public sector bodies. This has been described as involving a 'hollowing out' of the state. Yet it also suggests the state is performing an essentially different role – an enabling role, to borrow a term first used in Britain to describe the new role of local government, but which could equally well be applied to the role of the state as a whole. The key point is that the state is no longer necessarily providing services directly but 'enabling' others to do so – business, public–private partnerships, the voluntary sector, the community itself. An analogous term employed by the Americans Osborne and Gaebler (1992) is the notion of the state 'steering' rather 'rowing'. Governments should facilitate and coordinate rather than attempt to do everything themselves.

There are some obvious problems, including potentially serious difficulties of coordination. The new governance, with its myriad forms of organisation, its emphasis on partnership and networks, involves considerable institutional fragmentation. Responsi-

bility and accountability is blurred. Leading and coordinating require different and more demanding skills than those required of business managers or public officials in old hierarchical public sector organisations. It may seem more difficult to get things done. In devolving and decentralising, governments may lose effective control of service delivery, which is a major problem if they are judged on successful service delivery. Thus to achieve the goals they have proclaimed, governments may fall back on increased regulation.

The regulatory state

There is nothing essentially new in regulation. Governments have always been in the business of regulating, although the extent of regulatory activity and regulatory bodies seems to have increased dramatically over the last 30 years of so, sufficiently to justify the term 'regulatory state' which some writers have used (e.g. Loughlin and Scott, in Dunleavy *et al.*, 2002; Moran, 2000, 2001). Three kinds of state regulatory activity have attracted the attention of commentators:

- regulation of private sector bodies, of which there has long been some, but which has increased substantially of late because of specific problems, particularly in the financial sector
- regulation of recently privatised industries, particularly important where these retained substantial monopoly elements
- regulation of the public sector, which has intensified as a consequence of increased managerial delegation and decentralisation.

Important long-established bodies to regulate the private sector include the Monopolies and Mergers Commission (now the Competition Commission), and various planning, licensing and public health bodies that have an essentially regulatory role. The European Community/Union introduced further elements of regulation into British life, particularly with regard to health and safety, the workplace and the environment. For a long time the private sector chafed against state regulation, and the Conservative Party in particular stressed the importance of relaxing regulation to reduce the burden of bureaucracy on business enterprise and agriculture (Loughlin and Scott, in Dunleavy *et al.*, 1997: 210–11). Thus Michael Heseltine promised a 'bonfire of red tape' while planning regulations were progressively relaxed in the 1980s, and some of the closer regulation of farming was reduced. In general, internal voluntary self-regulation was reckoned to be preferable to the heavy hand of the state. More recently a succession of scandals and policy disasters have led to fresh demands for more regulation to protect the public. Moran (2000) links this with the decline of deference towards authority and trust in professions.

Despite repeated criticisms of the 'nanny state', 'red-tape' and 'over-regulation', problems in the private sector regularly provoke a media and popular outcry for the government to 'do something', and the creation of new watchdog bodies. Thus the BSE and foot-and-mouth disease crises, coupled with more general concerns over food safety, additives and quality have led to more rigorous inspection and regulation of food production and retailing through such bodies as the Food Standards Agency. The mis-selling of insurance, endowment mortgages and pension schemes provoked new demands for the regulation of the financial sector to protect the public. The Blair government created a new super-regulator, the Financial Services Authority, to take over regulatory functions previously performed (not too effectively, many would allege) by nine separate agencies, including the Bank of England which had until then had responsibility for regulating the commercial banks (Sinclair, in Seldon, 2001).

Privatisation of the former nationalised industries created a new raft of regulatory bodies, so that state ownership and control was effectively replaced by state regulation. This would perhaps not have been necessary had competition and market forces been reckoned sufficient to protect consumer interests. Yet in most cases a state monopoly was replaced by a privatised monopoly, or at best very imperfect competition. The unrestrained pursuit of profit in such circumstances would have led to considerable exploitation of consumers. Thus a series of regulatory bodies were established, primarily to control prices, but also to monitor service standards and investment, and deal with public complaints. These bodies have become memorably known by their new shorthand descriptions – such as Ofgas to regulate the gas industry, Oftel to regulate telecommunications, Offer to regulate electricity supply and Ofwat to regulate water. (Gas and electricity are now jointly regulated by the Ofgem, the Office of Gas and Electricity Markets.) Views of the effectiveness of the new regulatory regimes vary. Predictably the left think the new regulators are only cosmetic, while the industries themselves complain of over-regulation. Yet clearly regulation of these privatised industries is here to stay – and the pressures are for more rather than less state regulation.

One of the interesting aspects of privatisation is that the transfer of assets from the public to the private sector has not removed these industries from the sphere of public policy, or even significantly reduced pressures on government to remedy perceived problems. Thus government is still held to account for the problems and deficiencies of rail transport despite the removal of the industry from state ownership and control. This is hardly surprising, as whether state-owned, privatised or controlled by a not-for-profit organisation, the rail network still requires massive injections of public money which ultimately derive from taxpayers. Rail crashes provoke legitimate public concerns over rail safety, and demands for government action and tougher safety regimes. The state may divest itself of the ownership of troublesome industries, but not, it seems, of their problems.

However, the most substantial recent growth in state regulation has not been over the private or recently privatised sectors but over the activities of the state itself. Again, this is hardly new. In the 19th century central government departments established inspectorates to monitor services delivered by local government. More recently, from 1965 onwards a system of ombudsmen (as they are popularly known) was set up to cover complaints from the public against central government departments (the Parliamentary Commissioner for Administration), local government and the health service (see Chapter 15). Yet it is only in the last 20 years or so that that number of bodies to regulate the public sector has really exploded. Paradoxically pressures for decentralisation and delegation have increased the pressures on the centre closely to regulate and monitor service delivery. Managers of schools, hospitals and a whole range of devolved executive agencies have been given more autonomy and 'freedom to manage',

BOX 19.3

Some important regulatory bodies

Audit Commission: audits local authorities and health authorities.

Competition Commission (formerly Monopolies and Mergers Commission): promotes competition in the private sector. May declare that mergers are not in the public interest.

Financial Services Authority (FSA): regulates banks, building societies, insurance companies, stock exchange etc. Absorbed functions of nine former regulatory bodies.

Food Standards Agency: independent regulator to monitor the food production and supply industry, set up by the Blair government in the wake of the BSE scandal.

Health and Safety Executive: responsible for the whole range of health and safety (e.g. on railways).

National Audit Office: audits central government.

Office of Fair Trading (OFT): regulator charged with making markets work for consumers.

Office of Gas and Electricity Markets (Ofgem) (formerly Ofgas and Offer): regulates the gas and electricity industry.

Office of the Rail Regulator (ORR): regulation of train operators and rail network (prices, services etc.).

Office for Standards in Education (Ofsted): responsible for inspecting and raising standards in schools.

Office of Telecommunications (Oftel): regulates the privatised telecommunications industry.

Office of Water Services (Ofwat): regulates the privatised water industry.

Strategic Rail Authority: responsible for longer-term rail investment.

yet demands for improved services – for reduced class sizes or hospital waiting lists, for better exam results or improved treatment – lead to the setting of targets and the establishment of new regulatory bodies to measure performance. Thus schools, universities, hospitals, local authorities and other bodies not only have their performance measured against a wide range of criteria, but these performances are published and ranked in league tables.

Much of this is highly laudable. The measurement of performance enables generally valid comparisons to be made between institutions, authorities and areas. It leads to investigations into the reasons for variations in performance. It enables others to imitate the successful methods of the best providers. It puts pressure on poor performers to improve. Moreover, it is urged that the public have a right to know about service and performance levels, particularly where there is an element of public choice of service providers, for example where parents are choosing a school for their children. It serves the interests of public accountability and open government. From a government perspective it is crucial to be able to demonstrate that the money it is putting into a service, particularly if it is extra money, is achieving measurable improvements in standards, otherwise opposition parties will be able to allege that the money has been wasted and been swallowed up by more bureaucracy.

Yet measurement brings some problems. Some measures may be misleading. It does not necessarily follow that a school with better exam results than another has really performed better. To make a fair comparison it would be necessary to know much more about the two schools – for example their catchment areas, and the respective achievements of pupils when they entered the two schools, the support and facilities made available by their families, and any extra private coaching they received. Other measures may be manipulated. The most important things might not be measured anyway. Generally speaking, performance yardsticks focus on things that are easily quantifiable – class sizes, hospital waiting lists, offences notified to the police – rather than other aspects of a service that may be equally or more important, but are not so easily measured. Thus measurement may distort priorities.

Unsurprisingly, those who are regulated complain of increased pressure and the costs in time and money of compliance with the numerous controls and yard-sticks. Compliance costs may become a serious drain on resources, which sometimes might have been employed more productively. In some cases more resources may go into satisfying the regulators than serving consumers or users. This is hardly surprising, as the stakes are high. Poor scores reflect badly on a service or institution, which is competing for resources and sometimes effectively for clients. Thus a university department that scores badly on the research assessment exercise loses money for research, and will find it more difficult to recruit students and staff. It may lead to staff contracts not being renewed, or even the closure of the department. Considerable ingenuity will be devoted to impressing the assessors. Cheating is not unknown.

If regulation can be excessive and counter-productive, it can also be ineffective. 'Regulatory capture' is a term long used by the observers of regulatory agencies in the USA. A particular agency established to regulate a profession or industry may become effectively captured by the interests it is supposed to regulate, instead of looking after the interests of consumers or the wider public. Some observers would argue that some British regulatory bodies have similarly 'gone native', adopting the perspective of those whose activities they were expected to police. Indeed, some regulatory agencies have proved singularly ineffective in detecting and publicising dubious practices and preventing major scandals (Loughlin and Scott, in Dunleavy *et al.*, 2002; Moran, 2001).

Open government and the secret state

The British state has sometimes been described as a secret state. The term is perhaps most often used to describe the British secret services and other clandestine aspects of British government. There are certainly serious questions to ask about the power, accountability and performance of these services. However, the term can also be employed to characterise British government generally, as secretiveness has often appeared to be one of trademarks of the practice of government in the United Kingdom. The more recent commitment to 'open government' indeed reflects a recognition that government has been less than open in the

> **BOX 19.4**
> **Britain's security services**
>
> **MI5 (security service):** concerned with domestic security, primarily with internal threats to the British state, and countering 'serious crime'.
>
> **Special Branch:** the internal security arm of the police – works with MI5 to counter terrorism, protect VIPs, conduct surveillance etc.
>
> **MI6 (secret intelligence service):** gathers political, military and economic intelligence in foreign countries, combating serious crime – e.g. money laundering, drug smuggling, illicit arms deals, illegal immigration.
>
> **Government Communications Headquarters (GCHQ):** intercepts and decodes international communications.

past. However, the passage of a Freedom of Information Act by the Blair government does not satisfy critics that this is now a problem of the past. Many would argue that British government remains too secretive.

To begin with the narrower but important issue of the British security services, it would perhaps be conceded generally that all states may have to resort to clandestine operations in the interests of defence and internal security. Intelligence gathering on potential threats may save lives and prevent or deter serious threats. For example, better intelligence could have led the Thatcher government to anticipate and perhaps prevent an Argentine invasion of the Falklands, and conceivably rendered the task force to recover the islands unnecessary. More recently, better intelligence in the west might have detected and prevented the events of 11 September 2001. When the stakes are high, particularly in time of war, it would also be conceded that secret operations, including 'dirty tricks' to destabilise the enemy, are to be commended, particularly if they are shown materially to affect the outcome. Churchill established the Special Operations Executive (SOE) in the Second World War, and British agents who operated behind enemy lines are celebrated as heroes (although of course enemy agents are more commonly considered despicable). There is a continuing fascination and some admiration for the whole world of espionage. Yet there are also important civil liberties issues surrounding the activities of the security services. There is a delicate balance to be struck between protecting British citizens against internal and external threats to their well-being and safety, and violations of the fundamental human rights and freedoms of those same citizens.

However, although the British secret services are often viewed as glamorous, some hard questions may be asked about their record, overall effectiveness and value for money:

- The discovery in the 1950s and 1960s that some high-ranking members of the security services were double agents working for the Soviet Union undermined faith in the reliability of the services, and their recruitment and internal vetting. Doubts resurfaced in the 1970s and 1980s with further prosecutions and damaging (but unproved) allegations against senior figures.
- Ostensibly far-fetched allegations that some elements of MI5 were plotting against Prime Minister Harold Wilson and attempting to destabilise his government were shown to have an element of truth, and raised questions about the judgement, loyalty and political bias of the security services (Hennessy, 2000: 372–5).
- The alleged use of the security services for partisan purposes, including intelligence gathering on trade unions and industrial disputes in the 1980s, renewed allegations of inappropriate targeting of those with left-wing politics. Ironically, some senior members of Blair's government were themselves earlier subjects of surveillance by the security services (Jack Straw, Harriet Harman and Peter Mandelson, according to former MI5 officer, David Shayler).
- The Scott Inquiry (1996) into the arms to Iraq scandal raised some serious questions about the role of the security services and the coordination of intelligence (Tomkins, 1997).
- The failure of western intelligence services generally, including the British intelligence services, to anticipate and prevent the events of 11 September 2001 suggests that they are ill-equipped to counter the new global terrorism, and are too much locked into activities and methods of the cold war.
- The additional powers acquired by the government to counter terrorism and the detention without trial of suspects have provoked concerns of civil liberties in general and Islamophobia in particular.

Necessary as security services may be, the past record of the British security services does not inspire great confidence, even if some of the wilder conspiracy theories have not been substantiated. By their very nature there are bound to be problems with the accountability and control of secret services. However, in 1991 the appointment of a woman,

---

IN FOCUS 19.1
David Shayler

Former MI5 officer David Shayler, with his girlfriend, arrives at the Old Bailey where he was being prosecuted under the Official Secrets Act following newspaper interviews he had given five years earlier in which he criticised the efficiency of the security services. After initially fleeing to France he eventually returned to Britain, and was found guilty and given a short prison sentence in October 2002.

Photograph: PA Photos.

Stella Rimmington, to take charge of MI5 was announced by the Major government, while MI5 and GCHQ now have their own websites. Remarkably, Stella Rimmington has since published her own (rather unrevealing) memoirs. Yet all present and former employees of the security services are bound by the Official Secrets Act which they are obliged to sign, and can be prosecuted for breaches, as former MI5 officer David Shayler discovered.

Full accountability would require detailed publicity for activities which would no longer be secret. Information on the activities of the security services is thus confined to as few politicians as possible, on a 'need to know' basis, and overall responsibility lies with the prime minister alone. The most delicate secret operations have to be cleared with the prime minister personally (Hennessy, 2000: 83), although it is ironic in this respect that at least one prime minister, Harold Wilson, was himself the target of some malcontent members of the service. Yet some steps have been taken to improve the accountability of the security services, and more now is known about them than previously, partly because of official disclosure of information, and partly because of insider accounts and leaks (e.g. by Peter Wright in the Spycatcher affair, 1986–7, and more recently by David Shayler – see In Focus 19.1).

Beyond the fascinating world of the secret services proper there are however much wider questions about secrecy in British government. It is sometimes argued that the lack of open government and fuller accountability to Parliament and the public is the consequence of particular features of the uncodified British constitution. Thus British ministers and public servants formally serve the crown rather than 'the people' or 'the public interest'. As ministers, and particular the prime minister, have inherited most of the old prerogative powers of the Crown, in practice civil servants, and public officials generally, are expected to serve the government of the day. Advice to ministers is confidential. Civil servants are obliged to sign the Official Secrets Act, and can be prosecuted for unauthorised disclosure of classified information. No defence of the public interest is allowable.

However, both the Major and Blair governments made some moves in the direction of more open government. The Major government for the first time published the details of Cabinet committees, their membership and terms of reference (see Chapter 12), published the names of the heads of MI5 and MI6, provided a legal right of access to non-computerised personal files, and published a new 'Open Government Code of Practice' on information to be provided by government departments and agencies. Blair's government has maintained and in some respects extended the commitment to open government. However, although the Labour Party in opposition promised a Freedom of Information Act, and this promise was honoured in the sense that a Freedom of Information Act was eventually passed, critics argued that the initial proposals had been so substantially watered down to render the Act almost worthless. Austin (in Jowell and Oliver, 2000: 371) claims that Labour's Freedom of Information Act involved such an 'extraordinary list of exemptions' that it was 'a regime for open government only by consent of government ministers' and 'a denial of democracy'.

Yet some would question how far fully open government is practical or desirable. If for example formal Cabinet meetings were open to the public, it seems likely that the discussion would take place in secret pre-meetings, leaving the Cabinet simply to record decisions that had already effectively been taken elsewhere. There is a difference between the interests of government and opposition. While the media and opposition parties have a clear interest in open government, because it gives them more information on which to mount criticism, all governments retain an interest in maintaining some confidentiality for their internal deliberations. Many ideas that are tentatively floated by ministers or their advisers never come to fruition, and some are abandoned at an early stage, but the knowledge that they had even been contemplated, however briefly, could have damaging political repercussions. If all deliberations and all advice to ministers were made public, this would almost certainly inhibit the range of debate. Ministers would no longer dare to 'think the unthinkable' or come up with unpopular but perhaps necessary policy proposals because of the potential political damage. Governments might even become wary of making contingency plans to cope with threats or disasters from fear of creating public alarm and perhaps panic.

Table 19.4 From the old Westminster model to the new British governance

The Westminster model	The new British governance
The unitary state	The 'differentiated polity'
Parliamentary sovereignty	The devolution of power
Ministerial responsibility	Delegation of management
Central–local relations	Multi-level governance
Homogeneity, uniformity, 'Fordism'	Diversity, fragmentation, 'post-Fordism'

Source: adapted from Leach and Percy-Smith, 2001: 7.

The disintegration of the British state or towards multi-level governance?

Although writers may not fully agree over exactly how and why the British state has changed, there is widespread agreement that it has changed, and profoundly. Instead of a unified, highly centralised state whose traditional core institutions in Westminster and Whitehall had only changed gradually to accommodate modernity and democracy, there is a complex, fragmented, and multi-layered system of government of politics which is still seems to be in the process of evolving, although towards what remains unclear.

These trends clearly present a threat for those who cherish the traditional British state, British national independence, and the sovereignty of the UK Westminster Parliament and power of the old centralised core executive focused on the Cabinet and Whitehall. To them the growing importance of the European Union on the one hand (see Chapter 16), and the devolution of power to nation to sub-UK nations and regions on the other (see Chapter 17) represents a danger to the British state which could prove terminal. For those who, like Hobbes, believe that supreme power cannot be divided, the fragmentation of government spells disaster.

For others, the trend towards multi-level governance is natural and inevitable in the modern world, and it is the old nation-state that is obsolete (Giddens, 1998; Pierre and Peters, 2000; Pierre and Stoker, 2002). As far as Britain is concerned, the term 'multi-level governance' suggests that the process of governing is no longer exclusively, or even necessarily largely, restricted to the traditional heart of British government in Whitehall and Westminster, nor to the old binary distinction between 'central' and 'local' government implied in the term 'central–local relations'.

Instead a more complex pattern of governance operates at an increasing range of levels – international, European, UK, devolved national, regional, local and institutional. While some levels clearly remain much more important than others, the balance is clearly shifting over time. Key decisions affecting the lives of British citizens are made not

Table 19.5 The new multi-level governance, as applied to Britain

Level	Institutions
Global	United Nations, IMF, WTO, multi-national organisations & companies
Trans-Atlantic	North Atlantic Treaty Organisation
European	European Union, European Commission, European Parliament, European Court of Justice, Council of Europe, European Court of Human Rights
UK	Cabinet and core executive. Westminster Parliament
Devolved national	Scottish Parliament and executive, Welsh Assembly and executive, Northern Ireland Assembly and executive
Regional	Government offices, regional development agencies, regional chambers
Local	County, district, borough and parish councils, non-elected local government (learning and skills councils, police authorities etc.)
Institutional	Hospital trusts, universities and colleges, foundation schools etc.

just in London but in Brussels or Edinburgh or within hospital trusts, primary care trusts and learning and skills councils around Britain, and within a range of other devolved agencies, units and networks. The unitary state of the old 'Westminster model' of British government has been replaced by a 'differentiated polity' in which a variety of agencies and interests are involved in the framing and delivery of policy at a number of different but interdependent levels.

There is much that seems confusing and contradictory about this emerging system of multi-level governance, which explains some of the range of competing terms that have been employed to describe it. Is the new British politics all about devolution and decentralisation, or does it more plausibly involve a new concentration of power by a bunch of control freaks? Has the state been 'hollowed out' or 'joined up'? Has the welfare state been replaced by a regulatory state? Has representative democracy been effectively replaced by a new magistracy or quangocracy? Does the rhetoric about open government merely conceal the maintenance of a secret state? In part different answers reflect different assumptions and partisan viewpoints, yet they also reflect genuine uncertainty. Clearer answers to such questions may be available subsequently to historians with the benefit of hindsight, but it is difficult to spot the truly significant trends in an era of extensive political and institutional upheaval.

Partly the issue is what the most appropriate level of government is for functional effectiveness. While it might seem appropriate to decentralise some decision making down from the UK government level to local communities or even institutions in the interest of improved delivery of (for example) education and health services, there are other issues, such as international trade, disarmament, global pollution and conservation, that can only be tackled effectively at a supranational and global level. Yet for many services and activities there are many levels at which decisions may be appropriately taken, and multi-level governance appears almost inescapable.

However, issues of functional efficiency are bound up closely with the politics of identity and allegiance. The demands for closer European union, for a Scottish Parliament, and even for successive UK local government reorganisations were not driven just by expectations of more efficient government and service provision, but by political ideals and loyalties. Much of the debate over Europe or devolution, or local authority boundaries is ultimately about how people feel about who they are, and the communities they identify with. Do they feel part of Europe or the English-speaking world? Are they Scots or British? Do they identify with their city or county? Other identities – ethnic, religious, class – may cut across geographical boundaries. Some are comfortable with multiple overlapping identities and allegiances, but to others a particular identity may appear exclusive and all-important. For them we are either British or European, either Scots or British; we have to choose between UK national sovereignty or a European superstate, between allegiance to the United Kingdom or an independent Scotland. The whole notion of multi-level governance is hardly compatible with more exclusive identities and allegiances.

Further reading

On the attack on the post-war consensus and 'big government' see Kavanagh (1990). On quangos and the 'democratic deficit' see Weir and Hall (1994), Weir (1995), Skelcher (1998) and Weir and Beetham (1998). On privatisation and marketisation see Ascher (1987), Self (1993) and Walsh (1995).

On regulation and the regulatory state see Loughlin and Scott (in Dunleavy et al., 2002) and Moran (2000, 2001). On freedom of information see Austin (in Jowell and Oliver, 2000). The Freedom of Information Act was the responsibility of the Home Office (website: <www.homeoffice.uk>). The Campaign for Freedom of Information's website can be consulted: <www.cfoi.org.uk>. On the security services it is possible to access the official MI5 website <www.mi5.gov.uk> and the GCHQ website <www.gchq.gov.uk>.

On governance, see Rhodes (1997), Pierre and Stoker (2000), Pierre and Peters (2000), Leach and Percy-Smith (2001), Newman (2001) and Flinders (2002).

Part **V**

POLICIES AND ISSUES

Part V of this book considers some of the most pressing issues confronting contemporary government, and the most significant policies that have been devised to address them. Policy is examined in terms of both the process of policy making and the content of specific policies. Different theoretical approaches to policy making are considered (Chapter 20) together with New Labour's own practical approach to policy in terms of practising 'joined-up' government. Can new structures overcome the policy fragmentation resulting from traditional problems of 'departmentalitis', and does it really matter how government policy targets are met (see Chapter 22) as long as policy is successful?

Conventional wisdom deems that the most electorally significant policy is how successfully the government manages the economy. Yet the Conservatives were not rewarded by a grateful electorate for a steadily improving economy in 1997, when Labour was swept into power on a Parliamentary landslide (see Chapter 21). The economy during New Labour's first term provided a 'feel good' combination of increasing growth, falling unemployment, low inflation, low interest rates and, latterly, rising house prices and higher consumer spending. Britain has not, however, been able to avoid entirely the impact of downturn especially in the USA after the events of 11 September 2001, and there is considerable uncertainty about the timing and consequences of membership of the euro, if indeed a decision is taken to join.

Despite its claim to being the fourth largest economy in the world, poverty still exists in Britain and, as discussed in Chapter 23, it is concentrated disproportionately among certain groups. What is more, Britain's increasingly diverse society poses government with challenges in relation to race relations, gender and life-style entitlements, as well as tax and the distribution of wealth and income (see Chapter 24).

Chapters 25 and 26 concern what is sometimes referred to as the 'high' politics of external and international affairs rather than with the 'low' politics of domestic issues such as education or healthcare. While some environmental problems can be tackled locally, the most crucial, climate change, involves policy making on a global scale. In this respect, the making of environmental policy is more akin to the international diplomacy and alliance building of foreign affairs and defence than it is to inter-departmental wrangling over budgets. The making of foreign and defence policy, which is frequently less exposed to electoral pressures than is domestic policy, has revealed some interesting splits and cleavages. For while much policy making on domestic issues has become increasingly 'Europeanised', security policy has become increasingly 'Americanised'. Given the equivocation of national governments of the EU to pursue the wider war on terrorism following 11 September 2001, it seems unlikely that the tensions between Britain's relationships with the USA on the one hand and its European partners on the other will be resolved speedily.

Finally, Chapter 27 returns to the central issue of power and influence in modern Britain, pulling together some of the main themes in the book to review the present condition of British politics, and the prospects for the British state within the context of an evolving system of multi-level governance.

Chapter 20

The policy process

Policy making and decision making   345
The political agenda   346
Decision making theory   347
The policy making process   349
Policy analysis   350
'Joined-up' policy making   351
Modernising policy making   352
Political leadership   352
Sources of policy advice   355
Policy and implementation   356

> *Definitions*
> **Policy making** involves adopting a position on an issue or problem. It provides a framework for decision making. Thus an ethical foreign policy has implications for decisions on, for example, arms exports to particular countries.
> **Decision making** involves selecting what is considered the best (or least worst) option from a range of alternatives – for example, a decision for financing new investment in the London tube system. Such a decision would however normally be informed by broader policy on financing investment in public services.

Earlier chapters in this book have introduced the machinery of government and the wider political, social and economic environment within which it operates. This chapter examines how government works in terms of how it deals with political issues and the nature of the public policy that emerges. Why do some issues get high on the political agenda and become hotly debated while other seemingly more pressing or urgent issues remain excluded from political consideration? In this chapter we look at how governments make policy, and differences in policy making style between governments. Who participates in policy making? In what ways do they set about solving problems? How important is leadership to successful policy making? Some theoretical approaches are explored which will help in answering these questions.

Policy making and decision making

While it is important to define terms in the study of government and politics, this is particularly difficult when it comes to policy making and decision making. What is the difference, first, between a policy and a decision?

A basic distinction is that 'what to do' answers policy making questions, and 'how to do it' answers decision making questions. Policies are about objectives or ends, while decisions involve means towards ends. However the distinction between policy making and decision making is hardly clear-cut, but one of degree and interpretation. For example, was the replacement of rates with the community charge (or poll tax) a policy or a decision?

The term 'policy' is used freely for both government and opposition parties. However there is an important difference between the two, in so far as opposition policy is no more than a set of *aspirations* about what the party thinks it might do if in office, whereas government policy is *operational* since it is designed to be implemented. Some opposition 'policies' may involve little more than 'wish lists', for which they may never have to find money, or face the awkward problems of how to put them into practice. This implies that policy making is easier and relatively cost-free for opposition parties. However, an opposition will lose credibility if its policies are not costed, and possible snags ignored, and will be exposed to criticism if it fails to implement policies when and if it is returned to government. Thus opposition parties may find it safer to concentrate on criticising government policy rather than articulating their own distinctive policies. Yet an opposition that has not prepared for power by developing its own coherent policies will have no plan or purpose in government. Moreover it risks losing the political argument, for such a negative approach suggests there is no real alternative to what the government is doing. Opposition parties need a policy agenda of their own if they are to inspire enthusiasm and confidence, and preferably a big idea to seize public imagination.

The political agenda

Formal meetings for any purpose involve an agenda – a list of items for discussion and action. It is a common experience that lower items on long agendas may not be reached or may only receive perfunctory discussion, for time is usually short and only a limited number of items can be explored thoroughly. Thus an issue needs to be high on the agenda if it is to receive full attention. This is true of government also. At any one time there is a vast number of issues and problems facing people in Britain, yet the government will attempt to solve only some of them. Some issues will get on to the political agenda and be debated publicly, while others, which might be just as urgent for those concerned, fail to do so. Why is this?

First, some issues have more *salience* than others as far as the government is concerned. Salience 'can be regarded as roughly equivalent to the *immediate importance* attributed to an issue or element … salience can be equated with the *prominence* of the issue' (Frankel, 1970: 61). Joseph Frankel has suggested, for example, that one reason why Britain failed to seize the leadership of Western Europe in the post-war years (see Chapter 16) was because the Attlee government saw other issues as much more salient. During the late 1940s and 1950s the Labour government was preoccupied with what it saw as the more important policies of establishing the welfare state and nationalisation. In his study of environmental politics, Anthony Downs devised a somewhat similar model of the political process in terms of a five-stage issue-attention cycle, with issues gaining salience, moving up the political agenda, only to fade away in importance, for example as policy makers and the public realise the issue is more complex and less easy to resolve than initially imagined (see Box 25.1), and other more pressing concerns displace them on the policy agenda.

Governments may be able to dominate the terms of political debate if they have a 'big idea' which captures the public mood, and enables them to shape the political agenda. The 'big idea' of Margaret Thatcher was the free market, essentially the rediscovery of a very old idea, but one that seemed to match some public disillusion with 'big government', the welfare state and Keynesian economic policies. The free market was a simple idea with wide application to various policy areas. It was sufficiently dominant to shape the agenda for a decade or more, and Thatcher's insistence, 'There is no alternative' was widely believed. Yet increasingly, particularly under her successor, John Major, it became clear that Britain's economic problems had not been solved, while some of the problems of unrestricted free enterprise were rediscovered. Major attempted to refocus public attention away from economics with his 'back to basics' campaign (see Box 20.1), and had some success in transforming the political agenda, but in a way that ultimately backfired spectacularly to his party's disadvantage.

New Labour came to power in 1997 promising sleaze-free government, sound economic policy and modernisation. It did not offer a really simple and memorable 'big idea' to challenge Thatcherism, although various key buzzwords were employed, including 'stakeholding', 'community', 'partnership' and 'networks', all of which have featured in Blair's 'third way', a contentious term which lacks the appealing simplicity of the free market. Yet if Labour sometimes seemed to lack focus and its first-term performance disappointed many supporters, in the face of a divided opposition it was able to transform the terms of political debate by focusing on improvements in the delivery of public services, particularly healthcare.

Pluralist theorists have shown how group activity or the media can influence the political agenda, and push issues such as gun crime, dangerous dogs, paedophiles, hospital waiting, or GM foods to the top. Yet power and influence may also be evident in issues that are not considered or decisions that are not made, because they are kept off the political agenda. Peter Bachrach and Morton Baratz (1971) have argued that there are two faces of power, the power more or less visible in public decision making, and the more hidden face of power involved in

BOX 20.1
Reshaping the political agenda: 'back to basics'

Governments may attempt to reshape the political agenda in order to refocus public attention away from areas of policy failure. For example, following the bad economic news on 'Black Wednesday' when Britain was ejected from the European Exchange Rate Mechanism, John Major's Conservative government attempted to swing public debate away from economic management issues. Although the government cannot normally control the political agenda, it was on this occasion successful in manipulating public debate away from issues concerning the recession, unemployment and poverty on to issues concerning the family and the responsibility of parents, schools and churches in developing social awareness and morality. Yet while successful in the short term, this agenda manipulation backfired on Major's government in the years that followed, and the new morality agenda worked to the disadvantage of the Conservatives. Right-wing Conservatives converted their party's 'back to basics' platform into a moral campaign, which collapsed under the weight of sleaze scandals involving numerous Conservative politicians. The morality crisis, exaggerated by the media, ironically obscured the economic improvements towards the end of the Major government and worked to the advantage of the Labour Party, assisting the 1997 Labour landslide.

depressing physical environment, bad housing, high crime, high unemployment, family breakdown and related social problems, often ethnic tensions, and so on, but what are the root causes? These may be interpreted in terms of ideological assumptions. Thus the problems may be variously seen as the consequence of permissive society, or the destruction of communities, or poor education, or bad planning, or unrestricted immigration, or the decline of key industries. Professional people may be inclined to interpret the problem in terms of their own particular specialism. Different interests and pressure groups may seek to 'capture' the issue to support their own demands. Clearly, how this problem is interpreted will strongly shape the policies developed to deal with it, and may influence whether public spending is directed primarily towards physical regeneration of an area, or better policing and crime prevention, or promoting skills, or encouraging new investment, or promoting better community relations, or improving leisure facilities.

Decision making theory

How are decisions actually arrived at? There has been a great deal of research, particularly by American political scientists, into the process of decision making. The pioneers in this area of research include Herbert Simon, David Braybrooke, Charles Lindblom, Graham Allison and Amitai Etzioni. Between them, they have devised a number of 'models' or theories to help explain how decisions are made in the real world of politics and government.

Rational decision making

Most individuals want others to see them as 'rational'. The term 'rational' is used in a slightly different sense when it comes to decision making theory. A rational decision is one where decision makers consider all the possible courses of action, then work out the consequences that would follow each one, and finally evaluate all the consequences before selecting the 'best' choice, which is the one most likely to achieve their goals.

Herbert Simon, who first defined the rational decision, was criticised because in real-life situations

non-decisions, where important issues are ignored or suppressed, perhaps because of the effective veto of influential interests.

Issues may get on to the policy agenda, but they still have to be defined and interpreted, and this has important implications for analysis and action. Very different perceptions of a particular problem may be possible. Take the problems of Britain's inner cities, which have preoccupied governments from at least the 1960s onwards. There are many manifestations of the problems of deprived urban areas – a politicians rarely have all the information necessary to make rational decisions. Would Margaret Thatcher have pressed ahead with the poll tax, rejecting all compromises, had she known all its future political consequences? Even when governments make great efforts to collect all relevant information, rational decisions need not follow. For example, in the 1960s Britain was developing a sophisticated multi-role combat aircraft, the TSR-2, whilst the Americans were developing the rather similar swing-wing F-111 aircraft. A new Labour government reviewed the TSR-2 project, taking into account all information available at the time concerning the costs of the TSR-2 compared with the F-111, the defence needs of Britain's changing external role, and the likely decline in importance of manned aircraft in the 'age of the missile'. Labour Defence Secretary, Denis Healey, considered all options and took the *rational* decision in 1965 to cancel the TSR-2 and buy the much cheaper F-111, but was it the *right* decision? Subsequent events showed that the F-111 performed poorly, that manned aircraft were to remain important, and that the apparent costs of the TSR-2 were artificially high because they included development costs of two other aircraft, the Phantom and the Harrier.

Simon accepted the criticism that decision makers rarely have total information, and he modified his theory to one of *bounded rationality*. He acknowledged that real-life decision making is bounded by constraints and that usually a choice has to be made between poorly defined and ambiguous options, each with incomplete information. Under these circumstances, decision makers agree on what is an 'acceptable' decision. This is referred to as *satisficing*: in other words, decision makers do not select the 'best' rational decision, but one that is satisfactory in terms of being 'good enough'. Given the imperfect information about the TSR-2 and F-111 available to Denis Healey in 1965, his decision to cancel the project seems a better example of satisficing than of rational decision making.

Incrementalism

David Braybrooke and Charles Lindblom argued that decision making could be best understood in terms of what they termed *disjointed incremental-*

ism. This can be described as 'decision making through small or incremental moves on particular problems rather than through a comprehensive reform programme. It is also endless, it takes the form of an indefinite sequence of policy moves' (Braybrooke and Lindblom, 1963: 71).

Incrementalism seems to describe reasonably accurately much decision making practice, but it was also felt by Braybrooke and Lindblom to lead to better policy. Basically, it was argued that when a particular policy began failing and producing an unsatisfactory or undesirable situation, small changes in policy are made as decision makers move cautiously towards what they hope will be an improved situation. It is important to note that incremental decision making tends to move away from an undesirable situation rather than be directed towards predefined policy goals. In a later article, Braybrooke provocatively called incrementalism 'the science of muddling through'.

Mixed scanning

Amitai Etzioni has devised a decision making model, which is basically a compromise between the rational approach and incrementalism. Mixed scanning involves decision making being done in two distinct phases. In considering a problem, decision makers first make a broad sweep, or scan, of all the policy options available and assess them in terms of how far each would go toward meeting their objectives. Then decision making becomes more narrowly focused and incremental in nature as details are agreed on the selected policy option.

How might mixed scanning operate? A chancellor faced with a problem such as a budget deficit may consider a wide range of measures that are available. The decision might be to do nothing, or to raise taxes, or to cut public spending. Once it has been decided which option or option mix best matches the goals, then attention will focus on the detail of, say, which tax should be raised, by what percentage, starting from what date, and so on.

The organisational process model

In his study of the Cuban missile crisis of 1962 Graham Allison analysed events in terms of alternatives to the rational model. The first of these was the organisation process model in which decisions are seen as the outputs of large organisations functioning according to regular patterns of behaviour. Decisions emerge as the result of negotiation and bargaining between organisations. In the past, political scientists have pointed out how the organisation of government in Britain affected decisions concerning Northern Ireland (see Chapter 17). Until 1972 Northern Ireland was governed from Stormont, and Westminster took relatively little interest in the province's affairs until the 'Troubles' began. Unlike Scotland, there had been no separate government department concerned with its affairs. It is interesting to speculate how different the recent history of Northern Ireland might have been had there been greater Westminster involvement during the 1950s and 1960s.

The bureaucratic politics model

Graham Allison also analysed the Kennedy administration's decisions in terms of what he called the government politics model, which in the context of British politics is better understood as a bureaucratic politics model. Allison argued that what happened in 1962 was characterised as the result of various negotiations between those in government, with top civil servants playing a key role. Policy emerges from bargains and compromises made by ministers and their civil servants representing different departmental interests and priorities. In other words, decisions that emerge are not in the national interest but in the interests of particular bureaucracies. For example, Chapter 26 considers the impact of the large cuts made in Britain's armed forces during the early 1990s. Were these cuts in defence calculated by the Ministry of Defence in response to the reduced international threat resulting from the ending of the cold war? Or, as some suspected, were the defence cuts insisted on by the Treasury, which was determined to reduce spending on defence under the guise of the 'peace dividend'? They suspected that bureaucratic politics resulted in defence cuts providing public spending savings, which suited the needs of the Treasury rather than the defence needs of the country.

The policy making process

Having considered decision making theory, it is timely to examine how and where policies are made in Britain's political system. Figure 20.1 provides a very schematic representation of the political system, which is designed to be looked at in conjunction with the detailed discussion of earlier chapters.

At the heart of the system lies the Cabinet and Cabinet committee system. Chapter 12 examined power and decision making within the executive in terms of defining the role of the prime minister in the policy process and identifying the constraints on prime ministerial power. Chapter 13 explored the revolution that has taken place within the civil service as well as the power relationship between ministers and their civil servants. What is particularly notable about the British decision making process is the power of the Treasury to influence the policy proposed in every other ministry through its control over departmental spending.

It is possible to argue that when dealing with technical issues in which the public has little interest, these small and powerful elites make decisions in a rational manner. This is based on the big assumption, of course, that all members of the elite concerned are highly informed and share similar policy goals. In reality, this would be unlikely. It is normal for political tensions to exist between government departments and between ministers and their civil servants, in which case the organisation model and bureaucratic politics model will be more useful in explaining decision making than the rational model.

However, once an issue is placed on the political agenda by the mass media (Chapter 10), is discussed in Parliament (Chapter 14), considered by political parties (Chapter 8) and concerns public opinion (Chapter 7), so the issue will become increasingly politicised. Under these circumstances it is very unlikely that those involved in the policy debate will share similar political goals. Even members of the same political party will be divided into competing factions or tendencies, and it is commonplace for members of the same pressure group (Chapter 9) to have different political aspirations. Where policy emerges through the close involvement of sectional

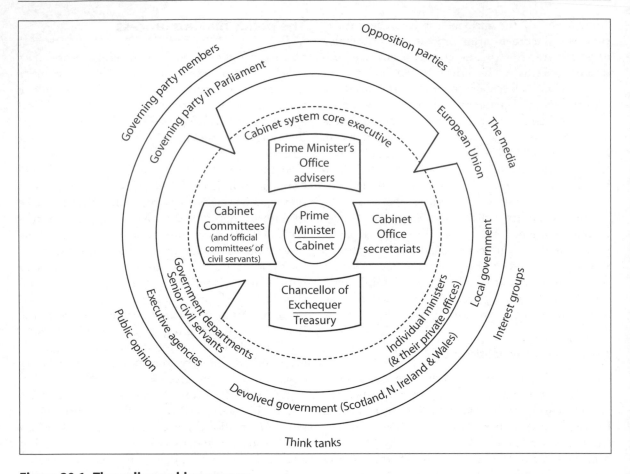

Figure 20.1 The policy making process

interest groups with government departments in a client or corporate relationship, or where policy emerges through a central–local dependency relationship (Chapter 18), then it is likely to have the characteristics of 'muddling through'.

Decisions will be the result of the interaction of participants in a power network. In order to reach agreement on issues they are likely to avoid setting out their political goals in detail, since this would be the cause of conflict. Policies and decisions that are ambiguous and understood differently by participants in the policy process generally contribute towards building a consensus and enabling progress to be made on an issue. In contrast, conviction politics based on explicit political goals generates conflict and maximises opposition. It is for this reason that incrementalism in policy making has been the general hallmark of contemporary British politics.

Policy analysis

Policy analysis is a specialist field within the study of politics and government. Policy analysts will research why certain issues have come to be seen as 'problems' for government to tackle and why some issues are ignored; how policies are made; the nature of the policies that are made, as well as the content of alternatives that were rejected; who influenced policy making and who did not (for example, whether policies were shaped to suit 'producers' or 'consumers'); how policies work in practice in terms of solving the original problem, as well as any other consequences, intended or unintended.

The main consensus amongst policy analysts is that making public policy tends to be incremental (see above). In other words, policy making can be seen as a series of small steps moving away from the original policy. Policy analysts point out that it is important to understand that past policies are always an important ingredient in the making of new policies. Policy making thus takes place in a number of stages, all of which make up a 'cycle' or 'process'. Figure 20.2 illustrates this process in relation to educational policy making.

'Joined-up' policy making

SOLACE (the Society of Local Authority Chief Executives) produced a useful framework for categorising examples of policy making. Policy making can be understood through the metaphor of lighthouses and spotlights: 'while the spotlight illuminates just a small field of vision, the lighthouse's beam covers a wide area. It also keeps you off the rocks' (Boatswain *et al.*, 1999). Greater use of market forces in policy making, through privatisation and contracting out, has led to fragmentation; in local government, for example, thousands of contracts are made each year which

deliver thousands of services. Is this like 'thousands of spotlights' each solving a separate problem but in so doing missing the 'big picture'? For there would be many dark spaces between the spotlights and in them, hidden from view, are interlinkages between different policy issues and problems.

A useful example is contained in Figure 20.2, where at the feedback stage of the policy process it is noted that schools are excluding many more pupils than was anticipated. Excluding troublesome pupils was a spotlight policy which made sense in the context of encouraging schools to raise educational standards. It was not anticipated that putting schools under the pressure of appearing in performance league tables would result in many more pupils being excluded from school, and that in turn this would result in higher juvenile crime rates. To understand how this happens requires the broad beam, or 'joined-up' approach to policy making (see Table 20.1).

Solving problems one at a time can miss the links between high educational standards, social exclusion

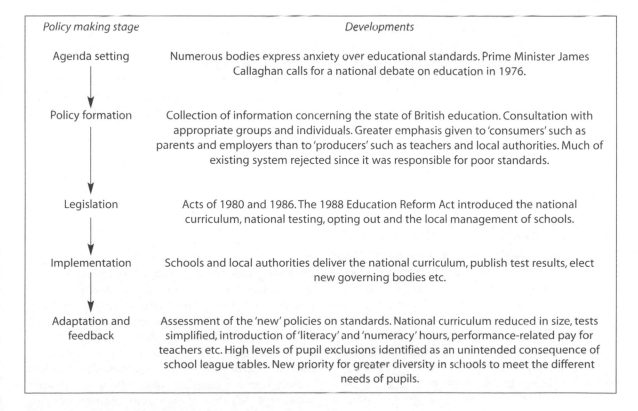

Policy making stage	Developments
Agenda setting	Numerous bodies express anxiety over educational standards. Prime Minister James Callaghan calls for a national debate on education in 1976.
Policy formation	Collection of information concerning the state of British education. Consultation with appropriate groups and individuals. Greater emphasis given to 'consumers' such as parents and employers than to 'producers' such as teachers and local authorities. Much of existing system rejected since it was responsible for poor standards.
Legislation	Acts of 1980 and 1986. The 1988 Education Reform Act introduced the national curriculum, national testing, opting out and the local management of schools.
Implementation	Schools and local authorities deliver the national curriculum, publish test results, elect new governing bodies etc.
Adaptation and feedback	Assessment of the 'new' policies on standards. National curriculum reduced in size, tests simplified, introduction of 'literacy' and 'numeracy' hours, performance-related pay for teachers etc. High levels of pupil exclusions identified as an unintended consequence of school league tables. New priority for greater diversity in schools to meet the different needs of pupils.

Figure 20.2 The educational policy making process

Table 20.1 Differing approaches to policy making

Single-issue policy making (the spotlight)	Joined-up policy making (the lighthouse beam)
Top down – centralised policy making to solve problems identified by the government	Bottom up – meeting local needs seen as crucial if policy is to be successful
Spotlight vision – misses the links between issues	Broad vision – recognises links and tackles causes, not symptoms
Fragmented policy making – many different agencies each pursuing its own policy. No overview of the whole of society.	Holistic – co-ordination and cooperation help meet needs for all in society and prevent 'unintended consequences'
Uniformity – centralised policy is identical throughout Britain	Context-sensitive – policy is flexible and adapts to local circumstances

and crime. The 'searchlight beam' approach would have revealed these connections which would be fed back into the policy making process. Another example, provided in the SOLACE paper, concerned a family buying their council house at a discount under the right to buy policy, but failing to keep up with their mortgage repayments. The house is repossessed and sold cheaply at auction to a private landlord. The family that will then live in this ex-council house will probably receive housing benefits in order to pay the rent. The end result will be that the original family has been put through a crisis and now has to be rehoused; taxpayers have lost the value of the right to buy discount; taxpayers have now to subsidise the higher rent for the same house by providing benefits for the new tenants. A joined-up approach to this problem, it was argued, could have prevented much personal misery as well as saving needless expenditure from the public purse.

Modernising policy making

The Thatcher governments introduced much change to the public sector, such as the introduction of market forces to education and health, as well as the conversion of most of the civil service into executive agencies. New Labour is also set on modernising the public sector. Its approach has been collaborative, and designed to develop a 'joined-up' approach to government associated with the 'searchlight' method of policy making discussed above.

It was argued that collaborative government would be better government. Tackling problems in a joined-up way would avoid many of the problems of 'departmentalitis'. In other words new units of collaborative government, created outside the old departmental boundaries, could link up and solve problems in a coordinated and inter-connected manner. The Social Exclusion Unit and to an extent the failed experiment with the so-called 'Drugs Czar' were new units created outside established departments.

Political leadership

Political scientists have paid considerable attention to the significance of leadership style in policy making. In particular there has been lengthy debate about the development of the office of prime minister into a presidential role. A recent contribution to this debate from Michael Foley considered issues such as the changing ways in which prime ministers and modern presidents communicate with the electorate and relate with other elements of government. A feature of the American political system is the political distance presidents put between themselves and Washington politics, a strategy which allows a president to remain an integral and even central part of government, while at the same time affording the opportunity to detach from government, and thereby relinquishing responsibility for much of what it does. Paradoxically, it might even be said that this sort of spatial detachment has become one of the most effective ways for a president to maintain a central position in government (Foley, 1993: 24–5).

BOX 20.2
The Phillips Inquiry: lessons about policy making

The 16-volume report of the BSE enquiry, chaired by Lord Phillips, was published in October 2000. Newspapers noted that the report did not blame individuals for the BSE disaster, it merely noted that policy making contained 'mistakes', showed a 'lack of rigour', was conducted in a 'culture of secrecy' with participants guilty of 'team failure'.

The Phillips Report does not make happy reading for all those people who ate beef during the 1980s. The tragedy began in a herd of cows on a Sussex farm in 1984 when cow 133 in the herd was suffering from an illness only previously seen in sheep. It appeared that feeding processed sheep and cattle brains to cows could result in their developing BSE ('mad cow disease'). Restrictions were eventually imposed on the use of brain and offal, and new safety procedures were devised for slaughter houses in order to prevent further health risks. Despite the mounting evidence, the Ministry of Agriculture, Fisheries and Food (MAFF) denied that BSE in cows could be transmitted to humans. In an ill-judged photo opportunity the Minister, John Gummer, fed his daughter a beef burger to reassure the public that beef was safe.

The media played a crucial watchdog role by setting an agenda that focused on the deaths of dairy farmers and butchers of vCJD, a disease closely related to BSE. Finally, in 1996, the Minister for Health informed the Commons that there could be a link between vCJD and BSE. The number of deaths resulting from BSE will not be known for many years but around 100, including many young people, have already occurred. Policy failure not only reached out to bring tragedy to many families, but also ruined a large sector of agriculture with billions of pounds lost in incomes, exports and compensation.

In addition to Whitehall's culture of secrecy, the report commented on a form of dependency culture which existed between officials and scientists to the detriment of policy making. Each 'shades their opinion' in order to obtain benefits from their respective superiors.

For example, the Agriculture Minister wanted 'good news' stories about agriculture in order to defend or strengthen his position in government, in Parliament, and with the media and public. His civil servants, therefore became desperate to supply their political master, the minister, with 'good news' stories about agriculture in Britain. Any news stories that

Ministers
want to receive 'good news' stories in order to promote or defend their political reputations.

findings

Civil servants
want to provide ministers with positive news. They control money needed by scientists to conduct their research.

 money   **findings**

Scientists
wishing to receive MAFF money are tempted to 'soften' or interpret their research findings in order to provide civil servants with positive results. This is known as 'shaded opinion'.

Figure 20.3 Shading opinion

might increase public anxiety were 'played down' as other, more positive stories, became emphasised. Many scientists relied on MAFF for money to carry out research. Civil servants who make decisions about research grants will tend to favour those scientists who help give them 'good news' stories which they could pass on to the minister. Thus scientists were naturally tempted to 'shade their opinion' about BSE in order to win bids for research grants and to avoid undertaking research projects that risked producing unwelcome findings.

The BSE disaster contributed to the restructuring of MAFF into DEFRA as well as the establishment of an independent Food Standards Agency. Other health issues, such as salmonella in eggs, *E. coli* in cooked meats and the impact of GM crops, had been the causes of public anxiety. Many felt that policy making had been shaped to reflect the fact that farming profits had priority over public safety. Early work by the FSA has involved licensing butchers' shops and reviewing sometimes meaningless information contained on food products, such as 'country-style' or 'farmhouse'. For more information see <www.bseinquiry.gov.uk>.

BOX 20.3
Contrasting the Thatcher and Blair approaches

Thatcher and Major	Blair
In the public sector their approach involves using new public management (NPM) which is based on *private sector* techniques – namely the *profit motive, market forces* and *competition* as a way of getting efficiency, economy and effectiveness.	In the public sector this approach is based on *collaboration* which is a highly active form of *cooperation* based on *partnerships* between government, private sector and the 'third' sector of voluntary bodies and charities.

In British politics, Prime Minister Margaret Thatcher frequently acted like an outsider in Number Ten, becoming engaged in a struggle against her Cabinet and Whitehall over the direction and content of policy. The outsider role enabled Thatcher to campaign against her own government ministers, implying that they lacked her vision and generally were not up to the job, while at the same time detaching herself from their policy failures and allowing her to dominate the machinery of government. The media attention given to the Labour leader, and the portrayal of new Labour as a Blairite party which rejected old Labour, gave the 1997 and 2001 general elections many features of presidential contests.

Leadership involves qualities in the exercise of power which are over and above prime ministerial and presidential styles. Within a given power structure, leadership can be exercised in a number of qualitatively different ways. For example, some prime ministers have played a 'hands off' role regarding policy making and issues of government, intervening only when a major problem arose or if a specific policy was failing consistently. As prime minister, Sir Alec Douglas-Home adopted a laissez-faire or 'hands off' form of leadership. He explained his leadership style in an interview, stating that 'a good prime minister, once he had selected his ministers and made it plain to them he was always accessible for comment or advice, should interfere with their departmental business as little as possible'.

Other prime ministers have played a more positive role in leading the government, making sure that policy kept the backbenchers relatively content. Sometimes this might involve the prime minister acting as broker to make compromises in policy; other times it might involve the prime minister as a wheeler-dealer satisfying one party faction in one policy area and another faction in another policy area. Sometimes this type of leadership is referred to as transactional, and Harold Wilson as Prime Minister provides an example of power being exercised in this manner.

Finally, some prime ministers have led in ways that were initially at odds with the wishes of their followers but won their support in the course of time. Charismatic personality and inspiration have frequently been important factors in gaining the support of others in the party who come to share the leader's vision of what sort of society should be created. This type of leadership is referred to as transformational. Margaret Thatcher's dislike of lengthy Cabinet discussions, which she saw as a waste of time, her distaste for consensus politics, which were at odds with her strong political convictions, together with her personal domination of the Cabinet and wider party, were preconditions for the Thatcher revolution, a contemporary example of transformational leadership in practice. Similarly Tony Blair accelerated the transformation of the Labour Party in opposition, changing its constitution, and in government has embarked on a radical programme of modernising the British constitution.

The way in which leadership is exercised has a considerable impact on the policy making process. The laissez-faire approach tends to result in strong continuity in policies which are made at departmental level. The prime minister's thinking is guided by the 'if it ain't broke, don't fix it' rule. Only when one department's policy works against other departments' policies or is failing in some other way, will the prime minister intervene in order to find a solution. Such a government's policies will reflect different departmental views, tend to be pragmatic in nature, and although coordinated at cabinet level, are unlikely to be unified through being based on the same ideological beliefs.

Prime ministers leading in a transactional way will play a much greater 'hands on' role in managing policy making. Harold Wilson once described the role of prime minister as being like the conductor of an orchestra; talented and ambitious players, many of whom will want to star as soloists, have to be brought together to play the same tune in harmony. In political terms, this means rewarding some people, disappointing others, whilst still keeping the support of as many as possible. Policy emerges heavily influenced by patronage and compromise. For example, Prime Minister Harold Wilson created a new ministry, the Department of Economic Affairs (DEA), as a long-term-thinking counterweight to the short-term-thinking Treasury. Clearly this initiative had the potential for making a considerable impact on Labour's economic policy making as well as challenging the Treasury's influence on other departments' policy making. But many suspected that Wilson created the DEA simply to provide his troublesome deputy, George Brown, with an apparently important role while preventing him from being foreign secretary, the job he really wanted. If this suspicion was true, then policy making was influenced by the way in which personal political ambitions in cabinet were satisfied and rewarded. It had little to do with counter-balancing the Treasury.

Transformational leadership is very much a 'hands on' approach to government, with the political vision of the inspirational leader providing the basis of all policy making. Departmental policies should be unified since they are all derived from the same ideological source. For example, Margaret Thatcher's convictions about the enterprise economy and competition, and her strong preference for free market solutions, provided the basis not only for economic policy, but also for education reforms, health service reforms, civil service reforms and local government reforms. The main danger for the transformational leader is policy that deviates from the vision. This happened for Thatcher when her chancellor took Britain into the ERM (see Chapter 21), a policy she believed doomed to failure since 'you can't buck the market' by having strict foreign currency controls. The main danger for others is that the ideology is flawed. If markets fail, if they produce too many losers who rebel against government, if people are not motivated by the profit motive, or if market forces result in corruption, then there would be massive policy failure. Policy would be characterised by what political scientists refer to as 'unintended consequences' which beyond a certain point result in a 'policy mess' at the level of implementation.

Sources of policy advice

Parties competing for office have wanted to win support on the basis of what has become known as the 'big idea'. In many ways, Thatcherism was the big idea that inspired a number of policy initiatives which prevented Conservative administrations from looking exhausted at successive general elections. Labour has conducted a policy review which has eliminated its traditional big idea – nationalisation – from its manifesto in favour of more centrist policies. In its place have emerged two big ideas which unite Labour policies: community and stakeholding. These ideas, or themes, enabled the party to present the electorate with fresh policies which put 'clear water' between Labour and Conservative programmes.

The Conservatives under Thatcher and Major were assisted in policy formulation by a constant stream of proposals from right-wing think tanks such as the Institute of Economic Affairs, the Centre for Policy Studies, the Adam Smith Institute, Policy Search and the Social Affairs Unit. The importance of these groups was that they were able to 'think the unthinkable' since their activities were conducted outside the party. If one of the think tanks floated a policy proposal that was widely criticised, it did not damage the reputation of the Conservative government. Damage was done, however, if a flawed think tank policy was adopted and implemented by government. The latter occurred when the Adam Smith Institute's idea of financing local government with a poll tax was adopted by Thatcher.

In the past Labour had the reputation of being a 'thinking party' capable of producing radical policies, but during the 1980s Labour's policy making was criticised for lacking fresh ideas. The Fabians did not play a very vigorous role in generating new ideas, nor were there individuals able to do this as Anthony Crosland had done in the past. However, during the 1990s it restored its reputation as a 'thinking party', drawing ideas from a reinvigorated

Fabian Society, the Institute for Public Policy Research, Charter 88, the Commission on Social Justice as well as deriving inspiration from theories and concepts discussed by Amitai Etzioni, J. K. Galbraith, John Kay and Will Hutton.

New Labour has made increasing use of political advisers and task forces as sources of policy advice. Political advisers are sometimes associated in the public mind with practitioners of 'spin' and attempts to manage the news media to the advantage of government. However political advisers play a wider role in the policy process, and played an influential role in decisions to implement devolution, give the Bank of England autonomy in setting interest rates, and set up the Social Exclusion Unit. Despite their numbers, taskforces have wielded patchy influence over New Labour policy making. Whilst some recommendations have been implemented, such as compulsory citizenship education in schools, others such as recommendations on urban renewal have been shelved.

It has been argued that civil servants, unlike their partisan counterparts in the United States, are poor sources of policy ideas. British civil servants are frequently portrayed as amateurs and generalists, living in a Whitehall village which is cut off from the real world of industry, commerce and those at the delivery end of the public sector. What civil servants are able to do skilfully, it is argued, is take on board policy advice from specialists – scientists, professional specialists and others with specific expertise – and blend it with what is politically feasible as the basis of advice for their ministers.

Many pressure groups have established networks which include Whitehall contacts. Groups with insider status frequently have the opportunity of influencing policy at the formulation stage, while less favoured outsider groups have to rely on influencing public opinion in their attempts to shape policy. The involvement of pressure groups in Whitehall can be seen as a feature of consensus politics, and it is therefore not a surprise that pressure groups played a smaller role in policy making during the Thatcher years. Indeed one of her ministers attacked pressure groups, describing them as 'strangling serpents' which increased the workload of ministers and got in the way of good government. In contrast, Labour has been more receptive to pressure group proposals.

Britain's membership of the European Union is an increasingly important source of policy. However, although Labour is not as divided as the Conservatives on the prospects of greater federalism and policy harmonisation, European policies, particularly whether or not to join the euro, are likely to present the government with some problems. Indeed, like its Conservative predecessors its approach to such policies could be a damage limitation exercise; much emphasis will be put on presentation, subsidiarity will be emphasised, with the comforting knowledge that there is little that backbenchers can do to change such policies.

Policy and implementation

Finally, something should be said about policy implementation. There are problems of definition, not dissimilar from the distinction between policy making and decision making at the beginning of this chapter. Thus what is policy and what is implementation (or administration) of policy is partly a matter of perspective. Most of the examples discussed in this chapter have focused on central government policy making, with the implication that other parts of the public sector are involved in implementing policy decisions made at the centre. This may often seem not far from the truth. Yet Part IV of this book has emphasised a shift towards multi-level governance, which implies that various levels of government can have a significant input into the policy process – both above the level of the UK government, particularly through the European Union, and below it. Certainly the new devolved administrations of Northern Ireland, Wales and (particularly) Scotland are involved in policy making. Local authorities may have lost powers, but they still have some significant discretion and on some issues retain a policy making role. Managerial devolution in the health service and education, and the changes in the civil service through the growth of executive agencies, have given more discretion to institutions and managers, ostensibly the whole point of the reforms. Even fairly lowly front-line workers may have some meaningful discretion, such as to justify the term 'street-level policy making' used by some academics.

This does, however, highlight one of the problems of implementation. Commonly central government relies on some other agency to implement policy – perhaps part of the public sector, such as an executive agency, quango, local authority or hospital trust. Yet there is no direct line management involved between the minister and any of these. Many local authorities will be controlled by other parties with other priorities, and in some cases downright hostile to central policy. In some services there is a tradition of professional autonomy which resents what is perceived as interference. Central government can issue circulars, publish targets, and back them up with financial sticks and carrots, regulation, and where necessary new legislation. Yet even this may not be enough to prevent recalcitrant local authorities from dragging their feet. Opposition from key workers may effectively sabotage government initiatives.

The problem is clearer still when the centre is relying on organisations and interests outside government altogether for successful implementation. This was one of the problems with the incomes policies pursued by both Conservative and Labour governments in the 1960s and 1970s, which depended on the cooperation of employers and trade unions. (Legislation was tried but this proved a rather ineffective blunt instrument.) Much industrial, agricultural and environmental policy relies on private sector firms if is to succeed. Much social policy depends heavily on local communities and the voluntary sector.

Even without such problems of cooperation there may be other difficulties with implementation. Commonly insufficient resources have been made available, and in particular there has been a lack of money. Local authorities often complain that they have not been given additional funds to finance new government initiatives. There may sometimes be a lack of qualified personnel, or physical resources. Governments may will the ends but not provide the means. Sometimes of course unexpected difficulties occur, leading to a tacit decision to downplay or even abandon a particular policy. For all kinds of reasons there may be what has been described as an 'implementation gap': a significant gap between policy objectives and policy outputs and outcomes.

Such 'implementation gaps' are not always to be deplored. They may reflect the inputs of other interests and agencies into the policy process, perhaps leading to a better or more realistic policy, and sometimes may avoid disaster which would follow from blind adherence to ill-thought-out objectives. Unexpected rising costs of implementation or unanticipated side-effects may lead to a reappraisal and a decision that the cost outweighs the benefits. Policy making is or should be an iterative process, as ministers and officials learn from experience. Problems of implementation may be the inspiration for new policy initiatives to remedy the deficiencies in existing policy.

Further reading

Hill (1997a) provides a good overview of the policy process, while Hill (1997b) is also an excellent reader. Wayne Parsons (1995) provides more extensive and detailed analysis of specific aspects.

Allison (1971) is a classic study in international decision making. Burns (1978) is a classic text exploring the concept of effective leadership. Foley (1993) gives an interesting interpretation of the changing role of the prime minister. Greenaway, Smith and Street (1992) provides an analysis of governmental decisions. For discussion of other issues see Richards (2000) and McKie (2000).

Chapter 21

Managing the economy

The tools of economic management   355
Management of the economy: the Thatcher
 and Major years   361
Economic management under New Labour 363
A prudent or a gambling chancellor? 366
Britain's open economy   367

Britain was the first country to have an industrial revolution and to develop a capitalist economy. Over 40 per cent of the world's trade once involved British goods. Two hundred years later Britain had an ailing economy and a 6 per cent share of world trade. For many years the economy has been in relative decline, with Britain apparently unable to shake off the reputation of being the 'sick man of Europe'. Successive governments seemed content to manage Britain's decline so as to soften the blows and mitigate its worst effects. Some were critical of this fatalistic attitude and argued that there was nothing inevitable about Britain's decline. They believed that Thatcherite economics would reverse Britain's fortunes. Were they justified in thinking this? When the economy began recovering during John Major's Conservative administration, why did the electorate refuse to reward his party by supporting it in the 1997 general election? Have the Conservatives lost their traditional reputation for economic competence to Labour? Is the Labour Chancellor presiding over the best performance of the British economy in living memory? These questions will be tackled by first examining the range of 'tools' available for a chancellor to use in managing the economy. Second, what are the political implications for a chancellor managing what is arguably the most 'open' of the major world economies?

The tools of economic management

The state of the economy and how it affects them personally is an important issue in influencing the way people vote. Because of this, political factors play a central role in the way government manages the economy. Past governments have been criticised for their 'stop-go' Keynesian economic policies which 'go' for growth during the period in the run-up to a general election, winning the approval of the electorate, but then 'stop' once the election has been held in order for the economy to cool down. In political terms it may represent a successful economic strategy, but businesspeople are critical of the damage done to the economy through the instability and uncertainty that 'stop-go' creates (Figure 21.1).

Intervention

Governments can manage the economy through direct controls and intervention. In directing the wartime economy, the government led by Winston Churchill assumed massive powers of intervention in controlling the labour force, deciding on the location of industry, requisitioning economic assets, rationing the supply of raw materials to factories, and so on. These controls largely disappeared during the 1950s, but nevertheless peacetime governments have attempted since to control aspects of the economy through intervention. For example, in the fight against inflation Labour and Conservative governments have implemented prices and incomes policies (see Box 21.1).

Both Labour and Conservative governments

> *Definition*
> **Keynesian economics** is based on the idea that government can and should manage total demand for goods and services in the economy to promote full employment, stable prices, growth and a healthy balance of payments, increasing public expenditure.

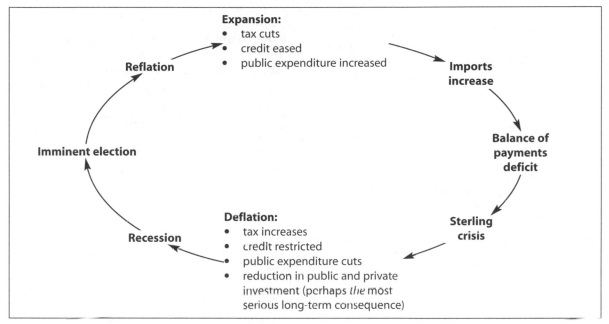

Figure 21.1 The 'stop–go' cycle of the political economy

BOX 21.1

Prices and incomes policies in the 1960s and 1970s

In 1961 a Conservative Chancellor, Selwyn-Lloyd, introduced the 'pay pause', a nine-month-long incomes policy designed to hold down pay awards. Between 1965 and 1969 Labour pursued a prices and incomes policy, and the Conservative government that followed converted an informal incomes policy into a statutory policy which controlled all incomes between 1972 and 1974. The Labour government returned to office in 1974 developed a voluntary incomes policy – known as the 'social contract' –under the leadership of James Callaghan, which finally broke down in the 'winter of discontent' of 1978–9. The industrial disputes during Labour's winter of discontent were an important factor in the Conservative election victory which saw Margaret Thatcher enter Number Ten promising economic management that would rely much more on market forces and far less on government intervention.

from 1945 through to 1979 pursued an industrial policy involving incentives to encourage investment and growth. Impressed by the success of economic planning in France, a Conservative government set up the National Economic Development Council (NEDC) – also known as 'Neddy' – in 1962 as a forum in which governments and both sides of industry discussed plans to improve Britain's industrial efficiency and international competitiveness. Later Labour governments set up other interventionist bodies – the Industrial Reorganisation Corporation (IRC) in 1966 and the National Enterprise Board (NEB) in 1975 – with a view to restructuring and strengthening Britain's industrial base.

By the 1990s all of these interventionist bodies had been abolished. During Thatcher's years in office her governments pursued a more free market and less interventionist approach to the problems of the British economy, cutting regional aid, and allowing unemployment to rise and manufacturing industry to contract.

Economically depressed areas of Britain can be stimulated and improved through an interventionist regional policy which attempts to attract new investment though grants and other financial incentives. Britain's industrial base would have been in an even worse state had it not been for the foreign investment – some £40 billion between 1988 and 1993 – which has created new manufacturing jobs. Today it is reckoned that around one in five of Britain's manufacturing jobs is in a foreign-owned factory.

Fiscal policy

Fiscal policy involves the government managing the economy through taxation and public spending. If the economy is depressed with high levels of unemployment, the government may (1) reduce taxes in order to stimulate the economy – income tax may be reduced so that employees will have more money to spend, or other taxes such as VAT or car tax may be reduced in order to make goods cheaper and thereby encourage more people to buy them; (2) increase public spending on, for example, new roads, hospitals and schools, in order to create new jobs which, as these new workers start spending more, will create yet more new jobs.

Other economic problems, such as a balance of payments deficit or a budget deficit, may be tackled by the government raising taxes and attempting to reduce public spending. Government may pursue other policies through taxation, such as promoting good health through taxing cigarettes or improving the environment through lower taxation of lead-free petrol.

Until 1992 governments announced taxation and spending plans as two separate but related exercises, but from thereon the budget and autumn statements were merged. In 1992, in the depths of a recession, the government was borrowing a massive £50 billion a year. Governments frequently spend more than they raise in taxes, and so have to borrow to fill this gap. The sum borrowed is known as the Public Sector Borrowing Requirement (PSBR).

Monetary controls

Monetary policy is carried out by the Bank of England and the Treasury in attempting to control the volume of money and purchasing power in the economy, and thereby influencing movements in the inflation rate and the level of consumer spending. The main tool of monetary control is the minimum lending rate (MLR),

Definition
Monetarism in a narrow sense involves controlling inflation by controlling the money supply. In a broader sense it involves the rejection of interventionist Keynesian policies which, monetarists argue, cause inflation, particularly if government spending is financed by borrowing. Monetarist policies emphasise the need to 'roll back the state' and reduce government spending to promote a healthy economy.

usually referred to by politicians and the public as simply the 'interest rate'. The level of interest rate determines the cost of borrowing money – a high interest rate makes borrowing expensive and lowers the demand for credit. It also means that mortgages become more expensive and so take more money out of the home-buyers' pockets, so they in turn will have less money available to spend on goods. A low interest rate means that money is cheap to borrow, encouraging consumers to purchase goods on credit. Lower mortgage payments also mean that home-buyers have more money available for consumer goods.

Interest rates gained a greater significance when Britain joined the Exchange Rate Mechanism (ERM) of the European Monetary System (EMS) in 1990. The ERM involved fixing the exchange rates of Community members so that they could move only marginally against each other. If sterling's international value slipped, then interest rates would be raised in order to make the pound more attractive and thereby increase its value on the foreign exchanges. Should demand for sterling push its value towards the upper limit of its ERM band, then the interest rate would be lowered in order to depress demand.

Margaret Thatcher was persuaded in 1990 that Britain should enter the ERM, although she did not believe in fixed exchange rates since 'you can't buck the market'. Her scepticism was justified to some extent on Wednesday 16 September 1992 when, within hours, interest rates were raised from 10 to 15 per cent to defend the falling pound, then reduced again to 10 per cent with the pound being withdrawn from the ERM. Furthermore, almost all Britain's foreign reserves had been spent in this unsuccessful defence of sterling.

Management of the economy: the Thatcher and Major years

Some have argued that the most distinctive features of Conservative economic management were to be found in the policies followed during the 1980s. In basic terms, previous post-war governments had identified unemployment as the biggest economic evil to be tackled, and thus they gave high priority to policies that reduced the number of people out of work. The Thatcher governments identified inflation as the biggest economic evil, and so governments followed policies that were designed to 'squeeze' inflation out of the economy. These policies were referred to as 'monetarism', and involved measures to reduce the levels of public spending, placing greater reliance on free market forces, and tighter control on the money supply. Under the leadership of John Major, and with the ERM policy in tatters, the Thatcher priorities were effectively abandoned and the creation of jobs became once more a central, if elusive, goal of economic policy.

The monetarist experiment

Monetarist policies were implemented during the period 1979–82. The Chancellor lowered the rate of income tax, doubled the level of VAT, and used high interest rates to limit the growth in the money supply. Inflation eventually began to fall but the high interest rate crippled many firms and caused a massive rise in unemployment. By 1982, one in five jobs in manufacturing had disappeared.

Some believed that mass unemployment was being used as a political weapon to curb trade union power. Previous governments that had used interventionist tools of economic management frequently relied on the cooperation of trade unions. But trade unions were not in a strong position to 'deliver' on deals made with the government, for what often seemed an acceptable agreement to trade union leaders was rejected by the rank and file. The attraction of monetarist policies to the government was that they could be implemented without the cooperation or consent of the trade

unions. Since the goodwill of the trade unions was no longer necessary to implement economic policy, the government felt able to erode the power and privileges until then enjoyed by unions. Unemployment weakened trade unions, particularly in the old traditional industries of the north most noted for their union militancy.

In the spring of 1988 the Chancellor, Nigel Lawson, was being described as 'the greatest chancellor of the century', but interest rates were to rise nine times before the end of the year and there was speculation that the Chancellor was in danger of being sacked. The economy was overheating; the Chancellor wished to slow down economic activity and bring an end to the consumer boom without causing a recession. Britain's economy now faced a massive balance of payments crisis accompanied by rising inflation and rising interest rates.

After a bitter row with Margaret Thatcher, Nigel Lawson resigned from the Cabinet and was replaced, briefly, by John Major. His task was to bring about what was referred to as a 'soft landing' in which the economy slowed down without sliding into recession. Sterling entered the ERM and it was recognised that this would cause some economic hardship in the short term, particularly if inflation made British goods uncompetitive abroad, but longer-term benefits of ERM membership would be low inflation and low interest rates. The government was taken by surprise by the depth and length of the recession which began in the late 1980s. At first it was described as a 'blip' in the economy; later it was clear that Britain was in the middle of the deepest recession since the 1930s. From December 1990 Chancellor Lamont began observing the 'green shoots of recovery' and reassured the public that the recession would be 'relatively short-lived and relatively shallow'.

By 1993 some economists were worried that Britain's recession was turning into a slump which was bankrupting or closing a firm every six minutes. The government argued that Britain's recession was not unique since the economics of all European countries were undergoing a prolonged period of recession. But critics argued that Britain's economy was experiencing both a longer and a deeper recession than our European partners.

After the dramatic events of September 1992, referred to above, some economists believed that

Britain's withdrawal from the ERM and subsequent devalued pound would stimulate the economy and bring about a recovery. The failure of free-market Thatcherism, and the collapse of the ERM policy left the government with no substantive economic policy.

Until Black Wednesday, the Conservatives had been seen by the electorate as more competent in managing the economy than Labour. In reality the

---

BOX 21.2
The pro-business party loses the support of business

In the months leading up to the 1997 general election, newspapers carried reports of increasing disillusionment in the business community with the performance of the Conservative government. The image of new Labour was no longer seen as a threat by businesspeople who, a decade earlier, would have feared the election of a Labour government. The chairs of top companies, such as Granada and Great Universal Stores, openly declared their support for Tony Blair. A poll of businesspeople revealed that 80 per cent were not at all worried by the prospects of a Labour government being elected, whilst 15 per cent actually believed that their businesses would do better under Labour. Another poll of business managers found that support for the Conservatives had dropped from 62 to 40 per cent over a five-year period.

It was not just the positive image of New Labour that won the support of many businesspeople, but also the poor performance of John Major's Conservative government. In many ways the old businessperson's political nightmare of a nationalising Labour government has been replaced by the new nightmare of a right-wing Conservative government hostile towards the European Union. European markets are important for British business, and the prospects of a Cabinet containing some ministers who would like Britain to withdraw from the EU was the main fear of businesspeople should the Conservatives be re-elected.

---

economy was in poor shape as a result of sterling being at too high a level in the ERM, which pushed up interest rates to keep sterling attractive, thereby encouraging low growth, high inflation and high unemployment. It was, however, the political panic surrounding Britain's withdrawal from the ERM that cost John Major's government its reputation for economic competence; David Sanders' research revealed that after Black Wednesday 'the competence graph plunges downwards and continues to trend downwards thereafter' (Sanders, 1995: 161). In many ways, John Major's Conservative government experienced the same political fate as Harold Wilson's Labour government, which never recovered its popularity after devaluation in 1967.

All the economic benefits of devaluation stimulated the economy after Black Wednesday: cheaper sterling led to a surge in export profits and Britain's worrying trade deficit narrowed; the economy grew; wages rose steadily but without risking the return of high inflation; and by autumn 1997 unemployment was below 1.5 million for the first time in 17 years. Polls recorded a return of economic optimism to the business community and signs of the 'feel good' factor returned to the electorate. Yet the Conservative government was not rewarded for these improvements, and its popularity ratings fell still further behind Labour.

Conservative reputations also suffered from the party promoting itself as the 'party of low taxation'. Whilst income tax had fallen, other indirect taxes had risen to the point where it was calculated that a typical family was paying £630 more tax a year in 1996 than in 1992. The main election promise of 1992 was broken. At the same time, New Labour, while still in opposition, was shedding its electorally damaging 'tax and spend' image which had dogged 'old' Labour. Labour neutralised potential Conservative attack by accepting Conservative public spending limits for two years and no income tax rises for five years. Labour also worked hard on what journalists called the 'prawn cocktail circuit', attending business lunches and other meetings, in order to convince the business community that New Labour was both 'business-friendly' and more competent than the Conservatives.

IN FOCUS 21.1 Blair and Brown

Prime Minister Tony Blair and Chancellor of the Exchequer, Gordon Brown, during a press conference, May 2001. Although Blair is generally reckoned to be a dominant, almost presidential Prime Minister, Brown has undisputed control over everything related to economic policy, and chairs several key Cabinet committees. Relations between the two men, formerly very close, reportedly soured when Blair leapfrogged over Brown in the Labour hierarchy to become Leader in 1994 and Prime Minister in 1997. The two are reported to be bitter rivals, and it is even alleged that Blair may have reneged on a deal to give way to Brown after a few years in power.

Photograph: PA Photos.

Economic management under New Labour

A favourable inheritance?

For the first time on entering office, in 1997 Labour inherited an economy that was performing relatively well. Compared with for example 1974, trends in inflation, growth, exports and unemployment were all moving in a favourable direction in 1997. Some of the strength in the economy resulted from Conservative policies which old Labour instincts had opposed. The position of trade unions had changed considerably; while they brought disruption to Labour in the mid-1970s, culminating in the 'winter of discontent', by 1997 they were much weaker and posed little threat to the economy. Many restrictive practices of the 1970s had also been swept away by Conservative governments, leaving Labour with a 'flexible labour force' much better able to compete for trade. Of course some problems remained, such as the decline in manufacturing, a relatively under-skilled working population, low levels of investment and an attitude of 'short-termism' towards business development.

A prudent chancellor?

Labour's new Chancellor, Gordon Brown, soon established a reputation for prudence. He was determined to keep Labour's pre-election pledge to stay within

Conservative taxing and spending plans for two years, and did so. Yet he immediately made another bold decision which was almost totally unexpected, particularly from a Labour government: he granted the Bank of England independence from government in setting the level of interest rates. This removed the temptation from government to manage the 'boom and bust' economic cycle to coincide with the 'electoral' cycle (see Coxall and Robins, 1998, ch. 9). The Bank of England, through its monetary committee, was now free to set interest rates as a weapon to combat inflation rather than the chancellor setting interest rates to help create an economic boom in the run-up to a general election. The government signalled its determination to keep inflation low by announcing a 2.5 per cent target rate, and Brown further announced his 'golden rule' of only borrowing to finance investment and keeping public debt at a stable and prudent proportion of national income over the economic cycle. These measures were generally well received, particularly in the City. By establishing Labour's credibility in managing the economy the Chancellor improved the prospects of long-term stability and growth.

Two further Labour pre-election pledges had caused some anxiety in the business community. One was the commitment to sign up to the Social Chapter of the Maastricht Treaty (Treaty of the European Union) from which Major had secured an opt-out. The other was to introduce a national minimum wage. Both

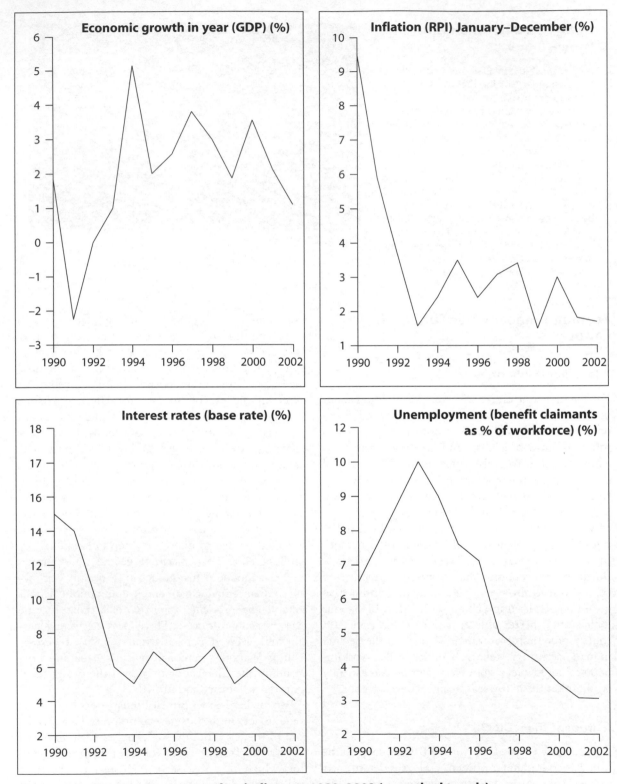

Figure 21.2 The British economy: key indicators, 1990–2002 (smoothed trends)

pledges were honoured, but neither proved as damaging to business as critics had feared. Labour's trade union allies were disappointed with the relatively low level at which the national minimum wage was set, and it had little if any measurable impact on inflation and unemployment. Indeed the Conservative Party, which had vigorously denounced the minimum wage in government, changed its stance in opposition and declared its support.

The commitment to keep within Tory spending plans and not increase income tax constrained Labour's policies in the first two years, although Brown did raise some additional revenue from a windfall tax on the privatised utilities to finance his 'new deal' (see below), raising National Insurance contributions, and removing some forms of tax relief. These 'stealth taxes', as the opposition called them, enabled him to pursue some redistribution of income, and inject some additional money into public services.

Beyond this the Chancellor emphasised 'supply side' reforms to improve the performance of the economy, and stimulate investment and employment. Most important of all was the 'new deal' to move the young unemployed 'from welfare to work'. Three billion pounds was earmarked to get them into jobs or training. There were additional tax and benefit incentives to make work financially worthwhile to single parents and poor families (e.g. through the working families tax credit). Investment was encouraged through the establishment of regional development agencies (with limited budgets however), and more controversially for Labour Party members and the trade unions, enthusiastic encouragement of the private finance initiative (PFI), developed under the previous government. A major attraction was that the use of PFIs enabled substantial additional much needed investment in the public sector without increasing the Public Sector Borrowing Requirement. Critics argued that it was more expensive than traditional public borrowing to finance investment in new hospitals, schools and prisons.

One very important issue was, however, ducked. All major parties had pledged a referendum before any final decision was taken on whether Britain should join the single European currency, for which plans were far advanced when Labour came to power. In the 1970s and early 1980s the Conservatives had been by far the more pro-Europe of the major parties. By 1997 the position was substantially reversed, and

BOX 21.3
Labour and the euro

From January 1999 11 members of the EU, but not including Britain, fixed their national currencies against the euro. The 11 were later joined by Greece, adjudged to meet the criteria for membership. From January 2002 the first euro notes and coins started replacing their national currencies in these 12 countries. A combined total of 290 million people inhabited 'Euroland' using the new single currency. Labour's policy is to support entry to the euro if five 'tests' or safeguards can be met: the convergence of British and European business cycles; assurances that the British economy can respond successfully to changes resulting from entry; and the impact on (1) investment; (2) financial services and (3) jobs. The Treasury has responsibility for making this assessment. Gordon Brown has appeared less enthusiastic about the euro than Blair, partly perhaps because of the bruising experience of Britain's brief membership of the ERM. However, the main problem is perhaps political: winning a referendum in the face of public opinion which remains hostile to the euro. Euro-sceptics, on the other hand, fear that the electorate will be bombarded with pro-euro propaganda to 'soften them up' before a referendum is held. One of the principal concerns will be the impact of a 'one size fits all' interest rate set by the European Central Bank. Different economies may require different interest rates to either encourage growth or dampen down inflation, but Euroland has to share the same rate. This means that the same rate applies to a country experiencing economic recession and unemployment (Germany in recent years) and one with high inflation (such as Ireland latterly). An additional problem for Labour is that some European politicians have argued that the euro provides an opportunity for the harmonisation of European taxes. Some influential European politicians have been committed to 'rapid progress' in tax harmonisation within Euroland.

the Conservatives were more Euro-sceptic than Labour. The new government was more favourable to the single currency than its predecessor, but there were reservations over its possible implications for the British economy and political doubts over whether a referendum was winnable (see Box 21.3).

A prudent or a gambling chancellor?

The British economy continued to perform relatively well throughout Labour's first term. The government had entered office in 1997 five years into a recovery and subsequently managed the economy in a manner which won considerable praise. Unemployment, inflation and interest rates had fallen, despite the dangers posed by fluctuating oil prices, a stock market collapse, the scandals in corporate America and the failing economies of the Far East and South America.

However, Gordon Brown's reputation for prudence suffered some questioning after Labour' second election landslide in 2001, when substantial extra sums were already being pumped into Britain's public services, particularly health and education (see Chapter 22). Against a continued downturn in the American economy, and in most of the western world, economic growth in Britain does not look like being as high as Treasury forecasts. Some economic commentators became increasingly worried that the healthy state of the British economy was too dependent on high consumer spending, fuelled in large part by rising house values and greater debt. Britain's productivity record remained poor, and manufacturing industry was further depressed by the high pound which adversely affected exports and led to a substantial balance of payments deficit. Brown and the government generally were determined, however, not to cut back on their ambitious spending plans, and Brown's 2002 budget appeared to gamble on the capacity of the British economy to avoid a slowdown (see Box 21.4).

While Brown's budget pleased the Labour Party it had a less positive impact on business. During the 1990s Labour made overtures to businesspeople to reassure them that a future Labour government would promote their interests. New Labour rebadged itself as a pro-enterprise party. Some doubts about the economic wisdom of New Labour

have been expressed by businesspeople, especially following the 2002 budget. For example the Director-General of the CBI, Digby Jones, argued that British businesses 'have already stumped up an additional £29 billion in tax during the past five years ... and are now expected to pay at least another £4 billion a year in employers' National Insurance contributions' (*Observer*, 21 April 2002). There seems little doubt that these increased costs will inevitably damage Britain's future international competitiveness.

There are also external threats to the continued good health of the British economy. By the end of 2002 Britain had experienced a consumer boom which had largely protected the economy from recession and, as some argued, masked a serious collapse in the manufacturing sector. But how far the economy can be protected from the global downturn remains a moot question. Japan's economy is currently suffering from deflation, which some economists now believe is an increasing threat to Germany, the USA and ultimately to Britain. Should this come to be the case, the Chancellor's 'tax, borrow and spend' budget may be appropriate for reasons other than those of its original redistributive purpose.

It is too early to assess Labour's handling of the economy. Budgets that are praised at the time are often subsequently criticised in the light of subsequent developments. Chancellors who win high marks in office may see their reputations tumble later. It has been said that there are only two kinds of chancellor – those who fail and those who get out in time. It remains to be seen whether Gordon Brown will upset this cynical judgment. It could be 10 or 20 years, or perhaps more, before it is possible to pass a reasoned verdict on Labour's economic record.

Assessing the distinctiveness of New Labour's management of the economy, Grant argued that the 'Blair government has built on the economic foundations established by Thatcher and Major, retaining an attachment to sound money, but giving a greater emphasis to sustained growth and to an element of redistribution' (Grant, 2002: 1–2). The 'third way' approach, conceptualised as not midway but beyond Thatcherism and old Labour, applies to New Labour's management of the economy. The economy is far more regulated than under Thatcher, with a minimum wage and redistribution via the tax system. But Labour has also given

BOX 21.4

The radical Labour budget of 2002

The Chancellor, Gordon Brown, delighted 'old' Labour by introducing what many political commentators described as a 'tax and spend' budget. He announced massive increases in funding totalling £40 billion for the NHS over a five-year period. This represented a 43 per cent rise by 2007 after taking inflation into account. Spending will rise by 7.4 per cent a year in real terms from £65.4 billion in 2001 to £105.6 billion in 2007. To express this increase in public spending another way, the percentage of GDP spent on health will rise from 7.7 per cent to 9.4 per cent. Significant increases in funding were also promised for education. The increased public spending will be paid for primarily by increasing National Insurance contributions from both employees and employers. The composition of public accounts is shown in Figure 21.3, with the difference between income and spending met by £11 billion of borrowing. However, some commentators argued that a consequence of global economic slowdown would be new tax rises in order to pay for increased public spending.

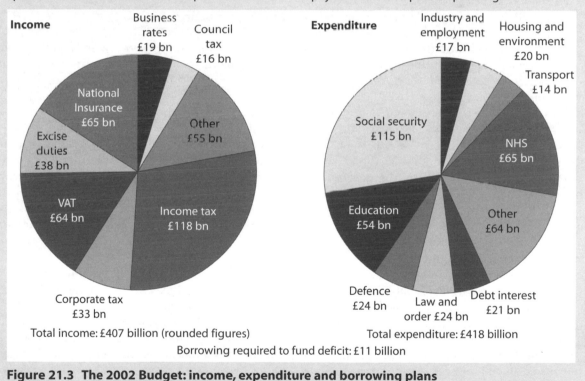

Total income: £407 billion (rounded figures)　　Total expenditure: £418 billion

Borrowing required to fund deficit: £11 billion

Figure 21.3 The 2002 Budget: income, expenditure and borrowing plans

Source: adapted from *Guardian*, 18 April 2002.

considerable encouragement to the private sector through its endorsement of the private finance initiative and its enthusiasm for public–private partnerships generally. Moreover, the Bank of England has been given near autonomy in the setting of base rates (a decision which would have been most unlikely under previous Labour governments).

Britain's open economy

Over and above the short-term performance of particular governments and chancellors there are broader questions about the British economy and its relationship with the world economy which affect any British government. The City of

London remains arguably the world's most important banking and finance centre. The health of Britain's economy depends in large part on attracting inward investment from large overseas companies and multi-nationals. Large and frequent capital flows, along with the internationalisation of credit, make it increasingly difficult for national governments to control aspects of economic policy making. For example, globalization 'makes it more difficult for governments and central banks to clearly identify, let alone control, the domestic money supply. These developments transform the capacity of governments to control effectively the money supply and interest rates, as well as the impact of both on output and inflation' (Held *et al.*, 1999: 229).

Many of Britain's biggest industries, including some recently privatised public utilities, are foreign owned. Many established British companies have moved their manufacturing to lower-wage economies in the developing world. Taking all these factors into account, Andrew Baker observed that 'Britain is now more heavily integrated into a global circuit of capital than any other country in the world' (Baker, 2000: 364). Furthermore, other policies of liberalising and deregulating, initiated by Thatcher governments and continued by the governments that followed, have resulted in complex changes to the political economy. 'Not only is the state less involved in the economy and the provision and distribution of material resources, the British economy is also increasingly internationalised' (ibid.: 365). In other words, seemingly domestic policies such as the privatisation of public sector assets deepen globalization 'since they involve the increasing interweaving of the domestic economy and the global economy' (Cerny, 1996: 134).

The so-called 'Washington consensus' has been constructed around the needs of international capital – free markets, low inflation, prudent government finances resulting in balanced budgets, and a preference for distancing economic policy making from electoral pressures. The decision to give the Bank of England autonomy on deciding base rates, and the move to balanced budgets, reflected such needs.

The degree to which the British economy is absorbed into an extensive global economy also presents a potential barrier to Britain's entry to the euro, for the economies of 'Euroland' are far less integrated into the global economy than is Britain's. Where a 'one size fits all' interest rate may arguably work for the relatively insulated economies of France, Germany and the other current members, it exposes Britain's economy to wider fluctuations, since the health of Britain's economy is more dependent on global trends in the first place.

Further reading

Grant (2002) examines economic policy and policy making in the post-war years. The economic management of earlier Labour governments is usefully discussed by Thomas (1992). Gamble (1994) examines the political context of Thatcherism, while Maynard (1988) provides an early assessment of the impact of Thatcherism on the economy. Thain (1992) gives a useful overview of economic management and mismanagement. New Labour's economic record is helpfully assessed by Grant (2002). Useful summaries are also provided by Gamble and Kelly (in Ludlam and Smith, 2001), Stephens (in Seldon, 2001) and Thain (in Dunleavy *et al.*, 2002).

British economic policy is examined within a global context by Baker (2000). See also Chapter 9 of Coxall and Robins (1998).

Useful official websites on economic policy include the Treasury <www.hm-treasury.gov.uk>, Downing Street <www.number-10.gov.uk>, the Cabinet Office <www.cabinet-office.gov.uk> and the Bank of England <www.bankofengland.co.uk>. Further analysis can be derived from the websites of think tanks, the financial press, business and trade unions.

Chapter 22

Delivering public services

The changing context of public service
    delivery   369
Investment in the public services   371
Delivering healthcare   372
Delivering market-led education   374
Delivering law and order   375
Problems with performance   376

Public services consume large sums of tax-payers' money, and it has been argued that these services under-perform and provide taxpayers with poor value for money. Recent government measures have attempted to improve the quality of these services, not only through the injection of more cash to make up for years of under-funding, but by making additional resources conditional on meeting tough performance requirements. The country's police forces, schools and hospitals are compared in their respective league tables and 'failures' are named and shamed. New managerial techniques of priority setting, performance indicators and targets supposedly guide each service towards achieving greater quality in delivery. How far are such techniques useful, if at all? This chapter considers the success of target setting on the delivery of healthcare, education, and law and order.

The changing context of public service delivery

The delivery of public services such as healthcare and education has changed considerably during the last 30 years or so; at the same time, the public's expectations concerning those services have also changed. A useful way of summing up many of these changes and developments is to consider the differing administrative cultures surrounding public service delivery through traditional public administration on the one hand and the new public management on the other (see Table 22.1).

New Right critics, who assume individuals pursue their own self interest, argue that in the absence of the profit motive, public sector managers require incentives to look after the interests of consumers and the public rather than their own working conditions and career prospects. The new public management reflects a more private sector managerial approach in which managers are motivated by a surrogate profit motive, usually a target defining success, as well as higher salaries. Public service organisations are increasingly modelled on, or shaped by, market forces with the aim of maximising competition and driving up standards. Individual service users are viewed as consumers, and the quality of public services to them is guaranteed in part through offering them greater choice.

Not only are public services provided in a private

Table 22.1 Contrasting administrative cultures

Traditional public administration	New public management
• Informed by a 'public service ethos'	• Informed by private sector management principles
• Services delivered according to written rules, minimum managerial discretion	• Services delivered more flexibly with more managerial autonomy
• All citizens in the same circumstances receive the same service – equity and uniformity	• Services tailored to the requirements of consumers – variations in services
• Service delivery audited to ensure strict legality – the spending of money as authorised	• Service delivery audited to measure economy, efficiency and effectiveness (the 3 Es)

sector-like culture, some have been contracted out to the private sector (see Chapter 18). Other services may be provided through complex patterns of part- nerships between the public, private and voluntary sectors (see Table 22.2). Some services previously regarded as part of the welfare state and provided free (most services for the elderly) or at least heavily subsidised (social housing) are now charged at commercial rates.

The new public management may have improved efficiency and customer choice, but importing commercial ethics into the public services has caused some problems. What are regarded as normal busi- ness practices often fall below traditional public sector standards of probity. For example, schools encouraged to behave more like businesses have sometimes contracted out work to family members or friends of the staff without taking sufficient safeguards.

Second, there may be conflict between the provision of public services on the basis of need, almost irre- spective of cost considerations particularly in the health service, and the importation of financial costs and benefit calculations into decisions on healthcare by accountants and business managers. While it could be argued that escalating demands on services compel some form of rationing in the public sector, doctors fear that their clinical autonomy has been eroded by such financial decision making. Patients may not be given the best treatment where there are cheaper if less effective alternatives. The elderly, with low life expectancy, may find they cannot receive certain forms of treatment at all.

Although Britain was a laboratory for much of the rethinking about the delivery of public services, it was two American authors who wrote the best-selling book, *Reinventing Government* (1992). David Osborne and Ted Gaebler argued that big monolithic government bureaucracies had failed and needed to be 'reinvented' to cope with new conditions and circum- stances. They argued that 'big' government was inef- ficient and must be replaced by entrepreneurial government. In the British context, the big post-war bureaucracies that administered the welfare state and the nationalised industries required breaking up in ways influenced by free market forces. To use their famous phrase, government should be 'steering, not rowing'. In other words, they saw it as the govern- ment's task to set policy goals, measure performance and monitor outcomes. But it was not the govern- ment's job directly to provide or manage services to the public.

Changing a culture from one based on a public sector ethos to one based on the principles of new public management is not easily achieved. Many public servants, particularly civil servants, are conser- vative with a small 'c' and they do not welcome change. The public sector has developed certain ways of doing things, cherishes long-held practices, all within a specific administrative culture. Under such circumstances, the natural inclination of public servants is to continue into the future the way it was in the past. Often this means coping with govern- ment reforms in order to minimise change. Tony Blair has expressed his frustration with the culture of the public sector since in his eyes it represents an aspect of the 'forces of conservatism' which he believes prevents Britain from becoming a fully modern state. New Labour's attempt to modernise the delivery of public services include:

- Greater use of IT to improve efficiency and lower costs.

Table 22.2 Welfare services: the market and the state

Public sector	Semi-autonomous public sector	Private sector
Healthcare:		
Directly managed units under the control of district health authorities	Trust status hospitals accountable directly to the secretary of state	Private hospitals
Non-fundholding GPs	Fundholding GPs	Private health insurance, such as BUPA
Education:		
Schools maintained by local authorities	Opted-out grant maintained schools	Private schools
	City technology colleges	Conservative assisted places scheme

IN FOCUS 22.1 Holding the purse strings

Gordon Brown, Chancellor of the Exchequer, has earmarked substantial additional funds for Britain's public services. Much of the money, however, comes with 'strings attached', dependent on government-approved reforms and the meeting of government targets. It has also proved difficult to spend some of the money, partly because of an immediate shortage of skilled labour. Recruiting, training and retaining new health workers, teachers and police officers cannot be done quickly.

- More movement of public sector employees in and out of the private sector. More top jobs should go to women and members of the ethnic minorities.
- Greater use of performance-related pay to motivate and reward effort.
- The setting of clear performance goals for the public services.

In demanding greater value for money from the spending departments the Treasury sets targets, sometimes referred to as 'public service agreements'. Typically, targets involve the police reducing crime levels, schools raising educational standards, hospitals providing quicker treatment, and local authorities recycling more waste. The Treasury has also facilitated improvements in the public services through releasing additional resources after a period of under-funding. Since the public services have been under-funded, it can be argued that increased resources alone will result in improvements. However, the Chancellor has made increased funding partly conditional on further reforms to service delivery.

Investment in the public services

The wider Labour party, including many trade unions, is opposed to the government over the increasing role it is allocating to the private sector in running public services. The major focus of controversy concerns what are known as public–private partnerships (PPPs). It was a Conservative Chancellor, Norman Lamont, who initially created the private finance initiative (PFI) in which private sector firms competed to win contracts to design, finance, build and run large public projects. The PFI has become the dominant long-term arrangement in which the public and private sectors cooperate to finance the building, and in many cases also management, of hospitals, prisons, schools and large civil engineering projects such as bridges or new roads.

Supporters of PFIs argue that 18 years of under-investment in the public sector during the Thatcher–Major years has resulted in a massive backlog of projects which cannot be financed solely from the public purse without unacceptable increases in public sector borrowing (see Chapter 21). In this sense, a PFI is somewhat similar to a mortgage, whereby much-needed new hospitals, schools and so on are supplied through using private sector resources which are repaid over the long term, commonly 25 or 30 years. PFIs are also claimed to bring the advantage of private sector skills to the public sector in the management of public services. The most cited example of a successful PFI is the Manchester Metro system.

Critics of these new arrangements argue that the private sector is primarily concerned about making profits out of PFI projects, which have too frequently resulted in poor design and shoddy building standards to keep costs low and thereby boost profits. Additionally, PPPs have been attacked for being a very expensive way for the government to borrow money, and therefore a 'poor deal' for taxpayers. For example, it has been estimated that the Edinburgh Royal Infirmary would have cost £180 million if it had been paid for directly but under PFI it will cost £900 million spread over 30 years. To its critics, PFIs result in 'higher taxes and worse public services' (*New Statesman*, 19 March 2001). This impression has been reinforced by some well-publicised PFI disasters such as the new Cumberland Infirmary which has experienced sewerage flooding, collapsing ceilings and dangerous electrical wiring.

The PFI issue had a dramatic impact in the 2001 general election with the election of Richard Taylor as MP for Wyre Forest, where he stood for the Independent Kidderminster Hospital and Health Concern Party. In the neighbouring constituency, Worcester Hospital was being rebuilt as a PFI project, and its building costs had already more than doubled from the original estimates. In order to help pay its share of these higher costs, the health authority closed down the accident and emergency services at the Kidderminster Hospital. For Kidderminster residents, then, PFI meant only the running down of local services, and they rebelled against Labour at the polls.

The future of many large-scale projects, such as the London tube and air traffic control, depends upon public–private partnerships which are being viewed with increasing public scepticism. Colouring perceptions of all public–private arrangements has been the privatisation of the railways, involving the break-up of an integrated system into numerous separate private companies. At the centre of the privatised system was Railtrack, responsible for managing stations and the tracks. Following serious train crashes at Southall, Ladbroke Grove and Hatfield, it looked as if Railtrack was more concerned with private profits than with public safety. Critics from the left, right and centre of the political spectrum argued that Railtrack had failed to invest sufficiently in maintenance to provide a reliable and safe service. The refusal of the government to provide a financial bail-out led to the insolvency of the company, which has been replaced by a new non-profit trust organisation, Network Rail.

BOX 22.1
Britain's largest PFI contracts (2002)

Health
University College London Hospitals
£404 million
Edinburgh Royal Infirmary £180 million
Norfolk and Norwich NHS Trust £158 million

Education
Stoke on Trent LEA £93 million
Liverpool City Council £72 million
London Borough of Haringey £62 million

Law and order
Metropolitan Police stations £100 million
Altcourse Prison, Liverpool £88 million
Parc Prison, Mid Glamorgan £74 million

Transport
Channel Tunnel Rail Link £4 billion
National Air Traffic Service £800 million
Birmingham Northern Relief Road £485 million

Delivering healthcare

The National Health Service established by Aneurin Bevan in Attlee's post-war Labour government has long been the most popular part of the welfare state, and the jewel in Labour's crown. Yet health service spending failed to keep pace with the rising demand fuelled by an ageing population on the one hand, and the development of new and often expensive forms of health treatment on the other. The consequence was that a smaller proportion of Britain's national income was devoted to health care than in most other leading western nations. Newspaper stories about bed shortages, waiting lists, and other NHS shortcomings became increasingly commonplace. It was reckoned that the service was seriously under-funded, with 15,000 more doctors, 38,000 more nurses and 42 new hospitals required by 2008. The Wanless Report into the long-term funding of healthcare influenced the Chancellor's decision in 2002 to allocate an additional £40 billion to health over a five-year period.

It remains to be seen how far this new money will translate into improved services. Because the government is aware that it will be judged on delivery, strenuous efforts have been made to establish clear targets to measure improvements in health care. Thus the performance of hospitals is measured by their success in meeting targets and winning star ratings in league tables. For example, for acute hospitals trusts there are 37 performance indicators, summarised in Box 22.2.

Assessed against these measures, 47 of England's 158 acute hospital trusts improved in 2002, 36 did worse and 75 remained the same. Any hospital deemed 'failing' is allowed up to 12 months to improve. Otherwise, failing hospitals risk being taken over by NHS management teams, voluntary organisations or private companies. Some hospitals whose position fell in the league tables claimed it was unclear whether their standards of healthcare had really declined or whether, more likely, there had been basic flaws in the ways they had measured their own performance. Others were more critical of hospital targets; for example, David Walker argued that the 'evidence is growing that both audit and targetry can be dysfunctional' and reduce the quality of healthcare (*Guardian*, 6 May 2002).

Should the Chancellor's huge increase in resources be sufficient alone to result in healthcare improvements, or is there a need for further reforms in the way the money is spent? This question has divided both Labour's front and backbenches. Labour has already reformed primary care, health care in the community, through replacing health authorities with primary care trusts, a measure which has devolved more power collectively to family doctors. It was in the area of secondary healthcare that the creation of new 'foundation' hospitals proved particularly vexing.

New Labour 'transformers' felt that some hospitals with high reputations should be free from Whitehall controls. The new foundation hospitals, with freedom to manage themselves, could ignore Whitehall targets. This independence would enable them to respond more positively to local needs, to set their own salary levels, to borrow money from financial institutions to build new wards or operating theatres, and to sell unwanted land and invest the proceeds in further improvements. It was argued that in the past top-down control had stifled local innovation. Foundation hospitals would compete with trust hospitals for primary care trust business, by offering reduced waiting times, which in turn would drive up improvements in the performance of rival trust hospitals.

Labour's 'consolidators' saw foundation hospitals as a reform too far since they reintroduced discredited Conservative market forces into healthcare which set 'hospital against hospital, doctor against doctor' (Frank Dobson, Radio 4 *World at One*, 7 August 2002). Also there was the danger of creating a two-tier health service if foundation hospitals could pay higher salaries and poach nurses from surrounding trust hospitals. Even the sale of surplus land was controversial since, under old arrangements, some of the proceeds of expensive hospital land sold in the south would benefit Midland and northern hospitals where land sales generated less money.

The Treasury was particularly concerned over the creation of foundation hospitals since, through the abandonment of targets, its control over these hospitals would be weakened. Also there was the fear that should a foundation hospital fall into the hands of poor local management and go 'bust', the Treasury would have pick up the unpaid bills. Finally, the greatest fear was that public resources

---

BOX 22.2

Nine key performance indicators for acute hospital trusts

- No patients waiting more than 18 months for inpatient treatment.
- Fewer patients waiting for more than 15 months for inpatient treatment.
- No patients waiting more than 26 weeks for outpatient treatment.
- Fewer patients waiting on trolleys for more than 12 hours.
- Less than 1 per cent of operations cancelled on the day.
- No patients with suspected cancer waiting more than two weeks to be seen in hospital.
- Improvements to the working lives of staff.
- Hospital cleanliness.
- A satisfactory financial position.

would be devoted to an independent hospital which, in maximising 'profits', would give greatest priority to attracting overseas and private patients rather than treating NHS patients. Such a situation might provide extremely poor value for money to the taxpayer.

Delivering market-led education

In 1976 Labour Prime Minister James Callaghan delivered a speech at Ruskin College, Oxford, which opened what is sometimes referred to as the 'great education debate'. Callaghan raised questions about education standards, including specifically levels of literacy and numeracy, the purpose of the school curriculum and the needs of industry. He also expressed unease about certain teaching methods:

> there is the unease felt by parents and teachers about the new informal methods of teaching which seem to produce excellent results when they are in well qualified hands but are much more dubious in their effects when they are not.... There is no virtue in producing socially well adjusted members of society who are unemployed because they do not have the skills.
>
> (James Callaghan, quoted in Bash and Coulby, 1989)

Education standards became a major political issue, and have remained so since. The educational left which had promoted comprehensive education and progressive methods was put on the defensive, enabling the right to take the initiative on education and largely take control of the political agenda. Under Thatcher, radical right-wing groups such as the Hillgate Group, the Adam Smith Institute, and the Institute for Economic Affairs, came to dominate the 'great debate', and in so doing redefined the purpose and means of schooling in Britain.

The political right argued that education had been subverted to the cause of social engineering rather than the pursuit of high academic standards. To repair the situation, the right argued that the influence of those responsible for causing the damage, those with professional vested interests, must

be reduced. At the same time the influence of those with the greatest interest in raising educational standards, parents and employers, must be increased. This, it was argued, could be best accomplished by making education more responsive to market forces. As Stewart Ranson stated, the:

> failures of education, it is argued, derive from professionals and (local) politicians appropriating control of the service from its proper source – the parents. The 'producers' have taken over and pursue their own purposes at the expense of the needs of the 'consumers' of the service.... The professionals create a technical language which serves only to bamboozle ordinary people and they organise the system for their convenience rather than to respond to the demands of consumers.... For consumers to fulfil their allotted role as quality controllers in the market place they require some diversity of product, information about the scope of choice and the quality of performance, as well as the opportunity to choose.
>
> (Ranson, 1990)

The radical right argued that a market-led system in education would mean that schools had to compete with each other for 'customers', and that this competition would lead to a general rise in standards. The creation of a market, however, meant that the 'producer' monopoly must be curtailed. First, it was argued, the influence of teachers must be reduced. Second, the influence of local education authorities must be reduced. In the event this occurred through delegating more financial and managerial responsibilities to individual schools, and through providing opportunities for schools to 'opt out' from local authority control. Having reduced the influence of the 'producers', the right argued that the creation of a market in education rested only on increasing the role of 'consumers' in terms of providing greater choice and control. Parental influence was increased through open enrolment, the provision of more information by schools, and a bigger role in the management of individual schools.

New Labour accepted the fundamentals of providing diversity and choice for parents, underpinned by market mechanisms designed to drive up educational standards. 'Bog-standard comprehensives', an unfortunate phrase originating in Number Ten, were to be restructured into a quality-delivering system of yet to be created advanced schools alongside foundation schools, city academies, specialist schools, beacon schools, training schools, grammar schools, fresh start schools and contract schools. Schools would be placed on a 'ladder of improvement' regarding accountability and incentives. Inherited from Thatcherite policies was the faith that competition with the best schools would lever up the standards of the rest.

The Chancellor allocated an additional £15 billion to schools over the coming years on condition that standards improve. Targets included literacy and numeracy attainment levels and an annual rise in the number of 16 year olds achieving five grade Cs or better at GCSE. There would be 'zero tolerance' of failing schools or authorities, which would be taken over by new leadership or closed altogether.

In practice, some of these education targets have been missed. Despite a massive increase in funding to raise primary school maths and reading standards, after some initial improvement standards actually fell in the two years following 2000; at Key Stage 2 only 75 per cent achieved level 4 or above for English, missing the 80 per cent target. For maths, the target was missed by 2 per cent. The government also missed its own target to reduce the size of infant classes by September 2002.

Delivering law and order

Crime statistics are notoriously difficult to interpret. For example the British Crime Survey, which is based on interviews with over 30,000 members of the public, reported that 13 million crimes had been committed in 2001. This figure is generally accepted as more accurate than the 5.5 million crimes reported to the police during the same period. The discrepancy between the two sets of figures results from a number of factors. Some forms of crime, particularly car crime, are reported for insurance purposes. Where this incentive is lacking, victims of crime often fail to inform the police, particularly if they believe the police are unlikely to take further action.

Contradictory trends were reported for 2001–2, with the Crime Survey reporting a 2 per cent fall in overall crime, while the police's adjusted figure showed a 2 per cent rise. But the pattern of crime was far from even: for example, police figures showed that street crime, including mugging, had risen 20 per cent nationally and in some areas as much as 77 per cent. This particular statistic resulted in the Prime Minister setting a new and highly publicised target for the police to halt this alarming trend in the ten worst hit areas in 2002.

As with the other public services discussed above, police forces are set targets (both nationally and locally), with subsequent league tables listing each force. Senior police officers have complained that their respective forces are set too many targets, frequently the targets are too ambitious, and they have the unintended effect of distorting policing. Examples of unrealistic targets include the Metropolitan Police's target to reduce robberies and other street crimes in London by 2 per cent: in reality, robberies rose by 38 per cent. The Somerset and Avon Force was set a target to maintain or reduce the current level of robberies: in reality, robberies rose by a massive 78 per cent. Overall, it has been calculated that the combined police forces have failed to meet 75 per cent of targets for cutting crime (*Sunday Times*, 4 August 2002).

It has been argued that government targets, league tables and the identification of 'failing' forces have demoralised officers on the beat. In addition, failure to meet a target is inevitable if a serious murder or search for a missing child consumes police resources and draws officers away from normal duties. It is suspected by senior police officers that governments are tempted to set tough targets for the purposes of political spin and electoral image, since the targets have relatively little meaning in the real world of policing. An anonymous police officer commenting on the impact of government targets observed, 'What can't be measured doesn't count and what doesn't count doesn't get done' (*Guardian*, 28 May 2002). Target setting has skewed police work away from essential, but long-term preventive efforts, such as community policing and work in schools, and towards ones that yield a short-term gain.

The targets for reducing crime are unlikely to be achieved by improvements in policing alone. More police officers and a better use of technology would

BOX 22.3
Law and order

Police: 127,231 officers in England and Wales operating from 1807 police stations.
Detection: 24 per cent of all reported crimes in England and Wales were solved in 2000. In 1980, the corresponding figure was 40 per cent.
Prison: There are 69,969 prisoners in England and Wales in 136 prisons. Prison numbers are rising – there were 5000 more prisoners added to the total during 2001–2.

Many crime statistics need a 'health warning' attached to them. The figure for the decline in detection rates (above) looks dire, indicating a drastic drop in the effectiveness of the police. Yet the figure is almost certainly grossly misleading, the consequence of changes in police procedure following the 1984 Police and Criminal Evidence Act (PACE). Before this, police officers were often able to persuade offenders to confess to other crimes which would be 'taken into consideration' when sentencing. These admissions enabled the police to 'clear up' many crimes that had not previously been detected. Following PACE, criminals were less prepared to cooperate with the police in admitting to other crimes beyond those for which they had been arrested (not surprisingly, because it might lead to an increase in sentence). The substantial reduction in the number of offences admitted and 'taken into consideration' goes a long way towards explaining the apparent drop in detection rates.

Problems with performance

The Labour government has committed substantial extra resources to public services. However, governments are not judged on the resources they commit to services, but on the perceived level and efficiency of those services. Hence the importance of delivery to any government, but to Labour in particular, which has boldly established ambitious targets for performance. Blair has staked the reputation of his government on the achievement of measurable improvements in health, education and law and order.

The Labour government faces problems at two levels concerning the delivery of public services. First, has the most appropriate model for delivery of high quality services been selected by policy makers? In other words, is the system being used the best system? Second, is target setting the most effective means of directing delivery? In other words, is there a better way of getting improvements in public services? To some extent, the first issue concerns 'rowing' whilst the second is more about 'steering'.

New Labour has faith in free markets being dynamic and efficient. They may be, but this does not mean every company that operates in the private sector shares these characteristics. The private sector, after all, is littered with the debris of wrecked companies. Furthermore, there is a danger for any reform-minded government that what appear to be crucial private sector reforms are simply the latest management fashion and may end up discredited, being found worse than the arrangements they replaced. In other words, the 'forces of conservatism', as Tony Blair has called his favourite targets, are sometimes justified in resisting changes. When organisations change needlessly it can result in both employees and clients not 'knowing their way around', and in the sort of chaos created by the privatised railways.

The second problem involves the effectiveness and credibility of government targets. For example, in 2002 the Treasury published 130 public service agreements to replace the 160 set two years earlier. While Labour claimed that nine out of ten of the original targets had been met, the opposition parties calculated that fewer than half had been met, underlining the problem in interpreting

help, but other measures taken in wider society would also contribute, such as responsible parenting, improved education, and improved rehabilitation in prisons. Even effective health education on diets would help reduce crime. A more effective Crown Prosecution Service, a reformed criminal justice system, and tougher sentencing might deter criminals from committing crimes. More controversially, decriminalising drugs might reduce crime levels.

statistics, especially where service providers have an incentive to manipulate them so as to appear to meet targets.

Targets can actually distort a public service in ways not anticipated by the target setter. Two targets mentioned above illustrate this point A health service target to reduce hospital waiting lists might result in the admission of patients whose operations can be done quickly, while more seriously ill patients might be kept off the waiting lists altogether and actually die before receiving treatment (*Sunday Times*, 5 May 2002). Similarly, headteachers wanting to meet the target of more pupils getting five or more grade Cs at GCSE might be tempted to divert resources such as the best teachers and scarce equipment away from both the most academically able pupils (who will do well under any circumstances) and the least able (who will struggle for one or two grade Es). Resources will be disproportionately concentrated on middle-ability pupils who are on the margin of getting five grade Cs.

The political stakes for Blair's government are high. Delivery of improved public services has been flagged as the key domestic issue for Labour's second term, with clear implications for the party's electoral prospects. The problem is that the government does not directly control policy implementation, but is reliant on other agencies and front-line workers, and cannot ensure delivery. Andrew Denham (in Dunleavy *et al.*, 2003: 283) argues that the government faces a choice in approach. It can continue to rely on the techniques it inherited and further developed from the Conservatives, involving targets and central monitoring of performance (an approach associated with Gordon Brown and the Treasury), or it can pursue the alternative radical decentralisation of public services, apparently favoured by some of the Prime Minister's advisers and particularly championed by the Health Secretary Alan Milburn.

Denham suggests that there are problems with both approaches. If the government seeks to impose its priorities through extra spending with strings attached in the form of detailed performance targets, this may produce wasteful and inefficient behaviour (as described above), erode the morale of front-line workers, and even threaten to destroy the ethos of the public service. However, decentralisation runs the risk that the government

is left with little effective control over the quality of the services it is funding. It also involves more variation in service levels, with implications for equity, and damaging criticisms of a postcode lottery or a two-tier service.

Whichever approach is adopted, if the substantial tax-funded additional sums now being spent on health and education do not achieve results, Labour may ultimately pay a high electoral price. Yet as Denham (2003: 289) goes on to point out in the case of health, the government is reliant, first on people – doctors, nurses and NHS managers – whom ministers do not and cannot control directly, and second on public perception of services, which may not always reflect the government's own claims of improvements. Labour not only has to deliver but must be seen to deliver. This is a formidable task. Statistics may be interpreted variously (as we have noted above), and public perceptions may be shaped more by anecdotal evidence, viewed through the distorting prism of tabloid journalism. One high-profile scandal may thus effectively offset less newsworthy marginal statistical improvements in a whole range of service level indicators. In such circumstances the apparent renewed public approval of tax and spend policies could prove short-lived.

Further reading

On educational reform, Bash and Coulby (1989) is a comprehensive account of the legislation; also see Ranson (1990). The seminal text on public sector reform is Osborne and Gaebler (1992). For the performance of the Labour government see the chapters by Morris (on crime and penal policy) and Smithers (on education) in Seldon (2001), and the chapter by McCaig (on education) in Ludlam and Smith (2001). For individual case studies see newspaper articles by Walker (2002) and Hough (2002). For commentaries on PPPs, see Cohen (2001), Walker (2001) and Macalister (2001).

Relevant government websites include those of the Department of Health <www.doh.gov.uk>, the Department for Education and Skills <www.des.gov.uk> and the Home Office <www.homeoffice.gov.uk>. The police have their own extensive website <www.police.uk>.

Chapter **23**

Tackling poverty and exclusion

Rich Britain, poor Britain   378
Explanations for poverty and inequality:
    family breakdown   379
Explanations for poverty and inequality:
    changes in the labour market – the
    30/30/40 society   381
Fresh approaches: community and
    stakeholding   381
New Labour's anti-poverty programme   383
Conservative rethinking   384
The pensions crisis and future poverty   385

In the 1940s Sir William Beveridge set out a blueprint for the government to follow which would banish the 'giant evils' of want, disease, squalor, ignorance and idleness from Britain. Half a century later, and despite the creation of a welfare state, Britain remains a society plagued by social inequalities. Britain has the fourth largest economy in the world and yet some of its people live impoverished lives in both town and country. Even with some of the trappings of affluence, their lives have all the characteristics of an excluded class. Should the existence of an excluded underclass, seemingly impervious to assistance from well-intentioned politicians, be accepted as inevitable, as in the old adage, 'the poor are always with us'? Or can government policy transform the lives of the poor by incorporating them into the mainstream of society? The chapter assesses the causes of poverty, examines New Labour policy, and concludes by considering what some argue is a new poverty crisis in the making. Are today's affluent workers destined to poverty in old age as a 'pensions gap' opens up for Britain's ageing population?

Rich Britain, poor Britain

The purpose of the Beveridge Report was to combat poverty and the social ills that accompanied it. Postwar governments of the 1950s, 1960s and 1970s accepted in general terms that a redistribution of resources in society from the better-off to the poor should be a central principle of social policy. Although governments, and the electorate, accepted that there would inevitably be rich people and poor people in society, it was also accepted that reducing these inequalities was politically and socially beneficial. Taxation was progressive, with the better-off paying much greater percentages of their incomes in tax than the less well-off. Tax revenues were used by governments to provide a welfare state – the equivalent of 'social wages' – to provide free education, free healthcare and other benefits to those who would not otherwise have been able to afford these basic needs. Local authorities provided subsidised housing. Although the redistributive principle did not always operate in the way intended, it was assumed that welfare benefits would be financed disproportionately by the better-off members of society but drawn disproportionately by the less well-off. Through such a redistribution of resources, it was intended that the worst impact of poverty would be softened, and that even the poorest members of society would be able to lead dignified lives in which they or their children would enjoy some equality of opportunity despite their relative poverty.

By the 1960s it was clear that the welfare state had not succeeded in eliminating poverty in Britain. There were regions of high unemployment in Northern Ireland, parts of Scotland and Wales and the north of England where average incomes were much lower than the rest of Britain. Even

---

Definition
Relative poverty rather than absolute poverty exists in Britain. Nearly all people are materially better off now than they were in the past, including the poor. Being poor does not mean going without food or basic clothing, but means not having enough money for the things that the rest of society enjoys.

Definition

Child poverty was re-identified as a major problem in the 1960s, but government policy failed to tackle it effectively. By 2000 it was estimated that around a third of all children experienced poverty, compared with 10 per cent in the 1960s. Labour made a commitment to cut child poverty by over a million in its first term and to eradicate it altogether by 2020.

---

within some relatively prosperous cities there were deprived areas where some experienced real poverty. The elderly dependent on inadequate state pension, large families headed by unemployed or low paid adults, and many one-parent families were among Britain's poor. Some on the right of the political spectrum argued that many of these had brought poverty on themselves, by 'feckless' behaviour, reviving a Victorian distinction between the 'deserving poor' (whose poverty was no fault of their own) and the 'undeserving poor'. Yet it was difficult to apply such distinctions to children. The rediscovery of child poverty in the 1960s shocked educated opinion and led to the formation of a major new pressure group, the Child Poverty Action Group (CPAG). Around the same time homelessness, which was widely reckoned to have been eliminated by the housing programme, was also rediscovered, and its effects poignantly demonstrated in the influential television drama *Cathy Come Home*.

Some attempt was made to alleviate child poverty in the 1970s, particularly through replacing child tax allowances (involving reductions on a father's tax payments) and the old family allowances with a new and more substantial child benefit paid to the mother. The Labour minister responsible, Barbara Castle, reckoned that this transfer 'from the wallet to the purse' would ensure that the money was more likely to benefit children. Yet the beneficial consequences of this and other changes to the tax and benefit system were soon more than offset by the rapid growth of unemployment in the 1980s to over 3 million, which sucked many more families into poverty and dependence on welfare. It also dramatically increased the social security budget, with adverse implications for public spending and taxation, making it difficult for

the Thatcher governments in power from 1979 onward to 'roll back the state' in accordance with New Right free market views.

It might be expected that the increase in poverty, the emergence of an underclass, the growth of 'cardboard cities' in many towns, together with an associated culture of crime and drug abuse, would be issues at the top of any government's political agenda. Yet the nature of poverty in Britain, as well as its causes and possible cures, divided right-wing from left-wing politicians as well as left-wing academics from their right-wing counterparts (see Box 23.1).

New Right ideas undermined the assumptions shared by earlier Conservative and Labour governments that poverty was an evil which should be tackled by government. Indeed it was argued that the high levels of taxation that were needed to finance the welfare state actually reduced people's incentive to be enterprising and to work hard. Furthermore, it was argued that a high level of welfare had a negative impact on the poor. For it produced a 'dependency culture' which sapped their determination and ability to lead independent lives. Cutting taxes and reducing welfare would, it was argued, release enterprise and energy, which would result in the creation of more wealth. The fear of poverty, no longer cushioned by generous welfare benefits, would encourage many poor people to reassess their lot and see them move back into the job market. Once in employment, the opportunity to keep more of their income by paying less tax would encourage them to work harder. In this way, it was argued, the existence of poverty has a beneficial effect on society through eventually creating more wealth. Even those in poverty who, for whatever reason, could not redirect their lives, would benefit from the 'trickle down' of prosperity from the richest to the poorest. In other words, the New Right argued that the creation of wealth was more socially beneficial than the redistribution of wealth.

Explanations for poverty and inequality: family breakdown

Some blamed the 'permissive society' and the decline of family life for growing poverty and inequality. Charles Murray, an American sociologist, argued

BOX 23.1
Political controversy over the meaning of poverty

There was a revealing political debate on the meaning of 'poverty' in Britain in the 1980s and 1990s. What the political left recognised as 'poverty', the right saw as 'inequality'. The right argued that the least well-off were not poor; they were just not as well off as the rest of society. It was argued that no one in Britain experienced genuine absolute poverty as did, for example, many people living in Ethiopia, Somalia or Bangladesh. In Britain those who were relatively poor never went hungry, and many owned possessions associated with affluence such as cars, videos, fridges and telephones. John Moore, once Margaret Thatcher's Secretary of State for Health and Social Security, attacked the left's claim that poverty existed in Britain, since according to the left's definition of poverty, there would be 'poverty in paradise'.

Paul Wilding (1993) argued that this New Right argument which redefined 'poverty' as simply 'inequality' was no more than a political convenience: 'since it lifted responsibility for action from the shoulders of government since inequality was not a matter for government ... responsibility for this so-called poverty was personal'. It was widely believed that the unemployed were really work-shy and that job vacancies existed if only they would 'get on their bikes' in search of them. It was also argued that the welfare state 'created poverty' by providing perverse incentives to secure welfare benefits (thus it was alleged that young single females became pregnant in order to obtain a council house). Wilding commented that 'blaming the victim' is an approach adopted by all governments when they are either unable or unwilling to tackle poverty.

that Britain had developed an underclass as a result of social disintegration caused by the breakdown of the two-parent family structure. He linked two factors together in ways that suggested that one was the cause of the other:

- The number of babies born outside marriage had risen sharply. He argued that 'as late as 1976, only 9 per cent of children were born out of wedlock ... by 1992 this had jumped to 31 per cent' (Murray, 1994b).
- The rising level of crime accompanied changes in the family structure: 'from 1987 to 1992, property crime in England and Wales rose by 42 per cent. The risks of being burgled in England is now more than twice that in the United States' (Murray, 1994b).

Murray continued to argue that national statistics obscured what was happening in different parts of society. For example, although the traditional family structure is breaking down across all classes, it is happening in different ways and to different extents. The percentage of children born outside marriage is twice as high in the low-skilled working class as in the professional middle class. His forecasts were that the middle class 'illegitimacy rate' would stabilise at around 15 per cent, while the lower working class rate would rise to over 70 per cent. He predicted that British society would polarise into extremes of what he called the 'new Victorians', affluent, well-educated people holding traditional moral values, and a 'new rabble' of poor, ill-educated people in moral disarray. Murray and others assumed that British society would develop in much the same way as the United States, in which case:

the children of the New Rabble will come to the school system undeveloped intellectually and unsocialised to norms of considerate behaviour. Once in school these children will attend irregularly and pose severe discipline problems when they do. The New Rabble will provide a large and lucrative market for violent and pornographic film, television and music. Their housing blocks will be characterised by graffiti and vandalism, their parks will be the venues for drugs and prostitution.

(Murray, 1994b)

The Conservative response to this and similar diagnoses was illustrated by John Major's call for a campaign to get Britain 'back to basics'. He rejected those who claimed 'the family was out of date' and that people should rely instead on 'the council and social workers' (Durham, 1994). Major argued that faced with the sort of problems outlined by Charles Murray, it was time to get back to the basics of self-discipline and respect for the law, to consideration of others, and individuals accepting responsibility for themselves and their families.

Explanations for poverty and inequality: changes in the labour market – the 30/30/40 society

Charles Murray's ideas were highly controversial. Although some on the left agreed privately with parts of his analysis, others rejected it as being alarmist and elitist. It was argued that it was Thatcherite policies which had caused poverty and social decay, and Charles Murray was simply diverting blame away from those policies by blaming the poor for their poverty. For example, Peter Townsend attacked him for using insulting terms, such as 'New Rabble' and 'out of wedlock' while ignoring the effects of mass unemployment, the casualisation of labour, the failure of skills training, the collapse of public housing and the growth of homelessness, and the destruction of public services.

> *Definition*
> **Social exclusion** is the experience of people who suffer from a combination of connected problems such as unemployment, poor education and poor skills, low incomes, poor housing in high-crime areas, bad health and family breakdown. Social exclusion includes poverty, but is a broader concept. However, some academics have challenged the association of social exclusion with the poor. Rather, they have argued, it is the rich who are isolated from the mainstream of society. In other words, there exists an 'overclass' of people who defend their privileges and are separated from the rest of society.

Will Hutton brought many of these developments together in a conception of society based on rapid changes taking place in the labour market. In contrast to Murray, he argued that:

> The British are increasingly at risk. The chances of their jobs disappearing, of their incomes falling, of their homes being repossessed or of being impossible to sell, of their families breaking up, of their networks of friendships disintegrating, have not been higher since the war.
> (*Guardian*, 30 October 1995)

Hutton (1995: 14) argued that the changes happening to British society were not simply a case of the rich getting richer and the poor getting poorer. They were more complex than this, for even some of the better-off were suffering from increased insecurity and stress. Drawing on the ideas of the American economist J. K. Galbraith, Hutton described a 30/30/40 society. At the bottom were the disadvantaged 30 per cent who were either unemployed or working for poverty wages. Another 30 per cent he reckoned were 'insecurely self-employed, involuntarily part-time or casual workers', with less effective trade union protection than in the past, leaving just 40 per cent in permanent full-time employment. Yet even some of this advantaged 40 per cent faced job insecurity, arising from business failures, relocations and takeovers in the private sector, and contracting out and privatisation in the public sector.

Fresh approaches: community and stakeholding

Labour's approach to solving the problems of social decay was based on ideas of communitarianism and stakeholding. Community is not a particularly new concept within Labour thinking – indeed it lies at the heart of the cooperative movement and collectivism – but it was reinvented as an approach to policy making that would stop and reverse the trend of more people falling into poverty, into alienation, and into anti-social behaviour and crime.

Labour's starting point was that Conservative policies, particularly those pursued by the Thatcher governments, had created much of the deprivation and criminality which was beginning to alarm the electorate. Cutting social security benefits, abolishing council house subsidies and creating mass unemployment had increased social inequality and produced what some called an 'underclass'. While the political right argued that it had been 'big' government and welfare dependency that had destroyed communities, the left argued that it was free market Thatcherism that had resulted in disintegration. Indeed, Margaret Thatcher once asserted that there was 'no such thing as society, only individuals and their families'. Thatcherite policies arguably contributed to weakening the institutions that existed between the state and the individual, in the 'space' that was 'community', such as trade unions, pressure groups and local government. The result of weakening these institutions had resulted in the fragmentation and disintegration of community and society. Margaret Thatcher preferred to expand the free market into the space previously occupied by these intermediate institutions, but uncontrolled free market forces resulted in exacerbating social problems.

New Labour policy makers were influenced by the 'big idea' of another American, Amitai Etzioni, who popularised the value of community (building on the work of major communitarian thinkers). He argued that a 'good' society was one in which people lived freely, take responsibility for themselves, their families and their communities. His view was that most problems can be solved at the individual, family or community levels; only when problems get too big to be solved at these levels should the state become involved.

Communitarianism takes as its starting point that neither the welfare state of 'old' Labour nor the right-wing free market Thatcherite policies have created a successful society. Thus a new social order is required, which should be based on restored communities. Communitarians argue that demands for more law and order and a return to traditional family values have not reduced poverty, crime or drug abuse in American cities. 'Back to basics', they argue, would also be a futile attempt to reverse poverty and crime in Britain.

Communitarians in the USA were particularly anxious to integrate young working class people back into their communities. As well as stressing the importance of the family, they also stressed the role of schools in instilling a sense of citizenship and responsibility in young people. Where necessary, the community must police its own young, by censoring films, videos and music that are available locally, by requiring young people to undertake community service, and by setting night-time curfews to take young people off the streets.

Critics of communitarian ideas as a means of creating a more inclusive society included feminists, who objected to the heavy emphasis on the role of wives and mothers imprisoned in the two-parent family structure; libertarians who objected to the authoritarian control exercised by communities over individuals; and those who believed that the idea of 'community' had been idealised since communities could also be very unpleasant, characterised by intolerance, bigotry and racism. Regardless of these criticisms of communitarianism, New Labour incorporated its essential themes into its 'third way' approach to policy and into its new updated Clause Four.

'Stakeholding' is another New Labour 'big idea' concerning the development of a more inclusive society, but again it is not a new idea. It was developed in the 1960s by American academics in books such as J. K. Galbraith's *The New Industrial State* and Robin Marriss's *The Theory of Managerial Capitalism*. Later ideas were developed in John Kay's *The Foundation of Corporate Success* and Will Hutton's *The State We're In* (1995).

Tony Blair, as Leader of the Opposition, made his first 'stakeholder' speech in Singapore. In many ways stakeholding can be seen as one New Labour answer to the problems posed by the inequalities of rich Britain: poor Britain which have been discussed above. Alongside the idea of a stakeholder economy was that of a stakeholder society in which no group or class should be set apart or excluded from the rest. A particular stakeholder welfare policy that attracted Labour's attention was Singapore's Central Provident Fund, a compulsory savings scheme for benefits and pensions. Unlike the British system where an individual's National Insurance payments disappear into the Treasury for recycling as benefits for other individuals, the Singapore system enables people to keep track of their contributions.

New Labour's anti-poverty programme

New Labour's anti-poverty programme draws upon ideas developed whilst the party was in opposition, such as aspects of communitarianism and stakeholding. Unlike its immediate predecessors in government, Labour has mounted a sustained programme aimed at reducing both poverty and social exclusion. But like its predecessors, it has adopted an authoritarian approach towards the poor, which takes the form of compulsion and punishment to enforce expected behaviours.

At the heart of Labour's thinking is the belief that employment, or paid work, is crucial in combating poverty and related exclusion. In this sense, 'work is the best welfare'. But employment may not always provide an adequate solution in the short term. Where unemployed people are in low-paid work, Labour accepts that the state will have to continue to support families with welfare benefits. However with continued help, in the longer term such family members may acquire skills which will lift them out of low-paid into higher-paid work, so ending the need for welfare.

Labour's anti-poverty measures are summarised in Box 23.2.

At the same time as introducing these measures, the government has facilitated the implementation

---

BOX 23.2

New Labour's main anti-poverty measures

- The Welfare to Work programme, funded by a £5.2 billion windfall tax on the profits of the privatised utilities. The programme funded some of the measures detailed below.
- SureStart, which was designed to help very young children in poor areas develop their language and other education-related skills at the normal rate, through ensuring children are monitored by health visitors and social workers. This provision enables the young to begin to learn socially and educationally, sometimes referred to as 'educare', at nurseries and playgroups. The aim of SureStart is to reduce the number of young children on at-risk registers and have fewer children excluded from school.
- Increases in child benefit, in real terms.
- Zero tolerance of poor educational standards in schools. By driving up both literacy and numeracy attainment levels, young people will be better prepared for both further education and further skills development, or employment.
- The New Deal for young people, single parents and the unemployed aged over 50. In practice, up to one-third of 18–24 year olds re-entered New Deal programmes rather than moving into employment. A complementary Step Up programme was designed for those most likely to enter the insecure 'intermediate labour market'.

- A New Deal for communities and employment zones to tackle persistent pockets of poverty.
- Step Up designed to help the most disadvantaged into more temporary jobs, but with training. It is easier to move into secure employment from the intermediate labour market than it is from unemployment. Individuals will exercise some choice over Step Up employment, but it will not be possible to turn down all offers and remain on benefits.
- The minimum wage was designed to reduce the extent and impact of low pay. Introduced in April 1999, it has increased the wages of around 1.5 million low-paid workers, the majority of whom were women.
- The working families tax credit was introduced in October 1999 as a replacement for family credit, providing a family with an average £24 a week increase.
- A 'baby bond' for each newborn child, which might mature into a 'life changing' amount in later adult life, for example helping with education costs. Older school pupils from poorer families will receive cash payments to remain at school.
- Changes in the tax system to reward work.
- Stakeholder pensions for the lower paid to secure more comfortable retirement.
- A macroeconomic policy resulting in falling unemployment has lifted many out of poverty.

BOX 23.3
A profile of poverty in Britain

A recent survey, based on government low income data, indicates that poverty rates have risen sharply. In 1983 14 per cent of households lacked three or more necessities because they could not afford them. That proportion had increased to 21 per cent in 1990 and to over 24 per cent by 1999. (Items defined as necessities are those that more than 50 per cent of the population believes 'all adults should be able to afford and which they should not have to do without'.) By the end of 1999 a quarter (26 per cent) of the British population was living in poverty, measured in terms of low income and multiple deprivation of necessities. Roughly 9.5 million people in Britain today cannot afford adequate housing conditions. About 8 million cannot afford one or more essential household goods. Almost 7.5 million people are too poor to engage in common social activities considered necessary by the majority of the population. About 2 million British children go without at least two things they need. About 6.5 million adults go without essential clothing. Around 4 million are not properly fed by today's standards. Over 10.5 million suffer from financial insecurity. One in six people (17 per cent) consider themselves and their families to be living in 'absolute poverty' as defined by the United Nations. Over 90 per cent of the population think that beds and bedding for everyone, heating to warm living areas of the home, a damp-free home, the ability to visit family and friends in hospital, two meals a day, and medicines prescribed by the doctor are necessities that adults should not have to do without because they cannot afford them. Less than 10 per cent of the population see a dishwasher, a mobile phone, Internet access or satellite television as necessities.

Source: <www.bris.ac.uk/Depts/SPS/docs/gafix11/PSE.pdf>. Research undertaken by researchers at the universities of Bristol, Loughborough, York and Heriot-Watt with fieldwork undertaken by the Office for National Statistics.

of communitarian ideas designed to improve the social fabric: parenting classes, home–work classes, the possibility of introducing youth curfews, the introduction of 'no alcohol' zones, and the introduction of citizenship into schools. Since anti-social behaviour orders had failed to tackle the damage that anti-social teenagers wreak on neighbourhoods, Labour began rethinking the links between welfare rights and social duties. Off the record briefings revealed that the Government was considering clawing back benefits, including child benefits, from the parents of persistent truants and anti-social hooligans. Where parents contributed to their children's delinquency, they too might be punished. In other words, welfare benefits are to be conditional on the good behaviour of recipients. Some poor, it seems, are deserving; others not.

Conservative rethinking

Under the leadership of Iain Duncan Smith the Conservative Party has moved towards Labour on poverty and social exclusion. Thatcherites either denied the existence of the poor or saw them as

BOX 23.4
Identifying the poor

The proportion of people in poverty is higher amongst:

- lone-parent households
- households dependent on income support/jobseeker's allowance
- households with no paid workers
- local authority and housing association tenants
- large families
- separated/divorced households
- families with a child under 11
- adults living in one-person households including single pensioners
- children and young people
- those who left school at 16 or under
- women.

playing a useful role as a warning to others of what might happen to them if they lost the work ethic. Shadow Conservative ministers now acknowledge 'there are millions of people in are country who are in need' (*Guardian*, 27 February 2002). The emerging Conservative policy is to target benefits to the poorest groups in society, such as pensioners and the families of young children. Also echoing communitarian themes, the Shadow Home Secretary has spoken of the need to create a more 'neighbourly society'.

The pensions crisis and future poverty

Many people at work in Britain today will find that their retirement income will only be a fraction of what they had been expecting (see Box 23.5). Even middle class employees will find that on retire-

ment, they are less well off than their parents a generation before. This situation results from a £27 billion gap between what people are currently saving for their retirement and what needs to be saved for a comfortable retirement.

In 2002 the government commissioned two reports into the looming pensions crisis. The Sandler Report recommended that private pensions, unit trusts and other savings accounts be made easier to understand and cheaper to buy. The Pickering Report recommended that it should be compulsory for employees to contribute to their employers' pension schemes. In order to encourage private companies to continue providing pensions, it was also recommended that schemes should become more flexible with provisions, such as the need to continue paying pensions to widows.

Others, approaching the crisis from different directions, offer alternative solutions. For example, some

---

BOX 23.5

The pensions crisis: key factors

- People are living longer, so they are pensioners for longer. The total pension bill is therefore getting bigger.
- The state pension which is funded from taxation is losing value in real terms since it is now linked to inflation rather than, as it once was, linked to wage levels.
- The stock market is volatile and company profits are not growing as once anticipated. Many insurance companies are cutting their final payouts when policies mature.
- Interest rates are low and look like remaining so for many years. This means that annuity rates are also low. Pensioners buying annuities will therefore receive much less income from them than in the past.
- Many companies are switching from final salary pension schemes to money purchase schemes. The former guarantees employees a fixed percentage – up to two-thirds – of their final salary, taking into account the number of years they have worked. Money purchase schemes are more risky because they depend upon the performance of the stock market as well as annuity rates at

retirement. Thus if the stock market is low when an individual retires, then his or her pension fund will be relatively small; and it is this fund that the retired person will use to buy an annuity which pays back a pension at a fixed rate of interest. If interest rates are low, then the annuity rate will be low, and the final pension will be very modest.
- The government's stakeholder pensions have attracted contributions from only 10 per cent of the low-paid employees for whom they were designed.
- The Chancellor has even contributed to the pensions crisis by ending certain tax reliefs on private pensions and savings accounts, which has reduced the final value of pensions.
- Finally, many of the public have lost confidence in pensions provided by the private sector following the mis-selling scandal of the Thatcher years and more recent events such as the collapse of Equitable Life. This further encourages individuals to ask 'what's the point?' of saving for their retirements if years of thrift make them no better off.

argue that since life expectancy has risen considerably in the last 50 years it is unrealistic to keep the retirement age at 65. If the age of retirement is raised to 70, or abolished altogether, older people could work longer and avoid the enforced poverty of retirement. Others have proposed that it be made compulsory for all individuals to contribute to their own pension scheme throughout their working lives.

Further reading

Ellison and Pierson (1998) have edited a useful collection of essays on social policy – see especially the chapter by David Piachaud for a discussion of poverty. Hutton (1996b) is a major source on the 30/30/40 society and stakeholding, both discussed in this chapter. Etzioni's (1995) influential analysis of community might also be consulted. Hutton *et al.* (1991) is a wide-ranging set of contributions based on an academic conference. Oppenheim (1990) and Wilding (1993) provide detailed statistics of poverty in Britain. For opposing accounts of poverty see Murray (1994a, 1994b) and Hutton (1995). For John Major's approach, see Durham (1994). New Labour's social policies are reviewed by Howard Glennester in Seldon (2001), by Claire Annesley in Ludlam and Smith (2001), and by Peter Alcok in Dunleavy *et al.* (2002). Details of the pensions crisis are included in Milner (2002).

Chapter 24

The politics of diversity

Black and British   387
Countering racism and discrimination   389
Institutional racism   391
Multi-cultural Britain?   392
Including women: the impact of the women's
      movement on policy   394
Achievements of the women's movement
      and areas of controversy   397
The diversity of alternative lifestyles:
      lesbian and gay rights   397

Fifty years ago, as we have already noted, political scientists could justifiably describe British society as relatively homogenous, with social class being the only politically significant division. National divisions were relatively invisible; little importance was placed on either regional or urban/rural differences; women lacked an ideology with which to express distinctive perspectives; those who led 'unconventional' lifestyles did so in secrecy; and with the possible exception of the Jewish community, ethnic minorities were so small as to be politically insignificant.

In sharp contrast, contemporary Britain is characterised by diversity, creating a whole range of new and complex demands on policy makers. This chapter explores aspects of cultural diversity and their impact on political life in general and policy making in particular. While some argue that London provides a successful model for multiculturalism, others argue that recent events in Britain's northern towns indicate that more integrationist policies are required. How far have events of 11 September 2001 focused prejudice found in all other ethnic communities on Muslims? How far do the institutions of the state unintentionally reinforce the prejudices found in wider society? Are women today only disadvantaged in relation to men in terms of the respective incomes they earn as they compete in the labour market, or are they still the victims of wider social and political discrimination? Finally, what has been the impact on the politics of diversity of the public's growing acceptance of alternative lifestyles?

Black and British

Britain has experienced considerable demographic change in terms of immigration and emigration. Numerous groups have settled in Britain – Irish, Jewish, Polish, Chinese, among others – while British-born people have set up new homes in countries such as Canada, Australia, New Zealand and South Africa. Britain has a long history of immigration and emigration, but a new pattern of immigration was established after the Second World War. The British Nationality Act 1948 allowed citizens of the Commonwealth to settle in Britain, and this facilitated a new era in which most of those people who made new homes in Britain were black.

'New Commonwealth' immigrants, as they were termed, formed numerous ethnic communities based on common language, religion and race. But unlike previous immigrants from countries such as Ireland or Poland who could 'blend in' with the way of life, immigrants from Pakistan, India and the West Indies remained visibly distinctive through skin colour. In other words, they were visible as 'strangers' and because of this many British people formed hostile attitudes towards them which, in turn, made it more difficult still for the new black immigrants to adapt to Britain's traditional culture. It was hoped that in the course of time, British-born blacks would not experience the isolation of their immigrant parents, but a survey conducted by the Runnymede Trust in 1986 found this was not the case. It was reported that fewer than 5 per cent of black schoolchildren had been invited into a white home, and although over 40 per cent said they had white friends at school, most felt that British society at large did not like them.

BOX 24.1
Blacks and Asians

The use of 'black' as a shorthand term in both everyday language and the social sciences can be misleading. At the immediate level, it is obvious that 'blacks' are no more black than 'whites' are white. But just as the term 'white' can embrace widely differing cultures, so the term 'black' disguises the diversity that exists amongst people from a relatively small number of countries in the new Commonwealth. Although general distinctions are made between the Afro-Caribbean and Asian communities, far greater diversity exists than is implied by this simple twofold categorisation, with some ethnic communities having surprisingly little in common. In Leicester, for example, two residents in five are members of what is popularly known as the 'Asian community'. Yet this community is actually made up of numerous groups based on seven main languages, further divided into numerous dialects. Some groups have to resort to a second language, such as English, in order to communicate at anything more than the most basic level with other groups. The Asian community is further fragmented by different religions, values, cultural practices and castes, as well as by the political tensions found in the politics of the Indian subcontinent. For our purposes, then, 'black' and Asian are general labels or 'political colours' which cover members of all ethnic communities who are located in a broadly similar position in society.

It is a sad fact that many individuals have negative attitudes towards others purely on the grounds of racial difference. Racial prejudice can be expressed by whites against blacks, blacks against whites, or indeed between minority ethnic groups, as in the case of Asian prejudice against West Indians (Mohapatra, 1999: 79). Clearly, however, the most politically significant prejudice is that expressed by the white majority against the black minority. Before such overtly discriminatory practices were outlawed, lodging houses for example could and did display 'No Blacks' signs in their front windows. There is little doubt that, despite legislation, some deliberate acts of racial discrimination still take place in British society. For the most part, however, such racial discrimination as has taken place in recent years has been practised by organisations in the public and private sectors which have unwittingly operated policies with a hidden bias against black people. Many bodies now practise race-monitoring in specific areas as a check against such unintentional discrimination.

In the late 1950s Britain experienced its first major race riots – as opposed to gang skirmishes – when whites attacked blacks in Notting Hill and Nottingham. These riots came as an unexpected shock, and the government adopted both a tough and tender response. The former represented a response to public anxiety about black immigration to Britain, while the latter was an attempt to promote racial harmony within Britain.

The Commonwealth Immigrants Act 1962 was the first of a number of Acts that restricted the entry of black first-time immigrants and their families to Britain. A second Commonwealth Immigrants Act was rushed through Parliament in 1968 to tighten up the 1962 Act, which did not apply to East African Asians. In that year, an extremely controversial intervention was made by Conservative MP Enoch Powell in which he called for a halt to black immigration and moves to repatriate blacks already settled in Britain. The Immigration Act 1971 tightened controls still further, although its restrictions were waived on humanitarian grounds to allow Asians expelled from Uganda to enter Britain freely. A new Nationality Act in 1981 represented even tighter restrictions. All this legislation, passed by both Conservative and Labour

Definition
Race: In the 19th century it was commonly believed that humankind was divided into five 'races' distinguished by skin colour (white, black, brown, yellow, red), and other characteristics. It is now clear that 'race' is a completely bogus scientific category. Indeed some writers (e.g. Miles) refuse to use the term, even in the context of 'race relations', because it appears to endorse a meaningless concept.

governments, has been criticised for being founded on racist principles. The prime goal has been not the restriction of immigrants who have claims to be British, but the restriction of *black* immigrants who have claims to British status.

Illiberal immigration policies towards blacks living outside Britain have been accompanied by liberal policies towards those already resident within Britain. The Race Relations Acts of 1965, 1968 and 1976 outlawed direct and indirect discrimination in widening areas of public life and provision such as housing, employment and education. What is sometimes disparagingly referred to as the 'race relations industry' was established, with complaints taken to the Race Relations Board, later replaced by the Commission for Racial Equality, with community relations councils operating at local level. The view expressed by many liberal-minded individuals of the time was that the 'race' problem would eventually wither away. It was felt that the children of immigrants would not suffer from the cultural problems and disadvantages of being newcomers, and given time, economic growth would provide benefits to all Britain's citizens. The blacks, at the end of the queue for prosperity, would be served in due course. How far have these early beliefs been justified by subsequent developments and trends?

Countering racism and discrimination

The Commission for Racial Equality supports the idea that employers in the public and private sectors should be obliged by law to monitor the ethnic composition of their various workforces in order to strengthen the working of the 1976 Race Relations Act. Some on the left have argued that Britain

---

Definition

Racism has been defined as 'any political or social belief that justifies treating people differently according to their racial origins' (Robertson, 1993: 120) 'Race' is commonly interpreted in terms of skin colour. A distinction is sometime drawn between the now discredited 'scientific racism' practised by the Nazis and a 'new racism' based on cultural differences.

---

should follow the American practice of 'affirmative action'. They cite Northern Ireland as an example of using positive action in order to penalise employers who discriminate on religious grounds by refusing to employ Catholics. It is argued that in much the same way, positive action could be used on the mainland to combat racial discrimination in the job market. The political right tends to dislike affirmative action on the grounds that it lowers the self-esteem of the ethnic minority communities; a minister recently argued against positive action because it had not worked well in the United States, and added 'People dislike it intensely. It doesn't do much for your morale if you think that you have been chosen for a job because you are black rather than because you are good. What people want is fair treatment' (*Independent on Sunday*, 7 July 1991).

These contrasting attitudes towards positive action reflect two distinct philosophies towards equal opportunities in Britain. The minister's viewpoint places the emphasis on equal treatment for all people so that no one is discriminated against. In the example of individuals applying for a job, no person should be discriminated against, with the job being offered to the 'best' candidate. As Dave Russell has stated, this liberal approach 'insists that equal opportunity laws and policies require people to be judged as *individuals* without regard to racial/ethnic group membership but only on his or her own qualities and performance. All individuals should be treated equally in a meritocratic, colour-blind, non-discriminatory manner' (Russell, 1990: 11). In other words, fair treatment is seen as the absence of racial discrimination.

In contrast to the liberal approach is what Russell refers to as the 'radical' approach to equal opportunities, which is more concerned with a fair distribution of resources than with fair procedures. The radical approach is more concerned with 'who gets what' in terms of different ethnic groups getting their fair proportional share of society's resources (jobs, houses, education etc.) As Russell stated:

This perspective puts the case for racial explicitness, arguing that people should be treated with regard to *group membership*, therefore directly going against the liberal principle of 'blind justice' whereby everyone is treated as an individual.... It also understands fairness to exist where members of different racial/ethnic groups are distributed in proportion to their presence in the wider population and in order to provoke a yardstick by which to measure the success for such a *redistributive* approach, equality 'targets' or 'quotas' are often established. This might involve some deliberate manipulation of selection procedures and standards in pursuit of proportionality whereby individuals can be selected for a job partly on the basis of group membership rather than because they are the best qualified candidate.

(Russell, 1990: 11; see Table 24.1)

Legislation concerning equal opportunities and anti-discrimination has embraced both the liberal and radical approaches. How effective has it been? The 1976 Race Relations Act included two important developments. The first was the introduction of the concept of indirect discrimination, based on the American model of affirmative action. This made unlawful actions that had an unintended adverse effect on members of ethnic minority communities even when formally they were being treated the same as everyone else. The second development was the setting up of the Commission for Racial Equality, with wide powers to impose sanctions against unlawful discrimination. It is fair to say that these two measures looked far more promising on paper than they have turned out to be in practice. Removing indirect discrimination has proved to be very difficult, and consequently this part of the 1976 Act has done little in removing racial inequalities from society. The Commission for Racial Equality has

Table 24.1 Liberal and radical approaches to equal opportunities

	Equal what?	Principles	Approach
Liberal	Equal **treatment** of individuals from different groups	People should be treated as individuals **without** regard to group membership	Regulatory and procedural e.g. all job applications subject to same rules
		Fairness = absence of discrimination	Prohibition of discriminatory forms of behaviour, e.g. insistence on minimum height for a job which may disadvantage certain minorities
		Free competition between individuals / Blind justice	Concern for processes favouring whoever is best qualified
Radical	Equal shares of scarce goods (jobs, housing)	People should be treated **with** regard to group membership	Positive discrimination in terms of making allowances for the disadvantages experienced by some minorities
		Fairness = proportionality in employment. If 10% of local community is Asian, then 10% of all firms' employees should be Asian.	Targeting particular groups who will benefit – setting quotas
		Social justice	Concern for outcomes

Source: based on Russell, 1990: 11.

been attacked from a number of different directions. In practical terms its success rate in combating discrimination has been low. Also right-wing critics have argued that the Commission follows multicultural policies which stress the differences between various groups rather than the similarities.

Since the overwhelming majority of ethnic minority families from the West Indies and the Indian sub-continent are among the most recent immigrants to settle in Britain, it was to be expected that a large proportion would initially find jobs in low paid and unskilled occupations. Is it possible, therefore, that what appears as the result of racial discrimination is no more than lingering social disadvantage? Alternatively, are ethnic minority communities discriminated against in ways that restrict their social mobility?

Statistics rarely present 'facts which speak for themselves', they have to be interpreted. Sometimes they are ambiguous or suggest contradictory developments. For example, although 56 per cent of ethnic minority communities are based in Britain's 44 most deprived local authorities, over 80 per cent of families own their own homes compared with the

white average of 65 per cent. Figure 24.1 shows that for employed males there is much differentiation in the type of employment. Indians enjoy the greatest 'success' in the labour market, with 40 per cent of their number in professional and managerial jobs. This compares with 37 per cent of whites, 29 per cent of blacks and only 18 per cent of Pakistanis and Bangladeshis. Is this pattern caused by the relative discrimination of employers? Or does it reflect patterns of immigration, with the most successful in Britain coming from the most successful families in the 'mother' country, and the least successful emigrating from poor and rural communities?

Institutional racism

Much of the discussion regarding the issue of law and order revolves around perceived racism in the police force and alleged high levels of criminality among a proportion of the young male members of the ethnic minorities. Statistics are available for public scrutiny, but as before they require careful interpretation.

The Metropolitan Police Commissioner, Sir Paul

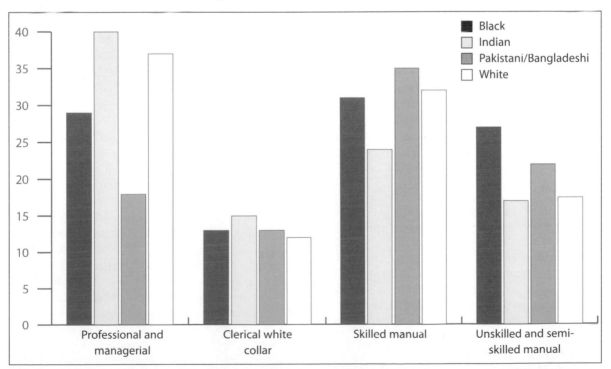

Figure 24.1 The social class of ethnic minority and white males (percentage of each ethnic group in each class)

Condon, appeared before an enquiry into the murder of teenager Stephen Lawrence. Sir Paul apologised for the police investigation into this racist killing, which he acknowledged had gone badly wrong in policing terms. He conceded that there was both unconscious and deliberate racism within London's police force, but argued that it did not add up to 'institutional racism'. Sir Paul argued that the Met was doing much to build up an anti-racist police force in terms of more specialised training and efforts to recruit from the ethnic minorities. He reported that 8 per cent of recent young recruits serving in London came from ethnic minorities, as against only 4 per cent of all serving officers.

The Macpherson Report into the killing of Stephen Lawrence concluded that the police had blundered with their enquiries, partly as a result of 'institutional racism'. While agreeing that racism in any form must be combatted, some argued that institutional racism was not a useful concept for improving race relations. For example, some applied the concept to schools. The Commission for Racial Equality argued that the fact that young black males were more than three times as likely to be excluded from schools as their white counterparts was evidence of institutional racism. Others disagreed, asking, if it was institutional racism that was responsible for Pakistani, Bangladeshi and Afro-Caribbean children doing less well in schools than their white counterparts, what was responsible for Indian and Chinese children doing much better? It is probably true to say that institutional racism as currently defined is too vague a concept, and fails to distinguish sufficiently between the unintentional and deliberate forms of discrimination.

In the year following Macpherson, stop-and-search incidents fell by 41 per cent in London.

Definition

Institutional racism is the collective failure of an organisation to provide an appropriate and professional service to people because of their colour, culture or ethnic origin. It can be detected in processes, attitudes and behaviour, and amounts to discrimination through unwitting prejudice, ignorance, thoughtlessness and racist stereotyping which disadvantages minority ethnic people.

Nevertheless, the disproportionality of black suspects remained. For example, while 7.5 per cent of Greater London's population is black, 57 per cent of all suspects arrested were black (*The Times*, 19 January 2001). In Greater Manchester, where 1.3 per cent of the population is black, 12 per cent of those arrested were black. These disproportional figures are also reflected in Britain's prison population, with 18 per cent of male and 25 per cent of female prisoners being black.

Fresh attempts made to monitor race relations in terms of the number of reported 'racist' incidents have resulted in farce. Following Macpherson, the Home Office defined a racist incident as 'any incident which is perceived to be racist by the victim or any other person'. This measurement was to prove of little use since, following Macpherson, many poor white victims of crime stated that their cases would have been taken more seriously by the police had they been black. Hence crimes in which there was no evidence of actual racism came to be reported as 'racist incidents'. Another study of racist incidents in Britain analysed the data according to the size of the ethnic communities. Surprisingly it found that the greatest perception of racist incidents by ethnic minorities was in the relatively rural areas of Northumbria, South Wales, Devon and Cornwall. Much lower in the ratings were London, the West Midlands, Greater Manchester and Leicester.

Multi-cultural Britain?

Ethnic minorities have contributed hugely to the British economy and many would argue that they have also enormously enriched Britain's culture. Not everyone, however, finds the idea of a 'multi-cultural Britain' so appealing. A Runnymede Trust report, *The Future of Multi-Ethnic Britain*, provoked an angry response from much of the British press, confirming that the politics of national identity was an emotional issue. Moreover riots in a number of northern towns in 2001 dramatised some of the continuing inter-community tensions. Lord Ouseley's subsequent report into the race relations in Bradford (see Box 24.2) pulled no punches.

An open debate took place reassessing the management of race relations in Britain. The dominant model, multi-culturalism, was portrayed as wanting.

BOX 24.2

Race riots in northern towns in Britain, 2001: the Ouseley Report

Britain's second major race riots took place in 2001, in the northern towns of Bradford, Burnley and Oldham, and were to become entangled with perceptions of international events such as 11 September 2001. After assuming that the race issue had fallen off the political agenda, many people representing all communities began asking what was now the best way to manage race relations in Britain. Commenting on reasons for sometimes fragile race relations in Britain, Lord Ouseley blamed failure in the school system to stimulate understanding of diversity in society. He was also concerned with 'the negative obsession with immigration and asylum seekers: the fear of being over run by outsiders'. Finally, he was disappointed by weak equality legislation and ineffectual political leadership in challenging racism (*Guardian*, 22 June 2001). He criticised local politicians for misplaced politically correct sensitivity and local Muslims for self-segregation from Bradford society, as well as turning a blind eye to the increasing criminal activities perpetrated by a minority of their community's youth.

It was argued that multi-culturalism was based on an article of faith – that all people of goodwill would want to live together, celebrating diversity, each community preserving its culture while respecting the culture of others. The reality was frequently very different. Bradford, Burnley and Oldham contained populations fragmented and polarised in terms of ethnicity. People from different ethnic backgrounds were segregated and leading 'parallel lives'. The lack of contact between different groups fuelled fear and suspicion, which was then easily exploited by political extremists. In these towns, multi-culturalism was little more than a 'consenting' form of apartheid. The Denham Report revealed the absence of 'shared values to unite diverse communities' in these towns. The implication was, therefore, that a more proactive form of managing race relations was called for.

The theme common to the Denham and Cantle reports into the riots, and the Home Office White Paper, was the need to build social cohesion. Central was the need for all to speak English. Secondary was the need to confront certain social practices that conflicted with basic British values. No doubt this will involve tackling the 'un-British' tradition of 'forced marriages' and the sometimes uncomfortably similar 'arranged marriages'.

The ethnic tensions in Britain's northern towns were the consequence of economic deprivation among both the majority and minority communities, exacerbated by social segregation over a period of years, and exploited by the BNP. The riots were a shock but they were largely the result of old problems which had been allowed to fester. However, ethnic tensions over much of Britain have been dangerously exacerbated by two more contemporary issues. One was ongoing political controversy in the late 20th and early 21st centuries over the numbers of people from outside the European Union (many belonging to ethnic minorities) seeking asylum in Britain; the second was the war against terror, for which the events of 11 September 2001 provided the dramatic catalyst.

Critics have suggested that the government has allowed Britain to become a 'soft touch' for asylum seekers. Substantial numbers have entered Britain illegally and then claimed asylum. The Conservative opposition has often drawn attention to the issue, and has sought a tougher response. It featured in the Conservatives' 2001 election campaign, in which it was argued that the number of applications, rising from 32,500 in 1997 to 76,000 in 2000, was unreasonable. The then party leader, William Hague, asked why so

Definition

Asylum seekers are strictly speaking those seeking political asylum as a consequence of persecution in their country of origin. Some argue that many asylum seekers are 'bogus' and are really 'economic migrants' seeking a higher standard of living. The term is sometimes indiscriminately applied to immigrants (particularly blacks or Asians) in a pejorative racist sense, although some asylum seekers are 'whites' from areas such as Eastern Europe.

many asylum seekers passed through safe European democracies just to reach Britain. The left has argued that the bulk of asylum seekers are fleeing from difficult or impossible conditions in their country of origin, and that their entry is beneficial to Britain's economy. They have accused those trying to stir up concern about asylum seekers of covert racism.

The government has sought to cut the flow of illegal immigration, to process applications for asylum faster, and to disperse the numbers of asylum seekers around the country, to prevent too great a concentration of numbers in London and Kent. This policy of dispersal has proved controversial, leading to tensions and some violence in host communities. Although the vast majority of asylum seekers want nothing more than the opportunity to stay and work peacefully in Britain, the war against terror has added a new dimension to concerns, particularly after terrorist suspects arrested in January 2003 proved to be asylum seekers, leading to renewed appeals from Conservative politicians and among sections of the media for tighter controls and more effective security screening.

The events of 11 September 2001 and the war against terror not only raised suspicions over asylum seekers, but caused massive problems for members of ethnic communities long settled in Britain. Britain's now substantial Muslim population have been victims of irrational panic reactions in what has been termed 'Islamophobia' (see Box 24.3).

The government's response to 'Islamophobia' has been to argue strenuously that it is involved in a war against terror not a war against Islam, and it has moved to secure the active support of moderate Muslims. Yet these new concerns have contributed to moving race relations policy firmly in an integrationist direction by stressing the uniting concept of citizenship (see Box 24.4). A Home Office White Paper, *Secure Borders, Safe Haven*, proposed that all new immigrants would require a working knowledge of English as well as a basic knowledge of UK culture and history. It was envisaged that new citizens would swear an oath of allegiance to Queen and Country. Furthermore, citizens could be stripped of their citizenship if they concealed any involvement with terrorism.

Photograph: PA Photos.

IN FOCUS 24.1 A war against terror or a war against Islam?

The Stop the War Coalition march in Parliament Square, central London, September 2002. The protesters opposed military action against Iraq by US President George W. Bush and Prime Minister Tony Blair. Although Blair has insisted that it is a war against terror rather than a war against Islam, it has caused particular problems for British Muslims, and has exacerbated Islamophobia.

Including women: the impact of the women's movement on policy

All contemporary societies are to varying degrees male-dominated. In Britain, as in other western countries, prestige is attached to 'men's work', be it the glamour of a professional career or the machismo of manual labour, while women's additional place of work is seen as being in the home. The difference is reflected in rewards; men's work earns a salary or wage while women's domestic

BOX 24.3
Islamophobia

Long before 11 September 2001, British Muslims were concerned that a stereotype was being reinforced by the mass media which linked Islam with political extremism. They felt that terrible events then occurring in Algeria, Iran and Luxor were reported in ways that fed the prejudices of some against British Muslims. British Muslims are not a particularly united group: Pakistan is the original country of origin for most, but many originate from India, Africa and the Middle East.

The late Dr Kalim Siddiqui set up a Muslim parliament in Britain which put views forward in a robust way. A new, more representative body, the Muslim Council for Britain, was set up in 1997. The Muslim Council is an umbrella body which represents around 250 organisations. It aims to counteract the extremist image of Islam by projecting a positive image based on the traditional values of peaceful cooperation, compassion for the poor and justice.

Western governments identified Osama Bin Laden and his al-Qaeda network of terrorists as responsible for the atrocities of 11 September. The US President and the British Prime Minister declared a 'war against terrorism' not 'a war against Islam'. The USA and UK organised a coalition of supporting governments for air and ground force attacks against the Taliban, who were protecting al-Qaeda in Afghanistan. These events resulted in politicians and political commentators discussing issues that previously they had ignored or seen as too sensitive to raise. Much of the debate focused on the relationship

between the values of Islam and the values of the west. For example, Ziauddin Sardar argued that political opposition was not legitimate in many Muslim societies, and that violence and terrorism are the only ways in which to express dissent. As a result, terrorism is rife in Pakistan, Algeria, Egypt, Saudi Arabia, Indonesia, Bangladesh, Lebanon and Iraq. He argued that terrorism was a problem in these Muslim countries mainly because their societies had not come to terms with modernity. Kanan Makiya argued that the USA had made diplomatic mistakes in dealing with the Arab and Muslim world in general, and with Palestine in particular. Nevertheless he concluded that the Muslim world had to change, embrace modernity, and cease blaming the USA for all its problems. Faisal Bodi disagreed with these views, arguing that the USA was a modern imperialist country attempting to dominate Muslim countries, and in a sense the west's war was against Islam rather than terrorism.

Other commentators have placed events in a more chilling context. The Fukuyama–Huntingdon debate (see Chapter 26), especially after 11 September, resulted in dreadful links being perceived between the al-Qaeda terrorists and young disaffected Muslim rioters in Britain. In reality, the overwhelming majority of British Muslims hold moderate views. Yet because of the actions of an extremist minority, the majority risk getting tarred with the same brush. Muslims argued that al-Qaeda was no more typical of Islam than the Ku Klux Klan was of Christianity.

labour is unpaid. When women enter paid employment, their average incomes are lower than men's. Part-time, unskilled and low-paid jobs are filled overwhelmingly by women. Despite the fact that women account for approximately half of Britain's total labour force, women receive far less promotion and career advancement than men. Also, the very nature of women's jobs makes them most vulnerable to automation, and it is women's jobs that are most likely to be lost first as a direct result of the introduction of new technologies.

The women's movement is not a formal political organisation in the sense that it has a national, regional and local structure which recruits members who, in turn, elect officials. It is informally organised and highly factionalised. The women's movement is made up of a network of small localised groups, some of which work within established organisations such as trade unions or political parties. Even so, the women's movement has had a significant impact on policy.

At the beginning of the century, the first wave of

BOX 24.4

The left, right and centre of good race relations

Race relations are both a controversial and emotional political issue. Sometimes discussion is constrained by 'political correctness', which on some occasions can help avoid offence but on others obscures sensible debate. Discussion of 'numbers' remains a politically sensitive topic. Although Home Office figures suggest the number of asylum seekers is dropping, Migration Watch UK, an allegedly non-political body, has argued that 2 million non-EU immigrants will settle in Britain over the next ten years, and expressed concern that Britain's already creaking infrastructure could not successfully absorb such numbers.

The following framework, drawn from numerous liberal sources, attempts to classify three basic models of race relations across a political spectrum:

Multi-culturalism	Integration	Assimilation
Race riots in Bradford, Burnley and Oldham led to doubts whether multi-culturalism could be successful. Critics argued that the separation of various faith-based communities resulted in 'consenting apartheid'. Lord Ousely criticised the self-imposed segregation of some Bradford Muslims, isolating themselves into 'Islamic ghettoes' with little or no contact with the wider British culture in order to preserve their traditional way of life.	Evidence of distinctive cultures but not segregated cultures. More emphasis given to social coherence: in other words, to the 'glue which binds us all together'. Promotion of citizenship values and English language to all groups. Demanding some competence in English for new immigrants is not seen as 'linguistic colonialism' but a means of making sure that ethnic minorities are able to find employment and avoid poverty.	Race relations approach favoured by the political right. The controversial MP John Townend complained that immigration had undermined Britain's 'homogenous Anglo-Saxon society'. He went on to argue that all ethnic minorities born in Britain should consider themselves British and not look to their parents' motherland for identity. They should, he said, adopt the English language and British culture. Lord Tebbit's 'cricket test' was another example of assimilation: he argued that Afro-Caribbeans should support the England team, not the Windies. This approach is a version of the US 'melting pot' in which all new arrivals surrender their traditional values in order to become British. Seen by many as a form of 'white supremacy'.
Peaceful coexistence of different values depends upon a high level of toleration by all groups. But traditional values, such as speaking only the language of the 'mother' country, can lead to social exclusion and encourage racism from others, especially whites.	All groups should develop a feeling of belonging to British society without feeling that their traditions are being threatened. In other words, white, Asian, Chinese, black communities etc. have distinctive cultures but at the same time share some basic values and feelings of being 'British'.	
Sample identity: 'Muslim living in Britain'	Sample identity: 'British Muslim'	Sample identity: 'British'

the movement exhibited 'moderate' and 'radical' wings and these survive today. 'Reformist' feminists argue that much of the battle against female inequality has been won. The Equal Pay Act 1970 stipulated equal pay for equal work and the Sex Discrimination Act 1975 ended discrimination against women in employment, education, housing, as well as in other service areas. The Act also established the Equal Opportunities Commission, a body to investigate infringements of the Equal Pay and Sex Discrimination Acts. Residual inequalities – in areas such as retirement and taxation – are being eliminated by subsequent legislation. Radical feminists point to the continued differences in average pay rates between men and women, the relative absence of women at the highest levels in business, politics and the judiciary, violence against women, and the exploitation of women in the family and home.

The women's movement has also made legislative advances in the area of abortion reform, which have however opened more divisions between feminists. The abortion issue is of great importance to many feminists since it symbolises a woman's 'right to choose'. On the other hand, many women, including Roman Catholics, put the 'right to life' above 'the woman's right to choose'.

Achievements of the women's movement and areas of controversy

The women's movement is not without its critics. Some of them point out that, despite feminist claims that gender is the fundamental division in society and causes inequalities above and beyond those caused by social class or race, the women's movement itself is a very middle class political phenomenon. It has failed to appeal to or to mobilise those women who suffer greatest social disadvantage, namely those found in the working class. It is argued that this proves that social class is a greater cause of inequality in society than is gender. In addition, critics contend that the women's movement has failed to win the support of all middle class women.

Some critics of the women's movement argue that feminists undervalue the traditional role of women in society and underestimate the political influence already wielded by women. For example, it is argued that some radical feminists neither recog-

nise the responsibilities involved in child-rearing nor understand the extent to which mothers shape the personalities and views of their children, be they boys or girls.

Some feminists now argue that the 'women's lib' thinking of the 1960s was flawed. Basically, what feminists then demanded was that women should achieve equality through being treated in exactly the same ways as men were treated. In other words, some feminists who once argued that men and women should be treated equally now believe that this was a political mistake.

The main reason for their change of mind has been the experience of areas where men and women have been treated equally; for it has inevitably been on male terms. For example, when women entered the world of business to pursue careers as executives, success generally depended on them acting like men. Feminists are now arguing that women are not like men; they have different needs, behave in different ways, and prefer to work in different environments. The early feminist goal of getting women treated in an equal way to men ignores all these differences. Some feel that the feminists of the 1960s fought hard but for the wrong things. They should have fought for the recognition of 'gender differences' as well as demanding 'gender equality'.

The diversity of alternative lifestyles: lesbian and gay rights

Until 1967 homosexual acts between consenting men were illegal. Since then there has been a near revolution in attitudes towards sexuality, with the social climate of the late 1990s being one in which many people with gay or lesbian preferences feel secure enough to 'come out'. Television has done much to promote changing attitudes, with gay people given positive rather than 'pansy' characters in soap operas and drama. An increasing number of MPs have 'come out', and other institutions, such

---

Definition
Feminism is a political ideology that explains women's role in the family, the workplace and wider society in terms of power held by men.

BOX 24.5
Women in Parliament

'Where power is, woman is not' has long been a feminist critique of both high and low politics. Indeed, the franchise did not extend to women on fully equal terms until 1928, and it was not until 1979 that Britain had its first female prime minister. The issue of the under-representation of women in Parliament has been tackled by the major Parliamentary parties, with varying degrees of success (see Figure 24.2).

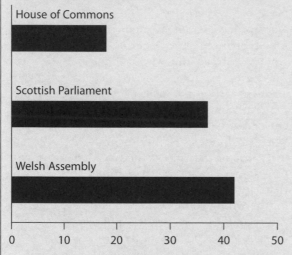

House of Commons

Scottish Parliament

Welsh Assembly

0   10   20   30   40   50

Figure 24.2 Female representation in British parliaments and assemblies as a percentage of the total

The result of having a more diverse Parliament, in which nearly one in five MPs is female, has been disputed. Some of Labour's new female MPs entered Parliament in 1997 thinking that they would challenge the traditional, male-dominated confrontational style of politics in preference for a politics of 'partnership'. Many quickly became disillusioned with MPs continuing to indulge in 'yah-boo nonsense, point scoring and silly games' which had little bearing on constituents' problems in the real world (*Guardian*, 20 June 2001). They felt that they had no impact, and some stood down.

Some felt that women MPs had 'feminised' the Commons, but in subtle ways. Women MPs, it was argued, were frequently more ambitious than their male counterparts and would not risk open confrontation with their front bench when they disagreed with official party policy. Rather they would write to the minister concerned, or attempt to arrange a private meeting, in which to communicate their concern, in a manner hidden from media attention. Others dismissed Labour's relatively large intake of female MPs, mostly selected from all-women shortlists, for being second rate Parliamentarians.

as the Church of England and armed forces, are redefining their traditional attitudes. For example, the Archbishop of Canterbury has argued that while God loves homosexuals, homosexuality remains a sin. Other bishops have taken a more liberal position and reconciled homosexuality with their religious beliefs.

The lesbian and gay lobby, Stonewall, has traditionally looked to the Labour Party in order to promote gay and lesbian political rights. Sometimes they have been disappointed, as when, in opposition, Labour supported the right of the armed forces not to enlist gay recruits. An ICM opinion poll (*Guardian*, 14 December 1995) found that Labour was not necessarily the natural ally of the gay community. Surprisingly, the poll found that Conservative

supporters were often more tolerant of gay relationships than Labour supporters; that women were more tolerant than men; and that the skilled working class was often more tolerant than the middle classes.

Revelations concerning the sexual orientation of politicians appear in newspapers from time to time. However, such reports have not appeared to damage their careers, as might have been the case even a decade ago. The contemporary social climate regarding gay and lesbian lifestyles is considerably more liberal than during the 1980s. Attitudes towards same-sex partners have become more tolerant, with political opinion shifting towards recognition of gay rights:

- The law lords have ruled that a homosexual couple living in a stable relationship could be defined as a family. This conferred new legal rights for gays and lesbians, such as the right of one partner to claim damages if he or she was dependent on the other partner, who died through a third party's negligence. Also, gays and lesbians now have the right to inherit tenancies that were in the name of their dead partners.

- The Children's Society has lifted its ban on gay and lesbian couples adopting children.
- The European Court of Human Rights ruled that the Ministry of Defence's policy of sacking gay members of the armed forces was 'inhuman and degrading'.
- A voluntary code on sexual orientation and discrimination in the workplace has been agreed. Section 28 of the Local Government Act (1988) which banned the 'promotion' of homosexuality in schools and colleges has been repealed.
- The age of consent is the same as in different-sex relationships.
- Legal rights only applicable to married couples are now claimed by same-sex couples.

Conservative attitudes, once criticised for being socially authoritarian and excessively homophobic, increasingly recognise the diversity of contemporary British society and now acknowledge the legitimacy

---

BOX 24.6
The New Feminism

In her book, *The New Feminism* (1999), Natasha Walter accepted that women had made enormous advances in society. Given such progress, therefore, is there still a need for a women's movement? She answered 'yes' to this question because of the continuing inequality experienced by women. Women are still poorer and less powerful than men. She argued that women have gained at the personal or cultural level rather than at the social and economic level. For example, a woman who feels she is treated as an equal by her male friends and colleagues might still find she is paid less than them and is therefore valued less by wider society (see Figure 24.3). The main goal of the new feminism was therefore total equality with men, particularly concerning incomes. Her research found that feminism had moved beyond middle class women to all women. It was no longer a minority political movement, for working class women in social classes D and E were more likely than AB women to say that feminism had been good for women. Walter claimed that new feminism was inclusive, no longer man-hating, since it could benefit men by accessing them to the female dominated spheres of the home and community.

Some feminists are less reluctant to give up the 'sex war' with men. For example, Germaine Greer dismissed the new feminists as little more than 'lipstick' feminists and continued to argue that gender conflict is still relevant in contemporary society. There are cultural arguments that lend some weight to this view. It has been argued that powerful male-dominated interests have usurped feminism, processed and deradicalised it, then sold it back to women at a profit. For example, in the 1930s tobacco companies wanted women to smoke more cigarettes. At the time, the prevailing cultural view was that smoking was a 'male/macho' habit and consequently there was a taboo against women smoking. Skilful marketing, however, transformed cigarettes into a symbol of freedom for women but 'of course, nicotine addiction didn't actually make women freer – cigarettes just made them feel freer' (*Guardian*, 5 June 2002). Similarly in contemporary society, shopping has been transformed into an 'empowering experience' for women. However, the true beneficiaries of smoking and shopping are male-dominated businesses, not women.

Others disagree with this sort of analysis. They have argued that feminism has given women genuine power over their lives. Contemporary young women can exercise choices not available to older generations of women. If a young woman pursues the traditional female role of motherhood it is not because it is what society expects of her, it is because that is her choice.

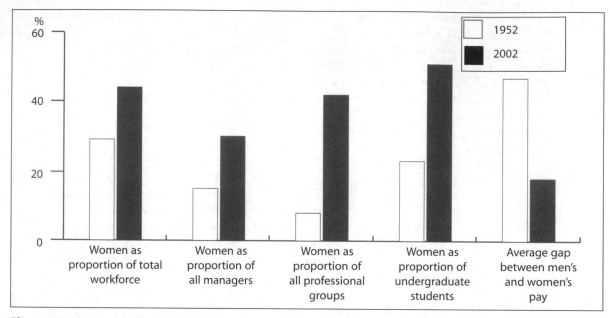

Figure 24.3 Women's employment and pay, 1952 and 2002

Source: Equal Opportunities Commission.

of political claims from minorities which previously were dismissed.

Further reading

Coxall (1992) is a useful account of post-war trends. Layton-Henry (1992) is a comprehensive account of 'race' in British politics. Lupton and Russell (in Savage and Robins, 1990) examines technical aspects of implementing EO policies. McIlroy (1989) is a useful overview of the area. Mohapatra (1999) provides some interesting insights into Leicester's Asian community. See also Ouseley (2001) and Hunt (1997), a useful overview. Maclean and Groves (1991) provides a feminist perspective on a wide range of issues. Oakley (1972) is an influential text and Randall (1987) gives a concise analysis of feminism. Individual statements are found in Kingham (2001), an account of a so-called 'Blair babe' who stood down, Walter (1998), and Viner (2002).

Chapter 25

Politics and the environment

The environmental debate 401
The 'tragedy of the commons' 402
Green ideology 402
The political agenda and the political
 process 403
The Green Party 404
The greening of mainstream political
 parties? 404
Britain and transnational pollution 406
The European Union and international
 commitments 407
The GM debate 408

What is meant by the term 'green politics'? How is it possible for the environment to have emerged as an important issue with the public, yet for the Green Party to have failed to win a single seat in Parliament? The major political parties now claim to have policies for the environment; how valid is this claim? Is the idea of sustainable development which has become the focus of Labour's environmental policy realistic? To what extent has the politics of the environment moved beyond being an issue of political debate to become a serious form of public policy? This chapter addresses these issues, and assesses the impact of the EU and other international commitments on Britain's environmental policy making. It concludes with an assessment of why the GM food issue climbed up the political agenda and how Labour dealt with it.

The environmental debate

In his book *The Closing Circle* (1971), Barry Commoner spelled out some basic 'laws of ecology': everything is connected to everything else; everything must go somewhere; nature knows best; and, finally, there is no such thing as a free lunch. We tend to see the simple acts that fill our everyday lives as inconsequential, even trivial, without realising how the laws of ecology operate and draw them together with what can be awesome impact. A simple example of changing the battery of a transistor radio makes the point. The old battery is thrown into the dustbin, is collected along with other domestic rubbish and taken to the council incinerator. 'But,' asked Professor Commoner, 'where does it really go?' The battery contains a heavy metal element, mercury, which cannot be destroyed but can only be combined with other elements. As the battery is heated in the incinerator it:

> produces mercury vapour which is emitted by the incinerator stack, and mercury vapour is toxic. Mercury vapour is carried by the wind, eventually brought down to earth in rain or snow. Entering a mountain lake, let us say, the mercury condenses and sinks to the bottom. Here it is acted on by bacteria which convert it to methyl mercury. This is soluble and taken up by fish; since it is not metabolised, the mercury accumulates in the organs and flesh of the fish. The fish is caught and eaten by a man and the mercury becomes deposited in his organs.
>
> (Commoner, 1971: 33–46)

The interconnection of seemingly unrelated yet commonplace acts – changing a battery and eating a fish; the fact that the mercury did not disappear but simply moved from one place to another; that anthropogenic (human-created) changes were detrimental to the environment; and that the benefits of a battery-operated radio are gained at the cost of pollution and possible ill-health – together illustrate the working of ecological laws. These laws are working across such a wide range of behaviour with such adverse effects that some scientists talk of there being an 'ecological crisis'. They believe that great damage has already been done to the thin skin of earth, water and air that clothes 'Planet Earth', with yet greater damage in store. The air is polluted by carbon dioxide resulting from the burning of coal and oil, and this is producing the 'greenhouse effect' as the atmosphere slowly heats up, because excessive carbon dioxide absorbs heat that previously would have radiated away. Some believe that this will result in climatic changes which will melt the polar ice-caps and transform the world's most fertile areas into deserts. Burning coal and oil also produces large quantities of sulphur dioxide in the atmosphere, resulting in acid rain which kills forests and water life. Nitrogen fertilisers used in increasing quantities by farmers have now been washed from the land and have found their way into drinking water, causing a major health hazard for young children. Nuclear testing has put radioactive substances into the bones of children for the first time in human history. Exposure to another heavy metal – lead – put into the atmosphere by car exhausts has resulted in the impaired mental development of many urban children. Cancers have been caused through exposure to asbestos. The thinning in the ozone layer which surrounds the earth has concerned the scientific community. This layer of gas acts as a vital filter which protects animals and plants from the sun's ultraviolet rays, and has almost disappeared altogether over Antarctica. This list of potential disasters seems endless, so why is global society not in a state of panic?

Environmentalists argue that many of the major ecological threats are recent, and their effects have not yet fully been understood or felt. They sometimes use the analogy of a pond which is gradually being covered by a weed. The area covered by the weed doubles each day, so that by the twelfth day half the pond is covered. Suddenly on the thirteenth day, the pond will be totally covered by weed. Environmentalists see a crisis creeping up on humanity and taking governments by surprise in a similar way. How has the political system responded to the relatively new environmental lobby, and with what results?

The 'tragedy of the commons'

The main idea behind this metaphor is that in the absence of regulations, greed by some leads to destruction for everyone. The 'commons' refers to the natural resources in the world that are used by everyone, such as atmosphere. The metaphor was first coined by British ecologist Garrett Hardin in 1968, when he used the scenario of a village green in medieval England to address the problems of over-exploitation facing the contemporary world. Imagine a green upon which the farmers of the village are free to graze their cattle. Each individual farmer has many cows, far too many for the green to feed. Acting out of self-interest and the profit motive, farmers begin to introduce as many cattle as possible to the green, since the lack of regulation enables them to do this. The total number of cattle overstretches the capacity of the green, and the result is that all the cows die from starvation. The metaphor suggests, first, that without restraints, multinational companies, governments and individuals will use the earth's resources to get rich quickly, with no concern for the environment; and second, that the remedy for the tragedy of the commons is international environmental protection treaties and agreements that prevent the plundering of natural resources. The work of Hardin and other ecologists has provided the basis for the concept of sustainable development, involving the notion of self-sacrifice for the general good. In a world of nation-states, some form of global regulation is needed to address the causal link between, for example, car driving habits, transport and energy policies found in Britain and other western countries 'and the changing agricultural fortunes of Bangladesh or sub-Saharan Africa and their internal politics' (Held *et al.*, 1999: 378).

Green ideology

Green politics has been described as 'new politics' in so far as it does not fit into the framework of conventional Parliamentary politics. Yet many aspects of green politics connect with aspects of pre-existing belief systems. In this sense, green politics is not really new. As Robinson has stated, 'Environmentalist rhetoric has drawn inspiration from such diverse ideological wells as Christian, Buddhist, Hindu, Taoist and Pagan religious belief systems, Anarchist, Marxist and Conservative political ideologies, the critical rationalist tradition in science from ecology to quantum physics, and the romantic reactions to post-Enlightenment social changes from Keats to Kerouac' (Robinson, 1992: 34).

Environmentalism, or Green thinking, is an eclectic ideology which is drawn from numerous and diverse sources (see also page 71). It rejects 'industrialisation' and the policies of economic growth that remain at the heart of both Conservative and Labour programmes. Environmentalists argue that the economy should produce no more than is necessary to meet people's essential needs, and in a society where people live simpler lives such needs will be met by local production (rather than by multinational companies). Seven basic principles underlie contemporary environmentalism:

- **A world approach.** All human activity should reflect appreciation of the world's finite resources and easily damaged ecology.
- **Respect for the rights of our descendants.** Our children have the right to inherit a beautiful and bountiful planet rather than an exhausted and polluted one.
- **Sufficiency.** We should be satisfied with 'enough' rather than constantly seeking 'more'.
- **A conserver rather than consumer economy.** We must conserve what we have rather than squander it through pursuit of high growth strategies.
- **Care and share.** Given that resources are limited we must shift our energies to sharing what we have and looking after all sections of society properly.
- **Self-reliance.** We should learn to provide for ourselves rather than surrendering responsibility to experts and specialised agencies.
- **Decentralise and democratise.** We must form smaller units of production, encourage cooperative enterprises and give people local power over their own affairs. At the same time international integration must move forward rapidly (Jones, 1989–90: 51).

Definition
Environmentalism (or Green thinking) is a broad approach to life on the planet which is concerned primarily with the impact of human beings on the environment of themselves and other species.

The political agenda and the political process

Much of the post-war consensus was built on the assumption common to both Labour and Conservative that it would be economic growth that would provide the extra resources needed by an expanding welfare state. Economic growth would improve the lives of the less well-off in society without the need to tax and redistribute wealth from the better-off. The major parties competed with each other principally in terms of which would be the most competent in managing the economy and maximising its growth. Many commentators look back at the period from the mid-1950s onwards as the 'age of affluence'.

It was not long after, Conservative Prime Minister Harold Macmillan assured voters that 'Most of our people have never had it so good' that the modern environmental debate began, in a modest undramatic way, with the publication of Rachel Carson's book *Silent Spring* in 1962. However, it was not until the 1970s that the 'first wave' of environmental concern challenged the assumptions that underlay the consensus about economic growth providing a politically painless way of meeting the rising expectations of the electorate. A report by the Massachusetts Institute of Technology for the Club of Rome, *The Limits to Growth*, examined patterns of growth for various elements, including industrialism and the consumption of non-renewable natural resources. The investigation concluded that (like the surface of the pond discussed earlier) within a short time-period a situation of great abundance can turn into one of scarcity.

The 'second wave' of environmental concern emerged during the 1980s as a response to a number of issues including Britain's greater dependence on military and civil nuclear power (the latter being a response to the energy crisis), with the risk of accidents demonstrated by the near-miss at Three Mile Island and the Chernobyl disaster; pollution and acid rain damage; the depletion of the ozone layer through CFC (chlorofluorocarbon) damage and the risks of global warming through increased carbon dioxide in the atmosphere.

In the USA Anthony Downs argued that political concern about the environment would pass through a five-stage process (Box 25.1). Downs's

BOX 25.1

Political concern about the environment: the five-stage cycle

- **Stage 1: the pre-problem stage.** The problem exists and may be severe but the public is unaware, the media uninterested and only interest groups are alarmed.
- **Stage 2: alarmed discovery and euphoric enthusiasm.** The problem is suddenly discovered as a result of some particular event, the public call for solutions, and politicians promise action.
- **Stage 3: realising the cost of significant progress.** This comes slowly and follows disclosure about the sacrifices necessary and the uncertainty of technological solutions.
- **Stage 4: gradual decline of public interest.** Public concern falls, through either boredom or rejection of the scale of the changes necessary or the costs involved.
- **Stage 5: post-problem stage.** The public forgets about the issue but most original problems remain; a few institutions devoted to the problem may survive, but on severely reduced funding.

Source: Bradbeer, in Savage and Robins, 1990.

model has proved to be generally accurate, in so far as public concern for environmental issues and governmental response has passed through the five-stage cycle twice: once with the first wave of environmental concern in the 1970s and again with the second wave in the 1980s. No doubt there will be a third wave of public concern in the future, with every chance that it too will pass through five stages.

The Green Party

Britain's Green Party has not enjoyed the electoral success of some of its European counterparts, although this is partly the consequence of the first-past-the-post electoral system which penalises smaller parties whose support is widely spread geographically (see Chapter 6). The Greens represent a 'new' politics and are to some extent opposed to conventional politics. The party has been and remains divided on both its strategy and its goals. Should it become an orthodox political party interested in winning political power, or not? 'Green 2000' was set up to relaunch the party as a real contender for power. But not all Greens agreed with this initiative, since they did not believe that the Green Party could operate within the conventional party political system. Dark-green fundamentalist party members saw 'Green 2000' as a sell-out to what they saw as the failed system of power politics. By the time of the 1997 general election, the Greens were operating more in the nature of a pressure group than a political party with Parliamentary aspirations. Following successes in PR elections, the Greens won two seats in the 1999 European Parliamentary elections, which resulted in the party taking a more conventional approach in the 2001 general election. It selected candidates for 145 constituencies and won an average of 2.45 per cent of the vote. (It did best in a Brighton constituency, where it polled 9.3 per cent.) Greens consider themselves to be 'the fourth party' behind the main three, and realise that only a system of PR could win them representation in general elections.

The greening of mainstream political parties?

How far have green ideas influenced policy making in the major parties? All of them claim to have coherent environmental policies. Margaret Thatcher startled her party by announcing her commitment to environmental protection and conservation in 1988.

We Conservatives … are not merely friends of the Earth – we are its guardians and trustees for generations to come. The core of Tory philosophy and the case for protecting the environment are the same. No generation has a freehold on this Earth. All we have is a life tenancy – with a full repairing lease. And this Government intends to meet the terms of this lease in full.

(Speech at Brighton, 14 October 1988)

Some Greens have acknowledged the impact of Thatcher's apparent conversion. The speeches of this mainstream party leader who had dominated politics for a decade effectively 'legitimised the environmental issue' and made many take notice who had ignored environmental pressure groups and the Green Party previously. Yet the rhetoric did not seem to have a marked effect on Conservative government policy (although John Major's government introduced the 'fuel escalator' involving regular above-inflation increases in fuel duty, ostensibly to encourage people to switch from their cars to public transport). Indeed the New Right emphasis on the free market and competition involved the relaxation of planning controls, which reduced scope for a positive environmental policy.

The Labour tradition is rather more favourable to intervention and environmental planning. Labour after all had pursued town and country planning, and had encouraged public transport as part of an integrated transport policy. New Labour made similar noises. Blair himself has re-emphasised the importance he and his party have attached to the environment:

> The evidence grows all around us daily of the danger of indifference to our duty to treat nature with respect, and care for the environment. I want these issues to occupy a central part of the British government's agenda in coming years.
>
> (6 March 2001; source <www.fco.gov.uk>)

Yet Labour was also a party traditionally wedded to industrial growth and full employment. Both old and New Labour would opt for living standards and jobs rather than environmental protection, if forced to choose. Moreover, New Labour is sensitive to the concerns of 'middle England' and only too aware of the electoral damage of the kind of anti-motorist policies advocated by Greens (see Box 25.2). Thus faced with major protests about fuel prices in September 2000, the government abandoned the fuel escalator. Moreover, in the aftermath of chaos on the railways following crashes and new safety restrictions, coupled with increased congestion on the roads, Labour has effected a U-turn and announced a new road building programme. Hostility to the congestion charges introduced by the

---

BOX 25.2
A Green transport policy?

Britain's road system is nearing crisis. It coped with 2 million vehicles in 1950, 9 million in 1963, 27 million in 1997, and will have to cope with an estimated 40 million within 20 years unless political action is taken. Some town centres have kept cars at bay through pedestrianisation, but the real solution rests in getting people out of the habit of using their cars and into the habit of using public transport. Environmentalists have argued that a 'stick and carrot' approach would be required to achieve such change. The 'stick' might include road pricing (drivers pay to use certain roads); congestion charges for motorists who enter town centres; lower speed limits on all urban and rural roads; much higher car tax, based on engine size; taxing companies on their car parks so that they begin to charge employees for parking at work, and much higher fuel prices. At the same time, government must continue to discourage out-of-town shopping centres, which generate car usage. The 'carrot' would have to include alternative means of public transport that were reliable, frequent, convenient, clean and cheap. One option is a scheme for making one journey with one ticket, even if a train and a bus trip are both involved.

---

maverick ex-Labour London Mayor Ken Livingstone in early 2003 may deter the government and Labour councils from imitating this initiative.

Of the major parties the Liberal Democrats have been perhaps the most Green in their outlook. Their 2001 election manifesto featured green coloured boxes on almost every page, headed 'Green Action', addressing a whole range of policy areas. Yet on transport policy, although they pledged themselves to 'reverse plans for new road building in environmentally sensitive areas' they made no commitment to increase fuel prices. They too have trimmed their environmental concerns to electoral arithmetic.

Critics argue that the policies of all mainstream parties are designed merely to reassure public opinion that problems are being tackled rather than to offer real solutions. In his study of green politics, Robinson concludes that the:

> main political parties are still chained to the idea that the natural ecosystem exists primarily as a resource for man's exploitation. Although, as a review of environmental policy documents of recent years show, the parties have begun to address issues of resource planning, future energy policy, recycling and the nascent concept of sustainability, the sacred cow of economic growth has not been sacrificed, nor is it likely to be in the near future.
>
> (Robinson, 1992: 217)

Britain and transnational pollution

Increasingly governments have come to realise that pollution can easily travel by means of wind, air and water and cause environmental damage many miles away; indeed often in a different country. The UK and Germany are the worst EU offenders in emitting sulphur and nitrogen-based compounds into the environment, which are carried by prevailing winds to fall as acid rain in Nordic countries. Because of the transnational nature of pollution, many states accept that the solutions to protecting the environment now lie in multilateral approaches. Labour supports global solutions to transnational pollution, with Tony Blair advocating a partnership approach to tackling environmental problems. This requires that all states work together on environmental issues, and crucially, all states must be prepared to make economic concessions to better the global environment.

The principal objective behind Labour's thinking on sustainable development is to expand income and wealth, but in ways that do not destroy the resources of the world. The concept was discussed widely following the Brundtland Report (Report of the World Commission on Environment and Development, 1987), which concluded that the world could not support the rising demands of an ever-increasing population. Sustainable development calls for new approaches to the issues of economic growth, resource management and the use of energy. Prior to the Brundtland Report, environmental protection

policy revolved around restrictive means that tended to slow or halt economic growth. This method of environmental protection was not seen as electorally viable by the British government, and while it attached certain environmental measures to policy areas, critics argued that the protection never went far. Sustainable development policies allow economic growth, but not at the expense of the environment. For example, John Major's Conservative government declared that 'Sustainable development does not mean having less economic development ... a healthy economy can better generate the resources to meet people's needs. New investment and environmental protection go hand in hand' (HM Government, 1994).

> It is time to accept firm limits for global warming. We are all in this together. No country can opt out of global warming or fence in its own private climate.
>
> (Tony Blair, quoted in Kegley and Wittkopf, 2000: 311)

Labour's approach to international sustainable development has been twofold: first, to encourage poorer states to meet their populations' needs without depleting their natural resources, and second, for richer states to alter their attitudes towards material abundance. With this is mind, it can be seen that achieving sustainable development will be difficult, and some would argue, politically impossible. For sustainable development cannot be attained without radical changes to social, political and economic structures, especially in the more developed countries. Individuals living in countries such as Britain and the USA must prove willing to abandon their current lifestyles for the future good. Despite the elusive nature of the concept, since 1994 sustainable development has been the focus of British environmental policy.

Since John Prescott launched Labour's strategy on sustainable development in 1999, little has been heard of it. There was no specific timetable or implementation plan, and the strategy merely committed the government to pursuing sustainable development in all areas of government policy. There is little doubt that the priority of economic growth per se has consistently trumped environmental protection policy based on sustainable

BOX 25.3
The Environment Agency

Created in 1997, the Environment Agency is a quango dealing with key areas of government policy initiatives on the environment. It has a staff of 10,500 and a budget of £625 million a year. The agency is concerned with issues of British environmental protection and the public's relation to them. The main objectives of the agency are to monitor water companies (it has insisted on the need for new sewerage systems), maintain the standard of rivers and clean up any river pollution, and monitor industrial pollution. Although the agency has a 'name and shame' policy for companies guilty of damaging the environment, some environmentalists have been disappointed that it has not played a more proactive and political role in protecting the environment.

development. Labour's Green critics argue that it is clear that economic growth is still the number one priority, and will frequently occur at the expense of the environment.

The European Union and international commitments

Britain's membership of the European Union (EU) has been an important source of influence on environmental policy. EU Directives have been designed to harmonise environmental policies throughout member states, especially important in equalising commercial costs in the single market. Although EU Directives are technically binding on member governments, their impact can in effect be avoided through blocking and delaying tactics. Nevertheless, the government has responded positively to many Directives, and where it has not, it has been embarrassed by the resulting publicity. For example, Directives on the quality of drinking water and bathing water around Britain's coasts received much publicity in the media. A more recent and controversial Directive in 2003 concerns the mandatory recycling of old cars. While this addresses the issue of environmental protection and

sustainability, some commentators, including the Institute for European Environmental Policy, fear that it will result in the 'unanticipated consequences' of thousands of abandoned and burnt-out cars littering both urban and rural areas.

British international commitments on environmental protection and sustainable development ensure that the government cannot escape its commitments on the environment. The majority of British environmental protection policy originates in the EU, and the EU is able to initiate environmental policy more effectively than the governments of member states since it is more insulated from domestic electoral pressures. While some attribute to the EU a predominant and successful role in shaping British environmental policy, others would accuse the EU of playing the major role in the environmental degradation of Europe. For the EU has been implicated in some of Europe's worst acts of 'environmental vandalism' (*Guardian*, 29 July 2002). EU funding has paid for a number of environmentally damaging civil engineering schemes, and numerous other policies (such as the Common Agricultural Policy) have allowed huge EU subsidies to create wide-scale intensive farming and drainage of wetlands. Others argue that the EU shapes only 'petty environmentalism' and has limited influence over 'major environmentalism', such as global climate change. As in the case of the 'tragedy of the commons' (see page 402), a globally accepted and implemented solution is the only way in which an issue such as climate change can be tackled. The EU can play an important role within the global context, but it is relatively powerless when acting unilaterally, although its impending enlargement should increase its world influence, while also extending its environmental regulations over some major polluting states in Eastern Europe.

Britain has participated in international regimes for conservation of the global commons such as the seabed, Antarctica and the oceans. The recent international initiatives in which Britain has featured prominently are the 1997 Kyoto Protocol on climate change and the UN Earth Summit. The Kyoto agreement aims to return 2000 levels of carbon dioxide to a percentage of 1990 levels. It arose from the 1992 Climate Change Treaty, but most states missed the targets set by this treaty due to a lack of enforcement and verification. However, some alarming reports from the scientific community has alerted governments of the need to act now in order to prevent a future catastrophe.

Domestic policy targets set by the government, however, sometimes appear as optimistic and ambitious, and environmentalists fear they will not be met. Labour has, for example, stated its determination to cut greenhouse gas emissions by 20 per cent by 2010. The government has taxed industry heavily in order to cut energy consumption, but at the same time cut VAT on domestic fuel, which will encourage energy consumption.

The UN Earth Summit meets every five years to re-commit governments to a broad range of environmental and development goals. The original Earth Summit held in 1992 in Rio de Janeiro has led to further meetings being referred to as 'Rio Plus Five/Ten'. The summit is concerned with sustainable development and attempts to reconcile international development. The later summits have placed the environment firmly on the international agenda. Such issues as climate change and transnational pollution can now be called high politics, when such a title was originally reserved for international diplomacy and militaristic matters.

The GM debate

When they first came into commercial circulation, genetically modified (GM) crops were largely uncontroversial with the wider public. Such crops were a commonplace feature of American agriculture throughout the late 1980s and 1990s. But in 1998 the British public became aware of the alleged risks of GM food and the confusion and distrust that followed demonstrated the gaps in Labour's policy on coordinating all departments of government on environmental policy. The GM problem was an environmental issue in the traditional sense. The government reacted to the crisis as it arose, rather than having a previously thought-out protocol for public discontent with GM food. The concern of the consumer triumphed in the GM debate, leading to government retraction and downplaying of previous statements on the safety of GM food.

In 1998 a decision by the US-based multinational corporation Monsanto sparked public concern in Britain over GM food. Monsanto planned to cease separating GM and non-GM soya beans, meaning the consumer could no longer choose between the two in food products that used Monsanto beans. Environmental groups such as Greenpeace played a big part in alerting the public to this, with public opinion consequently turning against GM crops as well as the companies that created and sold them. Also in 1998, some British scientists broke away from the government's official endorsement of GM crops and stated that there were, after all, potential dangers attached to the growing and consumption of GM crops. Major supermarkets capitalised on the public concern and offered GM-free products, and some, such as Ice-

---

BOX 25.4
The Kyoto Agreement

Negotiated in 1997, the Kyoto Agreement sets targets for 186 states (including 38 developed states) to bind them to reduce their emissions of carbon dioxide and other greenhouse gases by 2012. The EU will turn the Agreement into law for all member states; the target for UK reduction will be around 7–10 per cent, although the government has set itself a more ambitious target of 20 per cent. By planting new forests, states will be able to set 'credits' against the carbon dioxide reductions that the Agreement assigns to them. The rather vague language of the Agreement has allowed oppositional states like the USA to reinterpret terms such as 'goals' and 'targets' in their favour. It had seemed America would ratify the Agreement, since President Clinton was supportive of climate control, but the Senate rejected the Agreement. The election of George W. Bush was the final nail in the coffin for USA participation in climate change. Tony Blair criticised the USA for non-participation in the Agreement, and on matters of global environmental protection, Blair and Bush stand very far apart.

land, ensured that no GM crops were used in the products they sold.

The British government had initially been strong supporters of the biotechnology industry, as Britain was a world leader in GM research. The events of 1998 forced the government to back-track on its full support of GM food. Rather than rely on original scientific research, the government opted for a neutral position, claiming more research was needed. This did not ease public concern, as the trials of new GM crops across the British countryside led to fears that GM crops could cross-pollinate other species of plant. Greenpeace activists participated in the destruction of GM crops around Britain, claiming they had a moral duty to do so, and many were arrested. The government argued that such protests were anti-scientific and would never allow the truth to be known about GM food.

Further reading

Dobson (1995) is the best source on Green thinking, and Garner (2000) should be consulted on Green politics in Britain. Also useful are Bradbeer (in Savage and Atkinson, 2001), McCormick (1991) and Robinson (1992). The transport policy of Blair's Labour government is robustly discussed by Foster (in Seldon, 2001).

Useful websites include the government departments <www.defra.gov.uk> and <www.transport. gov.uk>, the Environment Agency <www.environment-agency.gov.uk>, the international pressure groups Friends of the Earth <www.foe.co.uk>, Greenpeace <www.greenpeace.org.uk>, the Council for the Protection of Rural England, <www. greenchannel.com/cpre>, and the web page of the radical environmentalist journalist George Monbiot: <www.monbiot.com>.

Chapter 26

Foreign and defence policies

The differing nature of external policy   410
The making of British foreign and defence
   policies   411
The basis of Britain's foreign policy   412
The Commonwealth   412
The special relationship with the USA   413
Britain in Europe   414
The EU versus NATO in British foreign and
   defence policies   414
From new world order to the war on terror   416
Britain and Europe's evolving relationship
   with Russia   416
An ethical foreign policy for Britain?   416
The war on terror   419
British foreign and defence policies in the
   21st century   419

Within the memory span of many middle-aged adults, Britain has moved from being a major world power to being a middle-sized regional power. What factors led to this decline? Britain's changed circumstances have forced policy makers into taking sometimes painful decisions. The EU has grown in importance in relation to British foreign policy, and at times this has created tensions in Britain's 'special relationship' with the USA. As a consequence, Britain is attempting to balance its links with both the USA and the EU. While British foreign and defence policies have traditionally reflected the interest of a small political elite rather than a wider political public, the media, non-governmental organisations and multi-national companies are becoming increasingly important actors in shaping external policy. The end of the cold war has not resulted in a 'new world order' as some politicians predicted, but in a new disorder which has involved Britain and its allies. Terrorism has emerged as a new threat after 11 September 2001, and the war on terrorism may yet replace inter-state conflict as the main means of defence policy in the 21st century: already British foreign and defence policy objectives have to prioritise homeland defence in its various forms.

The differing nature of external policy

External policy, such as foreign and defence policy, differs from internal or domestic policies in three important respects. First, foreign policy tends to be reactive rather than proactive. The government has far greater control over areas such as education or health, where it can direct policy through legislation and financial support. The day-to-day conduct of foreign policy tends to be in reaction to international politics made up of the actions of other governments and international organisations. During the cold war, foreign policy makers had a structure within which to create their foreign policies. There was a clear enemy, a technological arms race, and doctrine such as containment, mutually assured destruction and flexible response gave British foreign policy makers a framework within which to plan for foreign and defence policy scenarios. After the cold war, foreign policy makers no longer had a lexical structure to give meaning and frame action. Foreign policy does not need to be structured rigorously, but it does need a focus. To a large extent, the post cold war era was marked by the search for an adversary. The Gulf War in 1991 (and continued engagement with Iraq) gave British foreign policy a direction, but it was not until the attacks of 11 September 2001 that British foreign policy makers once again had a clear enemy (the war on terrorism) upon which to focus.

Second, public opinion tends to divide less on foreign policy issues than on domestic issues. On issues such as the economy, education or health, government policy tends to create 'winners' and 'losers'. A situation of zero-sum politics may exist in which the gains made by one section of society are at the direct expense of the losses incurred by another section. This is rarely the situation when government faces a foreign crisis or threat from abroad, when all sections of society feel the need to support their own government against the common foe. If armed conflict arises, as between British and Argentinian troops in 1982 over control of the Falklands, even to question the wisdom of one's own government may appear treacherous in the eyes of others.

Third, foreign and defence policy issues have, in the past, tended to interest only a small minority of the population. As a consequence, pressure groups, parties and the media played a minor role compared with their influence in shaping domestic policy. Even Parliament's role, despite the energetic work of various party groups and select committees in scrutinising policy, has been limited. William Wallace argued that in Britain 'as in other democratic countries, there is a long-established parliamentary tradition that foreign policy ought to be insulated from the rough-and-tumble of domestic debate' (Wallace, 1975: 1). Increasingly in the new millennium the British government is learning to cope with the greater input in the foreign policy making process from multinational companies (MNCs), non-governmental organisations, transnational civil society, and the

global media. The rise of globalization and the consequences of the phenomenon mean government and the state are no longer solely in charge of the making, direction and public perception of their foreign policy.

The making of British foreign and defence policies

In constitutional terms, responsibility for the conduct of foreign policy lies with the Secretary of State for Foreign Affairs. Normally the conduct of foreign affairs involves close liaison between his/her department, the Foreign and Commonwealth Office (FCO) and the Ministry of Defence, the FCO's 'closest cousin in Whitehall' (Clarke, 1992: 84). The FCO also works with other departments on issues of common interest, in which case 'the Foreign Secretary or his officials formulate policy in consultation with those Departments. These policies are implemented by the FCO,

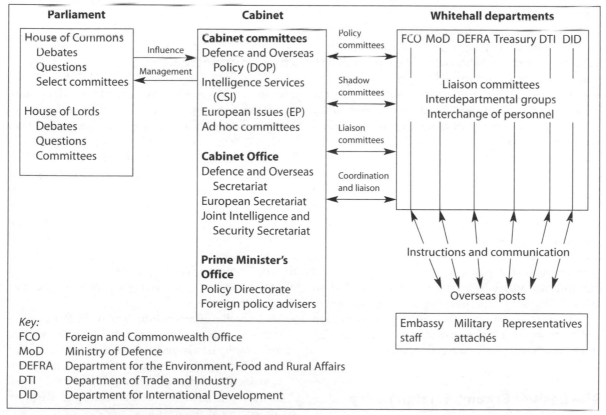

Figure 26.1 The British foreign policy making process

Source: adapted from Sanders, 1990 and Clarke, 1998.

either directly or through the agency of British embassies and missions abroad' (Wallace, 1975: 21).

Most academics have recognised the close political relationship between the foreign secretary and the prime minister. Of course in some cases the prime minister has previously held the post of foreign secretary, as did James Callaghan and John Major, and this may explain why in the past so many prime ministers intervened in the work of the FCO. But perhaps the main reason for intervention lies in the fact that the prime minister is expected to be a statesperson on the international stage and so has to have a command of foreign policy issues. As Prime Minister, Margaret Thatcher was noted for her long-running hostility towards the FCO and occasional bitter battles with the foreign secretary. There were complex reasons for this antagonism, but of central importance among them was the clash between Thatcher's Atlanticist foreign policy outlook and the Europeanism of the FCO.

Whatever foreign policy is pursued by ministers or their civil servants, it will inevitably be accompanied by claims that this decision or that treaty is 'in the national interest'. Yet this can mean very different things to different people. Some Labour and Tory MPs supported the Maastricht Treaty because they believed closer involvement in a potentially federal structure was in Britain's 'national interest'. At the same time others opposed Maastricht because they believed that it threatened Britain's sovereignty and therefore was against 'the national interest'. What then is meant by the term 'national interest'? As Joseph Frankel has stated, '"National interest" is a singularly vague concept. It assumes a variety of meanings in the various contexts in which it is used and, despite its fundamental importance, these meanings often cannot be reconciled' (Frankel, 1970: 15). Generally, national interest refers to 'the basic determinants that guide state policy in relation to the international environment' (Evans and Newnham, 1998: 344). 'National interest' applies only to sovereign states and relates specifically to foreign policy, as opposed to domestically contested policies, where the term 'public interest' is used.

The basis of Britain's foreign policy

Looking back, it is remarkable that until the 1960s this small country was one of the leading world powers. Britain was an independent nuclear power, held a permanent seat on the Security Council of the United Nations (as indeed it still does), and was responsible for policing much of the world. Britain, it was argued, had a unique contribution to make to world politics since it wielded influence in three distinct areas. Winston Churchill described Britain's role in terms of being at the intersection of 'three majestic circles'. The first was the Commonwealth circle which, being the legacy of Britain's imperial power, embraced much of Africa and Asia as well as the dominions of Canada, New Zealand and Australia. The second was Britain's 'special relationship' with the USA, and the third was Britain's close relationship with Western Europe, where armed forces were based as part of NATO's defences against the Soviet Union. But changes abroad such as the rise of nationalism in developing countries, as well as changes at home resulting from Britain's declining economic strength, have meant that Britain has had to adapt and make far-reaching changes in each of its 'foreign policy circles'.

The Commonwealth

The process of decolonisation, the transformation of the British Empire into the Commonwealth of Nations, began in the 1940s with India, Pakistan and Ceylon (Sri Lanka) gaining independence. In the 1960s what Prime Minister Harold Macmillan described as the 'winds of change' swept through Britain's African colonies. Country after country gained *self-determination*, with the exception of Rhodesia, which emerged as a problem when an experiment in multiracial government (the Central African Federation) failed, and South Africa, which left the Commonwealth in 1961. Britain retained a military presence in its former colonies in order to:

- Deter Soviet intervention. The main fear in London was that the Soviet Union would prey upon vulnerable newly-independent states, or states that British forces had left. British troops remained in the Mandate of Palestine until 1949, even though doing so damaged Britain's international reputation.
- Defend countries against insurgency, as in Malaya, though British forces were often

under-resourced and undermined in the bipolar world of the cold war.

- Defend western trade routes, from bases such as Simonstown in South Africa.

But the international role encapsulated by the Commonwealth 'circle' was to decline, and many historians see the Suez fiasco of 1956 as critical in eventually changing the direction of British foreign and defence policies (see Coxall and Robins (1998), ch. 11).

Labour Prime Minister Harold Wilson faced the familiar political problem of having to reduce public expenditure, and in 1968 his Cabinet decided that big savings must be made in the defence budget. Britain had 220,000 soldiers, 125,000 airmen and 95,000 sailors. Substantial costs would be saved, it was decided, by withdrawing British forces that were garrisoned east of the Suez Canal. This involved Britain pulling out of Singapore, Malaysia and the Gulf. Along with this, the Defence Secretary, Denis Healey, emphasised the ascending importance of Europe in strategic thinking: 'our army is well trained and superbly equipped, and has more recent and varied fighting experience than any other European army … We shall thus be able to contribute to the security of NATO on a scale corresponding with our efforts to forge closer political and economic links in Europe.'

The Commonwealth was dubbed the New Commonwealth which, rather than being dominated by Britain and the Dominions (as it had been previously), allowed all states to have an equal vote. This increased the legitimacy of the Commonwealth but further decreased Britain's global influence. Britain's responsibilities now involved only a handful of commitments: after the handback of Hong Kong to China in 1997, the most important are the Falklands, Gibraltar and Bermuda. Ten additional 'colonial outposts', such as Montserrat, the Pitcairn Islands, and Turks and Caicos Islands, are either too small or too poor to survive as independent states. The Commonwealth has long ceased to be a viable basis for Britain's foreign and defence policy, yet it has grown in importance for some other countries. It provides a useful diplomatic network for developing countries; South Africa has rejoined the Commonwealth, and Mozambique, which was a Portuguese colony and has no colonial links with Britain, joined it too.

The special relationship with the USA

The history, institutions and culture of Britain and the USA are intertwined, and out of the close cooperation during the Second World War developed the much-vaulted 'special relationship' that is claimed to exist between the two countries. Labour Foreign Secretary Ernest Bevin drew the USA into a post-war European defence commitment with the establishment of the North Atlantic Treaty Organisation (NATO). America continued to contribute directly to British defence forces when, after the failure of Britain's own nuclear weapons system, the USA provided Britain with the most modern systems in

---

BOX 26.1

Britain's 'special relationship' with the USA

Britain's 'special relationship' with the USA involved the leaders of both countries working together closely. It has perhaps always been an unequal relationship given the size and power of the USA, and has perhaps always meant more to the British.

The special relationship was strained during the Suez crisis and weakened considerably during the 1960s and 1970s. The withdrawal of forces east of Suez meant that Britain was unable to play its traditional role of junior world policeman alongside the USA. Britain refused to provide troops to fight alongside Americans in Vietnam, and Atlantic ties appeared less important as Prime Ministers Wilson, Callaghan and Heath looked increasingly towards Europe. Margaret Thatcher did not share the deep Europeanism of her predecessor and re-established a special relationship on a personal level with President Reagan. Both leaders held similar New Right views; both saw the Soviet Union, to use Reagan's words, as the 'evil Empire'; and sought to engage the Soviet Union in a new, accelerated arms race that would cripple the already overstretched Soviet economy. Blair and Clinton enjoyed cordial personal relations which were, despite differences, re-established with Clinton's successor in the White House, George W. Bush.

the shape of *Polaris* and *Trident*, advanced submarine-launched inter-continental ballistic missiles.

Britain in Europe

As the Commonwealth circle declined and the special relationship was redefined, so Britain adapted by giving greater prominence to the European circle. Britain's reluctant acceptance that its future lay in Europe generally, and in the EU in particular, has been examined in earlier chapters. Britain at first attempted without success to negotiate a wide free trade area, then established EFTA (the European Free Trade Association), before eventually deciding to apply for membership of the EEC. But, as the following sections illustrates, tensions still exist in British policy making between the demands of Atlanticism and Europeanism.

The impact of the EU on British government and politics is discussed in detail in Chapter 16. Here it is useful to consider two differing interpretations of Britain's involvement in the EU. On one hand, it is argued that British government is becoming 'Europeanised', with British practices becoming more like counterpart practices in Europe. Such similarities are not just the result of the conduct of policy through the EU or the integration that comes from Britain implementing EU Directives, but is much more the result of adopting the 'European way' of doing things. The counter-argument is that the EU is a limited organisation with a limited impact on British government. For example, most important policies including education, healthcare, social security and law and order are made by national governments. The EU is administered by relatively few bureaucrats, with the representatives of national governments making important EU decisions. In this sense, it is argued that the EU is an organisation with limited powers and few resources, which operates within a limited scope of policy making.

The EU versus NATO in British foreign and defence policies

In the recent past, British prime ministers have been classified as either being 'European' or 'Atlanticist' in their foreign policy outlook. Tony Blair seeks to reconcile the two, stating he is both a passionate European and a convinced pro-American. He sees British foreign policy having a main focus in both the USA and Europe, with Britain playing a bridging role in bringing cooperation between the political, economic and military superpower of the USA and the economic 'superpower' of the EU.

Since the EU was established as an economic association, it is not surprising that a common defence policy has been such an elusive goal. After the failure to establish a 'European Defence Community' in 1954, following the refusal by the French National Assembly to ratify it, the Western European Union (WEU), a ten-state military pact, symbolised the desire of western European states to act in unity on defence matters.

During the 1990s the European Union itself sought a more effective common foreign policy from the Maastricht Treaty onwards. The subsequent treaties of Amsterdam and Nice involved the development of a Common Foreign and Security Policy

---

BOX 26.2
The Western European Union

The Western European Union (WEU) has been an only occasionally influential body in European foreign and security policy since it was founded by the Treaty of Brussels in 1948, and later played a role in the creation of NATO. The failure of the European Defence Community in 1954 led to its revival, now including six member states of the European Coal and Steel Community (and soon the EEC) and the UK, but its relevance declined after the UK joined the EC in 1973. The WEU was reactivated in 1984. Portugal and Spain joined in 1990, and Greece in 1995 (making ten full members). There are also six Associate Members, all also members of NATO but (not yet) the EU, and five observers (members of the EU who are not members of NATO). The WEU has been a useful forum linking member states with NATO and other international organisations, and took an active role in the Balkans in the 1990s. The development of an EU Common Foreign and Security Policy (CFSP) and the on-going EU enlargement may reduce the scope for the WEU in future.

(CFSP). The European Council has determined that 'The Union must have the capacity for autonomous action, backed by credible military forces, the means to decide to use them, and a readiness to do so, in order to respond to international crises without prejudice to actions by NATO.' Part of the rationale for the capacity for EU military action was the experience of the problems in the former Yugoslavia, and the inability of the EU to deal with a crisis on its own doorstep. These plans received some criticism from the Conservative Party and sections of the media in Britain, which argued that this new EU initiative could lead to differences with NATO. To some extent, however, the CFSP reflected a realisation that the USA could not be expected to sort out all Europe's problems, and a fear, prior to 11 September 2001, that the USA might retreat into isolationism, as it had done previously between the wars.

However it has to be said that the EU has never played a large role in British foreign and defence policy. This is, perhaps, also because Britain and most other EU and WEU members are existing members of NATO. Many strategic thinkers do not believe that the EU structures have the potential for being the basis of Britain's foreign or defence policy. The EU has been described as an 'economic giant but a military worm' (Kegley and Wittkopf, 2000: 168). The massive spending gap between the USA and its Western European NATO allies sets the two apart. (See Figure 26.2.) In the 2002 budget, George W. Bush announced a further 14 per cent increase in US defence spending, creating a total annual defence budget of over $336 billion.

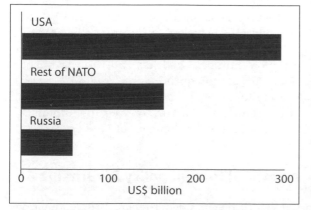

Figure 26.2 Defence expenditure, 2000

Source: data from *Guardian*, 13 February 2002.

Others have commented that a common security and defence policy, including Britain, remains impractical for the EU because it is too diverse an organisation. Having no robust defensive military role determines that, for the foreseeable future, Britain's external policies will remain played out within an Atlanticist framework with links to Europe. This tendency has been further reinforced by the 'war against terror' in which Blair's Britain has drawn closer to the USA and further apart from its European allies, especially over Iraq.

BOX 26.3
The views of Francis Fukuyama and Samuel Huntington

Francis Fukuyama is a leading American academic, noted for his 1989 essay *The End of History and the Last Man*. In many ways his ideas shaped the thinking of foreign and defence policy makers in the west in the immediate post cold war period. He observed that the 20th century was dominated by contests between communism, capitalism and fascism. With the end of fascism coming in 1945, and the end of communism in 1989 with the collapse of the Soviet Union, Fukuyama argued that we have reached the end of an historic contest in which liberalism and capitalism have succeeded: 'the century that began full of self-confidence in the ultimate triumph of Western liberal democracy seems at its close to be returning full circle to where it started: not to an "end of ideology" or a convergence between capitalism and socialism, as earlier predicted, but to the unabashed victory of economic and political liberalism' (Fukuyama, 1989: 3).

Following 11 September 2001, the ideas of Samuel P. Huntington assumed greater salience in thinking about the shape of the new world order. In *The Clash of Civilizations* (1996) he argued that ideological conflicts between superpowers would be replaced by broader struggles between cultures, such as between Islam and the west. His views are controversial and have been challenged by both American and British political scientists.

From new world order to the war on terror

The democratic revolutions that swept through Eastern Europe ended the ideological division of Europe which had existed since 1917. The old bipolar certainties of the cold war disappeared very rapidly; Germany reunited, the communist War-saw Treaty dissolved, and President Yeltsin announced that he wanted Russia to join NATO. History was moving fast and seemed to be leading to a new world order. But the Iraqi invasion of Kuwait, civil conflict in Serbia and Kosovo, the potential for ethnic turmoil within the Common-wealth as well as bloodshed in Central Africa, meant that aggression, instability and suffering remained the familiar ingredients of international politics. In many ways the stability of the cold war gave way to a new world disorder.

Britain and Europe's evolving relationship with Russia

NATO could have been seen as a redundant military alliance in the 1990s since its enemy, the communist Warsaw Pact countries, had collapsed. However NATO evolved, and found a new political and mili-tary purpose in enlargement and cooperation with former Warsaw Pact states. NATO remains impor-tant in European security affairs and is Britain's most important organisation for defence. In addition to being a defensive military organisation, NATO now has a role in crisis management, which means it can now respond to events in former Soviet republics in Central Asia as well as problems in its original Western European area.

In what ways might the reformed NATO bring increased political stability to Europe? First, NATO has enlarged its membership – to include Hungary, Poland and the Czech Republic – to help suppress nationalisms and bring both security and stability to Eastern Europe (see Box 26.4). Second, rather than isolate Russia, NATO has sought to include Russia in NATO affairs – but very much as a junior member. Russian membership of NATO is unlikely for the foreseeable future, as anti-NATO sentiment within Russia is still strong, especially among nationalists and communists in the state

Duma. The original Partnership for Peace (PfP) agreement for former Warsaw Pact members was replaced by the Euro-Atlantic Partnership Council (EAPC) and then became the landmark NATO-Russia Council (NATO-RC) in May 2002. This council gives Russia a full say in areas of NATO decision making but reserves full veto rights in some areas. Tony Blair initiated the idea of Russian involvement in NATO after meeting President Putin in 2001. The Pentagon initially balked at the idea, until after the terrorist attacks of 11 Septem-ber which gave the American military an entirely new perception of international threats facing America. It was then decided that closer ties with Russia could serve future American defence aims.

The three different organisations since 1990 that have included Warsaw Pact states (PfP, EAPC, NATO-RC) demonstrate the gradually developing closeness between Russia and NATO. Russia can now be called a partial member of NATO whereas 13 years ago Russia was the principal object of NATO's concern. Since 1997 Tony Blair has emphasised the need for Russia to receive distinct and separate relations with NATO, and not be 'bunched together' with other former Warsaw Pact states. Indeed, the British government had been at the forefront of aims to include Russia in NATO.

The USA, of course, remains the most important individual member of NATO, with American membership being crucial for NATO, yet America does not rely on NATO. The end of the cold war, continuing disarmament and subsequent decline in the importance of military might, as well as the new European members and the special relation-ship with Russia, have moved the alliance's 'centre of gravity' somewhat away from the America towards Europe. In other words, NATO is becom-ing more European and less American in orienta-tion. As a consequence, the Anglo-US special relationship is likely to become more important in Washington as a means of exerting diplomatic influence on the development of NATO.

An ethical foreign policy for Britain?

Can political values help to shape Britain's relations with other countries? In the past, Labour govern-ments found that socialist values were a poor guide

BOX 26.4
NATO membership status

Original 14 members

Belgium	Luxembourg
Canada	Netherlands
Denmark	Norway
France	Portugal
Germany	Spain
Iceland	United Kingdom
Italy	USA
Greece (1952)	Turkey (1952)

Original 14 members with Greece and Turkey joining in 1952. The alliance was created in 1949 to counter the Soviet-created European-based WTO. NATO is not specifically a collective security alliance but a military alliance that was formed to create an opposing bloc to the USSR. As an ideological alliance NATO needed a new purpose after the cold war. It found one in enlargement, while cooperation with WTO states replaced a policy of containment.

New members
Czech Republic
Hungary
Poland

Admitted in 1999. A landmark step seeing as all three were WTO members only ten years previously.

Future members
Bulgaria
Romania
Slovakia
Slovenia

These four states are expected to become full members in 5–15 years' time at varying stages. They are currently in accession talks with NATO.

Problematic future members
Estonia
Latvia
Lithuania

The Baltic republics began access negotiations with NATO in November 2002. The republics are keen for admission. Russia opposes full member status and would prefer partial membership for the republics. Russian concern is based around the isolated Russian port of Kaliningrad, which Baltic states membership would encircle by NATO states.

Russian relations
Belarus
Russia
Ukraine

These three can be called 'partial members' with NATO, although Russia and Ukraine are experiencing rapidly improving relations with NATO in the 21st century. Their changing relationship is reflected in their changing organisation: PfP ⇒ EAPC ⇒NATO-Russian Council. Belarus speaks of potential reunification with Russia and is not keen on NATO membership. Twenty-two others are involved with the EAPC including Croatia, Azerbaijan, Kazakhstan, Georgia and Modova.

to international politics (see Coxall and Robins,1988, ch. 11). When Blair's government took office in 1997 Labour's then Foreign Secretary, Robin Cook, declared that he wanted to put an ethical dimension into international politics by 'putting human rights at the heart of Britain's foreign policy'. The centrepiece of this approach was the promise not to sell arms to repressive regimes; in the hands of irresponsible governments imported arms have been used frequently to suppress the civilian population or aggressively against neighbouring countries.

Previous British ministers have been much less concerned over the moral arguments involved in selling arms abroad. Indeed, one minister was forthright in stating that he had few scruples about the consequences of arms sales when he declared his indifference: 'I don't really fill my mind much with what one set of foreigners is doing to another' (*Observer*, 18 May 1997). Other critics believe that Robin Cook's ethical foreign policy was merely political rhetoric, and indeed when the government faced the choice of promoting human rights abroad or saving thousands of jobs at home in the defence industry, the latter took priority. As with previous Labour governments, the Foreign Secretary's attempt to base policy on socialist values proved unworkable and was eventually discarded, only to be replaced by foreign policy based more on the 'realities' of what is in Britain's national interest, especially after Jack Straw replaced Cook as Foreign Secretary. Indeed Buller (in Ludlam and Smith, 2001: 231) concludes, 'Labour's record shows a rather depressing continuity with the activities of previous governments.'

The arms trade has shrunk globally since the end of the cold war. The need for arms to maintain a constant threat to an ideological enemy has evaporated. Since the demise of the Soviet Union, both Russia and the USA (as well as France and the UK) have made cuts in their stockpiles of nuclear warheads. The SORT agreement that replaced START-II in May 2002 cuts Russian and American nuclear warhead stockpiles by two-thirds. The demand for conventional military hardware (battle tanks, artillery, attack helicopters) has also diminished within NATO states and Russia. New markets have, however, opened up in the Third World which now consumes three-quarters of annual arms sales.

The arms trade is 'big business' for Britain which is the second largest supplier of arms in the world behind the USA. Contrary to the aspirations of Labour's ethical foreign policy, the realities of the international arms industry are that it is a highly competitive industry where there is little room for ethics. However, NGOs are pressuring governments to make their arms trade more transparent and to understand the consequences of where and to whom arms are sold. For New Labour, the difficulty of balancing the necessity of the arms trade against ethical considerations remains a largely unresolvable problem. Various solutions can ease the problem but

the arms trade will never be able to be labelled as truly ethical because of its inherent nature. Opening up the process of arms sales to inspection and scrutiny will make the trade more transparent: end-user licenses to ensure that arms reach their true destination and are not sold on is a new tactic being employed. Military hardware is now sold by British firms only if it meets certain guidelines (the guidelines are not legally but morally binding so it is possible for firms to contravene them) set down by the UN Register on Conventional Arms.

The New Labour government has, therefore, been more transparent than previous administrations regarding arms sales, but that has been a general trend in the post cold war trade in arms sales rather than a specific New Labour policy based on ethics. Over $280 billion of arms are sold globally each year. Britain (under John Major and continued under Tony Blair) has been at the forefront of international attempts to regulate and monitor international sales. The emphasis is still on monitoring sales rather than attempting to slow or decrease the amount of arms Britain sells each year. The UN Register on Conventional Arms and the Wassenaar Agreement require states to submit information on weapons in seven categories that they import and export. The Wassenaar Agreement has been described as an economic

---

BOX 26.5

The Ottawa Convention banning anti-personnel landmines

A component of New Labour's more ethically focused foreign policy was the signing and ratifying of the 1998 Ottawa Convention that bans the use, production, stockpiling and export of anti-personnel landmines (APLs). This major international treaty was a landmark in post cold war arms control because of its wide membership and quick negotiation (14 months). The presence of some 100–300 million APLs in 70 states worldwide was called an humanitarian disaster by the UN. APLs are not strategically vital for states like Britain, so signing and supporting the convention was an easy step to take, but one that supports New Labour's claims to be acting ethically in foreign policy.

arm of NATO, which seeks to regulate the sale of sensitive dual-use technology to states around the world.

The war on terror

It is generally agreed that potential for future world disorder lies in ethnic rivalries, guerrilla warfare and the international behaviour of the so-called 'axis of evil' regimes such as Iran, Iraq, Libya and North Korea. These states are clandestinely developing their biological, chemical and nuclear military capabilities in defiance of the Nuclear Non-Proliferation Treaty, the Chemical Weapons Convention and the Biological Weapons Convention. It has been estimated that 35 non-NATO countries now have ballistic missiles and that 18 of these have the capability of installing nuclear, biological or chemical warheads. As far as Britain and its western allies are concerned, this has resulted in a shift in US/NATO policy from trying to halt the proliferation of missile technology to trying to protect the west against a ballistic missile attack. The failure of the Missile Technology Control Regime has shown Britain and the west that unstable regimes can acquire missiles, and past defence doctrines such as mutually assured destruction (MAD) are no guarantees of security in such situations. The emphasis for Britain and NATO is now on defence rather than attempting to control the spread of technology.

The collapse of international communism in 1989 left a political vacuum in the global strategic order. Liberalism had triumphed, yet western governments including Britain were anxious about what would happen in the former republics of the Soviet Union. The majority of them turned to liberal democracy and painfully converted their collapsed economies into capitalist ones. This, coupled with China's rejection of isolationism and entrance into the World Trade Organisation, left Britain seeking a revised focus for policy making. After repeated military confrontation with Iraq from 1991 onwards, the question was answered on 11 September 2001 when Osama bin Laden and his al-Qaeda terrorist network struck the American homeland. This attack gave the USA, but also Britain, a new enemy on which to focus their defence policies.

Since his election in 2000, George W. Bush has followed more militaristic policies than his predecessor, while retaining the support of Britain. Bush has pursued a generally unilateralist foreign and defence policies under the banner of 'America First'. His administration identifies China and Russia as strategic competitors rather than partners, and has set out to tackle the threats posed by the so-called 'axis of evil' states. This new struggle not only justified the ballistic missile defence shield (BMD), but also demonstrated the more conflict-based world view held by Bush, which is not fully shared by either Britain or its EU partners. While the terrorist attack of 11 September has clearly reinforced the special relationship, it has taken on a clear senior–junior dynamic, with the US military and executive stating that British support is expected, but not necessary for US action. Blair's government, however, was directly involved in the war in Afghanistan and contributed to the massive military build-up in a show of strength over Iraq.

A major concern for British foreign policy makers following 11 September has been attempts to guide the USA into continued participation in the traditional western security frameworks. Although NATO allies were not consulted during the 2001 Afghan bombing campaign, Britain initially restrained US unilateral tendencies over Iraq, persuading the US government to pursue the UN route and weapons inspection. For Britain, then, a foreign policy priority post 11 September is to keep the USA involved in European and world affairs. While this has not yet affected the special relationship, it has made Tony Blair's relationship with Bush less close than that with Bill Clinton. Blair sees a multilateral approach to terrorism as most effective, with a more powerful UN enforcing international law. Bush prefers to override international institutions and act alone, or with the support of allies, but allies that are clearly subordinate. (See In Focus 26.1.)

British foreign and defence policies in the 21st century

There is no question that Britain has had to rethink its foreign and defence priorities after the events of 11 September 2001, especially as Britain was named as a possible target for further attack by al-Qaeda. On assuming office in 1997 Labour organised a

IN FOCUS 26.1 The special relationship survives?

Blair and Bush shake hands in a meeting in July 2001. It was widely assumed that the special relationship between Britain and the USA, which had thrived with Blair and Clinton, would cool after the inauguration of the Republican George W. Bush as President. Yet after the events of 11 September 2001 Blair emerged as the US administration's most dependable ally in the 'war against terror' both in Afghanistan and over Iraq. However, Blair's closeness to Bush in foreign policy, particularly over Iraq, has divided the UN, NATO, the EU and the Labour Party, and aroused massive hostile demonstrations in Britain.

Photograph: PA Photos.

strategic defence review (SDR), the first in 17 years. The SDR was aimed at structuring British foreign and defence commitments after the immense geopolitical shifts caused in 1989 by the end of the cold war. The SDR gave Britain a future defence outlook in regards to troop numbers, defence spending and the nuclear deterrent, but it became irrelevant in the changed global circumstances following 11 September. A particularly contentious part of the SDR was the cut in Territorial Army troops. Critics argued this could endanger home defence capabilities, a criticism raised four years before 11 September. The SDR did not consider the possibility of terrorist attack on the British mainland, or the threat of weapons of mass destruction being used by irresponsible regimes or terrorists.

There is no doubt that the consequences of 11 September have exposed gaps in the SDR and caused a rethink of British defence priorities. The focus for British policy in the 21st century is now twin-tracked. First, a priority of defence policy will be greatly increased homeland protection. This has two main paths: protecting the British homeland from potential attacks internationally, and terrorist attacks launched from within Britain. Protection from international threats will be secured through participation in the Bush administration's ballistic missile defence shield which calls for an upgraded early warning system to be built at Fylingdales.

The other path of homeland defence will be civilian defence and preparation against terrorist attacks. This will involve organised evacuations, protocol for chemical and biological weapon attacks by terrorists, as well the work of intelligence services in predicting and warning against attack such as that on the World Trade Center and the Pentagon on 11 September. Critics claim that currently there are massive gaps in British preparedness.

The second track priority involves pre-emptive military action against certain states in the world that pose a military threat. There has been talk of action against the 'axis of evil', perceived by Washington and London as dangerous regimes threatening the use of weapons of mass destruction. While there is no evidence that Iran, Iraq or North Korea could (or want to) reach the British homeland with ballistic missiles, there is a prevalent mood in defence decision makers' minds that action should be taken now rather than waiting until these states acquire a ballistic missile capability.

The twin-track approach to security for Britain poses the key dilemma in British foreign and defence policies of which track should take priority, for the inherent risk is for Britain to be preparing for the wrong war. By focusing on the 'axis of evil states' and BMD, British decision makers could be playing down the threat of terrorist attacks, and vice versa. Success in British defence policy in the

21st century will result from balancing priorities so as to meet potential threats from both rogue states and international terrorists. Critics of Blair's Iraq policy have argued that attacking Iraq, far from reducing the threat of terrorism, could actually increase it, if hostility to the USA and Britain intensified among Arabs and Muslims as a result, or if weapons of mass destruction fall into the hands of extremist factions amid the chaos of war.

Further reading

Berridge (1992) provides a useful account of the most important developments. Jones (1997) is a detailed examination of the importance of the USA in British politics. Sanders (1990) gives a comprehensive account of Britain's changing foreign policy. Accounts of the Blair Labour government's foreign and defence policies can be found in chapters by Christopher Hill and Lawrence Freedman in Seldon (2001), by Jim Buller in Ludlam and Smith (2001), and by Joanna Spear in Dunleavy et al. (2002).

Useful websites include the government departments the Foreign and Commonwealth Office <www.fco.gov.uk>, the Ministry of Defence <www.mod.gov.uk> and the Department for International Development <www.dfid.gov.uk>, and various international organisations such as NATO <www.nato.int>, the European Union <www. europa. eu.int>, the Western European Union <www.weu.int> and the United Nations <www. un.int>.

Chapter 27

Who governs? Power and the new British politics

Who gets what, when, how?	422
Top-down and bottom-up approaches to politics	423
Participating in politics	423
The power of the centre	424
Government and governance	426
Multi-level governance	427
The segmentation of public policy – policy communities	428
Governance and democracy	429
Democracy, equality and power	430
The future of British politics	431

In the opening chapter it was argued that politics was about power. At the end of this book are we any nearer to an answer to the question, who has power in Britain? Anyone who has read thus far should at least have learned how difficult it is to provide an easy answer to this apparently simple question. In this final chapter we will try to draw some of the principal themes of the book together, to recapitulate on some of the major questions surrounding British politics and government today, and to provide some tentative signposts to the future.

Who gets what, when, how?

Where then is power to be found in British politics today? One lesson is that power does not necessarily lie where it appears to lie. Back in the 19th century Walter Bagehot wrote a brilliant book in which he sought to strip away the illusions people had about British government (1963, originally published 1867). He distinguished between what he called the dignified and efficient parts of the constitution. His point was that some parts – the monarchy, and increasingly the House of Lords –

were largely for show; they no longer involved real power. For Bagehot the efficient secret of the constitution was the Cabinet. This was the real centre of power. Bagehot's readers found his account so convincing that it became the new orthodoxy. British government was Cabinet government. A book that began as an exercise in debunking old assumptions became the new received opinion.

Yet Bagehot, if he was right, had only provided a snapshot of British government at a particular moment in time. A century later another sceptical observer of British politics, Richard Crossman (1963), wrote an introduction to a new edition of Bagehot's work in which he argued that the Cabinet had joined the dignified elements of the British Constitution. Cabinet government had been replaced by prime ministerial government. Again, of course, he was not necessarily right. Crossman himself soon had first-hand experience as a leading member of Harold Wilson's government, and the evidence of his voluminous diaries is rather ambivalent on the issue of Cabinet government (Crossman, 1975/7).

From another perspective the arguments of Bagehot and Crossman on the role of the Cabinet tell us very little about real political power. Bagehot was a contemporary of another keen observer of politics, Karl Marx. Marx was hardly concerned at all with constitutional theory and the relative importance of particular governmental institutions. For Marx, political power reflected economic power. Power in 19th-century Britain lay with the capitalists (or bourgeoisie). The state and its political institutions served the interests of this ruling class. Parliament, for Marx, was simply a committee for discussing the common affairs of the bourgeoisie. It is very different view of politics and power. Had a 19th-century Jeremy Paxman managed to get Bagehot and Marx into the same studio, the encounter may have been fascinating but perhaps not very illuminating, as they were proceeding from such different theoretical assumptions, with few if any points of contact. A similar encounter between a modern Marxist such as the historian Eric Hobsbawm and a modern Bagehot, perhaps Peter Hennessy, would be in all probability equally unproductive.

Top-down and bottom-up approaches to politics

Peter Hennessy's book *The Prime Minister* (2000) exemplifies what might be called a top-down approach to politics. He is concerned with power at the centre. Thus in a series of diagrams and accompanying text he describes the changing circles of influence in Tony Blair's government – who's in and who's out. To some, this is the very stuff of politics. It reflects a widespread fascination with the men (and occasionally women) at the top of the greasy pole of politics, as demonstrated by the continuing market for the memoirs and biographies of dead and still-living leading British politicians. Nor is the interest necessarily misplaced. Personality matters. The decisions made (and sometimes ducked) by those at the top can have momentous consequences. If Churchill had not become Prime Minister Britain might well have made peace with Hitler, and the future of Britain and the world could have been very different. Eden's personal responsibility for Suez or Margaret Thatcher's for the Falklands or the poll tax are scarcely of the same order of magnitude, but they did have important consequences for British politics all the same, not least for those politicians themselves.

Yet a focus on great men and women has its limitations. For a start it grossly exaggerates their power to achieve change. Hitler's regime was not ultimately defeated by the big three of Churchill, Roosevelt and Stalin, but by millions of ordinary combatants and civilians. The final allied victory had much more to do with the endurance of Russian soldiers or the productivity of American factory workers than Churchillian rhetoric. Moreover, the focus on leaders seems to restrict the scope of politics. Politics, we are told, is a universal human activity. It should concern us all, yet many people

seem uninterested in, or, worse still, alienated by politics, especially, it seems, many young people. It may be because politics often seems to be about 'them' rather than 'us' – top people making decisions which, it often appears, we can do little to influence.

Other approaches to the study of history and politics focus on broader social and economic processes – on the masses rather than a handful of leaders, on the crowd rather than the individuals who seek to influence the crowd. E. P. Thompson (1963) charted the growth of a politically conscious English working class through the activities of small radical societies and groups of rural and urban artisans. Eric Hobsbawm (1984) began as a labour historian, examining groups and individuals who contributed to the rising political weight of trade unions and the labour movement.

It does not follow that one or other approach is necessarily right or wrong, although they are both inevitably partial. A full understanding of politics arguably has to involve both the view from top and from the grass roots. To an extent this is what most mainstream accounts of British politics (including this one) strive to provide. Thus we have sought to describe and explain both the broader political process in Part II and the apparently rather narrower governmental process, focusing first on the traditional centre of power in Whitehall and Westminster in Part II, and second on the developing system of multi-level governance in Part IV. The chapters on policy in Part V bring together, to varying degrees, both the top-down and bottom-up approaches to politics.

Participating in politics

One of the central concerns in Part II was the scope for popular participation in the political process and for effective influence in the framing and implementation of public policy – essentially the potential for effective democracy. While Chapter 5 reviewed various channels for citizen participation and possible reasons for alienation and apathy, Chapters 6 and 7 focused on elections and voting, central to the whole concept of representative as opposed to direct democracy. A key issue here was the extent to which the electoral system and participation through the ballot box enabled government and public policy to reflect the will of the people, or at least the will of the majority. Some questions were raised here over the fairness of the electoral machinery and over declining turnout levels.

Political parties, reviewed in Chapter 8, are still clearly important in terms of power as government remains party government. It remains to be seen whether the 1997 election marks a substantial turning point in the evolution of the British party system. The Conservatives could bounce back, as they have so frequently done in the past. Labour dominance may replace the Conservative dominance familiar for most of the 20th century. It is even possible that the Liberal Democrats could replace the Conservatives as the main opposition. Further electoral reform could increase the representation of minor parties and make coalition government the norm, as it already is throughout almost all the rest of Europe.

Yet it does not seem that the wider British public is any longer passionately involved in party futures. Once political parties provided a crucial link between the governors and the governed, for they offered a recognised and legitimate channel for participation by ordinary citizens in the political process, through their actively engaged mass membership. Of course, there were always questions about the effectiveness of that participation and the responsiveness of the leadership to the rank and file. Yet the problem today is not so much the extent of internal party democracy but the failure of the parties to engage with most people at all, for even the major parties have ceased to be mass parties in any meaningful sense.

Today, more people are prepared to engage in politics through organised groups than political parties. The scale and passion of some pressure group activity (discussed in Chapter 9) may be taken as an indication of a vibrant pluralist democracy. Some of the more dramatic or effective manifestations of pressure group politics have been cited earlier in this book – the anti-poll tax protests which contributed to the downfall of Margaret Thatcher, the Snowdrop petition (following the Dunblane massacre) which led to the ban on handguns, the fuel protests which shook the Blair government in 2000, the Countryside Alliance demonstration of September 2002, which was claimed to be the largest in living memory. It could be claimed that all these began as spontaneous popular protests from below. As one placard proclaimed at the Countryside Alliance, 'The peasants are revolting.' Yet sceptics might respond that many participants in that demonstration did not look much like peasants. One problem with pressure group politics is that they almost inevitably involve minorities, even if often sizeable and vociferous minorities, who are not necessarily representative of the majority.

Although parties and pressure groups both have some positive and negative characteristics (see Box 27.1), they perform different roles in the political process, and their contribution to democracy is perhaps best seen as complementary rather than competitive.

Among other issues discussed in Part II, the role of the mass media (examined in Chapter 10) in the relationship between rulers and ruled, or elite and mass, remains particularly contentious. The mass media are alternatively seen as the voice of the people or an elite instrument for manipulating and misrepresenting the views of the people, a crucial element in the democratic process or a key means by which the interests of the majority are negated or subverted. The answer to the question of media influence will tend to reflect assumptions derived from rival models of the role of the mass media in modern society, although some suggestive evidence on media ownership and case studies of media influence were reviewed in the chapter.

The power of the centre

Part III focused on those at the heart of government – prime ministers, ministers, top civil servants, MPs, members of the judiciary, those who form the cast lists of numerous memoirs and biographies. Here the emphasis was on the relationship between individuals and institutions among a small governing elite. Has prime ministerial government replaced Cabinet government? Are top civil servants more influential than elected politicians? Has the power of Parliament declined? Can the judiciary effectively restrain the executive? These questions are hardly new. They have figured in textbooks and in examination questions on British

BOX 27.1

Parties and pressure groups: power, influence and democracy

Political parties seek power:

- They engage directly in the democratic process by pursuing the support of majorities to secure the election of party candidates with the ultimate aim of establishing a party government and controlling public policy.
- Representative democracy would be virtually impossible without them.
- However, today they only engage the masses in the political process through elections.
- Few join parties and even fewer actively participate in them. Thus activists are unrepresentative of voters.
- Moreover, despite commitments to internal democracy, effective power is (perhaps inevitably) concentrated at the centre.

Pressure groups seek influence rather than power:

- While elections offer voters only an occasional highly limited and blunt choice, there is an almost limitless choice of groups for citizens to join.
- Group influence can be continuous in promoting specific interests and causes.
- Many more people are actively engaged in politics through groups than through parties.
- Groups thus play a crucial role in pluralist theories of democracy.
- However, groups serve sectional minority interests rather than the majority.
- There are significant inequalities in resources, organisational capacities and influence between groups.
- There are elitist tendencies within groups – leaders are generally unelected and may be unrepresentative of members.

government for half a century or more. They are in one sense perennial issues at the heart of government. This does not mean that nothing new can be said about them. Constitutional change and changes in the machinery of government, as well as more subtle changes in assumptions and behaviour, are likely to alter the balance of arguments over time. Changes in domestic and even global political circumstances may alter the scope of particular posts. Beyond that, much inevitably reflects the personalities and inter-relationship of individuals.

Some views are perhaps less fashionable than they were. To take one example, the bureaucratic model of power was influential 20 years or so, both among the political elite (partly through the persuasive public choice theory and bureaucratic over-supply model of Niskanen and others) and among the masses (largely perhaps through the popular television series *Yes, Minister* and *Yes, Prime Minister*). The arguments seem less persuasive now, partly because the civil service did not seem particularly effective at defending its own interests in the face of Conservative reforms in the 1980s and 1990s, and partly because those reforms have further limited the power and influence of leading civil servants. Indeed, the *Yes, Minister* thesis became widely accepted at the very time when it was already effectively destroyed. Today's political satire assumes that it is not the 'Sir Humphreys' of Whitehall who manipulate their elected leaders, but 'spin doctors' and press spokespersons, the Mandelsons and Campbells of New Labour (although this new cynical reality may also be already out of date). Yet if the power of the senior civil service now seems less obvious, the continuing inter-relationship of elected politicians and appointed civil servants at the heart of government remains an important issue.

Fashions in politics (as in clothes) come and go. Debates over prime ministerial power have waxed and waned through successive governments. Margaret Thatcher's dominance appeared to confirm the prime ministerial power thesis, until her abrupt fall apparently refuted it. Major's government appeared to confirm prime ministerial impotence in the face of open Cabinet dissent and backbench revolt, and inspired some wider speculation about the weakness of the office and the hollowing out of the centre of British government (Rhodes, 1997). Since 1997 there have been talk of a Blair presidency (Hennessy, 2000) and criticism of New

Labour 'control freaks'. The change does perhaps reflect some substance – the different personality of the holder, the altered electoral and Parliamentary circumstances after 1997, and perhaps some changes in the machinery of government. Yet the issues and arguments are much the same as they always were. It has long been the case that much depends on what the holder makes of the office, and on domestic and international political circumstances. All these has perhaps combine to enhance the perceived power of the prime minister. However, it was noted in Chapter 12 that Blair's power is less evident over the economy. Moreover, devolution involves some reduction in the scope of the UK prime minister, which could have further political implications if the British state moves further along the quasi-federal road.

All these issues and many more can be illuminated by a thorough survey of the different kinds of evidence, but it is virtually impossible to measure in any objective and effective way the distribution of political power. Sometimes it may appear from the focus on leaders that government is a closed shop, the concern of a limited elite – as indeed theorists like Pareto or Michels always maintained. Thus public policy can be explained largely in terms of the internal dynamics of government – who won which battle in Cabinet or Whitehall. Yet from another perspective the freedom of manoeuvre of governments can seem very limited. Wilson's government in 1967 and Major's in 1992 failed to defend the parity of the pound sterling, despite their best efforts. This might emphasise the impersonal power of the market, of currency dealers making their own assessment of the health and future of sterling, disregarding official government pronouncements. Other defining moments in post-war British political history may reflect the power of unions (e.g. the failure of the Wilson and Heath industrial relations reforms), or business, or public opinion, either expressed through the ballot box or in some other way.

Government and governance

To an extent the new governance literature (described particularly in Chapters 18 and 19 of Part III) transcends the traditional divide between

BOX 27.2
People power or business power?

Inevitably the answer to this question rests on initial assumptions. Much depends on the particular case studies selected, and even more on their interpretation. Business influence may be less visible and vocal than other interests, but may be more effective.

People power?
- Replacement of poll tax – 'people power' shown through demonstrations, tax evasion, the ballot box (local elections, Parliamentary by-elections) and opinion polls.
- Ban on handguns following Dunblane shooting – 'people power' shown through 'Snowdrop petition', other pressure group influence and opinion polls which persuaded the Major government to implement a partial ban and the Blair government a total ban.
- The fuel protests of September 2000 – a more dubious case, but apparent public support for the protest influenced the government to abandon planned further increases in fuel duty. (Note also, however, the ambivalent role of the fuel companies, and the kid glove treatment of blockades by the police.)

Business power?
- Edwina Currie's resignation over salmonella in eggs in 1988 – she was sacked as Health Minister following pressure from outraged producer and retailer interests, after she had declared that most egg production was infected by salmonella. (She may have been substantially correct at the time.)
- Compensation of Railtrack shareholders, 2001 – initially it appeared that Railtrack shareholders would receive little or no compensation following the collapse of the company in autumn 2001, but a compensation package was agreed after pressure from business and financial interests. It was suggested that the government would find it more difficult to raise private finance for other public investment if such compensation was refused.

the governmental and wider political process, or between governors and governed. Governance is an activity, not an institution. It is an activity in which ministers and civil servants may be involved but which also often involves businesses, voluntary organisations and community groups. It emphasises cooperation rather than coercion, networks rather than hierarchies, inclusion rather than exclusion. Power, by implication, is diffused rather than centralised.

Where does the new governance leave old government? In some respects government appears weaker. The shift towards 'governance' partly reflects an ideological reaction against the growth of government on the one hand and an increased realisation of the practical constraints on government on the other. This no longer involves just the issue of the location of power within government, but the power of government or the state itself, and the balance between the public sector and the private sector or between the state and civil society. There are limits to what governments can or should do. Governments should seek to enable rather than provide, 'steer' rather than 'row', and should work with the private and the voluntary sector in partnerships and networks. In the process the distinction between government and non-government is eroded. Instead of a clear dividing line between what is the state and what is not the state, there is subtle gradation running from government departments through semi-autonomous public agencies, quangos, public–private partnerships, voluntary organisations (sometimes partly funded by the state), professional bodies (often effectively licensed by the state), and private firms in a contractual relationship with some part of government (Rhodes, 1997).

In such a complex world the old boundaries are blurred and it is difficult to determine what exactly is government anymore. Moreover, there is no transparent chain of command, as there used to be in hierarchically organised departments. While it is possible to list the participants in partnerships and networks, it is much more difficult to be clear about the balance of power within and between them. Who calls the shots in the new governance? There is considerable divergence of views. Some argue that the state has been 'hollowed out', others that it has been 'filled in' (by, among other developments, the proliferation of task forces). Some suggest an increased governmental capacity to deliver policies, others emphasise the relative impotence of ministers and government collectively, partly because so many executive activities have been hived off to quasi-independent agencies. It could be argued that it is still too early to judge the results of some recent initiatives – the reforms in the NHS, the increased reliance on the private finance initiative for new investment in the public sector – and the balance of power and influence may be clearer in due course. Others see enhanced business power or professional dominance behind the new more complex structures.

Multi-level governance

Arguments over the location of power in the new British politics are further complicated by the increased importance of new levels of governance. Governance operates not only across sectors but at an increasing number of levels. As Part III of this book emphasised, power in government was once largely a matter of determining the current relationship between individuals and institutions at the centre of London, in the relatively small world of Westminster and Whitehall. The only other level of government that seemed to count at all was local government, in town or county halls. Although there was a continuing debate over 'central–local relations' and some apparent shifts over time, the general consensus was that local government was clearly subordinate and only enjoyed a very limited or qualified autonomy (see Chapter 18).

The position of local government may not have changed very much, or may even have grown more impotent, as many have argued. Its future remains clouded. However, there is no longer a simple bipolar relationship between British central and local government. On the one hand the European Union has become a steadily more important influence on British public policy since the UK joined in 1973. The power exercised in Westminster and Whitehall is increasingly constrained by decisions taken in Brussels, Strasbourg and Luxembourg. On the other hand, devolution within the United Kingdom has set up a series of national or provincial assemblies and executives, operating between Whitehall and town hall. The implications for the UK state are profound and contentious. If membership of the EU undermines UK national sovereignty, devolution could lead to the end of 'British' government and politics. Alternatively it could lead to a quasi-federal Britain, possibly including a significant English regional level of government. Yet already there has been some shift in power away from Whitehall and Westminster to Edinburgh, to Cardiff (to a markedly lesser degree) and (precariously) to Stormont. In Northern Ireland the peace process has initiated a significant shift in power relations within and between communities.

These changes are obvious and dramatic, even if their long-term implications remain far from clear. Yet multi-level governance is not just about the European Union and devolution but also involves a host of other changes in the process of governance, of which much of the public is only dimly aware. This is sometimes referred to in rather pejorative terms as 'quangocracy' or the 'new magistracy' or the 'regulatory state' (see Chapters 18 and 19). It involves certainly more managerial delegation, in keeping with the ideas of the new public management and theories of governance. Sometimes managerial delegation involves geographical decentralisation. Giving more authority over decisions to those in the front line of delivering services implies some decentralisation in the health and education services. In the case of education this has meant giving more power to the governing bodies of institutions (but arguably in practice to heads or principals) at the expense of local elected authorities. In the case of health it involves a transfer of power away from the centre (in theory at least) to hospital trusts and more recently primary care trusts. There has been a proliferation of other local bodies – housing associations, learning and skills councils, effectively autonomous police authorities. All this may be regretted as involving a bypassing of local government, but it appears to be an aspect more of the fragmentation of government (and power?) than of its centralisation. It is another dimension of multi-level governance. Decisions affecting the lives of citizens of the United Kingdom can now be taken at a number of levels, some local or institutional.

The segmentation of public policy – policy communities

The fragmentation of governance makes it rather more difficult to discuss British politics in terms of a single system of decision making or a single model of power. It is feasible that policy making and the distribution of power vary between services or functions, some of which were reviewed in Part V of this book.

Each major public service or area of public policy involves its own distinctive cast of players which constitute a policy community. Thus it could be argued that there is a health policy community, an education policy community, a transport policy community. Each of these policy communities may contain a major government department, several executive agencies, a range of quangos, local elected and/or appointed bodies, as well as a range of pressure groups representing managers, professionals, workers, client groups, and private sector and voluntary organisations. While it is possible that there is a similar distribution of power and influence within all the major communities, and they all fit one particular model, it is also possible that there are some significant variations. For example, it has been argued (rightly or wrongly) that elite specialisms within the medical profession used to dominate decision making in the health service, that the old Ministry of Agriculture, Fisheries and Food had been effectively captured by the National Farmers Union, and that the Department of Transport was dominated by motoring interests. Such judgements may be facile or perhaps outdated, but the fact that they have been made suggests that the balance of power and influence may vary within different policy communities.

However, the examples selected imply that there also may be significant changes over time in particular policy communities (as should be clear from the policy chapters in Part V). An ostensible aim of the Conservative reforms of the health service was to give more power to patients through market mechanisms. The extent of patient or consumer power in services like health or education is perhaps contentious, although it seems more significant than formerly. Moreover, it is widely conceded that managers on the one hand and other professional groups (such as nurses and paramedics) have gained

Table 27.1 The transport policy community in Britain: some key players

Government department and associated agencies	Department of Transport Highways Agency
Other government bodies	EU Transport Directorate (DG VII) Scottish and Welsh Transport Departments Regional English government (GOs, RDAs) Local authorities
Road interests	Society of Motor Manufacturers and Traders British Road Federation Road Haulage Association Road builders etc. Motoring organisations (AA, RAC etc.)
Rail interests	Train operating companies Network Rail Rail regulators Rail unions Passenger groups
Other transport and environmental interests	Transport 2000 British Waterways Countryside Alliance Ramblers Association

influence in health decision making at the expense of the old medical elite. With regard to transport, it is plausible that the replacement of a Conservative government by a Labour government has somewhat altered the weight attached to public transport as compared with motor manufacturing interests (although not enough, environmentalists would argue). Finally, with regard to agriculture it is at least arguable that a series of damaging food scares has reduced the influence of producer interests and forced government to pay more attention to consumer concerns, which were a significant factor in establishing the Food Standards Agency, and in 2001 replacing the old Ministry of Agriculture, Fisheries and Food with the new Department of the Environment, Food and Rural Affairs.

If the distribution of power and influence varies significantly between policy communities and over time then it is difficult to characterise British government and politics in terms of some single model – elitism, pluralism, consumer sovereignty, bureaucracy or whatever. Elected politicians may call the shots in one service, public sector bureaucrats in

another, business interests in a third. More plausibly, however, there is a more messy and fluctuating balance of interests and influences in each policy community.

Governance and democracy

If old-style British government may seem to enjoy less power, what are the implications for democracy under new-style governance? Is government's loss the people's gain? Once more the answer depends to a degree on initial assumptions. For those who have always seen government and the state as a real or potential threat to the freedom of the individual, the fragmentation of government and the new emphasis on governance are undoubted goods. Instead of one over-mighty state staffed by a powerful and self-seeking bureaucracy there is a diffusion of power, and a pluralist plethora of competing public, quasi-public, private and voluntary bodies. Social democrats, by contrast, have generally assumed that the state can be captured and effectively controlled to serve the interests of the majority. A weakening of the state thus weakens the capacity of the state to deliver services to the people, and particularly its capacity to achieve a significant redistribution of income and wealth. Yet this of course is precisely why free market liberals welcome the weakening of the state – they do not believe redistribution is a legitimate function of the state, but rather see redistribution as an illegitimate interference with individual freedom and property.

The rhetoric surrounding governance suggests that it is all about engaging and involving the public, devolving and delegating power to ordinary people as voters, citizens, consumers or patients. However, administrative and geographical decentralisation by itself, even if actively and sincerely pursued (and there has been some room for doubt on this score in Britain), does not necessarily entail more influence and participation for ordinary people. Partly this is just a restatement of the argument (above) about quangocracy and the new magistracy. Power may have been transferred, and sometimes transferred downwards, but often to appointed businesspeople, professionals or middle managers rather than elected representatives or the people themselves. There may be no effective accountability to the public or democratic control. Delegating power to front-line workers or some local appointed body does not necessarily give more power to people as voters, consumers or service users. It may even have the opposite effect if producer or professional interests are strengthened.

The language of governance suggests consultation, cooperation and compromise rather than coercion, and appears highly compatible with public participation, which offers the prospect of a richer form of democracy than through the limited mechanism of the ballot box. Partnerships and networks provide more scope for individuals to get involved in services and policy areas that affect or concern them. Yet periodic attempts to secure wider public participation have generally met with limited success. Critics argue that the public have generally been offered only token rather than genuine participation, and tokenism breeds apathy. Yet participation requires commitment, and entails costs, and it is difficult to sustain these on a longer-term basis.

In the last resort other forms of public involvement in the process of governance can only supplement

rather than replace representative democracy through the ballot box, for all its shortcomings (which have been amply documented in these pages). Multi-level governance, as we have seen, has provided some additional opportunities for voting, and led to the introduction of more proportional representation for devolved assemblies and the European Parliament. Yet despite, or conceivably partly because of, these reforms, turnout figures declined notably in the 1999 European elections and the 2001 general election. One possible explanation is that the proliferation of elections under the new multi-level governance has led to diminishing returns. Plausibly this is the result not just of apathy but of an understandable increasing confusion over who does what, exacerbated by the shifting boundaries and functions of public authorities. Devolution, delegation, the proliferation of agencies and task forces, the growth of networks and public–private partnership have all made it more difficult for ordinary members of the public to get to grips with government. Reforms intended to involve the public may sometimes have had the reverse effect. There are disturbing indications that a growing section of the electorate are becoming disengaged from mainstream politics.

Democracy, equality and power

From a radical left-wing or Marxist perspective, little of the above analysis is particularly relevant to the real location of power in government and society. The orthodox Marxist position would seem to have little to do with the argument over the functions and organisation of the state between free market neo-liberals and social democrats. After all, if political power reflects economic power, the way the state is organised hardly matters very much. Those with economic power will continue to control the political process at every level, European, UK, devolved national, regional and local. Corporate power will continue to call the shots, rather than the majority of voters at any level.

While both Marxists and social democrats favour some redistribution of income and wealth, Marxists, unlike social democrats, simply do not believe that the state will be able to achieve it to any significant degree in a capitalist economy and society. They have some evidence on their side. How far effective redistribution was taking place in the decades immediately after the Second World War is a matter of some dispute. What would be widely conceded by neo-liberals, social democrats and Marxists alike is that over the last quarter of a century or so, British society has not become more equal, but if anything inequality of income has widened. This, Marxists would argue, reflects the continuing power of business.

Neo-liberals do not dispute the extent of inequality, but argue that this is functional to enterprise and growth. A more equal society would be a more impoverished society. The gap between rich and poor might be reduced but people on average would be worse off. As it is, neo-liberal advocates of the free market argue, the prosperity of the rich in a free capitalist society 'trickles down' to benefit the poor. Social democrats might dispute this optimistic assumption, but have some problems in explaining why they have not been more successful in creating a more equal society.

For British social democrats, exclusion from power for 18 years after 1979 provides an alibi, although some controversy surrounds the aims and achievements of New Labour from 1997. Critics argue that Blair and New Labour have substituted equality of opportunity for equality of outcome, that they have deliberately sought to woo business and that this has ruled out redistribution. By contrast, both some New Labour apologists and critics on the right have claimed that New Labour has pursued redistribution by stealth – that Gordon Brown's budgets have had a significant redistributive effect. More recently, Blair himself has openly embraced the language of redistribution. It is still too early to tell how far expressed concerns are translated into reality. Yet how far a party in government is able to fulfil some of the aspirations of those who voted for it is one benchmark for measuring the impact of representative democracy.

The future of British politics

It has long been assumed that modern politics revolves around economic issues, and government performance on the economy. Yet some of the most passionate political differences now seems to revolve around what has been called the politics of identity rather than the politics of materialism. Of course, it may be the case that some of the differences that have arisen over issues of national, ethnic, cultural or religious identity reflect economic differences and material deprivation. Yet this does not seem to be the whole answer. Today identity politics seem to be increasingly at the heart of some of the major problems confronting the British government and state.

The future of British politics has been a recurring question throughout this book. Until very recently only a handful of revolutionaries, fanatical Europhobes or optimistic Celtic nationalists would have thought to ask whether British politics has a future. The fortunes of parties might fluctuate, some institutions might be reformed, but it was widely assumed the British state would survive for the imaginable future. It may do, but it can no longer be taken for granted that it will.

It used widely to be assumed that Britain was a nation, and the United Kingdom some kind of nation-state (albeit one with some peculiar features). Yet Britain and the symbol of Britannia were only reinvented in the 17th century, and more positively embraced in the 18th century after the Act of Union with Scotland. There is nothing particularly unusual about this. The forging of new national identities has been a feature of much of the world over the last few centuries. With the conspicuous exception of many Irish, allegiance to the British state was largely voluntary and enthusiastic, although it never fully replaced other older identities. Now the United Kingdom is itself a member of another much larger European Union, and rising support for Scottish and Welsh nationalism has led to meaningful political devolution to Edinburgh and Cardiff. Some fear that the European Union is developing into a superstate which will destroy British national sovereignty, others that devolution will prove a slippery slope towards the break-up of the United Kingdom. While disintegration is one possibility, another is that a federal Britain will become part of a federal Europe. At the very least, British politics and government have become more complex, and can no longer be related almost exclusively to the world of Westminster and Whitehall.

It may be argued that what is happening in Britain is happening in many other parts of the world. Other states too are faced with global and supranational pressures on the one hand and on the hand internal pressures to devolve more power and autonomy to nations or regions within their borders. Perhaps the whole concept of a world of sovereign independent nation-states is the product of a particular passing phase of historical development and has become outdated in the new world of global markets and global communications. Before the modern nation-state emerged, much of the world was familiar with a hierarchy of authority. Multi-level governance may be seen as a return to this older state of affairs. Multiple allegiances to different levels of government may be seen as matching the multiple identities which many seem to feel. Yet, as has been noted, nationalism with its claims to a more exclusive identity and allegiance has proved a remarkably resilient ideology.

Old national borders are not the only fault lines within British politics. Newer ethnic divisions cut across these older national allegiances. The total non-white population of the UK (now over 4 million) already exceeds the total population of Wales and Northern Ireland and is not far below that of Scotland. While the proportion of the population of England that is non-white is greater than the proportion in Scotland or Wales, ethnic tensions and racial prejudice are a feature of all three countries. In many respects these divisions seem to pose a more dangerous threat to the future of British politics. The recognition and willing acceptance of the new reality of a multi-cultural and multi-ethnic Britain seems the only realistic alternative to corrosive inter-community tensions. Yet the old notion of Britain as a 'mongrel race' may make multi-cultural Britain an easier concept to accept than a multi-cultural England or even a multi-cultural Europe.

Further reading

It is difficult to recommend further reading here, as most of this chapter has been concerned with picking up on themes developed earlier in the book. Most of the sources cited have already been mentioned before, some several times over in different chapters. For anyone seeking to understand British government and politics at the beginning of the 21st century, and where it might be heading, the following may be recommended or re-recommended, in no particular order. Will Hutton's *The State We're In* (1995) was an unexpected best-seller which sparked off renewed debate over the British economic and political system, and gave impetus to the debate over stakeholding. Some of the follow-up literature from Hutton and others is also worth looking at. Rod Rhodes' *Understanding Governance* (1997) is a collection of the author's articles which is still perhaps the best introduction to the governance debate and the ways in which the British state and political system may be changing. The debate over devolution and the future of Britain needs regular updating, but a fascinating if very weighty historical guide to the relationship between the peoples of the 'British' Isles is provided in Norman Davies' *The Isles* (2000). Those daunted by its size might try dipping into the later chapters and the extensive but well-chosen appendices. Antony Giddens' *The Third Way* (1998) is a very different kind of book, slim and broad-brush in approach, but which touches on many of the key concepts which have figured in recent and on-going political debate, including globalization, governance, exclusion, social investment and of course the 'third way'. As with Hutton's book, there is an extensive follow-up literature from Giddens himself and others.

Mention of the 'third way' leads on naturally to Blair and New Labour. None of these items featured in the index of the first edition of this book (1989) when Margaret Thatcher's Conservative government still reigned supreme, which emphasises how the political landscape can be transformed in a comparatively short time. Some of the best accounts of Thatcherism only appeared shortly before or after the end of Thatcher's long premiership, and almost certainly the best book on New Labour or 'Blairism' has yet to be written. In the interim, the collections of essays edited by Steve Ludlam and Martin Smith (*New Labour in Government*, 2001 and *Governing as New*

Labour, 2003) and by Anthony Seldon (2001) provide very useful guides, while Andrew Rawnsley's *Servants of the People* (2001) gives a readable and provocative narrative account of the first term. Peter Hennessy's book on *The Prime Minister* (2000) focuses on the premiership since 1945, but usefully discusses the debate over the Blair 'presidency' within that broader context. Such sources however can rapidly date, and readers are advised to refer to updating books such as the *Developments in British Politics* series (Palgrave) and the annual publication *Developments in Politics* (Causeway Press), as well as articles in journals and the quality press.

Bibliography

Adams, I. (1998) *Ideology and Politics in Britain Today* (Manchester: Manchester University Press).

Adonis, A. (1993) *Parliament Today*, 2nd edn (Manchester: Manchester University Press).

Alderman, K. (1995) 'The government whips', *Politics Review*, 4:4, April.

Allison, G. T. (1971) *Essence of Decision* (Boston: Little, Brown).

Almond, G. and Verba, S. (1965) *The Civic Culture* (Boston and Toronto: Little, Brown).

Anderson, A. (1997) *Media, Culture and Environment* (London: UCL Press).

Annual Abstract of Statistics (London: HMSO).

Arblaster, A. (1987) *Democracy* (Buckingham: Open University Press).

Ascher, K. (1987) *The Politics of Privatisation* (Basingstoke: Macmillan).

Bachrach, P. and Baratz, M. (1971) *Power and Poverty: Theory and Practice* (London: Oxford University Press).

Back, L. and Solomos, J. (2000) *Theories of Race and Racism: A Reader* (London: Routledge).

Bagehot, W. (1867/1963) *The English Constitution* (London: Fontana).

Baggott, R. (1995) *Pressure Groups Today* (Manchester: Manchester University Press).

Baker, A. (2000) 'Globalization and the British "residual state"', pp. 362–73 in R. Stubbs and G. Underhill (eds), *Political Economy and the Changing Global Order*, 2nd edn (Oxford: Oxford University Press).

Barberis, P. (ed.) (1996) *The Whitehall Reader* (Buckingham: Open University Press).

Barnett, A. (1997) *This Time: Our Constitutional Revolution* (London: Vintage, Random House).

Bash, L. and Coulby, D. (1989) *The Education Reform Act: Competition and Control* (London: Cassell).

Beer, S. (1982a) *Modern British Politics* (London: Faber and Faber).

Beer, S. (1982b) *Britain Against Itself: The Political Contradictions of Collectivism* (London: Faber and Faber).

Bell, D. (1960) *The End of Ideology* (New York: Free Press).

Benn, T. (1980) 'The case for a constitutional premiership', *Parliamentary Affairs*, 33:1, Winter.

Benn, T. (1982) *Parliament, Power and People* (London: Verso).

Berridge, G. R. (1992) *International Politics: States, Power and Conflict since 1945* (London: Harvester Wheatsheaf).

Berrington, H. (1995) 'The Nolan Report', *Government and Opposition*, 30:4, Autumn.

Bilton, T. *et al.* (2002) *Introductory Sociology*, 4th edn (Basingstoke: Palgrave).

Blackburn, R. and Plant, R. (eds) (1999) *Constitutional Reform* (London: Longman).

Blair, T. (1996) *New Britain: My Vision of a Young Country* (London: Fourth Estate).

Blair, T. (1998) *Leading the Way: A New Vision for Local Government* (London: Institute of Public Policy Research).

Bogdanor, V. (ed.) (1988) *Constitutions in Democratic Politics* (Aldershot: Gower).

Bolton, R. (1990) *Death on the Rock and Other Stories* (London: W. H. Allen).

Bottomore, T. (1991) *A Dictionary of Marxist Thought* (Oxford: Blackwell).

Braybrooke, D. and Lindblom, C. (1963) *A Strategy of Decision* (New York: Free Press).

Brazier, R. (1988) *Constitutional Practice* (Oxford: Clarendon).

Breuilly, J. (1993) *Nationalism and the State*, 2nd edn (Manchester: Manchester University Press).

Brittan, S. (1968) *Left or Right: The Bogus Dilemma* (London: Secker and Warburg).

Brooke, R. (1989) *Managing the Enabling Authority* (Harlow: Longman).

Bruce, S. (1986) *God Save Ulster: The Religion and Politics of Paisleyism* (Oxford: Oxford University Press).

Bryson, V. (1992) *Feminist Political Thought: An Introduction* (London: Macmillan Press – now Palgrave Macmillan).

Bryson, V. (1999) *Feminist Debates: Issues of Theory and Political Practice* (Basingstoke and New York: Palgrave – now Palgrave Macmillan)

Bryson, V. (2000) 'Men and sex equality', *Politics*, 20:1.

Bullock, A. and Stallybrass, O. (eds) (1977) *The Fontana Dictionary of Modern Thought* (London: Fontana).

Bulmer, M. and Solomos, J. (eds) (1999) *Racism* (Oxford: Oxford University Press).

Bulpitt, J. (1983) *Territory and Power in the United Kingdom: An Interpretation* (Manchester: Manchester University Press).

Burch, M. (1995) 'Prime Minister and Whitehall', in D. Shell and R. Hodder-Williams (eds), *Churchill to Major: The British Prime Ministership since 1945* (London: Hurst).

Burch, M. and Holliday, I. (1996) *The British Cabinet System* (London: Harvester Wheatsheaf).

Burke, E (1790/1969) *Reflections on the Revolution in France* (Harmondsworth: Penguin).

Burns, B. (1978) *Leadership* (New York: Harper and Row).

Butler, D., Adonis, A. and Travers, T. (1994) *Failure in British Government: The Politics of the Poll Tax* (Oxford: Oxford University Press).

Butler, D. and Kavanagh, D. (1997) *The British General Election of 1997* (London: Macmillan Press – now Palgrave Macmillan).

Butler, D. and Kavanagh, D. (2000) *The British General Election of 2001* (Basingstoke: Palgrave).

Byrne, P. (1997) *Social Movements in Britain* (London: Routledge).

Byrne, T. (2000) *Local Government in Britain*, 7th edn (Harmondsworth: Penguin).

Cabinet Office (1997) *Cabinet Practice: A Code of Conduct and Guidance on Procedure for Minister* (London: Cabinet Office, July).

Campbell, A., Converse, P. E., Miller, W.E. and Stokes, D. E. (1960) *The American Voter* (New York: Wiley).

Cantle, E. (2002) *Community Cohesion: A Report of the Independent Review Team Chaired by Ted Cantle* (London: Home Office).

Castle, B. (1980) *The Castle Diaries, 1974–1976* (London: Weidenfeld and Nicolson).

Cerny, P. (1996) 'What next for the state?' in E. Kofman and G. Youngs (eds), *Globalization: Theory and Practice* (London: Pinter).

Chalmers, M. (1985) *Paying for Defence* (London: Pluto).

Clarke, M. (1988) 'The policy-making process', in M. Smith, S. Smith and B. White (eds), *British Foreign Policy* (London: Unwin Hyman).

Clarke, M. (1992) *British External Policy-Making in the 1990s* (Basingstoke: Macmillan Press – now Palgrave Macmillan/RIIA).

Clarke, M. and Stewart, J. (1988) *The Enabling Council* (Luton: Local Government Training Board).

Cochrane, A. (1993) *Whatever Happened to Local Government?* (Buckingham: Open University Press).

Cockburn, C. (1977) *The Local State* (London: Pluto).

Cohen, N. (2001) 'How a hospital woke up to democracy', *New Statesman*, 19 March.

Coleman, S. (2001) 'Online campaigning', *Parliamentary Affairs*, 54.

Commoner, B. (1971) *The Closing Circle* (London: Jonathan Cape).

Cowling, D. (1997) 'A landslide without illusions', *New Statesman*, May Special Edn.

Coxall, B. (1992) 'The social context of British politics: class, gender and race in the two major parties, 1970–1990', in B. Jones and L. Robins (eds), *Two Decades in British Politics* (Manchester: Manchester University Press).

Coxall, B. (2001) *Pressure Groups in British Politics* (London: Pearson).

Coxall, B. and Robins, L. (1998) *British Politics Since the War* (London: Macmillan Press – now Palgrave Macmillan).

Cram, L., Dinan, D. and Nugent, N. (eds) (1999) *Developments in the European Union* (Basingstoke: Macmillan Press – now Palgrave Macmillan).

Crewe, I. (1996) '1979–1996', in A. Seldon (ed.), *How Tory Governments Fall* (London: Harper Collins).

Crewe, I. (2001) 'The opinion polls: still biased to Labour', *Parliamentary Affairs*, 54, pp. 650–65.

Crewe, I. and King, A. (1995) *SDP: The Birth, Life and Death of the Social Democratic Party* (Oxford: Oxford University Press).

Crick, B. (1993) *In Defence of Politics*, 4th edn (Harmondsworth: Penguin).

Crosland, C. A. R. (1956) *The Future of Socialism* (London: Jonathan Cape).

Crossman, R. (1963) 'Introduction' to W. Bagehot, *The English Constitution* (London: Fontana).

Crossman, R. (1975/7) *The Crossman Diaries*, 3 vols (London: Hamish Hamilton and Jonathan Cape).

Curran, J. and Seaton, J. (1990) *Power without Responsibility: The Press and Broadcasting in Britain* (London: Routledge).

Curtice, J. (1997) 'Anatomy of a non-landslide', *Politics Review*, 7:1, September.

Curtice, J. and Jowell, R. (1995) 'The sceptical electorate', in R. Jowell, J. Curtice, A. Park, L. Brook and D. Ahrendt (eds), *British Social Attitudes: The 12th Report* (Aldershot: Dartmouth).

Davies, A. J. (1996a) *We, The Nation: The Conservative Party and the Pursuit of Power* (London: Abacus).

Davies, A. J. (1996b) *To Build a New Jerusalem: The British Labour Party from Keir Hardie to Tony Blair* (London: Abacus).

Davies, D. (2000) *The Isles* (London, Macmillan).

Dearlove, J. (1973) *The Politics of Policy in Local Government* (London: Cambridge University Press).

Denham, Lord (2002) *Building Cohesive Communities: A Report of the Ministerial Group on Public Order and Community Cohesion* (London: Home Office).

Denham, A. (2003) 'Public services', in P. Dunleavy, A. Gamble, R. Heffernan and G. Peele, *Developments in British Politics 7* (Basingstoke: Palgrave Macmillan).

Denver, D. (1997) 'The 1997 general election results: lessons for teachers', *Talking Politics*, 10:1, Autumn.

Denver, D. (2002) *Elections and Voters in Britain* (Basingstoke and New York: Palgrave Macmillan).

Denver, D. and Hands, G. (1992) 'The political socialisation of young people', in B. Jones and L. Robins (eds), *Two Decades in British Politics* (Manchester: Manchester University Press).

de Smith, S. A. and Brazier, R. (1994) *Constitutional and Administrative Law* (Harmondsworth: Penguin).

Digby, A. (1989) *British Welfare Policy* (London: Faber and Faber).

Dobson, A. (1995) *Green Political Thought*, 2nd edn (London: Routledge).

Donoughue, B. (1987) *Prime Minister* (London: Jonathan Cape).

Donoughue, B. (1988) 'The Prime Minister's diary', *Contemporary Review*, 2:2.

Dorey, P. (1995) *British Politics Since 1945* (Oxford: Blackwell).

Dorey, P. (2002) 'The West Lothian question in British politics', *Talking Politics*, September.

Dowding, K. (1995) *The Civil Service* (London: Routledge).

Downs, A. (1957) *An Economic Theory of Democracy* (New York: Harper and Row).

Drewry, G. (1988) 'Legislation', in M. Ryle and P. Richard (eds), *The Commons Under Scrutiny* (London: Routledge).

Drewry, G. and Butcher, T. (1991) *The Civil Service Today*, 2nd edn (Oxford: Blackwell).

Driver, S. and Martell, L. (1998) *New Labour: Politics after Thatcherism* (Cambridge: Polity Press).

Dunleavy, P. (1991) *Democracy, Bureaucracy and Public Choice* (London: Harvester Wheatsheaf).

Dunleavy, P., Gamble, A., Holliday, I. and Peele, G. (eds) (1997) *Developments in British Politics 5* (London: Macmillan Press – now Palgrave Macmillan).

Dunleavy, P., Gamble, A., Heffernan, R., Holliday, I. and Peele, G. (2002) *Developments in British Politics 6* (rev. edn) (Basingstoke and New York: Palgrave Macmillan).

Dunleavy, P., Gamble, A., Heffernan, R. and Peele, G. (2003) *Developments in British Politics 7* (Basingstoke: Palgrave Macmillan).

Dunleavy, P. and Jones, G. W. (1993) 'Leaders, politics and institutional change: the decline of prime ministerial accountability to the House of Commons, 1868–1990', *British Journal of Political Science*, 23.

Dunleavy, P., Jones, G. W. and O'Leary, B. (1990) 'Prime ministers and the Commons: patterns of behaviour, 1868–1967', *Public Administration*, 68, Spring.

Durham, M. (1994) 'Major and morals: Back to Basics and the crisis of Conservatism', *Talking Politics*, 7:1.

Duverger, M. (1954) *Political Parties* (London: Methuen).

Duverger, M. (1972) *The Study of Politics*, trans. Wagoner (Sunbury on Thames: Nelson).

Eccleshall, R. (1986) *British Liberalism: Liberal Thought from the 1640s to the 1980s* (London: Longman).

Eccleshall, R. (1990) *English Conservatism since the Reformation: An Introduction and Anthology* (London: Unwin Hyman).

Eccleshall, R., Geoghegan, V., Jay, R., Kenny, M., MacKenzie, I. and Wilford, R. (1994) *Political Ideologies*, 2nd edn (London: Routledge).

Economist (1997) *Election Briefing, 1997* (London: Economist Publications).

Ellison, N. and Pierson, C. (eds) (1998) *Developments in British Social Policy* (Basingstoke: Macmillan).

Etzioni, A. (1968) *The Active Society: A Theory of Societal and Political Processes* (London: Collier-Macmillan).

Etzioni, A. (1995) *The Spirit of Community* (London: Fontana).

Evans, G. and Newnham, J. (1998) *Dictionary of International Relations* (London: Penguin).

Evans, R. and Hencke, D. (2001) 'Olympic star expelled as hunt lobby loses battle for RSPCA', *Guardian*, 15 June.

Eysenck, H. J. (1957) *Sense and Nonsense in Psychology* (Harmondsworth: Penguin).

Farrell, D. (1997) *Comparing Electoral Systems* (Hemel Hempstead: Prentice Hall/Harvester Wheatsheaf, now published by Basingstoke and New York: Palgrave Macmillan).

Farrell, D. (2001) *Electoral Systems: A Comparative Introduction* (Basingstoke and New York: Palgrave Macmillan).

Flinders, M. (2002) 'Governance in Whitehall', *Public Administration*, 80:1.

Foley, M. (1993) *The Rise of the British Presidency* (Manchester: Manchester University Press).

Frankel, J. (1970) *National Interest* (London: Pall Mall).

Frankel, J. (1975) *British Foreign Policy 1945–73* (London: RIIA/Oxford University Press).

Franklin, B. (1994) *Packaging Politics* (London: Edward Arnold).

Franklin, M. (1985) *The Decline of Class Voting* (Oxford: Oxford University Press).

Freeden, M. (1996) *Ideology and Political Theory* (Oxford: Clarendon Press).

Freeden, M. (1999) 'The ideology of New Labour', *Political Quarterly*, 70:1.

Freeman, M. (1997) 'Why rights matter', *Politics Review*, 7:1, September.

Fukuyama, F. (1992) *The End of History and the Last Man* (London: Hamish Hamilton).

Gamble, A. (1988, 2nd edn 1994) *The Free Economy and the Strong State: The Politics of Thatcherism* (Basingstoke: Macmillan Press – now Palgrave Macmillan).

Garner, R. (2000) *Environmental Politics*, 2nd edn (Basingstoke: Macmillan Press – now Palgrave Macmillan).

Garner, R. and Kelly, R. (1998) *British Political Parties Today*, 2nd edn (Manchester: Manchester University Press).

Gavin, N. and Sanders, D. (1997) 'The economy and voting', *Parliamentary Affairs*, 50:4, October.

Gellner, E. (1983) *Nations and Nationalism* (Oxford: Blackwell).

Giddens, A. (1998) *The Third Way: The Renewal of Social Democracy* (Cambridge: Polity).

Giddens, A. (2001) *Sociology*, 4th edn (Cambridge: Polity).

Gilmour, I. (1978) *Inside Right* (London: Quartet).

Gilmour, I. (1992) *Dancing with Dogma* (London: Simon and Schuster).

Gilmour, I and Garnett, M. (1997) *Whatever Happened to the Tories? The Conservatives since 1945* (London: Fourth Estate).

Glennerster, H., Power, A. and Travers, T. (1991) 'A new era for social policy: a new Enlightenment or a New Leviathan?', *Journal of Social Policy*, 20:3.

Golding, P. (1974) *The Mass Media* (London: Longman).

Graber, D. (1997) *Mass Media and American Politics* (Washington, D.C.: CQ/Press).

Grant, W. (1993) *Business and Politics in Britain*, 2nd edn (Basingstoke: Macmillan).

Grant, W. (1995) *Pressure Groups, Politics and Democracy in Britain*, 2nd edn (Hemel Hempstead: Prentice-Hall/Harvester Wheatsheaf).

Grant, W. (2000) *Pressure Groups and British Politics* (Basingstoke: Palgrave).

Grant, W. (2001) 'Pressure politics; from "insider" politics to direct action?' *Parliamentary Affairs*, 54, pp. 337–48.

Grant, W. (2002) *Economic Policy in Britain* (Basingstoke: Palgrave).

Gray, J. (1986) *Liberalism* (Buckingham: Open University Press).

Gray, P. (1996/7) 'When the minister won't resign', *Talking Politics*, 9:2.

Greenaway, J., Smith, S. and Street, J. (1992) *Deciding Factors in British Politics: A Case-Studies Approach* (London: Routledge):

Greenleaf, W. H. (1973) 'The character of modern British conservatism', in R. Benewick, R.N. Berkhi and B. Parekh (eds), *Knowledge and Belief in British Politics* (London: Allen and Unwin).

Greenleaf, W. H. (1983) *The British Political Tradition, Vol. 2: The Ideological Heritage* (London: Methuen).

Greenwood, J., Pyper, R. and Wilson, D. (2001) *New Public Administration in Britain* (London: Routledge).

Greenwood, J. and Robins, L. (2002) 'Citizenship tests and education: embedding a concept', *Parliamentary Affairs*, 55:3, pp. 505–22.

Griffith, J. A. G. (1997) *The Politics of the Judiciary* (London: Fontana).

Griffith, J. A. G. and Ryle, M. (1989) *Parliament* (London: Sweet and Maxwell).

Gyford, J. (1991) *Citizens, Consumers and Councils: Local Government and the Public* (London: Macmillan Press – now Palgrave Macmillan).

Hague, R. and Harrop, M. (2001) *Comparative Government and Politics* (Basingstoke: Palgrave – now Palgrave Macmillan).

Hall, W. and Weir, S. (1996) *The Untouchables: Power and Accountability in the Quango State* (London: Democratic Audit/Scarman Trust).

Harvie, C. (1994) *Scotland and Nationalism* (London: Routledge).

Hazell, R. (ed.) (1999) *Constitutional Futures: A History of the Next Ten Years* (Oxford: Oxford University Press).

Hazell, R. (ed.) (2000) *The State and the Nations* (Thorverton: Imprint Academic).

Hazell, R. (2001) 'Reforming the constitution', *Political Quarterly*, 72:1 (Jan.–March).

Hechter, M. (1975) *Internal Colonialism: The Celtic Fringe in British Colonial Development, 1536–1966* (London: Routledge and Kegan Paul).

Heclo, H. and Wildavsky, A. (1974) *The Private Government of Public Money* (London: Macmillan Press – now Palgrave Macmillan).

Heffernan, R. (2002) 'The possible as the art of politics: understanding consensus politics', *Political Studies*, 50.

Held, D. (1987) *Models of Democracy* (Oxford: Polity Press).

Held, D., McGrew, A., Goldblatt, D. and Perraton, J. (1999) *Global Transformations: Politics, Economics and Culture* (Cambridge: Polity Press).

Hennessy, P. (1990) *Whitehall*, 2nd edn (London: Fontana).

Hennessy, P. (2000) *The Prime Minister: The Office and its Holders Since 1945* (Harmondsworth: Allen Lane).

Heywood, A. (1997) *Politics*, 2nd edn (Basingstoke and New York: Palgrave Macmillan).

Her Majesty's Government (1994) *Sustainable Development: The UK Strategy*, CM 2426 (London: HMSO).

Heywood, A. (1998) *Political Ideologies: An Introduction*, 2nd edn (Basingstoke: Palgrave).

Hill, M. (1997a) *The Policy Process in the Modern State* (London: Harvester Wheatsheaf).

Hill, M. (1997b) *The Policy Process: A Reader*, 2nd edn (Hemel Hempstead: Prentice Hall).

Himmelweit, H., Humphrics, P. and Jaeger, M. (1984) *How Voters Decide* (Milton Keynes: Open University Press).

Hobsbawm, E. (1984) *Worlds of Labour: Further Studies in the History of Labour* (London: Weidenfeld and Nicolson).

Holland, R. (1991) *The Pursuit of Greatness: Britain and the World Role, 1900–1970* (London: Fontana).

Holliday, I. et al. (1999) *Fundamentals in British Politics* (Basingstoke: Palgrave Macmillan).

Holme, R. and Elliot, M. (eds) (1988) *1688–1988: Time for a New Constitution* (London: Macmillan).

Hood-Phillips, O., Jackson, P. and Leopard, P. (2001) *Constitutional and Administrative Law* (London: Sweet and Maxwell).

Hough, M. (2002) 'Partners in crime', *Guardian*, 28 May.

Hunt, K. (1997) 'Women and Politics', in B. Jones (ed.), *Political Issues in Britain Today* (Manchester: Manchester University Press).

Huntingdon, S. P. (1996) *The Clash of Civilizations and the Remaking of World Order* (New York: Simon and Schuster).

Hutton, J. et al. (eds) (1991) *Dependency to Enterprise* (London: Routledge).

Hutton, W. (1995) *The State We're In* (London: Jonathan Cape).

Hutton, W. (1996) 'High risk strategy', *Talking Politics*, 8:3, Spring.

Hutton, W. (1997) *The State to Come* (London: Vintage).

Ingle, S. (2000) *The British Party System* (London: Pinter).

James, S. (1992) *British Cabinet Government* (London: Routledge).

Jeffery, C. and Mawson, J. (2002) 'Introduction; beyond the White Paper on the English Regions', *Regional Studies*, 36:7 (Oct.).

Jenkins, R. (2001) *Churchill: A Biography* (Basingstoke: Macmillan).

Jennings, I. (1966) *The British Constitution*, 5th edn (Cambridge: Cambridge University Press).

Johnson, N. (1977) *In Search of the Constitution* (London: Methuen).

Jones, A. (1994) 'European Union electoral systems – an overview of the electoral systems of the European Parliament and the national legislatures', *Talking Politics*, 6:3, Winter.

Jones, B. (1989–90) 'Green thinking', *Talking Politics*, 2:2, Winter.

Jones, B. (ed.) (1999) *Political Issues in Britain Today*, 5th edn (Manchester: Manchester University Press).

Jones, B. and Robins, L. (eds) (1992) *Two Decades in British Politics* (Manchester: Manchester University Press).

Jones, G.W. (1990) 'Mrs Thatcher and the power of the prime minister', *Contemporary Record*, 3:4.

Jones, P. (1997) *America and the British Labour Party: The Special Relationship at Work* (London: Tauris Academic Studies).

Jordan, A. G. and Richardson, J. J. (1987) *Government and Pressure Groups in Britain* (Oxford: Clarendon).

Jowell, J. and Oliver, D. (2000) *The Changing Constitution* (Oxford: Oxford University Press).

Jowell, R., Curtice, J., Park, A., Brook, L. and Thomson, K. (eds) (1996) *British Social Attitudes: The 13th Report* (Aldershot: Dartmouth).

Jowell, R., Curtice, J., Park, A., Brook, L., Thomson, K. and Bryson, C. (eds) (1997) *British Social Attitudes: The 14th Report* (Aldershot: Ashgate).

Jowell, R., Witherspoon, S. and Brooke, L. (eds) (1987) *British Social Attitudes: The 5th Report* (Aldershot: Gower).

Judd, D. (1996) *Empire: The British Imperial Experience from 1765 to the Present* (London: Fontana).

Judge, D. (1993) *The Parliamentary State* (London: Sage).

Katz, R. S. and Mair, P. (eds) (1994) *How Parties Organise: Change and Adaptation in Policy Organisations in Western Democracies* (London: Sage).

Kavanagh, D. (1990) *Thatcherism and British Politics*, 2nd edn (Oxford: Oxford University Press).

Kavanagh, D. (1995) *Election Campaigning: The New Marketing of Politics* (Oxford: Blackwell).

Kavanagh, D. (1997) 'The Labour campaign', *Parliamentary Affairs*, 50:4, October.

Kavanagh, D. and Morris, P. (1994) *Consensus Politics from Attlee to Thatcher*, 2nd edn (Oxford: Blackwell).

Kegley, C. and Wittkopf, E. (1999) *World Politics* (New York: Worth).

Kellner, P. (1997a) 'PR paradox puts Paddy in a quandary', *Observer*, September 21.

Kellner, P. (1997b) 'Why the Tories were trounced', *Parliamentary Affairs*, 50:4, October.

Kellner, P. (2001) 'It was always mission impossible for Hague', *Observer*, 10 June.

Keynes, J. M. (1936) *The General Theory of Employment, Interest and Money* (London: Macmillan).

King, A. (ed.) (1985) *The British Prime Minister: A Reader,* 2nd edn (Basingstoke: Macmillan Press – now Palgrave Macmillan).

Kingham, T. (2001) 'Cheesed off by willy-jousters in a pointless Parliament', *Guardian*, 20 June.

Klein, N. (2000) *No Logo* (London: Harper Collins).

Klein, N. (2001) 'They call us violent agitators', *Guardian*, 23 March.

Klug, F., Starmer, K. and Weir, S. (1996) *The Three Pillars of Liberty* (London: Routledge).

Lane, J.-E. and Errson, S. (1999) *Politics and Society in Western Europe,* 4th edn (London: Sage).

Layton-Henry, Z. (1992) *Immigration and 'Race' Politics in Post-War Britain* (Oxford: Blackwell).

Leach, R. (1998) 'Local government reorganisation RIP?', *Political Quarterly*, 69:1.

Leach, R. (2002) *Political Ideology in Britain* (Basingstoke: Palgrave).

Leach, R. and Percy-Smith, J. (2001) *Local Governance in Britain* (Basingstoke: Palgrave).

Lee, J. M. (1995) 'The prime minister and international relations', in D. Shell and R. Hodder-Williams (eds), *Churchill to Major: The British Prime Ministership since 1945* (London: Hurst).

Liddell, P. H. (1994) 'The Public Accounts Committee and the audit of public expenditure', *Talking Politics*, 7:1, Autumn.

Loveland, I. (1993) 'Redefining Parliamentary sovereignty? A new perspective on the search for the meaning of law', *Parliamentary Affairs*, 46:3, July.

Loveland, I. (1997) 'The war against the judges', *Political Quarterly*, April–June.

Lovenduski, J. (1997) 'Gender politics: a breakthrough for women?', *Parliamentary Affairs*, 50:4, October.

Lovenduski, J. (2001) 'Apathetic landslide; the 2001 British general election', *Parliamentary Affairs*, 54, pp. 565–89.

Lovenduski, J. and Randall, V. (1993) *Contemporary Feminist Politics* (Oxford: Oxford University Press).

Lowe, R. (1998) *The Welfare State in Britain since 1945,* 2nd edn (London: Palgrave Macmillan).

Ludlam, S. and Smith, M. J. (eds) (1996) *Contemporary British Conservatism* (Basingstoke: Macmillan Press – now Palgrave Macmillan).

Ludlam, S. and Smith, M. (eds) (2001) *New Labour in Government* (Basingstoke and New York: Palgrave – now Palgrave Macmillan).

Ludlam, S. and Smith, M. (eds.) (2003) *Governing as New Labour* (Basingstoke and New York: Palgrave Macmillan).

Lynch, P. (2002) 'Goodbye ballot box, hello post box', *Talking Politics*, 15:1.

Macalister, T. (2001) 'Where PPP is not a dirty word', *Guardian*, 23 October.

Mac an Ghaill, M. (1999) *Contemporary Racisms and Ethnicities* (Buckingham: Open University Press).

Maclean, M. and Groves, D. (eds) (1991) *Women's Issues in Social Policy* (London: Routledge).

Macpherson, C. B. (1977) *The Life and Times of Liberal Democracy* (Oxford: Oxford University Press).

Macpherson, Sir W. (1999) *The Stephen Lawrence Inquiry* (Cm 4262) (London: The Stationery Office).

Madgwick, P. (1991) *British Government: The Central Executive Territory* (London: Philip Allan).

Madgwick, P. and Rawkins, P. (1982) 'The Welsh language in the policy process', in P. Madgwick and R. Rose (eds) *The Territorial Dimension in United Kingdom Politics* (London: Macmillan).

Madgwick, P. and Woodhouse, D. (1995) *The Law and Politics of the Constitution* (Hemel Hempstead: Harvester Wheatsheaf; now published by Basingstoke and New York: Palgrave Macmillan).

Mair, P. (1994) 'Party organizations: from civil society to state', in R. S. Katz and P. Mair (eds), *How Parties Organize: Change and Adaptation in Party Organizations in Western Democracies* (London: Sage).

Major, J. (1999) *The Autobiography* (London: Harper-Collins).

March, D. and Rhodes, R. (1992) *Policy Networks and British Government* (Oxford: Oxford University Press).

Marr, A. (1992) *The Battle for Scotland* (Harmondsworth: Penguin).

Marsh, D. and Rhodes, R. A. W. (eds) (1992) *Policy Networks in British Government* (Oxford: Oxford University Press).

Marsh, D. and Rhodes, R.A.W. (1996) 'The concept of policy networks in British political science: its development and utility', *Talking Politics*, 8:3, Spring.

Marshall, G. (ed.) (1989) *Ministerial Responsibility* (Oxford: Oxford University Press).

Marshall, G. (1991) 'The evolving practice of Parliament accountability', *Parliamentary Affairs*, 4:4.

Maynard, G. (1988) *The Economy Under Mrs Thatcher* (Oxford: Blackwell).

Mazey, S. and Richardson, J. J. (eds) (1993) *Lobbying in the European Community* (Oxford: Oxford University Press).

McCormick, J. (1991) *British Politics and the Environment* (London: Earthscan).

McIlroy, J. (1989) 'The politics of racism', in B. Jones (ed.), *Political Issues in Britain Today* (Manchester: Manchester University Press).

McKenzie, R. T. (1955 and subs. edns) *British Political Parties* (London: Heinemann).

McKie, D. (2000) 'Taskforces are dead and buried', *Guardian*, 1 February.

McLellan, D. (1995) *Ideology*, 2nd edn (Buckingham: Open University Press).

McNaughton, N. (2002) 'Prime ministerial government', *Talking Politics*, 15:1.

McQuail, D. (1987) *Mass Communications Theory* (Beverley Hills: Sage).

Michels, R. (1915) *Political Parties: A Sociological Study of the Oligarchical Tendencies of Modern Democracy* (London: Jarrold).

Milbrath, L. (1965) *Political Participation: How and Why People Get Involved in Politics* (Chicago: Rand McNally).

Miles, R. (1989) *Racism* (London: Routledge).

Miles, R. (1993) *Racism after Race Relations* (London: Routledge).

Miliband, R. (1972) *Parliamentary Socialism*, 2nd edn (London: Merlin).

Miliband, R. (1973) *The State in Capitalist Society* (London: Quartet).

Mill, J. S. (1869/1988) *The Subjection of Women*, ed. S. Okin (Indianapolis: Hackett).

Miller, W. *et al.* (1990) *How Voters Change* (Oxford: Clarendon).

Milner, M. (2002) 'A pension's for life', *Guardian*, 18 February.

Minkin, L. (1992) *The Contentious Alliance: Trade Unions and the Labour Party* (Edinburgh: Edinburgh University Press).

Mohapatra, U. (1999) *With Love, From Britain. A Mother Writes to her Children: Observations on Changing Overseas Indian Culture* (Mumbai: Bhavans Book University).

Moran, M. (2000) 'From command state to regulatory state', *Public Policy and Administration*, 15:4.

Moran, M. (2001) 'Not steering but drowning: policy catastrophes and the regulatory state', *Political Quarterly*, 72: 4.

Morgan, K. (1990) *The People's Peace: British History, 1945–1989* (Oxford: Oxford University Press).

Morgan, K. and Owen, K. (2001) *Britain Since 1945* (Oxford: Oxford University Press).

Mount, F. (1992) *The British Constitution Now* (London: Heinemann).

Mowlam, M. (2002) *Momentum: The Struggle for Peace, Politics and the People* (London: Hodder and Stoughton).

Murdoch, G. and Golding P. (1977) 'Beyond monopoly – mass communications in an age of conglomerates', in P. Beharell and G. Philo (eds) *Trade Unions and the Mass Media* (Basingstoke: Macmillan Press – now Palgrave Macmillan).

Murray, C. (1994a) 'Underclass', *Sunday Times*, 22 May.

Murray, C. (1994b) 'The new Victorians and the new rabble', *Sunday Times*, 29 May.

Nairn, T. (1981) *The Break-up of Britain* (London: NLB and Verso).

Nairn, T. (2000) *After Britain* (London: Granta Books).

Nairn, T. (2001) 'Post Ukania', *New Left Review*, Jan/Feb.

Newman, J. (2001) *Modernising Governance: New Labour, Policy and Society* (London: Sage).

Newton, K. (1976) *Second City Politics* (Oxford: Oxford University Press).

Nolan, Lord (Chair) (1995) *First Report of the Committee of Standards in Public Life* (London: HMSO).

Norris, P. (1991) 'Gender differences in political participation in Britain: traditional, radical and revisionist models', *Government and Opposition*, 26:1.

Norris, P. (1997) 'Anatomy of a landslide', *Parliamentary Affairs*, 50:4, October.

Norris, P. and Lovenduski, J. (1995) *Political Recruitment: Gender, Race and Class in the British Parliament* (Cambridge: Cambridge University Press).

Norton, P. (1990) 'Public legislation', in M. Rush (ed.), *Parliament and Pressure Politics* (Oxford: Oxford University Press).

Norton, P. (1992) 'The House of Commons: from overlooked to overworked', in B. Jones and L. Robins (eds), *Two Decades in British Politics* (Manchester: Manchester University Press).

Norton, P. (1994) 'Select committees in the House of Commons: watchdogs or poodles?', *Politics Review*, 4:2, November.

Norton, P. (1995a) 'Standing committees in the House of Commons', *Politics Review*, 4:4, April.

Norton, P. (1995b) 'National parliaments and the European Union', *Talking Politics*, 7:3, Spring.

Norton, P. (1995–6) 'Parliamentary Behaviour since 1945', *Talking Politics*, 8:2, winter.

Nugent, N. (2002) *The Government and Politics of the European Union*, 5th edn (London: Palgrave Macmillan).

Nutting, A. (1967) *No End of a Lesson: The Story of Suez* (London: Constable).

Oakley, A. (1972) *Sex, Gender and Society* (Hounslow: Temple Smith).

Oppenheim, C. (1990) *Poverty: The Facts* (London: CPAG).

Osborne, D. and Gaebler, T. (1992) *Reinventing Government* (Reading, Mass.: Addison-Wesley).

Ouseley, H. (2001) 'Brittle Britain', *Guardian*, 22 June.

Panebianco, A. (1988) *Political Parties: Organization and Power*, trans. M. Silver (Cambridge: Cambridge University Press).

Parekh, B. (2000) *Rethinking Multiculturalism: Cultural Diversity and Political Theory* (Basingstoke: Palgrave).

Parry, G. and Moyser, G. (1990) 'A map of political participation in Britain', *Government and Opposition*, 25:2.

Parry, G. and Moyser, G. (1993) 'Political participation in Britain', *Politics Review*, 3:2, November.

Parry, G., Moyser, G. and Day, N. (1992) *Political Participation and Democracy in Britain* (Cambridge: Cambridge University Press).

Paxman, J. (1998) *The English* (London: Michael Joseph).

Payne, G. (ed.) (2000) *Social Divisions* (Basingstoke: Palgrave).

Pierre, J. and Peters, B. G. (2000) *Governance, Politics and the State* (Basingstoke: Macmillan Press – now Palgrave Macmillan).

Pimlott, B. (1992) *Harold Wilson* (London: Harper Collins).

Pimlott, B. (1994) 'The myth of consensus', in *Frustrate Their Knavish Tricks* (London: Harper Collins).

Pinder, J. (2001) *The European Union* (Oxford: Oxford University Press).

Pliatzky, L. (1980) *Report on Non-Departmental Bodies*, Cmnd 7797 (London: HMSO).

Pliatzky, L. (1982) *Getting and Spending* (Oxford: Blackwell).

Political Quarterly (1997), Special Issue on *Human Rights in the UK*, 68:2, April–June.

Pulzer, P. (1967) *Representation and Elections in Britain* (London: Allen and Unwin).

Putnam, R. (2000) *Bowling Alone. The Collapse and Revival of the American Community* (New York: Simon and Schuster).

Pyper, R. (1991) 'Governments, 1964–1990: a survey', *Contemporary Record*, 5:2, Autumn.

Pyper, R. (1994) 'Individual ministerial responsibility: dissecting the doctrine', *Politics Review*, 4:1, September.

Pyper, R. (1995) *The British Civil Service* (London: Harvester Wheatsheaf; now published by Basingstoke and New York: Palgrave Macmillan).

Pyper, R. (2000) 'The civil service under Blair', *Politics Review*, 9.1.

Pyper, R. and Robins, L. (eds) (1995) *Governing the UK in the 1990s* (London: Macmillan).

Pyper, R. and Robins, L. (eds) (2000) *United Kingdom Governance* (Basingstoke: Macmillan Press – now Palgrave Macmillan).

Rallings, C. and Thrasher, M. (1997) 'The local elections', *Parliamentary Affairs*, 50:4, October.

Randall, V. (1987) *Women and Politics*, 2nd edn (London: Macmillan Press – now Palgrave Macmillan).

Ranson, S. (1990) 'From 1945 to 1988: education, citizenship and democracy', in M. Flude and M. Hammer (eds), *The Education Reform Act 1988: Its Origins and Implications* (London: Falmer).

Rawnsley, A. (2001) *Servants of the People: The Inside Story of New Labour* (Harmondsworth: Penguin).

Regional Studies (2002) Special Issue, 'Devolution and the English Question', 36:7, October.

Rentoul, J. (2001) *Tony Blair: Prime Minister* (London: Little, Brown).

Rex, J. (1986) *Race and Ethnicity* (Buckingham: Open University Press).

Reynolds, D. (1991) *Britannia Overruled: British Policy and World Power in the Twentieth Century* (London: Longman).

Rhodes, R. A. W. (1981) *Control and Power in Central–Local Relations* (Farnborough: Gower).

Rhodes, R. A. W. (1988) *Beyond Westminster and Whitehall: The Sub-Central Governments of Britain* (London: Unwin Hyman).

Rhodes, R. A. W. (1997) *Understanding Governance* (Buckingham: Open University Press).

Rhodes, R. A. W. (2000) 'The governance narrative', *Public Administration*, 78, pp. 345–63.

Rhodes, R. A. W. and Dunleavy, P. (eds) (1995) *Prime Minister, Cabinet and the Core Executive* (Basingstoke: Macmillan Press – now Palgrave Macmillan).

Richard, I. and Welfare, D. (1999) *Unfinished Business: Reforming the House of Lords* (London: Vintage).

Richards, S. (2000) 'The special advisers are here to stay', *New Statesman*, 17 January.

Richardson, J. J. (ed.) (1993) *Pressure Groups* (Oxford: Oxford University Press).

Ridley, F. F. and Rush, M. (eds) (1995) *British Government and Politics since 1945* (Oxford: Oxford University Press).

Robertson, D. (1993) *The Penguin Dictionary of Politics* (Harmondsworth: Penguin).

Robins, L., Blackmore, H. and Pyper, R. (eds) (1994) *Britain's Changing Party System* (London: Leicester University Press).

Robinson, M. (1992) *The Greening of British Party Politics* (Manchester: Manchester University Press).

Rose, R. and McAllister, I. (1990) *The Loyalties of Voters* (London: Sage).

Rousseau, J.-J. (1762/1968) *The Social Contract*, trans. Cranston (London: Penguin).

Rush, M. (ed.) (1990) *Parliament and Pressure Politics* (Oxford: Clarendon).

Russell, D. (1990) 'Equal opportunities and the politics of race', *Talking Politics*, 3:1, Autumn.

Saggar, S. (1997) 'Racial politics', *Parliamentary Affairs*, 50:4, October.

Saggar, S. (2001) 'The race card, again', *Parliamentary Affairs*, 54, pp. 759–74.

Sanders, D. (1990) *Losing an Empire, Finding a Role: British Foreign Policy Since 1945* (Basingstoke: Macmillan Press – now Palgrave Macmillan).

Sanders, D. (1995) '"It's the economy, stupid": the economy and support for the Conservative Party, 1979–1994', *Talking Politics*, 7:3, Spring.

Sanders, D., Clarke, H., Stewart, M. and Whiteley, P. (2001) 'The economy and voting', *Parliamentary Affairs*, 54, pp. 789–802.

Sartori, G. (1994) *Comparative Constitutional Engineering* (Basingstoke: Macmillan Press – now Palgrave Macmillan).

Saunders, P. (1980) *Urban Politics: A Sociological Interpretation* (Harmondsworth: Penguin).

Savage, S. and Atkinson, R. (2001) *Public Policy under Blair* (London: Palgrave Macmillan).

Savage, S. and Robins, L. (eds) (1990) *Public Policy under Thatcher* (London: Macmillan Press – now Palgrave Macmillan).

Saville, J. (1988) *The Labour Movement in Britain* (London: Faber and Faber).

Scruton, R. (1996) *A Dictionary of Political Thought* (London: Macmillan).

Sedgemore, B. (1980) *The Secret Constitution* (London: Hodder and Stoughton).

Seldon, A. (1990) 'The Cabinet Office and coordination', *Public Administration*, 68:1, Spring.

Seldon, A. (ed.) (2001) *The Blair Effect: The Labour Government 1997–2001* (London: Little, Brown).

Seldon, A. and Kavanagh, D. (eds) (1994) *The Major Effect* (London: Macmillan).

Self, P. (1993) *Government by the Market: The Politics of Public Choice* (Basingstoke: Macmillan Press – now Palgrave Macmillan).

Seliger, M. (1976) *Ideology and Politics* (London: Allen and Unwin).

Semetko, H. A., Scammell, M. and Goddard, P. (1997) 'Television', *Parliamentary Affairs*, 50:4, October.

Seyd, P. and Whiteley, P. (1992) *Labour's Grass Roots: The Politics of Party Membership* (Oxford: Clarendon).

Seymour-Ure, C. (1974) *The Political Impact of the Mass Media* (London: Constable).

Seymour-Ure, C. (1995) 'Prime minister and the public: managing media relations', in D. Shell and R. Hodder-Williams (eds), *Churchill to Major: The British Prime Ministership since 1945* (London: Hurst).

Shaw, E. (1996) *The Labour Party since 1945* (Oxford: Blackwell).

Shell, D. (1992) 'The House of Lords: the best second chamber we have got?', in B. Jones and L. Robins (eds), *Two Decades in British Politics* (Manchester: Manchester University Press).

Shell, D. (1998) *The House of Lords*, 2nd edn (London: Harvester Wheatsheaf).

Skelcher, C. (1998) *The Appointed State* (Buckingham: Open University Press).

Smith, M. J. (1995) *Pressure Politics* (Manchester: Baseline).

Smith, M. J. (1999) *The Core Executive in Britain* (Basingstoke: Macmillan Press – now Palgrave Macmillan).

Smith, M. J. and Ludlam, S. (eds) (1996) *Contemporary British Conservatism* (London: Macmillan Press – now Palgrave Macmillan).

Stanyer, J. (2002) 'A loss of political appetite', *Parliamentary Affairs*, 55.

Stoker, G. (1991) *The Politics of Local Government* (London: Macmillan Press – now Palgrave Macmillan).

Stoker, G. (1999) *The New Management of British Local Governance* (Basingstoke: Palgrave Macmillan).

Stoker, G. (2000) *The New Politics of British Local Governance* (Basingstoke: Palgrave Macmillan).

Stokes, J. and Reading, A. (eds) (1999) *The Media in Britain: Current Debates and Developments* (Basingstoke: Macmillan Press – now Palgrave Macmillan).

Tapper, T. and Bowles, N. (1982) 'Working class Tories: the search for theory', in L. Robins (ed.), *Topics in British Politics* (London: Politics Association).

Taylor, A. (2000) 'Hollowing out or filling in? Task forces and the management of cross-cutting issues in British government', *British Journal of Politics and International Relations*, 2:1.

Thain, C. (1992) 'Government and the economy' in B. Jones and L. Robins (eds), *Two Decades in British Politics* (Manchester: Manchester University Press).

Theakston, K. (1991–2) 'Ministers and mandarins', *Talking Politics*, 4:2, Winter.

Theakston, K. (1995) *The Civil Service since 1945* (Oxford: Blackwell).

Theakston, K. (1999) *Leadership in Whitehall* (London: Macmillan).

Thomas, G. (1992) *Government and the Economy* (Manchester: Manchester University Press).

Thompson, E. P. (1963) *The Making of the English Working Class* (London: Gollancz).

Thompson, K. (1993) 'Redressing grievances: the role of the Ombudsman', *Talking Politics*, 6:1, autumn.

Thucydides (1954) *History of the Peloponnesian War*, trans. R. Warner (Harmondsworth: Penguin).

Tomaney, J. (2002) 'The evolution of regionalism in England', *Regional Studies*, 36:7 (Oct.).

Tomkins, A. (1996) 'The Scott Report: the constitutional implications', *Politics Review*, 6:1, September.

Tomkins, A. (1997) 'Intelligence and government', *Parliamentary Affairs*, 50:1, January.

Tomlin, Lord (Chair) (1931) *Report of the Royal Commission on the Civil Service*, Cmd 3909 (London: HMSO).

Tunstall, J. and Machin, D. (1999) *The Anglo-American Media Connection* (Oxford, Oxford University Press).

Viner, K. (2002) 'How feminism lost its way', *Guardian*, 5 June.

Wade, H. W. R. (1988) *Administrative Law*, 6th edn (Oxford: Clarendon).

Wadham J. and Mountfield, H. (2000) *Human Rights Act, 1998*, 2nd edn (London: Blackstone).

Wakeham, Lord (2000) 'Lords reform', *Politics Review*, 10:2.

Walker, D. (2001) 'The right to change our minds,' *Guardian*, 16 October.

Walker, D. (2002) 'Stand by your beds', *Guardian*, 6 May.

Wallace, W. (1975) *The Foreign Policy Process in Britain* (London: RIIA/George Allen and Unwin).

Wallace, W. (1999) 'The sharing of sovereignty: the European paradox', *Political Studies*, 47, pp. 503–21.

Waller, R and Criddle, B. (2002) *The Almanac of British Politics* (London: Routledge)

Walsh, K. (1995) *Public Services and Market Mechanisms* (Basingstoke: Macmillan Press – now Palgrave Macmillan).

Walter, N. (1998) 'Girls! New feminism needs you!', *New Statesman*, 16 January.

Walter, N. (1999) *The New Feminism* (London: Virago).

Watts, D. (1997) 'The growing attractions of direct democracy', *Talking Politics*, 10:1, Autumn.

Weir, D. and Beetham, D. (1999) *Political Power and Democratic Control in Britain: The Democratic Audit of Great Britain* (London: Routledge).

Weir, S. (1995) 'Quangos: questions of democratic accountability', in F.F. Ridley and D. Wilson (eds), *The Quango Debate* (Oxford: Oxford University Press).

Weir, S. and Hall, W. (eds) (1994) *EGO TRIP: Extra Governmental Organisations in the UK and their Accountability* (University of Essex: Human Rights Centre).

Whale, J. (1977) *The Politics of the Media* (London: Fontana).

Whiteley, P., Seyd, P. and Richardson, J. (1994) *True Blues: The Politics of Conservative Party Membership* (Oxford: Clarendon).

Whiteley, P., Clarke, H., Sanders, D. and Stewart, M. (2001) 'Turnout', *Parliamentary Affairs*, 54, pp. 775–88.

Whiteley, P. and Winyard, S. (1987) *Pressure for the Poor* (London: Methuen).

Wilding, P. (1993) 'Poverty and government in Britain in the 1980s', *Talking Politics*, 5:3, Summer.

Williams, R. (1976) *Keywords: A Vocabulary of Culture and Society* (London: Fontana).

Wilson, D. and Game, C. (2002) *Local Government in the United Kingdom*, 3rd edn (Basingstoke: Palgrave).

Wollstonecraft, M. (1792/1982) *Vindication of the Rights of Woman*, ed. M. Kramnick (Harmondsworth: Penguin).

Woodhouse, D. (1994) *Ministers and Parliament: Accountability in Theory and Practice* (Oxford: Clarendon).

Woodhouse, D. (1995) 'Politicians and the judiciary: a changing relationship', *Parliamentary Affairs*, 48.

Woodhouse, D. (1996) 'Politicians and the judges', *Parliamentary Affairs*, 49.

Woodhouse, D. (1997) 'Judicial/executive relations in the 1990s', *Talking Politics*, 10:1, Autumn.

Wright, A. (1983) *British Socialism* (London: Longman).

Wright, A. (1997) 'Does Parliament work?', *Talking Politics*, 9:3, Spring.

Young, H. (1990) *One of Us*, expanded edn with new epilogue (London: Pan Macmillan).

Young, H. (1998) *This Blessed Plot: Britain and Europe, from Churchill to Blair* (London: Macmillan).

Younge, G. (2000) 'Barbour rebellion: back in the hunt', *Guardian*, 4 October.

Index

Note: entries in **bold** indicate a definition

abortion, 150, 397
Act, **233**
  Private Act, **233**
  Public Act, **233**
Act of Union (1707), 288, 297
Adam Smith Institute, 355
Adams, Gerry, 294
additional member system *see*
  proportional representation
administrative law, *see* law,
  administrative
administrative tribunal, 261–2
Afghanistan, 419
age
  and implications for politics,
    23–4
  and voting, 104–5
ageism, 23
agriculture, 353
Alliance Party (Northern
  Ireland), 294
Alliance, the Liberal-SDP
  Alliance, 56
al-Qaeda, 83, 419
alternative vote, 92
Amnesty International, 137
Amsterdam Treaty (1997), 273
Anglo-Irish Agreement, 294
Animal Liberation Front, 149
anti-capitalist protests, 143
Anti-Nazi League, 149
Anti-Poll Tax Federation, 82,
  149, 151
anti-Semitism, 68, 157
Aristotle, 3, 24
Armstrong Memorandum, 217
Armstrong, Sir Robert, 222
ASH (Action on Smoking and
  Health), 140

Ashdown, Paddy, 124
asylum seekers, **393**, 394
Atlanticism, 47
Attlee, Clement, 32, 34, 63–4
Audit Commission, 337
authority, **5**, 57, 59

'Back to Basics' campaign, 219,
  346–7, 381
Bagehot, Walter, 422
Banham Commission, 305, 313
Bank of England, 336, 360,
  363
Beacon Council scheme, 311
Bell, Daniel, 52
Benn, Tony, 65, 124, 224
Bevan, Aneurin, 64
Beveridge, William, 37, 54, 378
Bevin, Ernest, 33–4, 63
bill, **233**
  public bill, **233**
  private bill, **233**
  Private Member's bill, **233**,
    238
blacks and Asians, 14, 20–1, 68,
  213, 257, 387–94
'Black Wednesday' (1992) 43,
  109–10, 275, 360, 362
Blair, Tony, 32–3, 65–6, 107,
  363, 382, 405
  crime, 258
  environment, 405, 406
  European Union, 275–6, 414
  foreign policy, 47–8, 414,
    419, 420
  ideology, 45–47, 65–6, 382
  local government, 309,
    311–13
  Northern Ireland, 295–7

parliament, 193, 241, 243
party leader, 45–8, 66, 122
Prime Minister, 191, 192,
  195, 197, 198, 200, 354
public services, 376
'Bloody Sunday' (1972), 291
Blunkett, David, 258
Booth, Cherie, 158, 256
British Broadcasting
  Corporation (BBC), 157,
  163
British Empire 33–5, 270, 288
British-Irish Council, 295, 305
British Medical Association
  (BMA), 137, 140
British National Party (BNP),
  393
Brown, Gordon, 110, 363–7,
  371, 377, 431
BSE ('mad cow disease'), 141,
  353
budget, 367
bureaucracy, 211
  see also civil service
bureaucratic over-supply model,
  222, 224–5
Burke, Edmund, 56, 229
Bush, George W., 48, 408, 419,
  420
business influence, 8, 133, 366,
  426
Butler, R. A. ('Rab'), 3–4, 37
Butskellism, 37
Byers, Stephen, 219–20

Cabinet, 187–204
Cabinet committees, 196–7
Cabinet Office, 187, 197–8
Cabinet Secretary, 197

Callaghan, James, 32, 41, 42, 123, 127, 191, 374
Campaign for Nuclear Disarmament (CND), 42, 151
Campbell, Alastair, 164, 194
care in the community, 310
Carrington, Lord, 220
cause groups, *see* pressure groups
central–local relations, *see* local government
Centre for Policy Studies, 355
Chamberlain, Joseph, 57
Chamberlain, Neville, 57
Charter 88, 137, 183, 186
Chartists, 63
Child Poverty Action Group, 137, 379
Churchill, Sir Winston, 4, 32, 33, 270, 358, 412
Citizen's Charter, 45, 61, 86, 191, 215, 333
citizenship, 85–7
citizens' juries, 79
City, the, 151, 363, 367–8
civil liberties, 258–9
  see also human rights
civil rights, **258**
civil service, 191, **208**–17
civil society , **4**
Clarke, Kenneth, 125
class
  ruling, **8**, 9
  self-assigned, 28
  social, 26–8, 30
class dealignment, 100, **101**
class voting, 100–3
Clause Four, 26, 63–5, 119, 382
Clinton, Bill, 13, 408, 419
Code of Conduct and Guidance on Procedure for Ministers, 197, 218
Code of Conduct for Civil Servants, 217
cold war, 410, 416
collective responsibility, 197, **198**, 199, 220

Commission for Racial Equality, 330, 389–91
Common Agricultural Policy (CAP), 270, 273
Commoner, Barry, 401
Commonwealth, 33, 34–5, 270, 412–13
Communism, 34
communitarianism, **66**, 381–2
community, 381–2
community power debate, 316
Competition Commission, 337
compulsory competitive tendering (CCT), **309**, 310, 333
Confederation of British Industry (CBI), 137, 367
consensus politics, **33**, 40–1, 46–7, 52
conservatism, 56–62
  neo-conservatism, 60–1
  'One Nation', 56–8
  traditional, 56–7, **62**
Conservative Party, 56–62, 114–35, 181–2, 314
  1922 Committee, 126
constitution(s), 173–5, **174**
  American, 4, 174, 175
  British, 175–83
  French, 175
  typologies, 174–5
constitutional monarchy, 177–8
constitutional reform, 65, 183–6
consumption cleavages, 28
Continuity IRA, 294, 297
contracting out, 332–3
conventions, 177
Cook, Robin, 417–18
core executive, 187, 203–4
corporatism, **41**
  neo-corporatism, 138, **139**
Council for the Protection of Rural England (CPRE), 19
council house sales, 28, 59, 332–3
council tax, 324–5
Countryside Alliance, 19, 83, 140–1, 149, 151, 424
courts, 253–4

crime, 375–6
criminal law (*see* law, criminal)
Crosland, Anthony, 64
crossbenchers, 246, 248
'crossing the floor', 121, 230
Crossman, Richard, 422
Currie, Edwina, 219

Dalyell, Tam, 186, 303
Davies, Norman, 289
Davies, Ron, 300, 302–3
decision making, **345**
decision-making theory, 347–9
decommissioning of weapons, 296–7
defence policy, 348, 410–21
deference, 336
De Gaulle, General, 271
delegated legislation, **233**
Delors, Jacques, 43, 278
democracy, 5–7, 24, 75, 429–31
  direct, 5, **6**, 97
  participatory, 75
  representative, **6**, 7, 180
'democratic deficit', 280, 312, 328
democratic elitism, **8**
Democratic Unionist Party (DUP), 112, 293–7
departments of state, 206–9
departmental reorganisation, 207
departmental select committees (DSCs), 239–40
dependency culture, 379
de Tocqueville, Alexis, 311
devolution, 12, 30, **48**, 59, 67, 134–5, 184–6, 249–50, 288–307, **289**, 329, 342
Dewar, Donald, 299
Diana, Princess of Wales, 178
Dicey, A.V., 180–1
'differentiated polity', 341–2
Disraeli, Benjamin, 57
D-Notice system, 157
Douglas-Home, Sir Alec, 32, 354
Downs, Anthony, 118–9, 346, 403–4

Dugdale, Sir Thomas, 221
Duncan Smith, Iain, 61, 107, 125, 135, 384–5
Duverger, Maurice, 4

Ecclestone, Bernie, 133, 139–40, 158
economy
 decline of British, 36
 management of, 35–6, 40–2, 358–68
 performance of, 45
Eden, Anthony, 32
education policy, 351, 374–5
education action zones, 311
elections, 88–114
 for devolved parliaments and assemblies, 96
 for European Parliament, 89–90
 local, 312
 London, 92
 UK general, 88–91, 99–100, 102–14
electoral reform, 94–6, 135, 184 (see also proportional representation)
electoral system, 91–6
electoral volatility, 100
elite(s) and elitism, **8**, 9–10, 316, 426
employment zones, 311
enabling, 308, 335
England, 16–17, 288–90, 303–5
environment, 401–8
Environment Agency, 407
environmentalism, 71, 77, **403**
equality, 54
Equal Opportunities Commission, 330, 397
Equal Pay Act, 397
establishment, **8**
ethical foreign policy, 416–19
ethical socialism, **66**
ethnicity, 19–21
 and voting, 105
ethnic minorities, 19–21, 22, 68–9

see also blacks and Asians
Etzioni, Amitai, 347, 348, 382
euro (Single European Currency), 273, 275–7, 286–7, 365–6, 368
European Atomic Energy Authority (Euratom), 270
European Coal and Steel Community, 34, 270, 271
European Community (EC) and Union (EU), 11, 43–4, 47, 60–2, 270–87
 Common Agricultural Policy (CAP), 270, 273, 285
 COREPER, 281
 Council of Ministers, 277–8
 Economic and Social Committee, 284
 European Commission, 278, 284
 European Council, 277
 European Court of Justice (ECJ), 278–9
 European Monetary System, 43
 European Parliament, 249–50, 277, 279–81, 283
 enlargement, 271–2, 286
 environmental policy, 407
 Exchange Rate Mechanism (ERM), 44, 274–5, 360–2
 institutions, 277–83
 integration, 34–6, 273
 regional and social policy, 285, 325
 regulation, 335
 Social Chapter, 275–6, 363
 subsidiarity, principle of, 277
 UK involvement with, 39–40, 60–2, 273–6, 414–16
 UK referendum on, 274
European Convention on Human Rights, 65, 265, 282
European Court of Human Rights, 264–6
European Economic Community (EEC), 34, 39–40, 270
European Free Trade Association, 39, 270, 414

Euro-sceptics, 162, **274**, 275–6, 281–2, 284
executive, **187**
executive agencies, 181, 209, **210**, 215, 331
executive dominance (of parliament) 242–3

Fabian Society, 63, 356
factions, within political party, 120–1
Factortame case, 179
fair trade, 57
Falklands War, 43, 220
family breakdown, 380–1
family values, 59
fascism, 4, 69
federalism, 175, 176, **276**, 305–6
feminism, 4–5, 69, 70, 77, 395–7, **397**, 398, 399
 liberal, 69, **70**, 397
 Marxist, 69, **70**
 radical, **70**, 397
 socialist, 69
Financial Management Initiative (FMI), 214
Financial Services Authority, 336, 337
Firestone, Shulamith, 70
first past the post voting system, 90, 92, 312
fiscal policy, 36, 360
focus groups, 79
Food Standards Agency, 336, 337
foot and mouth epidemic (2001), 336
Foot, Michael, 65
Foreign and Commonwealth Office (FCO), 411–12
foreign policy, 33–6, 39–40, 43–4, 47–8, 410–21
foundation hospitals, 373
foundation schools, 310
free collective bargaining, 63
freedom of information, 328, 338
free market, 4, 44–5, 54, 59–62, 71–2, 370

free trade, 54, 57
Friedman, Milton, 56, 59
Friends of the Earth, 150
fuel protests, 82
Fukuyama, Francis, 52, 415
Fulton Report (1968), 211

Gaitskell, Hugh, 64
gay and lesbian rights, 397–400
gender, 23, 70, 77
    and judiciary, 255
    and Parliament, 229, 244,
        246, 398
    and participation, 77
    and voting, 103–4
General Strike, 63
Giscard d'Estaing, Valery, 281
Gladstone, William E., 123,
    291
global warming, 406–7
globalization, **11**, 48–9, 67,
    71–2, 329, 368
GM (genetically modified) food,
    83, 408–9
Goldsmith, Sir James, 97–8
Good Friday Agreement, 112,
    295
governance, 328, 426–7,
    429–30
    see also local governance,
    multi-level governance
Government Communications
    Headquarters (GCHQ),
    338
government offices for the
    regions (GOs or GORs),
    304–5
gradualism, 57, 60, 63
grant maintained schools, 310
Greater London Authority, 318
Green Paper, **234**
Green Party, 401, 404–5
Greenpeace, 83, 137, 150, 409
green politics, 401–9
green thinking, 71, 401–9
Greer, Germaine, 70
Gross Domestic Product (GDP),
    17
Gulf War, 410

Hague, William, 61–2, 107,
    125, 131
Haldane Report (1918), 207
Hamilton, Neil, 158, 233
Hattersley, Roy, 55
Hayek, Friedrich von, 56, 59,
    60
Healey, Dennis, 39, 40, 65, 124,
    413
health action zones, 311
Health and Safety Executive, 337
health policy, 372–4
Heath, Edward, 32, 40, 42, 123,
    291
Hennessy, Peter, 423
Heseltine, Michael, 219, 315,
    335–6
Hobsbawm, Eric, 423
homosexuality, 219, 299,
    397–400
hospital trusts, 309, 310, 373
House of Commons, 227–44
    composition, 228–33
    functions, 228–42
    reform, 243–4
    representation of interests,
        232–3
    representation of parties,
        230–2
    representation of society,
        228–9
House of Lords, 244–9
    as court, 253–4
    composition, 246
    functions, 244–6
    party affiliations, 248
    reform, 246–9
housing, 28–9
housing associations, 28–9, 309,
    334
Howard League for Penal
    Reform, 137, 151
Howard, Michael, 218
Howe, Sir Geoffrey, 60, 201
Human Rights Act, 184, 185,
    255, 264–6
Hume, John, 294
Huntington, Samuel, 415
Hutton, Will, 381

ideology, **51**, 51–3, 118–19
identity, 12, 16, 18–19, 30, 67,
    288–90, 329, 342, 431
immigration, 19–20, 387–9
income distribution, 25
incomes policy, 40
incrementalism, 348, 350
individualism, 54
industrial relations, 40, 42, 139
inequality, 24–5
inflation, 40
influence, **5**
Institute for Public Policy
    Research (IPPR), 356
Institute of Directors, 139
Institute of Economic Affairs
    (IEA), 355
institutional racism, **68**, 257
internal markets, 44, 333
Iraq, 419–20
Ireland, 11–12 (*see also*
    Northern Ireland)
Irish nationalism, 67, 290–7
Irish Republican Army (IRA),
    291–7
Irvine, Derry, 248
Islam, 22
Islamophobia, 21, 22, 68–9,
    394, 395
issue preferences (and voting)
    108–9

Jenkins, Roy, 65, 278
Jenkins Report, 95, 184
Jennings, Sir Ivor, 30, 289
'joined-up government', 331,
    351–2
judicial independence, **255**
judicial review, **260**, 260–1
judiciary, **187**, 254–6

Kennedy, Charles, 94
Keynes, John Maynard, 37, 51,
    54
Keynesian economics, **359**
Keynesianism, 36–7, 57, 59, 64
Kinnock, Neil, 45, 65, 278
'kitchen cabinet', 194
Kyoto Agreement, 407–8

Labour Party, 63–6, 118–35, 182–3, 314
labourism, 62–3, 65
Laden, Osama bin, 419
Lamont, Norman, 361
law
  administrative, 253
  civil, 253
  common, 177
  criminal, 253
  European, 249–50
  Scottish, 253
  statute, 177
Law Lords, 246–7
Lawson, Nigel, 60, 361
learning and skills councils, 309, 310
left and right, 52, 77
legislation, 233–8
legislative process, 234–7
legislature, **187**
liberal-bureaucratic model, 222
Liberal Democrats, 56, 94, 122, 124, 130, 131, 134, 182–3, 283, 314, 405
Liberal Party, 53–6, 118, 122–4, 182
Liberal-SDP Alliance, 56
liberalism, 53–6, **62**
  neo-liberalism, 56, 60–1
liberty, 54
Lincoln, Abraham, 6
Lindblom, Charles, 347, 348
Livingstone, Ken, 315, 317, 318, 333, 405
Lloyd George, David, 126, 133
lobby system, 168
local democracy, 311–13
local governance, 12, **308**, 309–26
local government, 12, 117, **308**, 309–26
  central–local relations, 325–6
  elected mayors, 315, 317, 318
  elected members, 314–15
  finance, 322–5
  officers, 314
  parties, 314–5
  reorganisation, 316–20

  services, 308–9, 320–2
  Scotland, 317, 320
  unitary authorities, 317–20
  Wales, 320–1
local management of schools (LMS), 310
London government, 302, 317, 318
loyalist paramilitaries, 292

MI5, 338–40
MI6, 338
Maastricht Treaty (Treaty of the European Union), 249, 273, 277, 412
McConnell, Jack, 299, 306
MacDonald, J. Ramsay, 132
McGuiness, Martin, 296
McKenzie, Robert, 119
MacLeish, Henry, 299
Macmillan, Harold, 32, 35, 36, 39, 57, 201, 271
Macpherson Inquiry, 257, 392
Major, John, 32–3, 42, 43, 61, 201, 219, 295, 274, 313, 361–2
majoritarian electoral systems, 91, 92
Malthus, Thomas, 24
Mandelson, Peter, 219, 296–7
manifestos, 122
marginal constituencies, 90
market testing, 333
Marx, Karl, 10, 26, 50, 62, 423–4
Marxist ideas, 9–10, 29, 430–1
mass media, **156**–69
  media and democracy, 157–9
  media as tool of ruling class, 159–62
  media ownership and control, 160–2
May, Sir Thomas Erskine, 177
mayors, see local government, London government
Michael, Alun, 300–1
Michels, Robert, 118, 131–2, 152
Militant Tendency, 65

Milburn, Alan, 377
Mill, John Stuart, 69, 79, 311
Millet, Kate, 70
Minimum Lending Rate (MLR), 360
minimum wage, 363–5
ministerial responsibility, **218**, 218–21
Ministry of Defence (MoD), 411
mixed economy, 36
Monarchy, 177–8
monetarism, **44**, **360**, 361–2
Monnet, Jean, 270, 278
Moore, Jo, 163, 219
Morgan, Rhodri, 300–1
Morris, Estelle, 220
Mowlam, Marjorie (Mo), 201–2, 295–7
Mozambique, 413
multiculturalism, 21, 392–3, 396
multi-level governance, 12–13, 341–2, 356, 289, 427–8, 432
multi-party system, 117
Murdoch, Rupert, 160–2, 165
Murray, Charles, 379–81
Muslims, 22, 68–9, 394, 395
mutually assured destruction (MAD), 419

Nairn, Tom, 300, 306
National Audit Office, 337
National Economic Development Council (NEDC), 359
National Executive Committee (NEC) of Labour Party, 118, 129–30
National Farmers' Union (NFU), 152
National Health Service, 37, 64, 330, 333, 372–4
national interest, 412
nationalisation, 36, 40, 63
nationalism, 66–8, 289–90
Neill Committee, 134
neo-conservatism, see conservatism

neo-corporatism, 138, **139**
neo-liberalism, 55–6, 59–61
Network Rail, 334
'New Commonwealth', 387, 413
'new deal' (from welfare to work), 365, 383
new deal for communities, 311
new feminism, 399
New Labour, 45–9, 65–6, 71, 119, 139–41, 184–6
new magistracy, **311**, 328, 331
new public management (NPM), 213, 308, 369, 370
New Right, 59–61
newspapers, 157–62
  coverage of elections, 167–8
  influence, 166–8
  ownership, 160–2
  readership, 165–6
Next Steps programme, 209, 214
Nice Treaty, 200
'nimby' (not in my back yard) groups, 150
Niskanen, William, 224
Nolan Lord, 232–3
Nolan Report, 217, 233
North Atlantic Treaty Organisation (NATO), 34, 413–17, 419
Northern Ireland, 16–17, 22, 112
Northern Ireland Assembly, 249–50
Nott, John, 220
nuclear weapons, 33, 34, 39, 418–20

Official Secrets Act, 340
Office of Fair Trading (OFT), 337
Ofgem (Office of Gas and Electricity Markets), 336, 337
Ofsted (Office for Standards in Education), 337
Oftel (Office of Telecommunications), 336, 337

Ofwat (Office of Water Services), 336, 337
Ombudsman, **263**, 263–4, 336
O'Neill, Terence, 291
open government, 328, 338–40
opinion polls, 113–14, 193
Ottawa Convention, 418
Owen, Robert, 62
Oxfam, 137

Paisley, Ian, 293, 295
Parliament, 227–50
parliamentarism, 63
parliamentary debates, 240–1
Parliamentary Labour Party (PLP), 118
parliamentary questions, 239, 240, 243
parliamentary scrutiny of executive, 238–40
parliamentary sovereignty, 178–**180**, 185, 306
participation, 73, **74**–87
parties, political, 52–3, 115–35
  cadre parties, 118
  conferences, 123, 128–9
  factions, 120–1
  finance, 133–4
  functions, 116
  image, 108
  leadership, 122–6
  manifestos, 122
  mass parties, 118, 132
  membership, 75, 76, 130–3
  parliamentary parties, 126–7, 230–2
  party discipline, 126–7, 231
  party systems, 115–17
  party typologies, 118–19
party identification, 100
party realignment, 134
patriarchy, 70
Patten, Chris, 296
peers
  hereditary, 246–8
  life, 246–8
  spiritual, 246–7
pensions crisis, 385–6

performance indicators, 373
permanent secretary, 208
Phillips Inquiry, 353
Plaid Cymru, 67, 299–302
Plato, 4, 24
Pliatzky Report, 330
pluralism, **8**, 9–10, 316, 338
  neo-pluralism, **8**
police and policing, 256–8
police authorities, 257, 309
Police Complaints Authority, 258
policy, 13–15
policy analysis, 351–2
policy communities, 428–9
policy implementation, 356–7
policy making, **345**
political agenda, 346–7, 404
political culture, **81**–5
political generations, 24, 84–5
political leadership, 107, 122–6, 352–5
political socialisation, 83–5, **84**, 101
politics, nature of **3**, 4–5, 15
poll tax (Community Charge), 59
Ponting, Clive, 256
popular capitalism, 29
popular sovereignty, 6, **180**
popular vote, **89**
post-Thatcherism, 60–2
poverty, 13–14, 24–5, 378–86
  child poverty, **379**
  relative poverty, **378**
Powell, J. Enoch, 281, 283, 388
Powell, Jonathan, 194
power, **5**, 7–10
power-bloc model, 222, 223, 224
'power dependence' model, 325–6
pragmatism, 51, 57, 66, 71
Prescott, John, 406
Presidents
  American, 201
  French, 201
pressure groups, 136–55
  and British government, 145–9

and democracy, 151–5
and European Union, 143–4
and Parliament, 146–8
cause (or promotional) groups, **137**
insider groups, **137**, 138
outsider groups, **137**, 138
primary groups, 137–8
secondary groups, 137–8
sectional (or defensive), **137**
prices and incomes policy, 359
Primary Care Trusts, 309
prime minister, **187**–93
Prime Minister's Office, 187, 194, 199
Prior, James, 294
Private Finance Initiative, 65, 333, **334**, 365, 371–2
Private Member's bills (see bills, Private Member's)
privatisation, **42**, 43, 59, 65, 332–3, 336
Prodi, Romano, 278
Profumo, John
proportionality (in elections), 90
proportional representation (PR), **91**, 93–4
additional member system, 93, 95–6, 298, 300–1
list systems, 93, 94
single transferable vote, 93, 94
psephology (and psephologists), **90**
public administration model, 222, 224–5
public opinion, 79–80
public opinion polls, 113–14
Public Sector Borrowing Requirement (PSBR), 333, 360, 365
public ownership, 63 (see also nationalisation)
public–private partnerships (PPPs), 46–7, 65, 326, 331, 333, **334**, 371–2
Putnam, Robert, 78

quangos, **329**, 330–2
quasi markets, 44

race, 68, **388**
Race Relations Acts, 389
race riots, 388, 392–3
racism, 68–9, **389**
institutional racism, **68**, 257, 391–2, **392**
Railtrack, 333, 372, 426
rates, domestic, 324
rationalism, 54–5, 56, 347–8
Rayner, Sir Derek (and Rayner scrutinies), 214
Real IRA, 294
redress of grievances, **259**, 259–66
Redwood, John, 124
Referendum Party, 98, 283
referendums, **96**, 96–8, 184, 185
continued membership of EC (1975), 274
devolution (1979), 298, 299
devolution (1997), 298, 299
Ireland (Easter agreement, 1998), 295
London government (1998), 318
Northern Ireland (1973), 291
Regional Development Agencies (RDAs), 184, 304
regional devolution, 184, 282, 304–5
regulation, 331, 335–8
regulatory capture, 338
regulatory state, 328, 335–8
Reid, John, 297
religion and politics, 21–2
republic, 178
rights, 258–9
civil rights, **258**, 259
human, **258**
natural, **258**
Rhodesia, 39
Ricardo, David, 54
Rimmington, Stella, 339–40
Rome Treaty, 270, 271, 274
Rousseau, Jean-Jacques, 6
Royal Society for the Prevention of Cruelty to Animals (RSPCA), 153

Royal Ulster Constabulary, 292, 296
rule of law, 180–1, **251**–3
ruling class, **8**, 9–10
Russia, 416

Salmond, Alex, 299
Schuman, Robert, 270
Scotland, 12, 16–18, 112–13, 253, 288–90, 297–9, 302–3, 306
Scottish Executive, 12, 299
Scottish National Party, 18, 67, 112, 297–9, 306
Scottish nationalism, 12, 18, 30, 297–9
Scottish Parliament, 249 250, 298–9
Scott Report, 221, 339
scrutiny of executive, 238–40
Section 28 of the Local Government Act, 98, 299
security services, 338–40
select committees, 238–40
September 11th (2001), 14, 68, 338–9, 387, 394, 410, 419, 420
Shayler, David, 256, 339–40
Sheehy Report, 258
Shelter, 137
Simon, Herbert, 347–8
Sinn Fein, 112, 293–7
Single European Act, 43, 274
single transferable vote (STV), 93
see also proportional representation
'sleaze', 133, 219
Smith, Adam, 54, 59
Smith, John, 45
Snowdrop campaign, 424, 426
social capital, **78**
Social Chapter, 273, 275
social democracy, 65
Social Democratic and Labour Party (SDLP), 112, 294–7
Social Democratic Party (SDP), 65, 124, 283

social exclusion, **381**
Social Exclusion Unit, 47, 331, 352
socialisation, *see* political socialisation
socialism, **62**
  British 62–6
  ethical, 63, **66**
  Fabian, 63
social movements, 141–3
Society for the Protection of the Unborn Child (SPUC), 145, 150
Society of Local Authority Chief Executives (SOLACE), 351–2
Souter, Brian, 98
South Africa, 412, 413
sovereignty, **175**
Soviet Union (USSR), 412
Special Branch, 338
special relationship with the United States, 33, 286–7, 410, 413–14
spin and spin-doctors, 50, 163–4, 194, 199–200, 219, 425
'stagflation', **40**, 41, 329
stakeholding, **66**, 382
standards in public life, 217
standing committees, 234–7
state, **4**
  independent sovereign state, **11**
statute law, 177
Statutory Inquiries, 262–3
Stonewall, 398
'stop–go' cycle, 359
strategic defence review (SDR), 420
Straw, Jack, 258
subsidiarity, *see* European Union, subsidiarity
Suez affair, 35, 270–1, 413
Sun, the, 161–2, 167, 168
Sunningdale Agreement, 294

supplementary vote, 92
sustainable development, 406–7
Swinney, John, 299

tactical voting, 90–**91**
targets, 375, 376–7
television and politics, 162–3
terrorism, 410
Thatcher government, 309–10
Thatcher, Margaret
  civil service, 213–15, 224
  environment, 404–5
  Europe, 43, 60, 274
  foreign policy, 412
  ideology, *see* Thatcherism, New Right
  party leader, 60, 124
  Prime Minister, 32, 42–3, 59–62, 191, 198, 202 , 354–5
  quangos, 329–30
Thatcherism, 42–5, 59–62, 86, 119, 139–40, 327, 330, 382
think tanks, 355–6
third way, 45, **66**, 71–2, 217–18, 284, 308
Thompson, E. P., 423
Toryism, 56, **62**
town planning, 64
trades unions, 42, 63, 133
Trades Union Congress (TUC), 41, 137, 145, 151
transport policy, 405, 428–9
trial by jury, 256
Trimble, David, 295–7
tripartism, **41**
Turnbull, Sir Andrew, 197
turnout, 75–6, 78–9, 89–90
two ballot electoral system, 92
two party system, 99–100

Ulster Unionist Party (UUP), 112, 291–7
unemployment, 21, 40, 45

unitary local authorities, 317–21
unitary state, 306, 341
United Kingdom, 12, 16–17, 288–90, 305–7
UK Independence Party, 135, 283
United States of America, 6

voluntary sector, 334–5
voting behaviour, 98–114

Wakeham Report, 248
Wales, 12, 17–19, 288–90, 299–303
war on terror, 394, 395, 415, 419
Weber, Max, 4, 5, 26
welfare state, 37–8, 44–5, 54, 64, 329, 370, 378
welfare to work, 383
Welsh Assembly, 249–50, 300–2, 303–4
Welsh Cabinet, 301
Welsh nationalism, 12, 18, 299–302
Western European Union, 414
'West Lothian question', 303–4, 306
White Paper, **234**
Whitehall, 209
'Whitehall village' model of civil service, 222–3, 226
Whitelaw, William, 294
Wilson, Harold, 32, 40, 42, 64–5, 127, 339, 340, 351, 354–5, 413
Wollstonecraft, Mary, 69, 70
women's movement, 70, 395–7
Women's Royal Voluntary Service (WRVS), 309
World Trade Organisation, 419

Zimbabwe, *see* Rhodesia
Zinoviev letter, 167